Review chapter summary.

Review tables.

See if you can answer the questions in the "key questions" section of the web chapter summary.

Write your own chapter summary. Then compare it to the web chapter summary.

Make your own concept map of the key terms, and compare it to the map on the chapter's website.

Write your own definitions of the key terms, and compare your definitions to the chapter's web glossary.

Do interactive web exercises.

Do end-of-chapter exercises.

Read web appendixes.

Follow links to interesting applications of the chapter material.

Follow links to tips and resources that will help you use the chapter material.

Research Design Explained

Research Design Explained

SIXTH EDITION

Mark L. Mitchell
Clarion University

Janina M. Jolley
Clarion University

THOMSON

™

WADSWORTH

Australia • Brazil • Canada • Mexico • Singapore • Spain
United Kingdom • United States

THOMSON
✳
™
WADSWORTH

Publisher: *Vicki Knight*
Assistant Editor: *Dan Moneypenny*
Editorial Assistant: *Sheila Walsh*
Technology Project Manager: *Adrian Paz*
Vice President, Director of Marketing: *Caroline Croley*
Marketing Assistant: *Natasha Coats*
Senior Marketing Communications
 Manager: *Kelley McAllister*
Content Project Manager: *Karol Jurado*
Creative Director: *Rob Hugel*
Senior Art Director: *Vernon Boes*

Senior Print Buyer: *Karen Hunt*
Senior Permissions Editor: *Sarah D'Stair*
Production Service: *Interactive Composition Corporation/*
 Scratchgravel Publishing Services
Copy Editor: *Mary Anne Shahidi*
Illustrator: *Interactive Composition Corporation*
Cover Designer: *Katherine Minerva*
Cover Image: *Peter Haigh/Alamy*
Cover Printer: *Coral Graphics*
Compositor: *Interactive Composition Corporation*
Printer: *RR Donnelley/Crawfordsville*

Thomson Higher Education
10 Davis Drive
Belmont, CA 94002-3098
USA

Library of Congress Control Number: 2006924110

Student Ed: ISBN-13: 978-0-495-09223-0
 ISBN-10: 0-495-09223-1

International
Student Edition: ISBN-13: 978-0-495-09362-6
 ISBN-10: 0-495-09362-9

We dedicate this book to our parents—Anna, Glen, Zoë, and Neal—and to our daughter, Moriah.

Brief Contents

Contents

CHAPTER 5   **MEASURING AND MANIPULATING VARIABLES: RELIABILITY AND VALIDITY   97**

CHAPTER 6   **BEYOND RELIABILITY AND VALIDITY: THE BEST MEASURE FOR YOUR STUDY   140**

CHAPTER 7 INTRODUCTION TO DESCRIPTIVE METHODS AND CORRELATIONAL RESEARCH   162

CHAPTER 10   **THE SIMPLE EXPERIMENT   279**

CHAPTER 11

EXPANDING THE SIMPLE EXPERIMENT: THE MULTIPLE-GROUP EXPERIMENT   321

CHAPTER 12

EXPANDING THE EXPERIMENT: FACTORIAL DESIGNS   350

CHAPTER 13   **MATCHED PAIRS, WITHIN-SUBJECTS, AND MIXED DESIGNS   392**

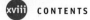

Preface

This book focuses on two goals: (1) helping students evaluate the internal, external, and construct validity of studies and (2) helping students write a good research proposal. To accomplish these goals, we use the following methods:

- We use numerous, clear examples—especially for concepts with which students have trouble, such as statistical significance and interactions.
- We focus on important, fundamental concepts; show students why those concepts are important; relate those concepts to what students already know; and directly attack common misconceptions about those concepts.
- We show the logic behind the process of research design so that students know more than just terminology—they learn how to think like research psychologists.
- We explain statistical concepts (not computations) because (a) students seem to have amnesia for what they learned in statistics class, (b) some understanding of statistics is necessary to understand journal articles, and (c) statistics need to be considered before doing research, not afterward.

Flexible Organization

We know that most professors share our goals of teaching students to be able to read, evaluate, defend, and produce scientific research. We also know that professors differ in how they go about achieving these goals and in the emphasis professors place on each of these goals. For example, about half of all research methods professors believe that the best way to help students understand design is to cover nonexperimental methods first, whereas the other half believe that students must understand experimental methods first. To accommodate professor differences, we have made the chapters relatively self-contained modules. Because each chapter focuses on ethics, construct validity, external validity, and internal validity, it is easy to skip chapters or cover them in different orders. For example, the first chapter that some professors assign is the last.

Changes to the Sixth Edition

Whereas the last edition was revised to help students write better research proposals and reports, this edition was revised to help students read journal articles. This new focus not only caused us to add more examples from interesting recent research but also affected the concepts we covered.

Chapter-by-Chapter Changes

Chapter 1, "Science, Psychology, and You," was split into two because teaching students about ethics, validity, what science is, and why psychology is a science was a lot to cover in one chapter. In the current Chapter 1, we explain the distinction between the scientific method and other ways of knowing, explain why psychology is a science, and explain how students can benefit from understanding research methods. The chapter also links to two Web Appendixes: (1) one on the value of research design for getting a job and getting into graduate school, and (2) another on Kuhn and other criticisms of science. We thank Dr. Jamie Phillips, an expert on the philosophy of science, for his extensive (7 single-spaced pages) comments on an earlier draft of this chapter.

Chapter 2, "Ethics and Validity," has been streamlined. The revised discussion of validity is not only easier to understand but also includes more information about techniques (e.g., random assignment, counterbalancing) to achieve validity. This chapter can be linked to the extensive discussion of how to deal with IRBs in our enhanced appendix on ethics (Appendix C).

Chapter 3, "Generating and Refining Research Hypotheses," was revised to give students even more help in developing experimental hypotheses. In addition, because so much research today involves either mediating or moderating variables, we expanded our discussion of the distinction between those two types of variables.

Chapter 4, "Reading and Evaluating Research," was improved by (a) placing more emphasis on the idea that "published does not mean perfect," (b) enhancing the box that shows students what questions they can ask of an article, and (c) addressing the "file drawer problem."

Chapter 5, "Measuring and Manipulating Variables: Reliability and Validity," was updated to include recently developed measures of unconscious prejudice and was shortened.

Chapter 6, "Beyond Reliability and Validity: The Best Measure for Your Study," was enlivened by adding several examples and visuals.

Chapter 7, "Introduction to Descriptive Methods and Correlational Research," was made clearer and more engaging by using more and better examples from current research and by providing more tips on how to develop descriptive hypotheses. The statistical material is more concise (especially the discussion of the coefficient of determination), more up-to date (consistent with APA's guidelines, we added material on confidence intervals), and more organized (much of the discussion is organized around the limits of significant results).

Chapter 8, "Survey Research," was enlivened by adding examples from recent research as well as from famous errors in political polls. It was also updated by adding material on web surveys (including Table 8-2, "Advantages and Disadvantages of Web Surveys") and information on how cell phones and answering machines have affected telephone surveys. It was made more useful to student researchers by adding (a) material on ethics in survey research (mostly on informed consent and confidentiality), (b) information to help students develop survey-appropriate hypotheses, (c) and a table that lists the main survey techniques, the advantages of each technique, and tips on how to use each technique. Finally, to help students understand journal articles, we added a very brief description of structural equation modeling.

Chapter 9, "Internal Validity," was improved by (a) using better and more realistic examples, especially of regression and selection, (b) being more explicit about the prerequisites for inferring causality, and (c) putting more emphasis on the value of causal research.

Chapter 10, "The Simple Experiment," was revised to help students (a) generate research ideas for simple experiments (by including more examples from research that illustrated how and why one should manipulate variables), (b) read and conduct analyses of simple experiments that do not involve the t test (by adding a very brief section on alternatives to the t test), and (c) understand that the validity of a statistical test depends on meeting the assumptions of that test (by adding a table on the impact of violating the t test's assumptions). In addition, because the issue of significance testing is not limited to simple experiments, we moved the box on the controversy surrounding significance testing to Appendix D.

Chapter 11, "Expanding the Simple Experiment: The Multiple-Group Experiment," was improved in three ways. First, we described more uses for multiple-group experiments. Second, we included many more examples of published multiple-group experiments, especially examples that illustrated value of control groups for (a) boosting construct validity and for (b) determining whether one group was scoring higher than another because of a positive effect of one treatment or because of a negative effect of another treatment. Third, we streamlined our discussion of ANOVA.

Chapter 12, "Expanding the Experiment: Factorial Designs," was made easier to understand by (a) assuming less background knowledge and thus providing a gentler introduction to factorial experiments, (b) simplifying computations, (c) spending more time explaining interactions in nonmathematical terms, (d) showing students simple ways to graph their results, (e) giving students a model for writing up their results, and (f) condensing our discussion of the distinction between ordinal and disordinal interactions (the extended discussion is available from the book's website).

Chapter 13, "Matched Pairs, Within-Subjects, and Mixed Designs" was made more interesting by adding a few examples from recent research and by shortening the chapter.

Chapter 14, "Single-n Designs and Quasi-Experiments," was shortened, and a better explanation of how single-n designs differ from case studies was added.

Chapter 15, "Putting It All Together: Writing Research Proposals and Reports," has been revised to help students evaluate their own writing.

Appendix A, "APA Format Checklist," is a new appendix. If you have your students hand in a filled-out copy of this checklist along with their paper, the quality of their papers will improve.

The old Appendix B, "Searching the Literature," has been put online so that students can access it while doing their online searches and to make it easier for students to use the links to other online resources. The new Appendix B, "Sample APA-Style Paper," is a good model for students to follow—and an interesting article to read.

Appendix C, "Practical Tips for Conducting an Ethical and Valid Study," is a radically revised version of our old "Ethics" appendix. This appendix not only discusses the APA ethical code and IRB issues but also gives practical advice for conducting an ethical and valid study.

Appendix D, "Introduction to Statistics" now provides an even better introduction to statistics. We have added (a) a box discussing the statistical significance controversy, (b) a detailed description of techniques researchers use to make the case for a mediator variable, and (c) explanation of how some correlational researchers make the case that a variable has an effect. In addition, we have made our discussion of multiple regression clearer and more informative.

Appendix E, "Statistics and Random Numbers Tables," contains statistical tables and instructions on how to use those tables. For example, Appendix E tells students how to draw random samples, randomly assign participants, and do post hoc tests.

Changes to the Student Website

The student website now includes many goodies that make it almost impossible for a diligent student to get lower than a "C" in the course. For each chapter, the site contains a concept map, learning objectives, a pretest and a posttest quiz for each chapter based on those learning objectives, and answers to the text's even-numbered exercises.

Changes to the Professor's Website

The major change to the professor's website was to add, for each chapter, a list of articles to assign, a summary of each article, and a "reading guide": a handout that defines terms, explains concepts, and translates particularly tough passages, allowing students to read and understand the article.

Acknowledgments

Writing *Research Design Explained* was a monumental task that required commitment, love, effort, and a high tolerance for frustration. If it had not been for the support of our friends, family, publisher, and students, we could not have met this challenge.

Robert Tremblay, a Boston journalist, and Lee Howard, a Connecticut journalist, have our undying gratitude for the many hours they spent critiquing the first five editions of this book. We are also grateful to Darlynn Fink, an English professor and Jamie Phillips, a philosophy professor, for their work on this edition. We also give special thanks to Vicki Knight, Sheila Walsh, and the rest of the folks at Wadsworth College Publishers for sharing and nurturing our vision. In addition to thanking Bob, Lee, Darlynn, Jamie, and Wadsworth College Publishers, we need to thank three groups of dedicated reviewers, all of whom were actually coauthors of this text.

First, we would like to thank the competent and conscientious professors who shared their insights with us. We are grateful to the reviewers whose constructive comments strengthened this sixth edition: Jeff Adams, Trent University; Anne DePrince, University of Denver; Karen Fragedakis, Campbell University; Glenn Geher, SUNY, New Paltz; Paula Goolkasian, University of North Carolina, Charlotte; Shelia Kennison, Oklahoma State University; Eugene Packer, William Paterson University; Jodie Royan, University of Victoria; and Donna Stuber-McEwen, Friends University. In addition, we thank the reviewers of past editions: Ruth Ault, Davidson College; Louis Banderet, Quinsigamond Community College; James H. Beaird, Western Oregon State College; John P. Brockway, Davidson College; Tracy L. Brown, University of North Carolina–Asheville; Edward Caropreso, Clarion University; Walter Chromiak, Dickinson College; James R. Council, North Dakota State University; Helen J. Crawford, University of Wyoming; Raymond Ditrichs, Northern Illinois University; Patricia Doerr, Louisiana State University; Linda Enloe, Idaho State University; Mary Ann Foley, Skidmore College; George Goedel, Northern Kentucky University; George L. Hampton III, University of Houston–Downtown; Robert Hoff, Mercyhurst College; Lynn Howerton, Arkansas State University; John C. Jahnke, Miami University; Randy Jones, Utah State University; Sue Kraus, Fort Lewis College; Scott A. Kuehn, Clarion University; R. Eric Landrum, Boise State University; Kenneth L. Leicht, Illinois State University; Charles A. Levin, Baldwin-Wallace College; Joel Lundack, Peru State College; Steven Meier, University of Idaho; Charles Meliska, University of Southern Indiana; Kenneth B. Melvin, University of Alabama; Stephen P. Mewaldt, Marshall University; John Nicoud, Marion College of Fond du Lac; Jamie Phillips, Clarion University; David Pittenger, Marietta College; Carl Ratner, Humboldt State University; Ray Reutzel, Brigham Young University; Anrea Richards, University of California–Los Angeles; Margaret Ruddy, Trenton State College; James J. Ryan, University of Wisconsin–La Crosse; Rick Scheidt, Kansas State University; Gerald Sparkman, University of Rio Grande; Sylvia Stalker, Clarion University; Ann Stearns, Clarion University; Sandra L. Stein, Rider College; Ellen P. Susman, Metropolitan State College of Denver; Russ A. Thompson, University of Nebraska; Benjamin Wallace, Cleveland State

University; Paul Wellman, Texas A&M University; and Christine Ziegler, Kennesaw State College.

Second, we would like to thank our student reviewers, especially Susanne Bingham, Mike Blum, Shannon Edmiston, Chris Fenn, Jess Frederick, Kris Glosser, Melissa Gregory, Barbara Olszanski, Shari Poza, Rosalyn Rapsinski, Katelin Speer, and Melissa Ustik.

Third, we would like to thank the English professors who critiqued the previous editions of our book: William Blazek, Patrick McLaughlin, and John Young. In addition to improving the writing style of the book, they also provided a valuable perspective—that of the intelligent, but naïve, reader.

Finally, we would like to thank our daughter Moriah for allowing us the time to complete this project.

About the Authors

After graduating summa cum laude from Washington and Lee University, Mark L. Mitchell received his M.A. and Ph.D. degrees in psychology at The Ohio State University. He is currently a professor at Clarion University.

Janina M. Jolley graduated with "Great Distinction" from California State University at Dominguez Hills and earned her M.A. and Ph.D. in psychology from The Ohio State University. She is currently an executive editor of *The Journal of Genetic Psychology* and *Genetic Psychology Monographs*. Her first book was *How to Write Psychology Papers: A Student's Survival Guide for Psychology and Related Fields,* which she wrote with J. D. Murray and Pete Keller.

In addition to working on this book for more than 98 (dog) years, Dr. Mitchell and Dr. Jolley coauthored *Developmental Psychology: A Topical Approach*. In addition, they collaborated with Robert O'Shea to write *Writing for Psychology: A Guide for Students*.

Dr. Mitchell and Dr. Jolley are married to research, teaching, and each other—not necessarily in that order. You can write to them at the Department of Psychology, Clarion University, Clarion, PA 16214, or send e-mail to them at either mmitchell@clarion.edu or jjolley@clarion.edu.

Research
Design
Explained

1

Science, Psychology, and You

The whole of science is nothing more than
a refinement of everyday thinking.

—*Albert Einstein*

Overview

They lived in a time when scientific giants like Galileo and Newton made tremendous discoveries. Yet, the people of this scientific age executed thousands of women for being witches (Robinson, 1997).

We live in a time just after the scientific giants Einstein and Skinner made tremendous discoveries. Yet, in the United States, a country considered the world's superpower, three-quarters of the citizens believe in astrology, millions believe in psychics, billions of dollars are spent on diets that do not work, billions are spent on health care that does not work, and much of what the United States does when it comes to attacking a wide range of problems—from fighting crime to treating the mentally ill—is based on superstition rather than fact.

As you can see, living in a scientific age does not guarantee that a person will engage in scientific rather than superstitious thinking. In fact, living in a scientific age does not even guarantee that a person will know what science is. For example, if you were to tell 100 people that psychology is a science, you would get the following reactions:

> "What's a science?"
> "No, it isn't."
> "That's what's wrong with it."
> "They do some science in the lab, but that has nothing to do with helping people."

In this chapter, we will address these common reactions to psychological science. We will begin by showing that science is a set of strategies that allows people to learn from experience. You will see how you can use science to think more clearly about real-world problems. Then, you will see why most psychologists believe that psychology is a science—and that if psychology is to continue to help people, it must continue to be a science. Finally, you will see why it is vital that when you become a professional, you embrace science rather than superstition.

Why Psychology Uses the Scientific Approach

Since humans were first able to reason, they have asked themselves, "Why are people the way they are?" A little more than 100 years ago, a few individuals tried a different approach to answering this question—the scientific approach: a way of using unbiased observation to form and test beliefs. As a result, psychology—the science of behavior—was born.

Today, the scientific approach is the foundation of all good science. In the next section, we will explore why psychologists and other legitimate scientists find the scientific approach so attractive.

The Characteristics of Science

Psychologists find the scientific approach attractive because it is a useful tool for getting accurate answers to important questions. Crime scene investigators (CSIs) use the scientific approach to solve crimes; biologists use the scientific approach to track down genes responsible for inherited disorders; and behavioral scientists use the scientific approach to unravel the mysteries of the human mind.

What is it about the scientific approach that makes it such a useful tool for people who want answers to important questions? As you will soon see, the eight strengths of the scientific approach are that it

1. finds general rules
2. collects objective evidence

3. makes testable statements
4. adopts a skeptical, questioning attitude about all claims
5. remains open-minded about new claims
6. is creative
7. is public
8. is productive

General Rules: Finding Patterns and Order

Just as CSIs assume that criminals have motives, scientists assume that events happen for reasons. Furthermore, scientists are optimistic that they can find general rules (unifying themes) that will allow them to see connections between seemingly disconnected events and thus better understand the world. They want to explain the most (things) with the fewest (principles). Their hope is that by finding the underlying reasons for events, they will find simplicity, order, and predictability in what often seems a complex, chaotic, and random universe. Thus, contrary to what happens in some science classes, the goal of science is not to make the world unnecessarily complicated and thus more confusing, but instead to make the world more understandable by finding simple, elegant rules that describe, predict, explain, and change behavior.

Objective: Seeing the Real World for What It Is

Scientists must be careful, however, not to let their desire to see the world as a simple and predictable place blind them to reality. (As Albert Einstein said, "Things should be made as simple as possible, but not any simpler.") We all know people who, in their desire to see the world as simple and predictable, "see" rules and patterns that reflect their prejudices and biases, rather than the facts. For example, some people think they can size up someone based on the person's race, astrological sign, attractiveness, handwriting, body build, or some other superficial characteristic. However, when we objectively test the ability of these people to predict other people's behavior, they fail miserably—as more than 100 studies have shown (Dawes, 1994).

Scientists believe in objective facts because human history shows that we can't always accept people's subjective opinions. In the past, physicians believed that destroying parts of patients' brains (lobotomies) made patients better. Some surgeons even issued reports about the number of patients who were "cured" and the number who were "better off"—but both "cured" and "better off" reflected the surgeon's subjective judgment rather than observable changes in the patients, such as patients returning to work (Shorter, 1997).

Unfortunately, not everyone understands the problems with subjective interpretations. Instead, too many people focus on the fact that their subjective interpretations "feel right" to them, rather than that their subjective interpretation may be wrong. Because many people ignore the possibility that their interpretations may be wrong or that other people may interpret events differently, we have

- individuals who think their biased view of themselves, their relationships, and other groups is reality
- lie detector professionals who do not realize that another lie detector professional would disagree with their judgment about whether the suspect is lying
- therapists who do not realize that another therapist would disagree with their interpretation of what a client's response to an inkblot means

To avoid being swept away by either unfounded speculations or biased perceptions, scientists tie their beliefs to concrete, observable, physical evidence that both independent observers and skeptics can double-check. Scientists look for *independent* evidence of their claim: objective evidence that does not depend on the scientist's theory or personal viewpoint. The scientific laws of gravity, magnetism, and operant conditioning are based on objective observations of physical evidence (Ruchlis & Oddo, 1990). Consequently, these laws are not opinions but facts.

Testable (Correctable): Could I Be Wrong?

Although we have attacked *unsupported* speculation, we are not saying that scientists don't speculate—they do. Like CSIs, scientists are encouraged to make bold, specific predictions and then to find evidence that either supports or refutes their speculations. In reflecting this "no guts, no glory" approach, psychologist Bob Zajonc says, "You don't do interesting research if you don't take risks. Period. If you prove the obvious, that's not interesting research."

Similarly, although we would argue that unsupported opinions, like unsupported speculations, are of limited value, we are not saying that scientists don't have opinions. Like everyone else, they do. However, unlike almost everyone else, scientists willingly put those opinions to the test and stand ready to publicly renounce their previous views if proved wrong.

At one level, you probably appreciate scientists' willingness to consider that they might be wrong. You may wish other people asked themselves the "Could I be wrong?" question more often.

At another level, you might ask, "Why should I risk finding out that a cherished opinion is wrong?" Scientists have at least two reasons. First, a major goal of science is to identify myths, superstitions, and false beliefs. Second, one of science's major strengths is that its methods allow scientists to learn from mistakes. Thus, to be a scientist, you do not need to start with intuitively accurate insights into how the world works. You just need to learn when your initial insights are wrong by making *testable statements:* statements that may possibly be shown to be wrong. The goal in making a testable statement is not to make a statement that will be wrong, but rather to put yourself in a position so that if you are wrong, you admit it and learn from your mistake. As Peter Doherty (2002, p. 89) writes, "The scientific method requires that you struggle exhaustively to disprove, or falsify, your best ideas. You actually try, again and again, to find the possible flaw in your hypothesis. We scientists are rather accustomed to falling flat on our faces!"

You probably still think it is strange to risk being wrong. To understand why it is okay to make statements that can potentially be proven false, let's see what happens when people don't make falsifiable statements. As you will see, people who ask "Am I right or am I right?" never find out that they are wrong. Those people do not allow facts to change their beliefs. For example, one individual predicted that the earth would be destroyed in 1998. Has he admitted his mistake? No, he claims that the earth, in fact, *was* destroyed in 1998, but that we are now living on an alternate earth in another dimension, and we are unaware of the destruction of our "previous" world. We can't prove him wrong.

We can, however, point out that he has made an untestable statement—a statement that no observation could possibly disprove. That is, we can point out that his prediction, like the prediction that "Our team will win, lose, or tie its next game," is so flexible that it can fit any result. Because his untestable prediction can fit any result, his belief can never be changed, refined, or corrected by the discovery of new facts. Because untestable statements do not allow scientists to test their beliefs, scientists try to avoid untestable statements. Scientists'

Figure 1-1   **Untestable Statements**

Vague predictions that are never wrong may be useless.

efforts to avoid being fooled by untestable statements lead scientists to be skeptical of (a) vague statements and (b) after-the-fact explanations.

Vague Statements May Be Untestable. Vague statements are as useless as they are untestable (see Figure 1-1). Thus, a CSI who claims that the murderer was born in this galaxy can neither be proven wrong nor given credit for solving the case.

Vague statements, because they are untestable, are often the province of "sucker bets" and of pseudosciences, such as palmistry and astrology. For example, suppose a stranger bets you that Wednesday will be a good day—but he doesn't define what a good day is. No matter what happened on Wednesday, the stranger may come back on Thursday, demanding payment because Wednesday, by the stranger's definition, was a good day. Similarly, one of the authors' horoscopes once read: "Take care today not to get involved with someone who is wrong for you and you for him or her. Trouble could result." This horoscope tells us nothing. No matter what happens, the astrologer could claim to have predicted it.

One reason the astrologer can be so slippery is that he or she used vaguely defined terms. For example, the astrologer does not give us a clue as to what "wrong for you" means. Thus, if trouble had resulted, the astrologer could say, "The person was wrong for you." If trouble had not resulted, the astrologer could say, "The person was right for you." Note that because the horoscope does not tell us anything, it is both unfalsifiable and useless.

One way that scientists avoid making vague statements is by defining their concepts in precise and objective terms. Instead of talking only in terms of vague, invisible, and hard-to-pin-down abstractions such as "love," psychologists talk in terms of the specific, observable procedures they use to measure love.

More technically, scientists use **operational definitions:** the specific, observable, concrete steps that are involved in measuring or manipulating the concept being studied. Thanks to operational definitions, researchers are not limited to talking about psychological variables such as stress, love, and intelligence in vague, abstract, and poetic ways. Instead, researchers can also talk about a psychological concept in terms of the specific recipes they have invented for measuring that variable.

As you will see in Chapter 5, these recipes may range from measuring brain wave activity to scoring a multiple-choice test. Some of these recipes will be clever and do a good job of capturing the psychological variable they are supposed to measure, whereas others will not be as good. But no matter what the recipe is, it is one that other scientists can follow. Because the operational definition is an objective recipe that anyone can follow, there is no disagreement about what each participant's score is.

When researchers state their predictions in such clear, concrete, and objective terms, they can objectively determine whether the evidence supports their predictions. For example, no matter what their biases, scientists can objectively establish whether scores on a given happiness test are correlated with scores on a certain IQ test.

If, contrary to the researchers' predictions, scores on the happiness test are correlated with scores on the IQ test, the researchers admit the prediction was wrong. If repeating the study in several different ways obtains the same result, the researchers will change their minds about the relationship between happiness and intelligence. Note that quacks, on the other hand, can avoid making testable predictions by avoiding operational definitions. For example, the quack can continue to insist that everyone the quack judges as intelligent is— in the quack's view—unhappy. By not making testable predictions, the quack will never have to admit being wrong. Another technique quacks can use to avoid having to change their minds is to avoid predictions and instead make after-the-fact explanations.

After-the-Fact Explanations May Be Untestable. After-the-fact explanations (sometimes called ad hoc explanations), like vague statements, are difficult to prove wrong. For example, if we say that a person committed a murder because of some event in his childhood, how can we be proven wrong? Most people would accept or reject our claim based on whether it sounded reasonable. The problem, however, with accepting "reasonable-sounding" explanations is that after something happens, almost anyone can generate a plausible-sounding explanation for why it happened.[1] Although these explanations may seem reasonable, they may be incorrect.

To dramatize how plausible-sounding explanations often turn out to be wrong, psychologists have asked people to explain numerous "facts," such as why "opposites attract," and why changing your original answer to a multiple-choice test question usually results in changing from a right answer to a wrong answer. Participants were able to generate logical, persuasive reasons for why the "facts" were true—even though all of the "facts" were false (Dawes, 1994; Myers, 1999; Slovic & Fischoff, 1977; Stanovich, 1990; Weiten, 1992).

Skeptical: What's the Evidence?

Scientists are not just skeptical about after-the-fact explanations. Scientists, like CSIs, are so skeptical that they want evidence before they believe even the most "obvious" of statements. As Carl Sagan (1993) noted, scientists have the courage to question conventional wisdom. For example, Galileo tested the obvious "fact" that heavier objects fall faster than lighter objects—and found it to be false. Like the skeptical CSI, scientists respond to claims by saying things like "Show me," "Let me see," "Let's take a look," and "Can you verify that?" Neither

---

[1]According to *Time,* Nancy Reagan's strong trust in an astrologer was cemented by the astrologer showing, *after the fact,* that "her charts could have foretold that period on or around March 30, 1981, would be extremely dangerous for the President." According to *The Skeptical Inquirer,* another individual tried to capitalize on the assassination attempt. That person, a self-proclaimed psychic, realized that predicting the assassination attempt would be persuasive evidence of her psychic powers. Consequently, she faked a videotape to make it look like she had predicted the assassination attempt on Ronald Reagan months in advance. However, analysis showed that the videotape was made the day after the assassination attempt (Nickell, 2005).

CSIs nor scientists accept notions merely because an authority says it's true or because everyone is sure that it is true. Instead, both CSIs and scientists demand objective evidence.

Even after scientists have objective evidence, they continue to be skeptical. They realize that having circumstantial evidence in support of a belief is not the same as having proof that the belief is correct. Consequently, scientists ask themselves two questions: "What is the evidence *against* this belief?" and "What other explanations are there for the evidence that seems to support this belief?" Scientists realize that if they looked only at the cases that support a belief, they could find plenty of evidence to confirm their pet hypotheses. For example, they could find cases and stories—anecdotal evidence—to "prove" that going to a physician is bad for your physical health (by looking only at malpractice cases) and that playing the lottery is good for your financial health (by looking only at lottery winners).

In addition to looking for evidence that might refute the belief, scientists look for alternative explanations for evidence that appears to support the belief. Consequently, scientists are experts at considering alternative explanations for events. For example, *malaria* means "bad air" ("mal" means bad, as in "malpractice," and "aria" means air) because people thought malaria was caused by breathing the bad-smelling air around swamps. People pointed out that malaria cases were more common around swamps and that swamps contained foul-smelling marsh gas. Scientists countered by pointing out that the presence of marsh gas is not the only difference between dry areas and swampy areas. For instance, there are more insects, such as mosquitoes, in swamps. As we now know, mosquitoes—not marsh gas—infect people with malaria.

Being skeptical also means realizing that "convincing proof" may merely be the result of a coincidence. A suspect may be near the victim's house on the night of the murder for perfectly innocent reasons; a patient may suddenly get better even after getting a "quack" treatment; a volcano may erupt exactly 20 years after an atomic bomb went off; and one cold winter does not disprove the "greenhouse effect." Scientists, as Robert Abelson (1995) says, "give chance a chance" to explain events.

Open-Minded

Despite being skeptical, good scientists are also open-minded. The same respect for the evidence that allows them to be skeptical of popular claims that are not supported by the evidence allows them to be open to unpopular claims that are supported by the evidence. But what happens when there isn't evidence for a claim?

Just as a good CSI initially—before the evidence is in—considers everyone a suspect, good scientists are willing to entertain all possibilities. Scientists have the courage to be open to the truth and to see the world as it is (Sagan, 1993). Consequently, scientists will not automatically dismiss new ideas as nonsense, not even ideas that seem to run counter to existing knowledge, such as telepathy. The willingness to consider odd ideas has led scientists to important discoveries, such as the finding that certain jungle plants have medicinal uses.

Creative

To test such ideas and to formulate new ideas to be tested, scientists must be creative. Unraveling the mysteries of the universe is not a boring, unimaginative, or routine task. Scientific giants such as Marie Curie (the discoverer of radium), Charles Darwin, and Friederich Kekule (who, while dreaming, solved the riddle of how carbon molecules are structured) are called creative geniuses.

We should point out, however, that you don't need to be "naturally creative" to think in a creative way. Indeed, Darwin, Einstein, and Edison did not attribute their creative success to natural creative ability, but to persistence. As Einstein said, "The most important thing to do is to not stop questioning."

Shares Findings

Science is able to capitalize on the work of individual geniuses like Einstein because scientists, by publishing their work, produce publicly shared knowledge. Most of this published work involves submitting reports of research studies. These reports allow other scientists to **replicate**—repeat, or duplicate—the original study.

One advantage of scientists publishing their work is that biases and errors can be spotted—and corrected. If a researcher publishes a biased study, rival investigators may replicate that study and get different results. If a researcher publishes a flawed study, critics may challenge the researcher's conclusions and research methods. Thus, publishing findings, along with using standard research methods, are ways to maintain objectivity by keeping individual scientist's biases in check (Haack, 2004).

A second advantage of scientists publishing their work is that researchers can build on each other's work. Nobody has to solve a problem alone. If a scientist doesn't have the time or energy to solve an entire puzzle, the scientist can work on a filling in one of the last remaining pieces of the puzzle that others have almost completed (Haack, 2004). If a scientist does not see how to go about solving the puzzle—or the scientist is going about it the wrong way—the scientist can take advantage of the viewpoint of individual geniuses such as Einstein as well as the wide variety of different viewpoints offered by all the other puzzle workers in the scientific community (Haack, 2004). Thus, by combining their time, energy, and viewpoints, the community of scientists can accomplish much more than if each had worked alone.

Without an open sharing of information, science doesn't work, as the debate on cold fusion illustrates. In 1989, two chemists announced at a press conference that they had invented a way of creating nuclear fusion, a potential source of safe electric power, without heating atoms to extreme temperatures. (Before the scientists' announcement, all known ways of producing nuclear fusion used more energy to heat atoms than the fusion reaction produced. Thus, nobody could seriously consider using nuclear fusion to produce electricity commercially.) However, the two scientists did not submit their research to peer-reviewed journals, and they failed to give details of their procedures. Thus, nobody could replicate their work.

All this secrecy worked against science's self-corrective and unbiased nature. By not sharing their work, the two chemists removed the checks and balances that make science a reliable source of evidence. Instead of letting others verify their findings, they expected people to accept claims made at a press conference. Fortunately, most reputable scientists refuse to accept claims as facts, even claims from other scientists, without objective evidence. Therefore, rather than accepting the chemists' claims, scientists tried to replicate the alleged effect. (Note that, consistent with the view that scientists are open-minded, scientists did not reject the claim outright. Instead, in a fair and open-minded way, they tested the claim.) So far, no one has succeeded in replicating cold fusion.

Thus far, we have skeptically assumed that cold fusion did not really happen. But what if it had? The researchers' lack of openness would still be unfortunate because science progresses only when scientists openly exchange findings.

Productive

Fortunately, scientists usually do share their findings and build on each other's work. As a result, theories are frequently revised, refined, or replaced, and, in some fields of science, knowledge doubles every 5 to 10 years. The evidence that science is a productive tool for

Figure 1-2	Productivity

*"Sometimes I wonder if there's more to life than
unlocking the mysteries of the universe."*

Science has made impressive progress.

making discoveries and advancing knowledge is all around us. The technology created by science has vaulted us a long way from the Dark Ages or even the pre–DVD, pre–personal computer, pre-microwave early 1970s.

The progress science has made is remarkable considering that it is a relatively new way of finding out about the world. As recently as the 1400s, people were punished for studying human anatomy and even for trying to get evidence on such basic matters as the number of teeth a horse has. As recently as the early 1800s, the scientific approach was not applied to medicine or psychology. Until that time, people were limited to relying on tradition, common sense, intuition, and logic for medical and psychological knowledge (and it was not a good idea to go to the doctor).

Once science gained greater acceptance, people used the scientific approach to test and refine commonsense notions, as well as notions derived from intuition, tradition, and logic. By supplementing other ways of knowing, science helped knowledge progress at an explosive rate.

Almost everyone would agree that science has allowed physics, chemistry, and biology to progress at a rapid rate (see Figure 1-2). Hardly anyone would argue that we could make more progress in understanding our physical world by abandoning science and going back to prescientific beliefs and methods, such as alchemy or philosophy (Dawkins, 1998). Indeed, it seems like every field wants to be labeled a science—from creation science to handwriting science to library science to military science to mortuary science (Haack, 2004).

The Characteristics of Psychology

Although few doubt the value of the older sciences, some doubt the value of psychological science. Some of the same individuals who would strongly object to chemists going back to alchemy have no objections to psychologists going back to phrenology: measuring individuals' personalities by measuring the bumps on their head and changing their personalities by moving those bumps.

Why do some individuals think the scientific method is wonderful for studying chemistry, biology, physics, and astronomy, but not for studying psychology? Often, they question whether psychology is a science. That is, they question whether psychologists

- find general rules
- collect objective evidence
- make testable statements
- are skeptical
- are open-minded
- are creative
- produce publicly shared knowledge that can be replicated
- are productive

General Rules

Perhaps the most serious question about psychology as a science is, "Can psychologists find general rules that will predict, control, and explain human behavior?" Cynics argue that although it is possible to find rules to explain the behavior of molecules, it is not possible to find rules to explain the behavior of people.

These cynics claim that, unlike molecules, people are not all alike. Psychologists respond by saying that even though people are not all alike, humans are genetically similar. Perhaps because of this similarity, we humans share many similarities, from our use of language to our tendency to try to repay those who help us. Furthermore, if people's behavior did not follow some basic and recognizable rules, human interactions (e.g., holding a conversation, driving down a road, playing a sport) would be extremely difficult, if not impossible.[2]

Cynics also claim that, unlike molecules, humans may spontaneously do something for no reason. Psychologists argue that most behavior does not just spontaneously appear. Instead, people usually do things for a reason—even if the reason isn't apparent.

Although both cynics and psychologists make logical arguments for their positions, psychologists have evidence to back up their arguments. That is, psychologists have not only argued that human behavior is governed by rules, they have also found many such rules (Kimble, 1990). For example, psychologists have discovered laws of operant and classical conditioning, laws of perception, laws of memory (Banaji & Crowder, 1989), and even laws of emotion (Frijda, 1988). (If you doubt that emotions follow rules, then ask yourself why people have fairly predictable reactions to certain movies. For example, most people cry or come close to tears the first time they see *Bambi*, whereas most people feel a nervous excitement the first time they see a horror film.)

Like psychology, medicine once faced resistance to the idea that general rules applied to humans. Until recently, people believed that one person's flu was caused by circumstances that were completely different from another's. As Burke (1985, p. 195) noted, "Each patient regarded his own suffering as unique (being caused by unique circumstances) and demanding unique remedies." Consequently, one patient's treatment was totally different from another's. Knowledge about cures was not shared, partly because what cured one person was supposed to be totally ineffective for curing anyone else. As a result, medicine did not

---

[2]We thank Dr. Jamie Phillips for this example.

progress, and many people died unnecessarily. It was only after physicians started to look for general causes of disease that successful cures (such as antibiotics) were found.

Nevertheless, general rules do not always work. A treatment that cures one person may not cure another. For example, one person may be cured by penicillin, whereas another may be allergic to it. It would be wrong, however, to say that reactions to drugs do not follow any rules. It's simply that an individual's response to a drug is affected by many rules, and predicting the response would require knowing at least the following: the individual's weight, family history of reactions to drugs, time of last meal, condition of vital organs, other drugs being taken, and level of dehydration.

Like human physiology, human behavior is governed by many factors. Because there are so many rules that may come into play in a given situation, predicting what a given individual will do in that situation would be difficult even if you knew all the rules. Psychologists agree with cynics that predicting an individual's behavior is difficult. However, they disagree with the cynic's assumption that there are no rules underlying behavior. Instead, psychologists know of rules that are useful for predicting the behavior of most people much of the time. As Sherlock Holmes said, "You can never foretell what any man will do, but you can say with precision what an average number will be up to. Individuals may vary, but percentages remain constant."

Some critics mistakenly argue that if you can't predict an individual instance of behavior, then the behavior does not follow general rules. Although this argument sounds convincing, think about trying to predict the outcome of a coin flip. We can't accurately predict the outcome of a coin flip. Why not? Is it because the outcome of a coin flip does not follow any rules? No, it follows very simple rules: The outcome depends on what side was up when the coin was flipped and how many times the coin turned over. Nevertheless, because we do not know how many times the coin will turn over, we can't know the outcome of a single coin toss. Similarly, most would agree that the weather is determined by specific events. However, because there are so many events and because we do not have data on all events, we can't predict the weather with perfect accuracy.

In short, just because a given behavior in a given situation can't be predicted, we should not conclude that the behavior does not follow rules. The behavior might be perfectly predictable—if we knew the rules and could precisely measure the relevant variables.[3]

Objective Evidence

A second question people raise about psychology's ability to be a science is, "Can psychologists collect objective evidence?" There are two reasons for this concern.

First, some people worry that the psychologists won't be able to keep researcher biases in check. The fear is that the typical researcher will notice information that is consistent with the hypothesis while ignoring information that is inconsistent with the hypothesis; interpret ambiguous evidence as being consistent with the hypothesis; induce participants to behave in a way that fits with the hypothesis; and, if the study still doesn't support the hypothesis, manipulate statistics to prove the hypothesis. If that were true, psychological researchers would "prove" whatever they wanted to prove and research would simply confirm researchers' pet theories and beliefs. Fortunately, psychologists have found ways to keep their biases in check. We can separate "the facts of life from wishful thinking" (Myers, 2002b, p. 28).

---

[3]In physics, for example, researchers working on chaos theory (also known as complexity theory) have shown that simple processes can produce a complex and hard-to-predict pattern of behavior.

Second, some people worry that psychologists won't be able to collect objective evidence about abstract mental concepts because psychologists can't see the mind. Although we can't directly measure abstract concepts such as love, attitudes, aggression, social influence, and memory, we can develop observable operational definitions of these concepts.

In the effort to measure the unobservable objectively, psychology can follow the lead of the older sciences, which have a long history of studying the unseen. Genetics was well advanced before anyone had seen a gene; and nobody has seen gravity, time, temperature, pressure, magnetism, or electrons. Unobservable events or states can be inferred from observable events: Gravity can be inferred from observing objects fall, electrons can be inferred from the tracks in a cloud chamber, and psychological variables such as love can be assessed by observable indicators such as how long a couple gazes into each other's eyes, pupil dilation at the sight of the partner, physiological arousal at the sight of the partner, passing up the opportunity to date attractive others, and responses on a love scale (Rubin, 1970).

According to one historian of science, psychology's reliance on operational definitions has made psychology more objective than physics (Porter, 1997). Another indication that psychologists have succeeded in making unbiased observations is that when psychologists replicate another's study, they are very likely to get the same pattern of results that the original investigator obtained—even when the reason for repeating the study was skepticism of the original study's results. In fact, the results of psychological research are just as likely to replicate as those of physics research (Hedges, 1987; Stanovich, 1990). In short, both logic and evidence suggest that psychological research is objective.

Testable

A third question people have about psychology is, "Can it make testable statements?" If it can't, then it would share the weaknesses of astrology. Fortunately, most published research articles in psychology make testable predictions. Indeed, our journals are full of articles in which predictions made by the investigators were disconfirmed. For example, to his surprise, Charles Kiesler (1982; Kiesler & Sibulkin, 1987) found that many mentally ill individuals are hurt, rather than helped, by being put into mental institutions. In summary, the fact that research frequently disproves researchers' predictions is proof that psychologists make testable statements (and further evidence of psychological research's objectivity).

Skeptical

A fourth question about psychology is, "Can psychologists be as skeptical as other scientists?" Some people worry that psychologists will accept, rather than test, existing beliefs about human behavior. After all, many of these beliefs seem logical and have the weight of either popular or expert opinion behind them. Consequently, some fear that, rather than seeing what the evidence says, psychologists will base their decisions about what is true on logic, popularity, or authority.

Although some therapists have ignored the objective evidence, scientific psychologists have been diligent about testing even the most "obviously true" of ideas. For example, Greenberger and Steinberg (1986) performed a series of studies testing the "obviously true" idea that teenagers who have jobs better understand the value of hard work. They found that—contrary to conventional wisdom—teenagers who work are more cynical about the value of hard work than nonworking teens. Similarly, Shedler and Block (1990) tested the "obviously true" idea that drug use is the cause of psychological problems. Their evidence suggested that conventional wisdom was wrong—heavy drug use was a symptom, rather than a cause, of psychological problems. Likewise, Coles (1993) found that "cocaine babies" were not as troubled as many people originally believed. Thus, "obviously true" ideas are often found to be false when objectively tested.

In addition to questioning conventional wisdom, psychologists question observable evidence. For example, psychologists may question the degree to which mental tests or other measures of behavior truly capture the psychological concepts that those instruments claim to capture. Psychologists are not easily convinced that a set of questions labeled as a "love scale" actually measures love or that an "intelligence test" measures intelligence. Instead, psychologists need evidence documenting that these tests really measure what the tests claim to measure.

Psychologists are skeptical about self-report measures because they realize that people do not always know their own mind (and, as we shall discuss in Chapter 8, even when people do know, they may not tell). Psychologists are skeptical about other measures because psychologists realize that we never have a direct pipeline into a person's mind. We can't see the mind; we can see only behavior. From observing behavior, we may be able to make educated guesses about what is going on in the mind. Unfortunately, we could be wrong. Consequently, we should never assume that we know what a behavior really means. In other words, there is often a gap between the operational definition of a concept and the concept. Therefore, we should always question how well the operational definition really matches the label that the investigator gives it.

Psychologists are also very skeptical about drawing cause–effect conclusions. They realize that it is hard to isolate the one factor that may be causing a certain behavior. Therefore, if they find that better students have personal computers, they do not leap to the conclusion that computers cause academic success. Instead, psychologists would consider at least two alternative explanations. First, psychologists realize that if students were given computers for doing well in school, computers would be the effect—rather than the cause—of academic success. Second, psychologists realize that the computer-owning students may be doing better than other students because the computer-owning students went to better preschools, had better nutrition, or received more parental encouragement. Until these and other explanations are eliminated, psychologists would not assume that computers cause academic success.

Finally, many psychologists are skeptical about the extent to which results from a study can be generalized to the real world. They do not assume that a study done in a particular setting with a particular group of people can be generalized to other kinds of participants in a different setting. For instance, they would not automatically assume that a study originally done with gifted 10-year-olds at a private school would obtain the same results if it were repeated with adult participants studied in the workplace.

To review, psychologists are extremely skeptical. What others see as proof, psychologists may see as circumstantial evidence. Thus, psychologists raise questions when people claim (a) to measure thoughts and feelings, (b) to know the causes of behavior, and (c) to be able to generalize the results of a study beyond the situation or population studied.

Open-Minded

Paralleling the concern that psychologists do not test "obvious facts" is the concern that psychologists are not open to ideas that run counter to common sense. These concerns are groundless. Psychological scientists are skeptical, but not closed-minded. Consequently, psychologists have tested all sorts of counterintuitive ideas, such as the idea that subliminal, backward messages (back-masking) on records can lead teens to Satanism (Custer, 1985); the idea that people can learn in their sleep; and the idea that ESP can be reliably used to send messages (Swets & Bjork, 1990). Although psychologists found no evidence for those particular ideas, psychologists' willingness to test virtually anything has led to tentative acceptance of some novel concepts, such as the idea that acupuncture may be effective in relieving pain and the idea that meditating helps people to live longer (Alexander, Langer, Newman, Chandler, & Davies, 1989).

Creative

Whereas psychologists' open-mindedness has been questioned, few have questioned psychologists' creativity. Most people realize that it takes creativity to come up with ideas for psychological research. Fortunately, with a little help, most people have the creativity to generate research ideas. If you follow the tips on idea generation in Chapter 3, you will be amazed at how creative your ideas can be.

Creativity is needed not only to generate a research idea but also to test it. For example, creativity is needed to develop accurate measures of the concepts the researcher plans to study. Imagine the challenge of developing measures of such concepts as love, intelligence, and helpfulness. Fortunately, to measure key variables, the individual researcher does not always have to rely on his or her own creativity. As you will see in Chapter 5, the researcher can often rely on the creativity of others. After all, why reinvent the wheel when creative psychologists have already developed ways of measuring all kinds of concepts—from practical intelligence (Sternberg, 1986), to level of moral reasoning (Kohlberg, 1981), to need for exciting stimulation (Zuckerman, 1993)?

Even after finding ways of measuring key concepts, researchers may need to use their creativity to develop a situation that will permit them to test their research idea. Like the inventors of the wind tunnel, psychological scientists may need to create a scaled-down model of a real-life situation that is simpler and more controllable than real life, yet still captures the key aspects of the real-life situation. For example, to study real-life competition, social psychologists have developed competitive games for participants to play. Similarly, to model the situation in which nothing you do seems to matter, Seligman (1990) had people try to solve unsolvable puzzles. In conclusion, psychologists have been very creative in their research.

Shares Findings

Psychologists have also been very good at sharing their ideas and findings with others in the field, as shown by the hundreds of journals in which they publish their work. Indeed, psychologists may enjoy more candor and cooperation than scientists in other fields because psychologists usually gain little by keeping results secret. For example, if you wanted to be the first to patent a new technology, it would pay to keep secrets from competitors. In such a race, if you were first, you might make millions. If you were second (like the poor guy who tried to patent the telephone 2 hours after Alexander Graham Bell did), you would make nothing. Although such races for dollars are common in chemistry, they are rare in psychology because psychologists produce few patents.

Productive

Perhaps because of this candor, psychologists have made tremendous progress. As Mynatt and Doherty (1999) point out, "A little over a 100 years ago, we started knowing nothing, but look where we are now! In the last 100 years, a few psychologists have learned more about human behavior than the rest of humanity learned in the previous 1,000 years." One hundred years ago, a person could know everything about every area of psychology. Today, even psychologists cannot know everything about their own area of psychology—and there are so many more areas of psychology than there were. We now have textbooks full of

BOX 1-1	The Inconsistency of Common Sense		
1. Absence makes the heart fonder.	BUT	Absence makes the heart wander.
2. Birds of a feather flock together.	BUT	Opposites attract.
3. Look before you leap.	BUT	He who hesitates is lost.
4. Too many cooks spoil the broth.	BUT	Two heads are better than one.
5. To know you is to love you.	BUT	Familiarity breeds contempt.

research-generated facts in applied areas such as consumer psychology, counseling psychology, political psychology, sports psychology, and organizational psychology. Reading recent research in cognitive, social, and developmental psychology can give you insights into almost any aspect about the human mind—from the unconscious mind to evil to happiness to intuition.

Much recent research has implications for real life. For example, accurate answers to questions like "How do I tell whether the couple I'm counseling will get divorced?" and "How do I tell when a suspect is lying?" have come from the research lab. Because psychological research has been so productive in generating answers to applied questions, professionals in applied areas—such as education, communication, marketing, economics,[4] and medicine—are enthusiastically embracing our research methods.

The Importance of Science to Psychology

The scientific method is responsible for the tremendous progress in psychology and is also largely responsible for psychology's uniqueness. Whereas many other fields—from astrology to philosophy—are concerned with the thoughts and behaviors of individuals, only psychologists study individuals scientifically (Stanovich, 1990). Thus, as Stanovich points out, it is no accident that every definition of psychology starts out "the science of. . . ."

What if psychology were not a science? Psychology would not be useful for helping and understanding people. Without science, psychology might merely be a branch of the popular pseudoscience of astrology (Stanovich, 1990). Without science, psychology might merely be common sense, even though common sense contradicts itself (see Box 1-1). Without science, psychologists might just do what tradition and logic tell us, even when tradition and logic tell us to do things that are actually harmful. For example, until psychological research showed that premature infants benefit from being held and massaged, physicians asserted that both logic and tradition dictated that premature infants should not be held or rubbed (Field, 1993).

Psychology is not the only science that has had to free itself from quackery, tradition, common sense, philosophy, and from the belief that its subject matter follows no rules. Since the beginning of recorded history, some people have argued that finding rules or laws that govern nature is impossible. For centuries, most people believed the stars followed no pattern. Not that long ago, it was believed that diseases followed no patterns. Even today, some people believe that human behavior follows no discernible pattern. Yet, each of these assumptions has been disproven. The stars, the planets, diseases, and humans behave for

---

[4]For an entertaining and elementary introduction to how one economist uses some of our methods, read the best-selling book *Freakonomics* (Levitt & Dubner, 2005).

Table 1-1	Psychology as a Science

CHARACTERISTIC	EXAMPLE
Finds general rules	Helps us understand human behavior through rules such as laws of operant and classical conditioning, laws of memory (meaningless information is hard to remember; memorizing similar information, such as Spanish and Italian, leads to memory errors; spreading out your studying leads to longer retention), lawful reactions to stress (general adaptation syndrome), and a wide range of theories from social learning theory to cognitive dissonance theory.
Collects objective evidence	Tests whether beliefs and theories are consistent with objective evidence. Obtains objective evidence by recording participants' behaviors: number of words written down on memory test, ratings made on an attitude scale, responses on personality test, reaction times, etc. One index of how effective we are at being objective is that our research findings are as replicable as research findings in physics.
Makes verifiable statements	Makes specific testable predictions that are sometimes found to be wrong (rewarding someone for doing a task will always increase their enjoyment of that task). That is, we use evidence to correct wrong beliefs.
Skeptical	Demands evidence for almost any statement. Challenges common sense and traditional notions. Does not take evidence (participants' statements or ratings) at face value. Considers alternative explanations for evidence (group given memory pill may do better than another on memory task because they had naturally better memories, because they were tested later in the day, or because they believed the pill would work).
Open-minded	Entertains virtually any hypothesis, from acupuncture relieving pain to meditation prolonging life.
Creative	Measures psychological concepts, generates hypotheses, and devises studies that rule out alternative explanations for findings.
Public	Allows scientists to check and build on each other's work because research is presented at conferences and published in journals.
Productive	Increases psychological knowledge at a dramatic rate.

reasons that we can understand. Admittedly, the rules determining human behavior may be complex and numerous—and it may even be that some behaviors do not follow rules. However, to this point, searching for rules of behavior has been fruitful (see Table 1-1).

Although science is only one way of knowing, it is our most objective way of knowing, and it can work in concert with a variety of other ways of knowing. Psychologists can use scientific methods to verify knowledge passed down by tradition or from an authoritative expert or to test knowledge obtained by intuition or common sense. By anchoring speculation in reality, psychologists can create, refine, or verify common sense and eliminate superstitions (Kohn, 1988). For example, consider the following 10 findings from research:

1. Punishment is not very effective in changing behavior.
2. Having teens work in low-wage jobs does not instill the "work ethic."
3. Absence makes the heart fonder only for couples who are already very much in love.
4. Pessimistic older people are less likely to get depressed.
5. Money does not buy happiness.

6. If you want to make yourself feel better, do charity work.

7. IQ tests predict life success better than tests of emotional intelligence.

8. Married couples' understanding of each other declines over the course of marriage.

9. Women don't have more empathic ability than men.

10. Nonverbal communication is not very helpful in letting people know what other people are thinking.

All of these findings are refinements of the common sense of a few years ago. All of these findings are, or will soon become, part of the common sense of this century.

In short, science is a powerful tool that can be used to solve human problems. If we have such a tool, why shouldn't psychologists use it—especially when it does not rule out the use of other tools?

Why You Should Understand Research Design

Thus far, we have explained why psychologists are interested in scientific research: they see research as a useful tool to obtain answers to their questions. But why should you know how to use this tool? After all, if you don't need to understand the science of agriculture to enjoy its fruits, why do you need to understand the science of psychology to take advantages of its products?

To Understand Psychology

The classic answer is that you can't really understand psychology—the science of behavior—unless you understand its methods. Without understanding psychology's scientific aspects, you may know some psychological facts and theories, but you will not understand the basis for those facts and theories. It would be like buying a house without inspecting its foundation to ensure that the structure is sound and free of serious faults such as cracks, termite damage, and rot.

Even if you trust that your psychological knowledge is based on a solid foundation, you will have trouble selling that knowledge if you can't explain why your advice is sound. Understanding the foundation on which psychological facts are based allows you to defend psychological facts from those who claim that such "facts" are really baseless opinions.

Beyond increasing your own credibility and that of your field, explaining the basis for psychological facts has practical implications. For example, suppose your organization or community is facing a problem (e.g., increased tensions between two groups). You know certain facts (e.g., increasing intergroup contact alone will not improve relations; the groups must work as equals toward a common goal) that could be applied to the problem. You want others to use these facts to improve the situation—you do not want them to dismiss these facts as "unsupported opinions" or "merely psychological theory." To convince people that your advice is sound, you must understand the foundation supporting those facts—the research process—so well that you can make others understand it.

We have just discussed the scenario in which psychology has the solution to a problem and your task is to sell that solution. But what if psychological science has not yet unearthed any facts that apply to the particular problem? This is often the case because as a young science, psychology does not have as large a knowledge base as some older sciences have. In such a case, it is even more important to understand psychological methods because the most useful thing psychology can offer is not a prepackaged answer to the problem based on established facts, but rather its method of getting answers to problems (Levy-Leboyer, 1988). Often, even when you cannot use psychology's research *findings* to tell you what will work, you can still use psychology's research *methods* to find out what works. Thus, understanding that psychology is both a knowledge base (a technology) and a way of getting knowledge (science) enables you to make better use of psychology.

To Read Research

When research addresses problems that interest you, you will want to take advantage of that research. To do so, you must be able to read and interpret scientific research reports. For instance, you may want to know something about the latest treatment for depression, the causes of shyness, factors that lead to better relationships, or new tips for improving workplace morale. If you need the most up-to-date information, if you want to draw your own conclusions, or if you want to look at everything that is known about a particular problem, you need to be able to read the research yourself.

You can't rely on reading about research in textbooks, magazines, or newspapers. Textbooks will give you only sketchy summaries of the few, often out-of-date studies selected by the textbook's authors. Magazine and newspaper articles, on the other hand, often cover up-to-date research, but these reports often do not accurately represent what happened (Anderson & Bushman, 2002; Brescoll & LaFrance, 2004; Bushman & Anderson, 2001). Knowing research terminology and logic allows you to bypass secondhand accounts of research, thus allowing you to read the original source and come to your own conclusions.

With psychology progressing at a rapid rate, you will need to keep up with the field. As an employee, you will want to make more money every year. How can you justify receiving raises if, with every year, your knowledge is more out-of-date? If you see clients, you should be giving them treatments that work, and you should be acting on the best information available. After all, you would not be pleased to go to a physician whose knowledge about your illness was 10 years out of date.

To Evaluate Research

If you understand research, you will not only be able to get recent, firsthand information, but you will also be in a position to evaluate that information. You may be able to evaluate many secondhand reports of research in magazines and newspapers, too.[5] Thus, you will be able to take full advantage of the knowledge that psychologists are giving away, knowledge that is available to you in libraries, in newspapers, and on television. Your critical abilities will also enable you to judge how much weight you should place on a particular research finding—a useful skill, especially when you encounter two conflicting research findings.

To Protect Yourself From "Quacks"

Perhaps more important than encountering conflicting research findings is the problem of identifying phony experts. Free speech protects quacks, just as the free market protected "snake oil" salespeople in the days before the United States government created the Food

---

[5]If the secondhand reports provide you with enough information about the study's procedures, you can evaluate the study. If they do not, you will have to read the original scientific publication.

and Drug Administration.[6] Back then, patent medicine vendors could sell the public almost anything, even pills that contained tapeworm segments (Park, 2000).

Today, "experts" are free to go on talk shows and the Internet to push "psychological tapeworms." Common psychological tapeworms include unproven and sometimes dangerous tips on how to lose weight, quit smoking, discipline children, and solve relationship problems.

We do not mean that all experts are giving bad advice. We mean that it's hard to tell what is good advice and what is not. Although the truth is out there, so are a lot of lies. Science, nonscience, pseudoscience, and common nonsense exist side by side on the shelves of the psychology section in the bookstore, on talk shows, on the Internet, and on televised newsmagazines. We live in the information age, but we also live in the *mis*information age. As a result, without some training in research design, it is hard to distinguish which "expert" information is helpful and which is potentially harmful.

To Be a Better Psychologist

In psychology, as in many fields, professionals who believe that science applies to their field do their job differently than colleagues who don't. Scientifically oriented detectives use fingerprints and DNA analysis, whereas other detectives rely on psychics and lie detectors. Scientifically oriented physicians treat patients based on what research has established as the most effective cure, whereas other physicians rely on their instincts and on alternative medicines. Scientifically oriented counselors treat patients based on what research has established as the most effective treatment, whereas other counselors sometimes use techniques shown to be ineffective and harmful.

In short, the professionals who rely on science-based treatments that have been shown to be effective, whereas the professionals who do not rely on science are quacks. We do not want you to be a quack.

To Be a Better Thinker

Understanding the scientific approach can improve both your access to psychological knowledge and your thinking. As you will see, Einstein was right when he said, "The whole of science is nothing more than the refinement of everyday thinking." The skills you learn in this course—problem-solving skills, decision-making skills, looking for objective information, and being able to judge and interpret information—are transferable to your everyday life. Consequently, the same scientific thinking skills you will learn in this book are taught in books that purport to raise your practical intelligence (e.g., Lewis & Greene, 1982), are measured by some tests of "practical intelligence" (N. Frederikson, 1986), and are used in real life. Indeed, research suggests that if you want to be able to apply scientific reasoning to everyday life, your best move would be to learn about psychological research methods rather than to learn about other sciences, such as chemistry (Lehman, Lempert, & Nisbett, 1988).

Put another way, people like to be able to separate fact from fiction. They like to believe that they will not accept statements without adequate proof (Beins, 1993; Forer, 1949). However, without understanding science, how can they know what adequate proof is?

---

[6]Although we now do have an FDA, "that agency's 40 analysts can't be counted on to evaluate the accuracy of the more than 30,000 ads and promotions that are made each year" (Schmit, 2005, p. 1A). Furthermore, some treatments (e.g., homeopathic remedies) are exempt from FDA review (Park, 2000).

To Be Scientifically Literate

Another reason to study psychological research methods is to learn how science works. Intelligent people are supposed to be able to profit from experience, and in today's world many of our experiences are shaped by scientific and technological changes. Yet, many people do not know how science works.

Some argue that this scientific illiteracy threatens our democracy—and they have a point. How can we make intelligent decisions about the so-called greenhouse effect if we can't properly interpret the data about global warming? How can juries correctly decide whether to convict an alleged murderer or award damages to people who have allegedly been harmed by a product if the jurors can't understand the scientific evidence (Kosko, 2002)? We would like to rely on experts, but experts may contradict each other. Furthermore, some "experts" may be quacks (Kosko, 2002). Therefore, if we are going to make an informed decision about global warming, address the crime problem or a host of other problems, we need to know how to interpret scientific research.

Regrettably, it appears that many people are scientifically illiterate. Most high school students (and some high-ranking politicians) believe in astrology. Furthermore, many of astrology's skeptics can easily become believers (Glick, Gottesman, & Jolton, 1989). In addition to astrology, other scientifically invalid procedures such as foot reflexology, numerology, and assessing personality via handwriting analysis also enjoy surprising popularity (Lardner, 1994).

Given this low level of scientific literacy, perhaps it is not surprising that hype often seems to carry more weight than objective facts. Politicians, for example, often say, "We don't need to do research on the problem; we know what we need to do," or "I don't care what the research says, I feel. . . ." Similarly, many consumers buy products that include "secret, ancient remedies" rather than products that have been proven to be effective through open, public, scientific testing. Thus, Americans spend billions of dollars each year on treatments and products that have been shown to be ineffective.

Even when people present us with evidence, their evidence could be weak and should be questioned. Leaders take credit for random or cyclical changes in the economy. Advertisers try to convince us that certain products make professional models attractive. Talk-show hosts periodically parade a few people who claim "success" as a result of some dieting or parenting technique. Advertisers still successfully hawk products using testimonials from a few satisfied users, and political leaders "prove" what our country needs by telling us stories about one or two individuals rather than "boring" us with facts (Kincher, 1992). Unfortunately, research shows that, to the naïve, these nonscientific and often misleading techniques are extremely persuasive (Nisbett & Ross, 1980).

Fortunately, after studying psychological research methods, you will know how to question evidence (Lawson, 1999). You will be more skeptical of misleading information and more receptive to scientific information. Consequently, you will be a better-informed citizen and consumer.

To Increase Your Marketability

Besides making you a more informed citizen and consumer, knowing about research makes you more employable. In today's job market, your being hired will probably not depend on what job-relevant information you have memorized. After all, such information is quickly obsolete and is often instantly accessible from a computer database. Instead, you will be hired because you can find, create, and judge information that your company needs. Like most workers in this century, you will probably be a "knowledge engineer," hired for your ability to evaluate and create information. That is, you will be hired for your analytical abilities rather than your knowledge of facts.

For example, even marketing majors are told that, at least for their first few years, their scientific skills, not their marketing intuition, are what will pave the way to future career success (Edwards, 1990). In other words, if you have the analytical skills that enable you to distinguish between good and bad information, and the ability to turn data into useful information, companies want you. These same analytical skills will, of course, also be helpful if you plan to go to graduate school in business, law, medicine, or psychology.

To Do Your Own Research

To increase your chances of getting into graduate school or getting a good job, you can conduct your own research. Completing a research project shows that you are organized, persistent, and capable of getting things done.

You may also need to do research as part of your job. Some of our former students have been surprised that they ended up doing research to get government grants or to get more staff for their social services agencies. Perhaps they should not have been surprised. More and more organizations—from Wal-Mart to museums—are doing research to find out whether what they are doing works (Ralof, 1998). Others do research to find out whether what they are planning to do will work. For example, movie moguls do research to determine whether a movie's ending is effective—and how to change the ending if it is not.

Beyond the employment angle, you may find that doing research is its own reward. Some students like research because it allows them to *do* psychology rather than simply read about it. Some enjoy the teamwork aspect of working with professors or other students. Some enjoy the creativity involved in designing a study, seeing it as similar to writing a script for a play. Some like the acting that is involved in conducting certain kinds of studies (some researchers claim that a valuable research skill is the ability to say "oops" convincingly). Some enjoy the challenges of solving the practical problems that go along with completing any project. Others enjoy the excitement of trying to discover the answers to questions about human behavior. They realize that there are so many interesting and important things about human behavior that we don't know—and that they can find out. Some enjoy the search so much that they even consider psychology research as "me-search" (Field, 1993).

Certainly, many have found the passion for discovery much more exciting than learning terms and definitions. Thus, not surprisingly, such poor-to-average students as John Watson (the father of behaviorism) and Charles Darwin enjoyed exploring the mysteries of human behavior. Once you start trying to answer one of the many unanswered questions about human behavior, we think you will understand what Rogers meant when he said, "We need to sharpen our vision of what is possible . . . to that most fascinating of all enterprises: the unearthing, the discovery, the pursuit of significant new knowledge" (1985, p. 1).

Concluding Remarks

No matter what you do in the future, understanding scientific research will be useful (see Table 1-2). The skills you learn will allow you to refine your critical thinking skills and become a scientifically literate citizen and consumer—almost necessities in our science-dominated world.

Table 1-2	Nine Reasons to Understand Psychological Research Methods

1. To understand psychology better
2. To keep up with recent discoveries by reading research
3. To evaluate research claims
4. To protect yourself from quacks and frauds
5. To be a better psychologist
6. To be a better thinker
7. To be scientifically literate and thus a better-educated citizen and consumer
8. To improve your marketability in our information age
9. To do your own research

Similarly, no matter what you do in the future, you may find it necessary to read and evaluate the merits of specific psychological research findings. If you become a counseling psychologist, you will want to use the best, most up-to-date treatments with your clients. Partly for this reason, licensing exams for counseling psychologists include questions about research design. If you become a manager, you will want to know the most effective management techniques. If you become a parent, you will want to evaluate the relative effectiveness of different child-rearing strategies. To get accurate answers in any of these areas, you will need to understand research. Unless you understand the research process, you may be limited by insufficient, out-of-date, or inaccurate information.

Finally, knowing about research will help you get the tools you need to get answers to your own questions. By reading this book, you will learn how to generate research ideas, manipulate and measure variables, collect data that are both objective and valid, choose the right design for your particular research question, treat participants ethically, interpret your results, and communicate your findings. We hope you will use this knowledge to join the most fascinating quest of our time—exploring the human mind.

SUMMARY

1. Psychologists use the scientific approach to unearth observable, objective evidence that either supports or refutes their preconceived notions.

2. Because scientists make their evidence public, they can check each other's work, as well as build on each other's work. Because of the public, group-oriented nature of science, scientific progress can be rapid.

3. Because scientists make their evidence public, informed people can make use of new discoveries.

4. Science is both open-minded and skeptical. It is skeptical of any idea that is not supported by objective evidence; it is open-minded about any idea that is supported by objective evidence.

5. One goal of science is to find simple, general rules that will make the world more understandable.

6. One reason psychological research is objective is that psychologists use concrete, operational definitions of abstract concepts.

7. Psychologists realize that concrete operational definitions may not capture the invisible concepts the operational definitions are intended to capture. Therefore, psychologists question the labels researchers give to measures and manipulations.

8. Psychologists realize that it is difficult to prove that a certain treatment causes an effect. Often, the alleged "proof" is only circumstantial evidence: other factors may be responsible for the change in behavior. Therefore, psychologists often question cause–effect statements.

9. Psychologists realize that what happens with one group of participants in one setting may not

generalize to another type of participant in a different setting. For example, they realize that a study done with one group of students in a lab setting may not apply to a group of people working in a factory. Therefore, psychologists are appropriately cautious about generalizing the results of a study to real-world situations.

10. There is no psychology without science (Stanovich, 1990). Without science, psychology would have fewer facts than it does now and would be little better than palmistry, astrology, graphology, or any other pseudoscience (Stanovich, 1990). More specifically, using the scientific approach in psychology has allowed psychologists to (a) improve

common sense, (b) disprove certain superstitions, and (c) make enormous progress in understanding how to help people.

11. Science is the best tool we have for obtaining objective and accurate information about the real world. Furthermore, science is a useful tool for testing the accuracy of common sense and intuition.

12. Scientific research is a logical and proven way to obtain important information about human behavior.

13. The skills you learn in this course can help you in the real world.

KEY TERMS

operational definition *(p. 5)*

replicate *(p. 8)*

EXERCISES

1. Give one example of a testable statement and one example of an untestable statement. Is your untestable statement untestable because (a) it is vague (possibly because it lacks operational definitions), (b) it is an after-the-fact explanation, or (c) some other reason? State at least one advantage of scientists making testable statements.

2. Give an example of an operational definition of a concept, such as love. How does your operational definition differ from a dictionary definition of that concept? How do operational definitions help psychology to
   a. be objective?
   b. make testable statements?
   c. be public?
   d. be productive?

3. How does the ability of psychologists to replicate each other's work help psychology to be
   a. skeptical?
   b. open-minded?
   c. productive?

4. Match the following to the qualities of science.

_____ testable	a. learning from mistakes
_____ skeptical	b. "show me the evidence"
_____ open-minded	c. avoid bias
_____ objective	d. publishing studies
_____ public	e. question authority
_____ productive	f. science works

5. List at least two similarities between a scientist and a detective.

6. Physicists can't accurately predict certain simple events. For example, physicists have trouble with such questions as, "If you drop a basketball from a table, how many times will it bounce—and what will be the pattern of those bounces?" Which characteristic of science is threatened by physicists' failure to answer this question? What implications, if any, does this failure have for psychology?

7. Some early psychologists studied and reported on their own thoughts. For example, a person would solve a mathematical problem and then report on everything that went on in his mind during the time that he worked on the problem. What quality of science was missing in these studies?

8. From what you know about astrology, grade it as "pass" or "fail" on the following scientific characteristics:
   a. Makes testable statements
   b. Is productive (knowledge refined, new discoveries made)
   c. Seeks objective, unbiased evidence to determine the accuracy of beliefs

9. According to some, iridology is the "science" of determining people's health by looking at their eyes. Practitioners tend not to publish research, they don't try to verify their diagnoses through other means, and different practitioners will diagnose the same patient very differently. What characteristics of science does iridology have? Where does it fall short?

10. Some claim that psychoanalysis is not a science. They attack it by claiming that it lacks certain characteristics of science. Following are three such attacks. For each attack, name the characteristic of science that psychoanalysis is being accused of failing to achieve.

a. "Psychoanalytic explanations for a person's behavior often fit with the facts but are generally made after the fact."
b. "The unconscious is impossible to observe."
c. "The effectiveness of psychoanalysis does not appear to have improved in the last 20 years."

WEB RESOURCES

1. Go to the Chapter 1 section of the book's student website and:
   a. Look over the concept map of the key terms.
   b. Test yourself on the key terms.
   c. Take the Chapter 1 Practice Quiz.
   d. Do the interactive end-of-chapter exercises.
   e. Download the Chapter 1 tutorial.

2. To learn more about how to market the skills you will develop in this course, read "Web Appendix: Marketing Your Research Design Skills."

3. To learn more about science, read "Web Appendix: Criticisms of Science."

INFOTRAC® COLLEGE EDITION EXPLORATIONS

To see that pseudoscience is not dead, do an InfoTrac College Edition keyword search on "pseudoscience."

Ethics and Validity

Science is not physics, biology, or chemistry . . . but a moral
imperative . . . whose purpose is to give perspective,
balance, and humility to learning.

—*Neil Postman*

Science is a long history of learning how not to fool ourselves.

—*Richard Feynman*

OUTLINE

Overview

Psychologists are excited about using the scientific method to understand and help people. However, whenever a researcher proposes testing a belief against the objective evidence, psychologists immediately ask two questions that may stop the study from being conducted.

First, psychologists ask, "Is it ethical to conduct the study?" Just because a researcher could do a study that would get objective evidence to test a prediction, doesn't mean the researcher *should* do that study. As you will see, ethics and morals affect what researchers do.

Second, even if the study would obtain objective evidence, psychologists ask, "Would that evidence be valid?" Just because the evidence is objective doesn't mean it provides an accurate answer to the research question.

In this chapter, you will learn how psychologists ask and answer these two questions. Specifically, you will learn (a) the ethical and validity problems that psychologists encounter when they try to apply traditional scientific techniques to the study of behavior and (b) some common strategies for dealing with those problems.

Questions About Applying Techniques From Older Sciences to Psychology

Although psychologists are excited about using a tool—the scientific method—that has been so successful in the older sciences, psychologists know that studying human and animal behavior is different from studying objects. To appreciate how sensitive psychologists are to the unique challenges and responsibilities involved in studying the behavior of living things, let's see how a psychologist would react if someone ignored those challenges and responsibilities. For instance, suppose that a novice investigator tried to model his psychological research after the following chemistry experiment:

> A chemist fills two test tubes with hydrogen and oxygen molecules. She leaves the first test tube alone. She heats the second over a flame. She observes that water forms only in the second test tube. She then comes to three conclusions. First, because there was only one difference between the two test tubes (the flame), she concludes that the flame caused the group of molecules in the second test tube to behave differently from the molecules in the first tube. Second, because she knows the flame was a pure manipulation of heat and because she knows that water's presence is a valid indicator that there was a reaction, she concludes that heat causes hydrogen and oxygen to react. Third, because she knows that oxygen molecules are all alike, hydrogen molecules are all alike, and that molecules do not change over time, she concludes that heat always causes hydrogen and oxygen to combine.

The novice investigator then conducts the following study:

> A novice investigator fills two rooms with people. He leaves the group in the first room alone. He heats up the second room. He "observes" that the second group behaves more aggressively than the first. He then concludes that "feeling hot" always makes people more "aggressive."

Because of the vast differences between humans and molecules, an experienced research psychologist would have four sets of questions about the novice investigator's study. The first three sets (summarized in Table 2-1) deal with the validity of the novice investigator's conclusions. First, did the treatment manipulation really *cause* one group to behave differently from the other? Second, did the investigator really manipulate and measure the two

Table 2-1	Common Threats to the Three Kinds of Validity		
TYPES OF VALIDITY	**MAJOR SOURCES OF PROBLEMS**	**MISTAKES TO AVOID**	**EXAMPLES OF PROBLEMS IN REAL LIFE**
Internal: Determining *cause–effect* relationship between manipulation and behavior *in* a given study; establishing that a certain observable event caused (was responsible for, influenced) a change in behavior.	Allowing factors other than the manipulation to vary. For example, if the treatment and the no-treatment group differ before the study begins, we can't conclusively establish that the treatment caused the difference in the groups' behavior.	Failing to ask the question, "Isn't there something other than the treatment that could cause the difference in behavior?"	Misidentifying the causes of a problem. Giving a new president credit or blame for changes in the economy, blaming a new dentist for your existing dental problems, claiming that a parent's child-rearing methods are responsible for the child's autism.
Construct: Accurately naming our measures and manipulations; making accurate inferences about both (a) what our participants' behaviors mean and (b) what psychological states our manipulations produce.	Faulty measures, resulting in mislabeling or misinterpreting behavior. Poor manipulations can also harm construct validity, as can participants figuring out and playing along with (or against) the hypothesis.	Accepting at face value that a test measures what its title claims it does. Anybody can type up some questions and call it an intelligence test—but that doesn't mean the test really measures intelligence.	Mislabeling a behavior. Thinking that a shy person is a snob, believing that what people *say* they think and feel is exactly what they think and feel, having complete confidence in lie detectors, "knowing" that a cat loves you because it sits in your chair after you get up.
External: Generalizing the study's results *outside* the study to other situations and participants.	Artificial situations, testing an unusual group of participants, and a small number of participants.	Believing that any survey, regardless of how small or biased, has external validity.	Stereotyping. For example, based on a limited sample, concluding that "They are all like that; seen one, seen them all."

psychological variables (feeling hot and being aggressive) that he claimed he did? Third, would the results *generalize* to other settings and participants? The fourth set of concerns is the most serious: Was it ethical to perform the study?

Internal Validity Questions: Did the Treatment Cause a Change in Behavior?

The first set of questions deals with the study's **internal validity:** the degree to which the study demonstrates that the treatment *caused* a change in behavior. If the study establishes that putting the participants into different rooms *caused* the one group to behave differently from the other group, the study has internal validity. If something else could be causing the groups to differ, the study does not have internal validity.

For the chemist, establishing internal validity is simple: If the flame condition yields water and the no-flame condition does not, the chemist knows that the flame manipulation caused the water to form. No other differences between the test tubes could have caused water to form in one tube but not the other.

Because oxygen molecules are pretty much all alike in terms of basic physical properties, the chemist does not have to worry that the oxygen molecules in the tube she heated were naturally more likely to combine with hydrogen than were the molecules in the other tube. Because oxygen molecules are stable in terms of their physical properties, the chemist does not have to worry that she put the flame to the oxygen molecules at a time of day when the molecules were in the mood to combine. Because the oxygen molecules can be isolated from other events by putting them in a test tube, she does not have to worry that something in the environment other than the heat—a noise, another chemical, or some other event—was responsible for the oxygen combining with hydrogen. In short, isolating the cause of a difference in molecular behavior is easy.

Isolating the cause of a difference in human behavior, on the other hand, is not easy. Thus, in the novice investigator's study, the experienced investigator would wonder whether the groups acted differently for reasons having nothing to do with the treatment manipulation. Specifically, she would have at least three questions.

First, instead of the treatment causing the groups to differ, could it be that the people assigned to the hot room group were naturally more hotheaded and aggressive than the people assigned to the other room? Before concluding that the hot room made the groups behave differently, the experienced investigator would need to know what steps the novice investigator had taken to rule out that the difference in the groups' behavior was not due to personality differences between the groups. The experienced investigator would hope that the novice investigator had used a specific type of study that psychologists refer to as an **experiment:** a study that allows researchers to disentangle treatment effects from natural differences between groups, usually by randomly assigning participants to treatment group. In this case, the experienced investigator would probably hope that (a) the novice investigator had used several hot room groups and several normal room groups and that (b) the novice investigator had used some random process (similar to flipping a coin) to determine whether a person was put in the hot room or the normal room.

Second, could it be that the groups behaved differently because the groups were tested at different times of day? For example, the experienced researcher would be worried if the normal room group had been tested in the morning and the hot room group was tested at night because (a) people tested at night may have had additional experiences, such as hearing the nightly news, watching a violent show, having a long day at work, or having some after-work drinks, that the group tested in the morning did not have, and (b) crime statistics suggest that people are more aggressive at night. Thus, the experienced investigator would hope that the novice investigator had controlled for time of testing by either testing all the participants at the same time or by making sure that there were no systematic differences between when the participants were tested.

A researcher could make sure there were no systematic differences between groups in time of testing by using several groups and then either (a) randomly determining, for each group, what time each group would be tested or (b) balancing out the time of testing by systematically trading off when the groups are tested (e.g., warm room participants are tested at 9:00 and 11:00 on Monday and 10:00 and 12:00 on Tuesday, whereas the normal room participants are tested at 10:00 and 12:00 on Monday, and 9:00 and 11:00 on Tuesday).

Third, could the groups have behaved differently because some event outside the lab, such as the voices of a few people cursing loudly in the hallway, penetrated the hot room, but not the normal room, during testing? For example, if the hot room group, but not the normal room group, is exposed to a jackhammer making noise outside or a thunderstorm starting, that event may cause the hot room group to behave more aggressively than the other group.

In summary, although the novice investigator *assumed* his study had internal validity (that it showed the treatment manipulation had an effect), the novice investigator failed to establish internal validity. To establish internal validity, the novice investigator would have had to show not only that the treatment group behaved differently than the no-treatment group but also that the treatment manipulation—rather than something else—was responsible for the difference in behavior. It is hard to establish internal validity because it is hard to rule out the possibility that the groups differ due to some factor other than the treatment. For example, even if the groups had the same personalities and the same experiences before the groups entered their rooms, the groups may still be exposed to different nontreatment events (such as the rumbles, light flashes, and negative ions of a thunderstorm) while in their rooms. Because establishing internal validity is so difficult, the experienced investigator is skeptical whenever people claim to establish that a treatment causes, increases, decreases, affects, influences, produces, brings about, triggers, or makes a change in a behavior.

Construct Validity Questions: Are the Variable Names Accurate?

As we have seen, the novice investigator naively assumed that the room manipulation caused the two groups of participants to behave differently. That is, he went from (a) *observing* that the participants in the room where he turned up the thermostat behaved differently from those in the other room to (b) *inferring* that "turning up the thermostat *caused* the two groups to behave differently." However, that was not the only questionable inference he made.

The novice investigator also went from (a) *observing* that the participants in the room where he turned up the thermostat behaved differently from those in the other room to (b) *inferring* that "participants who *felt hot* were more *aggressive*." In making the leap from observable events to talking about the world inside participants' heads, the novice investigator presumed that his manipulation made hot room participants feel hot and that he accurately measured aggression. In other words, the novice investigator assumed that he accurately manipulated and measured psychological **constructs**: characteristics of individuals that can't be directly observed, such as mental states (e.g., love, hunger, feeling hot), traits (e.g., agreeableness), abilities (e.g., intelligence), and intentions (e.g., aggression: the intent to harm another).

The novice investigator might wonder why others are challenging the names he gave his variables given that most scientists go beyond talking about the procedures they use. After all, a chemist's conclusions deal not with the actions the chemist performed but with the underlying variables that the chemist manipulated. For example, the chemist's conclusions would deal not with the effects of the chemist putting a test tube over a lit Bunsen burner but rather with the effects of the underlying variable—heat.

The experienced researcher would agree that the chemist, like most scientists, makes inferences. However, the experienced researcher would point out that it is not much of a leap to go from seeing a chemist put a test tube over a lit Bunsen burner to saying that the chemist is manipulating the heat of molecules in that test tube. The flame definitely heated the molecules, and it is unlikely that the burner has any other effects: The molecules do not notice the flame's color, do not hear the gas coming into the burner, and do not smell the gas. People, on the other hand, may not feel hot just because the novice investigator turned up the thermostat. People may notice that a room heater has done more than heat the room. For example, the noise or the odor coming from the heater may annoy people. Thus, manipulating the temperature of molecules is simpler than the "mind control" involved in

Figure 2-1	The Problem With Constructs

Because constructs can't be observed, knowing what participants do is not the same as knowing what they are thinking.

manipulating how people feel. Likewise, measuring the amount of water produced by a reaction is simpler than the "mind reading" needed to measure aggression.

If you are not careful, going from objective, observable, physical events to inferring invisible, subjective, psychological constructs may involve jumping to conclusions (see Figure 2-1). For instance, some people are quick to infer that a person who works slowly is unintelligent when the truth may be that the individual is cautious, ill, lazy, or unfamiliar with the task.

Psychologists are extremely cautious about inferring private mental states from publicly observable behavior. Therefore, the research psychologist would question the temperature study's **construct validity:** the degree to which the study measures and manipulates the underlying psychological elements that the researcher claims to be measuring and manipulating (see Figure 2-2). In this case, the research psychologist would look for at least three potential cracks in the study's construct validity:

1. The manipulation was poor, so the construct "feeling hot" was not manipulated adequately.
2. The measure was poor, so the construct "aggression" was not measured accurately.
3. Participants figured out what the hypothesis was and played along, so the high scores on the aggression measure were due to lying or acting rather than to feeling aggressive.

Construct Validity Problems Caused by the Manipulation: What Does the Treatment Really Manipulate?

The experienced researcher might start questioning the construct validity of the novice investigator's study by questioning the temperature manipulation's construct validity. She would ask herself, "Is it right to call this 'raising-the-thermostat' manipulation a 'feeling-hot' manipulation?"

Figure 2-2   **Linking the Invisible to the Visible: The Challenge of Construct Validity**

Constructs:
Unobservable, psychological, abstract variables such as love

Operational definitions:
Observable, physical, concrete measures and manipulations such as:

How much do you love your spouse?

1   2   3   4   5
not at all   very much

To begin answering that question, she would ask two other questions. First, "Did the manipulation make the warm group really feel hot?" Second, "Did the manipulation have any effect besides making the warm group feel hot?"

The answer to the first question is not as simple as you might think. You can't directly get inside participants' minds (a) to change how they feel and (b) to see whether you made a change. Instead, the only possible way for any researcher to manipulate participants' mental states is indirectly—by changing the physical environment. For any indirect manipulation to work, participants must mentally react to the manipulation in the way the researcher expects. Unfortunately, participants may interpret the manipulation differently from the way the researcher intended. Thus, putting one group of participants in a room that is, at the physical level, 10 degrees hotter than another is not the same as making one group, at the psychological level, feel hot. For example, participants may take off jackets and sweaters to cool off, they may find the room's temperature "comfortable," or they might not even notice the difference in temperature.

If the researcher decides that the manipulation does indeed make participants feel hot, she still has to answer the question, "Did the manipulation do anything besides make the warm group feel hotter than the other group?" Usually, manipulations are not so pure that their only effect is to change the one thing you intended to change. Instead, manipulations often contain extra ingredients that produce unwanted side effects. As we will see, these impurities can be physical or psychological.

The research psychologist might start her search for the manipulation's impurities at the physical level. She would ask, "What did turning up the thermostat do to the participants' environment besides make the room hotter?" She may find that turning up the thermostat also made the room noisier (because the heater was noisy) and decreased the room's air quality (because the heater's filter was dirty). If turning up the thermostat is a temperature manipulation, a noise manipulation, and an air-quality manipulation, how can the novice investigator justify labeling it as a "warmth" manipulation? It would be more accurate to call it a "temperature, noise, and air-quality" manipulation.

Even if the manipulation is pure at the physical level, it may not be pure at the psychological level. The novice investigator may have made the participants feel frustrated about being unable to open the windows to cool off the room, or he may have made participants feel angry with him for putting them in such an uncomfortable room. Therefore, in addition to being a manipulation of feeling hot, the treatment may have had the additional side effect of making people frustrated or angry. So, how can the novice investigator justify calling the room manipulation a warmth manipulation when it may actually be a frustration manipulation or an anger manipulation?

As you have seen, it is difficult to manipulate variables. Even seemingly straightforward manipulations may not be what they seem. For example, suppose that an "aspirin" manipulation involves giving aspirins to one group, but not to the other. On the surface, the "aspirin" label would seem to describe the manipulation accurately. However, many aspirin tablets also contain caffeine. Therefore, rather than being a pure manipulation of aspirin, the manipulation may be an "aspirin and caffeine" manipulation. What if getting the aspirin makes participants expect to feel better? Then, the manipulation is an "aspirin and positive expectations" manipulation.

In conclusion, you should always question the name that a researcher decides to attach to a manipulation. Because of the difficulties of manipulating what one wants to manipulate, the novice investigator should not expect skeptical scientists to take it on faith that he is manipulating the invisible mental state that he claims to be manipulating.

Construct Validity Problems Caused by the Measure: What Does the Measure Really Measure?

Even if the manipulation of "feeling hot" is valid, the measure of aggression may not be. Psychological constructs such as aggression are abstract, invisible, and therefore impossible to measure directly. Because we cannot see directly into participants' minds, the best we can do is to set up situations in which what they are thinking will be reflected in their behavior. Unfortunately, participants' behaviors may be mislabeled. For example, the novice investigator may have misinterpreted "kidding around" and attention-getting behaviors as aggression. Or, the novice investigator may have misinterpreted physiological reactions to being hot (sweating, flushed face) as signs of nonverbal aggression. Or, the novice investigator may have labeled assertive behavior as aggressive. Or, scores on the novice investigator's multiple-choice test of aggression may not have any relationship to aggression. In short, it is reckless to assume that a measure will perfectly capture the construct that the researcher is trying to measure.

Construct Validity Problems Caused by Participants: Is Their Behavior Genuine or an Act?

Even if the novice investigator had used a good manipulation and a good measure, the results may be misleading because participants may mask their feelings, especially if participants know they are in a research project. In the novice investigator's study, warm room participants may realize that they have been (a) deliberately placed in an abnormally warm room and then (b) given an opportunity to express aggression. In other words, they may figure out that the investigator wants them to be aggressive. If they like the investigator, they may mask their true feelings by acting aggressively just to try to help him.

Review: Comparing Internal Validity and Construct Validity

In conclusion, our novice investigator wants both internal and construct validity. If he can show both internal and construct validity, he can conclude that feeling hot causes aggression.

If his study had internal validity, but not construct validity, he couldn't legitimately make statements about constructs such as aggression. Therefore, the only thing he could safely conclude would be that his manipulation caused a change in participants' behavior. For example, he might be limited to concluding, "Turning up the thermostat caused a difference in how participants filled in circles on a multiple-choice answer sheet."

If, on the other hand, his study had construct validity, but not internal validity, he couldn't legitimately make cause–effect statements. He could conclude only that "the group that felt hot was more aggressive." He could not conclude that warmth caused aggression because it might be that individuals in the warm room group had more aggressive personalities than the people in the other group.

External Validity Questions: Can the Results Be Generalized?

Even if the novice investigator actually manipulated feeling warm and accurately measured aggression (construct validity) and established that differences between the two groups in this particular study were caused by the room manipulation (internal validity), the experienced researcher would still question the study's **external validity:** the degree to which the results could be generalized to different participants, settings, and times (see Figure 2-3). There are at least two reasons to question the aggression study's external validity.

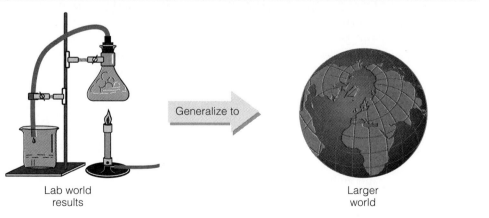

Figure 2-3   **External Validity**

Generalize to

Lab world
results

Larger
world

| Figure 2-4 | **Studying a Small, Unusual Sample Might Harm a Study's External Validity** |

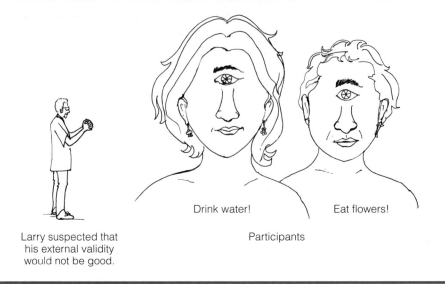

Drink water!   Eat flowers!

Larry suspected that   Participants
his external validity
would not be good.

Can the Results Be Generalized to Other Participants?

First, because people differ, a result that occurs with one group of people might not occur with a different group of people (see Figure 2-4). The novice investigator might have obtained different results had he studied Russian sixth graders instead of Midwestern college students; if he had studied people used to working in very warm conditions; or if he had studied less-aggressive individuals. To maximize external validity, the novice investigator should have tested a large, random sample of participants.

Can the Results Be Generalized to Other Settings?

Second, because people's behavior may change depending on the situation, the results might not hold in another setting.[1] For instance, suppose the novice investigator used a sterile laboratory setting to eliminate the effects of nontreatment factors. By isolating the treatment factor, the novice investigator may have succeeded in establishing internal validity. However, results obtained under such controlled situations may not generalize to more complex situations, such as the workplace or the home, where other factors, such as frustration and pressure, come into play. Thus, the investigator may have achieved internal validity at the expense of external validity.

In short, even if temperature did increase aggression in this particular lab, with this particular group of participants, at this particular time, the experienced researcher would not automatically assume that temperature would have the same effect in future studies conducted with different participants in different settings. Therefore, to maximize external validity, the experienced researcher might repeat the study using different types of participants and different situations.

[1]Researchers may use the terms "ecological validity" or "mundane realism" to refer to the degree to which a study's setting resembles a real-life setting.

Ethical Questions: Should the Study Be Conducted?

Before repeating the study—indeed, before performing it in the first place—the investigator would have to determine whether conducting the study was **ethical:** consistent with the American Psychological Association's principles of right and wrong. If the study could not be conducted ethically, it should not be done (see Figure 2-5).

In deciding whether the study was ethical, the researcher would consult the American Psychological Association's *Ethical Principles of Psychologists and Code of Conduct* (American Psychological Association [APA], 2002), often referred to as the *Principles.* A copy of the ethical guidelines from the *Principles* relating to research is included in Appendix C. In addition to the *Principles,* the researcher might also consult the American Psychological Association's *Ethical Principles in the Conduct of Research With Human Participants* (APA, 1982). By consulting both sources, the researcher should be able to make an informed decision about whether the participants' rights had been protected and whether the novice investigator had lived up to his responsibilities.

Has Potential Harm Been Minimized?

As the *Principles* point out, participants have the right to **informed consent:** to understand what will happen in the study and then agree to participate. Thus, according to the *Principles,* the novice investigator should have told participants that the study would involve sitting in a room that might be warm with a group of people for 30 minutes while filling out a questionnaire about their feelings toward the other participants. Knowing what the study was about, participants should have freely volunteered to be in the study and signed an

---

Figure 2-5   **The Decision to Do a Study Should Be Based on More Than Scientific Validity**

Not all studies should be performed. Note that the ethical consequences of a study are sometimes hard to predict.

informed consent form. That consent form, in addition to describing what the study was about and what the participant would do, should

1. explain the potential benefits of the research
2. explain any risks to the participant
3. describe what the researcher will do to protect the participant's privacy
4. explain that participation is voluntary
5. describe any compensation the participant will receive
6. explain that the participant will receive that compensation even if the participant withdraws from the study
7. make it clear to participants that they can quit the study at any point

(To learn more about informed consent and to see a sample consent form, see Appendix C.)

In addition to having the right to refuse to be in the study, participants have the right to confidentiality. Therefore, the novice investigator should have taken extensive precautions to ensure that no one other than the investigator found out how each participant behaved during the study. Common precautions include (a) using code numbers (e.g., "Participant 1's response")—rather than participants' actual names—when recording participants' responses, (b) storing data in a locked file cabinet, (c) password-protecting any data files stored on a computer, and (d) signing a pledge to keep all information about participants confidential.

The *Principles* not only address participant rights but also stress investigator responsibilities (see Table 2-2). According to the *Principles*, the investigator's responsibilities begin

---

Table 2-2   **Selected Ethical Guidelines for Studies Involving Human Participants**

1. Participants should volunteer to be in the study. They need to feel that they can refuse to be in the study. Consequently, bribing people by offering excessive rewards (including awarding extra credit points that a student could not earn by doing an alternative activity) for participation is forbidden.

2. Participants should have a general idea of what will happen to them if they choose to be in the study. In addition, they should be well-informed about anything that they might perceive as unpleasant. That is, they should know about anything that might cause them to decide not to participate. For example, they should be told about the number and length of sessions, and about any foreseeable risks.

3. Participants should be told that they can quit the study at any point and they should be encouraged to quit the study if, at any point, they find the study upsetting.

4. Investigators should keep each individual participant's responses confidential.

5. Investigators should make sure all people working for them behave ethically.

6. Investigators should try to anticipate all possible risks to participants and take steps to prevent these potential problems from occurring.

7. At the end of the study, investigators should probe participants for signs of harm and take steps to undo any harm detected.

8. At the end of the study, investigators should explain the purpose of the study and answer any questions participants may have.

9. Researchers should get approval from appropriate committees (for research with human participants, probably the school's internal review board [IRB], for research with nonhuman animals, probably the school's internal animal care and use committee [IACUC]).

well before the study begins. As part of the planning phase, the investigator should try to anticipate all possible risks to participants and then protect participants from these risks. In this study, the investigator should consult with physicians to be sure that the temperature was not too hot and to identify people who might have a bad physiological reaction to the heat. In addition, the investigator would have to determine how to ensure that the aggression induced by the heat would not get out of hand, leading to someone being harmed either physically or psychologically.

While the study is being conducted, the investigator is responsible for behaving in an ethical manner. Furthermore, under some circumstances, the investigator may also be responsible for ensuring that others behave ethically. For example, if the people working with or for the novice investigator on the aggression study had behaved unethically, the novice investigator would have been responsible for their behavior even if he was unaware of what the others were doing.

After each participant has finished taking part in the study, the investigator should **debrief** participants: explain the purpose of the study, answer any questions, address any concerns, and undo any harm that the participant may have experienced. During debriefing, the investigator should actively look for signs of harm because (a) some events that do not bother most people may be traumatic to some participants and (b) some participants may be reluctant to tell the investigator about that harm. If harm is detected, the researcher should try to undo it.

Fortunately, most studies do not harm participants. Thus, the main function of debriefing is usually to explain the study to participants. Educating participants about the study is the least an investigator can do to give something back to those who volunteered to be in the study.

Unfortunately, you can't determine that the novice investigator's study was ethical merely by observing that the novice investigator followed a few simple guidelines. Instead, as the introduction to *Ethical Principles in the Conduct of Research With Human Participants* (APA, 1982) states, "the decision to undertake research rests upon a considered judgment by the individual psychologist about *how to best contribute to psychological science and human welfare* [italics added]."

This statement has two important implications. First, it means that even if the novice investigator fulfilled all his responsibilities to the participants, the study might still be unethical if the study was unlikely to contribute to psychological science and human welfare. Second, it means that even if the novice investigator violated certain participant rights (such as not telling participants what the study is trying to find out), the study might still be ethical if the expected benefits of the study would compensate for those violations. Consequently, an important step in determining whether a study is ethical is determining the likelihood that the study will benefit humanity.

Have Potential Benefits Been Maximized?

The experienced researcher would begin to determine the likelihood that the study would benefit humanity by determining the importance of the research question. Unfortunately, determining the value of the research question is highly subjective. One person may find the idea very important, whereas another may find it unimportant. In the aggression study, the novice investigator may believe that determining the relationship between temperature and aggression is extremely valuable, arguing that it might lead to ways of preventing riots. Others, however, may disagree.

To further complicate the problem of assessing the potential value of a piece of research, no one knows what the researcher will discover. A study that looks promising may discover nothing. On the other hand, many scientific studies designed to answer one question have ended up answering a very important but unrelated question (Burke, 1978; Coile &

Miller, 1984). For example, Pavlov set out to discover the role of saliva in digestion, yet ended up discovering classical conditioning. Because it is so hard to judge the value of a research question, the researcher would probably acknowledge that the novice investigator's research question has some merit.

As you have seen, judging the importance of a research question is difficult. Therefore, to estimate the potential value of the novice investigator's study, the research psychologist would put less emphasis on her subjective impression of the importance of the research question and put more emphasis on the more objective judgment of how well the study would answer the research question. That is, she would ask, "Is the study likely to provide valid data?"

By "valid data," she would not necessarily mean that the study must have all three types of validity (i.e., construct, internal, and external). Indeed, few studies even attempt to have all three validities. Rather, her focus would be on determining whether the study has the validity or validities necessary to answer the research question. To illustrate that different research goals require different validities, let's look at three examples.

First, suppose that an investigator wants to describe what most people do in a given situation. In that case, the investigator is not interested in the causes of behavior and therefore would not strive for internal validity. However, because the investigator is interested in generalizing the results to most people, the investigator would strive for external validity.

Second, suppose that a researcher is trying to develop a test of social intelligence. If the researcher's only goal is to show that the test accurately measures the construct of social intelligence, the researcher needs only construct validity.

Third, suppose that an investigator is trying to explain or control behavior. In that case, the investigator needs to discover the causes of a behavior and therefore would need internal validity.

After the research psychologist evaluated the extent to which (a) the research question was important and (b) the study would provide a valid answer to that question, the research psychologist would be able to estimate the study's potential benefits. Then, the research psychologist would probably suggest changes that would either maximize the study's potential for benefiting humankind or minimize the study's potential for harming participants. If, after those changes were made, the researcher was satisfied that (a) the research's benefits outweighed the risks and (b) the planned precautions would minimize risks, then the researcher would conclude that conducting the study was ethical.

Has Permission to Conduct the Research Been Obtained?

Even if the researcher believed that the study was ethical, the researcher would not necessarily grant the novice investigator permission to conduct the study. Indeed, even if the researcher wanted to conduct the study herself, she would not just go out and do it. Instead, she—like most researchers—would consult with others before doing the research.

Consulting with others is vital for at least two reasons. First, when weighing the benefits of one's own research against the costs to participants, it is hard to be fair and impartial. Second, consulting with others may lead to insights about how to protect participants from harm.

Because consulting with others is so important, some researchers will not do a research study until their department's ethics committee has approved the study. At most schools, before conducting a study with human participants, researchers must obtain permission from the school's **internal review board (IRB):** a committee of at least five members—one of whom must be a nonscientist—that review proposed research and monitor approved research in an effort to protect research participants. As you can see from Figure 2-6, the IRB, when deciding whether to approve research, weighs the potential benefits of the research against the potential risks to participants. In addition to assessing the risks and

IRB Process

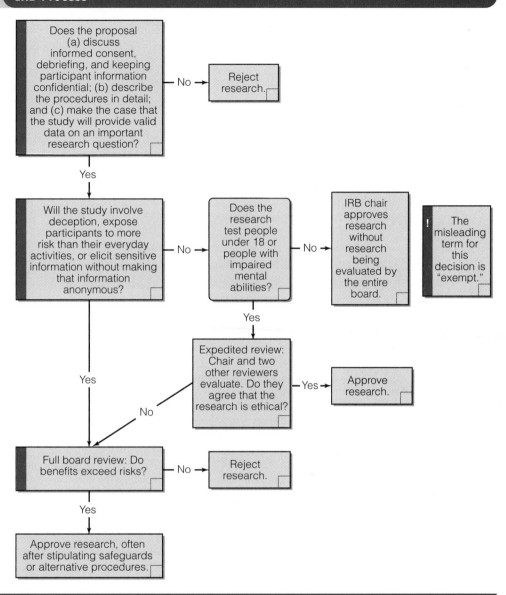

benefits of the research, the IRB might require additional steps to protect the participants. These steps might include having the investigator

1. make the informed consent form more specific and easier to understand

2. exclude individuals whose ability to give informed consent could be questioned, such as people under 18 or people with mental disabilities

3. exclude individuals who may be more at risk for negative reactions to the treatment, such as pregnant women

4. eliminate rewards for participation (e.g., extra credit) that might make participants feel obligated to be in the study

5. use alternative procedures that would involve less distress or deception

6. produce a detailed plan for dealing with participants who are upset or harmed by the study

7. take additional steps to protect the participants' privacy

If your school has an IRB, it is a violation of federal law to do research without first submitting that research to the IRB. In any event, a novice investigator should always get approval from a higher authority before conducting a study. *Never conduct a study without first obtaining approval from your professor!*

As you have seen, the psychological researcher's most important concerns about the novice investigator's aggression study are ethical concerns. Indeed, because ethical concerns include concerns about validity and human betterment, one could argue that ethical concerns are the researcher's only concerns (see Table 2-3).

Table 2-3	**Determining Whether a Research Study Is Ethical**

Does It Maximize the Potential Benefits to Psychological Science and Human Welfare?

1. Is the research question important?

2. Will the research study provide valid answers to the research question? The type of validity needed will depend on the research question.
   - If the research question concerns finding out whether a certain factor causes a change in behavior (e.g., "Does a certain type of school environment increase student attendance?"), the study should have internal validity. That is, the study should take steps to rule out the possibility that other factors may be responsible for the effect.
   - If answering the research question hinges on accurately measuring abstract psychological concepts, construct validity would be important. That is, the researchers should be able to make a strong case that the psychological variables they are talking about are the variables they actually measured. Construct validity would be the main concern in a research study that was trying to develop a psychological test.
   - If the main purpose of the research is to provide results that can be generalized to the real world, external validity would be important. In such a case, the researchers would want to show that their participants did not represent a limited sample of people. External validity is important for polls because polls try to determine how most people would respond to certain questions.

Does It Minimize the Potential for Harm to Participants?

1. Does it conform to the ethical principles of the American Psychological Association?
   - Are participants volunteers?
   - Did they know what the study involved before they agreed to participate?
   - Were participants told they could quit the study at any point?
   - Were participants debriefed?

2. If participants will be subjected to stress,
   - have less-stressful alternatives been considered?
   - has the amount of stress been minimized?
   - have procedures for helping distressed participants been established?

Table 2-4	Humane Care and Use of Animals in Research

The ethical standards that follow are considered enforceable rules of conduct. Violating these rules may result in being expelled from the American Psychological Association and being both sued and arrested.

8.09 Humane Care and Use of Animals in Research

a. Psychologists acquire, care for, use, and dispose of animals in compliance with current federal, state, and local laws and regulations, and with professional standards.

b. Psychologists trained in research methods and experienced in the care of laboratory animals supervise all procedures involving animals and are responsible for ensuring appropriate consideration of their comfort, health, and humane treatment.

c. Psychologists ensure that all individuals under their supervision who are using animals have received instruction in research methods and in the care, maintenance, and handling of the species being used, to the extent appropriate to their role.

d. Psychologists make reasonable efforts to minimize the discomfort, infection, illness, and pain of animal subjects.

e. Psychologists use a procedure subjecting animals to pain, stress, or privation only when an alternative procedure is unavailable and the goal is justified by its prospective scientific, educational, or applied value.

f. Psychologists perform surgical procedures under appropriate anesthesia and follow techniques to avoid infection and minimize pain during and after surgery.

g. When it is appropriate that an animal's life be terminated, psychologists proceed rapidly, with an effort to minimize pain and in accordance with accepted procedures.

Source: From *Ethical Principles of Psychologists and Code of Conduct* (2002). *American Psychologist, 57*, 1060–1073. Reprinted with the kind permission of the American Psychological Association.

But what if the novice investigator's study had used animals instead of human participants? In that case, some might think that the psychologist would not have been concerned about ethics. As you can see from Table 2-4, nothing could be further from the truth. Indeed, in recent years, animal rights have received more attention from the American Psychological Association than human rights. If the aggression study had used animals as participants, the researcher would have consulted the ethical standards listed in Table 2-4 (APA, 2002) as well as APA's 1996 booklet *Ethical Principles for the Care and Use of Animals*, a copy of which is included in Appendix C. In addition, the researcher would probably need to have the research approved by the school's internal animal care and use committee (IACUC). If the study had been done unethically, the investigator would be severely punished.

Concluding Remarks

You have seen that research psychologists are aware of the responsibilities and challenges of studying human and animal behavior. What you have not seen is the wide range of methods psychologists use to meet these challenges and responsibilities. Depending on ethical considerations, the type of validity the researcher is after, and the research problem, investigators may use a single participant or thousands of participants; human participants or animal participants; laboratory studies or field studies; experiments or surveys.

SUMMARY

1. Psychologists realize that measures and manipulations of invisible mental constructs may be flawed. Therefore, psychologists question the labels that researchers give to their measures and manipulations.

2. If investigators are studying the psychological and mental states they claim to be studying, their research has construct validity.

3. Two common threats to construct validity are poor measures of variables and poor manipulations. A third common threat to construct validity is participants figuring out the purpose of the research and acting how they think the researcher wants them to act. That is, participants may play a role rather than share their honest reactions.

4. Psychologists realize that it is hard to prove that a certain treatment causes an effect. Often, the so-called proof is only circumstantial evidence because factors other than the treatment may be responsible for the change in behavior. Therefore, psychologists often question cause–effect statements.

5. If a study establishes that a particular, observable, physical stimulus or manipulation causes a certain, observable response, it has internal validity.

6. Psychologists realize that what happens with one group of participants in one setting may not generalize to another type of participant or to a different setting. For example, they realize that a study done with one group of students in a lab setting may not apply to a group of people working in a factory. Therefore, they are appropriately cautious about generalizing the results of a study to real-world situations.

7. If a study's findings can be generalized to other people, places, and times, the study has external validity.

8. Human participants in research studies have many rights, including the right to decide whether they want to be in the study, the right to privacy, and the right to learn the study's purpose.

9. *Do not conduct a study without the approval of your professor.* In addition, obtain approval from the appropriate ethics committees. For example, if you are doing animal research, you may need approval from your school's internal animal care and use committee (IACUC). If you are doing research with human participants, you may need approval from your school's internal review board (IRB).

10. If you are involved with a study that harms a participant, you cannot avoid responsibility by arguing that you did not know the rules; that you did not mean to harm the person; that you were just doing what the lead investigator told you to do; or that your assistant, rather than you, caused the harm.

11. According to APA's ethical principles, the study's potential benefits should outweigh the study's potential for harm. Thus, there are two ways to increase the chances that your study is ethical: reduce the potential for harm, and maximize the potential gains of your research.

12. To maximize the gains of your research, you should make sure that your study has the kind of validity that your research question requires. Your research question will determine which type—or types—of validity you need.

13. If your research question is about whether something causes a certain effect, your study should have internal validity.

14. If your research question concerns what percentage of people engage in some behavior, you need a study that has external validity.

15. If your research question involves measuring or manipulating some state of mind (hunger, stress, learning, fear, motivation, love, etc.), you need construct validity.

KEY TERMS

internal validity *(p. 27)*

experiment *(p. 28)*

construct *(p. 29)*

construct validity *(p. 30)*

external validity *(p. 33)*

ethical *(p. 35)*

informed consent *(p. 35)*

debriefing *(p. 37)*

internal review board (IRB) *(p. 38)*

EXERCISES

1. Match the concept to the type of validity.
   _____ construct validity   **a.** generalize
   _____ external validity   **b.** cause–effect
   _____ internal validity   **c.** mental states

2. Match the threat to the type of validity.
   _____ construct validity   **a.** poor measure
   _____ external validity   **b.** reatment and no-
                                treatment groups
                                were unequal before
                                the study began
   _____ internal validity   **c.** small, biased sample
                                of participants

3. What type of validity are chemists most interested in? Why don't chemists do more research in natural settings like bakeries? What implications does this have for psychological research?

4. Is it ethical to treat a patient with a method that has not been scientifically tested? Why or why not? Is it ethical to withhold a treatment that is believed to work in order to find out if it does indeed work? Why or why not?

5. For one of the following television shows—*Survivor, Fear Factor, The Swan, Punk'd, Candid Camera,* and *America's Funniest Home Videos*—state which of the nine APA ethical principles listed in Table 2-2 are violated and explain—or provide an example of—how those principles are violated.

6. Two of the most ethically questionable studies in the history of psychology are Milgram's obedience study (in which participants were told to deliver dangerous shocks to an accomplice of the experimenter) and Zimbardo's prison study (in which well-adjusted students pretended to be either prisoners or guards). In both of these studies, there would have been no ethical problems at all if participants had behaved the way common sense told us they would; that is, no one would have obeyed the order to shock the accomplice, and none of the "guards" would have mistreated the prisoners.
   a. Does the inability to know how participants will react to a research project mean that research should not be done?
   b. Does people's inability to know how they and others will react in many situations mean that certain kinds of research should be performed so we can find out the answers to these important questions?
   c. What ethical principles, if any, were violated in Milgram's shock experiment? (See Table 2-2.)
   d. What ethical principles, if any, were violated in Zimbardo's prison study? (See Table 2-2.)

7. Assume that a participant in a study in which you were involved suffered intense distress. According to the APA ethical guidelines, which of the following are legitimate excuses that would relieve you of responsibility? Explain your answers.
   a. "I was just following orders."
   b. "My assistant conducted the session and behaved inappropriately, not me."
   c. "I didn't notice that the participant was upset."
   d. "I just didn't think that we had to tell participants that they would get mild electrical shocks."
   e. "I didn't think that asking questions about suicide would be upsetting—and for most of my participants it wasn't."
   f. "When the participant got upset, it surprised me. I just didn't know what to do and so I didn't do anything."
   g. "Our subjects were mice. We can cause mice whatever distress we want."

WEB RESOURCES

1. Go to the Chapter 2 section of the book's student website and:
   a. Look over the concept map of the key terms.
   b. Test yourself on the key terms.
   c. Take the Chapter 2 Practice Quiz.
   d. Do the interactive end-of-chapter exercises.
   e. Download the Chapter 2 tutorial.

2. To learn more about IRBs, getting IRB approval for research, and the ethical issues in conducting research, use the "Ethics" link.

INFOTRAC COLLEGE EDITION EXPLORATIONS

To see how difficult it is for an untrained person to distinguish truth from fiction, do an InfoTrac College Edition search on the "Mozart effect." What are your conclusions about that effect?

Generating and Refining Research Hypotheses

In good science, questions come first. Science is just a tool for answering those questions.

—*John Bargh*

It is better to know some of the questions than all of the answers.

—*James Thurber*

Overview

Research does not begin with variables, equipment, or participants. It begins with questions.

In this chapter, you will learn how to generate questions. Then, you will learn how to develop your questions into workable research **hypotheses:** testable predictions about the relationship between two or more variables.

Generating Research Ideas From Common Sense

Many students find developing a research hypothesis intimidating. They ask, "How can I find out something that people don't already know?" One solution is to adopt the skeptical attitude that characterizes science by asking whether what people already "know" is supported by the objective evidence. You can begin your questioning by doubting the effectiveness of "time-tested" treatments as well as new treatments. These treatments may range from palm-reading courses to the value of the Internet for teaching.

Another avenue for your skepticism is to test common sense. Galileo is famous for his experiments testing the commonsense assumption that heavier objects fall faster than lighter objects and for his skepticism about the commonsense belief that the sun revolved around the unmoving earth. Likewise, several psychologists have won Nobel Prizes for testing the assumption that humans are rational decision makers. Thus, testing commonsense assumptions ("myth busting") is valuable. Indeed, one scientist (Stern, 1993) believes that a major goal of psychology should be to "separate common sense from common nonsense."

Psychologists have a long history of testing common sense by testing old sayings. For example, Schachter (1959) tested the saying that "misery loves company." Zajonc (1968) found the saying "familiarity breeds contempt" to be false in many situations. Berscheid and her colleagues (1971) discovered that "birds of a feather flock together." D. Byrne (1971) found that opposites don't attract. Latane, Williams, and Harkins (1979) found evidence for the idea that "too many cooks spoil the broth." Pennebaker et al. (1979) learned that "the girls do get prettier at closing time." Wilson and Schooler (1991) discovered evidence against the saying "look before you leap."

More recently, researchers have been testing sayings related to happiness. For example:

- Seligman (2002) found support for the saying "happiness is like a butterfly, if you chase it, you won't catch it" (or, if you prefer Eleanor Roosevelt's version, "happiness isn't a goal, it's a byproduct").
- Emmons and McCullough (2003) discovered evidence to support the saying "focus on what's right in your world instead of what's wrong."

If we cited a saying that you were planning to test, do not automatically abandon plans to test that saying. Sayings are usually broad enough that all aspects of them can't be completely tested in a single study. For example, consider Wohlford's (1970) finding that, as would be expected from the saying "like father, like son," fathers who smoked were more likely to have sons who smoked. Researchers still—more than 35 years later—do not have definitive answers about the extent to which a son's behaviors (other than smoking) are modeled after his father's. Similarly, even though in 1971, Byrne found evidence that opposites (in terms of attitudes) don't attract, it wasn't until 7 years later that researchers found that opposites—in the form of psychologically "masculine" males and psychologically "feminine" females—don't attract in short-term blind dates (Ickes & Barnes, 1978). And it wasn't until 12 years later that researchers discovered that psychologically "masculine" males and psychologically "feminine" females don't attract in long-term marriage relationships (Antill, 1983). Thus, you can test a saying that has already been partially tested. However, if you want to test completely untested sayings, there are many from which to choose.

Where do you find a commonsense assumption that you could dispute? You might find one in a fortune cookie, in a package of Salada tea (Dillon, 1990), in a book of quotations, in a self-help or advice book such as *Life's Little Instruction Book,* in a song, in an ad, on a bumper sticker, on a T-shirt, or an editorial column, or a news event that doesn't seem to make sense. For example, much of what we know about helping someone in trouble comes from two people's efforts to understand why at least 38 people stood by and did nothing while Kitty Genovese was murdered. Darley and Latané (1968) questioned the common view that the reason the bystanders did not help was because New Yorkers were cold and alienated. Their research suggests that, rather than saying nobody helped *despite* the presence of 38 other witnesses, it would be more accurate to say that nobody helped *because* there were 38 other witnesses.

Another way to find an assumption you want to test is to talk to a person who always seems to disagree with you. If both of you make sensible arguments, but neither one of you can prove that the other is wrong, it is time to get objective evidence to show that your acquaintance is wrong.

Yet another way to find questionable assumptions is to attack a real-life, practical problem (cheating, prejudice, rudeness, apathy, too many false fire alarms in the dorms, etc.). Usually, you will find that different people have different "solutions" to almost any practical problem. You could collect objective evidence to find out which of these "solutions" work best.

If you decide to attack a practical problem, you may find that you have two research projects. The first is to document that a problem really exists; the second is to compare the effectiveness of different approaches to solving the problem. For example, you might first conduct a study to find out how prevalent the problem of cheating (or prejudice, apathy, superstitious thinking, etc.) is on your campus. Then, your second study might see which approaches to solving the problem are most effective. For instance, you might see if any of the following five methods designed to stop students from cheating on exams are more effective than what teachers normally do:

1. having a presenter emphasize the ways that cheating harms the cheater
2. having students discuss—in groups that you have set up so that most of the members in the group oppose cheating—whether cheating is unfair to other students
3. having students write an essay about why it is wrong to cheat and then having students read that essay aloud to students in a freshman English class
4. having more serious penalties for cheaters
5. having observers walking around during the exam

In summary, questioning common sense is a time-tested way to generate research ideas. In the distant past, famous discoveries—such as that the earth revolves around the sun and that light objects fall just as fast as heavy objects—came from researchers who were willing to question common sense. More recently, a fourth grader made national news by doing research that questioned whether a "healing technique" adopted by over 100 nursing schools was effective (Rosa, Rosa, Sarner, & Barrett, 1998). Even more recently, Cialdini (2005)

BOX 3-1 | **Six Ways to Tap Your Intuition**

1. Base your idea on "old sayings," assumptions or predictions made in songs, assumptions made in classic or popular literature, or statements made by experts, by asking:

   a. Is it true?
   b. Is there anything I know that seems to contradict that?
   c. When isn't it true? When is it more likely to be true?
   d. Is it true only in moderation?
   e. Why is it true? (What is the cause–effect relationship? What changes in thoughts, feelings, or physiological reactions does the cause trigger that, in turn, cause the change in behavior?)
   f. Why do people believe it's true?

2. Collect data on your own behavior, try to find rules that govern your behavior, and then see if those rules apply to other people.

3. Transform an argument into a research idea—find facts to settle a battle between two opinions.

4. Ask six key questions about any interesting phenomenon:

   a. What precisely is the behavior?
   b. Who does the behavior?
   c. How do people who are high performers and low performers of the behavior differ?
   d. When (under what circumstances) is the behavior most likely to occur?
   e. Why do people engage in the behavior?
   f. What are the long- and short-term effects of the behavior?

5. Determine why bad/irrational actions occur.

6. Attack a practical problem (ecology, illiteracy, prejudice, apathy, alcoholism, violence).

   a. Document that it exists.
   b. Evaluate the effectiveness of potential cures for the problem.

---

questioned the persuasiveness of the cards used by thousands of hotels that urge guests to reuse towels.

As you can see from these examples, just by being skeptical, people have been able to generate important research ideas. If you are naturally somewhat skeptical and use Box 3-1, you too can generate an important research idea. However, testing your own insights is not the only—or even the most preferred—way to generate research ideas.

Generating Research Ideas From Previous Research

A more preferred way to generate research ideas is to base an idea on previous research. Most advances in science come from scientists building on each other's work. For a beginning researcher, basing an idea on previous research has at least three major advantages.

First, a hypothesis based on previous research is more than a guess, it is an educated guess. Consequently, you have a reasonable chance of obtaining results that support your hypothesis.

Second, regardless of whether your hypothesis is supported, your study will be relevant to what other scientists have done. Consequently, your research will not produce an isolated, trivial fact.

Third, doing research based on other people's work is easier than starting from scratch, especially when you are a beginning researcher. Just as a beginning cook might find it intimidating to make a pizza from scratch without a recipe, some beginning researchers find it intimidating to design a study from scratch. However, just as the beginning cook would feel comfortable adding a few toppings to a store-bought pizza, a beginning researcher might feel comfortable building on someone else's study.

Specific Strategies

You have seen that there are advantages to developing research ideas from previous research. But how can you take advantage of other people's work?

Repeat Studies

The simplest way to take advantage of other people's work is to repeat (replicate) someone else's study. Because science relies on skepticism, you should repeat studies when you find the study's results difficult to believe—especially when those results conflict with results from other studies, seem inconsistent with established theory, or have not been replicated.

Do a Study Suggested by a Journal Article's Author(s)

Almost as simple as replicating a study is doing a study suggested by an article's authors. At the end of many research articles, the authors suggest additional studies that should be done. Often, they point out that the research should be repeated either using a different sample of participants or using a different setting.

Improve the Study's External Validity

Even if the researchers do not suggest it, you may decide to test the external validity (generality) of their findings. For example, you might ask:

1. Should I redo a study, but include types of participants that were not adequately represented in the original sample? If you have specific reasons to believe that the original study's results would *not* apply to most people— for example, to most women, or to most members of some other group—you probably should.

2. Should I redo a lab study by taking it outside of the lab and into the real world? In other words, is there any important element of real life that was not only left out of the study but that might moderate (modify) the relationship found in the original study?

3. Should I repeat the study using stimulus materials more like stimuli that people are exposed to in real life? Sometimes, stimuli in research are highly artificial. For example, many studies have asked participants to form impressions of a person based on reading a list of traits that supposedly describe that person, and many have asked participants to memorize lists of nonsense syllables. You could replace the list of words, nonsense syllables, or traits that participants saw in the original study with a videotape of a real-life event.

4. Should I see whether the effect is long lasting? Short lab studies document that a treatment has a short-term effect, but do not document whether the treatment has a long-term effect. An action that produces a positive short-term reaction may produce no long-term reaction—or even a negative long-term reaction. For example, you may know an ill-tempered person who feels good while throwing a tantrum but who regrets it later.

5. Can I think of any other situations in which the relationship between the variables observed in the original study may not hold? For example, consider the relationship between group size and helping: The *more* people available to help a victim, the *less* likely the victim is to get help. Can you think of some situation—such as an

unexpected disaster or some other event that increases group identity or makes people feel the desire to make their lives seem worthwhile—that would weaken or reverse the relationship between group size and helping?

Improve the Study's Internal Validity

Instead of improving a study's external validity, you may choose to improve its internal validity. As you learned in Chapter 2, establishing that one factor caused an effect is very difficult, partly because it is hard to control other factors. For example, Gladue and Delaney (1990) argued that a study finding that "girls get prettier at closing time" at bars (Pennebaker et al., 1979) left unanswered the question of whether time or alcohol consumption was responsible for increased perceptions of attractiveness. Therefore, they modified the original study to control for the effects of alcohol consumption.

Similarly, although Frank and Gilovich (1988) found that teams switching to black uniforms were called for more penalties, their finding did not prove that wearing black causes a team to get more penalties. After all, it could be that aggressive coaches like to have their teams wear black. Therefore, as you can see in Appendix B, Frank and Gilovich devised a study that allowed them to make sure that uniform color was the only difference between their teams. Consequently, they were able to isolate black as the cause of the increased aggression.

Improve the Study's Construct Validity

Rather than improving a study's external or internal validity, you may choose to improve a study's construct validity. As you learned in Chapter 2, researchers who try to guess what is going on inside participants' minds may guess wrong. Usually, the problem is either that the researchers used poor operational definitions of their constructs (the manipulation or measure was poor) or the participants figured out the hypothesis and that discovery affected their responses.

When thinking about improving a study's construct validity, start by asking whether you can use a better manipulation or measure than the original researchers used. Is there a better "stress" manipulation than the one the original researchers used? Was their "conformity" measure really a measure of cooperativeness?

Even if the researchers used a relatively good measure of the construct they wanted to measure, it is unlikely that any single measure of a broad construct such as conformity, intelligence, aggression, or memory will fully capture the entire construct. Therefore, if the original study finds a relationship using one set of operational definitions, it may pay to replicate the study using different operational definitions of the construct(s). For example, when early research suggested that men have greater "spatial ability" than women, critics questioned whether the tasks used to measure spatial ability fully captured the construct of spatial ability. This questioning led to further research. That research has given us a better picture of how men and women differ on spatial ability. (On the average, men are much faster than women at mentally rotating objects, are slightly better at picking out figures that are hidden in a complex background, and are not nearly as good at remembering where objects are.)

Even when the measures and manipulations are fine, a study's construct validity will be poor if participants figure out what the hypothesis is. Therefore, when reading a study, you should ask, "If I were a participant, would I know what results the researcher expected?" If your answer to this question is "yes," you may decide to repeat the study but improve it by reducing the biasing effects of participants' expectations.

One way to avoid the biasing effects of participants' expectations is to use the **double-blind technique:** the tactic of keeping both the participants and the research assistants who interact with the participants from knowing which treatment the participants are getting. You are probably most familiar with the double-blind technique from studies examining the effects of new drugs. In such studies, the participants all receive a pill, but only some of the pills contain the drug being tested. Because neither the physician nor the participants know who has received the drug, differences between the medicated group and placebo group will be due to the drug itself rather than to the patients' or physician's belief that the drug will work.

Look for Practical Implications of the Research

Even if you are satisfied with the original study's validity, the study will still leave many questions unanswered. If the study involves basic (nonapplied) research, do the findings apply to a practical situation? For example, can a technique that helps participants remember more words on a list in a laboratory experiment be used to help students on academic probation? Similarly, if a study finds that a treatment affects the way people think, you could do a study to see whether the same treatment also affects what people actually do. It is one thing to show that a treatment helps participants remember certain information, feel more sympathy for a crime victim, or produce more of a certain kind of chemical; it is something else to show that the treatment changes the way participants actually act in real-life situations.

Try to Reconcile Studies That Produce Conflicting Results

When you find studies that produce conflicting results, try to reconcile the apparent contradictions. One strategy for resolving the contradictions is to look for subtle differences in how the studies were conducted. What do the studies that find one pattern of results have in common? What do the studies that find a different pattern have in common? Asking these questions may alert you to a possible **moderator variable:** a variable that intensifies, weakens, or reverses the relationship between two other variables.

For example, consider the relationship between argument quality and persuasion. Generally, ads that contain strong arguments are more persuasive than ads with weak arguments. However, humor might moderate that relationship, by either weakening it or intensifying it. If humor distracts people from thinking about the ad's arguments, humorous ads containing strong arguments might not be any more effective than humorous ads containing weak arguments. If, in contrast, humor makes people process ads more deeply, argument quality might be even more important for humorous ads than it is for nonhumorous ads.

Trying to uncover the moderator variable is a creative and potentially productive task. For example, consider the research on the effect of having people observe you. Many studies found a "social facilitation" effect—the presence of an audience improved performance. Many other studies, however, found a "social inhibition" effect—the presence of others decreased performance. By studying both the studies that found a "social facilitation effect" and the studies that found a "social inhibition" effect, Robert Zajonc (Zajonc, 1965; Zajonc & Sales, 1966) discovered how the two sets of studies differed: studies finding social facilitation involved tasks that were easy for participants to do, whereas studies finding social inhibition involved tasks that were hard for participants to do. Zajonc then designed several studies in which he varied both the presence of others and task difficulty. His results supported the hypothesis that task difficulty was a moderator variable. That is, the effect that other people's presence had on task performance depended on how difficult the task was.

Conclusions About Generating Research Ideas From Previous Research

In conclusion, existing research is a rich source of research ideas. At the very least, you can always just repeat the original study. If you wish to modify the existing study, you have numerous options. You could improve its internal, construct, or external validity. Or, you may decide to pursue the practical applications of the study. Or, try to find situations where the findings would not hold. Or, try reconciling a study's findings with a study that obtained different findings.

Not only does using existing research help you generate ideas, but it also helps you test those ideas. If you decide to repeat a study, reading the original study will tell you almost everything you need to know. If you want to improve or build on a study, reading the original article will still help you determine how to measure your variables, what to say to your participants, and so forth.

Converting an Idea Into a Research Hypothesis

If you used any of the strategies we have discussed thus far, you should have some research ideas. However, you still may not have a research hypothesis: a testable prediction about the relationship between two or more variables. Note that a research hypothesis is not a research topic, not a vague question you have, but a short, specific statement of how two or more variables will be related. Although converting an idea into a workable research hypothesis can be difficult, it is essential because the goal of all research is to test hypotheses.

Admittedly, different types of research may test different kinds of hypotheses. For example, experiments test hypotheses about whether a treatment *causes* a certain *effect*. Testing experimental hypotheses help us understand *why* a certain behavior occurs. Survey research, on the other hand, tests hypotheses about *what* factors are correlated (associated) with a certain behavior. Thus, rather than finding out why a certain behavior occurs, survey research might focus on finding out who is most likely to do that certain behavior, what other behaviors they tend to do, and when, where, and how they are likely to do that behavior. For example, an experimenter's hypothesis may involve seeing whether a given intervention stops people from cheating on their spouses, whereas a survey researcher's hypothesis may deal with finding out whether men are more likely to cheat than women. Despite their differences, however, both researchers will have hypotheses.

All researchers should have hypotheses *before* they conduct their research. If they started their research without having a hypothesis to help them know what to look for, it is unlikely that they would have found anything. Consequently, before they will even consider allowing you to do research, most professors and many ethics committees require you to state the hypothesis you plan to test. Because having a hypothesis is so important, the rest of this chapter is devoted to helping you generate a workable research hypothesis.

Make It Testable

When converting an idea into a hypothesis, you must be sure that your hypothesis is testable. In general, a testable hypothesis has the same basic characteristics as a fair bet.

As with any bet, you must be able to define your terms. For example, if you bet that "Pat will be in a bad mood today," you need some publicly observable way of determining what a bad mood is. Similarly, if you hypothesize a relationship between two variables, you must be able to obtain operational definitions of your key variables. Thus, if you plan to measure the effects of physical attractiveness on how much a person is liked, you must be able to define both attractiveness and liking according to publicly observable, objective criteria.

Also, as with any bet, your prediction should be specific so that it is clear what patterns of results would indicate that your hypothesis "won" and what results would indicate that your hypothesis "lost." You do not want to conduct a study and then have to debate whether the results supported or refuted your hypothesis. Usually the easiest way to avoid such disputes is to make your hypothesis as specific as possible. Therefore, when stating your hypothesis, specify not only a relationship between two or more variables, but also the direction of that relationship. That is, rather than saying, *aggression will vary with temperature*, it would be better to say, *increases in aggression will correspond to increases in temperature*. Ideally, you would be even more specific. For example, you might predict that *increasing the temperature from 80 to 90 degrees Fahrenheit will increase aggression more than increasing the temperature from 70 to 80 degrees*. To check that your prediction is precise enough, ask yourself, "What kind of result would disconfirm my prediction?" and "What kind of result would support my prediction?" Then, graph both of these patterns of results.

By being specific, you can avoid making predictions that are so vague that no pattern of results will disprove them. Unlike some fortunetellers and unscrupulous gamblers, you want to be fair by giving yourself the opportunity to be proven wrong.

Make It Supportable

Besides giving your hypothesis a chance to be refuted, you also want to give your hypothesis the opportunity to be supported. That is, you not only have to beware of making bets you can't lose, but also of bets you can't win.

You must be especially wary of one kind of bet you can never win—trying to prove the **null hypothesis:** a prediction that there is no relationship between your variables. Even if your treatment group scores exactly the same as the no-treatment group, you have not proven the null hypothesis.

To understand why you can't prove the null hypothesis, suppose you hypothesize no relationship between attraction and liking. Even if you find no relationship, you can't say that there isn't a relationship. You can only say that you didn't find the relationship. Failing to find something—whether it be your keys, a murder weapon, a planet, or a relationship between variables—is hardly proof that the thing doesn't exist.[1]

The fact that you can't prove the null hypothesis has two important implications. First, you can't do a study to prove that a treatment has no effect. If you find no difference between your treatment group and no-treatment group, you can't say that your treatment has no effect: You can say only that you *failed* to find a treatment effect. Second, you can't do a study to prove that two treatments have the same effect. That is, if you find no difference between your two treatment groups, you can't say that the treatments have the same effect: You can say only that you *failed* to find a difference between them.

Be Sure to Have a Rationale: How Theory Can Help

In addition to making sure that your hypothesis is testable, make sure that you have a solid rationale for your hypothesis. If you can't think of a good reason why your hypothesis should

---

[1]But why might you fail to find an effect? We'll answer that question in detail in Chapter 10. For now, just realize that we can't say "there is no effect." Instead, we can only say "no effect has been found."

be correct, your hypothesis is probably a "bad bet." For example, if you hypothesized, without giving any rationale, that people would be more creative after drinking seven glasses of water, it is doubtful that your prediction would pan out. Instead, it would appear that you were simply going on a hopeless fishing expedition. Therefore, always write out the reasons for making your prediction. Your rationale can come from previous research that has found results similar to what you are hypothesizing, common sense, or **theory:** a set of principles that explain existing research findings and that can be used to make new predictions that can lead to new research findings.

Do not overlook the fact that theory can provide a rationale for your hypothesis, even when your hypothesis did not originally come from theory. For example, suppose that, on a hunch, you predicted that taking care of a plant would cause the elderly to be more mentally alert and healthy. You might then use theory to help you clearly articulate a logical rationale for your prediction. For example, according to learned helplessness theory, a lack of control over outcomes may cause depression. Therefore, taking care of a plant may give one more of a sense of control and thus make one less vulnerable to helplessness (Langer & Rodin, 1976).

Demonstrate Its Relevance: Theory Versus Trivia

In addition to giving yourself a reasonable chance of finding support for your hypothesis, you should explain how your research fits in with existing theory and research or how it solves a practical problem. Thus, the hypothesis about what would happen if one gave people seven glasses of water—as well as any other hypothesis in which the only rationale for the hypothesis is "let's expose people to an unusual circumstance and see what happens"—is not only a bad bet but also a silly and trivial bet. Scientists frown on doing research just to find isolated bits of trivia. For example, without any other rationale, doing a study to show that alcohol decreases Ping-Pong performance is meaningless, except possibly to people who bet on Ping-Pong. Psychological research should not be a trivial pursuit.

To see how theory can transform your hypothesis from trivial to relevant., consider the following two examples. First, consider this hypothesis: *Around age 7, children stop believing in Santa Claus.* In its own right, this is a relatively trivial hypothesis. However, when put in the context of Piaget's theory, which states that around age 7, children are able to think logically about concrete events (and thus realize that Santa Claus can't be everywhere at once and can't carry that many toys), the finding has deeper significance. Now, rather than being just an isolated fact about children's thinking, it is evidence supporting an explanation of how children think (Piaget's theory).

Second, suppose you were to make a hypothesis about a gender difference. For example, suppose that, like Haselton, Buss, Oubaid, and Angleitner (2005), you predicted that women would be more upset than men to discover that their dating partner was not as wealthy as they were led to believe. At first, such a hypothesis might seem trivial. If you were, however, able to tie your hypothesis to the theory of evolution, your hypothesis would be more interesting.

How could you tie a hypothesis about gender differences to the theory of evolution? The key is to assume that although both genders have the evolutionary goal of bringing as many offspring into adulthood as possible, the strategies that men will use to achieve this aim are different from the strategies that women will use (Buss, 1994). Consequently, it is consistent with the theory of evolution that men would be more

- promiscuous (They have virtually no limit on the number of offspring they can have.)
- jealous (Before DNA testing, men could not be sure that they were the biological parent.)

- impressed by youth (Younger women are more fertile than older women.)
- influenced by physical attractiveness (Attractiveness is a rough indicator of health, and the woman's health is vital because the potential offspring will live inside the woman's body for 9 months.)

You are not limited to using a single theory to make your hypothesis seem relevant. Indeed, the most interesting hypotheses are the ones in which you can show that one theory predicts one outcome, whereas a second theory predicts the opposite outcome. For example, researchers tested the psychoanalytic prediction that if you express hostility toward a person, you'll release pent-up anger and consequently feel better about the person. They pointed out that cognitive dissonance theory, on the other hand, predicts that if John is mad at Bob and then hurts Bob, John will justify his aggression by viewing Bob in a negative way. That is, according to dissonance theory, after you express aggression toward a person, you will feel more hostility toward that person. Experiments support the dissonance prediction (Aronson, 1990).

Refine It: 10 Time-Tested Tips

One reason you may have trouble demonstrating your hypothesis's relevance is that you are not used to using past research and theory to justify testing an idea. However, another reason you may have trouble selling people on the value of testing your idea is that you need a better hypothesis to sell. The following 10 tips have helped students improve their hypotheses.

1. Don't Be Afraid to Be Wrong

Some beginning researchers mistakenly believe that a good hypothesis is one that is guaranteed to be right (e.g., *alcohol will slow down reaction time*). However, if we already know your hypothesis is true before you test it, testing your hypothesis won't tell us anything new. Remember, research is supposed to produce *new* knowledge. To get new knowledge, you, as a researcher-explorer, need to leave the safety of the shore (established facts) and venture into uncharted waters. If your predictions about what will happen in these uncharted waters is wrong, that's okay: Scientists are allowed to make mistakes. Indeed, scientists often learn more from predictions that do not turn out than from those that do. As the saying goes, "no guts, no glory."

2. Don't Be Afraid to Deal With Constructs

Some beginning researchers are so concerned about making sure they can measure their hypothesis's key variables that they design their hypothesis around what they can easily observe (e.g., alcohol consumption and reaction time) rather than around the constructs that interest them (e.g., mood and creativity). If you avoid constructs, you may propose a hypothesis that is easy to test but hard to find interesting, such as *alcohol slows down reaction time*. To avoid proposing hypotheses that lack both constructs and excitement, realize that there are valid ways to manipulate and measure constructs (as you will see in Chapter 5). In short, scientists study what they are interested in—and so should you.

3. Don't Avoid Theory

Good theory explains existing findings and leads to testable new insights. Theory can help you make the leap from just having a general topic to having a specific prediction, especially if your topic is an applied problem. As Kurt Lewin said, "There is nothing so practical as a good theory."

Figure 3-1 | **Cognitive Dissonance**

Dilbert reprinted by permission of United Features Syndicate, Inc.

Table 3-1 | **Basic Propositions of Cognitive Dissonance Theory**

1. If an individual has two thoughts that the individual considers inconsistent, then that individual will experience dissonance.
2. Dissonance is an unpleasant state, like anxiety or hunger.
3. An individual will try to reduce dissonance.
4. Changing one of the thoughts to make it consistent with the other is one way of reducing dissonance.

Before seeing how theory can help you attack a practical problem, let's first look at cognitive dissonance theory (see Figure 3-1). According to this theory, if a person holds two thoughts that the person considers contradictory, the person will experience an unpleasant state called dissonance (see Table 3-1). Because dissonance is unpleasant, the person will try to reduce it, much as the person would try to reduce hunger, thirst, or anxiety (Aronson, 1990).

To better understand cognitive dissonance theory, suppose a woman thinks she is generous, but also knows she doesn't give money to charity. If she notices and perceives that these two thoughts are inconsistent, this inconsistency will bother her. In other words, she will feel dissonance. To reduce this dissonance, she may change her thoughts or her actions. To reconcile the perceived inconsistency, she may decide that she is not generous, that the charities she refused were not worthwhile, or that she will give some money to charity.

Now that you have some understanding of cognitive dissonance theory, let's see how two sets of researchers used dissonance theory to go from a general practical problem to a specific prediction. The first set of researchers were concerned with the general problem of how to get people to buy condoms. According to cognitive dissonance theory, people will buy condoms if doing so will reduce their feelings of cognitive dissonance. That is, if John is aware that he has two contradictory thoughts ("I believe that people should use condoms when having sex," and "I have had sex without condoms"), John will feel dissonance. To reduce that dissonance, he can perform an action that will be consistent with what he has just preached—buy condoms. Thus, cognitive dissonance theory led to this hypothesis: Participants will be motivated to buy condoms if researchers (a) have participants publicly advocate the importance of safe sex and then (b) remind each participant about times when that participant had failed to use condoms. As predicted, participants who were made to see that their past behavior was inconsistent with their publicly stated position were more likely to buy condoms (Stone, Aronson, Crain, Winslow, & Fried, 1994).

The second set of dissonance researchers were concerned about the general problem of getting introductory psychology students to believe that it was important to learn about research methods. Although many general psychology professors have worried about the problem, Miller, Wozniak, Rust, Miller, & Slezak (1996) seem to be the first ones to use cognitive dissonance theory to find a solution. The hypothesis suggested by cognitive dissonance theory was that having students write essays about why it was important to know about research methods would be more effective than lecturing to students about the value of research. This hypothesis was supported: Students were more likely to believe in the value of research methods when they had "convinced themselves."

You have seen that theory can be useful. A theory, however, can help you only if you know about it and understand it. How can you get to know a theory?

Your first step to getting introduced to a theory might be to read textbook summaries of theories. These summaries will allow you to select a theory that can help you. Once you have selected a theory, you must go beyond textbook summaries because such summaries may oversimplify the theory. The researcher who relies exclusively on textbook summaries may be accused of ignoring key propositions of the theory or of using a **straw theory:** an exaggerated, oversimplified caricature of the theory. Therefore, in addition to reading textbook summaries, you should also see how other researchers have summarized the theory by consulting journal articles that describe studies based on the theory (e.g., "Elation and depression: A test of opponent process theory"). The beginnings of these articles usually include a brief description of the theory that the study tests.

Once you have selected a theory, read the original statement of the theory (the citation will be in the texts or articles that you read). Then, to keep up to date about changes in the theory, use *Psychological Abstracts* or *Social Sciences Citation Index* to find books and review articles devoted to the theory. (For more information on how to conduct a literature review, see Web Appendix B.)

4. Be Manipulative: Use True Independent Variables

Rather than trying to describe what happens, try to change what happens. That is, think about how you can manipulate variables. For example, the authors of the sample article in Appendix B, like many other people, observed that wearing dark uniforms was associated with aggression. They went beyond what others had done, however, by manipulating whether participants wore black or white uniforms and observing its effect on aggressiveness.

To see another example of how and why experimenters manipulate variables, consider a study in which experimenters *manipulated* participants' expectations of how likely it was that Bush would be elected president (Kay, Jimenez, & Jost, 2002). To manipulate participants' expectations, the experimenters first created five reports that were allegedly based on valid scientific analyses of polling data. The experimenters then manipulated (via random assignment) whether the participant read the report, which concluded that (a) Bush would win in a landslide, (b) Bush would win a narrow victory, (c) there would be a tie, (d) Gore would win a narrow victory, or (e) Gore would win in a landslide. Kay, Jimenez, and Jost found that expecting Bush to win caused people to like Bush. Note what the researchers would have lost if, instead of manipulating expectations, the researchers had merely asked participants (a) who they expected to win and (b) how much they liked Bush. In that case, if the researchers found that participants who expected Bush to win liked Bush more than those who expected Bush to lose, the researchers could *not* conclude that expecting Bush to win caused participants to like Bush. After all, it might be the reverse: Liking Bush might cause people to expect Bush to win.

The big lesson here is that if you want to have internal validity and more interesting research ideas, rather than looking for participants who already differ in some way, start with participants who do not differ in that way and then manipulate a factor that will make them differ in that way. In technical terminology, you need to use an **independent variable:** a treatment (an intervention or manipulation of a variable) that you administer to some individuals but not to others.

Using independent variables allows you to find out why people do things. Consequently, many professors will require your hypothesis to be in the form, "_____ affects scores on _____," with the first blank containing the name of your independent variable (the factor you are manipulating) and second blank containing the name of your **dependent variable (dependent measure)**: the participant's response that the researcher is measuring.

If you are having trouble thinking of hypotheses that involve independent variables, remember that one reason people do things is because of the immediate environment—and you can manipulate the immediate environment. You can tell people things, show people things, and set up situations that will change how they feel, think, and act. That is, although you may tend to think that individuals do certain things because of the type of person they are, research clearly shows that, in many cases, the immediate environment is much more important in determining individuals' moods, mental states, and behavior than what type of person the individual is. For example:

- People studying to be ministers are much less likely to stop and help a person if they are led to believe that they might be late to give their speech—even when that speech is on the Good Samaritan parable, about the virtue of the person who stopped and helped a person in need (Darley & Batson, 1973).
- When playing a game called "The Community Game," students judged by their dorm counselors to be highly competitive are not any more competitive than students judged to be highly cooperative. Similarly, when playing a game called "Wall Street," students considered highly cooperative are just as competitive as students considered highly competitive. What makes this finding more remarkable is that it is the same game—only the name has been changed (Liberman, Samuels, & Ross, 2004).
- In his study that involved a simulated prison, Zimbardo and colleagues (Zimbardo, Haney, Banks, & Jaffe, 1975) found that when well-adjusted undergraduates were assigned to play the role of prison inmate, they became dependent, but when they were assigned to play the role of prison guard, they became sadistic.

5. Look for Other Effects: Use Other Dependent Variables

Almost any treatment will have more than one effect. Effects can be short term, , long term, behavioral, physiological, emotional, cognitive, good, bad, and side. So, if people are looking at the good effects of pursuing the American dream, you could look for the bad effects. Similarly, if others look for the good effects of attractiveness, you could look at the bad effects. The key is to realize that a treatment has many more effects (on beliefs, feelings, actions, and bodily reactions) and a predictor may predict many more events than you would first think.

Thinking of the many possible effects of a treatment is perhaps the most important skill that an evaluation researcher—a person who looks at the effect of a program (e.g., a training program, an advertising campaign, a new law)—has. The ability to think of many events that might be related to a variable is a useful skill for any researcher.

For example, Dabbs believed that testosterone levels had an effect on people's behavior. To bolster his case, he found that high levels of testosterone in one's saliva correlated with

- phony-looking smiles
- rough tactics in domestic disputes
- premeditated murder
- greater apparent confidence when meeting strangers
- moodiness in children
- aggression and crudeness among fraternity men
- higher rates of marriage
- higher rates of divorce
- being a trial lawyer rather than a non–trial lawyer
- being in prison
- lower levels of career achievement

6. Reverse Cause and Effect: Switch Independent and Dependent Variables

Suppose you have a rather ordinary hypothesis such as *if a person is attractive, participants will be more likely to help that person than if the person is not attractive. That is, being attractive causes one to be helped.* Your idea is to make a friend look either moderately attractive or very attractive and see if the friend is helped more when she looks very attractive. You could make this hypothesis more interesting by changing which variable is the cause and which is the effect. That is, you could hypothesize that *being helped leads to being perceived as attractive.* For example, you might give some participants a chance to do your friend a favor and see if those participants rate your friend as being more attractive than those who are not given that opportunity.

Many psychologists have made important contributions by doing studies that reversed conventional cause–effect hypotheses. For example:

- Rather than looking at attitude change leading to behavior change, Festinger and Carlsmith (1959) found that behavior change led to attitude change.
- Rather than looking at the finger pulling the trigger, Berkowitz (1981) found that the trigger can pull the finger.
- Rather than looking at how seeing leads to believing, some perception researchers have found, as Myers (2002a) puts it, that "believing leads to seeing."
- Rather than looking at how stress on the body affects mental health, many researchers have looked at how mental stress affects physical health.
- Rather than looking at whether increased income leads to happiness, Diener and Seligman (2004) have looked at whether happiness leads to increased income.

7. Look for Mediating Variables

If you have a hypothesis about the relationship between two variables that is too obvious and too well documented, you might look for the relationship's **mediating variable:** the mental or biological mechanism by which the stimulus affects the response. Understanding the mediating processes inside the participant that come between the observable stimulus and the observable response allows you to understand *how* a cause has its effects. That is, a stimulus often has an effect by first changing some mediating variable inside the participant (thoughts, feelings, or physiological reactions), which, in turn, triggers a change in the participant's behavior (see Figure 3-2). For example, A (an environmental event, such as working with a large group of people) may affect B (a mediating process, such as the belief that nobody will know how hard you worked), which, in turn, may lead to C (the consequence that you do not work very hard).

Even the most mundane hypothesis may become quite interesting by focusing on the "behind the scenes" mediating processes that are responsible for the proposed relationship. For example, the hypothesis that football fans feel bad when their team loses is not that interesting. It is interesting, however, to hypothesize about the bodily or psychological *mechanisms* that create this effect. What inside the person causes him to feel badly? Is the

Figure 3-2   Mediating Variables

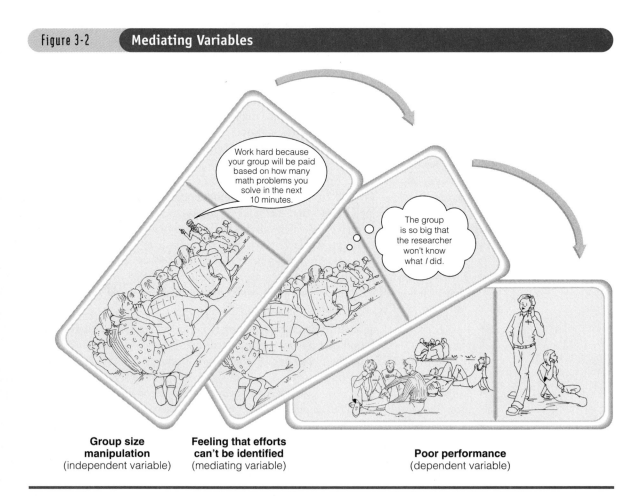

| Group size manipulation (independent variable) | Feeling that efforts can't be identified (mediating variable) | Poor performance (dependent variable) |

mediating physiological process a decrease in testosterone (Bernhardt, Dabbs, Fielden, & Lutter, 1998)? Is the mediating cognitive psychological process a change in self-concept?

Similarly, the hypothesis *increasing the room temperature will cause people to be more aggressive* (room temperature is the independent variable; aggressive, the dependent variable) is not that interesting. It is more interesting to find out *how* warm temperatures increase aggression. What mediates that relationship? Once you have the answer to that question, you have a hypothesis about a mediating variable. For example, if your answer to that question was "liking" (others in the room), your hypothesis might be *increasing the room temperature, by making people like each other less, causes increased aggression.*

If you suspect that a mediating variable (e.g., liking) is responsible for the effect of a certain factor, you may want to do a study that measures the mediating variable. However, showing that an effective treatment causes changes in an alleged mediating variable does not establish that the variable is mediating the effect: Rather than being the underlying cause of the effect, the variable might be a side effect of the treatment.

For example, suppose you found that the less acupuncture patients sweat during a session, the more effective the acupuncture is at relieving their pain. In such a case, you would not assume that acupuncture leads to less sweating (mediating variable), which leads to less pain. Instead, you would suspect that less pain leads to less sweating. Because reduced sweating might be a byproduct of reduced pain rather than the cause of reduced pain, you would not conclude that sweating was the mediator of acupuncture's pain-reducing effect.

To establish that a variable is the mediator of the treatment's effect rather than a mere byproduct of the treatment, you should do an experiment that manipulates the mediating variable (Sigall & Mills, 1998). In such an experiment, you might show that the treatment is not effective when you block the underlying mediating process. For example, researchers showed that acupuncture was effective in relieving pain—unless the researchers gave participants a drug that blocked the effect of endorphins. In that case, acupuncture was ineffective. Therefore, they concluded that acupuncture worked via endorphins.

8. Look for Moderator Variables

Any treatment that manipulates a mediating variable is also a moderator variable. As you may recall, a moderator variable is a variable that can modify (strengthen, weaken, or reverse) the relationship between two other variables (see Figure 3-3).[2] For example, suppose you suspect that the reason individuals loaf when they are in a group (the "social loafing effect") is that they do not think that their efforts can be identified. In that case, perceived identifiability would be the mediating variable (large group leads to low perceived identifiability, which leads to loafing).

If your hypothesis is correct, variables that affect perceived identifiability should moderate the social loafing effect (Williams, Nida, Baca, & Latané, 1989). For example, manipulations that make individuals think they are more identifiable (e.g., having observers record each individual's performance, making an individual responsible for one section of a report, making the group smaller) should weaken the social loafing effect because those manipulations make it so that increasing group size leads to less of an effect on perceived identifiability, which leads to less of an effect on loafing.

---

[2]A mediating variable is an inner mental (e.g., perceived identifiability) or biological (e.g., physiological arousal) mechanism that is triggered by an outside cause (e.g., group size) and is responsible for the cause's observable effect (e.g., less work). A moderator variable is a variable that modifies ("moderates") another variable's effect.

Figure 3-3 **How Moderator Variables May Affect a Relationship Between Two Variables**

A. Original relationship

B. Modifier boosting treatment's original effect

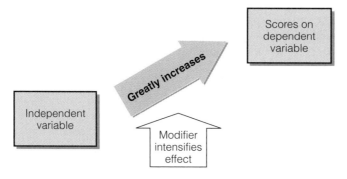

C. Modifier reversing treatment's original effect

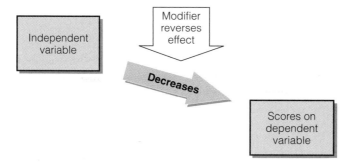

D. Modifier neutralizing treatment's original effect

Note that moderator variables are not the same as mediating variables and that not all efforts to find moderating variables involve looking for variables that might manipulate an underlying mediating variable (Baron & Kenny, 1986). For example, the following moderating factors weaken the social loafing effect yet have nothing to do with the mediating variable of individual identifiability: competing with another group, liking the other group members, and liking the task (Myers, 2002a). Thus, even if you do not have any hypotheses about variables that may mediate a relationship, you may still have a hypothesis about a variable that might moderate that relationship.

If you have a hypothesis about the relationship between two variables that is too obvious and too well documented, you may be able to rescue your hypothesis by adding a moderator variable. For example, whereas the hypothesis *increasing group size will decrease effort* has already been extensively tested, the hypothesis *increasing group size will decrease effort when anxiety is low but not when anxiety is high* has not. Even if your hypothesis does not need to be rescued, chances are good that your hypothesis can be improved by adding a moderating variable.

To find a potential moderator variable, ask yourself, "Under what circumstances doesn't this relationship hold?" Think of exceptions to the rule—and then try to see how these exceptions to the rule may suggest an addition to the old rule. For instance, imagine that Zebrowitz had decided to test the old saying "people from a different race all look alike." This hypothesis would not be that interesting because much research has shown support for it. Instead, she and her colleagues thought about exceptions to that rule. She and her colleagues (Zebrowitz, Montepare, & Lee, 1993) found that, under certain conditions, people could do a good job of distinguishing among members of other racial groups. For example, they found that attractiveness moderated the "all look alike" effect: People could distinguish between attractive and unattractive members of a different race.

In addition to looking for moderating variables that allow you to state conditions under which commonsense rules are wrong, you could look for moderator variables that allow you to reconcile conflicts among commonsense rules. For example, when does "like attract like," and when do "opposites attract"? When does "absence make the heart grow fonder," and when does absence mean "out of sight, out of mind"? Under what circumstances are "two heads better than one," and under what circumstances is it better to do it yourself (after all, "too many cooks spoil the broth" and "nothing is worse than a committee")?

One type of moderator variable you might look for could be your intervention program. For example, you might predict that people who went through your "how to work better in groups" training program might follow the "two heads are better than one" rule, whereas those who had not would follow the "too many cooks spoil the broth" rule. In other words, untrained people might work better alone, whereas trained people might work better in groups.

9. Be More Precise About the Relationship Between Your Variables

Sometimes, you can improve your hypothesis by being more precise about the relationship between your variables. For instance, the hypothesis that exercise reduces stress is, by itself, not that interesting. However, it would be interesting and valuable to graph the relationship between exercise and stress so that we could quantify how much exercise leads to how much stress reduction. This graph would allow you to answer questions such as:

- Can you get away with exercising for 15 minutes, or do you need an hour to get the full effect?
- Is exercising for 2 hours twice as effective as exercising for 1 hour?
- Is exercising for 3 hours better, worse, or the same as exercising for 1 hour?

For many treatments, people would like to know how much is too little, how much is too much, and how much is just right. Some would argue that the hallmark of a useful science is the ability to make precise, specific predictions about the effects of treatment. The best way to estimate the effects of different amounts (doses) of a treatment is to map the shape of the **functional relationship:** the extent to which changes in one variable are accompanied by changes in another variable.

10. Study Individual Dimensions of Multidimensional Constructs

In addition to changing a hypothesis by being more specific about what *amounts* of one variable had what effect, you can change a hypothesis by being more specific about what *aspect* of a variable had what effect. Thus, if your hypothesis involves a general construct, you may be able to improve your hypothesis by breaking that multidimensional construct down into its individual dimensions and then making hypotheses involving those individual components (see Figure 3-4). For example, rather than hypothesizing that love will increase over time, you might hypothesize that certain aspects of love (commitment, intimacy) will increase over time, whereas other parts (passionate love) will not. Similarly, rather than saying that stress will interfere with memory, you might try to find what part of memory is most affected by stress. Is it encoding, rehearsal, organization, or retrieval? The component strategy has been useful for

Figure 3-4	**Two Examples of How Component Measures Generate New Relationships to Explore**

Without component measures, there is only one relationship to explore.

Without component measures, there is only one relationship to explore.

With component measures, there are many relationships to explore.

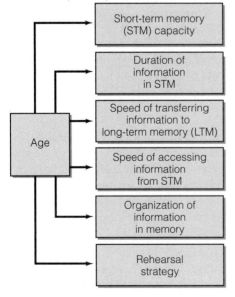

With component measures, there are many relationships to explore.

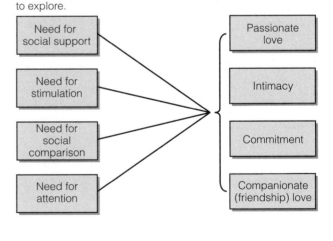

personality psychologists who have broken down global (overall) self-esteem into different types (body self-esteem, academic self-esteem, social self-esteem, etc.), and social psychologists who have broken down prejudice into its conscious and unconscious dimensions.

Make Sure That Testing the Hypothesis Is Both Practical and Ethical

Once your hypothesis is testable, reasonable, and relevant, you must still ask two additional questions. The first question is, "*Can* your hypothesis be tested?" Sometimes you may not have the skills or the resources to test it. For example, testing some hypotheses in physiological psychology may require equipment or surgical skills that you do not have. The second question is, "*Should* your hypothesis be tested?" That is, can the hypothesis be tested in an ethical manner?

You have a serious obligation to make sure that your study is ethical. Clearly, you do not have the right to physically or psychologically harm another. Reading Appendix C can help you decide whether your study can be done in an ethical manner. However, because conducting ethical research is so important, do not make the decision to conduct research without consulting others. Before doing a study, you and your professor will probably need to have your project reviewed by an ethics committee. In any event, *never conduct a study without your professor's approval!* (See Table 3-2.)

Table 3-2	Questions to Ask About a Potential Hypothesis

1. Can it be proven wrong?
   - Can you obtain operational definitions of the variables?
   - Is the prediction specific?
2. Can it be supported?
   - Are you predicting that you will find an effect or a difference? (Remember, your results can never prove the null hypothesis.)
3. Are there logical reasons for expecting the prediction to be correct?
   - Is it predicted by theory?
   - Is it consistent with past research findings?
   - Does it follow from common sense?
4. Would the results of the test of your prediction be relevant to
   - previous research?
   - existing theory?
   - a practical problem?
5. Is it practical and ethical to test your prediction?
   - Do you have the physical and financial resources to test this idea?
   - Would testing the hypothesis cause physical or psychological harm to the participants? (See Appendix C.)
   - Do you have approval from your professor?
   - If you are planning on doing research with human participants and your school has an internal research review board (IRB), do you have approval from that board?
   - If you are planning on doing research with nonhuman animals and your school has an internal animal care and use committee (IACUC), do you have approval from that committee?

Changing Unethical and Impractical Ideas Into Research Hypotheses

In their present form, some of your ideas may be impractical or unethical. However, with a little ingenuity, many of your ideas can be converted into workable research hypotheses. As you will see, many practical and ethical obstacles can be overcome by making the key variables more abstract, constructing a smaller scale model of the situation, toning down the strength of the manipulation, or not using manipulations.

To understand how these principles can turn even the most impractical and unethical idea into a viable research hypothesis, consider the following hypothesis: *Receiving severe beatings causes one to be a murderer.* How could we convert this idea into a workable research hypothesis?

Make Variables More General

One possibility is to consider your original variables as specific instances of more general variables and then reformulate your hypothesis using these more abstract variables. In our murder example, you could view murder as a more specific instance of aggression and view beating as a specific instance of either aggression, pain, or punishment. Thus, you now have three research hypotheses that have been studied in controlled settings: (1) *aggression leads to more aggression*, (2) *pain causes aggression*, and (3) *punishment causes aggression*.

Use Smaller Scale Models of the Situation

Of course, you are not going to have human participants hitting each other to measure aggression. Instead, you may give participants an opportunity to destroy something that supposedly belongs to the target of their anger, an opportunity to write a negative evaluation, an opportunity to press a button that supposedly (but doesn't really) delivers a mild shock to another person, and so on. As you can imagine, working with a small-scale model of aggressive situations is more ethical than manipulating real-life aggression.

Smaller scale models of the situation not only have ethical advantages, but also have practical advantages as well. For example, if you are interested in the effects of temperature on aggression, you can't manipulate the temperature outside. However, you can manipulate the temperature in a room. Similarly, you can't manipulate the size of a crowd at a college football game to see the effect of crowd size on performance, but you can manipulate audience size at a dart contest that you sponsor. By using a dart contest, testing your audience-size hypothesis is not only possible, but also practical. For instance, if audience size has an effect, you could probably find it by varying the size of the audience from zero (when you are hiding behind a one-way mirror) to three (yourself and two friends).

Once you have a small-scale model of a phenomenon, you can test all kinds of ideas that previously seemed impossible to test. For example, can you imagine using the dart contest situation to test the effects of audience involvement or size of reward on performance?

Because smaller scale models of situations are so valuable, researchers often review research literature to discover if someone else has already made a smaller scale model of the phenomenon they wish to study. That is, just as an airplane designer may use a wind tunnel to test new airplane designs, researchers may use someone else's model of a situation to see if their ideas fly.

Carefully Screen Potential Participants

In some research, you might decrease the ethical problems by choosing participants who are unlikely to be harmed by the manipulation. Therefore, if you were to do a frustration-aggression study, you might only use participants who

1. were, according to a recently administered personality profile, well-adjusted
2. were physically healthy
3. volunteered after knowing about the degree of discomfort they would experience

Use "Moderate" Manipulations

Not only can you limit who will be in the study, but you can also limit how much of the manipulation you use. By reducing the extent to which you use unpleasant stimuli, you reduce the harm to participants. Thus, if you were to induce frustration to observe its effect on aggression, you might decide not to use a very high level of frustration. Even though a high level of frustration would be more likely to produce aggression, you might decide to use lower levels of frustration to lower the risks of harming your participants.

Do Not Manipulate Variables

Finally, you may decide not to manipulate the variables at all. To understand the basic advantages and disadvantages of not manipulating variables, let's return to the original hypothesis: *Receiving severe beatings causes one to be a murderer.* You might pursue this idea by interviewing murderers and nonmurderers to see whether murderers were more likely to report being beaten as children. Unfortunately, even if you found that murderers were more likely than nonmurderers to have been beaten, your results would not necessarily mean that the beatings caused the murders. Beatings may have no impact on murders. Instead, murderers may have been beaten more than nonmurderers because, even when they were younger, murderers were more aggressive and more disobedient than nonmurderers. Although interviewing wouldn't allow you to discover whether beatings cause children to become murderers, it might allow you to address a related research hypothesis: *Murderers are more likely to claim to be beaten by their parents than nonmurderers.*[3]

Concluding Remarks

In this chapter, you have learned how to generate research ideas. Consequently, if you spend a little time reviewing this chapter, you should be able to generate several hypotheses about how two or more variables are related.

Now that you have a hypothesis about how two or more variables are related, you have several choices about your next step. If your most immediate concern is how to obtain or generate valid measures and manipulations of your variables, skip ahead to Chapter 5. If you think you may need a new research hypothesis—or if you want to see how others have tested related hypotheses—read Chapter 4. If you like your hypothesis, but you either need to

---

[3]Unfortunately, you will not know whether murderers actually were beaten more than other people because murders may exaggerate the extent to which they were beaten.

refine or write up the rationale for your hypothesis, skip ahead to Chapter 15. If your most immediate concern is that you want to know how to actually go about conducting a study to test your hypothesis, read Appendix C: "Practical Tips for Conducting an Ethical and Valid Study." If you are pretty sure you want to use a survey to test your hypothesis and your most immediate concern is how to conduct such a survey, skip ahead to Chapter 8.

SUMMARY

1. The purpose of scientific research is to test ideas. One way to get research ideas is to test common-sense ideas.

2. Hypothetical constructs are abstract variables that can't be directly observed (love, learning, thirst, etc.). Researchers can deal with abstract constructs by devising "recipes" for these variables called operational definitions: concrete ways of manipulating or measuring abstract constructs.

3. Building on other people's research is an easy way to get good research ideas.

4. Strategies for developing research ideas from previous research include improving the original study's external, internal, or construct validity; repeating the study; seeing if the finding has any practical implications; doing a follow-up study suggested by the study's authors; and trying to determine why two studies produced conflicting findings.

5. You can sometimes improve a study's construct validity by using the double-blind technique.

6. Never do a study without first obtaining your professor's permission.

7. A null hypothesis states that there is no relationship between two variables. Although the null hypothesis can be disproven, it can't be proven.

8. When possible, use theory and past research to provide a rationale for your prediction and to show that the results of your study may have implications for evaluating theory and previous research findings.

9. If your hypothesis involves a prediction that one variable influences a second variable, you can refine that hypothesis by (a) studying the functional relationship between those two variables, (b) trying to find the physiological or mental variable mediating that relationship, or (c) finding a variable that moderates that relationship.

10. A research hypothesis must be testable and must be testable in an ethical manner.

11. Even the most impractical and unethical of ideas may be converted into a practical and ethical hypothesis if you carefully screen your participants, use a small-scale model of the phenomenon you wish to study, make key variables more general or abstract, tone down the intensity of your manipulation, or don't use manipulations.

KEY TERMS

hypothesis *(p. 46)*

double-blind technique *(p. 51)*

moderator variable *(p. 51)*

null hypothesis *(p. 53)*

theory *(p. 54)*

straw theory *(p. 57)*

independent variable *(p. 58)*

dependent variable (dependent measure) *(p. 58)*

mediating variable *(p. 60)*

functional relationship *(p. 64)*

EXERCISES

1. Look up a research study that tests a commonsense notion or proverb. (If you are having difficulty finding an article, consult Web Appendix B.) What is the title of the article? What are its main conclusions?

2. Writing an essay that expresses opinions that go against your beliefs may cause you to change your beliefs. According to dissonance theory, what factors may moderate the effect of writing such a counterattitudinal essay?

3. According to dissonance theory, what is an important variable that mediates attitude change?

4. Find a research article that tests a hypothesis derived from theory. Give the citation for the article, and describe the main findings.

5. Describe the relationship between moderator variables and external validity.

6. Design a study to improve the construct validity of the study reported in Appendix B.

7. Design a study to test the generalizability of the findings of the study reported in Appendix B.

8. The study reported in Appendix B finds a relationship between two variables. Design a study to map out the functional relationship between those two variables.

9. Design a study to test the practical implications of the findings from the study reported in Appendix B.

10. Taking into account the problems with the null hypothesis, discuss what is wrong with the following research conclusions:
    a. There is no difference in outcome among the different psychological therapies.
    b. Viewing television violence is not related to aggression.
    c. There are no gender differences in emotional responsiveness.

WEB RESOURCES

1. Go to the Chapter 3 section of the book's student website and:
   a. Look over the concept map of the key terms.
   b. Test yourself on the key terms.
   c. Take the Chapter 3 Practice Quiz.
   d. Do the interactive end-of-chapter exercises.
   e. Download the "Idea Generator," and develop a research idea.
   f. Use the "C3Tester" link to help spell out your predictions.
   g. Practice evaluating hypotheses using the "C3Evaluator" link.

2. Get a better sense of what research is like by using Chapter 3's "Participate in a Study" link.

3. Get more ideas on how to use theory to support your hypothesis by reading "Web Appendix: Using Theory to Generate Ideas."

4. If you have a research hypothesis that you want to test, use Chapter 3's "Getting Started on Writing Your Introduction" link.

INFOTRAC COLLEGE EDITION EXPLORATIONS

1. To find some examples of research that tests theory, do an InfoTrac College Edition keyword search using the phrase "test of theory and psychology."

2. To see some examples of hypotheses involving moderating variables, do an InfoTrac College Edition keyword search for "moderator."

3. To get a better understanding of the distinction between mediators and moderators, do an InfoTrac College Edition keyword search using the phrase "moderators and mediators."

4

Reading and Evaluating Research

It's not what you don't know that's the problem.
It's what you know that just ain't so.

—*Will Rogers*

Overview

Nobody can know everything. Thus, there is much you will never know. Furthermore, thanks in part to the disinformation campaigns waged by advertisers, the media, politicians, and others, some of what you think you know will be false. Most of the time, what you don't know won't hurt you. However, there are times—when making a decision about a medical test or treatment, when deciding on a way to help a child, when deciding what charity to support, when deciding whether a country has nuclear weapons, when deciding about what problems social security has—when not knowing the facts can have life-changing, and even life-ending, consequences.

When you do need the best information, you need to read the research and question that research. In this chapter, we will focus on helping you read and question psychological research presented in journal articles. We chose psychological research articles because they are rich gold mines of information about a wide variety of topics: from how to be happier or healthier to how the genders differ to how the mind works. However, if you wish to use the critical thinking skills we discuss in this chapter to help you mine other original sources that are relevant to making informed purchasing or political decisions, you will be able to do so.

We will start by learning how to make sense of a research article. Then, you will learn how to spot flaws and limitations in research. Finally, you will learn how you can get research ideas by reading research: You will see how ideas breed ideas. Thus, the aim of this chapter is to make you an intelligent consumer and producer of research.

Reading for Understanding

You wouldn't find a "how to" manual about how to download ring tones for your cell phone very useful unless you were reading it while you were downloading rings. Similarly, you will find this "how to read an article" chapter little more than a review of what you already know unless you read it while you are reading an article. Therefore, before you finish the next section, get an article.

Choosing an Article

Do not get just any article. To repeat, don't just read the first article you find! Because critically evaluating an article involves actively applying what you have learned about research design, get an article that will motivate you to apply what you know about research design. Specifically, choose an article that uses a design you understand and that deals with an area that you find interesting.

To start your quest for such an article, you could:

1. Look at sections of texts that you find particularly interesting, and look up the articles they reference. For example, you might want to look up a study referenced in this textbook, such as the study by Wilson and Schooler (1991) on situations when thinking about why we like something hurts our ability to know how much we like it.

2. Consult Web Appendix B, "Searching the Literature," to learn how to search for articles on a topic that interests you or by a researcher whose work interests you.

3. Browse the table of contents of current journals.

Your first clue to whether an article is interesting is its title. Almost any title will tell you what the general topic or research question was. A good title will also contain the study's key variables. For example, in articles describing an experiment, the main manipulated factor (the main independent variable) and the outcome variable (the dependent measure) may be in the title. In some cases, the title may hint at what the hypothesis was or even what the main findings were.

Once you find an article that has an interesting title, the next step is to read a brief, one-paragraph summary of that article. This one-paragraph summary of the research's purpose, methodology, and results is called the **abstract.**

Even if you don't have the original article, you can read its abstract—provided you have access to one of the resources described in Web Appendix B, such as *Psychological Abstracts* or *PsycINFO* (the computerized version of *Psychological Abstracts*). If you have the original article, the only problem in finding the abstract is that it is usually not labeled. To find the abstract, turn to the article's first page. Right under the title, you will see a paragraph that stands apart from the rest of the article. Although *it might not be labeled*, this one-paragraph summary of the study is called the abstract.[1]

Reading the Abstract

By reading the abstract, you should get a general sense of what the researchers' hypotheses were, how they tried to test those hypotheses, and whether the results supported those hypotheses. But most importantly, you will get an idea about whether you want to read the article. To reiterate, you will probably not want to read the first article that you find. Indeed, when we have students analyze an article, we find that the students who look at more than five abstracts before choosing an article are the happiest with their articles.

Reading the Introduction

Once you find an article that has an interesting title and abstract, you are ready to start reading the rest of the article. For the beginning student, the best place to start reading an article is at the beginning. Although unlabeled, the beginning of the article is called the **introduction.** The introduction is the most difficult, most time consuming, and most important part of the article to understand. You must understand the introduction because it is where the authors tell you

1. how they came up with the hypothesis, including reasons why they think the hypothesis will be supported
2. reasons why the hypothesis might not be correct
3. why the hypothesis is important
4. why the authors' way of testing the hypothesis is the best way to test the hypothesis (see Figure 4-1)

One way of thinking of the introduction is as a commercial for the article. The authors try to sell you on the importance of their research. They may try to sell you on their study by claiming that, relative to previous research ("our competitor's brands"), their methodology is "clearly superior."

---

[1]Some older articles do not have an abstract but do contain a summary placed at the end of the article.

Figure 4-1 | **General Flow Chart of an Introduction**

1	Overview of general topic
2	Rationale for study in terms of flaws or gaps in past research
3	Reasons to believe hypothesis will be supported
4	Reasons to doubt that hypothesis will be supported
5	Clear statement of specific research hypothesis
6	Arguments for why the author's method is the best way to test the hypothesis

Sometimes they argue that their methodology is superior because their study has better construct validity. For example, they may argue that they use a better measure, a better manipulation, or a better way of preventing participants and experimenters from biasing the results.

Sometimes they argue that their methodology is superior because their study has more internal validity. For example, they may argue that they, unlike previous researchers, are able to demonstrate that the treatment, rather than some other factor, caused changes in the participants because they, unlike previous researchers, used an **experimental design:** a design in which (a) a treatment manipulation is administered and (b) that manipulation is the only variable that systematically varies between treatment conditions.[2]

---

[2]As you will see in Chapters 10-13, the only factors that systematically vary in an experimental design are the treatment factors. Therefore, in an experiment, if manipulating a treatment is followed by a significant behavioral change, the experimenter can be confident that the behavioral change is due to the treatment. As you will also see in Chapters 10-13, one key to making sure other variables do not systematically vary along with the treatment is random assignment. In its simplest form, random assignment involves using a coin flip or some other random process to determine which of two treatments a participant receives.

Sometimes researchers argue that their study is superior to previous research in terms of external validity. To argue that their study has more generalizability than previous research, they will stress that they are using a more representative sample of participants, a broader range of participants, or more naturalistic settings.

Sometimes researchers argue that their study is superior to previous research in terms of **power:** the ability to detect differences between conditions. A powerful study may find relationships that a less powerful study fails to find. To argue that their study has more power, they may stress that they are using a more sensitive design, more sensitive measures, or more participants than the original study.

If the authors don't try to sell you on the methodological superiority of their study, they may try to sell you on their study by telling you that, relative to previous hypotheses, their hypothesis is "new and improved" because it has a special ingredient that other hypotheses don't have. Thus, they will try to get you to say, "It's incredible that people have done all this other, related research, but not tested this hypothesis! Why didn't anyone else think of this?" Often, such studies extend existing research by

1. using a different sample than previous research (e.g., women versus men)
2. looking at a different behavior (e.g., manner of walking instead of facial expression, gambling rather than bar-pressing)
3. looking at a variable, such as experience, ability, or motivation, that might moderate or alter a previously discovered relationship
4. looking at cognitive (e.g., feelings of being overwhelmed) or physiological (e.g., blood pressure) variables that may mediate a previously discovered relationship
5. testing a competing explanation for a treatment's effect (e.g., biological versus cultural)
6. attempting to reconcile the fact that studies have produced apparently conflicting results

A second way to look at the introduction is as a preview to the rest of the article. The authors start by giving you an overview of the research area. Then, they go into more detail about what other researchers have found in exploring a specific research topic. Next, the researchers point to some problem with past research. This problem may be a gap in past research, such as a research hypothesis being tested in only a couple of studies—or by none at all. This problem may be a flaw in past research, such as the failure to control for key variables or the production of contradictory findings. The authors will use the problem as the rationale for their study and then state the research question. Finally, the authors may explain why their method for testing the hypothesis is the best way (see Figure 4-1 on page 73). For example, they may justify their choice of design, their choice of measures, and their choice of participants. Consequently, if you understand the introduction, you should be able to anticipate what will be said in the rest of the article.

Unfortunately, understanding the introduction is not always easy. The main reason the introduction may be hard for you to understand is that the authors are not writing it with you in mind. Instead, they are writing it to other experts in the field. Their belief that the reader is an expert has two important consequences for how they write their research. First, because they assume that the reader is an expert in the field, they do not think that they have

| Table 4-1 | **Deciphering Journal Articles** |

Even experts may need to read a journal article several times to understand it fully. During your first reading, highlight any terms or concepts that you do not understand on a photocopy of the article. The highlighting shows you what you don't understand (if you highlight the entire article, maybe you should find another article). Once you identify the terms that you don't understand, decipher those terms by using one of the techniques listed below.

To Decipher Highlighted Terms

- Consult an introductory psychology text.
- Consult an advanced psychology text.
- Consult a psychological dictionary or encyclopedia.
- Consult a professor.
- Consult general sources such as *Psychological Science, Psychological Bulletin, Annual Review,* and *American Psychologist*—to better understand key theories.
- Consult other articles that were referenced in the article.
- Look up the term in a search engine, such as http://www.google.com or http://scholar.google.com.

to give in-depth descriptions of the published articles they discuss. In fact, authors often assume that just mentioning the authors and the year of work (for instance, Miller & Smudgekins, 2006) will make the reader instantly recall the essentials of that article. Second, because they assume that the reader is an expert, they do not think they have to define the field's concepts and theories.

Because you are not an expert in the field, the authors' failure to describe studies and define concepts may make it difficult to understand what they are trying to say. Fortunately, you can compensate for not having the background the authors think you have by doing two things. First, read the abstracts of the articles that the authors mention. Second, look up unfamiliar terms or theories in a textbook. If you can't find the term in a textbook, consult the sources listed in Table 4-1.

To encourage yourself to look up all relevant terms and theories, make a photocopy of your article. On the photocopy, use a yellow highlighter to mark any terms or concepts you do not understand (Brewer, 1990). Do some background reading on those highlighted concepts, and then reread the introduction. As you reread it, highlight any terms or concepts you do not understand with a pink marker. Do some more background reading to get a better understanding of those terms. Then, reread the introduction using a green marker to highlight terms you still do not understand (Brewer, 1990).

By the third time you go through the introduction, you should see much less green than yellow, visually demonstrating that you are making progress (Brewer, 1990). However, even if you know all the individual terms, how do you know that you understand the introduction? One test is to try to describe the logic behind the hypothesis in your own words. A more rigorous test is to design a study to test the hypothesis and then describe the impact of those results for current theory and further research. If you can do that, you not only understand the introduction, but you probably also have a good idea of what the authors are going to say in their discussion section. To reiterate, do not simply skim the introduction and then move on to the method section. The first time through the introduction, ask yourself two questions:

1. What concepts do I need to look up?
2. What references do I need to read?

Then, after doing your background reading, reread the introduction. Do not move on to the method section until you can answer these six questions:

1. What variables are the authors interested in?
2. What is the prediction (hypothesis) involving those variables? (What is being studied?)
3. Why does the prediction (hypothesis) make sense?
4. How do the authors plan to test their prediction? Why does their plan seem to be a reasonable one?
5. Does the study correct a weakness in previous research? If so, what was that weakness? That is, where did others go wrong?
6. Does the study fill a gap in previous research? If so, what was that gap? That is, what did others overlook?

Reading the Method Section

After you are clear about what the authors predicted and why the authors made those predictions, read the method section to find out what the authors did.

In the **method section,** the authors will tell you what was done in terms of

1. who the participants were and how they were selected
2. what measures and equipment were used
3. what the researchers said and did to the participants

An efficient way to tell you about each of these three aspects of the method is to devote a section to each aspect. Although many method sections are subdivided into these three subsections—participants, apparatus (or measures), and procedure—some have fewer and some have more.

Studies with more sections have an overview subsection. You are most likely to see an overview subsection if the article reports several studies, all of which use similar procedures. By using an overview section, the author of a four-experiment paper can describe the aspects of the method that are the same for all four studies once, rather than repeating those details in all four method sections. You may also see a brief overview section for any method section that is so long or so detailed that readers need to see a general outline of the methods before they can make sense of the procedure section.

Some method sections have a separate design subsection. For instance, the design sub-section might tell you whether the design was a between-subjects design, a within-subjects design (often referred to as a repeated-measures design), or a mixed design (to learn more about within-subjects designs and mixed designs, see Chapter 13). However, authors do not need to include a separate design section. Instead, they may put information about the design in the participants section, in some other section, or even leave design information out of the method section entirely.

Just as authors often do not include a design subsection, authors often do not include either a materials or an apparatus section. Instead, they may incorporate information about the apparatus or materials in the procedure section.

In short, there is no one rule for how many subsections a method section should have. Many will have only two: a participants section and a procedure section. Others may have an overview section, a participants and design section, a procedure section, and a dependent-measures section. Other method sections will use still different formats.

Regardless of its structure, the method section should be the easiest to understand for two reasons. First, the only purpose of the method section is to tell you what happened in the study—who the participants were, how many participants there were, and how they were treated. The authors should make it easy for you to imagine what it would be like to be a participant in the study. Indeed, some good procedure sections almost make you feel like you are watching a video, shot from the participants' perspective, of what happened in the study.

Second, the method section should be easy to understand because the introduction should have foreshadowed how the authors planned to test the hypothesis.[3] Therefore, the only trouble you may have in understanding a method section is if you are unfamiliar with some task (for example, a Stroop task) or piece of equipment (such as a tachistoscope) that the researchers used.

What should you do if you encounter an unfamiliar apparatus or measure? Look up any unfamiliar apparatus in the index of either an advanced textbook or a laboratory equipment catalog. If that fails, ask your professor. If you encounter an unfamiliar measure, find a source that describes the measure in detail. Such a source should be cited in the original article where the measure is first mentioned and that source should be referenced in the original article's reference section. If the source is not referenced in the original article, look up the measure in the index of one or more textbooks. If that fails, look up the concept the measure is claiming to assess in *Psychological Abstracts*. The *Abstracts* should lead you to an article that will describe the measure.

After reading the method section, take a few moments to think about what it would have been like to be a participant in each of the study's conditions. Then, think about what it would have been like to be the researcher.

Realize that the method section contains the information you need to evaluate the study's internal, external, and construct validity. Consequently, to critique a study, you will need to reread the method section (see Box 4-1).

When evaluating the study's internal validity, you will want to know

- whether random assignment was attempted and properly executed
- whether an apparent effect might be due to more people dropping out of one condition than another

When evaluating external validity, you will want to know

- the population from which the sample was drawn
- what criteria were used to exclude people from the study
- whether random sampling was used
- what the dropout rate was
- what the gender, age, racial, and ethnic composition of the sample was

---

[3]We do not mean that all method sections are easy to read. We mean that authors should be able to write a clear, understandable method section. Unfortunately, authors sometimes do not write coherent method sections. Therefore, if you do not understand a method section, it is probably not your fault. It is the fault of the author and editor. In such cases, professors are usually quite willing to help you translate a poorly written method section.

BOX 4-1 Questions to Ask of a Study

Questions About Construct Validity

1. Was the manipulation valid (does it manipulate what it claims to manipulate)?

   a. Is the manipulation consistent with definitions of the construct that is allegedly being manipulated?

   b. If the treatment manipulation involved using a sample of specific stimuli (e.g., particular men's names and women's names) to represent a broad, general variable that has many members (e.g., all men's and all women's names), did the researcher use a good enough sample of stimuli to make the case that the difference between conditions was due to differences in the underlying construct? For example, if "David" produced a different reaction than "Dana," that difference might be due to some factor other than gender ("David" is longer, more common, and more closely associated with the Bible's King David). Thus, we would be more confident saying that the effect was due to gender of the name if the researcher had obtained the same effect using several other pairs of names (e.g., "Larry" and "Mary"). Similarly, if the researchers used one male experimenter and one female experimenter and then talked about a gender of experimenter effect, the manipulation's effect may be due to some other difference between the experimenters besides gender.

   c. Did the researchers use a **manipulation check:** a question or set of questions designed to determine whether participants perceived the manipulation in the way that the researcher intended? (For more on manipulation checks, see Chapter 5.)

   d. Are *more* or *better* control (no-treatment) conditions needed? (The control condition[s] and the experimental [treatment] condition[s] should be identical except for those aspects directly related to the construct being manipulated.)

2. Is the measure **valid:** does it measure what it claims to measure?

   a. Is it **reliable:** does it produce stable, consistent scores that are not strongly influenced by random error? Reliability is a prerequisite for validity. One index of reliability—called test–retest reliability—assesses whether participants score about the same when they are retested as when they were originally tested. If test–retest reliability is below .70, the measure is not very reliable. Indeed, many people are displeased with test–retest reliabilities below .80.

   Even if the authors do not provide the measure's test–retest reliability—an index of the measure's overall resistance to random error—the authors may provide indexes of the measure's vulnerability to specific sources of random error. The specific index of reliability you would want would depend on what specific sources of unreliability concerned you the most. For example, if the measure involved making raters judge something, you should be concerned that the raters might not be reliable. Therefore, look for evidence that different raters judging the same thing made similar judgments. Percentage of times judges agreed, correlations between raters, and Cohen's kappa might all serve as evidence of observer agreement. If, on the other hand, participants are filling out a rating scale measure, you are not worried about inconsistency due to unreliable scoring. Instead, you are worried about unreliability due to inconsistencies in the questions. To get at your concern that the questions may not be measuring the same concept, you would want some index of internal consistency (sometimes called internal reliability) such as inter-item correlations (which should be above .30) or Cronbach's alpha (which should be above .80).

   b. Did research show that it correlated with other measures of that same construct?

   c. Did research show that it was uncorrelated with measures of unrelated constructs?

   d. Was the measure consistent with accepted definitions of the construct?

3. Could the researchers have biased the study's results?

   a. Were researchers "blind"—or did they know which participants were expected to score higher?

   b. Did the lack of detailed and clearly spelled out procedures make it easy for researchers to bias the results?

4. Could participants have figured out the hypothesis? If so, they might have tried to "help" the researcher get the "right" results.

   a. Could participants have learned about the study from former participants?

   b. Were participants experienced enough to figure out the hypothesis (for instance, senior psychology majors who had participated in several studies)?

c. Was the hypothesis a fairly easy one to figure out?

d. Did the research use a no-treatment (empty) control group—rather than a control group that got a fake (placebo) treatment?

e. Did the researcher fail to make the study a double-blind study, thus allowing either the participants or the researcher to know which treatment the participants were receiving?

f. Was it obvious to participants what was being measured? (For example, did participants fill out a self-report scale?)

g. Did the study lack **experimental (research) realism:** the ability to psychologically involve participants in the task so that they would not merely be playing the role of cooperative participant?

h. Did the researchers fail to have an effective "cover story" that disguised the true purpose of the study?

Questions About External Validity

1. Would results apply to the average person?
   a. Were participants human?
   b. Were participants distinct in any way?
   c. Were the participants too homogeneous? That is, were there certain types of individuals (women, minorities) who were not included in the study?
   d. Was the dropout rate high—or high among certain groups (for example, participants over 65 years of age)? If so, the results apply only to those who stayed in the study.
   e. Is there any specific reason to suspect that the results would not apply to a different group of participants?
   f. If the researchers used a survey and tried to generalize their results to a wider group
      i. what was that larger group?
      ii. did they have a large and random sample from that group?

2. Would the results generalize to different settings? Can you pinpoint a difference between the research setting and a real-life setting and give a specific reason why this difference would prevent the results from applying to real life?

3. Would the results generalize to different levels of the treatment variable?
   a. Was a wide range of treatment levels tested?
   b. Were realistic levels of the treatment variable tested?
   c. Were enough (at least three) levels of the treatment variable used to allow one to generalize to untested levels?

Questions About Internal Validity

1. Was an experimental design used? If not, the study probably does not have internal validity. To help determine whether a study is an experiment, realize that (a) all experiments involve manipulating the treatment and (b) most experiments involve randomly assigning participants to condition (using a random process, such as a random number table, to determine which treatment a participant receives). Random assignment allows researchers to make a strong case that the difference between the actions of participants in the different conditions is due to the treatment manipulation rather than to nontreatment factors. In the experiment,
   a. Was there a difference between the scores in the different conditions? If not, there is no evidence of an effect, so there is no point in talking about its cause.
   b. What steps did the experimenter take to make it unlikely that the difference between conditions was due to nontreatment factors? Usually, experimenters will deal with nontreatment factors in at least one of the following three ways:
      i. Keeping the nontreatment factor constant. Thus, to control for time of day, the researcher might test all participants at the same time of day.
      ii. Using random assignment or some other technique to randomize—and then statistically account for—nontreatment variables. Thus, to control for time of day, the researcher would randomly assign participants to condition. With random assignment, there would be no systematic difference between participants in terms of when they were tested. Instead, any differences in time of testing would be unsystematic differences. Consequently, if the difference between groups' scores was statistically significant, it is unlikely that the difference in scores is due solely to time of day—or to any other—unsystematic, chance difference.
      iii. Counterbalancing—systematically rotating which condition received which level of the nontreatment variable—to balance out the effect of that variable. Thus, to control for time of day, the researcher might alternate testing sessions. For example, on the first day,

(continued)

BOX 4-1 (*continued*)

the treatment group might be tested in the morning and the no-treatment group might be tested in the afternoon. On the next day, the situation would be reversed.

c. Did more participants drop out of the treatment group than the control group? If so, this dropout may mimic a treatment effect.

2. If the study was not an experiment, the study probably does not have internal validity. Note that
   a. In some nonexperimental research, what the researcher thinks is a cause may actually be an effect. For example, surveys show that people that watch more television tend to have lower self-esteem. If a researcher concluded that television-viewing caused low self-esteem, the researcher could be wrong. It might be that low self-esteem causes people to watch television (Moskalenko & Heine, 2003).
   b. In some nonexperimental research, two variables may be statistically related because both are effects of some other variable. For example, consider the relationship between low self-esteem and television-viewing. Both may be side effects of having few friends: people who have few friends may have low self-esteem and may watch a lot of television (Moskalenko & Heine, 2003).

Questions About Power (The Study's Ability to Find Differences)

1. If the study failed to find a difference between groups or conditions, ask:
   a. Were measures sensitive enough? Sensitive measures tend to be reliable (for more about reliability, see "Reliability" under construct validity), valid, and provide a range of scores (for more on sensitivity, see Chapter 6).
   b. Was the study sufficiently standardized? That is, did lack of standardization and lack of control over the testing environment create so much noise (error variance) that the treatment effect was overlooked?
   c. Were enough participants used?
   d. Did conditions differ enough on the treatment/predictor variable?
   e. Were participants homogeneous enough—or did between-subject differences hide the treatment effect?
   f. Could the failure to find a difference be due to a floor or ceiling effect?

i. In a floor effect, a problem with the measure makes it so participants who are very low on the variable do not score lower on the measure of the variable than people who are merely low on the variable. Because participants are not scoring differently from one another, the researcher may not find differences between conditions. Suspect a floor effect if everyone is scoring low on the measure or if the scores in the lower scoring group are less spread out (have a much smaller standard deviation) than scores in the higher scoring group.

ii. The ceiling effect is the reverse of the floor effect. Everyone is scoring so high on the measure that participants who are, in reality, very high on the variable can't score higher on the measure of the variable than participants who are somewhat high on that variable. As a consequence of participants "maxing" out the scale, the researcher may not find differences between conditions. For example, if all the participants scored 100% on a memory test, the participants who have a memory for the information that is better than the average participant's are not able to show their better memory on this test. Thus, even if every participant in the treatment group had a better memory for the material than any one in the no-treatment group, there would be no difference between the groups on the measure: Both groups would average 100%. Suspect a ceiling effect if everyone is scoring high on the measure or if the scores in the higher scoring group are less spread out (have a much smaller standard deviation) than scores in the lower scoring group.

Questions About Statistical Analyses

1. Do the data meet the assumptions of the statistical test? For example, if the researchers did an independent-groups t test, were participants' responses unaffected by how other participants responded and were data at least interval scale? (To learn about interval scale data, see Chapter 6; to learn more about the independent-groups t test, see Chapter 10 or Appendix D.)

2. Are the researchers running a high risk of making a **Type 1 error:** declaring a difference significant even though, in reality, there is not a reliable difference?
   a. Are they doing multiple statistical tests without correcting for the fact that their reported significance level is only valid if they are doing a single test? For example, if they use a .05 (5%) significance level, but do 100 tests, 5 tests could turn out significant by chance alone.
   b. Are they using unconventionally high significance levels (the higher the significance level, the higher the risk of a Type 1 error)? For example, if they are using a .20 level rather than the traditional are $p < .05$ level, they are taking more than 4 times the risk of making a Type I error than most researchers take.
   c. Has the study been replicated? Replication, rather than statistical significance, is the best evidence that the findings are reliable. If you know of failures to replicate, or if you suspect a file drawer problem (see page 87), the significant results of the study may reflect a Type 1 error.

3. Did the authors represent differences between two means as real even though
   a. A statistical test had been performed and the differences were not statistically significant?
   b. No statistical significance test had been performed that directly tested whether those two means were significantly different from each other?

4. Did the authors represent statistically significant differences as being large without providing effect size indexes (e. g., r, r^2, eta squared [η^2], omega-squared [ω^2], Cohen's d) to support their position that those differences were large? Effect size measures, not significance tests, are what tell you the size of the effect. (These effect size measures should be not be derived from statistical analyses where the F for the numerator was greater than 1.)

5. If the authors used regression analysis, realize that regression involves fitting a regression model to data. Like the farmer who shot at the barn and then painted the target where most of the shots were, regression models can be misleading. Be suspicious that the model's fit would not be so good if the model had to predict the data if
   a. the authors used stepwise regression; or
   b. the ratio of participants to predictors was less than 15 to 1.

When evaluating the construct validity of a study, you will want to know

- the reliability and validity of the measure
- the degree to which the researcher has used techniques to prevent researcher and participant bias, such as (a) having the dependent measure collected and coded by assistants who do not know what condition the participant is in and (b) having the treatment administered by assistants who do not know what the hypothesis is

Although you will probably return to the method section, do not leave it to go on to the results section until you understand what happened well enough that you could act out the roles of both researcher and participant. More specifically, do not go on to the results section until you can answer these five questions:

1. What were the participants like (species, gender, age), and how did they come to be in the study?

2. What was done to the participants?

3. What tasks or actions did the participants perform?

4. What were the key variables in this study, and how did the researcher operationally define those variables? For example, how was the dependent variable measured?

5. What was the design?

Reading the Results Section

Now, turn to the results section of the article you selected to find out what happened. Just like a sports box score tells you how your team did, the **results section** tells you how the hypotheses did.

Like a box score, the results section tells you more than whether the hypothesis "won." You probably could have determined whether the hypothesis was supported just from reading the article's title, just like you could tell whether your team won merely from reading the headline. The results section, like the box score, provides a more in-depth analysis of the results.

Of course, there are many differences between box scores and results sections. One difference is that authors of box scores do not have to explain what the numbers in the box scores mean. For example, any baseball fan knows that a "1" in the "HR" column means that the batter hit one home run. But in a study, what does it mean that the participants averaged a "6"? The meaning of a 6 would depend on the study; therefore, at the beginning of the results section (if they did not do so in the method section), the authors will briefly explain how they got the numbers that they later put into the statistical analysis. That is, they will describe how they scored participants' responses. Often, the scoring process is straightforward. For example, researchers may say, "The data were the number of correctly recalled words."

Occasionally, computing a score for each participant involves a little more work. In one study, researchers were looking at whether participants believed a person had a mental illness (Hilton & von Hippel, 1990). To measure these beliefs, the researchers had participants answer two questions. First, participants answered either "yes" or "no" to a question about whether the person had a mental illness. Then, researchers had participants rate, on a 1-to-9 scale, how confident participants were of their decision. How did the researchers turn these two responses into a single score? To quote the authors,

> In creating this scale, a value of −1 was assigned to "no" responses and a value of +1 was assigned to "yes" responses. The confidence ratings were then multiplied by these numbers. All ratings were then converted to a positive scale by adding 10 to the product. This transformation led to a scale in which 1 indicates a high degree of confidence that the person is normal and 19 represents a high degree of confidence that the person is pathological.

Do not merely glance at the brief section describing the scores to be used. Before leaving that section, be sure you know what a low score indicates and what a high score indicates. If you do not understand what the numbers being analyzed represent, you will not be able to understand the results of analyses based on those numbers.

After explaining how they got the scores for each participant, the authors may explain how those scores were analyzed. For example, they may write, "The prison sentence the participant recommended was divided by the maximum prison sentence that the participant could have recommended to obtain a score on the dependent measure. These scores were then subjected to a 2 (attractiveness) × 3 (type of crime) between subjects analysis of variance (ANOVA)." (To learn more about ANOVA, see Appendix D.)

Both the kind and the number of analyses will depend on the study. Depending on the study, the authors will usually report anywhere from one to four kinds of results.

Basic Descriptive Statistics

The first kind of analysis that may be reported—but often is not—is an analysis focusing on basic, descriptive statistics that summarize the sample's scores on one or more measures. Typically, authors will describe the average score using the mean (which they will abbreviate as M), a measure of the variability (spread) in scores such as the range of scores or, more commonly, the standard deviation (abbreviated SD), and the degree to which the scores were normally distributed (normally distributed usually indicates that [a] the most common score is the mean, [b] most scores are near the mean, [c] as many scores are above the mean as below the mean, and [d] plotting the scores on the graph produces a symmetrical, bell-shaped pattern). For instance, authors may report, "Overall, recall was fairly good ($M = 12.89$, $SD = 2.68$) and recall scores were normally distributed."

Knowing that the data are normally distributed is useful because many statistical tests, such as the t test and ANOVA, assume that data are normally distributed. If the data are not normally distributed, the researcher has three choices. First, the researcher may do the test and hope that violating the normality assumption will not unduly affect the results. Second, the researcher can decide to use a statistical test that does not assume that scores are normally distributed (often, such tests are called "nonparametric tests"). Third, the researcher may be able to perform some mathematical operation (transformation) on the scores to get a more normal distribution (hence, the joke that statisticians are not normal, but can be transformed). Occasionally, the mathematical operation that makes the distribution normal is relatively simple. For instance, rather than analyze how much *time* it took participants to scan a word, a researcher may analyze the scanning *speed*. The time-to-speed transformation involves inverting the time scores. Thus, a scanning time of half a second per word may become a speed of 2 words per second (2/1).

If a new measure is used, the authors may report evidence suggesting that the measure has one prerequisite for validity: reliability. Reliability means that the scores are not unduly influenced by random error and thus may be influenced by the stable characteristic the researchers want to measure. One way to provide evidence that the measure is reliable is to show that the measure produces stable, consistent scores by showing that people taking the test twice score about the same both times. Thus, authors may report, "test–retest reliability was .90."

In addition to—or instead of—using test–retest reliability to show that the measure is "random error free," the authors may show that the measure is free of certain kinds of random error. To provide evidence that the measure is free of random error due to inconsistent raters, the authors might show that raters agreed with one another by reporting inter-rater agreement (e.g., "Raters agreed on 96% of the ratings") or inter-rater reliability ("Inter-rater reliability was extremely high [$r = .98$]"). To provide evidence that the measure is free of random error due to participants' answers to some questions being inconsistent (disagreeing) with answers to other questions on the same scale, the authors may report some measure of internal consistency. For example, the authors might report that the scale had a "coefficient alpha of .91."

In addition to providing evidence for the measure's reliability, the authors may provide evidence for the measure's validity. For instance, authors may report that their emotional intelligence test

a. correlates with other tests of emotional intelligence

b. predicts a behavior associated with the construct (e.g., people scoring higher on the emotional intelligence test have more positive interactions with friends)

c. is not a measure of a related construct (e.g., it does not correlate highly with measures of traditional IQ)

Results of the Manipulation Checks

The next type of results that may be reported would be in a section that describes the results of the manipulation check. The manipulation check is a question or set of questions designed to determine whether participants perceived the manipulation in the way that the researcher intended.

Usually, these results will be statistically significant (unlikely to be due to chance alone and, thus, probably due to the treatment) and unsurprising. For example, if a study manipulates attractiveness of defendant, the researchers might report that: "Participants rated the attractive defendant ($M = 6.2$ on a 1–7 scale) as significantly more attractive than the unattractive defendant ($M = 1.8$), $F(1,44) = 11.56, p < .05$."[4] After the authors have shown you that they manipulated the factor they said they manipulated, they are ready to discuss the effects of that factor.

Results Relating to Hypotheses

The next findings the authors would discuss are the findings that every author discusses—those that relate to the hypotheses. The authors try to connect the results to the hypotheses so that the reader can easily tell how the hypotheses fared. For example, if the hypothesis was that attractive defendants would receive lighter sentences than unattractive defendants, then the author would report what the data said about this hypothesis:

> The hypothesis that attractive defendants would receive lighter sentences was not supported. Attractive defendants received an average sentence of 6.1 years whereas the average sentence for the unattractive defendants was 6.2 years. This difference was not significant, $F(1,32) = 1.00$, *ns*.[5]

Other Significant Results

After reporting results relating to the hypothesis (whether or not the results are statistically significant), authors will dutifully report any other statistically significant results. Even if the results are unwanted and make no sense to the investigator, significant results must be reported. Therefore, you may read things like, "There was an unanticipated interaction between attractiveness and type of crime. Unattractive defendants received heavier sentences for violent crimes whereas attractive defendants received heavier sentences for nonviolent crimes, $F(1,32) = 18.62, p < .05$." Or, you may read, "There was also a significant four-way interaction between attractiveness of defendant, age of defendant, sex of defendant, and type of crime. This interaction was uninterpretable." Typically, these results will be presented last. Although an author is obligated to report these unexpected and unwelcomed findings, an author is not obligated to emphasize them.

Conclusions About Reading the Results Section

In conclusion, depending on the statistics involved, reading the results section may be difficult. The first time through the results section, you may not understand everything. However, before moving on to the discussion section, you should be able to answer these five questions:

1. What are the scores they are putting into the analysis?

---

[4]"$F(1,44) = 11.56$" means that a statistical test called an F test was calculated and the value of that test was 11.56; $p < .05$ means that, if there was no effect for the manipulation, the chances of finding a difference between the groups of that size or larger is less than 5 in a 100. Traditionally, if p is less than 5 in 100, the difference is considered reliable and is described as "statistically significant."

[5]The abbreviation *ns* stands for "not statistically significant." To learn more about statistical significance, see Appendix D.

2. What are the average scores for the different groups? Which types of participants score higher? Lower?

3. Do I understand all the tables and figures that contain descriptive statistics, such as tables of means, percentages, correlations, and so on?

4. What type of statistical analysis did the authors use?

5. Do the results appear to support the authors' hypothesis? Why or why not?

Reading the Discussion

Finally, read the **discussion.** The relationship between the discussion and the results section is not that different from the relationship between a sports article and the box score. The article about the game reiterates key points from the box score, but focuses on putting the game in a larger context—what the team's performance means for the team's playoff hopes, the team's place in history, or even for the league itself. Similarly, the discussion section relates the results to the real world, theory, and future research. Whereas the results section analyzes the results in relationship to the hypothesis, the discussion section interprets the results in light of the bigger picture.

The discussion section should hold few surprises. In fact, before reading the discussion, you could probably write a reasonable outline of it if you take the following three steps.

1. Jot down the main findings.

2. Relate these findings to the introduction.

3. Speculate about the reasons for any surprising results.

Because many discussion sections follow this three-step formula, the discussion is mostly a reiteration of the highlights of the introduction and results sections. If the authors get the results they expect, the focus of these highlights will be on the consistency between the introduction and the results. If, on the other hand, the results are unexpected, the discussion section will attempt to reconcile the introduction and results sections.

After discussing the relationship between the introduction and the results, the authors will provide some general conclusions about the significance of their research and offer suggestions for future research. Consequently, by the time you finish the discussion section, you should be able to answer these five questions:

1. How well do the authors think the results matched their predictions?

2. How do the authors explain any discrepancies between their results and their predictions?

3. Do the authors admit that their study was flawed or limited in any way? If so, how?

4. What additional studies, if any, do the authors recommend?

5. What are the authors' main conclusions?

Developing Research Ideas From Existing Research

Once you understand the article, you can take advantage of what you have learned in previous chapters to question the article's conclusions. For example, you can question the study's power (its ability to detect differences between conditions) as well as its internal, external, and construct validity.

As you can see from Box 4-1, there are many questions you can ask of any study. Asking these questions of a study pays off in at least two ways.

First, because you become aware of the study's limitations, you avoid the mistake of believing that something has been found to be true when it has not. Consequently, you are less likely to act on misinformation and thus less likely to make poor choices when buying products, voting in elections, making business decisions, or treating clients.

Second, because you are aware that no single study answers every question, you realize that additional studies should be done. In other words, a common result of asking questions about research is that you end up designing additional studies that will document, destroy, or build on the previous research. Thus, familiarity with research breeds more research.

The Direct Replication

Whenever you read a study, one obvious research idea always comes to mind—repeat the study. In other words, do a **direct or exact replication:** a copy of the original study.

One reason to do a direct replication is to develop research skills. Many professors—in chemistry, biology, and physics, as well as in psychology—have their students repeat studies to help students develop research skills.

But, from a research standpoint, isn't repeating a study fruitless? Isn't it inevitable that you will get the same results the author reported? Not necessarily—especially if there was an error in the original study. Unfortunately, there are at least three reasons why the results reported in the original study may be misleading: fraud, Type 1 errors, and Type 2 errors.

Combatting Fraud

Although scientific fraud is rare, it does occur. Some cheat for personal fame; others cheat because they believe their ideas are right, even though their results fail to reach the traditional $p < .05$ level of significance.

Although thousands of researchers want to be published, cheating is unusual because the would-be cheat knows that others may replicate the study. If these replications don't get the results the cheat reported, the credibility of the cheat and of the original study would be questioned. Thus, the threat of direct replication keeps would-be cheats in line. Some scientists, however, worry that science's fraud detectors are becoming ineffective because people are not doing replications as often as they once did (Broad & Wade, 1982).

Combatting Type 1 Errors

Although fraud is one reason that some findings in the literature are probably inaccurate (Broad & Wade, 1982), perhaps more common sources of nonreplicable findings are Type 1 and Type 2 errors. Type 1 errors occur when variables are not really related, even though the statistical test suggests that they are. That is, Type 1 errors are statistical "false alarms" that involve mistaking a coincidence for a real relationship. **Type 2 errors,** on the other hand, occur when the statistical test fails to detect that the variables are related. Partly because of psychologists' concerns about Type 1 and Type 2 errors, some journals solicit and accept studies that replicate—or fail to replicate—previously published research.

To understand how the original study's results may have been significant because of a Type 1 error, imagine that you are a crusty journal editor who allows only simple experiments that are significant at the $p = .05$ level to be published in your journal. If you accept an article, you believe that the chances are only about 5 in 100 that the article will contain a Type 1 error (the error of mistakenly declaring that a chance difference is a real difference). Thus, you are appropriately cautious. But what happens once you publish 100 articles? Then, you may have published five articles that have Type 1 errors.

In fact, you may have many more Type 1 errors than that because people do not send you nonsignificant results. They may have done the same experiment eight different times, but they send you the results of the eighth replication—the one that came out significant. Or, if 20 different teams of investigators do basically the same experiment, only the team that gets significant results (the team with the Type 1 error) will submit their study to your journal. The other teams will just keep their nonsignificant results in their filing cabinets. As a result, you have created what is called the **file drawer problem:** a situation in which the research not affected by Type 1 errors languishes in researchers' file cabinets, whereas the Type 1 errors are published.

To see how the "file drawer problem" might bias published ESP research, imagine you do a study looking for an effect of ESP. If you fail to find an effect, your study would not be published (the data would probably never make it out of your file cabinet). However, if, because of a Type 1 error, you found an effect, your study could be published, thereby contributing to a "file drawer problem."

Knowing about the file drawer problem can prevent you from contributing to the problem. For example, while serving as editor for the *Journal of Personality and Social Psychology,* Anthony Greenwald received an article that found a significant effect for ESP. Because Dr. Greenwald was aware that many other researchers had done ESP experiments that had not obtained significant results, he asked for a replication. The authors could not replicate their results. Thus, the original study was not published because the original results were probably the result of a Type 1 error.

Combatting Type 2 Errors

Just as studies that find significant effects may be victimized by Type 1 errors, studies that fail to find significant effects may be victimized by Type 2 errors. Indeed, Type 2 errors (the failure to find a significant difference when a reliable difference exists) are probably more common than Type 1 errors. Realize that, in a typical study, the chance of a Type 1 error is usually about 5%. However, in most studies, the chance of a Type 2 error is much higher. To give you an idea of how much higher, Jacob Cohen, who has urged psychologists to make their studies much less vulnerable to Type 2 errors than they currently are, wants psychologists to set the chance of a Type 2 error at about 20%. Even if researchers would reach Dr. Cohen's relatively high standards, the risk of making a Type 2 error in a study would be at least four times higher than the risk of making a Type 1 error!

Few researchers conduct studies that come close to Cohen's standards. Cohen (1990) reports that, even in some highly esteemed journals, the studies published ran more than a 50% chance of making a Type 2 error. Put another way, their power (the ability to avoid Type 2 errors) was less than 50%. Similarly, when reviewing the literature on the link between attributions and depression, Robins (1988) found that only 8 of 87 published analyses had the level of power that Cohen recommends. No wonder some studies found relationships between attributions and depression whereas others did not! Thus, when a study fails to find a significant effect, do not assume that a direct replication would also fail to find a significant effect. Repeating the study may yield statistically significant results.

The Systematic Replication

Rather than merely repeating the study, you could do a **systematic replication:** a study that varies in some systematic way from the original study. Usually, your systematic replication will differ from the original in one of two ways.

First, you may refine the design or methodology of the previous study. For example, your systematic replication may use more participants, more standardized procedures, or more objective methods of coding behavior than the original study used.

Second, you may make different tradeoffs than the original researcher. Whereas the original researcher sacrificed construct validity to get power, you may sacrifice power to get construct validity.

You now know what a systematic replication is, but why should you do one? There are two basic reasons.

First, as we suggested earlier, you might do a systematic replication for any of the reasons you would do a direct replication. Because the systematic replication is similar to the original study, the systematic replication, like the direct replication, can help verify that the results reported by the original author are not due to a Type 1 error, a Type 2 error, or to fraud.

Second, you might do a systematic replication to make new discoveries. The systematic replication may uncover new information because it will either do things differently or do things better than the original study. Because you can always make different tradeoffs than the original researcher and because most studies can be improved, you can almost always do a useful systematic replication.

In the next few sections, we will show you how to design a useful systematic replication. Specifically, we will show you how to design systematic replications that have more power, more external validity, or more construct validity than the original. We will begin by showing you how to change the original study to create a systematic replication that has more power than the original.

Improving Power by Tightening the Design

As we suggested earlier, if a study fails to find a relationship, that failure could reflect a Type 2 error—and that Type 2 error could be due to the study's lack of power. Therefore, you may want to repeat the study, but add a few minor refinements to increase the study's power to detect relationships (see Table 4-2). If you chose to improve your study's power to pick out a small effect's faint signal, you could:

- Reduce "background noise" (random error) due to variations in the testing environment by having researchers follow a detailed script or having a computer present the stimuli.

Table 4-2	**How to Devise a Systematic Replication That Will Have More Power Than the Original Study**

1. Improve standardization of procedures.
2. Use more participants.
3. Use more homogeneous participants.
4. Use more extreme levels of treatment or predictor variables.
5. Use a more sensitive dependent measure.

- Test more participants to give the signal more chances to be heard through the noise.
- Reduce noise due to individual differences by using participants who are very similar to one another.
- Use a sensitive measure that can "hear" even a faint signal.
- Reduce noise due to individual differences by using a within-subjects design (also called a repeated measures design) that compares participants who received one treatment with those same participants when they received a different treatment.

Alternatively, you might improve your study's power by generating a bigger effect. Often, your best bet for getting a bigger effect is to use a more powerful manipulation. For example, when Frederickson et al. (1998) had men sit in a room with a mirror while wearing a bathing suit, the men did not do worse on a math test than men wearing a sweater. Thus, there was no evidence that wearing swimsuits made men self-conscious about their bodies. However, Hebl, King, and Lin (2004) noted that the men wore swim trunks rather than very brief Speedo swimsuits. When Hebl, King, and Lin replicated the study by having men wear Speedo swimsuits, the men did do poorer on a math test.

Improving External Validity

If the original study had adequate power, this power to obtain a statistically significant result may have come at the expense of other valued characteristics (see Table 4-3), such as external validity. To illustrate, let's look at two cases in which attempts to help power hurt the generalizability of the results.

Table 4-3	Tradeoffs Involving Power
CONFLICT	**STEPS TO IMPROVE POWER**
Power versus construct validity	Using empty control group, despite its failure to control for placebo effects.
	Using sensitive measure, despite its vulnerability to self-report biases.
	Using a matched pairs design or a within-subjects design even though using that design alerted participants to the hypothesis.
Power versus internal validity	Using a restricted sample of participants to reduce random error due to differences among participants.
	Using a simple, controlled environment to reduce random error due to uncontrolled situational variables.
	Using a within-subjects design even though—in real life—individuals rarely receive more than one level of the treatment.
	Maximizing the number of participants per group by decreasing the number of groups. That is, you may choose to do a simple experiment rather than multilevel or factorial experiment. Consequently, the degree to which the results generalize to various levels of treatment or across different factors is hard to assess.
Power versus internal validity	Using a within-participants design even when a between-participants design would have more internal validity (see Chapter 13).
Power versus statistical conclusion validity	Increasing the risk of a Type 1 error to increase power.

In the first case, a researcher is worried that noise—random error due to individual differences among the participants—will mask the treatment effect. Therefore, the researcher tries to reduce the impact of individual differences on the study by choosing a group of individuals who are homogenous (all similar). The researcher knows that studying participants who are all alike will tend to boost power: The researcher is more likely to obtain a statistically significant result. However, choosing homogeneous participants will decrease the extent to which the results can be generalized to other kinds of participants. What applies to a particular group of 18-year-old White, middle-class, first-year college participants may not apply to other groups of people, such as retirees, members of the working class, and members of minority groups.

In the second case, a researcher is worried that random, real-life events would create so much noise in the data (error variance) that it would hide the treatment effect. Thus, to reduce error variance, the researcher performs the study in a lab rather than in the field. The problem is that we do not know whether the results would generalize outside of this artificial environment.

Suppose you find a study that you believe lacks external validity. For example, suppose that some students performed a lab experiment at their college to examine the effects of defendant attractiveness. There are at least four things you can do to improve the study's generalizabilty (see Table 4-4).

First, you can systematically vary the kinds of participants used. If their study tested only men, you might test only women.

Second, you can change a lab experiment into a field experiment. For example, suppose that the defendant study used college students as participants. By moving the defendant study to the field, you might be able to use real jurors as participants rather than college students.

Third, you can use different levels of the independent (treatment) variable to see whether the effects will generalize to different levels of the independent variable. In the defendant study, researchers may have only compared attractive versus unattractive defendants. Therefore, you might replicate the study to see whether extremely attractive defendants have an advantage over moderately attractive defendants.

Fourth, you can wait a while before collecting the dependent measure to see whether the effect lasts. Fearing the effect will wear off, researchers often measure the dependent variable almost immediately after the participant gets the treatment to maximize their chances of finding a significant effect. However, in real life, there may be a gap between treatment and opportunity to act.

Table 4-4	How to Devise a Systematic Replication That Will Have More External Validity Than the Original Study

1. Use a more heterogeneous group of participants or use a participant group (for instance, women) that was not represented in the original study.

2. Repeat a lab experiment as a field experiment (to see how, go to the field experiment section of our website).

3. Use more levels of the independent or predictor variable.

4. Delay measurement of the dependent variable to see if the treatment effect persists over time.

Table 4-5	How to Devise a Systematic Replication That Will Have More Construct Validity Than the Original Study

1. Replace an empty control group (a no-treatment group) with a placebo treatment group (a fake treatment group).
2. Use more than two levels of the independent variable.
3. Alter the study so that it is a double-blind study.
4. Add a cover story or improve the existing cover story.
5. Replicate it as a field study.

Improving Construct Validity

We have discussed doing a systematic replication to improve a study's power and external validity. You can also do a systematic replication to improve a study's construct validity by making some minor changes that will reduce the threat of your findings being the result of participants guessing your hypothesis and playing along with that hypothesis (see Table 4-5).

To illustrate, imagine a two-group lab experiment in which one group gets caffeine (in a cola), whereas the other group gets nothing (an empty control group). You could design a study that had more construct validity by:

- Replacing the empty control group with a placebo treatment (a caffeine-free cola) and making the study a double-blind experiment.
- Misleading the participants about the purpose of the study by giving them a clever cover story (e.g., they are doing a taste test).
- Not letting them know they were in a study by doing your study in the real world: If participants do not know they are in a study, they will probably not guess the hypothesis.

In short, the systematic replication accomplishes everything a direct replication does and more. By making some slight modifications in the study, you can improve the original study's power, external validity, or construct validity.

The Conceptual Replication

Suppose you believe there were problems with the original study's construct validity—problems that cannot be solved by making minor procedural changes. Then, you should perform a **conceptual replication**: a study that is based on the original study but uses different methods to better assess the true relationships between the variables. In a conceptual replication, you might use a different manipulation or a different measure.

Because there is no such thing as a perfect measure or manipulation, virtually every study's construct validity can be questioned. Because the validity of a finding is increased when the same basic result is found using other measures or manipulations, virtually any study can benefit from conceptual replication. Therefore, you should have little trouble finding a study you wish to redo as a conceptual replication.

There are a variety of ways to design a conceptual replication (see Table 4-6). For example, you could use a different way of manipulating the treatment variable. The more manipulations of a construct that find the same effect, the more confident we can be that

Table 4-6	How to Devise a Conceptual Replication That Will Have More Construct Validity Than the Original Study

1. Use a different manipulation of the treatment variable, and add a manipulation check.
2. Use a different dependent measure, such as one that
   a. is closer to accepted definitions of the construct.
   b. is less vulnerable to social desirability biases and demand characteristics, such as
      i. a measure of overt behavior (actual helping rather than reports of willingness to help)
      ii. a measure that is unobtrusive (how far people sit from each other, rather than reports of how much they like each other).

the construct actually has that effect. Indeed, you might use two or three manipulations of your treatment variable and use the type of manipulation as a factor in your design.

For instance, suppose a study used photos of a particular woman dressed in either a "masculine" or "feminine" manner to manipulate the variable "masculine versus feminine style." You might use the original experiment's photos for one set of conditions, but also add two other conditions that use your own photos. Then, your statistical analysis would tell you whether your manipulation had a different impact from the original study's manipulation.

Realize that you are not limited to using the same type of manipulation as the original study. Thus, instead of manipulating masculine versus feminine by dress, you might manipulate masculine versus feminine by voice (masculine-sounding versus feminine-sounding voices).

Although varying the treatment variable for variety's sake is worthwhile, changing the manipulation to make it better is even more worthwhile. One way of improving a treatment manipulation is to make it more consistent with the definition of the construct. Thus, in our previous example, you might feel that the original picture manipulated "fashion sense" rather than masculine versus feminine style. Consequently, your manipulation might involve two photos: one photo of a woman fashionably dressed in a feminine way, one of a woman fashionably dressed in a masculine manner. To see whether you really were manipulating masculinity–femininity instead of fashion sense or attractiveness, you might add a manipulation check. Specifically, you might ask participants to rate the masculine and feminine photos in terms of attractiveness, fashion sense, and masculinity–femininity.

Because no manipulation is perfect, replicating a study using a different treatment manipulation is valuable. Similarly, because no measure is perfect, replicating a study using a different measure is valuable. Often, you can increase the construct validity of a study by replacing a self-report measure (e.g., making a rating on a 1 (*unlikely*) to 7 (*likely*) scale in response to the question, "How likely would you be to help?") with a behavioral measure (e.g., seeing whether participants actually helped). By replacing a self-report measure with a behavioral measure, you don't have to worry as much about participants lying, misremembering, providing answers that please the researcher, or providing answers that make the participant look good.

The Value of Replications

Replications are important for advancing science. Direct replications are essential for guaranteeing that the science of psychology is rooted in solid, documented fact. Systematic replications are essential for making psychology a science that applies to all people. Conceptual replications are essential for making psychology a science that can make accurate statements about constructs. Conceptual replications help us go beyond talking about the relationship between specific procedures and scores on specific measures to knowing about the relationships between broad, universal constructs such as stress and mental health.

In addition to replicating previous research, systematic and conceptual replications extend previous research. Consider, for a moment, the conceptual replication that uses a better measure of the dependent variable or the systematic replication that shows the finding occurs in real-world settings. Such conceptual and systematic replications can transcend the original research.

Extending Research

Systematic and conceptual replications are not the only ways to extend published research. Of the many other ways to extend published research (see Table 4-7), let's briefly discuss the two easiest.

First, you could both replicate and extend research by repeating the original study while adding a variable that you think might moderate the observed effect. For instance, if you

Table 4-7	Extending Research

1. Replicate the research, but add a factor (participant or situational variable) that may moderate the effect. That is, pin down under what situations and for whom the effect is most powerful.

2. Conduct studies suggested by authors in their discussion section.

3. Look for variables that may mediate the relationship. That is, look for cognitive or physiological mechanisms that may be the underlying causes of the effect.

4. Look for related treatments that might have similar effects. For example, if additional time to rehearse is assumed to improve memory by promoting the use of more effective rehearsal strategies, consider other variables that should promote the use of more effective rehearsal strategies, such as training in the use of effective rehearsal strategies.

5. See if the effects last. For example, many persuasion and memory studies look only at short-term effects.

6. Instead of using a measure of a general construct, use a measure that will tap a specific aspect of that construct. This focused measure will allow you to pinpoint exactly what the treatment's effect is. For example, if the original study used a general measure of memory, replicating the study with a measure that could pinpoint what aspect of memory (encoding, storage, or retrieval) was being affected would allow a more precise understanding of what happened.

7. If the study involves basic (nonapplied) research, see if the finding can be applied to a practical situation. For example, can a memory effect demonstrated in the lab be used to help students on academic probation?

8. If the study describes a correlational relationship between two variables, do an experiment to determine whether one variable causes the other. For example, after finding out that teams wearing black were more likely to be penalized, the authors of this textbook's sample paper (Appendix B) did an experiment to find out whether wearing black causes one to be more violent.

9. Do a study to test a competing explanation for the study's results. For example, if the researchers argue that people wearing black are more likely to be violent, you might argue that there is an alternative explanation: People wearing black are more likely to be *perceived* as violent.

think that being attractive would hurt a defendant if the defendant had already been convicted of another crime, you might add the factor of whether or not the defendant had been previously convicted of a crime.

Second, you could extend the research by doing the follow-up studies that the authors suggest in their discussion section. Sometimes, authors will describe follow-up studies in a subsection of the discussion titled "Directions for Future Research." At other times, authors will hint at follow-up studies in the part of the discussion section in which they talk about the research's limitations. Thus, if the authors say that a limitation of the study was that it covered only a short period, they are suggesting a replication involving a longer period. If they say that a limitation was that they used self-report measures, they are suggesting a replication using other types of measures.

In short, much of the work done by scientists is a reaction to reading other scientists' work. Sometimes, the researcher gets excited because she thinks the authors are onto something special, so she follows up on that work. Other times, she thinks that the authors are wrong, so she designs a study to prove them wrong. Regardless of the reaction, the outcome is the same: The publication of an article not only communicates information but also creates new questions. As a result of scientists reacting to each others' work, science progresses.

Concluding Remarks

After reading this chapter, you can be one of the scientists who reacts to another's work and helps science progress. You know how to criticize research as well as how to improve it. Thus, every time you read an article, you should get at least one research idea.

SUMMARY

1. Not all articles are equally easy and interesting to read. Therefore, if you are given an assignment to read any article, you should look at several articles before committing to one.

2. Reading the title and the abstract can help you choose an article that you will want to read.

3. The abstract is a short, one-paragraph summary of the article. In journals, the abstract is the paragraph immediately following the authors' names and affiliations.

4. In the article's introduction, the authors tell you what the hypothesis is, why it is important, and justify their method of testing it.

5. To understand the introduction, you may need to refer to theory and previous research.

6. The method section tells you who the participants were, how many participants there were, and how they were treated.

7. In the results section, authors should report any results relating to their hypotheses and any statistically significant results.

8. The discussion section either reiterates the introduction and results sections or tries to reconcile the introduction and results sections.

9. When you critique the introduction, question whether (a) testing the hypothesis is vital, (b) the hypothesis follows logically from theory or past research, and (c) the authors have found the best way to test the hypothesis.

10. When you critique the method section, question the construct validity of the measures and manipulations, and ask how easy it would have been for participants to have played along with the hypothesis.

11. When you look at the results section, question any null (nonsignificant) results. The failure to find a significant result may be due to the study failing to have enough power.

12. In the discussion section, question the authors' interpretation of the results, try to explain results that the authors have failed to explain, find a way to test your explanation, and note any weaknesses that the authors concede.

13. The possibility of Type 1 error, Type 2 error, or fraud may justify doing a direct replication.

14. You can do a systematic replication to improve power, external validity, or construct validity.

15. If minor changes can't fix problems with a study's construct validity, you should do a conceptual replication.

16. Replications are vital for the advancement of psychology as a science.

17. Reading research should stimulate research ideas.

KEY TERMS

abstract *(p. 72)*

Psychological Abstracts (p. 72)

PsycINFO (p. 72)

introduction *(p. 72)*

experimental design *(p. 73)*

power *(p. 74)*

method section *(p. 76)*

manipulation check *(p. 78)*

valid *(p. 78)*

reliable *(p. 78)*

experimental realism *(p. 79)*

Type 1 error *(p. 81)*

results section *(p. 82)*

discussion *(p. 85)*

direct or exact replication *(p. 86)*

Type 2 error *(p. 86)*

file drawer problem *(p. 87)*

systematic replication *(p. 88)*

conceptual replication *(p. 91)*

EXERCISES

1. Find an article to critique. If you are having trouble finding an article, consult Web Appendix B (Searching the Literature) or critique the article in Appendix B. Using Box 4-1, critique the article you selected.

2. What are the main strengths and weaknesses of the study you critiqued?

3. Design a direct replication of the study you critiqued. Do you think your replication would yield the same results as the original? Why or why not?

4. Design a systematic replication based on the study you critiqued. Describe your study. Why is your systematic replication an improvement over the original study?

5. Design a conceptual replication based on the study you critiqued. Describe your study. Why is your conceptual replication an improvement over the original study?

WEB RESOURCES

1. Go to the Chapter 4 section of the book's student website and:
   a. Look over the concept map of the key terms.
   b. Test yourself on the key terms.
   c. Take the Chapter 4 Practice Quiz.

2. Get a better idea of the steps involved in actually conducting a study by reading "Appendix C: Practical Tips for Conducting an Ethical and Valid Study."

3. To learn more about how to use *PsycINFO* and other databases to find articles, go to Chapter 4's "Computerized Searches" link.

4. To use InfoTrac College Edition to find articles, go to Chapter 4's "InfoTrac College Edition" link.

5. To learn more about the value of reading the original source, click on Chapter 4's "Misinformation from Textbooks, Newspaper Articles, and Other Secondhand Sources" link.

6. If you want to read articles that are available on the web (including articles written by students), click on Chapter 4's "Web Articles" link.

7. If you want to start writing the introduction to either your research proposal or your research report, use Chapter 4's "Getting Started on Writing Your Introduction" link.

INFOTRAC COLLEGE EDITION EXPLORATIONS

1. To find examples of published research that involve replication (and some that need to be replicated), do an InfoTrac College Edition keyword search using the phrase "replication and psychology."

2. To see how some people look for flaws in research, do an InfoTrac College Edition keyword search using the phrase "breastfeeding and intelligence," and read Jain, Concato, and Leventhal's (2002) article.

5

Measuring and Manipulating Variables

Reliability and Validity

Science begins with measurement.

—*Lord Kelvin*

Overview

To state a hypothesis, you usually propose a relationship between two or more variables. For example, you might propose that "bliss causes ignorance." To test this hypothesis, you must define the vague, general, abstract, and invisible variables "ignorance" and "bliss" in terms of **operational definitions:** clear, specific, concrete, and visible procedures to follow to manipulate or measure variables.

Because operational definitions are objective recipes for variables, they allow you to talk about your variables in objective, rather than subjective, terms. Thus, rather than saying, "My opinion is that they are happy," you can say, "They scored 94 on the happiness scale." By letting you talk about facts rather than opinions, operational definitions make it possible for you to test your hypothesis objectively. In addition, because they are specific recipes that others can follow, operational definitions make it possible for others to repeat (replicate) your study.

Most people recognize that the ability of psychology to test hypotheses objectively and to produce publicly observable facts—in short, its ability to be a science—depends on the psychologists' ability to develop publicly observable ways to measure psychological variables objectively and accurately. Unfortunately, most people also believe one of two myths about measuring psychological variables.

At one extreme are cynics who believe the myth that psychological variables cannot be measured. For example, they believe personality can't be measured by a standardized personality test such as the Big Five Inventory and that arousal can't be measured by increases in heart rate or changes in brain waves. These people think that psychology is not—and cannot—be a science.

At the other extreme are very trusting souls who believe the myth that psychological variables are easy to measure and that anyone who claims to be measuring a psychological variable is doing so. For example, they believe that the polygraph (lie detector) test accurately measures lying and that tests in popular magazines accurately measure personality. Because these individuals can't distinguish accurate (valid) measures from inaccurate (invalid) measures, these individuals can't distinguish between scientific and pseudoscientific claims.

The truth is that developing measures and manipulations of psychological variables is not easy. However, developing objective measures of abstract constructs such as love, motivation, shyness, religious devotion, or attention span is not impossible. By the end of this chapter, you will know not only how to develop operational definitions of such abstract concepts but also how to determine whether such operational definitions have a high degree of construct validity. Put another way, by the end of this chapter, you will have completed a short course in psychological testing.

Choosing a Behavior to Measure

If your hypothesis is about a specific behavior, such as smoking, yawning, jaywalking, typing, exercising, or picking one's nose, then your hypothesis (e.g., people will be more likely to smoke after being told that they should not be allowed to smoke) tells you what behavior to measure. Indeed, your hypothesis may even spell out whether you should measure the behavior's

- rate (how fast—if you're measuring smoking, rate might be measured by how many cigarettes the participant smoked in 2 hours)
- duration (how long—if you're measuring smoking, duration might be measured by how many minutes the participant smoked)

- cumulative frequency (how many—if you're measuring smoking, cumulative frequency might be measured by the total number of cigarettes the participant smoked during the observation period)
- intensity (how vigorously—if you're measuring smoking, intensity might be measured by how much smoke the participant inhaled with each puff; if you're measuring exercise, intensity might be measured by how high the participant's heart rate was during exercise)
- latency (how quickly the behavior began—if you're measuring smoking, latency [also called either response time or reaction time] might be measured by how much time passed before the participant lit up a cigarette)
- accuracy (how mistake-free—if you're measuring typing, accuracy might be measured by number of typos)

Regardless, if you have a hypothesis about a specific behavior, your main challenge is to measure that behavior accurately.

But what if your hypothesis is about an abstract construct? At first, objectively measuring a construct may seem impossible: You cannot see abstract, invisible, psychological states such as love. As much as you might want to see what people are feeling, you can see only what they do. Fortunately, what they do may give you an indication of what they feel. Thus, although you cannot see love, you may be able to see love reflected in one of four types of behavior:

1. verbal behavior—what participants say, write, rate, or report, such as how a person fills out a "love scale"

2. overt actions—what participants do, such as the extent to which a person passes up opportunities to date attractive others

3. nonverbal behavior—participants' body language, such as the amount of time a person spends gazing into a partner's eyes

4. physiological responses—participants' bodily functions, such as brain wave activity, heart rate, sweating, pupil dilation, the degree to which a person's blood pressure increases when the partner approaches (Rubin, 1970)

To choose a specific behavior that is a valid indicator of your construct, you will probably need to consult theory and research. If you fail at this first step, your measure will not be valid. After all, if you are measuring a construct and you choose a behavior that is not a valid marker of that construct, your measure will not be valid. For example, if you choose self-reported social intelligence as a measure of actual social intelligence, handwriting as a sign of personality, or blood pressure as a gauge of lying, you are in trouble because those behaviors aren't strongly related to those constructs.

Errors in Measuring Behavior

If you have chosen a behavior that is a valid indicator of your construct—or if you are interested in measuring a certain behavior (e.g., smoking) rather than a construct—your search for a measure is off to a good start. However, it is only a start—you don't have a measure yet.

To understand why choosing a measure involves more than choosing a relevant behavior, imagine that you want to measure how fast participants run a 40-yard dash. To measure this behavior, (1) you must set the stage for the behavior to occur, (2) participants must perform the behavior, and (3) you must record the behavior. What happens at each of these three stages will affect what time you write down as the participant's 40-yard dash time.

First, by controlling the testing conditions, you, as the person administering the "test," will affect how fast a participant runs. For example, the instructions you give, the clothes the participant wears, whether the test is indoors or outdoors, whether the participant is tested on a grass field or on a track, the temperature at the time of the test, and how many people are watching will all affect how fast the participant runs. Thus, the accuracy of participants' times will depend on keeping the testing conditions constant.

Second, the participant will affect how fast he or she runs. For example, the participant's mood, health, energy level, and desire will affect how fast he or she runs.

Third, you, as observer, will determine the participant's *recorded* time by what time you write down, and the time you write down will usually be affected by when you start and stop the stopwatch. For instance, if you stop the stopwatch before a participant crosses the finish line, that participant's recorded time will be faster than the participant's actual time.

All three of these factors—testing conditions, participants, and observers—can vary. Testing conditions, such as weather conditions and what instructions the researcher gives, may not be the same from day to day, moment to moment, and participant to participant. Likewise, participants and their energy levels, efforts, and expectations may vary, as can the timer's accuracy.

Overview of Two Types of Measurement Errors: Bias and Random Error

When the three factors in the 40-yard-dash example (testing conditions, participants, and observers) vary, participants' scores vary. The way these three factors affect participants' scores depends on whether these factors vary (a) systematically or (b) randomly.

Bias

If these factors vary systematically (in a way that pushes scores in a certain direction), the result is **bias.** Bias may cause a researcher to "find" whatever he or she expects to find. For example, suppose a researcher believes that one group of individuals—the individuals given a special treatment—will run faster than the no-treatment group. The researcher could unintentionally bias the results in at least three ways.

First, the researcher could create biased testing conditions by consistently giving the participants who received the treatment more time to warm up than the other participants. Second, the researcher could bias the participants' expectations by letting only those participants who received the treatment know that they had received a special treatment that should improve their performance. Third, the researcher could bias observations by clicking off the stopwatch just *before* the participants who received the treatment reach the finish line, but clicking off the stopwatch just *after* the other participants reach the finish line. If the researcher does any of these things, the researcher will "find" that the group that was expected to run faster will have faster recorded times than the other group.

Random Error

You have seen that if the testing conditions, the researcher's expectations, or the scoring of the test consistently favor one group, the result is systematic bias. But what if testing conditions, researcher's expectations, and the scoring of the test do not consistently favor any group? Then, the result is unsystematic **random error** of measurement. For instance, suppose the wind at the time participants run the race varies in an unsystematic way. It unpredictably blows at the back of some runners, in the face of other runners, but, on the average, it does not substantially aid the runners receiving the treatment more than the other runners.

This random measurement error makes individual scores less trustworthy. Some runners' times will benefit from the gusts of wind, whereas other runners' times will be hurt by the wind. Thus, if there is a substantial amount of random measurement error, individual scores may be misleading.

Although random measurement error has a strong effect on individual scores, it has little effect on a group's average score. Why? Because random measurement error, like all random error—and unlike bias—does *not* consistently push scores in a given direction. To be more specific and technical, *random error tends to average out to zero* (see Figure 5-1).

Because random error tends to balance out to zero, if a group is large enough (e.g., more than 60), the seconds random error added to some members' times will be balanced out by the seconds random error subtracted from other members' times. Consequently, random error's average effect on the group will tend to be near zero. Because random measurement error will probably have little to no effect on either the treatment group's or the no-treatment group's average score, random measurement error will probably not create significant differences between those groups. For example, random gusts of wind, rather than helping the runners who received the treatment much more than runners who did not receive the treatment, will tend to balance out.

Admittedly, random measurement error will probably not balance out perfectly: The wind may help one group slightly more than the other. Fortunately, however, you can use statistical techniques to estimate the extent to which random measurement error might fail

| Figure 5-1 | **Random Error Balancing Out to 0** |

```
              H H H T
          H H H H H T T T T T
      H H H H H H H H T T T T T T T T
  H H H H H H H H H H H H H T T T T T T T T T T T T T
H H H H H H H H H H H H H H H H H H T T T T T T T T T T T T T T T T T T
```

Notes:

1. These are the results of 90 coin flips. "H" stands for heads, "T" stands for tails." Of the first four flips (see the first row), three were heads. However, of the next 26 flips (see the second and third rows), 13 were heads and 13 were tails. Thus, whereas 75% of our first four flips were heads, only 53% of our first 30 flips were heads. Put another way, when we had only four flips, random error exerted an enormous affect (changing the percentage of heads we should have had—50%—by 25% to what we obtained—75%), but when we had 30 flips, random error had a near zero effect (changing the percentage we should have had from 50% to 53%).

2. In our example, after 90 flips, we had 45 heads and 45 tails. This is an unusual result, especially given that we started out with 3 heads and 1 tail. Regardless of what happened in the first four flips, we would have expected to obtain approximately 43 heads and 43 tails in our next 86 flips. Thus, given that we started out with two more heads than tails, we would have expected—after 90 flips—to still have two more heads than tails. That is, we don't expect the coin to have a memory and for it (or chance) to correct for past errors. If we had obtained 43 heads and 43 tails in the next 86 flips, our total number of heads would have been 46, which is 51% heads, which is 1% more than the 50% we would get without random error. Thus, it might be best for you to think of random error balancing out *toward*—rather than to—zero.

to balance out. To appreciate the value of such statistical analyses, imagine that a statistical analysis told you that all sources of random error combined (variations in wind, variations in instructions, variations in scoring, etc.) would probably not cause the groups to differ by more than 5 seconds.

In that case, if your groups' average times differed by 10 seconds, you could conclude that the difference between the groups is due to something more than random error—the treatment. But what if the groups differed by 4 seconds?

The good news is that if this 4-second difference is due solely to random error, you will not be fooled into saying that the groups really differ. You know, thanks to the statistical analysis, that the groups could reasonably be expected to differ by as much as 5 seconds by chance alone.

The bad news is that if some of this 4-second difference is due to a real difference between the groups, you will *fail* to say that the groups really differ. You are not going to claim that the observed difference of 4 seconds represents a treatment effect when you know, thanks to the statistical analysis, that the groups could reasonably be expected to differ by as much as 5 seconds by chance alone. In such a case, unsystematic random measurement error would hide true differences between groups.

To see the benefits of reducing random measurement error, suppose you had reduced random measurement error to the point that it was unlikely that wind and other random error would have caused the groups to differ by more than 2 seconds. Then, because your observed difference (4) was more than the 2 seconds that chance could account for, you would be able to see that the groups really did differ.

The Difference Between Bias and Random Error

In short, although random measurement error and bias in measurement are both measurement errors, the two errors are different. Bias is systematic (it pushes scores in a certain direction), and statistics cannot account for its effects. Thus, bias can often fool you into thinking that two groups differ when they do not. Random error, on the other hand, is unsystematic, and statistics can partially account for its effects. Thus, if you use statistics, you will rarely mistake the effects of random error for a genuine difference between your groups—no matter how much random error in your measurements.

To better understand the difference between bias and random error, imagine that two people are weighing themselves over a period of days. Although neither is losing weight, the first is content with her weight, whereas the second is trying to lose weight. They might record the following data:

DAY	PERSON 1	PERSON 2
Day 1	150	151
Day 2	149	150
Day 3	151	149

In the case of Person 1, the errors are random; the errors do not make it look like she is losing weight. Despite the errors, we know that her weight is around 150 pounds. Although the weight of the clothes she is wearing while being weighed, the time of day she weighs herself, and how she reads the needle on the scale are not exactly the same from measurement to measurement, they do not vary in a systematic way. In the case of Person 2, on the other hand, the errors are systematic; they follow a pattern that makes it look like he is losing weight. Maybe the pattern is due to moving the scale to a more sympathetic part of the floor, maybe the pattern is due to weighing himself at a time of day when he tends to weigh less (before meals), or maybe the pattern is due to his optimistic reading of the scale's needle. Regardless of how he is biasing his measurements, the point is that he is seeing what he wants to see: He is not being objective.

Errors Due to the Observer: Bias and Random Error

To help you better understand the distinction between systematic errors (biases) and unsystematic, random errors, we will show you how these two types of errors can come from the following three sources: (1) the person administering the measure and that person's failure to create testing conditions that are the same for all participants, (2) the participant, and (3) the person scoring the measure. We will begin by discussing how bias and random error come into play as people observe, score, and record behavior.

Observer Bias (Scorer Bias)

The first, and by far the most serious, observer error occurs when people's subjective biases prevent them from making objective observations. Observers may be more likely to count, remember, or see data that support their original point of view. In other words, a measure of behavior may be victimized by **observer bias:** observers recording what they expect participants will do rather than what participants are actually doing.

To see how serious a problem observer bias can be, suppose that biased observers record the cigarette-smoking behavior of smokers before and after the smokers go through a "stop smoking" seminar. Before a smoker entered the program, if she took one puff from a cigarette, the observer counted that as smoking an entire cigarette. However, after completing the program, the observer did not score "only one puff" as smoking an entire cigarette. In such a case, observer bias would be systematically pushing cigarette-smoking scores in a given direction—down. By decreasing the average smoking score, observer bias may lead us to believe that a smoking prevention program worked—even when it did not.

If we can't control observer bias, we can't do scientific research. There is no point in doing a study if, regardless of what actually happens, you are going to "see" the results you want to see. Thus without objective measures, we go from the scientific ideal of believing whatever we see to seeing whatever we believe.[1] If, on the other hand, we can control observer bias, we move toward the scientific ideal that the findings will be the same no matter who does the study.

Random Observer Error

The second type of mistake that observers make in scoring behavior is unsystematic random errors that will inconsistently increase and decrease individual's scores. For example, a participant who should get a score of 3 could get a score of 2 one moment but a 4 the next.

If your observers are that inconsistent, the bad news is that you can't trust individual scores. You can't say "Participant X scored a 3, so Participant X's true score is a 3." Instead, the most you can do is use the observed score to estimate the range of scores in which the

---

[1]Fortunately, science does have a safeguard against subjective measures: replication. If a skeptic with different beliefs replicates the study, the skeptic will obtain different results—results consistent with the skeptic's beliefs. The failure to replicate the original study's results may expose the flaw in the measure.

participant's true score might fall.[2] For instance, you might say, "Participant X scored a 3, but random observer error may easily have added or subtracted a point from that score. Because random observer error has made that score inaccurate, we shouldn't think of it as a 3, but as a score somewhere between 2 and 4."

The good news is that because random errors are unsystematic, they will probably not substantially affect a *group's* overall average score. The points that random observer errors add to some group members' scores will tend to be balanced out by the points that random errors subtract from other group members' scores. Thus, unlike observer bias, random observer error will probably not substantially change a group's average score.

Minimizing Observer Errors

Although we would like to reduce the influence of both observer bias and random observer error, reducing observer bias is more important than reducing random error.

Why It Is More Important to Reduce Observer Bias Than Random Error. To understand why observer bias is more of a problem than random error, let's consider two error-prone basketball referees. The first makes many random errors; the other is biased. Which would you want to referee your team's big game?

Your first reaction might be to say, "Neither!" After all, the referee who makes many random errors is aggravating. Who wants an inattentive, inconsistent, and generally incompetent ref? However, in the course of a game, that ref's errors will tend to balance out. Consequently, neither team will be given a substantial advantage. On the other hand, a referee who is biased against your team will consistently give the opposing team a several-point advantage. Thus, if you had to choose between the two error-prone officials, which one would you pick? Most of us would pick the one who made many random errors over the one who was biased against us.

Eliminating Human Observer Errors by Eliminating the Human Observer. Often, we don't have to choose between minimizing random error and minimizing observer bias because the steps that reduce observer bias also tend to reduce random observer error. For example, one way to eliminate observer bias is to replace the human observer with scientific instruments, such as computers and other automated data recorders. Note that eliminating the human observer not only eliminates bias due to the human observer, but it also eliminates random error due to the human observer.

Limiting Human Observer Errors by Limiting the Human Observer's Role. If you can't eliminate observer error by eliminating the observer, you may still be able to reduce observer error by reducing the observer's role. For instance, rather than having observers interpret participants' answers to essay questions, you could limit the observers' role to recording participants' answers to multiple-choice questions. Similarly, rather than having observers rate how aggressive a participant's behavior was, observer's could simply decide whether that

---

[2]To calculate how big the range will be, first use the formula for the standard error of measurement (*SEM*): standard deviation (*SD*) $\times \sqrt{1 - \text{reliability}}$. For example, if the *SD* was 10 and the reliability was .84, the *SEM* would be $10 \times \sqrt{1 - .84} = 10 \times \sqrt{.16} = 10 \times .4 = 4$. Next, determine how confident you want to be that your range includes the true score. You can be 68% confident that the true score is within 1 *SEM* of the observed score, 95% confident that the true score is within 2 *SEM*s of the observed score, and 99% confident that the true score is within 3 *SEM*s of the observed score. Thus, with a SEM of 4, we could be 68% confident that the person's true score was within 4 points of the observed score. Put another way, our range would extend 8 points—from 4 points below the observed score to 4 points above.

Table 5-1	Techniques That Reduce Both Random Observer Error and Observer Bias

1. Use machines (such as computers and automatic counters) rather than humans to observe and record behavior.

2. Simplify the observer's task:

   a. Use objective measures such as multiple-choice tests rather than essay tests

   b. Replace tasks that require observers to judge a behavior's intensity with tasks that merely count how many times the behavior occurs

   c. Reduce the possibility for memory errors by making it very easy to immediately record their observations. For example, give your observers checklists so they can check off a behavior when it occurs, or give observers mechanical counters that observers can click every time a behavior occurs

3. Tell observers that they are to record and judge observable behavior rather than invisible psychological states.

4. Photograph, tape record, or videotape each participant's behavior so that observers can recheck their original observations.

5. Carefully define your categories so that all observations will be interpreted according to a consistent, uniform set of criteria.

6. Train raters, and motivate them to be accurate.

7. Use only those raters who were consistent during training.

8. Keep observation sessions short so observers don't get tired.

---

behavior was aggressive. For more tips on how to reduce both random observer bias and random observer error by making the observer's job easier, see Table 5-1.

Reducing Observer Bias by Making Observers "Blind." Although Table 5-1 includes a wide variety of strategies that will help reduce observer bias, those tactics may not eliminate it. To understand why, suppose you were having observers judge essays to determine whether men or women used more "aggressive" words. Even if you conducted a thorough training program for your raters, the raters might still be biased. For example, if they knew that the writer was a man, they might rate the passage as more aggressive than if they thought the same passage was written by a woman.

To reduce such bias, you should not let your raters know whether an essay was written by a man or a woman. Instead, you should make your raters **blind** (also called **masked**): unaware of the participant's characteristics and situation.

The importance of making observers blind has been illustrated in several studies. In one such study, people rated a baby in a videotape as much more troubled when they were told they were watching a baby whose mother had used cocaine during pregnancy than when they were not told such a story (Woods, Eyler, Conlon, Behnke, & Wobie, 1998).

Conclusions About Reducing Observer Bias. Reducing observer bias is critical. It is a big reason behind the popularity of measures that do not require an observer, such as multiple-choice tests, rating scale measures, and reaction time measures.

Most of the tactics you would use to reduce observer bias are the same tactics a professor would use to avoid favoritism in grading: She would not determine students' grades solely by sitting down at the end of the term and trying to recall the quality of each student's class participation. Instead, the professor would probably give multiple-choice tests that were computer scored. If the favoritism-conscious professor were to give an essay exam, she would establish clear-cut criteria for scoring the essays, follow those criteria to the letter, and not look at students' names while grading the papers.

Conclusions About the Relationship Between Reducing Observer Bias and Reducing Random Error. Making observers blind should eliminate observer bias, but it will not eliminate random observer error. Blind observers can still be careless, inattentive, forgetful, or inconsistent about how they interpret behavior. Suppose, for example, that a history professor grades 100 essay exams over the weekend. Even if the professor avoids bias by grading all those exams "blind," he may still fail to grade consistently from test to test. Thus, random error can creep in due to variations in how closely the professor reads each paper, variations in how much partial credit he gives for a certain essay answer, and even in variations (errors) in adding up all the points.

We do not mean to imply that the steps you take to reduce observer bias will never reduce random observer error. On the contrary, except for the blind technique, every step that you take to reduce observer bias will also tend to reduce random observer error.

Errors in Administering the Measure: Bias and Random Error

By using blind procedures and by reducing the observer's role, you can reduce the amount of measurement error that is due to scoring errors. However, not all errors in measurement are due to the scorer. Some errors are made in administering the measure. As was the case with scoring, there are two kinds of errors that people can make in administering the measure: bias and random error.

When you administer the measure, you hope to avoid introducing either bias or random error. But to avoid both these errors completely, you would have to keep everything in the testing environment the same from session to session. For example, if you were administering an IQ test, you would have to make sure that noise level, lighting, instructions to participants, your facial expressions, your gestures, and the rate, loudness, and pitch at which you spoke did not vary from session to session.

Keeping all these factors perfectly constant is impossible. However, most researchers—and people who administer psychological tests—strive for a high level of **standardization:** treating each participant in the same (standard) way. Thus, you should try to test all your participants in the same soundproof, temperature-controlled setting. You should also write out a detailed description of how you are going to test your participants and stick to those procedures. For example, you might write down whatever instructions you were going to give participants and read those instructions to every participant. To further standardize procedures, you might present your instructions on videotape, put the instructions and measures in a booklet, or you might even have a computer program present the instructions and administer the measure.

Because perfect standardization is usually impossible, there will usually be some measurement error due to imperfect standardization. If you must have such error, you would prefer that this error be random error rather than bias. It would be disastrous, for example, if you biased the results by being more attentive, enthusiastic, and patient when administering the test to the treatment group than to the no-treatment group.

To prevent bias from creeping in when your measure is administered, you should try to keep the person who administers the measure blind. You might have one researcher administer the treatment and a second researcher—who is blind to what the first researcher did—administer the measure.

Errors Due to the Participant: Bias and Random Error

To this point, we have focused on two sources of measurement error: errors made by the person administering the measure and errors made by the person scoring the measure. We will now turn to a third source of both random error and bias—participants.

Random Participant Error

Participants may produce responses that don't perfectly reflect their true behavior or feelings because they themselves are not perfectly consistent. Their behavior is variable, and some of this variability is random. One moment they may perform well, and the next moment they may perform poorly. For example, participants may misread questions, lose their concentration, or make lucky guesses.

One way to overcome this random variability in participants' behavior is to get a large sample of their behavior. For example, if you wanted to know how good a free-throw shooter someone was, you wouldn't have her shoot just 2 free throws. Instead, you would probably have her shoot at least 20. Similarly, if you wanted to know how outgoing she was, you wouldn't base your conclusion on a 2-item test. Instead, you would probably use a test that had at least 20 questions on it so that random participant error would tend to balance out.

Because psychologists want to give random participant error a chance to balance out, they often avoid trying to measure a construct with a single question. Instead, they tend to use multiple-item psychological tests. Indeed, if you have filled out a psychological test, you may have wondered, "Why is it so long—and why are they asking me what seems to be the same questions over and over?" Now you know one answer to your question: to balance out random participant error.

Subject Biases

Although random participant error is a problem, a more troublesome reason that participants' actions may not reflect their true selves is **subject (participant) bias.** That is, participants may change their behavior to impress you or to help you (or, perhaps, to thwart you).

One of the earliest documented examples of the problem of subject bias was the case of Clever Hans, the mathematical horse (Pfungst, 1911). Hans would answer mathematical problems by tapping his hoof the correct number of times. For example, if Hans's owner asked Hans what 3 times 3 was, Hans would tap his hoof 9 times. Hans's secret was that he watched his owner. His owner would stop looking at Hans's feet when Hans had reached the right answer. Although people believed Hans's hoof tapping meant that Hans was performing mathematical calculations, his hoof tapping only meant that Hans was reacting to his owner's gaze. Hans didn't know math, but he did know how to give the "right" answer.

If animals can produce the right answer when they know what you are measuring, so can humans. In fact, for humans, there are two kinds of right (biased) responses: (1) obeying demand characteristics and (2) social desirability.

Obeying Demand Characteristics. The first kind of right answer is the one that makes you, the researcher, look good by ensuring that your hypothesis is supported. Orne (1962) believed that participants are so eager to give researchers whatever results the researcher wants that participants look for hints as to what responses will support the researcher's hypothesis. According to Orne, if a participant finds a hint, the participant will follow that hint as surely as if the researcher had demanded that the participant follow it. Orne refers to such hints as **demand characteristics.**

To give you some idea of the power of demand characteristics, consider how they operate in everyday life. Imagine you and a friend are at a restaurant. The service is slow, and the food is bad. You and your friend grumble about the food through much of the meal. Then, at the end of the meal, your server asks you, "Was everything all right?" Do you share your complaints, or do you give in to demand characteristics and say that everything was fine?

To see how demand characteristics might affect the results of a study, imagine that you do the following study. First, you have participants rate how much they love their partner. Next, you give them fake feedback, supposedly from their partner, showing that their partner loves them intensely. Finally, you have participants rate how much they love their partner a second time. Participants may realize that they are supposed to rate their love higher the second time. Therefore, if participants reported that they loved their partner more the second time, you would not know whether learning about their partners' devotion changed participants' feelings or whether participants merely obeyed the study's demand characteristics.

How did participants know what you wanted them to do? Your measure made it obvious that you were trying to measure love. Once participants knew that you were trying to measure love, they were able to guess why you showed them their partners' ratings. You gave them all the clues (demand characteristics) they needed to figure out what you would consider a "good" response, and you made it easy for them to give that response.

You can use measures that make it more difficult for participants (a) to figure out what the hypothesis is or (b) to play along with that hypothesis. As Table 5-2 shows, there are at least two ways you could make it hard for participants to figure out the hypothesis by making it hard for them to figure out what you are measuring. Unfortunately, both ways raise ethical questions because they both involve compromising the principle of **informed consent:** Participants should freely decide whether to participate in the study only after being told what is going to happen to them.[3]

Table 5-2	**Ways to Avoid Subject Biases When Measuring Love**
TECHNIQUE	**EXAMPLE**
Measure participants in nonlaboratory settings	Observe hand-holding in the college cafeteria.
Unobtrusive observation	Observe hand-holding in the lab through a one-way mirror.
Unobtrusive measures (nonverbal)	Observe how much time partners spend gazing into each other's eyes.
Unobtrusive measures (physical traces)	Measure how close together the couple sat by measuring the distance between their chairs.
Unexpected measures	Lead participant to believe that partner has damaged something by accidentally knocking over something, and then ask participant to repair the alleged damage.
Disguised measures	Ask participants to rate themselves and their partners on several characteristics. Then, infer love from the extent to which they rate their partner as being similar to themselves.
Physiological responses	Measure pupil dilation to see if it increases when their partner comes into the room.
Important behavior	See if the participant passes up the opportunity to date a very attractive person.

---

[3]In the next chapter, we discuss the ethical issues involved in choosing a measure.

BOX 5-1   The Logic of a Disguised Prejudice Measure

Saucier and Miller (2003) had participants rate, for 16 different paragraphs and conclusions, how well each paragraph supported its conclusion. Although participants were asked to rate how logical the argument for a position was (e.g., spending more money on research to find a cure for sickle-cell anemia), the researchers were using participants' ratings as a measure of prejudice. For example, participants scored high on prejudice to the degree that they (a) gave low ratings on the degree to which the paragraph supported a conclusion when those conclusions were favorable toward Blacks and (b) gave high ratings on the degree to which the paragraph supported a conclusion when those conclusions were unfavorable toward Blacks.

After reading this chapter, you may want to read Saucier and Miller's (2003) article to see how they made the case that their measure really did measure prejudice. As you might expect, they found that participant's ratings of how logical the argument was correlated with the degree to which participant's agreed with the argument's conclusion. Also, as you might expect, they correlated their measure with other measures of prejudice to see whether their measure predicted prejudiced behavior. In addition, they tried to show that their measure was not strongly affected by (a) random error or (b) social desirability bias.

The first way involves making it hard for participants to know that you are observing them. In technical terminology, you use **unobtrusive measurement:** recording a particular behavior without the participants knowing you are measuring that behavior. For example, you might spy on them when they are in the real world or you might spy on them through a one-way mirror when they are in either the lab or in the waiting room.

The second way involves disguising your measure. You might let participants think you were measuring one thing when you were actually measuring something else. For instance, you might take advantage of the fact that people in love tend to overestimate how similar they are to their partner. Therefore, you could have participants rate themselves and their partners on a variety of characteristics. Participants would probably think you are interested in how accurately or positively they rate their partners. Instead, you'd be seeing the extent to which participants believed that they were similar to their partner—and using perceived similarity as a measure of love. (To see how this disguised technique can be used to measure prejudice, see Box 5-1.)

But what if you can't stop your participants from figuring out the hypothesis? Even if participants figure out the hypothesis, you can still do two things to prevent participants from playing along with it.

First, you could make it almost impossible for participants to play along with the hypothesis. For instance, you might use a physiological measure of love, such as brain wave activity, pupil dilation, or contraction of certain facial muscles that are associated with happiness and that most people can't voluntarily control. If you wanted to use a nonphysiological measure, you might use reaction time measures because those measures are also hard for participants to fake. (To see how reaction time measures can be used to measure prejudice, see Box 5-2.)

Second, you could make it costly for participants to play along with the hypothesis. For example, if you made it so participants would have to spend more time performing a dull task (watching people fill out questionnaires) to help out their partner, many would not be willing to play along with the hypothesis that learning of their partner's positive feelings toward them will cause them to help their partner.

BOX 5-2 | **The Implicit Attitude Test (IAT): A Reaction Time Measure That Is Hard to Fake**

Imagine that you are a White person and that you consider yourself unprejudiced. You go to the Implicit Association Test website (https://implicit.harvard.edu/implicit/) and take a test designed to measure whether you are biased toward Blacks. At first, the task is ridiculously easy: When you see a Black face, hit a key on the left (e.g., the letter "e" key); when you see a White face, hit a key on the right (e.g., the letter "i" key). Then, you have yet another easy task: When you see a positive word (e.g., "good") hit a key on the left; when you see a negative word (e.g., "bad), hit a right key. In the next phase, the task becomes slightly more challenging. Now, you have to deal with two categories at once. If you see either a White face or a positive word, you have to hit the left key. If you see either a Black face or a negative word, you have to hit the right key. You're still doing fine—responding accurately and quickly. In the final phase, the rules are changed. Now, if you see either a Black face or a positive word, you have to hit the left key. If you see either a White face or a negative word, you have to hit the right key. If you are like most (88%) of Whites, you will find the last task the hardest and perform it the slowest, indicating some degree of bias against Blacks.

How do researchers know that slower reaction times on this last task indicate implicit bias? Researchers know because, among other things, studies have shown that:

- Blacks are less likely than Whites to have slower reaction times on this last task.
- Conservatives are more likely than liberals to have slower reaction times on this last task.
- People in favor of racial profiling are more likely than others to have slower reaction times on this last task.
- Whites with slower reaction times on this last task are less likely to choose to work with a Black partner.
- Scores on the test do not correlate with hand-eye coordination.

Social Desirability Bias. Unfortunately, subject bias does not stop at participants trying to give you the results they think you want. In addition to wanting you to look good, participants also want themselves to look good. This kind of subject bias is called the **social desirability bias:** the participant acting in a way that makes the participant look good.

Participants want to look good, and on most questionnaires, it is easy for participants to choose the answer that makes them look good. Consequently, many studies have shown that people claim to be much more helpful (Latané & Darley, 1970) and less conforming (Milgram, 1974) than they really are.

The same two tactics that reduce the problem of demand characteristics also reduce the problem of social desirability. Participants won't try to impress the researcher if (a) they don't know they are being watched or (b) showing off is difficult. For example, they probably won't try to be more generous than they are if they don't know you are watching them or if it costs them time and money to show how generous they are.

Despite the effectiveness of those two techniques, the easiest and most commonly used tactic to deal with the social desirability bias is to have participants not put their names on their answer sheets so that their responses are anonymous. If participants cannot get credit for their answers, they cannot impress the researcher by putting down exaggerated or false information. Therefore, anonymous participants should not be motivated to make socially desirable, but false, responses.[4]

---

[4]Unfortunately, anonymous participants may still give false or misleading information. For example, some adolescents may display a sense of humor or a sense of rebelliousness by putting outrageous answers on an anonymous questionnaire.

| Figure 5-2 | Sources and Types of Measurement Error |

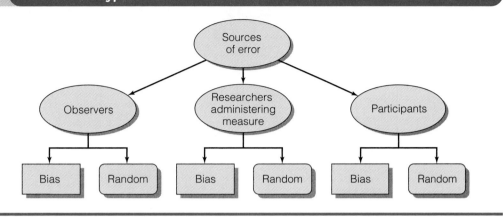

Conclusions About Reducing Subject Biases

Note that making responses anonymous—the most commonly used method to reduce social desirability bias—was not mentioned as a method to reduce bias caused by following demand characteristics. Making responses anonymous does not necessarily eliminate the bias caused by obeying demand characteristics because even though anonymous participants can't make themselves look good, they can still try to make you look good by producing results that they think will support your hypothesis.

Summary of the Three Sources and Two Types of Measurement Error

We have discussed three major sources of measurement error: errors due to the person scoring the measure, errors due to the person administering the measure, and errors due to the participant. We have also stressed that each of these sources can contribute two types of measurement error: random error and systematic bias (see Figure 5-2). Furthermore, we stressed that bias is a much more serious threat to validity than random error. We showed how observer bias was worse than random observer error, how researcher bias was worse than random errors in administering a measure, and how subject bias was worse than random participant error. To combat bias, we advocated using two strategies that specifically target bias—blind (masked) techniques and unobtrusive measurement (see Table 5-2)—and two strategies that reduce both bias and random error: standardizing how the measure is administered and simplifying how the measure is scored (see Table 5-1).

Reliability: The (Relative) Absence of Random Error

As you have seen, bias is a much more serious threat to a measure's validity than random error (see Figure 5-3). Indeed, at this point, you might be saying to yourself, "Bias is bad. I should try to eliminate it. Random error, on the other hand, doesn't seem that serious. Why should we bother to develop a measure that is free of random error?" In the next section, we will answer that question by explaining why you want a measure that is **reliable:** producing stable, consistent scores that are not strongly influenced by random error (chance).

Figure 5-3	**Bias Poisons a Measure's Validity, Random Error Merely Dilutes a Measure's Validity**

| Pure, valid measure | Bias | Random error |

If you loved pure orange juice, you wouldn't want your juice to be poisoned or watered down. However, if you had the choice, you would rather have your drink watered down than poisoned. Similarly, if you have to have error in your measure, you would prefer that the error be random error (which dilutes your measure's validity) rather than bias (which poisons your measure's validity).

The Importance of Being Reliable: Reliability as a Prerequisite to Validity

You want scores on your measure to be stable over time when you are measuring a construct that, rather than changing from minute to minute, is stable over time. Thus, if you are accurately measuring a person's intelligence, shyness, or height at two different times, you should get the same results each time. For example, if someone is 5 feet tall (152 cm) and your measure is valid (accurate), you should consistently (reliably) measure that person as 5 feet (152 cm) tall. In short, if your measure of height or any other stable characteristic is valid, your measurements must be reliable.

We have shown that, when talking about a stable characteristic, *validity guarantees reliability*. But what does reliability do for validity? Although reliability doesn't guarantee validity, *reliability is a prerequisite for validity*.

To be more specific, *reliability puts a ceiling on how high validity can be*. That is, only to the degree that your measurements of a stable trait are stable can your measurements of that stable trait be accurate. For example, suppose you measure a person's height twice. If you measure the person as 5' 5" (165 cm) both times, your measure's reliability is perfect and— if the person is 5' 5" tall (165 cm)—your measure's validity is also perfect. However, suppose your measurements are less than perfectly reliable. For example, suppose you measure the person as 5' 4" (162 cm) one time and 5' 6" (167 cm) the next. In that case, your average error of measurement would be at least 1 inch (2.54 cm). If your measurements were so unreliable that you measured someone's height to be 5' 0" (152 cm) one day and 5' 10" (175 cm) the next, your average error of measurement would be at least 5 inches (12.70 cm).

You have seen that the *less* reliable your measurements, the *more* random error your measurements contain. The more scores are affected by unstable, unsystematic random factors (random error), the less opportunity scores have to be affected by the stable factor

Figure 5-4 | **Reliability Puts a Ceiling on Validity**

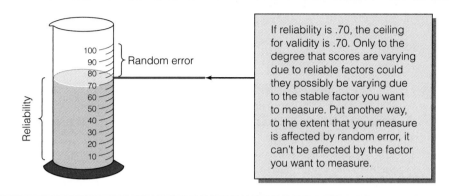

If reliability is .70, the ceiling for validity is .70. Only to the degree that scores are varying due to reliable factors could they possibly be varying due to the stable factor you want to measure. Put another way, to the extent that your measure is affected by random error, it can't be affected by the factor you want to measure.

(e.g., height) that you want to measure. Because reliability puts a ceiling on validity (see Figure 5-4), you want a reliable measure: one that produces scores that will not be bounced around by the erratic winds of chance. But how can you know the extent to which your measure is contaminated by random error?

Using Test–Retest Reliability to Assess Overall Reliability: To What Degree Is a Measure "Random Error Free"?

To find out to what extent your measurements are contaminated by random error, you should find out the measure's reliability. Perhaps the most straightforward way to find out the degree to which the measure produces consistent results that are stable and repeatable over time is to obtain the measure's **test–retest reliability.**

As the name suggests, test–retest reliability requires participants to be tested and then retested. For example, a psychological test developer may test participants on a measure and then test those same participants again on the same measure 3 months later. The developer would then calculate a test–retest coefficient by comparing the scores that participants received the first time they took the test with the scores participants received the second time.

The more that participants' scores on the first measurement correspond to their scores on the second measurement, the higher the test–retest coefficient. Although test–retest coefficients can range from 0 (no reliability) to 1 (perfect reliability), most are between .60 and .98.[5]

The test–retest coefficient tells you the percentage of variation in scores that is stable and consistent from test to retest. Thus, a test–retest coefficient of 1.00 would mean that there was a perfect (100%) correspondence between the first and second time of

---

[5]The test–retest reliability coefficient is usually not a correlation coefficient. If it were, it could range from −1 to +1. Instead, the test–retest reliability coefficient is usually the square of the test–retest reliability correlation (Anastasi, 1982). This squared term represents the percentage of variation that is *not* due to random error. To find out how much of the variation of scores is due to random error, you subtract the test–retest coefficient from 1. Thus, if your test–retest coefficient is 1, none (0%) of the variation in your scores is due to random error (because $1 - 1 = 0$). If, on the other hand, your test–retest coefficient is 0, then all (100%) of the variation in your scores is due to random error (because $1 - 0 = 1 = 100\%$).

measurement—all those who scored high the first time also scored high the second time. The data that follow reflect a 1.00 test–retest coefficient.

PARTICIPANT	SCORE FIRST TIME	SCORE SECOND TIME
Carol	3	3
Mary	4	4
Tom	5	5

Put another way, the test–retest coefficient tells you the *percentage* of variation in scores that is *not* due to random error. Thus, a test–retest coefficient of 1.00 tells us that 100% of the differences between scores are *not* due to random error. The measure is 100% (completely) free from random error.

What if a measure, rather than being perfectly reliable, was perfectly unreliable? Then, the measure would have a test–retest coefficient of 0, meaning that there was absolutely no (0%) relationship between scores participants received the first time they took the test and the scores they received when they were retested. In the next table, we have displayed data from a measure with a zero test–retest coefficient. As you can see, there is no connection between a participant's test and retest scores: The only way a participant gets the same score on both the test and retest is by chance. Put another way, in the case of a measure with a 0 reliability coefficient, scores are 0% (not at all) free from random error.

PARTICIPANT	SCORE FIRST TIME	SCORE SECOND TIME
Carol	3	4
Mary	4	3
Tom	5	4

Note that because this measure is being completely affected by random error, it can't be affected by the stable trait it is supposed to measure. Put another way, because it has zero reliability, it has zero validity: Because it is so unstable that it does not even correlate with itself, it can't correlate with the stable trait it is supposed to measure.

What if, rather than having zero reliability, the measure has .40 reliability? In that case, because only 40% of the variability in scores is not due to random error, only 40% of the variation in scores could possibly be due to the stable trait the measure is supposed to measure. Put another way, because it has .40 reliability, it can't have more than .40 validity. To express the idea that a measure can't correlate with what it is supposed to measure (validity) more than it correlates with itself (reliability), experts often say that "reliability puts a ceiling on validity."

Because reliability puts a ceiling on validity, you would like to know your measure's reliability. If you are examining a previously published measure, somebody may have already calculated its test–retest reliability coefficient for you. To find that correlation, check the article in which the measure was published. If the measure was not published in an article, check articles that used the measure or the *Directory of Unpublished Experimental Mental Measures* (Goldman & Mitchell, 1990). If you are using a psychological test and you still can't find the test–retest reliability, check the test's manual, *Mental Measurements Yearbook* (Kramer & Conoley, 1992), *Test Critiques* (Keyser & Sweetland, 1984), or *Tests in Print* (Mitchell, 1983).

When interpreting a measure's test–retest reliability coefficients, remember that these coefficients are telling you the extent to which the measure is *not* affected by random error. To find out the extent to which the measure is affected by random error, you have to subtract the reliability coefficient from 1. Like the ads that boast that their product is 70% fat-free

Figure 5-5 | **Reliability and Random Error Are Opposites**

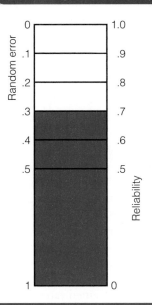

If the reliability coefficient is .70, random error makes up .30 of the variation in scores. How much variation in scores would be due to random error if the reliability coefficient was (a) 1.0? (b) 0? (c) .5? (d) .8?

rather than saying it is 30% fat (1.00 – .70 = .30 = 30%), and like the optimist who sees the glass as 70% full rather than as 30% empty, the test–retest reliability coefficient focuses on the positive by telling us how random–error free the measure is.

However, if you are trying to avoid using a poor measure, you may need to focus on the negative. For example, although a test–retest coefficient of .70 does not sound bad, it means two things. First, it means that your validity can't possibly be above .70 (because reliability puts a ceiling on validity). Second, it means that 30% (1.00 – .70 = .30 = 30%) of the differences between participants' scores on the measure are due to random error (see Figure 5-5).

Normally, you would not choose a measure in which more than 30% of the differences between participants' scores was due to random error. In other words, you would probably not choose a measure that had a test–retest reliability coefficient below .70.

Identifying (and Then Dealing With) the Main Source of a Measure's Reliability Problems

What if your measure's test–retest reliability is below .70? Then, more than 30% of the variation in scores is due to random error. Where is this random error coming from? The three likely sources are

1. random error due to the observer
2. random error due to the participant
3. random error due to the way the measure is administered

If you knew which of these possible sources was the main source of a measure's unreliability, you might be able to fix the measurement's reliability problem at the source. If the main reason your participants' scores were not consistent was because your observers were inconsistent, you would work on making your observers more consistent. On the other hand, if inconsistent scores were due to inconsistencies in how the measure was administered, you would work on administering the measure the same way every time. But how do you determine which of the three likely sources is most to blame for the measure's poor reliability?

Are Observers to Blame for Low Test–Retest Reliability?
Assessing Observer Reliability

Most researchers start by seeing whether the observer is to blame for a measure's poor reliability. Often, researchers can immediately determine that the scorer is *not* a major source of random error because the scoring system is relatively objective. For example, in a multiple-choice test, observers are probably not going to make many errors.

But what about when observers rate behavior? Then, you should determine the extent to which random observer error is lowering our test–retest reliability.

The first step to estimating the extent to which random observer error is a problem is to have two or more observers independently (without talking to one another) rate the same behavior. If the observers come up with similar scores (they agree), you don't have an observer-related problem. If, however, the two trained raters score the same behavior differently, these differences are due to random observer error. For instance, two observers may produce different scores because one or both observers guessed about which category to put the behavior in, misread the stopwatch, failed to pay attention, wrote down one number when they meant to write down another, or made any number of other random mistakes.

The second step is to calculate an index of the degree to which observers agree. Two of the most common indexes that researchers use are interobserver agreement and interobserver reliability.

Sometimes, researchers will report the **interobserver (judge) agreement:** the percentage of times the raters agree. For example, the researchers might report that the raters agreed 98% of the time. Interobserver agreement is simple to calculate and understand. If observers are agreeing 100% of the time, there is no random error due to the observer.

Rather than report percentage of times the raters agree, most researchers will report some index of interobserver reliability. They may use Cohen's kappa or Krippendorf's alpha. However, most of the time, they use the simplest index of interobserver reliability: the **interobserver (scorer) reliability coefficient.** To obtain the interobserver reliability coefficient, researchers calculate a correlation coefficient between the different raters' judgments of the same behaviors and then square that correlation.[6]

Like test–retest reliability coefficients, interobserver reliability coefficients can range from 0 to 1. An interobserver reliability coefficient of 1.00 means there is a 100% correspondence between the raters. Knowing how one observer rated a behavior allows you to

---

[6]To show you the connection between interobserver agreement and interobserver reliability, imagine that we are having observers rate whether a behavior falls into one of two categories. If observers were just flipping a coin to determine what category the behavior belonged, they would agree 50% of the time. Thus, if the observers' judgments are completely affected by chance, interobserver agreement would be 50% and the interobserver reliability coefficient would be zero. If, on the other hand, random error had no effect on judgments, interobserver agreement would be 100% and the interobserver reliability coefficient would be 1.00.

know perfectly (with 100% accuracy) how the other observer rated the behavior. The following data reflect an interobserver reliability coefficient of 1.00.

PARTICIPANT	OBSERVER 1'S RATING	OBSERVER 2'S RATING
Tom	1	1
Nia	2	2
Sue	3	3
Malik	4	4
Robert	5	5
Maria	6	6

The 1.00 interobserver reliability coefficient tells you the extent to which your measure is not affected by random observer error. Specifically, the 1.00 interobserver reliability coefficient shows that the measure is 100% (completely) random observer error free.

An interobserver reliability coefficient of zero, on the other hand, indicates that there is no relationship between the observers' ratings. Knowing how one observer rated a behavior gives you no idea about how the other observer rated the same behavior. With an interobserver reliability of zero, you could say either that the variation in scores is (a) not at all (0%) free from random observer error or (b) completely (100%) due to random observer error. To see a case in which observers' judgments are completely a function of random error, look at the data in the next table.

PARTICIPANT	OBSERVER 1'S RATING	OBSERVER 2'S RATING
Tom	1	3
Nia	2	5
Sue	4	3
Malik	5	3
Robert	2	3
Maria	6	4

As you can see, there is no connection between Observer 1's ratings and Observer 2's ratings. Because scores are completely a function of random observer error, the measure has no interobserver reliability.

Because observers usually agree to some extent, and because journal editors will usually publish only articles that have a high degree of interobserver reliability, you will almost never see a published study that includes an interobserver reliability coefficient below .60.[7] Therefore, when reading a study, your question will not be, "Did the observers agree?" but rather, "To what extent did the observers agree?" Generally, you will expect interobserver reliability coefficients of around .90.

You want a measure with a high interobserver reliability coefficient for two reasons. First, you want your measure to be objective—you want trained raters to report the same scores. Second, *interobserver reliability puts a ceiling on overall (test–retest) reliability.* For example, if interobserver reliability is .60, test–retest reliability can't be above .60.

If interobserver reliability is low, then you probably need to reduce random observer error. Sometimes, you can reduce random observer error by training or motivating your observers. Often, however, the most effective way to reduce—and prevent—random observer error is to simplify the observer's job.

---

[7]Usually, observer reliability coefficients—or Cohen Kappa's—below .70 are considered unacceptable.

To illustrate the benefits of simplifying the observer's job, consider Ickes (2003) research on "everyday mind reading." One way he studies such mind reading is by having two strangers interact. He tapes the interaction and then has each participant view the tape. Participants are to stop the tape at different points and say what they are thinking. Then, participants see the tape again and are to stop it at different points and write down what their interaction partner was thinking at that point. Observers rate the degree to which the participant's guess about what the partner was thinking matches what the partner was actually thinking. Ickes could have had observers make their judgments on a 0 (*not at all*) to 100 (*completely*) scale. However, he had observers use a 3-point scale with "0" being "essentially different content," "1" being "similar, but not the same, content," and "3" being "essentially the same content." By using fewer categories, raters found the job of rating easier and raters were able to make reliable ratings.

Ickes knew the observers' ratings were agreeing with each other because he calculated interobserver reliabilities. He was able to calculate inter-rater reliabilities because he had more than one person rate each participant.

Being able to calculate inter-rater reliabilities is one benefit of having more than one observer rate each participant. Another benefit is that rather than each participant's score being based on a single observer's rating, each participant's score can be based on the average of two or more observers' ratings.

The advantage of average ratings is that they are more reliable (more stable; less influenced by random observer error) than individual ratings. Average ratings are more reliable than individual ratings because observer error, like all random error, tends to average out to 0. That is, random errors made by one observer tend to be cancelled out by random errors made by another. Thus, even if Ickes had low interobserver reliability, random observer error would not have been a huge problem for his study because he was basing participants' scores on the *average* of 5 observers' ratings.

If you can't get multiple observers to rate each behavior and you can't get reliable ratings, you may need to find a way of measuring behavior that does not involve observers. One reason multiple-choice tests and rating scale measures are so popular in research is that these measures essentially eliminate human observers, thereby eliminating the random observer error that human observers produce.

Estimating Random Error Due to Participants

So far, we have discussed a situation in which interobserver reliability is low, thus dooming test–retest reliability to be low. But what if interobserver reliability is high, yet test–retest reliability is still low? For example, suppose you have the following data:

	TEST		RETEST	
Participant	Observer 1	Observer 2	Observer 1	Observer 2
Jordan	3	3	5	5
Asia	4	4	3	3
Deja	5	5	5	5

In such a case, you know your low test–retest reliability is not due to erratic observers, but instead must be due to inconsistencies in (a) how the measure was administered and/or (b) the participant.

Ideally, you would figure out how much of the random error was due to poor standardization and how much was due to random changes in the participant. Unfortunately, it is impossible to directly assess how much random error is due to poor standardization, and it is difficult to assess how much of the random error is due to the participant. However, there is a way to get a rough index of how much random error is due to the participant—if you are using a test, scale, or survey that can be objectively scored.

Internal Consistency: Test Questions Should Agree With Each Other. How can we determine how much random error on a test is due to the participant? The key is to assume that each question on the test is measuring the same thing. For example, let's assume that all questions on a shyness test are measuring shyness. If this assumption is correct, people who score "shy" on one question should score shy on all the other questions. In other words, the test should agree with itself. But what if it doesn't? What if a participant is shy according to the participants' answers to some questions but outgoing according to the participant's answers to other questions?

If our assumption that all the questions are measuring the same thing is correct, this inconsistency between how questions are answered is due to random error. As you may recall, random error, ordinarily, could be due to one or more of the following:

1. the observer
2. the testing environment
3. the participant

Random Error Due to Participants May Cause Low Internal Consistency. We can rule out observers as the source of the random error if we use an objective, multiple-choice test. In such a case, we can also rule out the testing environment as a cause of random fluctuations in the participant's behavior because the testing environment and instructions are probably not changing *during* the testing session. That is, we expect that the testing environment is the same when the participant answers question 2 as it is when the participant answers question 3. If the random error is not due to the scorer or to the testing environment, it must be due to

1. ~~the observer~~
2. ~~the testing environment~~
3. the participant

Specifically, the measure's inconsistency may reflect (a) participants experiencing random, momentary variations in mood or concentration, or (b) participants randomly guessing at the answers to some questions.

Two Solutions to Problems Caused by Random Participant Error

If your measure's reliability problems are due to the participant, what can you do? Your plan of attack will depend on whether the inconsistency is due to participants changing from moment to moment or to participants guessing at the answers to questions.

Add Questions to Let Random Participant Error Balance Out. If participants fluctuate considerably from moment to moment in how they think or feel, the best you can do is make sure your measure has many questions. By having participants provide many responses, you allow random fluctuations to balance out. Asking numerous questions should also help balance out the effects of guessing. For example, suppose you are unprepared for a physics quiz and the only thing you can do is guess at the answers. If the quiz is composed of one multiple-choice question, you might get 100% just by guessing. However, if the quiz is composed of 100 multiple-choice questions, random guessing is not going to get you a high score.

Ask Better Questions to Reduce Random Participant Error. Asking more questions is not the only way to deal with the problem of guessing. Sometimes the solution is to ask better questions. Your participants may be guessing at the answers because some questions are so poorly worded that participants are guessing at what those questions mean. You may be able to reduce random error due to guessing by rewording or eliminating those questions, thereby boosting your measure's **internal consistency:** the degree to which answers to each question correlate with the overall test score.

Measuring Internal Consistency

But how would you know whether you have boosted your measure's internal consistency? How would you know whether your measure's internal consistency was poor in the first place?

To estimate your measure's internal consistency, you would find or calculate an index of internal consistency, such as an average inter-item correlation, a split-half reliability, or Cronbach's alpha (often abbreviated as alpha, Cronbach's α, or just α). All of these indexes measure the degree to which answers to one item (question) of the test correspond to answers given to other items on the test. Thus, the following data would produce a high score on any index of internal consistency:

PARTICIPANT	QUESTION 1	QUESTION 2	QUESTION 3
Tyrone	1	1	1
Kiara	3	3	3
Susan	5	5	5

Average Inter-Item Correlations as Indexes of Internal Consistency. One index that directly assesses the extent to which answers to one test item (question) correlate with answers to other test items is the average inter-item correlation. As the name suggests, this index involves computing a correlation between the answers to each question (item) and then averaging those correlation coefficients.

Depending on how you average those correlation coefficients, you will either have the mean inter-item correlation or the median inter-item correlation. If you use the mean as your average (you add up all the correlation coefficients and divide by the number of correlation coefficients), you have the *mean inter-item correlation.* If your average is the median (you arrange the correlation coefficients from lowest to highest and pick the middle one), you have the *median inter-item correlation.*

Usually, there is little difference between the median inter-item correlation and the mean inter-item correlation. For example, if you had a three-item test, you might find the following:

Correlation of item 1 with item 2	.2
Correlation of item 1 with item 3	.3
Correlation of item 2 with item 3	.4
Mean inter-item correlation:	.3
Median inter-item correlation:	.3

Split-Half Reliability Coefficients as Indexes of Internal Consistency. Other indexes of internal consistency are less direct than the average inter-item correlation. Many rely on essentially splitting the test in half and comparing how participants scored on one half versus how they scored on the other half. For instance, researchers may (a) calculate each participant's score for the first half of the test, (b) calculate each participant's score for the second half of the test, and then (c) correlate scores on the first half of the test with scores on the last half of the test. This correlation between the score for the first half of the test and the score for the second half is a type of split-half reliability. Thus, the following data would yield a perfect (1.00) split-half reliability and suggest that the scale was internally consistent:

PARTICIPANT	SCORE ON FIRST 10 QUESTIONS	SCORE ON LAST 10 QUESTIONS
Joshua	50	50
Jasmine	10	10
Susan	30	30

Another type of split-half reliability involves splitting the test in half by comparing answers to the odd-numbered questions (1, 3, 5, etc.) with answers to the even-numbered questions (2, 4, 6, etc.). Specifically, researchers may calculate a score based on only the answers to the odd-numbered questions, a score based only on the answers to even-numbered questions, and then correlate each participant's "odds" score with that participant's "evens" score. That correlation would be the measure's "odd–even correlation."

Additional Indexes of Internal Consistency. In addition to the measures of internal consistency that we have described, there are more mathematically sophisticated measures of internal consistency, such as Cronbach's alpha and Kuder-Richardson reliabilities. At this point, we do not want you to know the advantages and disadvantages of each measure of internal consistency. Instead, we want you to realize whenever you see odd-even correlations, average inter-item correlations, Cronbach's alpha, split-half reliabilities, or Kuder-Richardson reliabilities, the researchers are just trying to tell you the extent to which their measure is internally consistent.

In general, you can treat these indexes of internal consistency as all being pretty much alike—except that the score suggesting good internal consistency is different for the average inter-item correlations than for the other indexes of internal consistency. For the other indexes we have mentioned, you need a score of at least .70 (and preferably above .80) to say that the measure is internally consistent. Therefore, you would probably not use a measure with an odd–even correlation of .60 or a Cronbach's alpha of .50. However, the cutoff for acceptable internal consistency of the average (mean or median) inter-item correlation index is .30. Thus, most experts would say that a measure that has a median inter-item correlation of .35 has an adequate degree of internal consistency.

Conclusions About Internal Consistency's Relationship to Reliability

An adequate degree of internal consistency suggests that your measure's reliability problems are not due to its questions. Nor are your reliability problems due to minute-to-minute fluctuations in your participants. Instead, your reliability problems, if you have any, are probably due to participants changing over time or to improper standardization.

Low internal consistency, on the other hand, suggests that there are problems with the questions on your test. These problems will tend to hurt your test's overall reliability, especially if your test is relatively short. Therefore, you may want to boost your test's internal consistency by eliminating or refining some of your test's less reliable questions.

Conclusions About Reliability

Up to now, this chapter has focused on reliability. We have shown you why reliability is important, how to determine if a measure has sufficient reliability, and how to determine where a measure's reliability is breaking down (for a review, see Table 5-3, Table 5-4, and Figure 5-6). Specifically, we have stressed that:

1. Reliability is a prerequisite for validity.
2. Test–retest reliability tells you the total extent to which random error is influencing your measure.
3. Low test–retest reliability should encourage you to calculate other types of reliability coefficients such as interobserver reliability and internal consistency to pinpoint the main source of the measure's unreliability.

Table 5-3   Reliability Index and the Type of Random Error They Detect

	RANDOM ERROR DUE TO THE OBSERVER	RANDOM ERROR DUE TO RANDOM CHANGES IN PARTICIPANTS	RANDOM ERROR DUE TO RANDOM CHANGES IN THE TESTING SITUATION
Measures of observer reliability (Cohen's kappa, Krippendorf's alpha, interobserver reliability coefficient)	Yes	No	No
Measures of internal consistency (Cronbach's alpha, split-half reliability, Kuder-Richardson reliability, mean inter-item correlation, median inter-item correlations)	No	Only for changes that occur during a testing session	Only for changes that occur during a testing session
Test–retest reliability	Yes	Yes	Yes

Table 5-4   Key Points to Remember About Reliability

1. Two major *avoidable* sources of unreliability are
   a. random fluctuations in the measurement environment
   b. random fluctuations in how observers interpret and code observations
2. All reliability coefficients are not the same.
3. Test–retest reliability tells you the total extent to which random error is influencing your measure.
4. Other types of reliability can help you find the source of the measure's unreliability. For example, a low interobserver reliability coefficient tells you that random observer error is seriously reducing your measure's overall reliability.
5. Reliability is necessary for construct validity: Valid measures are reliable.
6. Reliability does not guarantee construct validity: Reliable measures are not always valid.
7. Unreliability weakens a measure's validity but does not introduce systematic bias into the measure.
8. Reliability is an important, but not all-important, consideration in choosing a measure.

Figure 5-6   **Determining Whether—and How—to Improve a Measure's Reliability**

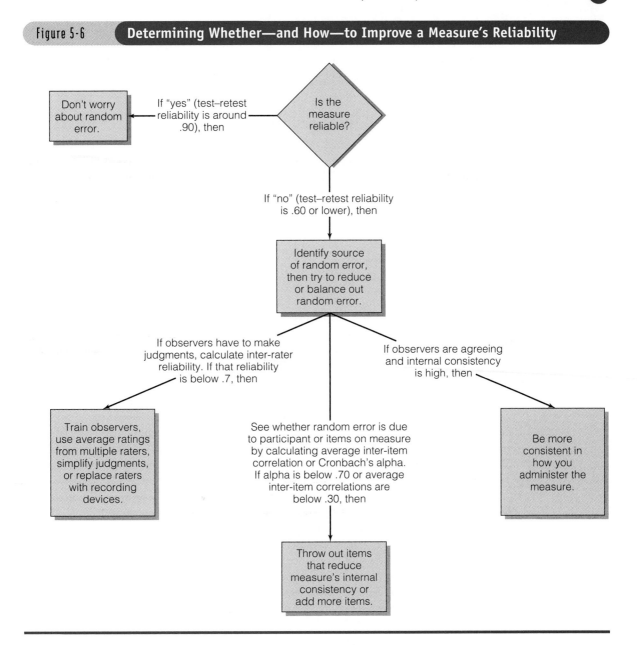

However, we have not emphasized the main limitation of reliability: *Reliability does not guarantee validity.* For example, consider the following data:

PARTICIPANT	SCORE ON PHYSICAL AGGRESSION TEST	SCORE ON RETEST	NUMBER OF FIGHTS
Darnell	50	50	3
Christopher	60	60	4
Alexus	70	70	1

As you can see, individuals score the same when retested as they did when they were first tested. Thus, the test has high test–retest reliability. However, individuals' scores on the test do not correspond with how many fights they have. Thus, the test is not a valid measure of physical aggression. Consequently, the measure is reliable but not valid.[8]

Beyond Reliability: Establishing Construct Validity

One reason a reliable measure may not be valid is that it is reliably and consistently measuring the wrong thing. How can we know that a measure has **construct validity:** the degree to which the measure is measuring the construct that it claims to measure?

We can never know that our measure has construct validity. However, we can make a case for a measure's construct validity, especially if it has good

- content validity
- internal consistency
- convergent validity
- discriminant validity

Content Validity: Does Your Test Have the Right Stuff?

Often, the first step in devising a valid test is to establish its **content validity:** the extent to which it represents a balanced and adequate sampling of relevant dimensions, knowledge, and skills. Before even writing any test questions, you should consult the established theories and definitions of the concept you wanted to measure. Your definition will guide you in writing your questions. For example, if you define love as, "feeling sexual attraction toward a person and a willingness to make sacrifices for that person," you would make sure your measure had questions that measured both sexual attraction and willingness to sacrifice. In fact, to make sure that you had an adequate number of both types of questions, you might break your scale into two subscales: a "sexual attraction" subscale and a "sacrifices" subscale.

As you can see, there are two main points to content validity: (1) having *content* (questions) tapping every dimension of your construct and (2) having enough questions to provide an adequate *sampling* of questions from each of those content areas. Consequently, content validity is sometimes called *content sampling*.

When evaluating classroom tests and other tests of knowledge or skills, content validity may be extremely important. For instance, a test to assess everything you have learned about psychology should not consist of only one multiple-choice question. Beyond having many questions, such a test should cover all areas of psychology, not just one. For example, if such a test consisted of 500 questions about classical conditioning, it would not have content validity.

Internal Consistency Revisited: Evidence That You Are Measuring One Characteristic

Content validity is important. If you can't argue that your measure logically follows from an accepted definition of the concept, few would accept your measure as valid. However, you must do more than claim that you have sets of questions that measure each important aspect of your construct: You need objective, statistical evidence of that claim. For example, if you

---

[8]As one reviewer pointed out, a classic example of a measure that would be reliable but not valid is using head circumference as a measure of IQ.

write some questions that you believe reflect the willingness to sacrifice for one's partner and call it a "personal sacrifices for partner scale," scientists are not going to accept your scale as valid without more evidence.

A first step toward making the case that your measure really is measuring the right thing (your construct) is to show that all the questions making up that instrument are measuring the same thing. To do this, you have to show that your scale is internally consistent: that participants who score a certain way on one of the "personal sacrifices for partner" subscale questions should score similarly to all the other "personal sacrifices for partner" questions. For example, if the answer to one question suggests a participant is willing to sacrifice for his partner, the answers to the other questions should echo that suggestion.

To understand the value of internal consistency, you may want to think of each question as a judge of whether participants have a certain characteristic. If one judge's scores are far apart from everyone else's, you would doubt that judge's competence. You might ask, "Was she watching the same thing everybody else was?" Similarly, if answers to a certain question on the test do not correspond to answers to the other questions, you would have doubts about that question. Because low internal consistency raises doubts about our questions, we want our measure to have high internal consistency.

As we mentioned earlier, there are several ways you can determine whether a measure has high internal consistency. If you found high inter-item correlations, split-half reliabilities, or Cronbach's alphas, you would be more confident that all the questions on the test were measuring the same construct. The following data would support the view that the questions agree with each other:

PARTICIPANT	QUESTION 1	QUESTION 2	QUESTION 3
Joe	1	1	1
Destiny	3	3	3
Ruby	5	5	5

However, what if the data were like this?

PARTICIPANT	QUESTION 1	QUESTION 2	QUESTION 3
Joe	1	1	5
Destiny	3	3	1
Ruby	5	5	3

Then, you would probably want to reword or eliminate question 3.

By eliminating and rewording questions, you should be able to achieve a reasonable level of internal consistency. Thus, if you were to take participants' scores on the first half of a 20-question test and correlate them with their scores on the last half of the test, you should find a high degree of agreement, like this:

PARTICIPANT	SCORE ON FIRST 10 QUESTIONS	SCORE ON LAST 10 QUESTIONS
Joe	50	50
Destiny	10	10
Ruby	30	30

These data strongly suggest that the test is measuring one thing. Thus, internal consistency seems like a good idea if you are measuring a simple construct that has only one dimension.

But what if you are measuring a complex construct that you think has two separate aspects? For example, suppose you want to measure love and you think that love has two different dimensions (sexual attraction and willingness to sacrifice for the other). You also believe that these dimensions are relatively independent: You believe that people who are high on sexual attraction are not much more likely to be high on willingness to sacrifice than people who are low on sexual attraction. In such a case, you don't expect a high level of internal consistency for your scale as a whole because your scale is measuring two different things.

One solution would be to make up a love scale that had two different subscales. You would then expect that each of the individual subscales would have a high degree of internal consistency but that the subscales would not correlate highly with each other. That is, all the responses to questions related to sexual attraction should correlate with one another; all the responses to items related to sacrifice should correlate with one another; but the sexual attraction scale should not correlate highly with the sacrifice scale.[9] The following results would support the case that your two subscales were measuring two different constructs:

Split-half reliability for Sacrifice Subscale	.84
Split-half reliability for Sexual Attraction Subscale	.89
Correlation between the Sacrifice and Sexual Attraction Subscales	.10

Convergent Validation Strategies: Statistical Evidence That You Are Measuring the Right Construct

Internal consistency can help you build the case that you are measuring the number of constructs you claim to be measuring. The data just presented strongly suggest that the test is measuring two things, but do not tell us what those two things are.

The data does not give us objective evidence that we are measuring "sacrifice" and "sexual attraction." Indeed, if one subscale was measuring intelligence and the other scale was measuring political attitudes, we might obtain those same data.

To make a case that your measure is measuring a certain construct, you should obtain evidence for its **convergent validity:** the extent to which your measure correlates with other indicators of the construct. The general idea is that your measure correlates with these other indicators because it and these other indicators are all converging on the same thing—your construct.

Perhaps the most obvious step in convergent validation is to show that your measure correlates with other measures of the same construct. Thus, if you were measuring love, you might correlate your measure with another measure of love, such as Rubin's Love Scale (Rubin, 1970). Because both measures are supposed to be measuring the same thing, the two measures should correlate highly with one another. That is, participants scoring high on your love measure should score high on the other love measure, and participants scoring low on your love measure should score low on the other love measure. Ideally, you would find a convergent validity correlation between your measure and the existing measure of .80 or higher, as in this example:

---

[9]Another commonly used strategy (discussed at the end of Appendix D) is to use factor analysis. In this case, you would want at least three outcomes from that factor analysis. First, you want the factor analysis to extract two independent factors (sacrifice and sexual attraction) that together accounted for much (over 60%) of the variability in scores. Second, you want items in the sacrifice subscale to correlate with (load heavily on-have factor loadings above .4) the factor you labeled sacrifice and not load on the factor you labeled sexual attraction. Third, you want items in the sexual attraction subscale to load heavily on the factor you labeled sexual attraction and not load heavily on the factor you labeled sacrifice.

PARTICIPANT	ESTABLISHED LOVE MEASURE	YOUR MEASURE
Basil	100	100
Maria	20	20
Pat	60	60

Another obvious convergent validity tactic is to find two groups: one known to possess a high degree of the characteristic you want to measure and one known to possess a low degree of that characteristic. You would hope that participants known to have a high level of the construct would score higher on your measure than participants known to have a low level of the construct. This tactic is called the **known-groups technique.** Thus, in validating your love scale, you might give your scale to two groups—one that is known to be in love (dating couples) and one that is known not to be in love (strangers). Scores on the love scale might approximate the following:

STRANGERS	DATING COUPLES
55	90

In addition to seeing whether different existing groups score differently on your measure, you could see whether individual scores on your measure predict future group membership. For instance, you might see if your measure could predict which dating couples would get engaged and which would soon split up (like Rubin did).

You could also see if your measure distinguishes between two groups exposed to different experimental manipulations. For example, if you had an experimental group that was expecting a shock and a control group that was not, you would expect the experimental group to score higher on your measure of anxiety than the control group.

Finally, you could determine whether your measure correlated with other indicators of the concept. Thus, you might correlate scores on the love scale with a behavior that lovers tend to do, such as look into each other's eyes, and find that couples with low scores on the love scale were less likely to gaze at each other than couples with high scores (like Rubin did).

Discriminant Validation Strategies: Showing That You Are Not Measuring the Wrong Construct

Convergent validity uses the "if it looks like a duck and walks like a duck, it must be a duck" approach to building the case for construct validity. Unfortunately, something may look like a duck and walk like a duck, but actually be a goose or other related bird. An "intelligence test," despite correlating with some measures of intelligence, may really measure mathematical knowledge. A lie detector measure that correlates with lying may merely be measuring nervousness. Similarly, a "love measure" that has some convergent validity with other measures of love may be measuring liking rather than love.

To illustrate the limits of convergent validity, suppose you correlate your love scale with another love scale. Imagine you have the following data:

PERSON	SCORE ON YOUR SCALE	SCORE ON OTHER LOVE SCALE
Basil	30	38
Maria	52	49
Pat	70	60

You have some good evidence for convergent validity because people who score one way on your test score about the same way on an established love test. But are you really measuring love? Before you say "yes," let's look at a table that combines data from the previous table with data from a liking scale:

PERSON	LIKING SCALE	YOUR SCALE	OTHER LOVE SCALE
Basil	30	30	38
Maria	52	52	49
Pat	70	70	60

As you can see from this new table, your scale seems to be measuring liking rather than love. Because you cannot show that your so-called love measure is different from a liking measure, you cannot say that the "love" measure is valid.

The moral of the two tables is that convergent validity alone is not enough to establish construct validity. It is not enough to show, as the first table did, that a measure correlates with measures of the right construct. We must also show that our measure has **discriminant validity:** showing that it is *not* measuring a different construct. Typically, you establish discriminant validity by showing that your measure does not correlate too highly with measures of different constructs.

What does it mean that your measure should not correlate *too highly* with measures of different constructs? In other words, what pattern of results would support the idea that your measure has discriminant validity? This is a tricky question, because it depends on whether you are trying to show discriminant validity relative to a related construct or whether you are trying to show discriminant validity relative to an unrelated construct.

Showing Discriminant Validity Relative to Unrelated Constructs

If you need to show discriminant validity relative to a construct that is unrelated, unassociated, and irrelevant to your construct, you would need a near-zero (anywhere from $-.20$ to $+.20$) correlation between your measure and a measure of the unrelated construct. For example, you, like most test developers, may need to show that your measure is not affected by social desirability bias. How would you do that?

The first step is to have participants complete your scale and a social desirability scale. Social desirability scales, sometimes called "lie scales," measure the degree to which the participant gives answers that—rather than being truthful—would impress most people. Basically, a social desirability scale consists of questions that ask you to describe yourself by choosing between two responses:

1. a socially desirable response ("Yes, I always help people out") that makes a good impression but is not honest
2. a less impressive response ("No, I do not always help people out") that is honest

People who lie by picking the socially correct responses will score high on the social desirability scale; people who pick the truthful, but less flattering, answers will score low in social desirability.

After administering both your measure and the social desirability scale, you would correlate the two measures. A correlation of around zero (between $-.20$ and $+.20$) would suggest that your measure is not strongly influenced by the social desirability bias. That is, a near-zero correlation between your scale and a social desirability scale suggests that you are measuring people's true feelings rather than people's willingness to make a good impression.

If, on the other hand, scores on the social desirability scale correlate highly with responses on your scale, your scale may be strongly affected by social desirability bias: Rather than measuring what people really think, you may just be measuring their willingness to make a good impression. For example, do you think the following data support the idea that the "friendliness test" really measures friendliness?

PERSON	FRIENDLINESS SCORE	SOCIAL DESIRABILITY SCORE
Basil	30	30
Maria	52	52
Pat	70	70

These data don't support the idea that the so-called friendliness test is measuring friendliness. Instead, they suggest that the so-called friendliness test is really a measure of social desirability.

As you can imagine, showing that a new measure has a near-zero correlation with social desirability is often one of the first steps that researchers take in establishing discriminant validity. However, in addition to showing that you are not measuring social desirability, you will also need to show that your measure has discriminant validity relative to a variety of other constructs.

Showing Discriminant Validity Relative to Related Constructs

For example, if you have a love measure, you may have to show that it does not correlate too highly with measures of related constructs such as liking, lust, loyalty, and trust. When trying to show discriminant validity relative to a related construct, you do not need a zero correlation between your measure and a measure of that related construct. Indeed, you would expect that scores on your measure would be somewhat related to scores on a measure of that related construct. For instance, you might expect that your love scale would correlate moderately (.60) with the liking scale because people who love each other tend to like each other. However, if your love scale correlated very highly with the liking scale, then you would be worried that you were measuring liking instead of love. You would especially be concerned if your scale correlated more highly with a liking scale than it did with other love scales.

Similarly, if you had a measure of practical intelligence, you would not be alarmed if it correlated moderately with a measure of conventional intelligence. However, if the correlation was around .80 (about as high as different IQ tests correlate with each other), you would have a hard time arguing that you had devised a test of a different type of intelligence. Instead, the evidence would suggest that you had devised yet another measure of conventional intelligence.

Conclusions About Discriminant Validity

In short, to make a convincing case that a measure really measures the construct it is supposed to measure (construct validity), you need to show that it really isn't measuring a construct that it shouldn't be measuring (disciminant validity). Therefore, when trying to decide whether to use a certain measure, you should ask two questions:

1. What other constructs might this measure be measuring?
2. Is there evidence that this measure does not measure those other constructs?

If you are trying to show that you are not measuring an unrelated construct, you need to show that there is a near-zero correlation between your measure and a measure of the unrelated construct. If, on the other hand, you are trying to show that you are not measuring a related construct, even a moderately high correlation of .60 might provide evidence of discriminant validity—as long as that was significantly lower than your measure's convergent validity correlations.[10]

Summary of Construct Validity

As you can see from Figure 5-7 and Table 5-5, building a strong case for your measure's construct validity is several research projects in itself. To assess convergent validity, researchers often have to consult theory and past research to see what manipulations would affect their

Figure 5-7 **Steps to Validity**

Strategy	How Accomplished
Measures more than random error	Test–retest reliability
Logical reasons to expect measure is valid	Content validity
Questions measuring same thing	Internal consistency
Measure corresponds with other measures of the right construct	Convergent validity
Measure does *not* correspond closely to measures of different constructs	Discriminant validity

[10]Two common ways of showing that a measure is not measuring a related construct are (1) partial correlations and (2) tests of the differences between correlations. Partial correlations are correlations between two variables that try to control for the possibility that the correlation between those two variables is due to some third variable. For example, suppose a social intelligence test correlated .60 with grades. One might wonder whether the social intelligence test was just another intelligence test. To find out, one could compute a partial correlation between social intelligence and grades that would control for IQ scores. If the partial correlation between social intelligence and grades was now zero, we would conclude that the social intelligence test did *not* have discriminant validity relative to conventional intelligence tests. If, on the other hand, the partial correlation was significantly different from zero, we would conclude that the social intelligence measure did have discriminant validity relative to conventional intelligence. The test between correlations might involve doing a statistical significance test to determine whether the correlation between your social intelligence test and another social intelligence test was significantly higher than the correlation between your social intelligence test and a conventional intelligence test.

Table 5-5	Validating a Love Measure: Rubin's Love Scale
REQUIREMENTS FOR CONSTRUCT VALIDITY	HOW RUBIN MET THE REQUIREMENT
Reliability	Showed that the measure was not excessively affected by random error: Test–Retest Reliability of .85.
Content validity	All three dimensions of love are represented (predisposition to help, dependency, and possessiveness).
Convergent validity	Predicts how much two individuals will gaze at each other.
	Predicts probability that individuals will eventually get married.
	People who are engaged score higher than people who are casually dating.
Discriminant validity	Love scores correlate only moderately with scores on a liking scale, suggesting that the scale is not a measure of liking.

construct and then see whether those manipulations affect scores on their own measure. In addition, researchers may need to consult theory and past research to see what behaviors correlate with high levels of the construct and then see whether people scoring high on their measure exhibit those behaviors. To assess discriminant validity, researchers have to correlate their measure with measures of other constructs. To assess internal consistency, researchers need to administer the measure and calculate some measure of internal consistency. Because validating a measure takes so much time and because most researchers are interested in finding out new things about a construct rather than finding new ways to measure it, most researchers do not invent their own measures. Instead, researchers use measures that others have already validated. (In fact, while reading about what it would take to validate your own love scale, you may have been saying to yourself, "Let's use Rubin's Love Scale instead.")

Manipulating Variables

There are two reasons we have devoted most of this chapter to measuring, rather than manipulating, variables. First, all research involves measuring variables, whereas not all research involves manipulating variables. For example, if a researcher wants to know whether people who tend to exercise are happier than people who don't, researchers can just measure both variables. Even if a researcher wanted to know whether exercise *causes* one to be happier, the researcher would still measure happiness—although the researcher would also have to *manipulate* how much participants exercise. Second, as you can see from both Table 5-6 and the next section of this chapter, many of the things you should think about when measuring variables also apply to manipulating variables.

Common Threats to a Manipulation's Validity

When evaluating manipulations, you have the same concerns as you have when you measure variables:

1. Can we reduce random error?
2. Can we reduce bias due to the researcher?

Table 5-6	Similarities Between Measuring and Manipulating Variables

MEASURE	MANIPULATION
Reduce random error by standardizing administration of the measure.	Reduce random error by standardizing administration of the manipulation.
Reduce observer bias by training, standardization, instruments, and making researcher "blind" to the participant's condition.	Reduce researcher bias by training, standardization, instruments, and making the researcher "blind" to the participant's condition.
Participants may figure out what the measure is measuring and then act in such a way as to make a good impression or give the researcher the "right" results. Sometimes, the problem of subject biases is dealt with by not letting participants know what the measure is or what the hypothesis is.	Participants may figure out what the manipulation is designed to do and then act in such a way as to make a good impression or to give the researcher the "right" results. Sometimes, the problem of subject biases is dealt with by not letting participants know what the manipulation is or what the hypothesis is.
Show that your operational definition is consistent with the theory's definition of the construct.	Show that your operational definition is consistent with the theory's definition of the construct.
Convergent validity is shown by correlating the measure with other measures of the construct.	Convergent validity is sometimes demonstrated by showing that the manipulation has the same effect that other manipulations of the construct have and that it has an effect on the manipulation check.

3. Can we reduce bias due to the participant?
4. Can we provide evidence that the operational definition we are using is valid?

Random Error

Just as you want to minimize random error when measuring variables, you want to minimize random error when manipulating variables. Therefore, just as you standardized the administration of your measure, you want to standardize the administration of your treatment. You want to administer the treatment the same way every time.

Experimenter Bias

Just as you were worried about researchers being biased in their observations, you will also be worried about **experimenter bias:** experimenters being biased when they administer the treatment. For instance, researchers may be friendlier to the participants who are getting the treatment. As was the case with observer bias, you can reduce researcher bias by

- using scientific equipment to administer the manipulations
- using written or computerized instructions
- standardizing procedures
- making the researcher *blind* to what treatment the participant received

Subject Biases

Just as you were concerned that your *measure* might tip off participants to how they should behave, you should also be concerned that your *manipulation* might tip off participants as to how they should behave. One of the most frequently cited examples of how a treatment could lead to demand characteristics was a series of studies begun in the 1920s at the

Hawthorne Electric Plant. The investigators, Roethlisberger and Dickson (1939), were looking at the effects of lighting on productivity. At first, everything seemed to go as expected: Increasing illumination increased productivity. However, when they reduced illumination, productivity continued to increase. The researchers concluded that the treatment group was reacting to the special attention rather than to the treatment itself. This effect became known as the **Hawthorne effect.**

Although many experts now believe that Roethlisberger and Dickson's results were not due to the Hawthorne effect, no one disputes that participants may act differently simply because they think they are getting a treatment. Therefore, researchers use a wide variety of techniques to avoid the Hawthorne effect. Some of these techniques are similar to the techniques used to make a measure less vulnerable to subject biases. Just as researchers may reduce subject biases by measuring participants in nonresearch settings, experimenters may reduce subject biases by manipulating the treatment in a nonresearch setting.

A more common way of reducing subject biases is to give the "no-treatment" group a **placebo treatment:** a treatment that is known to have no effect. For example, in most studies examining the effect of a drug, some participants get the pill that contains the drug (the treatment), whereas others get a sugar pill (the placebo). If both groups improve equally, researchers would be concerned that the treatment group's improvement might be due to participants expecting to get better. If, however, the treatment group improves more than the placebo group, we know that the improvement was not due to participants' expectations.

Evidence Used to Argue for a Manipulation's Construct Validity

As with measures, you would like to provide evidence that your treatment is doing what you claim it is. The difference is that making a case for the validity of a treatment is usually less involved than making a case for the validity of a measure.

The two most common ways of establishing validity are (1) to argue that your treatment is consistent with a theory's definition of the construct and (2) to use a **manipulation check:** a question or set of questions designed to determine whether participants perceived the manipulation in the way that the researcher intended.

Consistency With Theory

To illustrate the value of these two ways of establishing construct validity, suppose that you wanted to manipulate cognitive dissonance: a state of arousal caused when participants are aware of having two inconsistent beliefs. So you ask a group of smokers to write an essay about why people shouldn't smoke. You would want to argue that your manipulation meets three general criteria that dissonance theory says must be met for dissonance to be induced:

1. Participants must believe they are voluntarily performing an action that is inconsistent with their attitudes (a smoker writing an essay about why people shouldn't smoke).

2. Participants should believe that the action is public and will have consequences (before writing the essay, participants must believe that others will not only read their essay but know that the participant wrote it).

3. Participants must not feel that they engaged in the behavior for a reward (that they are being bribed to write an essay that goes against their beliefs).

To make the case that the manipulation is consistent with dissonance theory, you might argue that:

1. You told participants their cooperation was voluntary and they could refuse.
2. You told them that their essay would be signed and that children who were thinking about smoking would read it.
3. You did not pay participants for writing an antismoking essay.

Manipulation Checks

Your procedures would seem to induce the mental state of dissonance—assuming that participants perceived the manipulation as you intended. To check on that assumption, you might use a manipulation check. For example, you might ask participants whether they felt aroused and uncomfortable, coerced, that their attitudes and behavior were inconsistent, that their behavior was public, whether they foresaw the consequences of their behavior, and so on. Many researchers believe that you should always use a manipulation check when doing research on human participants (Sigall & Mills, 1998).

But what if the manipulation check tips off participants to the study's hypothesis? In that case, manipulation check advocates would say to use the manipulation check—but only after the participant has responded to your measure. Or, you might conduct a mini-study in which the only thing that happens is that participants receive the manipulation and then respond to the manipulation check.

But what if it's obvious that you are manipulating whatever you think you are manipulating (physical attractiveness, concrete versus abstract words, etc.)? Even then, manipulation check advocates would urge you to go ahead with a manipulation check for two important reasons. First, a manipulation check could establish the discriminant validity of your treatment. For example, wouldn't it be nice if you could show that your attractiveness manipulation increased perceptions of attractiveness but did not change perceptions of age or wealth? Second, because you are doing research to test assumptions rather than to make assumptions, you should be willing to test the assumption that you are manipulating what you think you are manipulating.

Pros and Cons of Three Common Types of Manipulations

Choosing a manipulation usually involves making tradeoffs because there is no such thing as the perfect manipulation. Different manipulations have different strengths and weaknesses. In the next sections, we will briefly highlight the strengths and weaknesses of three common ways of giving participants in different conditions different experiences: (1) giving them different instructions (instructional manipulations), (2) changing their physical environment (environmental manipulations), and (3) varying the behavior of their "co-participants"—research assistants pretending to be participants (stooge manipulations).

Instructional Manipulations

Perhaps the most common treatment manipulation is the **instructional manipulation:** manipulating the variable by giving written or oral instructions. One advantage of an instructional manipulation is that you can standardize your manipulation easily. Often, all you have to do is give each participant in the treatment condition one photocopied sheet of instructions and give each participant in the no-treatment condition another sheet of instructions. If you use a computer to compose the different sets of instructions, you can easily ensure that the instructions are identical except for the manipulation. If you have a cover sheet for the instructions, the person handing out the instructions can be blind to which set of instructions the participant receives. Because written instructions are easily standardized and because written instructions allow you to make the researcher blind, written instructions can reduce both random error and experimenter bias.

However, just because you can consistently present instructions to participants, don't assume that your instructions will be perceived the same way every time. Participants may ignore, forget, or misinterpret instructions.

To reduce random error due to participants interpreting your instructions differently, "hit participants over the head" with your manipulation by repeating and paraphrasing your most important instructions. Thus, if you were manipulating anonymity, you would make a big deal of forbidding participants from writing their name on any of the materials, and you would tell them that their responses will be anonymous, confidential, private, and that no one will know how they responded. In the public condition, you would do just the opposite: You would make a big deal of making participants write their names on their paper, and you would tell them that many people would see their paper.

If participants do not understand or do not pay attention to the manipulation, the instructional manipulation will have little effect on your participants. However, by making the instructions clear, repeating the instructions, and quizzing participants about the instructions, you can overcome the problem of participants not noticing or not understanding your manipulation.

If, on the other hand, participants understand your manipulation too well, they may figure out what you are trying to manipulate and then play along. Fortunately, you can reduce this threat to your study's construct validity by using placebo treatments, counterintuitive hypotheses (hypotheses that make a prediction that is opposite of what most people—and most participants—would predict), and clever ways of measuring your construct. (To see examples of clever measures, see Table 5-2.)

Environmental Manipulations

If you are concerned that participants will play along with an instructional manipulation, you might use an **environmental manipulation:** changing the participants' surroundings. Some environmental manipulations take the form of "accidents." For instance, smoke may fill a room, the participant may be induced to break something, or the participant may "overhear" some remark.

When considering an environmental manipulation, ask two questions. First, will participants notice the manipulation? Even when manipulations have involved dramatic changes in participants' environments (smoke filling a room), a sizable proportion of participants report not noticing the manipulation (Latané & Darley, 1970).

Second, can you present the manipulation the same way every time? Fortunately, many environmental manipulations can be presented in a consistent, standardized way. Most animal research, for example, involves environmental manipulations that can be consistently presented (food deprivation). Likewise, research in perception, sensory processing, cognition, and verbal learning usually involves environmental manipulations (presenting illusions or other stimuli). These manipulations vary from the routine—presentation of visual stimuli by computer, tachistoscope, memory drum, or automated slide projector—to the exotic. For example, Neisser (1984) has done studies in which the manipulation consists of silently moving the walls of the participant's cubicle.

Table 5-7	Comparing the Advantages and Disadvantages of Three Different Kinds of Manipulations		

INSTRUCTIONAL	ENVIRONMENTAL	STOOGES
Easy to do.	Not as easy to do.	Hardest to do.
Easily standardized.	Not as easily standardized.	Hardest to standardize.
Reduces:	May lead to concerns about:	May lead to concerns about:
1. Random error	1. Random error	1. Random error
2. Potential for experimenter biases	2. Potential for experimenter biases	2. Potential for experimenter biases
Vulnerable to subject biases.	Less vulnerable to subject biases.	Least vulnerable to subject biases.

Manipulations Involving Stooges

A special kind of environmental manipulation employs **stooges (confederates):** actors who pretend to be participants but are actually the researcher's assistants. By using stooges, social psychologists and others get participants to respond openly, thus avoiding the demand characteristics that accompany instructional manipulations. However, there are two problems with using stooges.

First, using stooges raises ethical questions because by deceiving your participants, you are violating the principle of informed consent. Your attempt to reduce demand characteristics is coming at the cost of participants' rights. The decision to try to deceive participants should be made only after careful consideration of the alternatives. Thus, for ethical reasons, you, your professor, or your school's ethics committee may decide that you shouldn't use stooges (for more on ethics, see Appendix C).

Second, it's hard to standardize the performance of a stooge. At best, inconsistent performances by stooges create unnecessary random error. At worst, stooges may bias the results. Some researchers solve the standardization problem by having participants listen to tapes of actors rather than relying on stooges to give exactly the same performance time after time. For example, both Aronson and Carlsmith (1968) and Latané and Darley (1970) made participants believe they were listening to people talking over an intercom when participants were actually listening to a tape recording.

As you can see from Table 5-7, choosing manipulations usually means making trade-offs. To choose the right manipulation for your study, you must determine what your study needs most. Is experimenter bias your biggest concern? Then, you might use an instructional manipulation. Is subject bias your biggest concern? Then, you might use an environmental manipulation.

Conclusions About Manipulating Variables

As you have seen, when manipulating variables, you have many of the same concerns you have when measuring variables. However, when manipulating variables, you have one set of concerns that you don't have when measuring variables: How many different amounts or types of the treatment should you have, how different should these amounts be, and who gets which amount? We will deal with these important issues in Chapters 10 and 11.

Concluding Remarks

In Chapter 3, you developed a research idea: a prediction about how two or more variables were related. In this chapter, you learned how to determine whether you had valid operational definitions of those variables. Now that you have the raw materials to build a research design, you can take advantage of the rest of this book.

SUMMARY

1. *Reliability* refers to whether you are getting consistent, stable measurements. Reliable measures are relatively free of random error.

2. A way to measure the extent to which a measure is free of random error is to compute its test–retest reliability.

3. Three major sources of unreliability are random errors in scoring the behavior, random variations in how the measure is administered, and random fluctuations in the participant's performance.

4. You can assess the degree to which random errors due to the observer are affecting scores by computing an interobserver reliability coefficient. Interobserver reliability puts a ceiling on test–retest reliability.

5. For objective tests, you may get some idea about the degree to which scores are affected by random, moment-to-moment fluctuations in the participant's behavior by using an index of internal consistency. Popular indexes of internal consistency are Cronbach's alpha, split-half reliabilities, and average inter-item correlations.

6. Random error is different from bias. Bias is a more serious threat to validity. In a sense, random error dilutes validity, whereas bias poisons validity.

7. *Validity of a measure* refers to whether you are measuring what you claim you are measuring.

8. Reliability puts a ceiling on validity; therefore, an unreliable measure cannot be valid. However, reliability does not guarantee validity; therefore, a reliable measure may be invalid.

9. A valid measure must have some degree of reliability and be relatively free of observer bias and subject biases.

10. Two common subject biases are social desirability (trying to make a good impression) and obeying the study's demand characteristics (trying to make the researcher look good by producing results that support the hypothesis).

11. By not letting participants know what you are measuring (unobtrusive measurement), you may be able to reduce subject biases (see Table 5-2).

12. Establishing internal consistency, discriminant validity, convergent validity, and content validity are all ways of building the case for a measure's construct validity.

13. Choosing a manipulation involves many of the same steps as choosing a measure.

14. Placebo treatments and unobtrusive measurement can reduce subject bias.

15. "Blind" procedures and standardization can reduce experimenter bias.

16. You can use manipulation checks to make a case for your manipulation's validity.

KEY TERMS

operational definition *(p. 98)*

bias *(p. 100)*

random error *(p. 100)*

observer bias *(p. 103)*

blind (masked) *(p. 105)*

standardization *(p. 106)*

subject bias *(p. 107)*

demand characteristics *(p. 107)*

informed consent *(p. 108)*

unobtrusive measurement *(p. 109)*

social desirability bias *(p. 110)*

reliable, reliability *(p. 111)*

test–retest reliability *(p. 113)*

interobserver (judge) agreement *(p. 116)*

interobserver (scorer) reliability coefficient *(p. 116)*

internal consistency *(p. 120)*

construct validity *(p. 124)*

content validity *(p. 124)*

convergent validity *(p. 126)*

known-groups technique *(p. 127)*

discriminant validity *(p. 128)*

experimenter bias *(p. 132)*

Hawthorne effect *(p. 133)*

placebo treatment *(p. 133)*

manipulation check *(p. 133)*

instructional manipulation *(p. 134)*

environmental manipulation *(p. 135)*

stooges (confederates) *(p. 136)*

EXERCISES

1. Why is bias considered more serious than random error?

2. What are the two primary types of subject bias? What are the differences between these two sources?

3. What is discriminant validity? Why is it necessary?

4. What is the value of internal consistency?

5. What is content validity? For what measures is it most important?

6. Swann and Rentfrow (2001) wanted to develop a test "that measures the extent to which people respond to others quickly and effusively." In their view, high scorers would tend to blurt out their thoughts to others immediately and low scorers would be slow to respond.
   a. How would you use the known groups technique to get evidence of your measure's construct validity?
   b. What measures would you correlate with your scale to make the case for your measure's discriminant validity? Why? In what range would the correlation coefficients between those measures and your measure have to be to provide evidence of discriminant validity? Why?
   c. To provide evidence of convergent validity, you could correlate scores on your measure with a behavior typical of people who blurt out their thoughts. What behavior would you choose? Why?

7. A researcher wants to measure "aggressive tendencies" and is trying to decide between a paper-and-pencil test of aggression and observing actual aggression.
   a. What problems might there be with observing aggressive behavior?
   b. What would probably be the most serious threat to the validity of a paper-and-pencil test of aggression? What information about the test would suggest that the test is a good instrument?

8. Think of a construct you would like to measure.
   a. Name that construct.
   b. Define that construct.
   c. Locate a published measure of that concept (if you are having trouble finding a published example, see Web Appendix B), and write down the reference for that source.
   d. Develop a measure of that construct.
   e. What could you do to improve or evaluate your measure's reliability?
   f. If you had a year to try to validate your measure, how would you go about it? (Hint: Refer to the different kinds of validities discussed in this chapter.)
   g. How vulnerable is your measure to subject and observer bias? Why? Can you change your measure to make it more resistant to these threats?

9. What problems do you see with measuring "athletic ability" as 40-yard-dash speed? What steps would you take to improve this measure? (Hint: Think

about solving the problems of bias and random error).

10. Think of a factor that you would like to manipulate.
   a. Define this factor as specifically as you can.
   b. Find one example of this factor being manipulated in a published study (if you are having trouble finding a published example, see Web Appendix B). Write down the reference citation for that source.
   c. Would you use an environmental or instructional manipulation? Why?
   d. How would you manipulate that factor? Why?
   e. How could you perform a manipulation check on the factor you want to manipulate? Would it be useful to perform a manipulation check? Why or why not?

WEB RESOURCES

1. Go to the Chapter 5 section of the book's student website and:
   a. Look over the concept map of the key terms.
   b. Test yourself on the key terms.
   c. Take the Chapter 5 Practice Quiz.
   d. Do the interactive end-of-chapter exercises.

2. If you are ready to draft a method section, click on the "Method Section Tips" link.

3. If you want to have a better understanding of correlation coefficients, click on the "Correlator" link.

INFOTRAC COLLEGE EDITION EXPLORATIONS

1. To get a better understanding of how researchers validate measures, do the following InfoTrac College Edition keyword searches: "convergent validity," "discriminant validity," "content validity," and "reliability and validity."

2. Look at some psychological tests by doing an InfoTrac College Edition keyword search for "psychological tests."

3. Look at how a measure can stimulate research by doing an InfoTrac College Edition keyword search for the phrase "Stroop and enduring" to find Bower's (1992) report on the Stroop effect.

6

Beyond Reliability and Validity

The Best Measure for Your Study

When possible, make the decisions now, even if action is in the future. A reviewed decision usually is better than one reached at the last moment.

—*William B. Given, Jr.*

Overview

Some people buy the most powerful software available, only to find out that it doesn't work well for them. The program may be incompatible with other software they have, or it may not have a certain feature they want. As a result, they have a decent program, but one that doesn't work well for what they want to do. Similarly, when selecting a measure, some people choose the most valid measuring instrument available, yet find out that it doesn't work well for what they want to do.

At first, choosing the most valid measure seems perfectly sensible. After all, who wouldn't want to make sure that their instrument measures what it is supposed to measure?

After giving it some thought, however, you probably realize that most important decisions involve weighing more than one factor. Every measure, like every computer program, has weaknesses. The key is to find the measure whose weaknesses are least likely to get in the way of what you want to do.

To choose the measure whose weaknesses won't stop you from doing what you want to do, you need to know not only the measure's weaknesses but also what you want to do. For example, imagine that you find three measures that, although they have similar overall levels of validity, have different specific weaknesses in terms of validity. The first measure is vulnerable only to biased observers. The second measure is a rating scale measure vulnerable only to subject biases. The third measure's only weakness is unreliability. Which measure should you choose? The answer depends on your particular study.

If your observers could not bias the results in favor of the treatment group because you kept them *blind* (you didn't let them know whether the participant they were rating was in the treatment group or in the no-treatment group), you would choose the measure that is vulnerable only to observer bias.

If you had a hypothesis that is easy to figure out, you would avoid the measure that is vulnerable to subject bias. Suppose, for example, you hypothesized that participants would like a product more after seeing an ad for the product. Unfortunately, even if the ad was ineffective, participants may still rate the product higher after seeing the ad because they thought you wanted the ad to be effective. In this case, the combination of a hypothesis that is easy to guess and a rating scale measure that is easy to fake would be deadly to your study's construct validity. Therefore, you would not use the rating scale measure. Suppose, however, you had a hypothesis that participants probably wouldn't figure out. For example, suppose your hypothesis was that the ad would actually decrease liking for the product. In that case, you might choose the rating scale measure because its vulnerability to subject biases might not hurt you.

Finally, if you were concerned about avoiding both subject and observer bias, you would choose the measure that was unbiased but unreliable. Admittedly, such a measure would have limited validity—and its random error would make it difficult for you to obtain a statistically reliable difference between your treatment and no-treatment groups. However, if you found a significant difference between the treatment and no-treatment groups, you could be confident that the difference wasn't due to bias.

As you can see, even if validity were your only concern, you would not always choose the measure that, in general, was most valid. Instead, you would choose the measure that would be most valid for your particular study. But validity should never be your only concern. For starters, ethical concerns (e.g., the degree to which using the measure deceives participants or makes them feel uncomfortable), and practical concerns (e.g., how expensive the measure is, how long it takes to test participants, how difficult it is to administer) will always affect your choice of measure. Furthermore, you should also choose a measure based on whether it will allow you to answer your research question.

Sensitivity: Will the Measure Be Able to Detect the Differences You Need to Detect?

To understand how a measure could prevent you from answering your research question, imagine a cell biologist's reaction to being told that she could use only a magnifying glass. Obviously, she would be surprised. Without a microscope, the cell biologist could not detect small differences between cells.

Like cell biologists, psychologists often look for subtle differences. Consequently, like cell biologists, psychologists usually want their measure to be **sensitive:** to have the ability to detect differences among participants on a given variable. For example, we might try to increase participants' empathy for others. Realistically, we realize that one short treatment is probably not going to have enormous effects on a trait that has been shaped by heredity and a lifetime of experiences. If we have been able to make even a small improvement in this characteristic, we want to know about it.

Achieving the Necessary Level of Sensitivity

How can you find or develop a sensitive measure? Often, you can evaluate or improve a measure's sensitivity by using common sense. For instance, if participants must receive either a score of "1" or "2," the measure will not be sensitive to subtle differences among participants (just as "weighing" people as either "light" or "heavy" would skip over subtle differences, such as differences between people who weigh 110 pounds and people who weigh 120 pounds). But beyond such commonsense considerations, look at the measure's validity and reliability: As you will soon see, the more valid and reliable the measure, the more sensitive it will tend to be.

Look for High Validity

The desire for sensitivity is a major reason that researchers often insist on having the most valid measure available. Even though they have several valid measures to choose from, they want the most valid one because it will tend to be the most sensitive.

Why does the most valid measure tend to be the most sensitive? To answer this question, keep two related facts in mind. First, the most valid measure is the one in which scores are least affected by factors that are irrelevant to what you are trying to measure. Second, the less a measure's scores are affected by irrelevant factors, the more it will be sensitive to changes in the relevant factor. For example, if you were weighing people to determine whether a diet had an effect, you would be more likely to find the diet's effect if participants were weighed unclothed rather than clothed. Both the clothed and unclothed measures would be valid. However, because the unclothed measure is not assessing the weight of the clothes, it is more valid and more sensitive to actual weight changes.

For similar reasons, measures that involve fewer inferences tend to be both more valid and more sensitive. Consequently, scientists would prefer to measure a person's weight on a scale rather than by the depth of the impression the person's footprint left in the sand. Likewise, they would prefer to measure body fat using calipers rather than by estimating it from overall body weight.

Given what you have just learned about how to increase validity and about how increasing validity often increases sensitivity, you will probably want to take the following two steps. First, spend the time to figure out precisely what it is you want to measure. When you initially come up with a research idea, you may have a general sense of what you want to measure. For example, you may start out thinking that you want to measure attraction. Upon reflection, however, you may decide that you really want to measure lust. One way of helping you focus on what you want to measure is to look up the term you think you want to measure in the *Psychological Thesaurus* (see Web Appendix B). The *Thesaurus* will help you clarify what you want to measure by alerting you to more specific terms, as well as related terms.

Second, ask if there is a more direct way of measuring your construct. For instance, if you are interested in measuring aggression in football, do not simply measure how many penalties a team gets. Instead, measure how many penalties they get for unsportsmanlike conduct. Similarly, rather than assuming that fear will lead children to sit closer to each other and then measuring fear by how closely children sit to each other, take the more direct approach of asking children how afraid they are. By thinking about the simplest, most direct way to measure what you want to measure, you can often reduce the extent to which your measure is affected by things you don't want to measure, thereby increasing sensitivity.

Look for High Reliability

One thing you don't want to measure is random error. When you are measuring random error, you aren't measuring the quality you wish to measure. The less reliable the measure, the more scores on that measure are being influenced by random error. Therefore, all other things being equal, the less reliable the measure, the less sensitive it will be at detecting different amounts of the quality you wish to measure.[1]

To illustrate that unreliability hurts sensitivity, imagine that you weighed yourself every day on a highly unreliable scale. Then, suppose you had gained 2 pounds. Some days your scale would make it seem like you had gained 6 pounds, whereas on other days your scale would make it seem like you had lost 2 pounds. Instead of realizing that you'd gained weight, you might think that the different readings on the scale were due entirely to random error.

As this example suggests, unreliability in your data is like static interfering with your ability to hear a radio news program. With a little static, you can still hear the program. But as the static increases, you will find it increasingly difficult to make out what is being said. Similarly, with a lot of random error in your measurements, it becomes hard to pick up the news your data are sending you. Consequently, if you see that your groups score quite differently on an unreliable measure, you may not know whether those large differences are due to random measurement error or whether they represent actual differences.

To visualize how random error makes it hard to see the message in your data, imagine you were measuring the time it took two different rats to run a maze. Suppose that Rat A and Rat B ran the maze four times each. Their actual times were:

	TRIAL 1	TRIAL 2	TRIAL 3	TRIAL 4
Rat A	6 seconds	6 seconds	6 seconds	6 seconds
Rat B	5 seconds	5 seconds	5 seconds	5 seconds

If you had obtained these data, you could clearly see that Rat B was the faster rat. However, suppose your measuring system was unreliable. For example, suppose you were having

---

[1]The less reliable the measure, the more it is affected by random error—provided that you are measuring a stable characteristic. If you are measuring intelligence—and if intelligence is stable—any unreliability in your measure reflects random error. If, however, you are measuring something that changes (knowledge about research methods), unreliability might not reflect random error.

some problems with the stopwatch or you weren't always paying close attention. Then, you might record the rats' times as follows:

	TRIAL **1**	TRIAL **2**	TRIAL **3**	TRIAL **4**
Rat A	7 seconds	6 seconds	5 seconds	6 seconds
Rat B	8 seconds	4 seconds	6 seconds	2 seconds

Despite the random error in your measurements, you correctly calculated that Rat A averages 6 seconds to run the maze and Rat B averages 5 seconds to run the maze. Thus, random error does not bias your observations. However, because of the unreliable, erratic nature of your measuring system, it is hard to determine whether Rat B really is the faster rat. The unreliability of the measuring system causes static that makes it harder to get a clear picture of the message your data should be sending you.

You have seen that too much random error in your measuring system can prevent you from detecting true differences between participants. In other words, all other things being equal, the more reliable the measure is, the more sensitive it is. Therefore, if you want to have a sensitive measure, you should probably choose a measure that has a high (above .80) test–retest reliability coefficient.

Find Measures That Provide a Variety of Scores

Thus far, we have discussed cases in which you could increase sensitivity by increasing both reliability and validity. The more scores on the measure are affected by the characteristic you want to measure (rather than by bias, a different trait, or random error), the more the measure is likely to be sensitive to differences between individuals on that characteristic. A reliable and valid measure might still be insensitive, though, because—like a scale that will measure you only to the nearest 100 pounds—it fails to allow participants who differ slightly on a trait to receive different scores (see Figure 6-1).

Figure 6-1 **An Insensitive But Potentially Reliable Measure**

Having only two scale points (light and heavy) makes this scale insensitive. Adding scale points (e.g., marks for every pound or every half a kilogram) would make the scale more sensitive.

If a measure is to be sensitive to subtle differences between participants, participants who differ on the characteristic must get different scores. Thus, if you measured participants who varied widely on the characteristic, you should get a wide range of scores. Some participants should get extremely low scores, and others should get extremely high scores. Few participants should get the same score.

Avoid Behaviors That Are Resistant to Change. What could prevent a valid measure from producing the wide variety of scores necessary to reflect the full extent of the variation among your participants? To answer this question, let's imagine that you are trying to detect small changes in how much a man loves a woman. What could stop you from detecting changes in the man's love?

One reason you might be unable to detect small changes in love is that you chose to measure a behavior that is resistant to change. Measures based on such behaviors are insensitive; therefore, if sensitivity is a big concern, you should not choose to measure a behavior that is resistant to change. What behaviors are resistant to change?

Important behaviors, such as proposing marriage or buying a car, and well-ingrained habits, such as smoking or cursing, are resistant to change. Such behaviors are especially insensitive to subtle changes in a construct. For example, suppose your measure of love was whether a man asked a woman to marry him. Because a man would ask a woman to marry him only after his love had reached an extremely high level, this measure would be insensitive to many subtle changes. It would not be able to detect a man's love changing from a near-zero level of love to a moderate level.

So, if you are interested in sensitivity, stay away from measures that cannot detect low levels of a construct. Don't use death as a measure of stress, tile erosion in front of a painting as a measure of the painting's popularity, quitting smoking as a measure of willpower, or any other measure that stays at zero until a high level of the variable is present.

Avoid "All or Nothing" Measures. A second thing that could prevent you from distinguishing between the subtly different levels of the man's love is if your measure did not represent all these different levels. Consequently, a second reason that a marriage proposal is an insensitive measure is that there are only two scores the man could receive (asked or didn't ask). You are trying to distinguish between numerous subtly differing degrees of love, but you are letting your participant respond in only two different ways. If a measure is going to discriminate between many different degrees of love, participants must be able to give many different responses.

Ask "How Much" Instead of "Whether." One obvious way to allow participants to get a variety of scores on a measure is to add scale points to your measure. Adding scale points to your measure may increase its sensitivity just as adding 1/2-inch marks to a yardstick makes the yardstick more useful for detecting subtle differences in the lengths of boards. So, if you are measuring generosity, don't just record whether someone gave to charity. Instead, record how often she donated, or how much she gave, or how long you had to talk to her before she was willing to give. Similarly, if you are using maze running to measure motivation, don't simply record whether or not the rat ran the maze. Instead, record how fast the rat ran the maze.

Using scientific equipment can help you add scale points to your measure. For instance, with the proper instruments, you can measure reaction time to the nearest thousandth of a second. Or, by using a sound meter to measure how loudly a person is speaking, you can specify exactly how many decibels the person produced.

Add Scale Points to a Rating Scale. Often, you should add scale points to self-report measures. For example, rather than measuring love by asking the question: "Are you in love? (1—no, 2—yes)," ask "How much in love are you? (1—not at all, 2—slightly, 3—moderately,

4—extremely).” Similarly, rather than having an observer rate whether a child was aggressive, you could have the observer rate the extent to which the child was aggressive.

There comes a point, however, where adding scale points to a measure will not enhance sensitivity. Asking people to report their weight to the nearest 1/1,000th of a pound or asking them to report their love on a 1,000-point scale will probably not boost sensitivity. After a certain point, any apparent gains in precision are wiped out by the fact that responses are unreliable guesses. Besides, such questions may cause participants to be frustrated or to doubt your competence. To boost sensitivity without frustrating your participants, you should not add scale points beyond a certain point. But what is that point?

According to conventional wisdom, that point could be after you reach 3 points or after you reach 11 points, depending on the kind of question you are asking. If you are asking about something that your participants think about a lot, you might be able to use an 11-point scale. If, however, you are asking about an issue that your participants are relatively ignorant of (or uninterested in), you may be fine with a 3-point scale. When in doubt, use either a 5- or 7-point scale.

Pilot Test Your Measure. If you have followed our advice, you now have a measure that potentially provides a range of scores. But, just because there are many possible scores a participant *could* get on your measure, it does not mean there are many different scores that your participants *will* get.

To determine whether scores will actually vary, *pilot test* your measure: Try out your study and your measure on a few participants before conducting a full-blown study. If you do a pilot test, you will often find that participants' scores on the measure do not vary as much as you expected.

If you do not conduct a pilot test, you will discover the problem with your measure only after you have completed the study. For example, one investigator performed an experiment to see whether participants reading a story while also watching the story on video (the reading plus video group) would remember more about the story than participants who only read the story (the reading only group).

To measure memory, she asked the children 24 questions about the story. She thought participants' scores might range from almost 0 (none correct) to 24 (all correct). Unfortunately, the questions were so hard that all of the children got all of the questions wrong. Put another way, the measure's *floor* (the lowest score participants could get) was too high. Because of the high floor, all of the children got the same score (0), even though the children probably did differ in terms of how well they knew the story. Consequently, the investigator didn't know whether the video had no effect or whether the measure's high floor prevented her from detecting the effect.

The previous example points out why you might pilot test a measure that you devised. But should you pilot test a published measure? To answer this question, suppose our student researcher had, instead of devising her own measure, found a published measure that appeared to be sensitive and that consisted of 24 questions about a story.

If her participants were less skilled readers than the participants in the published study, all her participants might have scored near the bottom (the floor) of the measure. In that case, if participants' memories were worse in the videotape condition, this decrease in memory wouldn't be detected because participants couldn't score worse than they did in the no-videotape condition. In technical terminology, if adding the videotape had a negative effect on memory, this harmful effect would probably be hidden by a **floor effect:** the effect of a treatment or combination of treatments being underestimated because the measure is not sensitive to values below a certain level. In such a case, if the investigator had pilot tested the measure, she would have known that she needed to either abandon the measure or to modify it by making the questions easier.

What if her participants had been better readers than the participants in the published study? In that case, pilot testing would still have been useful. Although she would not need pilot testing to avoid floor effects, she might need pilot testing to avoid the opposite problem: All of her participants might have scored close to 24—the measure's ceiling.

To see why there are problems when most of the participants score near or at the ceiling, suppose that all the participants in the reading only group are scoring at the ceiling. Even if the reading plus videotape group remembered the story better than the other group, the reading plus videotape group can't show it on this measure. To show that they remember the material better, they have to get a higher score than the other group—and the other group is getting a perfect score. Clearly, the reading plus videotape can't score higher than the measure's ceiling—the highest score the measure allows. In technical terminology, the reading plus videotape group's superiority would have been hidden by a **ceiling effect:** the effects of the treatment or combination of treatments being underestimated because the measure places too low a ceiling on what the highest response can be (for more on floor and ceiling effects, see Figure 6-2).

If the researcher had pilot tested the measure, she would have known that she would need to either abandon the measure or modify it by making the questions more difficult.

If participants' scores vary widely on the pilot test, you probably will not have to worry about your measure's sensitivity being ruined by floor effects, ceiling effects, or some other factor that restricts the range of scores. However, you may still need to worry about your measure's sensitivity being ruined by random error. Even if you are using a measure that was highly reliable in one study, that measure may not be so reliable when you administer it to

| Figure 6-2 | **Measures May Lead to Ceiling or Floor Effects** |

If we were looking at the effects of exercise on how much people weigh, the scale on the left would lead to a floor effect (because everyone under 500 pounds would get the lowest reading), whereas the one on the right would lead to ceiling effects (because everyone would weigh more than the scale's higest reading of 20 pounds).

your participants (Wilkinson and the Task Force on Statistical Inference, 1999). Therefore, as part of pilot testing the measure, you may wish to collect some data to determine how reliable the measure is with your participants.

Conclusions About Sensitivity

You have seen that if a measure is to be sensitive to differences between participants, participants must differ on the measure. It is not enough that different participants get different scores, however. Different participants must get different scores because they differ on what you are trying to measure. If participants are getting different scores due to random error, the measure will not be sensitive. For example, if you have people respond, on a 100-point scale, to a question they don't understand, you will get a wide range of scores, but your measure will be insensitive. In general, to the extent that participants' scores vary because of factors unrelated to your construct, the measure is not sensitive.

To boost sensitivity, you should minimize the extent to which participants' scores vary because of factors unrelated to your construct. Thus, if you use simple, anonymous behaviors as measures (such as self-rating scales like "How much do you like your partner?"), you may be more likely to detect differences between participants than if you observe complex, public behaviors (such as time spent with partner) that are influenced by many factors other than your construct.

As you can imagine, the goal of sensitivity sometimes conflicts with the goal of validity. For example, to avoid subject biases, you might want to use a complex, public behavior (sacrificing for one's partner) as your measure of love. However, to have a sensitive measure, you might want to use a simple rating scale. Do you choose the complex behavior that might be insensitive? Or, do you use the rating scale, even though it would be invalid if participants simply give you the ratings they think you want?

In certain situations, some researchers would choose the more sensitive rating scale. To understand why, realize that a sensitive measure can help you find small differences so that you can make discoveries. An insensitive measure, on the other hand, may stop you from making discoveries. Consequently, some scientists might select a more sensitive measure and worry about construct validity only after they have found differences. They would prefer debating what a difference meant to not finding any differences at all.

In short, even though validity is important, it is not the only factor to consider when selecting a measure. Depending on the circumstances, having the ability to detect subtle differences may be equally important. After all, an insensitive measure may—by preventing you from finding anything—prevent you from being able to answer your research question.

Scales of Measurement: Will the Measure Allow You to Make the Kinds of Comparisons You Need to Make?

Whereas an insensitive measure may prevent you from answering your research question because it fails to detect the answer, other measures may prevent you from answering the question because they fail to provide a specific enough answer. That is, some measures won't allow you to make the kind of comparison you need to make.

The kind of comparison you need to make is determined by your research question. For example, consider these four questions:

1. Do the two groups *differ* on the quality?
2. Does one group have *more* of the quality than the other?

3. *How much more* of the quality does one group have than the other group?

4. Does one group have *more than three times as much* of the quality as the other group?

All four of these questions could be answered by using numbers—and all measures can provide numbers. However, very few measures could help you answer the fourth question. Why?

The answer lies in the fact that not all measures produce the same kinds of numbers. To repeat, *not all numbers are alike.* Just as some descriptive phrases are more informative and specific than others ("Joe doesn't look the same as Tom" versus "Joe is twice as attractive as Tom"), some numbers are more informative than others.

The Four Different Scales of Measurement

Rather than saying that some numbers provide more specific information than other numbers, researchers say that some numbers represent a *higher scale of measurement* than others. To be more specific, social scientists have identified four different kinds of numbers. In the next few sections, we will show you

- how numbers representing different scales of measurement differ
- why some measures provide more informative numbers than others
- how to determine what kind of numbers you need

Nominal Numbers: Different Numbers Representing Different States

The least informative numbers are **nominal scale numbers (data):** numbers that do not represent different amounts of a characteristic but instead represent different kinds of characteristics (qualities, types, or categories); numbers that substitute for names. Like names, nominal numbers can be used to identify, label, and categorize things. Things having the same number are alike (they belong in the same category); things having different numbers are different (they belong to different categories).

Like names, nominal numbers cannot be ordered meaningfully. Just as we do not say that *Jane* is a bigger name than *Jim,* we do not say that someone having the uniform number 36 is better than someone wearing number *35.*

In everyday life, we often see these name-like, orderless, nominal numbers. For example, social security numbers, charge card numbers, license plate numbers, and serial code numbers are all nominal numbers.

In psychological research, the best use of nominal numbers is when the participants can be clearly classified as either having a certain quality (e.g., married) or not. In those cases, we can use numbers to substitute for category names. For example, we may put people into categories such as male/female or student/faculty. This most basic way of using numbers is ideal for when you aren't interested in measuring different *amounts,* but are interested in different *kinds* or *types.* For instance, if you were measuring types of love, someone scoring a "1" might think of love as an addiction, a person scoring a "2" might think of love as a business partnership, a person scoring a "3" might think of love as a game, and a person scoring a "4" might think of love as "lust" (Sternberg, 1994).

Unfortunately, sometimes we are interested in measuring different amounts of a construct, but we are stuck with nominal numbers because the measuring system is too crude. That is, in the early stages of developing a measure, we may have such a poor idea of what scores on the measure mean that we can't even say that a high score means we have more of a construct than a low score. Suppose that when participants see their partner, some participants produce one pattern of brain waves, whereas others produce a different pattern. Labeling the first brain wave pattern "1" and the other pattern "2" is arbitrary. We could have just as easily labeled the first pattern "2" and the other pattern "1." Consequently, we have nominal scale measurement because we do not know whether "2" indicates a greater reaction than "1." We only know that "2" is a different pattern than "1."

Once we find out that one pattern indicates more love than another, it would be meaningful to give that pattern the higher number. At that point, we would have moved beyond nominal scale measurement.

Ordinal Numbers: When Bigger Means More

As you shall see, we often want to move beyond nominal scale measurement. Rather than always being limited to saying only that participants getting different numbers differ, we often want to say that participants receiving higher scores have more of a given quality. Rather than being limited to saying only that people scoring "3" are similar to each other and are different from people scoring "1," we also want to say that people scoring "3" have *more* of a certain quality than those scoring "1." In other words, we may want to be able to meaningfully *order* scores from lowest to highest, with higher scores indicating more of the quality. For example, we would often like to say that people scoring a "5" feel more love than people scoring "4," who feel more love than people scoring "3," and so on.

If you can assume that higher numbers indicate more love than lower numbers, your measure is producing at least **ordinal scale numbers (data):** numbers that can be meaningfully ordered from lowest to highest. When you assume that you have ordinal data, you are making a very simple assumption: The numbers are ordered.

One way to get ordinal numbers is to rank participants. For example, if you record runners' times according to what place (first, second, third, etc.) they finished, you have an ordinal measure of time. Runners getting the higher numbers (e.g., "third") took more time to finish the race than runners getting lower numbers (e.g., "first"). Note, however, that you are not assuming that the difference in time between the runner who finished first and the runner who finished second is the same as the difference between the runner who finished second and the runner who finished third. For example, there might be a tenth of a second difference between the first and second runners but a 2-second difference between the second and third runners.

To illustrate what ordinal scaling does and does not assume, suppose you successfully ranked 10 couples in terms of how much they loved each other. Because the numbers can be ordered meaningfully from highest to lowest, these are definitely ordinal data. Yet, because they are ordinal data, the psychological difference between "1" and "2" may be very different from the psychological difference between "9" and "10." For example, there might be little difference between the couple getting rank 1 and the couple getting rank 2, but there might be an enormous difference between the couple getting rank 9 and the couple getting rank 10. In short, ranked data, like all ordinal data, can tell you whether one participant has more of a quality than another, but are limited in that they can't tell you how much more of a quality one participant has than another (see Figure 6-3).

Interval Scale Numbers: Knowing How Much More

Because of the limitations of ordinal numbers, you may decide you want a higher scale of measurement. For instance, in addition to assuming that numbers can be ordered, you might also want to be able to assume that the psychological distance (the difference in participants'

Figure 6-3	An Ordinal Scale

This ordinal scale lets us know which weighed more—but not how much more.

minds) between a score of "1" and "2" is exactly the same as the psychological difference between "2" and "3," which is the same as the psychological distance between any two consecutive whole numbers. In technical terminology, you want to be able to assume that you have **interval scale numbers (data):** The numbers can be ordered from lowest to highest and equal numerical intervals (distances) represent equal psychological intervals.

Although you may want to assume that you have an interval scale measure, be aware that the assumption of equal intervals is not easy to defend—no matter what measure you use. As we have seen, ranked data are typically assumed to be only ordinal—not interval. If you use a measure of nonverbal behavior, you could still fail to meet the assumption of equal intervals.

Suppose, for example, that during the 10 minutes you had couples wait in a small room, you recorded the total amount of time the couple stared into each other's eyes. It would be risky to assume that the difference in love between a couple who looks for 360 seconds and a couple who looks for 300 seconds is the same as the difference between a couple who looks for a total of 60 seconds and a couple who does not look at all.

Likewise, if you use a physiological measure, it is hard to justify the assumption that equal changes in bodily responses correspond to equal changes in psychological states. It seems unlikely that changes in the body correspond perfectly and directly to changes in the mind. For example, if, on seeing their partners, one participant's blood pressure increases from 200 to 210 and another's goes from 90 to 100, would you say that both were equally in love?

How could you possibly get interval scale data? One possibility is to ask participants to do the scaling for you. That is, ask participants to rate their feelings on a scale, trusting that participants will view the distances between each scale point as equal psychological distances.

Although many psychologists assume that rating scales produce interval scale data, this assumption of equal intervals is controversial. To see why this assumption is hard to justify, suppose you had people rate how they felt about their spouse on a -30 (hate intensely) to a $+30$ (love intensely) scale. Would you be sure that someone who changed from -1 to $+1$ had changed to the same degree as someone who had changed from $+12$ to $+14$?

Ratio Scales: Zeroing in on Perfection
If you are extremely demanding, it may not be enough for you to assume that your measure's numbers can be meaningfully ordered from lowest to highest and that equal intervals

between numbers represent equal psychological distances. You may want to make one last, additional assumption—that your measure has an absolute zero. In other words, you might assume that someone scoring a zero on your measure feels absolutely no love. If a score of zero on your love measure represented absolutely no love, and you had equal intervals, then you could make ratio statements such as: "The couple who scored a '1' on the love measure was 1:2 (a ratio of 1 to 2) as much in love as the couple scoring a '2.'" In technical terminology, you can make ratio statements because your measure provides **ratio scale numbers (data):** It has both (a) an absolute zero and (b) equal intervals.

Meeting one key assumption of ratio scale measurement—the assumption of having an absolute zero—is not easy. Indeed, even when measuring physical reality, you may not have an absolute zero. To illustrate, 0 degrees Fahrenheit doesn't mean the absence of (zero) temperature. If 0 degrees Fahrenheit meant no temperature, we could make ratio statements such as saying that 50 degrees is half as hot as 100 degrees. Similarly, if you were timing a runner using a handheld stopwatch, even if the runner somehow took zero seconds to cross the finish line, you would time the runner at about .1 seconds because it takes you time (a) to react to the runner crossing the finish line and (b) to push the stop button. Thus, your measure of time would provide interval rather than ratio scale data. To get near ratio scale data, you would need to use automated electronic timers.

Note that if our measure of zero is off by even a little bit, it may prevent us from making make accurate ratio statements. To illustrate, suppose you have a 2-pound weight and a 1-pound weight. If your scale's zero point is off by one-quarter of a pound, instead of seeing a 2:1 ratio between the weights, you will "find" a $2^1/_4$ to $1^1/_4$ (1.8 to 1) ratio. Furthermore, note that any inaccuracy in our measurements may prevent us from making accurate ratio statements. Even if we weigh the 1-pound weight with perfect accuracy, if we measure the 2 pound weight as 1.9 pounds, our statement about the ratio between the weights would be inaccurate. In other words, to make perfectly accurate ratio statements, we need perfectly accurate measurements.

Although meeting the assumptions of ratio scale measurement is difficult when measuring physical reality, it is even more difficult to meet those requirements when measuring a psychological characteristic. It is difficult to say that a zero score means a complete absence of a psychological characteristic or that the numbers generated by a measure correspond *perfectly* to psychological reality. It's tough enough to have some degree of correspondence between scores on a measure and psychological reality, much less to achieve perfection.

Because of the difficulty of achieving ratio scale measurements, most researchers do not ask participants to try to make ratio scale judgments. They usually do not ask participants to think of "zero" as the absence of the quality. Indeed, they often do not even let participants have a zero point. Instead, participants are more likely to be asked to make their ratings on a 1-to-5 scale than on a 0-to-4 scale. Furthermore, even when participants rate on a 0-to-4 scale, they are rarely asked to think of "2" as having twice as much of the quality as "1," "3" as three times "1," and "4" as four times as much as "1."

Occasionally, however, participants are asked to make ratio scale judgments, using a process called *magnitude estimation*. For example, participants might be told that the average amount of liking that people feel for a roommate is a "50." If they feel one-fifth as much liking toward their roommate as that, they should estimate the magnitude of their liking toward their roommate as 10. If they like their best friend twice as much as they think most people like their roommates, they should estimate the magnitude of their liking for their best friend as 100. Participants would then be asked to rate the magnitude of their liking for a variety of people.

Magnitude estimation doesn't always involve using numbers. Instead, participants might draw lines. For example, they may be shown a line and told to imagine that the length of that line represents the average extent to which people like their roommates. Then, they may be asked to draw lines of different lengths to express how much they like various people. If a participant likes Person A three times as much as Person B, the participant's line representing his or her liking for Person A should be three times longer than their Person B line.

Advocates of magnitude estimation believe that the numbers or line lengths that participants produce provide ratio scale data. However, as you might imagine, critics have doubts. Even when participants are asked to make ratio scale judgments in magnitude estimation, there is no guarantee that participants will be able to do so.

Why Our Numbers Do Not Always Measure Up

You can see why ratings and even subjective estimates of magnitude might not provide ratio scale numbers. But why don't you get ratio scale numbers from your behavioral measures of love? For example, why isn't time staring into each other's eyes a ratio scale measure of love?

If you were interested only in gazing behavior, time spent gazing would be a ratio scale measure: Zero would be the complete absence of gazing and 3 seconds of gazing would be three times as much gazing as 1 second. However, suppose you were not interested in gazing for gazing's sake. Instead, you were interested in love. You were using gazing behavior (an observable behavior) as an indicator of love (an unobservable psychological state). As an indirect, imperfect reflection of love, time of gaze does not allow you to estimate amount of love experienced with ratio scale precision (see Box 6-1). Similarly, although we can all agree

---

BOX 6-1   **Numbers and the Toll Ticket**

The toll ticket shows us many kinds of numbers in action. For example, the numbers representing vehicle class (1–4) at the top of the ticket (under toll by vehicle class) are nominal numbers. The only reason the toll people used numbers instead of names is that numbers take less room. So, instead of writing "car," "16-wheeled truck," "small truck," and so on, they wrote 1, 2, 3, and 4. There's no particular order to these numbers as shown by the fact that a "3" is charged more than any other number.

On this toll ticket, the exit numbers refer to the order in which the exits appear. Thus, a "1" on the toll ticket refers to the first exit and "7" refers to the seventh exit. The exits, when used as an index of distance, represent ordinal data. You know that if you have to get off at exit 5, you will have to go farther than if you get off at exit 4, but—without looking at the miles column—you don't know how much farther. When you do check the miles column, you realize that missing exit 4 isn't too bad—the next exit is only 4 miles away. Missing exit 6, on the other hand, is terrible—the next exit is 66 miles farther down the road!

Money, as a measure of miles, is also an ordinal measure. Although you know that the more money you spend on tolls, the farther you have gone, you can't

figure out how much farther you have gone merely by looking at how much money the toll was. For example, if you are vehicle class number 1, it costs you 25 cents to go 3 miles, 15 cents more to go 7 additional miles, and only 10 more cents gets you 30 additional miles.

As you have seen, both the amount of money spent and the number of exits passed are just ordinal measures when they are used to try to estimate the amount of another variable (distance). Similarly, some behavioral and physiological measures (eye-gazing or blood pressure increases) may merely be ordinal measures when used to estimate the amount of another variable, such as the invisible psychological state of love.

TOLL (IN DOLLARS) BY VEHICLE CLASS

Exit No.	No. of Miles	VEHICLE CLASS			
		1	2	3	4
1	3	0.25	0.35	0.60	0.35
2	10	0.40	0.45	1.00	0.60
3	40	0.50	0.60	1.35	0.80
4	45	0.80	0.90	2.15	1.30
5	49	0.90	1.10	2.65	1.55
6	51	1.45	1.65	3.65	2.15
7	117	3.60	4.15	9.95	5.85

that a heart rate of 60 beats per minute is twice as fast as a heart rate of 30 beats per minute, we can't all agree that a person with a heart rate of 60 beats per minute is twice as excited as a person with a heart rate of 30 beats per minute.

Likewise, we can all agree that a person who donates $2.00 to our cause has given twice as much as a person who gives us $1.00. We have a ratio scale measure of how much money has been given. If, however, we are using dollars given as a measure of construct such as "generosity," "kindness," "empathy," or "gullibility," we do not have a ratio scale measure. The person who gives $2.00 is not necessarily twice as kind as the person who gives $1.00.

To reiterate, you cannot measure generosity, excitement, love, or any other construct directly. You can measure constructs only indirectly. It is unlikely that your indirect measure of a construct will measure that construct with the perfect accuracy that ratio scale measurement requires.

Which Level of Measurement Do You Need?

You have seen that there are four different levels of measurement: nominal scale, ordinal scale, interval scale, and ratio scale. As you go up the scale from nominal to ordinal to interval to ratio scale measurement, the numbers become increasingly more informative (for a review, see Table 6-1 and Figure 6-4).

You have also seen that as you go up the scale, it becomes harder to find a measure that provides the required level of measurement. For instance, if you need ordinal data, you can use almost any measuring system—from ranked data to magnitude estimation. However, if you need ratio scale data, magnitude estimation might be your only option; you cannot use a measure that involves ranking participants from lowest to highest—no matter how valid that ranking system is. In that case, the scale of measurement you need, rather than validity, will determine what measure you should use.

The scale of measurement you need to test your hypothesis should always influence what measure you use. Therefore, when choosing a measure for a study, you should ask two questions:

1. What scale of measurement do I need to answer the research question?
2. Which of the measures that I am considering will give me this level of measurement?

The next sections and Tables 6-2 and 6-3 will help you answer these two key questions.

When You Need Ratio Scale Data

Suppose you want to find out whether engaged couples are twice as much in love as dating couples who are not engaged. Because you are hypothesizing a 2-to-1 ratio, you need a measure that gives you ratio scale numbers. As Table 6-3 indicates, there are few measures that you can use if you need ratio scale numbers. If you want a ratio scale measure of a construct (e.g., happiness), you probably need to use magnitude estimation. If you want a ratio scale measure of behavior (e.g., number of cigarettes smoked), you need to measure that behavior with perfect accuracy. Fortunately, you need ratio scale level of measurement only if you are trying to make ratio statements like "Married women are twice as happy as widows."

When You Need at Least Interval Scale Data

Because you will probably not be comparing groups to find out whether one group is twice as much in love as another group, you will rarely need to assume that your measure has ratio

| Table 6-1 | The Meaning and Limitations of Different Scales of Measurement |||

SCALE	WHAT DIFFERENT SCORES REPRESENT	WHAT WE CAN SAY	WHAT WE CAN'T SAY
Nominal	**a.** Different scores represent *different* amounts, kinds, or types.	People scoring a "3" experience a different kind (or amount) of love than people scoring a "1."	Because there is no order to nominal numbers, we can't say that "3" indicates *more* love than "1."
Ordinal	**a.** Different scores indicate different amounts *and* **b.** higher scores represent greater amounts of the measured variable.	People scoring a "3" are more in love than people scoring a "1."	Because the distances between numbers do not correspond to psychological reality, we can't say *how much* more of a quality one participant has than another.
Interval	**a.** Different scores indicate different amounts *and* **b.** higher scores represent greater amounts of the measured variable. *and* **c.** equal distances between numbers represent equal psychological differences.	We can say *how much* more love one participant feels than another. For example, people scoring "3" are more in love than people scoring "1" to the same extent that people scoring "5" are more in love than people scoring "3."	Because we do not have an absolute zero, we cannot say *how many more times* love one participant has than another.
Ratio	**a.** Different scores indicate different amounts, *and* **b.** higher scores represent greater amounts of the measured variable. *and* **c.** equal distances between numbers represent equal psychological differences. *and* **d.** zero means a complete absence of the measured variable.	The mathematical ratio between two scores perfectly corresponds to reality. People scoring "3" are three *times as much* in love as people scoring "1."	None.

properties. You may, however, have to assume that your measure does have interval properties. Suppose you are trying to estimate the effects of therapy on relationships. Before relationship counseling is offered on your campus, you measure the degree to which couples are in love. Next, you observe who goes to counseling and who doesn't. Finally, at the end of the term, you measure the couples' love again. Let's say that you got the following pattern of results:

	BEGINNING OF TERM	END OF TERM
Didn't go to counseling	3.0	4.0
Went to counseling	5.0	7.0

(The higher the score, the more in love. Scores could range from 1 to 9.)

Figure 6-4 **Different Scales of Measurements as Rulers**

a. Ratio Scale Ruler: Absolute zero and equal intervals. We have perfect measurement and we can make ratio statements such as, "The object we measured as '4' is two times as long as the object we measured as '2.'"

b. Interval Scale Ruler: No absolute zero but equal intervals. Because we do not have an absolute zero, we shouldn't say, "The object we measured as '4' is twice as long as the object we measured as '2.'" Because we have equal intervals, we can say, "The difference between the object we measured as '7' and the object we measured as '6' is the same as the difference between the object we measured as '4' and the object we measured as '3.'"

c. Ordinal Scale Ruler: Order but not equal intervals. Because we do not have equal intervals, we shouldn't say, "The difference between the object we measured as '7' and the object we measured as '6' is the same as the difference between the object we measured as '4' and the object we measured as '3.'" Because we do have order, we can say, "The object we measured as '6' is longer than the object we measured as '5.'"

d. Nominal Scale Ruler: No order—higher numbers (e.g., "3") represent a different length than lower numbers (e.g., "1") but not more length. Because we do have order, we can't say, "The object we measured as '6' is longer than the object we measured as '5.'" However, we can say, "The object we measured as '6' has a different length than the object we measured as '5.'"

Did the couples who went for counseling change more than those who didn't? At first glance, the answer seems obvious. The no-counseling group changed 1 unit and the counseling group changed 2 units, so isn't 2 units more than 1 unit? Not necessarily.

If we have interval or ratio scale data, we can assume that each unit of change represents the same psychological distance. Therefore, we can say that, psychologically, 2 units of change is more than 1 unit of change. Thus, if we have interval or ratio scale data, we can say that the counseling group changed more than the no-counseling group.

Table 6-2	Different Research Questions Require Different Levels of Measurement

RESEARCH QUESTION	SCALE OF MEASUREMENT REQUIRED
Can more members of Group A be categorized as _____ (in love, neurotic, etc.) than members of Group B?	At least nominal
Is Group A more _____ than Group B?	At least ordinal
Did Group A change more than Group B?	At least interval
Is the difference between Group 1 and Group 2 more than the difference between Group 3 and Group 4?	At least interval
Is Group A three times more _____ than Group B?	Ratio

Table 6-3	Measuring Instruments and the Kind of Data They Produce

SCALE OF MEASUREMENT	MEASURING TACTICS ASSUMED TO PRODUCE THOSE KINDS OF NUMBERS
Ratio	Magnitude estimation
Interval	Rating scales
	(Magnitude estimation)
Ordinal	Ranks (e.g., first, second, etc.)
	Nonverbal measures
	Physiological measures
	(Rating scales)
	(Magnitude estimation)
Nominal	Any valid measure
	(All of the above)

Note: Any measurement technique that provides data that meet a certain level of measurement also provides data that meet the less stringent requirements of lower levels of measurement. Thus, a measure that provides data that meet the requirements of interval scale measurement also provides data that meet the requirements of ordinal and nominal scale measurement.

But what if we had nominal or ordinal data? With nominal or ordinal data, we can't safely assume that each unit of change represents the same psychological distance. If our data were nominal or ordinal, the psychological distance between 3 and 4 could be much more than the psychological distance between 5 and 7. Thus, if we had nominal or ordinal data, we would *not* be able to answer the question, "Did couples who went for counseling change more than those who didn't?" As you can see from this example, if your research question involves asking whether one group changed more than another group, then you must use a measure, such as a rating scale, that has at least interval properties.

When Ordinal Data Are Sufficient

Suppose you don't care how much more in love one group is than the other. All you want to know is which group is most in love. For example, suppose you want to be able to order these three groups in terms of amount of love:

Didn't go to counseling at all	3.0
Went to counseling for 1 week	5.0
Went to counseling for 8 weeks	7.0

(The higher the score, the more in love. Scores could range from 1 to 9.)

If you had ordinal data, you could conclude that participants who went to counseling for 8 weeks were most in love, those who went for 1 week were less in love, and those who didn't go to counseling were least in love. So, if you simply want to know which group is higher on a variable and which group is lower, all you need is ordinal data. If that's the case, you are in luck. As you can see from Table 6-3, most measures produce data that meet or exceed the requirements of ordinal level measurement.

When You Need Only Nominal Data

It's conceivable that you aren't interested in discovering which group is more in love. Instead, you might have the less ambitious goal of trying to find out whether the different groups differ in terms of their love for each other. If that's the case, nominal data are all you need. Because you need to make only the least demanding and safest assumption about your numbers (that different numbers represent different things), any valid measure you choose will measure up.

Conclusions About Scales of Measurement

As you have seen, different research questions require different scales of measurement. If you are asking only whether two groups *differ,* any scale of measurement, even *nominal,* will do. If, however, you are asking whether one group has *more* of a quality than another, you need at least *ordinal* level data. If your research question involves asking *how much* more of a quality one group has than another, you need to use a measure that provides at least *interval* data. If you need to find out *how many times more* of a quality one group has than another, you need *ratio* level data.

If your research question requires a given level of measurement, you must use a measure that provides that level of measurement. Consequently, you may find that the type of data you need will dictate the measure you choose and that the only measure that will give you the type of data you want is not as sensitive or as free from biases as another measure.

Let's look at one example that illustrates this point. Suppose you want to know whether a treatment is more effective for couples who are less in love than it is for couples who are more in love. You are reluctant to use a rating scale measure because rating scale measures are extremely vulnerable to subjects biases, such as participants lying to impress the researcher or participants providing the answers that they think will support the researcher's hypothesis. However, rating scale measures are commonly assumed to produce interval data—and your research question requires at least interval scale data.

To illustrate why you require interval data, imagine that a problem couple's score on the measure goes from a "1" to a "3," whereas a high love couple's increases from an "8" to a "9." To say that the problem couple experienced more improvement, you must assume that the difference between "1" and "3" is greater than the difference between "8" and "9." This is *not* an assumption you can make if you have either nominal or ordinal data. It is, however, an assumption you can make if you have interval data (because with interval data, the psychological distance between "1" and "2" is the same as the distance between "8" and "9").

Because your research question requires interval data, you must use a measure that provides at least interval data. Consequently, if the rating scale is the only measure that gives you interval scale data, you will have to use it—despite its vulnerability to subject bias—because it is the only measure that will allow you to answer your research question.

Ethical and Practical Considerations

Clearly, you want to use a measure that will allow you to answer your research question. However, there may be times when you decide not to use a certain measure even though that measure allows you to answer your research question. For example, suppose you have a measure that gives you the right scale of measurement and is more valid than other measures because it is not vulnerable to subject biases. However, it avoids subject bias by surprising or tricking participants. In such a case, you may decide against using that measure because you believe participants should be fully informed about the study before they agree to participate. Similarly, you may reject field observation because you feel those tactics violate participants' rights to privacy.

When choosing a measure, you should always be concerned about ethical issues (see Appendix C). In addition, at times you may also have to be concerned about practical issues. You may have to reject a measure because it is simply too time consuming or expensive to use. Practical concerns may even force you to either reject or use a measure based on its **face validity:** the extent to which a measure looks, on the face of it, to be valid. But because face validity has nothing to do with actual, scientific validity, normally you would not choose a measure for its face validity any more than you would judge a book by its cover. Typically, you would choose a measure based on a careful evaluation of scientific evidence, rather than on participants' opinions.

Indeed, under many circumstances, high face validity could harm real validity. To illustrate, if people think that questions from a "test" in a popular magazine are measuring a certain construct, people can "fake" the test to get the results they want. Conversely, a measure with no face validity may be valid precisely because participants don't see what it is measuring.

As we have pointed out, when evaluating the validity of a measure, you will usually have little use for face validity. However, face validity may be important to the consumer (or the sponsor) of your research. For example, imagine you are doing research on factors that affect effort. How loud a person yells and how many widgets a person produces may be equally valid measures of effort. But if you were going to get a factory manager to take your research seriously, which measure would you use?

Concluding Remarks

In this chapter, you have seen that choosing a measure is a complex decision. It is not enough to pick the most valid measure. Instead, you need to pick the measure that will be most likely to answer your research question. For your particular study, you must decide what threats to validity are most serious, decide how much sensitivity you need, decide what level of measurement your research question requires, and carefully weigh both ethical and practical considerations.

In designing a research project, choosing a measure is an important decision. However, it is only one of several decisions you will make. For example, you must decide whether to do a survey, an experiment, or some other type of research. Then, if you decide to do an experiment, you must decide on what type of experiment to do. In the next few chapters, you will learn how to make these key design decisions.

SUMMARY

1. Because no measure is perfect, choosing a measure involves making tradeoffs.

2. Sensitivity, reliability, and validity are highly valued in a measure.

3. Sensitivity is a measure's ability to detect small differences.

4. Because reliability is a prerequisite for sensitivity, an unreliable measure cannot be sensitive. However, because reliability doesn't guarantee sensitivity, a reliable measure could be insensitive.

5. You may be able to increase a measure's sensitivity by asking "how much" rather than "whether," by knowing what you want to measure, by avoiding unnecessary inferences, and by using common sense.

6. Different kinds of measures produce different kinds of numbers. These numbers range from the least informative (nominal) to the most informative (ratio).

7. Nominal numbers let you say only that participants differ on a characteristic, but they do not let you say that one participant has more of a characteristic than another. With nominal measurement, higher numbers don't mean more of a quality because the number you assign to a category is arbitrary. For example, if you coded men as "1" and women as "2," your coding is entirely arbitrary. You could even go back and recode women as "1" and men as "2."

8. Ordinal numbers let you say that one participant has more of a quality than another. However, ordinal numbers do not allow you to talk about specific amounts of a quality. They let you talk only about having more of it or less of it, but not about how much more or less.

9. Interval and ratio numbers let you say how much more of a quality one participant has than another.

10. Ratio scale numbers let you say how many times more of a quality one participant has relative to another.

11. Depending on the research question, a measure's sensitivity and its level of measurement may be almost as important as validity.

12. You must always consider ethical and practical issues when choosing a measure.

KEY TERMS

sensitive, sensitivity *(p. 142)*

floor effect *(p. 146)*

ceiling effect *(p. 147)*

nominal scale numbers (data) *(p. 149)*

ordinal scale numbers (data) *(p. 150)*

interval scale numbers (data) *(p. 151)*

ratio scale numbers (data) *(p. 152)*

face validity *(p. 159)*

EXERCISES

1. Suppose that in a study involving only 40 participants, researchers look at self-esteem differences between two groups. They find a small, but statistically significant, difference between the self-esteem of the two groups. Based on this information, would you infer that the measure's reliability was low or high? Why?

2. List the scales of measurement in order from least to most accurate and informative.

3. Becky wants to know how much students drink.
   a. What level of measurement could Becky get? Why?
   b. Becky asks participants: How much do you drink?
      1. 0–1 drinks
      2. 1–3 drinks
      3. 3–4 drinks
      4. more than 4 drinks

      What scale of measurement does she have?
   c. Becky ranks participants according to how much they drink. What scale of measurement does she have?
   d. Becky assigns participants a "0" if they do not drink, a "1" if they primarily drink wine, and a "2" if they primarily drink beer. What scale of measurement is this?
   e. Becky asks participants: How much do you drink?
      1. 0–1 drinks
      2. 1–3 drinks
      3. 3–4 drinks
      4. more than 4 drinks
      5. don't know

      What scale of measurement does she have? Why?

4. Assume that facial tension is a measure of thinking.
   a. How would you measure facial tension?
   b. What scale of measurement is it on? Why?
   c. How sensitive do you think this measure would be? Why?

5. Suppose a researcher is investigating the effectiveness of drug awareness programs.
   a. What scale of measurement would the investigator need if she were trying to discover whether one drug awareness program was more effective than another?
   b. What scale of measurement would the investigator need if she were trying to discover whether one program is better for informing the relatively ignorant than it is for informing the fairly well informed?

6. In an ideal world, car gas gauges would be on what scale of measurement? Why? In practice, what is the scale of measurement for most gas gauges? Why do you say that?

7. Find or invent a measure.
   a. Describe the measure.
   b. Discuss how you could improve its sensitivity.
   c. What kind of data (nominal, ordinal, interval, or ratio) do you think that measure would produce? Why?

WEB RESOURCES

1. Go to the Chapter 6 section of the book's student website and
   a. Look over the concept map of the key terms.
   b. Test yourself on the key terms.
   c. Take the Chapter 6 Practice Quiz.

2. Go to the "Measure Chooser" link to practice choosing the right measure for the situation.

3. Download the "Scales of Measurement" tutorial.

INFOTRAC COLLEGE EDITION EXPLORATIONS

1. To get another view of the advantages and disadvantages of rating scales, do an InfoTrac College Edition keyword search using the phrase "advantages of rating scales."

2. To see some advantages to using more than one measure in a study, do an InfoTrac College Edition keyword search for the word "multimethod."

7

Introduction to Descriptive Methods and Correlational Research

The invalid assumption that correlation implies cause is probably among the two or three most serious and common errors of human reasoning.

—Stephen Jay Gould

Overview

In this chapter, you will be introduced to descriptive methods. Some methods, such as asking people questions and observing people, are systematic, organized, and objective ways to answer questions in your everyday life. Some, such as looking at diaries, marriage records, hospital records, police reports, and newspaper reports, are routinely used by detectives. However, despite descriptive research's similarity to everyday life, descriptive research is scientific.

Like all research, the goal of descriptive research is to test hypotheses and answer questions. However, unlike experimental research, it is not equipped to test cause–effect hypotheses. Because of this, it does not allow researchers to answer questions about the "whys" (causes) of behavior. Although descriptive research is not equipped to answer "why" questions, it can help us answer "what," "who," "when,"and "where" questions.

Descriptive researchers often start off by trying to answer "what" questions about a single variable, such as "What is the behavior?" and "What percentage of people have that characteristic?" For example, the earliest research on flirting focused on what people did when flirting; early work on laughter dealt with describing laughter; the earliest work on unconscious prejudice focused on seeing what percentage of people held these prejudices; and the earliest work on happiness counted how many people were happy.

Usually, descriptive researchers quickly expand their focus from "what"—questions about a single variable—to "who," "when," and "where"—questions about how that variable is related to other variables. Thus, soon after researchers had described laughter, they were finding factors that related to it, such as who laughs (women more than men), where people laugh (in public), and when (women laugh when listening to a man they like; Provine, 2004). Similarly, happiness researchers quickly went from finding out that most people were happy (Diener & Diener, 1996) to finding (a) factors that predict happiness, such as exercise, extroversion, marriage, and religious faith, as well as (b) factors that happiness seems to predict, such as a longer life (Danner, Snowden, & Friesen, 2001). Because researchers using descriptive methods almost always look at relationships between two or more variables to see whether those variables covary (*correlate),* most research using descriptive methods is called *correlational* research.

Uses and Limitations of Descriptive Methods

When you use descriptive methods, you gain the ability to test hypotheses about virtually any variable in virtually any situation. For example, you can use them even when you can't— for either practical or ethical reasons—manipulate variables. You can use descriptive methods even when you can neither control irrelevant variables nor account for their effects. In short, if your hypothesis is that two or more variables are related (e.g., soccer playing and IQ scores, being spanked and aggressive behavior, parental warmth and autism, mother's skill at reading her child's mind and child's self-esteem, smoking and hyperactivity, cheating and level of moral development, church attendance and happiness), descriptive methods give you the flexibility to test that hypothesis.

Descriptive Research and Causality

But this flexibility comes at a cost. Without being able to manipulate variables and account for the effects of irrelevant variables, you cannot legitimately make cause–effect statements.

In other words, you can find out that two variables are related, but you cannot find out why they are related. For example, if you find a relationship between church attendance and happiness, you cannot say *why* church attendance and happiness are related. Certainly, you cannot say that church attendance causes people to be happy.

Why Descriptive Methods Cannot Test Causal Hypotheses

Why not? There are two reasons.

First, rather than church attendance being a cause of happiness, church attendance may be an effect of happiness. Because you did not manipulate variables, you don't know which variable came first—happiness or church attendance—and thus, you don't know which variable caused which. You may believe church attendance causes happiness, but you may have it backward: Maybe happiness causes church attendance. For example, happy people may be more likely to be out of bed and ready to face the outside world in time to go to church than unhappy people.

Second, rather than church attendance being a cause of happiness, both church attendance and happiness may be effects of some other variable. Because you have neither controlled for nor accounted for any other factors that might lead both to being happy and to going to church, many factors might be responsible for the relationship between happiness and church attendance. Just a few of those possible factors are listed here:

- Disciplined people may be happier and more likely to go to church.
- People who like structured social activities may be more likely to be happy and more likely to go to church.
- Having genes that predispose one to be conventional and outgoing may cause one to be happy and go to church.
- Having church-going friends may cause one to be happy and to go to church.
- Married people may be more likely to be happy and more likely to go to church than unmarried people.
- Unhealthy people may be both less likely to make it to church and less likely to be happy.
- Optimistic people may be more likely to go to church (perhaps because they are more likely to believe in an afterlife) and may be more likely to be happy.

To repeat a key point, correlational methods do not have internal validity, so they do not allow you to make cause–effect statements. When you use a correlational method to find a relationship between two variables, you do not know whether the relationship is due to (1) changes in the first variable causing changes in the second variable; (2) changes in the "second" variable[1] causing changes in the "first" variable; or (3) a third variable causing the changes in both variables (see Figure 7-1).

How Descriptive Methods Can Stimulate Causal Hypotheses

Although data from descriptive research cannot allow you to make cause–effect assertions, such data may raise cause–effect questions. As you can see from Table 7-1 on page 166, correlational methods may stimulate causal hypotheses in two ways.

---

[1] Often, you don't know which variable came first, so labeling one variable the "first" variable and the other the "second" is arbitrary. Given that you don't know which variable is really the first, you can't say which caused which (the situation is like the "Which came first—the chicken or the egg?" question).

Figure 7-1

Three Basic Possibilities for an Observed Relationship Between Low Self-Esteem and Television-Viewing

1. The "first" factor causes a change in the "second" factor.

2. The "second" factor causes a change in the "first" factor.

3. Some "third" factor could cause a change in both the "first" and "second" factors.

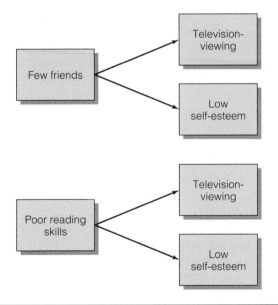

Note that there are many "third" factors that might account for the relationship. We have listed only two (friends and reading skills).

First, if you find a relationship between two variables, you may want to do an experiment to determine whether the relationship is a cause–effect relationship. For instance, knowing that there was a correlation between smoking and lung cancer led to experiments that tested whether smoking caused lung cancer.

Second, even if you know that the two factors do not directly influence each other, you may try to find out what causes them to be statistically related. In other words, you may try

Table 7-1	**Generating Causal Hypotheses From Correlational Data**

For each correlational finding listed here, develop an experimental hypothesis.

1. Listeners of country music tend to be more depressed than people who listen to other types of music.

2. There is a correlation between school attendance and good grades.

3. Attractive people earn higher salaries than less attractive people.

4. In restaurants, large groups tend to leave lower tips (in terms of percentage of bill) than individuals.

5. Teams that wear black uniforms are penalized more often than other teams.

6. People report being more often persuaded by newspaper editorials than by television editorials.

7. Students report that they would be less likely to cheat if professors walked around the classroom more during exams.

8. Students who take notes in outline form get better grades than those who don't.

to find out what third factor accounts for their relationship. Suppose you find that in general, students who study more have lower grade-point averages. This finding may suggest the following idea: Perhaps some students are using study strategies that are both time-consuming and ineffective. This idea may lead you to do experiments to test whether some study strategies are more effective than others. Alternatively, if you think the relationship is due to poorer students being poorer readers, you might design an experiment to see whether training in reading skills improves grades.

In summary, descriptive research does *not* allow you to infer causality (see Table 7-2). However, descriptive research may *stimulate* experimental research that will allow you to infer causality: Once you use a *descriptive* design to find out *what* happens, you can use an *experimental* design to try to find out *why* it happens.

Description for Description's Sake

By hinting at possible causal relationships, descriptive research can indirectly help psychologists achieve two goals of psychology—explaining behavior and controlling behavior. But the main purpose of descriptive research is to achieve another important goal of psychology—describing behavior.

Is description really an important scientific goal? Yes; in fact, description is a major goal of every science. What is chemistry's famed periodic table but a description of the elements? What is biology's system of classifying plants and animals into kingdom, phylum, genus, and species but a way of describing living organisms? What is astronomy's mapping of the stars but a description of outer space? What is science but systematic observation and measurement? Thus, one reason psychologists value descriptive methods is that description is the cornerstone of science. Besides, psychologists, like everyone else, want to be able to describe what people think, feel, and do.

Description for Prediction's Sake

Psychologists also like descriptive methods because knowing what *is* happening helps us predict what *will* happen. In the case of suicide, for example, psychologists discovered that certain signals (giving away precious possessions, abrupt changes in personality) were

Table 7-2	Questions That Must Be Answered to Establish That Two Variables Are Causally Related

Is There a Relationship Between the Two Variables in the Sample?

- Did the researchers accurately measure the two variables?
- Did the researchers accurately record the two variables?
- Did the researchers accurately perceive the degree to which the variables were related?

If the Variables Are Related in the Sample, Are the Variables Related in the Population?

- Is the sample a random sample of the population?
- Even if the sample is a random sample of the population, is the sample large enough—and the relationship strong enough—that we can be confident that the relationship really occurs in the population?

If the Variables Are Related, Did the Predictor Variable Cause Changes in the Criterion?

- Is it possible that the "criterion" (outcome) variable caused changes in the predictor variable? In other words, is our "cause" really the effect?
- Do we know which variable came first?
- Do we have data that suggest to us which came first? For example, if we are looking at self-esteem and delinquency, high school records might provide information about self-esteem before becoming criminals. If there is no difference between delinquents and nondelinquents' self-esteem prior to committing crimes, we would be more confident that self-esteem was not a cause of delinquency.
- Can we logically rule out the possibility that one variable preceded the other? For example, if height and being a delinquent were correlated, we can make a good case that the person's height was established before he or she became a delinquent.
- Is it possible that a third variable could be responsible for the relationship? That is, neither variable may directly influence (cause) the other. Instead, the two variables might be statistically related because they are both effects of some other variable. For example, increases in assaults and ice cream consumption may both be consequences of temperature.
- Were all other variables randomized or held constant? (This control over other variables happens only in experimental designs [we discuss experimental designs in Chapters 10–14].)
- Does the researcher know what the potential third variables are? If so, the researcher may be able to statistically control for those variables. However, it is virtually impossible to know and measure every potential third variable.

associated with suicide. Consequently, psychologists now realize that people sending out those signals are more likely to attempt suicide than people not behaving that way.

Why We Need Science to Describe Behavior

Certainly, describing behavior is an important goal of psychology. But do we need to use scientific methods to describe what's all around us? Yes! Intuition alone cannot achieve all four steps necessary to accurately describe behavior:

1. Objectively measure variables.
2. Keep track of these measurements.

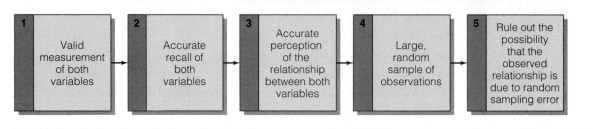

Figure 7-2

Five Steps Involved in Determining Whether There Is a Relationship Between Two Variables

1	2	3	4	5
Valid measurement of both variables	Accurate recall of both variables	Accurate perception of the relationship between both variables	Large, random sample of observations	Rule out the possibility that the observed relationship is due to random sampling error

People who draw conclusions based on their own personal experience could be making mistakes at every single one of these steps. Do you know anyone who executes all 5 steps correctly? Probably not—even some scientific studies fail to execute all 5 steps correctly.

3. Use these measurements to accurately determine the degree to which variables are related.

4. Accurately infer that the observed pattern of results reflects what typically happens (see Figure 7-2).

Indeed, intuition alone fails at each of these four steps. Thus, as you will soon see, we need science to measure variables, keep track of those measurements, determine the degree to which variables are related, and to accurately infer the extent to which the observed pattern of results reflects what typically happens.

We Need Scientific Measurement

We need scientific methods to accurately measure the variables we want to measure. As you saw in Chapter 5, reliable and valid measurement of psychological variables is not automatic. If you are to observe psychological variables in a systematic, objective, and unbiased way, you must use scientific methods. Imagine using intuition to measure a person's level of motivation, intelligence, or some other psychological variable!

We Need Systematic, Scientific Record-Keeping

Even if you could intuitively get accurate measurements of psychological variables, you could not rely on your memory to keep track of your observations. Your memory can fool you, especially when it comes to estimating how often things occur. For example, our memories may fool us into believing that more people die from plane crashes than actually do, that sharks kill more people than falling coconuts, and that more words start with r than have r as their third letter (Myers, 2002b). Therefore, if you are to describe behavior accurately, you need to record your observations systematically so that your conclusions are not biased by memory's selectivity.

We Need Objective Ways to Determine Whether Variables Are Related

Obviously, if you're poor at keeping track of observations of one variable, you are going to be even worse at keeping track of two variables—plus the relationship between them. Therefore, you cannot rely on your judgment to determine whether two things are related.

People are so eager to see relationships that they sometimes "see" variables as being related, even when those variables are not related. In several experiments on illusory correlation (Chapman & Chapman, 1967; Ward & Jenkins, 1965), researchers showed participants some data that did not follow any pattern and that did not indicate any relationship among variables. Remarkably, participants usually "found" patterns in these patternless data and found relationships (**illusory correlations**) between the unrelated variables.

Out of the lab, we know that people see systematic patterns in the stock market, even though the stock market behaves in an essentially random fashion (Shefrin & Statman, 1986). Similarly, many people believe that the interview is an invaluable selection device, even though research shows that interviews have virtually no validity (Dawes, 1994; Schultz & Schultz, 1990).

Even when there is a relationship between two variables, the relationship people perceive between those two variables may be exactly opposite of the relationship that exists. To illustrate, basketball coaches swear that if a player makes a shot, that player will be more likely to make the next shot. However, as Gilovich, Vallone, and Tversky (1985) have discovered, a shooter is less likely to make the next shot if he has made the previous shot.

Coaches are not the only ones to misperceive relationships. Many bosses and parents swear that rewarding people doesn't work whereas punishing them does, even though research shows that rewards are more effective than punishments. Many students swear that cramming for exams is more effective than studying consistently, even though research contradicts this claim. In short, because people may misperceive the relationship between variables, we need to do research to determine the real relationship between variables.

We Need Scientific Methods to Generalize From Experience

Even if you accurately describe your own experience, how can you generalize the results of that experience? After all, your experience is based on a limited and small sample of behavior.

One problem with small samples is that they may cause you to overlook a real relationship. Thus, it's not surprising that one man wrote to "Dear Abby" to inform her that lung cancer and smoking were not related: He knew many smokers and none had lung cancer.

Another problem with small samples is that the relationship that exists in the sample may not reflect what typically happens in the population. Thus, our experiences may represent the exception rather than the rule. In other words, the relationship you observe may be due simply to a coincidence. For example, if we go by some people's experiences, playing the lottery is a great investment.

As you have seen, even if you accurately observe a pattern in your experiences, you must take one additional step—determining whether that pattern is simply a coincidence. But how can you determine the likelihood that a pattern of results is due to a coincidence?

To discount the role of coincidence, you need to do two things. First, you need to have a reasonably large and random sample of behavior. Second, you need to use probability theory to determine the likelihood that your results are due to random error. Thus, even if you were an intuitive statistician, you would still face one big question: What's to say that your experience is a large, random sample of behavior? Your experience may be a small and biased sample of behavior. Results from such biased samples are apt to be wrong. For example, several years ago, George Bush senior defeated Michael Dukakis by one of the biggest margins in the history of U.S. presidential elections. However, right up to election eve, some ardent Dukakis supporters thought that Dukakis would beat George Bush. Why? Because everybody they knew was voting for Dukakis.

In summary, generalizations based on personal experience are often wrong. These informal generalizations are error prone because they (1) are based on small or biased samples and (2) are based on the assumption that what happens in one's experience happens in all cases. To avoid these problems, researchers who make generalizations about how people typically act or think (1) study a large, random sample and then (2) use statistics to determine how likely it is that the pattern observed in the sample holds in the population.

Conclusions About Why We Need Descriptive Research

As you can see, we need descriptive research if we are to accurately describe and predict what people think, feel, or do. Fortunately, descriptive research is relatively easy to do. To describe how two variables are related, you need to get a representative sample of behavior, accurately measure both variables, and then objectively assess the association between those variables. The bottom line in doing descriptive research is getting accurate measurements from a representative sample.

The key to getting a representative sample is to get a large and random sample. But how can you get accurate measurements from such a sample?

Sources of Data

In the next few sections, we'll look at several ways to get measurements. We'll start by examining ways of making use of data that have already been collected, then we'll move to going out and collecting new data.

Ex Post Facto Data: Data You Previously Collected

One possible source of data for descriptive research is data that you have already collected. For example, you may have done an experiment looking at the effects of time pressure on performance on a verbal task. At the time you did the study, you may not have cared about the age, gender, personality type, or other personal characteristics of your participants. For testing your experimental hypothesis (that the treatment had an effect), these individual difference variables were irrelevant. Indeed, experimenters often call such individual difference variables "nuisance variables." However, you collected this individual difference information anyway.

After the experiment is over, you might want to go back and look for relationships between these nuisance variables and task performance. This kind of research is called **ex post facto research:** research done after the fact.

External Validity

Suppose your ex post facto research revealed that women did better than men on the verbal task. Although this finding is interesting, you should be careful about generalizing your results. Unless the men and women in your study are a random sample drawn from the entire population of men and women, you cannot say that women do better at this verbal task than men do. Your effect may simply be due to sampling men of average intelligence and women of above-average intelligence. This sampling bias could easily occur, especially if your school was one that had higher admissions standards for women than for men. (Some schools did this when they switched from being all-women colleges to coeducational institutions.)

You could have a bit more confidence that your results were not due to sampling error if you had also included a mathematical task and found that although women did better than men on the verbal task, men did better on the mathematical task. If, in this case, your results are due to sampling error, they aren't due to simply having sampled women who are above average in intelligence. Instead, your sampling error would have to be due to something rather strange, such as sampling women who were better than the average woman in verbal ability but who were worse than the average woman in mathematical ability. Although such a sampling bias is possible, it is not as likely as having merely sampled women who are above average in intelligence. Therefore, with this pattern of results, you would be a little more confident that your results were not due to sampling bias.

Construct Validity

Even if you could show that your results are not due to sampling error, you could not automatically conclude that women had greater verbal ability than men. To make this claim, you would have to show that your measure was a valid measure of verbal ability and that the measure was just as valid for men as it was for women. For example, if your verbal ability measure used vocabulary terms relating to different colors, women's fashions, and ballet, critics would argue that your measure was biased against men.

Internal Validity

If you had carefully chosen a valid measure and, if, by randomly sampling from a representative sample, you had carefully selected a representative sample, you might be able to claim that women had better verbal ability than men. However, you could not say why women had superior verbal ability. As you'll recall, correlational methods are not useful for inferring causality. Therefore, you could not say whether the difference in men's and women's verbal ability was due to inborn differences between men and women or due to differences in how men and women are socialized.

Conclusions About Ex Post Facto Research

In summary, ex post facto research takes advantage of data you have already collected. Therefore, the quality of ex post facto research depends on the quantity and quality of data you collect during the original study. The more information you collect about your participants' personal characteristics, the more ex post facto hypotheses you can examine. The more valid your measures, the more construct validity your conclusions will have. The more representative your sample of participants, the more external validity your results will have. Therefore, if you are doing a study, and there's any possibility that you will do ex post facto research, you should prepare for that possibility by using a random sample of participants and collecting a lot of data about each participant's personal characteristics.

Archival Data

Rather than use data that you have collected, you can use **archival data:** data that someone else has already collected. Basically, there are two kinds of archival data—coded data and uncoded data.

Collected and Coded Data

Whereas uncoded data might simply be videotapes of behavior, coded data involves scoring (coding) the behavior: assigning a number to the behavior. Market researchers, news organizations, behavioral scientists, and government researchers are all collecting and tabulating data. How much data? To give you some idea, more than 5,000 Americans are surveyed every day—and surveys are just one way that these researchers collect data. Not only can you get access to some of these survey results but you can also get access to many statistics relating to people's behaviors—including statistics on accidents, attendance (church, school, sporting events, etc.), bankruptcy, baseball, chess, crime, mental health, income, IQ, literacy, mortality, movie viewing, obesity, voting, and all kinds of sales and spending.

Sometimes, to test a hypothesis, you need to comb through records and collate (pull together; assemble; compile) the data. For example, three psychologists found support for the idea that hotter temperatures are associated with aggression by looking through the baseball and weather sections of newspapers and finding there was a relationship between game time temperature and how many batters were hit by pitches (Reifman, Larrick, & Fein, 1991).

Many times, the data have already been collated (brought together and organized) for you. You simply need to make the connection between the data and your hypothesis—and that often involves making the connection between two different sources of data. For example, using existing measures of wealth (inflation-adjusted U.S. gross national product) and life satisfaction, Diener and Seligman (2004) found that although U.S. citizens became wealthier from 1950 to 1998, U.S. citizens did not become happier during that time.

Sometimes, collated data can help you test hypotheses derived from theory. To test the limits of modeling theory, David Phillips (1979) used suicide and traffic accident statistics to find that both suicides and one-car accidents increased after a well-publicized suicide—but only among people who were similar in age to the person who committed suicide. To test a hypothesis derived from social loafing theory—that songwriters would not work as hard on group-authored songs as they would on their own solo efforts—two music-loving graduate students looked at the equivalent of Top 40 charts. Specifically, the students found that songs written by members of the 1960s rock band The Beatles were better (measured by popularity in terms of chart rankings from *Billboard Magazine*) when written alone than when jointly written (Jackson & Padgett, 1982). Using a hypothesis derived from the theory of evolution—that left-handedness survives because it is helpful in hand-to-hand combat—two researchers found that, in eight societies that use knives rather than guns as weapons, the societies that had the most killings had the most left-handed people (Faurie & Raymond, 2005).

Sometimes, the data have been collected and collated but not published. In that case, you just need to ask for the information. For example, a journalist wanted to test the hypothesis that many heads are better than two by seeing whether the opinion expressed by the majority of the studio audience on the game show *Who Wants to Be a Millionaire?* is more accurate than the opinion given by the "expert" friend the contestant has selected. The journalist did not have to look at tapes of all the shows to compile the relevant data. Instead, because the show had already compiled that data, just interviewing the show's spokesperson gave him the information he needed: The answers provided by the friend-selected experts were right 65% of the time, whereas the answers provided by the studio audience were right 91% of the time (Surowiecki, 2004).

There is good news and bad news about archival data that have been coded for you. The good news is that if you can get access to archival data, you can often look at data that you would never have collected yourself because you wouldn't have had the time or resources to do so—and it has already been coded for you. The bad news is that most archival data are data that you would never have collected yourself because they were collected in a way that is inappropriate for answering your research question—and even those data you would have collected, you wouldn't have coded that way.

Collected but Uncoded Data

If you are willing to code the data yourself, you can avoid the problem of inappropriately coded data. You will also gain access to a vast amount and variety of preserved records of behavior, including

- letters to the editor
- transcripts of congressional hearings
- videotapes of television shows
- yearbook photos (which you can code for smiling and type of smile)
- diaries and autobiographies
- *Playboy* centerfolds (an indicator of the physical characteristics that *Playboy* readers consider ideal)
- comments made in Internet chat rooms and discussion groups
- personal ads for a dating partner

The main advantage of using records of behavior is that the basic data have already been collected for you. All you have to do is code them—and you can code them to suit your needs. If you want to study happiness, for example, you can code a wide range of data, such as:

- Videotapes. By having students rate the happiness of Olympic athletes on the podium during medal ceremonies, Medvec, Madey, and Gilovich (1995) coded videotapes and found that Bronze (third place) winners were happier than Silver (second place) winners.
- College yearbook photos. Using a coding strategy that involved looking at the position of two facial muscles, Harker and Keltner (2001) judged the happiness expressed by people in their college yearbook photos and found that the students who were rated as showing more positive emotion in their yearbooks were, 30 years later, more likely to be happily married.
- Essays. By coding the happiness expressed in short essays that nuns wrote when they were first accepted into the sisterhood, Danner, Snowden, and Friesen (2001) found that the nuns expressing the most happiness lived the longest.

Content Analysis: Objectively Coding the Uncoded. The challenge of using such data is that you must convert the photos, videotapes, transcripts, or other records into a form that you can meaningfully and objectively analyze. To succeed at this task, use **content analysis.**

Content analysis has been used to categorize a wide range of free responses—from determining whether a threatening letter is from a terrorist to determining whether someone's response to an ambiguous picture shows that they have a high need for achievement. In content analysis, you code behavior according to whether it belongs to a certain category (aggressive, sexist, superstitious, etc.).

To successfully use content analysis, you must first carefully define your coding categories. To do so, you should review the research to find out how others have coded those categories. If you can't borrow or adapt someone else's coding scheme, do a mini-study (often called a pilot study) to get an idea of the types of behavior you will be coding, which should help you choose and define the categories you will use to code the data.

After you have defined your categories, you should provide examples of behavior that would fit into each of your categories. Then, train your raters to use these categories.

The primary aim in content analysis is to define your categories as objectively as possible. Some researchers define their categories so objectively that all the coder has to do is count the number of times certain words come up. For example, to get an indication of America's mood, a researcher might count the number of times words like *war, fight,* and so on appear in *The New York Times.* These word-counting schemes are so easy to use that even a computer can do them. In fact, one set of researchers invented a computer program that can tell genuine suicide notes from fake ones (Stone, Smith, Dunphy, & Ogilvie, 1966), and another set invented a computer program that can, with a fair degree of accuracy, tell poetry written by poets who committed suicide from poetry written by poets who did not (Stirman & Pennebaker, 2001). Thus, objective coding can be simple and have construct validity.

Is Objective Coding Valid? Unfortunately, objective criteria are not always so valid. To get totally objective criteria, you often have to ignore the context—yet the meaning of behavior often depends on the context. For example, you might use the number of times the word *war* appears in the paper as a measure of how eager we are for war. This method would be objective, but what if the newspaper was merely reporting wars in other countries? Or, what if the newspaper was full of editorials urging us to avoid war or urging us to expand the war on poverty? In that case, our measure would be objective, but invalid.

Indeed, context is so important that completely objective scoring criteria of certain variables is virtually impossible. Whether a remark is sarcastic, humorous, or sexist may depend more on when, where, and how the statement is made than on what is said. However, despite the difficulties of objectively and accurately coding archival data, researchers often have successfully developed highly objective ways of coding archival data.

An Example of Archival Research

To get a clearer picture of both the advantages and disadvantages of archival research, suppose you wanted to know whether people were more superstitious when they were worried about the economy. As your measure of concern about the economy, you use government statistics on unemployment. As your measure of how superstitious people are, you have the computer count the number of key words such as *magic, superstition,* and *voodoo* that appear in local newspapers and then divide this number by the total number of words in the newspaper. This would give you the percentage of superstitious words in local newspapers.

Internal Validity

Once you had your measures of both economic concern and of superstitiousness, you would correlate the two. Suppose you found that the higher the unemployment rate is, the more superstitious words were used in the newspaper. Because you have done a correlational study, you cannot say why the two variables are related. That is, you do not know whether:

1. The economy caused people to become superstitious.
2. Superstitious beliefs caused the downfall of the economy.
3. Some other factor (bad weather ruining crops) is responsible for both an increase in superstitious beliefs and a decline in the economy.

Construct Validity

In addition to the internal validity problems that you have anytime you use correlational data, you have several construct validity problems specific to archival data. You are using measures of a construct, not because they are the best, but because they are the only measures that someone else bothered to collect. Although you are using unemployment records as an index of how insecure people felt about the economy, you would have preferred to ask people how they felt about the economy. To the degree that the relationship between how many people are unemployed and how people feel about the economy is questionable, your measure's construct validity is questionable.

Even if there is a strong relationship between actual unemployment and feelings about the economy, your measure may not be valid because it may not accurately assess unemployment because of **instrumentation bias:** scores on the measure changing due to (1) changes in the measure itself, (2) changes in how the measure is scored, or (3) changes in who is being measured and recorded.

In measuring unemployment, we would be most concerned about two sources of instrumentation bias: changes in the definition (scoring) of unemployment and changes in whose data is included when calculating the unemployment statistics. A change in scoring, such as the government changing the definition of unemployment from "being unemployed" to "being unemployed for 6 weeks and showing documentation that he or she looks for three jobs every week," would reduce the number of people recorded as unemployed.

Any change in how thoroughly data are collected and collated could affect unemployment statistics. For example, because of the introduction of unemployment compensation in 1935 and more recent computerization of national statistics, current unemployment statistics are more complete than they were in the early 1900s. Thus, better record keeping may increase the number of people currently recorded as unemployed. Another change might be found in data collection: Because the people who would collect unemployment statistics— social workers and other government workers—are sometimes laid off during hard economic times, unemployment statistics might be less complete during periods of high unemployment. Still another change that would reduce the number of people labeled as unemployed would be if some politicians distorted unemployment data to make things seem better than they were.[2]

To illustrate how the three sources of instrumentation bias (changes in the instrument, changes in scoring, and changes in sampling and tabulating) can make it difficult to do a meaningful study, imagine you wanted to compare average SAT scores from 2005 with average SAT scores of 20 years ago. Your first problem is that the SAT instrument has changed. The types of questions the current SAT asks are different from the ones used in the past. In 2005, a section on analogies was dropped from the test, an essay section was added, and the math segment went through a major change. Your second problem is that the way the instrument is scored has changed. For example, in 1985, the SAT was based on a perfect score of 1,600. However, in 2005, the new perfect score is 2,400. Your third problem is that the sample of students that are measured has changed. Specifically, a greater percentage of high school students took the SAT in 2005 (at one time, only the very best high school students took the SAT; in 2005, about half of all high school students took it).

---

[2]According to Levitt and Dubner (2005, p. 92), violent crime statistics in Atlanta were altered as part of that city's attempt to host the 1996 Olympics.

Thus, even if we developed a formula to compare 1985 scores with 2005 scores, we would have difficulty making meaningful comparisons. For instance, if scores on the SAT went down, we would not conclude that students were learning less in high school because (a) rather than testing what it once did, the test is testing different knowledge and (b) rather than testing the top 10% of students, the test is testing the top 50%. If, on the other hand, scores on the SAT went up, we couldn't conclude that students were learning more in high school because (a) the test is testing different knowledge and (b) the scoring system has been changed.

Although you don't have to worry about instrumentation bias ruining your superstition measure, you still have to worry about your superstition measure's construct validity. Is the number of times superstitious terms are mentioned in newspapers a good index of superstition? Perhaps these articles sell papers, and major newspapers stoop to using these articles only when sales are low. Rather than relying on the number of times "superstition" appears in papers, you would prefer to have results of some nationwide survey that questioned people directly about their superstitious beliefs. However, your measure has one advantage over the poll—it is a **nonreactive measure:** Collecting it does not change participants' behavior.

External Validity

Because you can collect so much data so easily, your results should have good external validity. In some cases, your results may apply to millions of people because you have data from millions of people. Specifically, you can easily get unemployment statistics for the entire United States. Furthermore, because you can collect data for a period of years rather than for just the immediate present, you should be able to generalize your results across time.

The Limits of Aggregate Data

Gaining access to group data (for instance, the unemployment rate for the entire United States for 1931) is convenient and may aid external validity. However, as psychologists, we are interested in what individuals do; therefore, we want individual data. Consequently, even if we find that there is a correlation between unemployment for the nation as a whole and superstition for the nation as a whole, we are still troubled because we do not know which individuals are superstitious. Are the individuals who are unemployed the ones who are superstitious? Or, are the superstitious ones the people whose friends have been laid off? Or, are the superstitious ones the people who are doing quite well? With aggregate data, we can't say.

Conclusions About Archival Research

By using archival data, you can gain access to a great deal of data that you did not have to collect, which may allow you to test hypotheses you would otherwise be unable or unwilling to test. For example, you can test hypotheses about relationships between type of prison and violence in prisons (Briggs, 2001), color of uniform and violence in professional sports (Frank & Gilovich, 1988), economic conditions and what men want women to look like (Pettijohn & Jungeberg, 2004), and competitiveness and violence in Detroit (Wilson & Daly, 1985). Because archival data often summarize the behavior of thousands of people across a period of years, your results may have impressive external validity.

Relying on others to collect data has its drawbacks. You may find that others used measures that have less construct validity than the measures you would have used. You may find that others did not collect the data as carefully and as consistently as you would have. You may find that you have data about groups but no data about individuals. Because the data that others collected will usually not be ideal for answering the question you want to answer, you may decide to collect your own data.

Observation

One way to collect your own data is through observation. As the name implies, observation involves watching (observing) behavior.

Observation can play a role in experiments. For example, an experimenter administering different levels of a drug to rats might observe and categorize each rat's behavior. Similarly, an experimenter manipulating levels of televised violence might observe and categorize each participant's behavior.

Observation is also of interest for its own sake. Describing behavior is a vital concern of every field of psychology. Developmental psychologists use observation to describe child–parent interactions, social psychologists to describe cults, clinical psychologists to describe abnormal behavior, counseling psychologists to describe human sexual behavior, and comparative psychologists to describe animal behavior.

Types of Observational Research

There are three basic types of observation: laboratory observation, naturalistic observation, and participant observation. In both naturalistic and participant observation, you study real behavior in the real world. In contrast, laboratory observation, as the name suggests, occurs in a laboratory.

Laboratory observation, however, is not always as artificial as you might think. The lab experience is often very real to participants—and participants' behavior may strongly relate to real-world behavior. For example, consider Mary Ainsworth's "strange situation." To oversimplify, a mother and her 1-year-old child enter the lab. The child has a chance to explore the room. Next, a stranger enters. Then, the mother leaves. Later, the mother reunites with the child (Ainsworth & Bell, 1970). This situation is very real to the child. Many children were extremely upset when their mother left and very happy when she returned. How children behave in the strange situation also seems to relate to how the child behaves in real life and even relates to the child's social skills and self-confidence 10 years later (Elicker, Englund, & Sroufe, 1992).

The lab experience can be real to adults as well. For example, Ickes and some of his students (Ickes, Robertson, Tooke, & Teng, 1986) brought pairs of opposite-sex strangers to the lab. The strangers sat down next to each other on a couch, supposedly to view slides that they were to judge. As the slide projector warmed up, the projector bulb appeared to pop. As the researcher left to find a bulb, the students began to talk—and their talking was what Ickes observed. The situation was quite real to the students—and not that different from real-life situations in which two students who arrive early to class find themselves talking to each other.

Even when people know they are being videotaped and have sensors clipped to their ears and fingers, they may behave naturally. For example, under these conditions, married couples argue with each other freely—and their behavior predicts with greater than 94% accuracy whether they will be married 15 years later (Carrere & Gottman, 1999). Yet, despite the impressive generalizability of lab observation, many researchers want to observe behavior in a more realistic setting. Such researchers use either naturalistic observation or participant observation.

In **naturalistic observation,** you try to observe the participants in a natural setting *unobtrusively:* without letting them know you are observing them. Often, naturalistic observation involves keeping your distance—both physically and psychologically.

In **participant observation,** on the other hand, you actively interact with your participants. In a sense, you become "one of them."

Both types of observation can lead to ethical problems because both may involve collecting data without participants' informed consent.[3] Whereas naturalistic observation may involve spying on your participants from a distance, participant observation may involve spying on a group that you have infiltrated. Because the participant observer is more likely to have a direct effect on participants, most people consider participant observation to present more ethical problems than naturalistic observation.

But which method provides more valid data? Not everyone agrees on the answer to this question. Advocates of participant observation claim that you get more "inside" information by using participant observation. Advocates of naturalistic observation counter that the information you get through participant observation may be tainted. As a participant, you are in a position to influence (bias) what your participants do. Furthermore, as an active participant, you may be unable to sit back and record behavior as it occurs. Instead, you may have to rely on your (faulty) memory of what happened.

Problems With Observation

Whether you use participant or naturalistic observation, you face two major problems. First, if participants know they are being watched, they may not behave in their normal, characteristic way. Thus, participants in observational research, unlike archival research, may react to being watched. Second, even if participants act "natural," you may fail to objectively record their behavior. That is, your personality and motives may affect what things you ignore and how you interpret those things you do pay attention to.

Dealing With Effects of the Observer on the Observed. To deal with the first problem, the problem of changing behavior by observing it, you might observe participants unobtrusively (without their knowledge). For example, you might want to observe participants through a one-way mirror.

If you can't be unobtrusive, try becoming less noticeable. One way to do this is to observe participants from a distance, hoping that they will ignore you. Another way is to let participants become familiar with you, hoping that they will eventually get used to you. Once participants are used to you, they may forget that you are there and revert back to normal behavior.

Dealing With Difficulties in Objectively Coding Behavior. Unfortunately, steps you might take to make observers less reactive, such as observing participants from a distance, may make observers less accurate. For example, if observers can't easily see or hear participants, they may record what they expected the participant to do rather than reporting what the participant actually did. However, even when observers can observe behavior at close range, observations make lack objectivity. That is, as with archival research (indirect observation), one problem with observation is that different observers may code the same behavior differently.

---

[3] According to most ethical guidelines, people in studies should be volunteers who know what they have volunteered for. If the people in your study did not volunteer, they are not really participants—people who participated in the research— but rather subjects (objects of study). For more on ethics, see Chapter 2 and Appendix C.

As with archival data, one way to check whether different observers are coding the same behavior differently is to have more than one observer rate the same behavior and then obtain some index (percent of times they agree, correlation between raters, Cohen's kappa) of interjudge reliability. As was the case with archival data, the way to maximize interjudge agreement is to use a clear coding scheme. You need to

1. define your categories in terms of specific target behaviors
2. develop a check sheet to mark off each time a target behavior is exhibited
3. train and motivate raters to use your check sheet

Training and motivating your raters are even more important in observational research than in archival research because in observational research, there are often no permanent records of the behavior. Thus, unmotivated or disorganized raters do not get a second chance to rate a behavior they missed: There is no instant replay. Furthermore, without permanent records, you cannot check or correct a rater's work.

We have shown you why training is so important. But how do you train observers to categorize behavior? Training should involve at least three steps. First, you should spell out what each category means, giving both a definition of each category and some examples of behaviors that belong and do not belong in each category. Second, you should have your observers rate several videotaped examples of behavior, and you should tell them why their ratings are right or wrong. Third, you should continue the training until each rater is at least 90% accurate.

Conclusions About Observation

In conclusion, observation can be a powerful technique for finding out what people do. However, observers may let you down by changing the behavior of the individuals they are observing or by letting their biases affect what they record.

Tests

If you do not want to rely on observers, you may decide to use tests. Tests are especially useful if you want to measure ability, knowledge, or personality variables. For instance, you might correlate scores on an extroversion test with scores on a happiness test.

External Validity

As was the case with ex post facto research, the external validity of a study that uses tests depends on the representativeness of the sample. You cannot generalize your results to a population unless you have a random sample of that population. Therefore, you cannot say that women score more extroverted on an extroversion test than men unless you have a random sample of all men and women. Similarly, you cannot say that extroverts are happier than introverts unless you have a random sample of all introverts and extroverts.

Internal Validity

As is the case with all correlational research, if you find a relationship between test scores, that relationship is not necessarily a causal relationship. For example, if extroverts are happier than introverts, we don't know whether extroversion causes happiness, happiness causes extroversion, or some other factor (supportive parents, social skills, etc.) causes both extroversion and happiness.

Table 7-3	Comparing Different Correlational Methods			
VALIDITY	**EX POST FACTO**	**ARCHIVAL**	**OBSERVATION**	**TESTS**
Internal validity	Poor	Poor[a]	Poor	Poor
Construct validity	Fair	Fair to poor	Fair to poor	Fair to good
Objective—Avoids observer bias	Good	May be good	May be poor	Good
Nonreactive—Avoids subject bias	Often a problem	Often good	Can be poor	Reactive—But steps can be taken to control for subject biases
Operational definition is consistent with definition of the construct	Fair to good	Often poor	Fair	Good
External validity				
Ease of getting a large representative sample	Depends on original study	May be easy	Difficult	May be easy

[a]Internal validity will be poor unless you find a situation in which a random process determines what treatment people receive. For example, two anthropologists found that Olympians who were randomly assigned to wear red were more likely to win than those who were randomly assigned to wear blue. Similarly, by comparing losers and winners of a lottery in which winners would get to go to the Chicago public school of their choice, an economist was able to determine that going to a better school didn't have noticeable long-term effects (Levitt & Dubner, 2005).

The fact that correlation does not prove causation is important to keep in mind. Without an understanding of this concept, you may mistake circumstantial evidence for proof. For example, certain authors try to show a genetic basis for some characteristic (career preferences, schizophrenia, introversion, etc.) by showing that identical twins score similarly on a test of a particular trait. However, identical twins could be similar on the trait because they share a similar environment or because they have influenced one another.

Conclusions About Using Tests

By using tests, you can take advantage of measures that other people have spent years developing. As a result, construct validity is usually less of a problem than if you had devised your own measures. Furthermore, tests are often easier to use than other measures. Because of these advantages, tests are often used in experimental as well as nonexperimental research. When used in nonexperimental research, however, this research has the same weaknesses as other correlational research: It doesn't allow you to establish causality, and the generalizability of your results will only be as good as the representativeness of your sample (to compare different descriptive designs, see Table 7-3).

Analyzing Data From Descriptive Studies: Looking at Individual Variables

Once you have coded your data, you want to compile and summarize them. You want to know what your data "look like."

You may start by describing participants' scores on one or more key variables. Often, summarizing those scores will involve calculating both (a) the average score as well as (b) an index of the degree to which scores vary from either that average or from each other. For example, you might report that the mean (average based on adding up all the scores and then dividing by the number of scores) score on the personality test was 78 and the *range* (the highest score minus the lowest score) was 50. Instead of reporting the range, you will probably report the **standard deviation (SD):** an index of the extent to which individual scores differ (deviate) from the mean; a measure of the degree of scatter in the scores.[4] For example, you might say that the mean was 78 and the standard deviation was 10.

Researchers must mention both the average score and an index (like the range or, better yet, the standard deviation) of the extent to which scores vary. If researchers mentioned only the average score, it would lead to many problems. One problem would be that descriptive research, rather than providing a deeper and richer appreciation of people, might lead to labeling, stereotyping, and other oversimplifications. For example, consider the problems caused by people knowing that the average age that infants talk is 12 months. The problem is that half of all infants are going to talk later than that. Many of those infants' parents, not understanding the wide range at which children begin to talk, needlessly worry that their child's development is delayed. Similarly, take the research suggesting that the average teenager today is as stressed as the average teenager in therapy in the 1950s (Twenge, 2002). Without considering the variability, knowing this fact might cause some people to stereotype today's teenagers as all being neurotic kids.

One way to describe the variability of scores is to make a **frequency distribution:** a graph on which the frequency of each score is plotted. The possible scores are arranged from lowest (leftmost) to highest (rightmost) on the bottom of the graph. The frequency of the scores are indicated by how high the line is above a given score. If there is no line above a score—or the line above the score is at the bottom of the graph—no one had that score (the score's frequency is zero). The highest point on the graph will be above the score having the highest frequency (the mode).

To draw a crude frequency distribution, start near the left edge of a sheet of paper and draw a line straight down almost to the bottom of the page. This vertical line is called the *y*-axis. Because you will use this line to represent how frequently scores occur, label this line "frequency" (see Figure 7-3a).

Your next step is to draw a line that goes from the bottom of the *y*-axis straight across to the right side of the page. (If you are using lined paper, you may be able to trace over one horizontal lines.) This horizontal line is called the *x*-axis and will represent your scores, so label this *x*-axis with numbers representing possible scores on your measure (see Figure 7-3b). For example, if the scores could range from 0 to 10, the bottom left-hand part of the graph would be labeled "0" and the bottom right-hand part of the graph would be labeled "10." Then, find the **mode:** the score that occurred most often; the most frequent score. For each

---

[4]The lowest the standard deviation can be is zero. You would get a zero only if everyone in the group scored at the mean. In that case, there would be zero (no) deviations from the mean. If you want a rough estimate of the standard deviation, divide the range by 6. If you want a more precise estimate of a population's standard deviation and you have a random sample from that population, (a) get the differences between each score and the mean by subtracting each score from the mean, (b) get the squared differences between each score and the mean by squaring each of those differences, (c) get the sum of squared differences (also called "sum of squares") by adding (summing) up all those squared differences, (d) get the variance by dividing the sum of the squared differences by one less than the number of scores, and (e) get the standard deviation by taking the square root of the variance. For more on calculating and using the standard deviation, see Appendix D.

| Figure 7-3 | **Making a Frequency Distribution** |

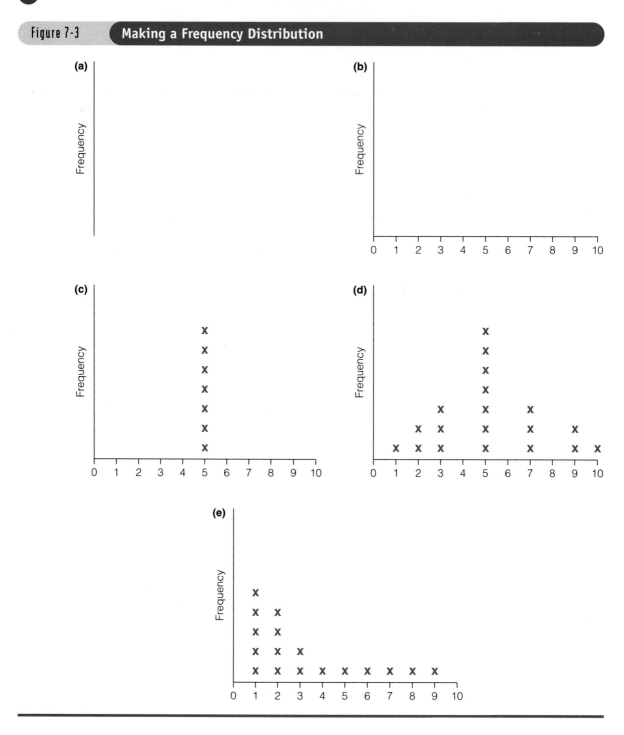

person who scored at the mode, put an "x" above the mode (see Figure 7-3c). After making a column of "x's" at the mode (each "x" representing one person who scored at the mode), repeat the process for the rest of the possible scores.

Once you are done plotting the scores, your distribution will probably look like the normal distribution in Figure 7-3d. This bell-shaped distribution shares at least three characteristics with every normal distribution.

First, the center of the distribution is at the mean. One indication that the mean is at the middle of the distribution is that the mean is the most common score. In other words, the mean is also the mode, as indicated by the fact that the tallest row of "x's" is above the mean. A stronger indication that the mean is the distribution's middle point is that just as many scores are above the mean as below the mean: If you count the "x's" below the mean, you will know how many are above the mean. In other words, for the normal curve, the mean is the same as the **median:** the middle score, the score at which just as many scores are above as are below (just as the median of the highway is in the middle of the road, the median of a set of scores is in the middle of the scores).

Second, not only is the distribution balanced on the mean, but the distribution is symmetrical. That is, if you fold the distribution in half at the mean, the two halves will match.

Third, the distribution extends for about three standard deviations in both directions from the mean, with about 2/3 of the scores being within one standard deviation of the mean. Relatively few of the scores (less than 5%) are more than two standard deviations from the mean.

But what if your frequency distribution does not look like a normal distribution? That is, what if, instead of having a symmetrical normal distribution, your frequency distribution is skewed (tilted) to one side of the mean, like the distribution in Figure 7-3e? Such a skewed distribution is likely if you use a reaction time measure—and reaction times are used to measure many constructs, from unconscious prejudice to intelligence to personality (Robinson, Vargas, Tamir, & Solberg, 2004).

One problem with skewed distributions is that a few extreme scores (those causing the skew) can distort (skew) the mean. For example, if a participant's reaction times were 0.1, 0.1, 0.1, 0.2, and 5 seconds, the participant's mean score would be 1.1 seconds. Note that although the one extreme score (the 5-second reaction time) throws off the mean, it does not throw off the median score (0.1). Therefore, if the researcher has a skewed distribution, the researcher may want to use the median (middle) score rather than the mean.[5]

If you put people into categories such as helped or didn't help, you have have nominal (qualitative, categorical) data. Calculating a mean on qualitative data makes little sense. For example, it doesn't make sense to say that "mean helping was 0.4." With categorical (nominal) data, you should use percentages (e.g., "40% of people helped") to summarize your data. If you had to use an average, use the mode (e.g., "the most common [modal] behavior was to avoid eye contact with the person needing help").

In short, the most appropriate average score for your data could be a mean, a median, or a mode. However, most of the time, the most appropriate average will be the mean.

---

[5]Some researchers still use the mean with reaction-time data. However, these researchers often (a) throw out reaction times that are abnormally long (or replace those times with a certain value, such as 4 seconds) and (b) use some mathematical transformation of the data to make the data normally distributed.

If your mean is based on a random sample of a larger group, you may want to estimate the mean of that population.[6] For example, Brescoll and LaFrance (2004), using a random sample of major U.S. newspapers, looked at the degree—on a scale of 1 (extremely opposed) to 5 (extremely in favor of)—to which newspapers opposed or supported women being allowed to enter military academies. The average rating for the newspaper editorials in their sample was 3.48. Thus, the best guess about the average extent to which all editorials in all 50 major newspapers opposed or supported women being allowed to enter military academies—the population mean—would also be 3.48.

This best guess of the population average, the sample mean, probably differs from the population average. Therefore, you may want to establish a range in which the population mean is likely to fall. Often, researchers establish a **95% confidence interval:** a range in which you can be 95% sure that the population mean falls. You can establish 95% confidence intervals for any population mean from the sample mean if you know the **standard error of the mean.**[7] You establish the lower limit of your confidence interval by subtracting approximately two standard errors from the sample mean.[8] Then, you establish the upper limit of your confidence interval by adding approximately two standard errors to the sample mean.

In this example, because the average was 3.48 and the standard error was .06, we can be 95% confident that the true population mean is somewhere between 3.36 and 3.60. Because 3.60, the upper limit of our confidence interval, is below 4, we can be very confident that the true population mean is below 4. The fact that the true population mean is below 4 is of interest because 4 represented supporting the women's right to go to a military academy—but with reservations. Consequently, the results suggest that there is a conservative bias in newspapers, at least as far as women's rights are concerned.

We used confidence intervals in this example to show that a sample mean (the average rating of newspaper editorials) is different from a certain score. However, we could have used the one-sample t test to find that the mean extent to which newspapers supported women

---

[6] If you have categorical data (e.g., number of people who helped), you can still use the confidence interval technique we describe below. The only differences are that (a) instead of the mean, you use the proportion of participants who did the behavior (e.g., .40 [40%] of the participants helped) and (b) instead of basing your standard error on the standard deviation, you calculate it by multiplying p by $(1 - p)$, dividing that quantity by n, and then taking the square root. For example, suppose p was .40 and you had 24 observations. Your sample mean equivalent is p, which is .40. Now you need the standard error, which you can calculate in three steps. The first step would be to multiply p by $1 - p$. That would be $.4 \times (1 - .4)$ or $.4 \times .6$, which is .24. The second step would be to divide .24 by 24, which would give you .01. The third step would be to take the square root of .01, which would be .10. Once you have the standard error, setting up the confidence interval for proportion is just like doing the confidence interval for the mean. Thus, in this case, the confidence interval for the population proportion would go from approximately 2 standard errors below the sample proportion to approximately 2 standard errors above the sample proportion. To be more specific, it would go from .03 to .45 $(.24 \pm .21)$.

[7] Many calculators and web pages can calculate the standard error of the mean for you. If you need to calculate the standard error, take the standard deviation and divide it by the square root of the number of observations. If you don't have the standard deviation, you can calculate it by following the steps in footnote 4 or by using the formula $\sqrt{\Sigma(X - M)^2/(N - 1)}$. In this case, the standard deviation was 1.11 and the number of observations was 326. Thus, the standard error was .06 (or $1.11/\sqrt{326} = 1.11/18.06 = .06$).

[8] The exact number will usually vary from 1.96 to 2.776, depending on how many participants you have. To be more precise, the exact number will depend on your degrees of freedom (df)—and your df will be 1 less than your number of participants. Thus, if you have a mean based on 11 participants' scores, your df will be 10. Once you have calculated your df, go to the t table (Table E-1) in Appendix E. In that table, look under the .05 column (it starts with 12.706) and find the entry corresponding to your df. Thus, if you have a df of 10, you would multiply your standard error by 2.228; if you had a df of 120, you would multiply your standard error by 1.98.

being allowed to enter military academies was significantly (reliably) different from 4. The results of such an analysis might be reported as, "The mean rating of 3.48 was significantly less than 4, $t(325) = 8.46, p < .05$."[9]

Should you use confidence intervals or one-sample t tests? To answer that question, let's compare the results of the confidence interval and one-sample t tests. The one sample t test told us one thing that the confidence interval told us: that it was unlikely that the true mean of our sample was 4.0. However, the t test failed to tell us two things that the confidence interval did.

First, it didn't tell us how close or far our population mean could be to 4—it told us only that the population mean is reliably different from 4. Whether our confidence interval was from 1 to 2 or from 2.97 to 3.99, the one-sample t test would say the same thing: that the results were significantly different from 4. Put another way, the t test may tell us what the mean probably isn't, but it doesn't tell us what the mean might be.

Second, the one-sample t test didn't tell us how accurate our estimate of the population mean was. For instance, the t test doesn't tell us whether our estimate is probably highly accurate, as indicated by a narrow confidence interval, such as one between 3.4 and 3.5, or whether the estimate is imprecise, as indicated by a wide interval, such as one between 1.1 and 3.9. In conclusion, despite the one-sample t test's popularity, it really doesn't tell you anything more than a confidence interval does—and it sometimes tells you less (Cumming & Finch, 2005).[10]

Analyzing Data From Descriptive Studies: Looking at Relationships Between Variables

Although you can answer an interesting question by describing how one group of participants scored on one measure, you will usually answer more interesting questions if you also look at how participants' scores on one measure relate to their scores on some other measure. For example, rather than just knowing at what ages children talk, you may want to know what relationship age of talking has with future success. Similarly, rather than knowing the average anxiety levels of teenagers, you might want to know whether boys are less anxious than girls. Sometimes, the simplest way to describe relationships between two variables is to look at two means. For example, you might compare the means for men and the means for women on your measure. Or, you might compare the happiness of a group of lottery winners against a group of people who, other than winning the lottery, seem similar to those lottery winners.

Comparing Two Means

To begin to compare the two means, you could subtract the smaller means from the larger means to find the difference between means. Then, you could calculate a 95% confidence

---

[9]"Significantly" means reliably. The t of 8.46 was calculated by subtracting the observed mean (3.48) from 4 and then dividing by the standard error of the mean (.06). If the real mean was 4, the chances of getting an observed mean as low or lower than 3.48 are fewer than 5 in 100 ($p < .05$). The "325" refers to the degrees of freedom (df) for the test, which is number of observations minus one (one df is lost computing the one sample mean).

[10]Both analyses involve comparing the mean and the standard error, so they both are similar. Indeed, you could use some algebra on the formula for confidence intervals to get the t.

interval for the difference between the means.[11] You would be interested in seeing whether the confidence interval included 0 because 0 would indicate no (0) difference between the two means. If your confidence interval did not include 0 (e.g., the lower and upper limits were both positive, or the lower and upper limits were both negative), you would be relatively confident that the difference between the means is not zero. In that case, you could say that the means are reliably different. If, on the other hand, your confidence interval included 0 (e.g., the confidence interval includes both a negative number and a positive number), there may be no (0) real difference between your means. In that case, you couldn't say that the means were reliably different.

Rather than—or in addition to—the confidence interval, you could compute an independent (between) groups *t* test.[12] Like confidence intervals that did not include 0, a significant *t* test would tell you that the groups were reliably different. However, note what the significant *t* test does not tell you. Whereas a confidence interval might tell you about how big the difference was (e.g., between .1 and .2 points or between 3 and 5 points), a significant *t* test tells you only that the difference was probably not zero.

The *t* test is even less informative when it is not significant. In that case, its results are completely inconclusive. In contrast, using confidence intervals on the same data will tell you two things.

First, as was the case with a significant *t*, confidence intervals give you some idea about how big the relationship might be. That is, a confidence interval between −.1 and +.1 indicates the relationship, even if it exists, is small. A confidence interval between −.1 and 10, on the other hand, hints that a sizable relationship may exist.

Second, we have some idea about whether our failure to find a relationship was due to random error causing our estimates of the difference between means to be inaccurate. For example, if our confidence interval is between −.1 and +.1, we probably have done a good job of dealing with random error. In such a case, we would probably conclude that the difference either doesn't exist or, if it does, is too small to be of interest. Therefore, we would probably not redo the study to see if we could find a difference. If, on the other hand, our confidence interval is between −20 and +20, our failure to find a difference may be due to having an imprecise estimate of the difference between the means. Therefore, we might try to redo the study by making changes that would reduce random error, such as making our measures more reliable, or that would balance out random error's effects, such as studying more participants.

In short, just as confidence intervals of means provide more information than one-sample *t* tests, confidence intervals of differences between means provide more

---

[11] To estimate the 95% confidence interval, you would (a) multiply the standard error of the differences by 2, (b) subtract that number from the mean to get the lower limit of the confidence interval, and (c) add that number to the mean to get the upper limit of the confidence interval. To get the exact confidence interval, rather than multiplying by 2, you would multiply by the number in the .05 column of the *t* table (Table E-1) in Appendix E corresponding to your degrees of freedom (*df*), where your *df* is 2 less than your number of participants. Thus, if you had 12 participants, you would have a *df* of 10 (12-2), and you would multiply your standard error of the differences by 2.228. If you need to calculate the standard error of the differences and you have the same number of participants in each group, you can simply (a) square the standard error of the mean of each group, (b) add those squared terms together, and (c) take the square root. If you need help calculating the standard error of the mean, see footnote 7.

[12] To compute a *t*, you would subtract your two group means and then divide by the standard error of the differences. To calculate the standard error of the differences by hand, you can (a) use the formula: standard error of the mean = $\sqrt{(s_1^2/N_1) + (s_2^2/N_2)}$, where s = standard deviation and N = number of participants, and where $_1$ refers to group 1 and $_2$ refers to group 2, (b) follow the brief instructions in footnote 11, or (c) follow the more detailed set of instructions in Appendix D.

information than independent group t tests. However, independent group *t* tests are useful and popular.

Doing a Median Split to Set Up the *t* Test

To do an independent groups *t* test, you need two groups. But what if you don't have two groups? For example, what if you have just participants' self-esteem scores and grade-point averages (GPA)? In that case, you could use participants' self-esteem scores to create two groups: participants scoring in the top half on the self-esteem measure ("highs"), and participants scoring in the bottom half ("lows"). Then, you would compare the GPA of the highs to the GPA of the lows. Dividing participants into two groups depending on whether they scored above or below the median (the middle score) on a predictor variable is called a **median split.**

Doing a median split and then conducting a *t* test is a common way of analyzing correlational data. You will frequently encounter such analyses in published articles (MacCallum, Zhang, Preacher, & Rucker, 2002).

The Case Against Doing a Median Split. Although the median split is popular, most statisticians argue that there are many reasons not to do it (MacCallum et al., 2002). The main reason is that using a *t* test based on median splits reduces your ability to find relationships (Cohen, 1990). This is because you have less information with which to work. Put another way, you have less power—ability to find differences—because you are recoding data in a way that hides differences. Instead of using participants' specific scores, you are using the median split to lump together all the participants who scored above average. Thus, a participant who scores 1 point above average gets the same score—as far as the analysis is concerned—as a participant who scores 50 points above average. Similarly, you are lumping together everyone who scored below average, despite the differences in their scores. In a sense, you are deliberately throwing away information about participants' scores.

Not surprisingly, some experts object to this waste. Cohen (1990), for example, argues that researchers should not lose power and information by "mutilating" variables. Instead of "throwing away" the information regarding a participant's specific score by doing a median split, Cohen believes that researchers should do correlational analyses that use participants' actual scores.

Graphing Scores

To begin using participants' actual scores, graph your data. Start by labeling the *x*-axis (the line that goes straight across the page) with the name of your predictor variable. More specifically, go a few spaces below the bottom of the graph and then write the name of your predictor variable. Next, label the other axis, the *y*-axis (the vertical line on the left side of the graph), with the name of your criterion (outcome) measure. Then, plot each observation.

For example, suppose we were were trying to see whether we could use self-esteem to predict grade-point average (GPA). Figure 7-4 shows the beginning of such a graph. As you can see, we have plotted the score of our first participant, a student who has a score of 4 on the self-esteem scale and a 2.0 GPA. As we plot more and more of our data, the points will be scattered throughout the graph. Not surprisingly, then, our graph will be called a **scatterplot.** There are four basic relationships that the scatterplot could reveal.

A Positive Relationship

The scatterplot in Figure 7-5 shows a pattern that indicates that the higher one's self-esteem, the higher one's grade-point average is likely to be. Put another way, the lower one's

Figure 7-4	The Beginning of a Scatterplot

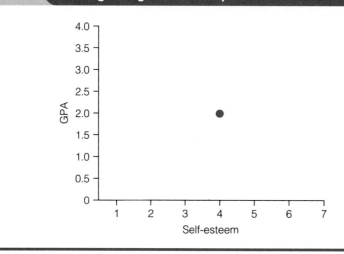

Figure 7-5	Scatterplots Revealing Positive Correlations

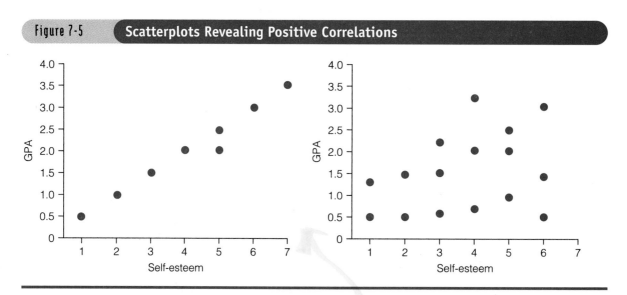

The graph on the left indicates a strong positive correlation; the graph on the right indicates a weak positive correlation.

self-esteem, the lower one's grade-point average will be. This kind of relationship indicates a **positive correlation** between the variables. One common example of a positive correlation is the relationship between height and weight: The taller you are, the more you are likely to weigh. Intriguing psychological examples are that smoking is positively correlated with sex drive, coffee drinking, stress, risky behavior, external locus of control (feeling that outside events control your life), negative affect (being in a bad mood), having problems in school, and rebelliousness.

Figure 7-6   **Scatterplots Revealing Negative Correlations**

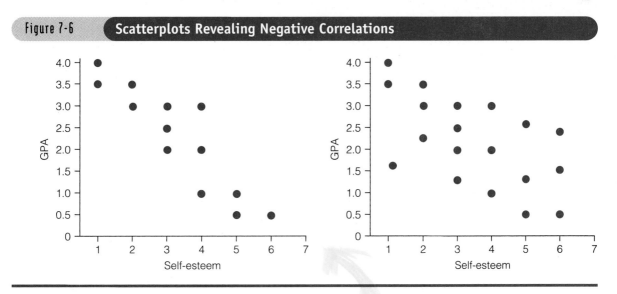

The graph on the left indicates a **strong negative correlation**; the graph on the right indicates a **weak negative correlation**.

A Negative Relationship

The scatterplot in Figure 7-6 shows a second pattern: The higher one's self-esteem, the lower one's grade-point average tends to be. Put another way, the lower one's self-esteem, the higher one's grade-point average tends to be. This relationship indicates a **negative correlation** between the variables. Many variables are negatively (inversely) related. One common example of a negative correlation is the relationship between miles run and weight: The more miles you run, the less you tend to weigh. Smoking is negatively correlated with internal locus of control (feeling in control of your life), positive affect (being in a good mood), doing well in school, and conformity.

Note that whether we have a positive or a negative relationship may depend on how we label or measure our variables. For example, suppose that people with high self-esteem answer math questions more quickly than people with low self-esteem. If we research this relationship, the type of correlation (positive or negative) we obtain will depend on whether we measure quickness in terms of speed (number of questions answered in 1 minute) or in terms of time (average time it takes to answer one question). If we used speed, we would find a positive correlation between self-esteem and speed (higher self-esteem, higher speed; higher self-esteem, more questions answered in one minute). If, on the other hand, we used time, we would find a negative correlation between self-esteem and time (more self-esteem, less time to answer a question). Similarly, if high self-esteem individuals did better on math tests, we would find a positive correlation between self-esteem and questions correct (higher self-esteem, higher percentage correct), but a negative correlation between self-esteem and questions missed (higher self-esteem, fewer questions missed).

No Relationship

The scatterplot in Figure 7-7 shows a third pattern: no relationship between self-esteem and grade-point average. This pattern reflects a **zero correlation** between the two variables.

Figure 7-7 | **A Scatterplot Revealing a Zero Correlation**

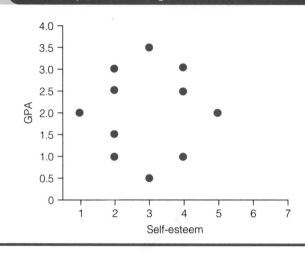

Figure 7-8 | **A Scatterplot Revealing a Nonlinear Relationship**

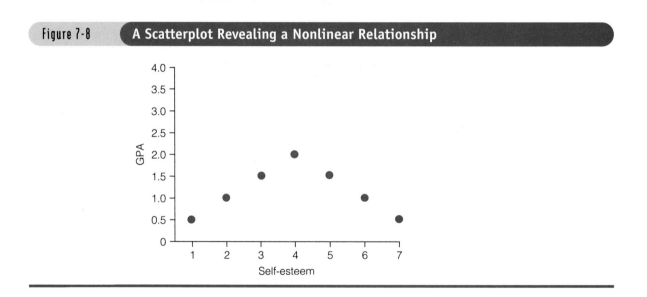

A Nonlinear Relationship

The scatterplot in Figure 7-8 shows a fourth pattern: a nonlinear relationship between self-esteem and grade-point average (GPA). As you can see, in a complex, nonlinear relationship, the relationship between self-esteem and GPA may vary, depending on the level of the variables. Thus, in the low ranges of self-esteem, self-esteem may be positively correlated with GPA, but in the high ranges, self-esteem may be negatively correlated with GPA. Such a pattern could emerge in any situation in which a low amount of a variable could be too little, a medium amount of a variable could be just right, and a high level of the variable could be too much. For example, with too little motivation, performance may be poor; with a moderate amount of motivation, performance could be good; and with too much motivation, performance might be poor.

Correlation Coefficients

Although a graph gives a good picture of your data, you may want to summarize your data with a single number that expresses the "go-togetherness" of the two variables: a **correlation coefficient.** The kind of correlation coefficient you use will depend on the nature of your data (see Table 7-4). Probably, you will use the most commonly calculated correlation coefficient—the Pearson r.

The Pearson r, like most correlation coefficients, ranges from -1 to $+1$. More importantly, like all correlation coefficients, the Pearson r summarizes the relationship described in a scatterplot with a single number.

The Pearson r will be consistent with the data in your scatterplot. When your scatterplot indicates a positive correlation between the two variables, your correlation coefficient will also be positive. When the scatterplot indicates that your variables are not related, your

Table 7-4	Different Kinds of Correlation Coefficients

When reading journal articles, you may come across correlation coefficients other than the Pearson r. In addition, you may be called on to compute correlations other than the Pearson r. This table should help you understand the distinctions among these different coefficients.

Although this table focuses on the differences between these correlation coefficients, these coefficients share commonalities. For example, all of them yield coefficients between -1 (a perfect negative correlation) and $+1$ (a perfect positive correlation). Furthermore, as Cohen and Cohen (1983, pp. 38–39) point out, the Pearson r, the point biserial, the phi coefficient, and Spearman's rho can all be computed using the same formula. That formula is the formula for the Pearson r. The difference in calculating them comes from what data are entered into that formula (see fourth column of the table). For example, if you were calculating Spearman's rho, you would not enter participants' actual scores into the formula. Instead, you would convert those scores to ranks and then enter those ranks into the formula.

NAME OF COEFFICIENT	LEVEL OF MEASUREMENT REQUIRED	EXAMPLE	DATA ENTERED	SIGNIFICANCE TEST
Pearson product-moment correlation (r)	Both variables must be at least interval	Height with weight	Actual scores	t test[a]
Point biserial (r_{pb})	One variable is interval, the other nominal or dichotomous (having only two values)	Weight with gender	Actual scores for the interval variable, 0 or 1 for the nominal variable	t test
Spearman's rho (r_s)	Ordinal data	High school rank with military rank	Ranks	Chi-square test
Phi coefficient (ϕ)	Nominal data	Race with learning style	Zeros and ones: zero if the participant is not a member of a category; 1 if the participant is a member of that category	Chi-square test

[a]$t = r/\sqrt{(1 - r^2)/(n - 2)}$

correlation coefficient will be close to zero. Finally, when your variables are negatively correlated (inversely related), the correlation coefficient will be negative.

Pearson *r* and the Definition of Correlation

If you want to compute a Pearson *r*, you can use a computer, a calculator, or either of the following two formulas.[13]

1. $$r = \frac{\Sigma(X - X) \times (Y - Y)}{\Sigma(X - X)^2 \times (Y - Y)^2}$$

2. $$r = \frac{N \times (\Sigma(X \times Y)) - (\Sigma X) \times (\Sigma Y)}{\sqrt{(N \times \Sigma X^2 - (\Sigma X)^2 \times (N \times \Sigma Y^2 - (\Sigma Y)^2)}}$$

At this point, however, we do not want you to focus on how to compute the Pearson *r*. Instead, we want you to focus on understanding the logic behind the Pearson *r*. Basically, there are two ways to think about that logic: (1) in terms of the definition of correlation, and (2) in terms of a scatterplot of the data.

As you know, the correlation coefficient is a number that describes the relationship between two variables. If the variables are positively correlated, then, when one variable is above average, the other is usually above average. In addition, when one variable is below average, the other tends to be below average. If the variables are negatively correlated, the reverse happens: When one is above average, the other is usually below average.

To see how the Pearson *r* mathematically matches that description, suppose that we have a pair of scores for each of 20 students: (a) one score telling us whether that student scored above or below average on a vocabulary test that was based on words that a teacher had just tried to teach, and (b) a second score telling us whether that student scored above or below average on a test of picking up on nonverbal cues.[14] To see whether student learning is correlated with sensitivity to nonverbal cues, we go through a two-step process.

First, we add one point for each student whose pair of scores match and subtract a point for each student whose two scores do not match.[15] Given that we have 20 participants, our total could range from −20 (mismatches between the pairs of scores for all 20 participants) to 20 (matches between the pairs of scores for all 20 participants).

Second, to give us a number that could range from −1 to +1, we divide our total by 20 (the number of participants). This number would be a crude index of correlation.

If most students' scores on the one test correspond with their scores on the other test, our correlation will be positive. If all students' scores on one test correspond to their scores on the other test, as in the case below, our correlation would equal +1.

---

[13]*X* refers to scores on the first variable, *Y* refers to scores on the second variable, and *N* refers to the number of pairs of scores. For step-by-step directions for computing Pearson *r*, see Appendix D.

[14]For a published example of a Pearson *r* calculated on these two variables, see Bernieri, 1990.

[15]Mathematically, we could do this by first giving each student either a "+1" if they were above average on the test of definitions or a "−1" if they were below average. Then, we would give them either a "+1" if they were above average on the reading nonverbal cues test or a "−1" if they were below average. Finally, we would multiply each person's scores together. If the person scored the same on both tests, the result would be +1 (because +1 × +1 = 1 as does −1 × −1). If the person scored differently on the two tests, the result would be −1 (because +1 × −1 = −1).

	SENSITIVITY TO NONVERBAL CUES	
Words Learned	**Below Average**	**Above Average**
Below Average	10	0
Above Average	0	10

Conversely, if participants who are above average on one variable are usually below average on the other variable, we will end up with a negative correlation. Indeed, if everyone who is high on one variable is also low on the other, as is the case below, our correlation index would equal −1.

	SENSITIVITY TO NONVERBAL CUES	
Words Learned	**Below Average**	**Above Average**
Below Average	0	10
Above Average	10	0

Finally, consider the case below in which there is no relationship between the variables. In that case, the mismatches (−1's) cancel out the matches (+1's), so the sum of the points is 0, and our coefficient will end up being 0.

	SENSITIVITY TO NONVERBAL CUES	
Words Learned	**Below Average**	**Above Average**
Below Average	5	5
Above Average	5	5

Mathematically, the Pearson *r* is a little more complicated than what we have described. However, if you understand our description, you understand the basic logic behind the Pearson *r*.

Pearson *r* and the Scatterplot

We have discussed how the Pearson *r* produces a number that is consistent with either a verbal description or a table of the data. Now, we will show how the Pearson *r* produces a number that is consistent with a graph of the data.

Pearson *r* could be estimated by drawing a straight line through the points in your scatterplot. If the line slopes upward, the correlation is positive. If the line slopes upward and every point in your scatterplot fits on that line, you have a perfect positive relationship, reflected by a +1.00 correlation. Usually, however, there are points that are not on the line. For each point that is not on the line, the correlation coefficient is made closer to zero by subtracting a value from the coefficient. The farther the point is from the line, the larger the value that is subtracted. Once all the misfit points are accounted for, you end up with the correlation coefficient.

If, on the other hand, the line that fits the points slopes downward, the correlation is negative. If every point fits on that line, you have a perfect negative relationship, reflected by a −1.00 correlation. However, perfect negative relationships are rare. Most of the time, many points will not be on that line. For each point that is not on the line, the correlation coefficient is made closer to zero by adding a value to the coefficient. The farther the point is from the line, the larger the value that is added. After all the misfit points are accounted for, you end up with the correlation coefficient.

As we have just discussed, the correlation coefficient describes how well the points on the scatterplot fit a straight *line.* That is, the correlation coefficient describes the nature of the *linear* relationship between your variables. But what if the relationship between your variables is not described by a straight line, but by a curved line? For example, suppose the relationship between your variables was *nonlinear,* like the nonlinear relationship depicted in Figure 7-8.

The fact that the correlation coefficient examines only the degree to which variables are linearly related is not as severe a drawback as you may think. Why? First, totally nonlinear relationships among variables are rare. Second, even if you encounter a nonlinear relationship, you would know that you had such a relationship by looking at your scatterplot. That is, you would notice that the points on your scatterplot fit a nonlinear pattern, such as a U-shaped curve.

If there is a linear relationship between your variables, the correlation coefficient can tell you how strong this relationship is—if you know what to look for and what to ignore. Ignore the sign of the coefficient. The *sign* tells you only the *kind* of relationship you have (positive or negative). The sign does not tell you how strong the relationship is.

To get a general idea of how strong the relationship is, look at how far the correlation coefficient is from zero. The further the correlation coefficient is from zero (no relationship), the stronger the relationship. Thus, because $-.4$ is further from 0 than $+.2$, a $-.4$ correlation indicates a stronger relationship than a $+.2$ correlation.

The Coefficient of Determination

To get a better idea of the strength of relationship between two variables, square the correlation coefficient to get the **coefficient of determination:** an index of the degree to which knowing participants' scores on one variable helps in predicting what their scores will be on the other variable; the percentage of variance in the predicted scores that is accounted for by the predictor. When we square the correlation coefficients from our previous example, we find that the coefficient of determination for the relationship described by a $-.4$ correlation (.16) is much bigger than the coefficient of determination for the relationship described by a .2 correlation (.04). In journal articles, researchers might describe the first relationship by saying that 16% ($-.4^2 = .16 = 16\%$) of the variability in scores was explained (accounted) for by the relationship between the variables and might describe the second relationship by saying that the relationship explained only 4% ($.2^2 = .04 = 4\%$) of the variance.

Note how small a coefficient of determination of .04 is. It is close to the lowest possible value: 0 (knowing participants' scores on one variable is absolutely no help in predicting what their scores will be on the other variable; the predictor accounts for 0% of the variation in the other variable). It is far away from the highest possible value: $+1.00$ (knowing participants' scores on one variable allows you to know exactly what their scores will be on the other variable; the predictor accounts for 100% of the variation in the other variable). Note that correlation coefficients between $-.2$ and $+.2$ will produce coefficients of determination of .04 or below. Thus, if the correlation between your predictor and outcome variables is between $-.2$ and $+.2$, basing your predictions on your predictor will be only slightly better than simply predicting that everyone will score at the mean.

Determining Whether a Correlation Coefficient Is Statistically Significant

Occasionally, you may want to describe—but not generalize from—a particular sample. If you just want to describe the relationship between self-esteem and grade-point average in one particular class during one particular term, scatterplots, correlation coefficients, and coefficients of determination are all you need.

Most of the time, however, you are interested in generalizing the results obtained in a limited sample to a larger population. You know what happened in this sample, but you want to know what would happen in other samples.

To generalize your results to a larger population, you first need a random sample of that population. If you want to generalize results based on observing a few students in your class to all the students in your class, the participants you examine should be a random sample of class members. If you want to generalize the results based on measuring a few people to all Americans, you must have measured a random sample of Americans. If you want to generalize results based on observing two rats for an hour a day to all the times that the rats are awake, the times you observe the rats must be a random sample from the rats' waking hours.[16]

Random samples, however, are not perfect samples. Even with a random sample, you are going to have sampling error. For example, suppose you studied a random sample of sophomores at your school and found a correlation of −.30 between grade-point average and self-esteem. Clearly, you found a negative correlation in your random sample. However, you can't say that if you had studied all sophomores at your school, you would have obtained a negative correlation coefficient.

To convince yourself that what happens in a sample does not necessarily mirror what happens in the population, you could conduct the following study. Find three people. Have each person flip a coin one time. Record each person's height and the number of "heads" (0 or 1) the person flipped. Do this for 10 different "samples" of three individuals. Then, graph each sample individually. Even though there is no reliable relationship between a person's height and how many "heads" he or she will flip, some of your graphs will reveal a positive correlation, whereas others will reveal a negative correlation.

As you have seen, even if the two variables are not related, they will appear to be related in some samples. That is, *a relationship that exists in a particular sample may not exist in the population.* Consequently, if you observe a relationship in your sample, you will want to know if you have observed (a) a real pattern that is characteristic of the population or (b) a mirage caused by random sampling error alone.

Fortunately, there is a way to determine whether what is true of your sample is true of the population: Use inferential statistics. Inferential statistics will allow you to determine how likely it is that the relationship you saw in your sample could be due to random error. Specifically, inferential statistics allow you to ask the question: "If there is no relationship between these variables in the population, how likely is it that I would get a correlation coefficient this large in this particular random sample?"

If the answer to this question is "not very likely," you can be relatively confident that the correlation coefficient in the population is not zero. Therefore, you would conclude that the variables are related. To use proper terminology, you would conclude that your correlation coefficient is *significantly* (reliably) different from zero (see Figure 7-9).

---

[16]Many researchers do not randomly sample from a population, but they still generalize their results. How? They argue that their sample could be considered a random sample of an unknown population. Then, they use statistics to determine whether the results are due to sampling error or whether the results hold in the larger population. If their results are statistically significant, they argue the results hold in this unspecified population. (The "unspecified population" might be "participants I would study at my institution.")

| Figure 7-9 | **Necessary Conditions for Producing Generalizable Results** |

Precisely which test you use to determine if a correlation coefficient is statistically different from zero depends on which kind of correlation coefficient you have (see Table 7-4). However, regardless of which test you use, the test will determine how unlikely it is that your sample's correlation coefficient came from a population in which the coefficient between those variables was zero. To determine whether your correlation coefficient comes from such a population, the test will take advantage of two facts about random samples from populations in which the correlation is zero.

First, if the population correlation coefficient is zero, the sample's correlation coefficient will tend to be near zero. Consequently, *the further the sample's correlation coefficient is from zero, the less likely the population coefficient is zero.* Thus, a correlation coefficient of .8 is more likely to be significantly different from zero than a correlation coefficient of .2.

Second, if the population correlation coefficient is zero, the larger the sample, the more likely that the sample's correlation coefficient will be near zero. Therefore, *the larger the sample, the more likely that a nonzero correlation coefficient indicates that the variables are related in the population.* Consequently, a correlation coefficient of .30 is more likely to be significantly different from zero if it comes from a sample of 100 observations than if it comes from a sample of 10 observations.

Interpreting Significant Correlation Coefficients

If a correlation coefficient is significantly different from zero, it should mean that there is a relationship between your variables. That is, the relationship between your variables, rather than being due to random error, is a reliable relationship (see Table 7-5). Note that we have *not* said that statistically significant results

- Have external validity
- Allow you to make cause–effect statements
- Always indicate a reliable relationship
- Are large

Significant Results May Not Have External Validity

A significant correlation indicates that the relationship you observed probably also exists in the population from which you randomly sampled. So, in your random sample of everyone in your country, if you find a significant correlation, you can generalize your results to your population—everyone in your country. If, however, your random sample is of students in your class—or if you didn't use a random sample—significant results do not necessarily generalize to a larger population.

Table 7-5	The Different Meanings of Statistical Significance	
QUESTION ASKED ABOUT A STATISTICALLY SIGNIFICANT RESULT	ANSWER IF YOU CONDUCT A CORRELATIONAL STUDY	ANSWER IF YOU CONDUCT AN EXPERIMENT
Are the variables related?	Yes	Yes
Do we know whether the predictor variable *caused* changes in the criterion variable?	No	Yes 1. The experimental design guaranteed that the treatment came before the change in the criterion (dependent) variable. 2. The experimental design also guaranteed that the treatment was the only systematic difference between treatment conditions. Thus, the relationships between the variables could not be due to some third factor.

Significant Results Do Not Allow You to Make Cause–Effect Statements

Ideally, statistical significance allows you to say that two variables are really related: The relationship you observed is not merely the result of a coincidence. However, even if you know that two variables are related, you do not know that they are causally related. As we said earlier in this chapter, to establish a cause–effect relationship between two variables, you must do much more than establish that your variables are statistically related.

For example, to infer that self-esteem caused low grade-point averages, you would have to show not only that self-esteem and grade-point average are related, but also that:

1. The low self-esteem students had low self-esteem before they got low grades, whereas the high self-esteem students had high self-esteem before they got high grades.

2. No other differences between your high and low self-esteem individuals could account for this relationship (there were no differences between groups in terms of parental encouragement, IQ, ability to delay gratification, etc.).

Significant Results May Be False Alarms

As we've seen, significant results in correlational research do not mean that changes in one variable *caused* a change in the other. At best, significant results mean only that both variables are correlated. However, all too often, significant results don't even prove that two variables are correlated.

To understand why they don't, suppose that a researcher is trying to determine whether two variables are correlated. The researcher uses the conventional $p < .05$ significance level, suggesting that a significant result means that if there is no relationship between these variables in the population, the probability (p) of obtaining a correlation coefficient this large or larger in this particular random sample is less than 5 in 100. Suppose further that, in

Figure 7-10

When People Do Multiple Tests, There May Be Something Fishy About Significant Results

What they are implying   What they may have done

reality, the variables aren't correlated. What are the chances that the researcher will obtain significant results?

You might be tempted to say "about 5%." You would be correct—if the researcher had conducted only one statistical test. However, because correlational data are often easy to obtain, the researcher might correlate hundreds of variables with hundreds of other variables. If the researcher does hundreds of statistical tests, many of these tests will be significant by chance alone.[17] Put another way, if the researcher uses a $p = .05$ level of significance and does 100 tests, the researcher should expect to obtain 5 significant results, even if none of the variables were related. Thus, if you aren't careful, disciplined, and ethical, you will "find" relationships that are really statistical errors (see Figure 7-10). Therefore, we urge you to resist temptation to have the computer calculate every possible correlation coefficient and then pick out the ones that are significant. Instead, decide which correlation coefficients relate to your hypotheses and test to see whether those correlation coefficients differ from zero.

If you are doing more than one statistical test, there are at least two things you can do to avoid mistaking a coincidence for a correlation. One option is to make your significance level more conservative than the traditional $p < .05$ level. For example, use a $p < .01$ or even a $p < .001$ level. A second option is to repeat your study with another random sample of participants to see whether the correlation coefficients that were significantly different from zero in the first study are still significant in a second study.

---

[17]The exception is if they use a sophisticated multivariate statistical test that controls for making multiple comparisons.

Significant Results May Be Tiny and Insignificant:
Bigger than Nothing Isn't Everything

Even if you do establish that the relationship between the variables is reliably different from zero, that does not mean that the relationship is large or important. If you had enough observations, a tiny correlation of .02 could be statistically significant.

In many cases, the issue is not whether there is a relationship, but whether the relationship is large enough. Put another way, the question you should be asking is often not "Are they completely unrelated?" but rather "Are they strongly related?" For example, if you have two people rating the same behavior, the question usually isn't "Do the raters agree at all?" but rather "To what extent do the raters agree?" Thus, experts would not be reassured by a correlation between raters of .10 that was significantly different from zero. Instead, they would usually want correlation of at least .85.

Similarly, if you correlate your measure of a construct with another measure of the same construct, the question isn't whether the correlation is greater than zero but rather whether the correlation is strong enough to suggest that the two measures are measuring the same thing: You're not trying to show that there is some overlap between what the two tests measure; you are trying to show that there is considerable overlap. A correlation of .20 between two measures does not suggest that the two measures are measuring the same thing; a correlation of .80 does.

Finally, if you find a significant correlation between responses on two questionnaires you handed out, few psychologists will be impressed. This is because if both your measures are affected to any degree by the same response bias, scores on the measure will correlate to some extent because of response bias. For example, if giving socially acceptable answers tends to increase scores on both your scales, people who are more likely to give such answers will tend to score higher than the other people on both measures. Likewise, if an individual tends to agree with items, this may make their responses on one questionnaire similar to their responses on another. Thus, if you find a small correlation between two questionnaires, the correlation may be due to both measures being vulnerable to the same response bias rather than to the measures assessing two related variables.

In short, do not just look at whether a correlation is significantly different from zero. Instead, also look at the correlation's size, especially its coefficient of determination. Also, consider testing whether your correlation coefficient is significantly (reliably) greater than a certain meaningful value (e.g., .60) rather than whether it is greater than zero.

Interpreting Null (Nonsignificant) Correlation Coefficients

If your results are not statistically significant, it means that you failed to show that any correlations you observed were due to anything other than random error. It does not mean your variables are unrelated—it means only that you have failed to establish that they were related. If there is a relationship, why would you fail to find it? There are four main reasons.

First, you may not have had enough observations. Even if you observed a fairly strong relationship in your sample, unless your sample is big enough, it's hard to say that your observed relationship is not a fluke.

Second, you may have failed to find a significant relationship because of **restriction of range:** You sampled from a population in which everyone is similar on one of the variables. Restriction of range is a problem because to say that both variables vary together, you need both variables to vary. If both variables don't vary, you end up with correlations of zero. For example, suppose you were looking at the relationship between IQ and grade-point average, but everyone in your sample scored between 125 and 130 on the IQ test. In this case, the correlation between IQ and grade-point average would be pretty small; consequently, the correlation might not be significant. If your participants' IQs had ranged from 85 to 185, however, you would probably have a sizable and statistically significant correlation between IQ and GPA.

Third, you may fail to find a significant relationship because you had insensitive measures. By preventing you from seeing how one variable varies, an insensitive measure also prevents you from seeing how that variable covaries with another variable.

Fourth, your variables may be related in a nonlinear way. This is a problem because your statistical tests are most sensitive to detecting straight-line (linear) relationships. Fortunately, you can easily tell whether you have a nonlinear relationship by looking at a scatterplot of your data. If you can draw a straight line through the points of your scatterplot, you don't have a nonlinear relationship. If, on the other hand, a graph of your data revealed a nonlinear relationship, such as a definite U-shaped curve, you would know that a conventional correlation coefficient underestimates the strength of the relationship between your variables.

Nonlinear Relationships Between Two Variables

What if the scatterplot suggests that your variables are related in a nonlinear way? Or, suppose that you hypothesized that there was a nonlinear (curvilinear) relationship between two variables, such as temperature and aggression. That is, suppose you don't believe that with each degree the temperature rises, aggression increases. Instead, you think there is some curvilinear relationship (see Figure 7-11). You might think that temperature only increases aggression after the temperature goes above 70 degrees Fahrenheit (21°C), or you might think that when the temperature goes over 90 degrees (32°C), aggression declines.

Other cases in which you might look for—and be likely to find—a curvilinear relationship include:

- Accuracy of married couples in reading each other's minds increases during the first few years of marriage and then decreases (Thomas, Fletcher, & Lange, 1997).
- Happiness increases rapidly as income increases until income is above the poverty level, above which point there is little to no relationship between income and happiness (Helliwell, 2003).
- Marital satisfaction is highest among couples who have the most similar personality profiles (Luo & Klohnen, 2005).

To test these kinds of curvilinear hypotheses, experts will often use a type of correlational analysis that uses each person's actual scores.[18] However, you might test for these relationships by using a less sensitive test that looks for differences between group means. Specifically, you could use a more flexible version of the *t* test: analysis of variance (ANOVA). (To see the similarities between the *t* test, ANOVA, and determining whether a correlation is statistically significant, see Box 7-1).

To set up your ANOVA, you would divide your participants into three or more groups based on their scores on your predictor. For example, if you were studying self-esteem's relationship to GPA, you might divide participants into three groups: (1) a low self-esteem group, (2) moderate self-esteem group, and (3) a high self-esteem group. Then, you would compare the means of the three groups. If there was a curvilinear relationship, you might

---

[18]The technique is called polynomial regression. Normal regression, called linear regression, enters values on the predictor and looks for the best straight line that can fit the outcome variable. By also adding in the square (the value to the second power) of each value on the predictor to the equation, a researcher can look at the best line with one bend in it that can fit the data. By also adding the cube of each value of the predictor (the value to the third power), a researcher can look at the best line with 2 bends in it that can fit the data. By taking predictors to even higher powers, researchers can see how well even more complex curves fit the data.

Figure 7-11	**Two Potential Nonlinear Relationships Between Temperature and Aggression**

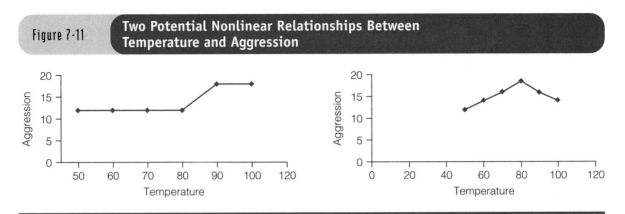

BOX 7-1	**The Similarities Between a *t* Test, an ANOVA, and a Test to Determine Whether a Correlation Coefficient Is Significantly Above Zero**

When you have only two groups, doing a *t* test, an *F* test, and an analysis of correlation is essentially the same. Thus, in the simple experiment, the three procedures are quite similar. In all three cases, you are seeing whether there is a relationship between the treatment and the dependent variable—that is, whether the treatment and the dependent variable covary.

The only difference is in how you measure the extent to which the treatment and dependent measure covary. In the *t* test, you use the difference between means of the two groups as your measure of covariation; in the *F* test, you use a variance between means of the two groups as the measure of covariation; and in testing the significance of a correlation, you use the correlation between the treatment and the dependent variable as the measure of covariation. Consequently, regardless of which technique you use to analyze the results of a simple experiment, significant results will allow you to make cause–effect statements. Furthermore, regardless of which technique you use to analyze the results of a correlational study, significant results will not allow you to make cause–effect statements.

To show you that the three analyses are the same, we have done these three analyses of the same data.

t TEST ANALYSIS

GROUP	N	MEAN	df	t	PROBABILITY[a]
Group 1	59	9.429	115	.87	.3859
Group 2	58	8.938			

Standard error of the difference = .565

$$t = \frac{9.429 - 8.938}{.565} = \frac{.491}{.565} = .87$$

[a]Probability (often abbreviated as *p*) refers to the chances of finding a relationship in your sample that is as large as the one you found if the two variables were really unrelated in the population. Thus, the smaller *p* is, the less likely it is that the relationship observed in your sample is just a fluke—and the more likely it is that the variables really are related in the population.

ANALYSIS OF VARIANCE

SOURCE	df	SUM OF SQUARES	MS	F VALUE	PROBABILITY
Treatment	1	4.155	4.155	.758	.3859
Error	115	630.768	5.485		

CORRELATIONAL ANALYSIS

COUNT	R	PROBABILITY
117	.081	.3859[b]

[b]Note that the probability (*p*) value is exactly the same, no matter what the analysis. That is, our *p* is .3859 whether we do a *t* test, *F* test, or a correlational analysis. The *t* that led to this probability value is 0.87, just as it was when we calculated the *t* between group means. However, because we were testing a correlation, we used a different formula. Applying that formula ($t = [r \times \sqrt{(N-2)}]/ \sqrt{(1 - [r \times r])}$) to our data led to the following computations:

$$t = \frac{.081 \times \sqrt{115}}{\sqrt{.993}} = \frac{.868}{.996} = 0.87$$

| Figure 7-12 | A Curvilinear Relationship Between Self-Esteem and GPA |

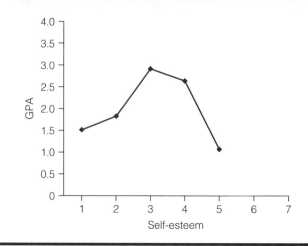

find that the group with moderate self-esteem had higher GPAs than the groups with either low or high self-esteem (see Figure 7-12).

To find out whether the curvilinear pattern you observed was reliable, you would first do an ANOVA. Using a computer program or statistical calculator, you would enter each person's group number (a "1" if they were in the low self-esteem group, a "2" if they were in the moderate self-esteem group, or a "3" if they were in the high self-esteem group) as the predictor and each person's GPA as the dependent measure. If your ANOVA was statistically significant, you would know that there was a relationship between self-esteem and GPA. Then, you could do a follow-up test to see whether the relationship was curvilinear by following the instructions in Table E-4 in Appendix E.

Relationships Involving More Than Two Variables

You can also use ANOVA to look at hypotheses involving two or more predictors. For example, with ANOVA, you could look at how self-esteem and gender together predict grade-point average. Specifically, an ANOVA would allow you to compare the grade-point averages of (1) women with low self-esteem, (2) women with high self-esteem, (3) men with low self-esteem, and (4) men with high self-esteem. By doing this analysis, you might find that high self-esteem is related to high grade-point averages for women, but that high self-esteem is related to low grade-point averages for men. In such a case, gender would be a **moderator variable:** a variable that specifies when certain relationships between other variables will hold; a variable whose presence modfies (strengthens, weakens, reverses) the relationship between two other variables.

If you want to look for moderating variables, you do not have to use ANOVA. Instead, you can use multiple regression. In multiple regression, the computer uses a few predictors (in this case, gender, self-esteem, and a variable that represents the combined effects of both variables) to try to predict participants' scores on the dependent measure. For more information on multiple regression, see Appendix D.

ANOVA and multiple regression are similar. Indeed, if you have a computer do an ANOVA for you, the devious computer will probably actually do a multiple regression and then just format the output to make it look like it did an ANOVA analysis. Because ANOVA is similar to multiple regression, many people do an ANOVA with correlational data. However, with most correlational data, multiple regression is a more powerful technique than ANOVA.

Multiple regression is more powerful than ANOVA for the same reason a test of the significance of a correlation coefficient is more powerful than a *t* test based on a median split: Multiple regression uses each individual's actual score on the predictor rather than ANOVA's trick of giving everyone in the group the same score. For example, in multiple regression, if someone scores 17 on the self-esteem test, that's the score that is put in the analysis. In ANOVA, on the other hand, you artificially create groups (e.g., "a low self-esteem group" and a "high self-esteem group") and give everyone in a group the same score on the predictor (e.g., all "lows" get a 1 on self-esteem, and all "highs" get a 2). The costs of lumping together participants into arbitrary groups is that you lose information about the extent to which participants differ on your predictors—and that loss of information, in turn, causes you to lose power (see Table 7-6 for a summary of the advantages and disadvantages of using ANOVA to analyze the results of correlational research).

Table 7-6	Advantages and Disadvantages of Using ANOVA to Analyze the Results From a Correlational Study

ADVANTAGES

- Allows you to perform two important analyses fairly easily.
  1. You can do more than look at the simple relationships between two variables. Instead, you can look at the relationship among three or more variables at once.
  2. You could determine whether the relationship between variables is nonlinear.

- You can minimize the problem of losing detail by dividing scores into more groups. That is, you are not limited to just comparing the top half versus the bottom half. Instead, you could compare the top fifth versus the second fifth, versus the third fifth, versus the fourth fifth, versus the bottom fifth. Because you would be entering more detailed information into your analysis, you would have reasonable power.

- Provides a convenient way to analyze data.

- Is a familiar way to analyze data.

DISADVANTAGES

- You have less power than testing the statistical correlation coefficient because ANOVA doesn't use actual scores. Instead, it uses much less detailed information. For example, if you use a two-level ANOVA, you are recording only whether the score is in the top half or the bottom half of the distribution. Furthermore, you can examine both complex relationships among variables and nonlinear relationships without ANOVA.

- You still do not have as much detail and power as if you had used participants' actual scores.

- It may not be so convenient if you have an unequal number of participants in each group. In that case, you would have what is called an unbalanced ANOVA. Many computer programs can't accurately compute statistics for an unbalanced ANOVA.

- Because it is a conventional way to analyze experimental data, people may falsely conclude that significant results mean that one variable causes changes in the other.

Concluding Remarks

In this chapter, you have been introduced to the logic of descriptive research. You have seen that although descriptive research cannot answer "why" (cause–effect) questions, it can answer "what," "when," and "where" questions. Furthermore, you have seen that such questions can be grounded in theory and can involve more than simple relationships between two variables. Although you have learned a great deal about descriptive research, you have not learned about the most common method of doing descriptive research: asking questions. Therefore, the next chapter is devoted to showing you how to conduct surveys.

SUMMARY

1. Descriptive research allows you to describe behavior accurately. The key to descriptive research is to measure and record your variables accurately using a representative sample.

2. Although descriptive research cannot tell you whether one variable causes changes in another, it may suggest cause–effect (causal) hypotheses that you could test in an experiment.

3. Description is an important goal of science. Description also paves the way for prediction.

4. Ex post facto research uses data that you collected before you came up with your hypothesis.

5. Archival research uses data collected and sometimes coded by someone else.

6. With both ex post facto and archival research, data may not have been measured, collected, or coded in a way appropriate for testing your hypothesis.

7. Observational methods are used in both correlational and experimental research.

8. In both naturalistic observation and participant observation, the researcher must be careful that the observer does not affect the observed and that coding is objective.

9. Using preexisting, validated tests in your correlational research may increase the construct validity of your study. As with all research, the external validity of testing research depends on the representativeness of your sample.

10. Using a scatterplot to graph your correlational data will tell you the direction of the relationship (positive or negative) and give you an idea of the strength of the relationship.

11. Correlational coefficients give you one number that represents the direction of the relationship (positive or negative). These numbers range from -1.00 to $+1.00$.

12. A positive correlation between two variables indicates that if a participant scores high on one of the variables, the participant will probably also score high on the other.

13. A negative correlation between two variables indicates that if a participant scores high on one of the variables, the participant will probably score low on the other variable.

14. A zero correlation between two variables indicates there is no relationship between how a participant scores on one variable and how that participant will score on another variable. The further a correlation coefficient is away from zero, the stronger the relationship. Thus, a $-.4$ correlation is stronger than a $+.3$.

15. By squaring the correlation coefficient, you get the coefficient of determination, which tells you the strength of the relationship between two variables. The coefficient of determination can range from 0 (no relationship) to 1 (perfect relationship). Note that the coefficient of determination of both a $+1$ and a -1 correlation coefficient is 1.

16. If your results are based on a random sample, you may want to use inferential statistics to analyze your data.

17. Remember, statistical significance means only that your results can be generalized to the population from which you randomly sampled. Statistical significance does *not* mean that you have found a cause–effect relationship.

18. Beware of doing too many tests of significance. Remember, if you do 100 tests and use a .05 level of significance, 5 of those tests might be significant by chance alone.

19. You may obtain null (nonsignificant) results even though your variables are related. Common culprits are insufficient number of observations, nonlinear relationships, restriction of range, and insensitive measures.

KEY TERMS

illusory correlation *(p. 169)*

ex post facto research *(p. 170)*

archival data *(p. 171)*

content analysis *(p. 173)*

instrumentation bias *(p. 175)*

nonreactive measure *(p. 176)*

laboratory observation *(p. 177)*

naturalistic observation *(p. 178)*

participant observation *(p. 178)*

standard deviation *(p. 181)*

frequency distribution *(p. 181)*

mode *(p. 181)*

median *(p. 183)*

95% confidence interval *(p. 184)*

standard error of the mean *(p. 184)*

median split *(p. 187)*

scatterplot *(p. 187)*

positive correlation *(p. 188)*

negative correlation *(p. 189)*

zero correlation *(p. 189)*

correlation coefficient *(p. 194)*

coefficient of determination *(p. 194)*

restriction of range *(p. 199)*

moderator variable *(p. 202)*

EXERCISES

1. Steinberg and Dornbusch (1991) found that there is a positive correlation between class-cutting and hours of week that adolescents work. In addition, they find a negative correlation between grade-point average and number of hours worked.
   a. In your own words, describe what the relationship is between class-cutting and hours of week that adolescents work.
   b. In your own words, describe what the relationship is between grade-point average and hours of week that adolescents work.
   c. What conclusions can you draw about the *effects* of work? Why?
   d. If you had been analyzing their data, what analysis would you use? Why?

2. Steinberg and Dornbusch (1991) also reported that the correlation between hours of employment and interest in school was statistically significant. Specifically, they reported that $r(3,989) = -.06$, $p < .001$. [Note that the $r(3,989)$ means that they had 3,989 participants in their study.] Interpret this finding.

3. Brown (1991) found that a measure of aerobic fitness correlated +.28 with a self-report measure of how much people exercised. He also found that the measure of aerobic fitness correlated $-.41$ with resting heart rate. Is resting heart rate or self-report of exercise more closely related to the aerobic fitness measure?

4. In the same study, gender was coded as 1 = male, 2 = female. The correlation between gender and aerobic fitness was $-.58$, which was statistically significant at the $p < .01$ level.
   a. In this study, were men or women more fit?
   b. What would the correlation have been if gender had been coded as 1 = female and 2 = male?
   c. From the information here, can you conclude that one gender tends to be more aerobically fit than the other? Why or why not?

5. Suppose you wanted to see whether men differed from women in terms of the self-descriptions they put in personal ads. How would you get your sample of ads? How would you code your ads? That is, what would your content analysis scheme look like?

6. Suppose that a physician looked at 26 instances of crib death in a certain town and found that some of

these deaths were due to parents suffocating their children. As a result, the physician concluded that most crib deaths in this country are due not to problems in brain development, but to parental abuse and neglect. What problems do you have with the physician's conclusions?

7. Researchers began by looking at how a sample of 5-year-olds were treated by their parents. Thirty-six years later, when the participants were 41-year-olds, the study examined the degree to which these individuals were socially accomplished. The investigators then looked at the relationship between childrearing practices when the child was 5 and how socially accomplished the person was at 41 (Franz, McClelland, & Weinberger, 1991). They concluded that having a warm and affectionate father or mother was significantly associated with "adult social accomplishment."

a. What advantages does this prospective study have over a study that asks 41-year-olds to reflect back on their childhood?

b. How would you measure adult social accomplishment?

c. How would you measure parental warmth? Why?

d. Assume, for the moment, that the study clearly established a relationship between parenting practices and adult social accomplishment. Could we then conclude that parenting practices account for (cause) adult social accomplishment? Why or why not?

e. Imagine that the researchers had failed to find a significant relationship between the variables of adult social accomplishment and parental warmth. What might have caused their results to fail to reach significance?

WEB RESOURCES

1. Go to the Chapter 7 section of the book's student website and
   a. Look over the concept map of the key terms.
   b. Test yourself on the key terms.
   c. Take the Chapter 7 Practice Quiz.

2. Get a better sense of what descriptive research is like by using the "Participate in a Descriptive Study" link.

3. Become more comfortable with correlation coefficients by:
   a. Going through the "Correlator" tutorial.
   b. Computing correlation coefficients using a statistical calculator, accessible from the "Statistical Calculator" link.

4. Get a better sense of the coefficient of determination by clicking on the "Coefficient of Determination" link.

INFOTRAC COLLEGE EDITION EXPLORATIONS

1. To read a very clever archival study by Coulumb and Pfister (1998) about aggression in sports, do an InfoTrac College Edition keyword search using the phrase "archival research and psychology."

2. To see how a variety of descriptive methods have been used to study sex differences in smiling, do an InfoTrac College Edition keyword search using the phrase "sex and smiling."

3. To understand the challenges of trying to make cause–effect statements from correlational evidence, do an InfoTrac College Edition keyword search using the phrase "correlation and causation and lead" to find Needleman and Gatsonis's (1990) meta-analysis of studies examining the relationship between lead exposure and IQ.

8

Survey Research

A fool can ask more questions in an hour than a wise man can answer in seven years.

—*English Proverb*

OUTLINE

Overview

If you want to know *why* people do what they do or think what they think, you should use an *experimental* design. If, on the other hand, you want to know *what* people are thinking, feeling, or doing, you should use a *nonexperimental* design, such as a **survey.**

To conduct a successful survey, you must meet three objectives. First, you must know what your research hypotheses are so that you know what you want to measure. Second, your questionnaire, test, or interview must accurately measure the thoughts, feelings, or behaviors that you want to measure. Third, you must be able to generalize your results to a certain, specific group. This group, called a **population,** could be anything from all U.S. citizens to all employees at a local company.

Survey research that fails to meet these three objectives will be flawed. Thus, there are three ways survey research can go wrong.

First, survey research may be flawed because the researchers did not know what they wanted to find out. If you don't know what you're looking for, you probably won't find it. Instead, you will probably be overwhelmed by irrelevant data.

Second, survey research may be flawed because the questionnaire, test, or interview measure has poor construct validity. This occurs when:

1. The questions demand knowledge that your respondents don't have.
2. By hinting at the answers the researcher wants to hear, the questions invite respondents to lie.
3. The respondents misinterpret the questions.
4. The researcher misinterprets or miscodes respondents' answers.

Third, survey research may have little external validity because the people who were questioned do not represent the target population. For example, the results of a survey will have little external validity if the sample of people surveyed was biased.

As you can see, there is more to survey research than asking some people some questions that you jotted down. Instead, survey research, like all research, requires careful planning. You have to determine whether the survey design is appropriate for your research problem. Then, decide what questions you are going to ask, why you are going to ask those questions, to whom you are going to ask those questions, how you are going to ask those questions, and how you are going to analyze the answers to those questions.

Unfortunately, few people engage in the careful planning necessary to conduct sound survey research. Consequently, even though the survey is by far the most commonly used research method, it is also the most commonly abused. By reading this chapter, you can become one of the few people who knows how to conduct sound and ethical survey research.

Questions to Ask Before Doing Survey Research

The most obvious—but least asked—question in survey research is, "Should I use a survey?" To answer this question correctly, you must answer these five questions:

1. What is my hypothesis?
2. Will I know what to do with the data after the survey is finished?
3. Am I interested only in describing and predicting behavior, or do I want to make cause–effect statements?

4. Can I trust respondents' answers?

5. Do my results apply only to those people who responded to the survey, or do the results apply to a larger group?

What Is Your Hypothesis?

The first question to ask is, "What is my hypothesis?" Because good research begins with a good hypothesis, you might think that everyone would ask this question. Unfortunately, many inexperienced researchers try to write their survey questions without clear research questions. What they haven't learned is that you can't ask pertinent questions if you don't know what you want to ask. Therefore, before you write your first survey question, make sure you have a clear hypothesis on which to base your questions.

Do Your Questions Relate to Your Hypothesis?

Having a hypothesis doesn't do you much good unless you are disciplined enough to focus your questions on that hypothesis. If you don't focus your questions on your hypothesis, you may end up with an overwhelming amount of data—and still not find out what you wanted to know. For example, the now-defunct United States Football League (USFL) spent millions of dollars on surveys to find out whether it should be a spring or fall league. Despite the fact that it took more than 20 books to summarize the survey results, the surveys did not answer the research question ("Injury Quiets," 1984). So don't be seduced by how easy it is to ask a question. Instead, ask questions that address the purpose of your research.

Asking useful questions involves two steps. First, determine what analyses you plan to do *before* you administer the questionnaire. You can do this by constructing a table like Table 8-1, the table we used to help develop the survey displayed in Box 8-1. If you don't plan on doing any analyses involving responses to a specific question and the question serves no other purpose, you get rid of that question.

Second, with the remaining questions, imagine participants responding in a variety of ways. For example, you may graph the results you predict and results that are completely opposite of what you would predict. If you find that no pattern of answers to a question would give us useful information, eliminate that question. Thus, when doing a survey to test hypotheses, eliminate a question if you determine that no matter how participants answer the question, it wouldn't disprove any of your hypotheses. Similarly, when doing a survey to help an organization, eliminate a question if you determine that no matter how participants answer the question, it wouldn't change how that organization runs its business.

Do You Have a Cause–Effect Hypothesis?

If your questions focus on the research hypothesis, your survey will be able to address that hypothesis—as long as you do *not* have a cause–effect hypothesis. To do survey research, you must have a **descriptive hypothesis:** a hypothesis about a group's characteristics or about the correlations between variables. Usually, you will test one of the following four types of descriptive hypotheses.

First, you may do a survey to find out how many people have a certain characteristic or support a certain position. For example, a social worker may do a survey to find out what percentage of adolescents in the community have contemplated suicide. Similarly, a politician may do a survey to find out what percentage of the voters in her district support a certain position.

Table 8-1	Table to Determine Value of Including Questions From Box 8-1 in the Final Survey		
QUESTION NUMBER	**PURPOSE(S) OF QUESTION**	**PREDICTIONS REGARDING QUESTION**	**ANALYSES TO TEST PREDICTION**
1	**1.** Qualify. **2.** See whether sample reflects population.	Percent of instructors in sample will be the same as in the population.	Compare percentages of sample at each rank with school's report of percentages of total faculty at each rank.
2–3	Find out computer use without using a leading question.	**1.** Average computer use will be fewer than 5 hours per week. **2.** Computer users will be more sympathetic to students. **3.** Male faculty members will use computers more than female faculty members. **4.** Younger faculty members will use computers more than older faculty members.	**1.** Compute mean and confidence intervals. **2.** Correlate Question 3 with the sum of Questions 6–11. (Graph data to see whether there is a curvilinear relationship.) **3.** Correlate this question with Question 16. **4.** Correlate this question with Question 15.
4–5	Engage respondent and aid transition to next section.		
6–11	Scale to measure attitudes toward students.	**1.** Faculty members will have positive attitudes toward students. **2.** See predictions made under Questions 2–3.	**1.** Compute average and confidence intervals for Question 11 and for sum of scale (sum of items 6–11). See whether the mean is significantly above the sale's midpoint. **2.** See analyses described under Questions 2–3.
12–16	See if sample reflects the population.	Sample will reflect the population.	Compare sample's demographic characteristics against the demographic characteristics of the school's faculty.

Second, you may do a survey to develop a detailed profile of certain groups. You might use surveys to develop a list of differences between those who support gun control and those who don't or between those who like computers and those who don't.

Third, you may do a survey to examine the relationships between two or more variables. For example:

- Davis, Shaver, and Vernon (2004) used a survey to test the hypothesis that attachment styles (being securely attached, being anxiously attached, or being insecurely attached) are related to sex drive and to reasons for having sex.
- Haselton, Buss, Oubaid, and Angleitner (2005) used surveys to test the hypothesis that how upset people will be when their partner lies to them will be related both to the type of lie and to gender. Specifically, the researchers hypothesized that

BOX 8-1   Sample Telephone Survey

Hello, my name is ____. I am conducting a survey for my Research Design class at Bromo Tech. Your name was drawn as a part of a random sample of university faculty. I would greatly appreciate it if you would answer a few questions about your job and your use of computers. The survey should take only 5 minutes. You can skip any questions you wish and you can terminate the interview at any time. If you agree to participate, your answers will be kept confidential. Will you help me?

1. **What is your position at Bromo Tech?** (read as an open-ended question)

   _____ Instructor
   _____ Assistant Professor
   _____ Associate Professor
   _____ Full Professor
   _____ Other (If other, terminate interview)

2. **Do you use computers?**

   _____ Yes
   _____ No (put "0" in slot for Question 3, and skip to 4)

3. **How many hours a week do you estimate you use computers?** (read as open-ended question)

   _____ (Write hours, then put a check next to the appropriate box. If exact hours are not given, read categories and check appropriate box.)
   _____ < 1 hour
   _____ 2–4 hours
   _____ 5–9 hours
   _____ 10–14 hours
   _____ 15–19 hours
   _____ > 20 hours

Please indicate how much you agree or disagree with the following statements. State whether you strongly agree (SA), agree (A), are undecided (U), disagree (D), or strongly disagree (SD).

4. **Computers have made the job of the average professor less stressful.**

   SA   A   U   D   SD

5. **Computers have made the average student's life less stressful.**

   SA   A   U   D   SD

6. **College is stressful for students.**

   SA   A   U   D   SD

7. **Colleges need to spend more time on students' emotional development.**

   SA   A   U   D   SD

8. **Colleges need to spend more time on students' physical development.**

   SA   A   U   D   SD

9. **College students should be allowed to postpone tests when they are sick.**

   SA   A   U   D   SD

10. **College students work hard on their studies.**

    SA   A   U   D   SD

11. **I like college students.**

    SA   A   U   D   SD

Demographics

Finally, I have just a few more questions to ensure that we get opinions from a variety of people.

12. **How long have you been teaching at Bromo Tech?***

    _____ (Write years, then check the appropriate box. If exact years are not given, read categories and check appropriate box.)
    _____ 0–4 years
    _____ 5–9 years
    _____ 10–14 years
    _____ 15–19 years
    _____ 20 or more years

13. **What department do you teach in?**

    _____ Anthropology
    _____ Art
    _____ Biology
    _____ Business
    _____ Chemistry
    _____ English
    _____ History
    _____ Math

*Questions 12–15 can be read as open-ended questions.

continued

BOX 8-1 *(continued)*

_____ Physical education
_____ Physics
_____ Political science
_____ Psychology
_____ Sociology
_____ Other _____

14. What is the highest academic degree you have earned?

_____ B.A./ B.S.
_____ M.A./ M.D.
_____ Ph.D./ Ed.D.
_____ Other _____

15. How old are you?

_____ (Write age, then check the appropriate box. If exact years not given, read categories and check appropriate box.)

_____ < 25
_____ 26–34
_____ 35–44
_____ 45–54
_____ 55–64
_____ > 65
_____ Refused

Thank you for your help.

Note: Complete the following after the interview is finished. Do not read item 16 (below) to the participant.

16. Gender (don't ask)

_____ Male
_____ Female

---

women will be more upset by men lying about their income, whereas men will be more upset about women lying about their past sexual history.

- Swann and Rentfrow (2001) used surveys to test the hypothesis that blirtatiousness—the degree to which a person tends to quickly respond to others by saying whatever thoughts pop in the person's head—is positively correlated with self-esteem and impulsivity but negatively correlated with shyness.

Fourth, you might want to describe people's intentions so that you can predict their behavior. For example, news organizations do surveys to predict how people will vote in an election, and market researchers do surveys to find out what products people will buy.

As we have discussed, the survey is a useful tool for finding out what people plan to do. However, the survey is *not* a useful tool for finding out *why* people do what they do. Like all nonexperimental designs, the survey design does not allow you to establish causality. Therefore, if you have a cause–effect hypothesis, do not use a survey.

To illustrate why you cannot make causal inferences from a survey design, let's imagine that you find that professors are more sympathetic toward students than college administrators are. In that case, you cannot say that being an administrator causes people to have less sympathy for students. It could be that professors who didn't like students became administrators; or, it could be that some other factor (like being bossy) causes one to be an administrator and that factor is also associated with having less sympathy toward students (see Figure 8-1).

Even among students who realize that nonexperimental methods cannot establish causality, some try to use survey methods to establish causality. They argue that all they have to do to establish causality is ask people why they behaved in a certain manner. However, those students are wrong: People do not necessarily know the causes of their behavior. For example, Nisbett and Wilson (1977) demonstrated that when participants are shown a row of identical television sets, they will prefer the TV farthest to the right. Yet, when asked why they preferred the TV on the right, nobody says, "I like it because it's on the right."

Figure 8-1 **Correlation Does Not Establish Causality**

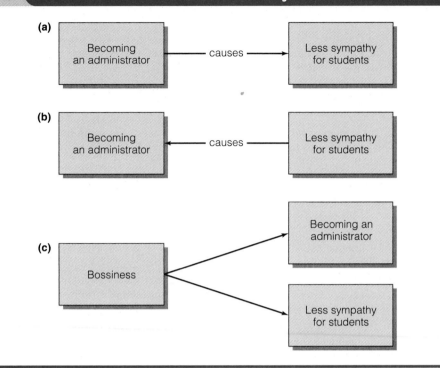

As you can see, finding that professors who became administrators are less sympathetic to students than other professors is not proof that becoming an administrator causes a loss of sympathy for students. There are at least two other possibilities.

Can Self-Report Provide Accurate Answers?

Nisbett and Wilson's research illustrates a general problem with questioning people: People's answers may not reflect the truth. People's self-reports may be inaccurate for four reasons:

1. Participants never knew, and never will know, the answer to your question.
2. Participants no longer remember the information needed to correctly answer your question.
3. Participants do not yet know the correct answer to your question.
4. Participants know the correct answer to your question, but they don't give you the correct answer.

Are You Asking People to Tell More Than They Know?

As we have discussed, when you ask people why they did something or how they feel about something, they often don't know. As research has shown, people are, in a sense, "strangers to themselves" (Wilson, 2002). For example, people may not know why they like (or dislike) broccoli, why they call "heads" more often than "tails," why they usually wake up right before their alarm goes off, or why they find some comedians funnier than others. In short, although asking people questions about why they behave the way they do is interesting, you can't accept their answers at face value.

Are You Asking More Than Participants Can Accurately Remember?

As Nisbett and Wilson's study showed, when people do not know the real cause, they make up a reason—and they believe that reason. Similarly, even though people have forgotten certain facts, they may still think they remember. For example, obese people tend to underreport what they have eaten, and students tend to overreport how much they study. Both groups are surprised when they actually record their own behavior (R. L. Williams & Long, 1983).

Because memory is error prone, you should be careful when interpreting responses that place heavy demands on participants' memories. If you aren't skeptical about the meaning of those responses, be assured that your critics will be. Indeed, one of the most commonly heard criticisms of research is that the results are questionable because they are based on **retrospective self-reports**: participants' statements about their past behavior.

Are You Asking Participants to Look Into a Crystal Ball?

As bad as people are at remembering the past, they can be even worse about predicting the future. Thus, asking people "What would you do in _____ situation?" may make for interesting conversation, but the answers will often have little to do with what people would actually do if they were in that situation (S. J. Sherman, 1980). For instance, most people claim that, if they were in a conformity experiment, they would not conform. If we relied on what people told us they would do in a certain situation, virtually none of the participants in the classic conformity experiments would conform. In reality, however, 60–80% of participants conform. For example, nearly two-thirds of Milgram's participants went along with an experimenter's orders to give high-intensity shocks to another person (Milgram, 1974).

As you might expect, people are particularly bad at predicting how they will react to a situation they haven't experienced. For example, when a committee surveyed high school girls in Illinois to help it decide whether establishing high school volleyball teams in that state would be a waste of time, the surveys indicated that girls had virtually no interest in the sport. But when the committee went ahead and set up leagues, volleyball was the most popular girls' high school sport in that state (Brennan, 2005).

If Participants Know, Will They Tell?

To this point, we have discussed cases in which participants aren't giving you the right answer because they don't know the right answer. However, even when participants know the right answer, they may not share that answer with you because they want to impress you, they want to please you, or they don't want to think about the question.

Social Desirability Bias. If you ask participants questions, you need to be concerned about **social desirability bias:** participants understating, exaggerating, or lying to give an answer that will make them look good. For instance, if you went by U.S. adults' survey responses, 40% of U.S. adults attended religious services in the early 1990s. However, research looking at actual attendance suggests that actual attendance was about half that (Hadaway, Marler, & Chaves, 1993). Participants are most likely to commit the social desirability bias when the survey is not anonymous and the question is extremely personal (e.g., "Have you cheated on your spouse?").

Obeying Demand Characteristics. Sometimes, participants will give you the answer they think you want to hear. Their behavior may be similar to yours when, after having a lousy meal, the server asks you, "Was everything okay?" In such a case, rather than telling the server everything was lousy and ruining his day, you say what you think he wants to hear—"Yes, everything was okay." In technical terms, you are obeying the **demand characteristics** of the situation.

Following Response Sets. Rather than think about what answer you want, participants may not give their answers any serious thought. Instead, they may follow a **response set:** a habit of responding in a certain, set way, regardless of what the question says. Participants who use the "agree" or "strongly agree" option in response to every rating scale question are following a *"yea-saying"* response set. Participants who respond "disagree" or "strongly disagree" to every statement are following a *"nay-saying"* response set. Participants who always choose the "neutral" or "neither agree nor disagree" option are following the *central tendency* response set.

To Whom Will Your Results Apply?

Even if you have a good set of questions that are all focused on your hypotheses, and you can get accurate answers to those questions, your work is probably not done. Usually, you want to generalize your results beyond the people who responded to your survey. For example, you might survey a couple of classes at your university, not because you want to know what the people in those particular classes believe, but because you hope those classes are a representative sample of your college as a whole. But are they? Unfortunately, they probably aren't. For example, if you selected a first-year English course because "everybody has to take it," your sample may exclude seniors. As you will see, obtaining an unbiased sample is difficult.

Even if you start out with an unbiased sample, by the end of the study, your sample may become biased because not everyone in your sample will fill out your questionnaire. In fact, if you do a mail or e-mail survey, don't be surprised if only 5% of your sample returns the survey. Unfortunately, the 5% who responded are probably not typical of your population. Those 5% probably feel more strongly about the issue than the 95% who did not bother to respond. As a result of (a) so many people refusing to take part in surveys and (b) the real possibility that those who respond are different from those who do not respond, **nonresponse bias** (members of a sample refusing to participate in the study) is one of the most serious threats to the survey design's external validity.

Conclusions About the Advantages and Disadvantages of Survey Research

A survey can be a relatively inexpensive way to get information about people's attitudes, beliefs, and behaviors. With a survey, you can collect a lot of information on a large sample in a short period of time.

Although surveys can be valuable, recognize that if participants' self-reports are inaccurate, the survey will have poor construct validity. If the sample is biased, the survey will have poor external validity. Finally, no matter what, the survey will have poor internal validity because it cannot reveal why something happened: If you want to know what causes a certain effect, don't use a survey design.

The Advantages and Disadvantages of Different Survey Instruments

If you decide that a survey is the best approach for your research question, then you need to decide what type of survey instrument you are going to use. Basically, you can choose from two types of survey instruments: (1) **questionnaire** surveys in which participants read the questions and then write their responses, and (2) **interview** surveys in which participants hear the questions and speak their responses.

Written Instruments

If you are considering a questionnaire survey, you have essentially three options: self-administered questionnaires, investigator-administered questionnaires, and psychological tests. In this section, we will discuss the advantages and disadvantages of these three written instruments.

Self-Administered Questionnaires

A **self-administered questionnaire,** as the name suggests, is filled out by participants in the absence of an investigator. Behavioral scientists, as well as manufacturers, special-interest groups, and magazine publishers, all use self-administered questionnaires. You probably have seen some of these questionnaires in your mail, on the Internet (see Table 8-2), at restaurant tables, and in magazines.

Self-administered questionnaires have two main advantages. First, self-administered questionnaires are easily distributed to a large number of people. Second, self-administered

Table 8-2	Advantages and Disadvantages of Web Surveys—and Strategies for Dealing With the Disadvantages		
CHARACTERISTIC	**ADVANTAGES**	**DISADVANTAGES**	**COMMENTS/ SOLUTIONS**
Participants can be anonymous.	• Less social desirability bias (Gosling, Vazire, Srivasta, & John, 2004; Lin, 2004).	• Participants may be underage, may take the survey several times, or may even take it as a group (Nosek, Banaji, & Greenwald, 2002). • Because a passerby could see responses while the participant is taking the survey, responses may not be anonymous (Nosek, Banaji, & Greenwald, 2002).	• You can delete surveys that come from the same IP address—or ones that come from the same IP address and have similar characteristics (Gosling, Vazire, Srivasta, & John, 2004). • You can ask participants whether they have taken the survey before (Gosling, Vazire, Srivasta, & John, 2004). • You can ask participants whether they are alone at the computer (Gosling, Vazire, Srivasta, & John, 2004). • Participants don't have to be anonymous: You can require them to register for the study (Nosek, Banaji, & Greenwald, 2002). • Internet surveys seem to get the same pattern of results as paper-and-pencil surveys. You can compare your results to an off-line sample (Gosling, Vazire, Srivasta, & John, 2004).

Table 8-2 *(continued)*

CHARACTERISTIC	ADVANTAGES	DISADVANTAGES	COMMENTS/ SOLUTIONS
Researcher exerts less control over participants.	• Fewer ethical problems that are due to researcher influencing participant to continue the study (Nosek, Banaji, & Greenwald, 2002).	• Participants might be distracted while filling out the survey and not pay attention to the questions. • Participants may not complete the survey. • Participants might not get comforted or debriefed (Nosek, Banaji, & Greenwald, 2002).	• Research finds that the reliability of a measure when administered over the Internet is equivalent to its reliability when administered via paper and pencil (Gosling, Vazire, Srivasta, & John, 2004; Miller et al., 2002; Riva, Teruzzi, & Anolli, 2003). Thus, participants seem to be focusing on the questions. • Keeping the survey short can decrease dropout rate.
Can survey anyone with a computer.	• Geography is not a boundary (Gosling, Vazire, Srivasta, & John, 2004). • Large samples possible, meaning that statistical inferences can be made about even groups that make up only a small percentage of the population (Gosling, Vazire, Srivasta, & John, 2004). • Can target groups that have special interests or characteristics by targeting members of online discussion groups (Nosek, Banaji, & Greenwald, 2002).	• Older people are less likely to be sampled (Gosling, Vazire, Srivasta, & John, 2004). • Web samples are usually not representative of the population (Gosling, Vazire, Srivasta, & John, 2004).	• Web samples are often a more representative sample than most lab surveys (Gosling, Vazire, Srivasta, & John, 2004).

questionnaires often allow anonymity. Allowing respondents to be anonymous may be important if you want honest answers to highly personal questions.

Using a self-administered questionnaire can be a cheap and easy way to get honest answers from thousands of people. However, using a self-administered questionnaire has at least two major drawbacks.

First, surveys that rely on self-administered questionnaires usually have a low return rate. Because the few individuals who return the questionnaire may not be typical of the people you tried to survey, you may have a biased sample. In other words, nonresponse bias is a serious problem with self-administered questionnaires.

Second, because the researcher and the respondent are not interacting, problems with the questionnaire can't be corrected. Thus, if the survey contains an ambiguous question, the researcher can't help the respondent understand the question. For example, suppose we ask people to rate the degree to which they agree with the statement, "College students work hard." One respondent might think this question refers to a job a student might hold in addition to school. Another respondent might interpret this to mean, "Students work hard at their studies." Because respondent and researcher are not interacting, the researcher will have no idea that these two respondents are, in a sense, answering two different questions.

Investigator-Administered Questionnaires

To avoid the self-administered questionnaire's weaknesses, some researchers use the investigator-administered questionnaire. The investigator-administered questionnaire is filled out in the presence of a researcher.

Investigator-administered questionnaires share many of the advantages of the self-administered questionnaire. With both types of measures, many respondents can be surveyed at the same time. With both types of measures, surveys can be conducted in a variety of locations, including the lab, the street, in class, over the phone, and at respondents' homes.

A major advantage of having an investigator present is that the investigator can clarify questions for the respondent. In addition, the investigator's presence encourages participants to respond. As a result, surveys that use investigator-administered questionnaires have a higher response rate than surveys using self-administered questionnaires.

Unfortunately, the investigator's presence may do more than just increase response rates. The investigator-administered questionnaire may reduce perceived anonymity. Because such respondents feel their answers are less anonymous, respondents to investigator-administered surveys may be less open and honest than respondents to self-administered surveys (see Figure 8-2).

| Figure 8-2 | **Participant Bias in an Investigator-Administered Survey** |

DILBERT reprinted by permission of United Feature Syndicate, Inc.

Psychological Tests: Borrowing From the Best

An extremely refined form of the investigator-administered questionnaire is the psychological test. Whereas questionnaires are often developed in a matter of days, psychological tests are painstakingly developed over months, years, and, in some cases, decades. Nevertheless, the distinction between questionnaires and tests is sometimes blurred.

One reason there is not always a clear-cut difference between questionnaires and tests is that questionnaires often incorporate questions from psychological tests. For example, in a study of people's concern about body weight, Pliner, Chaiken, and Flett (1990) incorporated two psychological tests into their questionnaire: Garner and Garfinkel's (1979) Eating Attitudes Test (EAT) and Janis and Field's (1959) Feeling of Social Inadequacy Scale.

Even if you do not include a test as part of your questionnaire, try to incorporate the best aspects of psychological tests into your questionnaire. To make your questionnaire as valid as a test, try to follow these seven steps:

1. Pretest your questionnaire.

2. Standardize the way you administer the questionnaire.

3. Balance out the effects of response-set biases, such as "yea-saying" (always agreeing) and "nay-saying" (always disagreeing) by asking the same question in a variety of ways. For example, you might ask, "How much do you like the President?" as well as, "How much do you dislike the President?"

4. Use as many "objective" questions (such as multiple-choice questions) that do not require the person scoring the test to interpret the participant's response as possible.

5. Prevent scorer bias on those questions that do require the scorer to interpret responses by (a) developing a detailed scoring key for such responses and (b) not letting scorers know the identity of the respondent. If the hypothesis is that male respondents will be more aggressive, for example, do not let coders know whether the survey they are scoring is a man's or a woman's.

6. Make a case for your measure's reliability. About a month after you surveyed your respondents, administer the survey to them again, and see whether they score similarly both times. Finding a strong positive correlation between the two times of measurement would suggest that scores reflect some stable characteristic rather than random error.

7. Make a case for your measure's validity by correlating it with measures that do not depend on self-report. For example, Steinberg and Dornbusch (1991) justified using self-reported grade-point average (GPA) rather than actual grade-point average by establishing that previous research had shown that school-reported and self-reported GPA were highly correlated.

Written Instruments: A Summary

To review, an investigator-administered survey is generally better than a self-administered survey because administering the survey gives you higher response rates and more control over how the questionnaire is administered. If you follow our seven additional steps to make your questionnaire more like a test, your investigator-administered questionnaire may have almost as much construct validity as a psychological test has.

Interviews

At one level, there is very little difference between the questionnaire and the interview. In both cases, the investigator is interested in participants' responses to questions. However, in an interview, rather than having respondents provide written answers to written questions, the interviewer records respondents' spoken answers to spoken questions. As subtle as these differences seem to be, they have important consequences.

One important consequence is that interviews are more time consuming than questionnaires because whereas you can administer a written questionnaire to many people at once, you should not interview more than one person at a time. You should not interview several people at a time, because each individual's response would not be independent of what others said. Instead, what one participant said might depend on what other participants had already said. For example, participants might go along with the group rather than disclosing their true opinions.

Because interviews are more time consuming than questionnaires, they are also more expensive. However, some researchers think interviews are worth the extra expense.

Advantages of Interviews

The added expense of the interview buys you additional interaction with the participant. This additional interaction lets you clarify questions that the respondents don't understand and lets you follow up on responses you do not understand or did not expect—a tremendous asset in exploratory studies in which you have not yet identified all the important variables. The additional personal interaction may also increase your response rate.

Two Methodological Disadvantages of Interviews

Unfortunately, the personal nature of the interview creates two major problems. First, there is the problem of **interviewer bias:** The interviewer may influence respondents' responses by verbally or nonverbally signaling approval of "correct" answers.

Second, participants may try to impress the interviewer. As a result, rather than telling the truth, participants may give socially desirable responses that would make the interviewer like them or think well of them. Thus, answers may be tainted by the social desirability bias (de Leeuw, 1992).

Advantages of Telephone Interviews

Psychologists have found that the telephone interview is less affected by interviewer bias and social desirability bias than the personal interview. Furthermore, the telephone interview may have fewer problems with sampling bias than other survey methods.

Because the telephone interviewer can't see the respondents, the interviewer cannot bias respondents' responses via subtle visual cues such as frowns, smiles, and eye contact. Furthermore, by monitoring and tape-recording all the interviews, you can discourage interviewers from saying anything that might bias respondents' answers. For example, you could prevent interviewers from changing the wording or order of questions or from giving more enthusiastic and positive verbal feedback (e.g., "Great!") for answers that support your hypothesis and less enthusiastic feedback (e.g., "Okay") for answers that do not support your hypothesis.

Because the telephone interviewer can't see the participants, participants feel more anonymous, which, in turn, appears to reduce desirability bias (Groves & Kahn, 1979). Thus, thanks to the lack of nonverbal cues, the telephone survey may be less vulnerable to both interviewer bias and respondent biases than the personal interview.

The telephone survey also reduces sampling bias by making it easy to get a representative sample. If you have a list of your population's phone numbers, you can randomly select numbers from that list. If you don't have a list of the population's phone numbers, you may still be able to get a random sample of your population by **random digit dialing:** taking the area code and the 3-digit prefixes that you are interested in and then adding random digits to the end to create 10-digit phone numbers. Note, however, that with random digit dialing, you call many fax numbers and disconnected or unused numbers. Furthermore, you will not contact people who either have no phone or whose only phone is a cell phone (although it would be technologically possible to call people's cell phones, the ethical problems—from participants having to pay for the cost of the call, to participants feeling their privacy has been invaded, to a participant potentially getting in a car accident while answering your call—are immense).

Thus far, we have discussed two basic advantages of telephone interviews. First, partly because there are no visual, nonverbal cues, the telephone survey is superior to the personal interview for reducing both respondent biases and interviewer biases. Second, because it is easy to get a large random sample, the telephone survey may give you the best sample of any survey method. However, the main reason for the popularity of the telephone interview is practicality: The telephone survey is more convenient, less time consuming, and cheaper than the personal interview.

Disadvantages of Telephone Interviews

Although there are many advantages to using the telephone interview, you should be aware of its four most serious limitations. First, as with any survey method, there is the possibility of sampling bias. Even if you followed proper random sampling techniques, telephone interviews are limited to those households with landline phones. Although this limitation may not seem serious, realize that some households have cell phones instead of landline phones, and some people do not have any kind of phone. Furthermore, if you are drawing your random sample from listed phone numbers, realize that many people (more than 25% of U.S. households) have unlisted numbers (Dillman, 2000).

Second, as with any survey method, nonresponse bias can be a problem. Some people will, after screening their calls through an answering machine or through "caller ID," choose not to respond to your survey. Indeed, one study reported that 25% of men between the ages of 25 and 34 screen all their calls (Honomichl, 1990). Even when a person does answer the phone, he or she may refuse to answer your questions. In fact, some people get angry when they receive a phone call regarding a telephone survey. We have been yelled at on more than one occasion by people who believe that telephone interviews are a violation of their privacy.

Third, telephone surveys limit you to asking simple and short questions. Rather than answering your questions, participants' attention may be focused on the television show they are watching, the ice cream that is melting, or the baby who is crying.

Fourth, by using the telephone survey, you limit yourself to learning only what participants tell you. You can't see anything for yourself. Thus, if you want to know what race the respondent is, you must ask. You can't see the respondent or the respondent's environment—and the respondent knows you can't. Therefore, a 70-year-old bachelor living in a shack could tell you he's a 35-year-old millionaire with a wife and five kids. He knows you have no easy way of verifying his fable.

How to Conduct a Telephone Survey

After weighing the pros and cons of the different surveys (see Table 8-3), you've decided to conduct a telephone survey. How do you go about it?

	PERSONAL INTERVIEW	PHONE INTERVIEW	INVESTIGATOR-ADMINISTERED (TO A GROUP)	SELF-ADMINISTERED (INCLUDES MAIL SURVEYS, E-MAIL SURVEYS, WEB SURVEYS)
Quality of Answers				
Interviewer bias	Facial expressions and tone of voice could affect responses. However, monitoring interview sessions (e.g., videotaping them or watching them through a one-way mirror) could prevent and detect interviewer bias.	Tone of voice could affect responses. However, having a supervisor monitor interview sessions or taping sessions could prevent and detect interviewer bias.	Minimal interaction with investigator, so little chance of interviewer bias.	No interviewer, no interviewer bias.
Social desirability bias	Participant may want to impress interviewer.	Participants often feel anonymous.	Participants often feel anonymous.[a]	Participants are anonymous.
Problems due to participants misunderstanding questions	Interviewer can clarify questions.	Interviewer can clarify questions.	In a group setting, participants are unlikely to ask questions even when they don't understand.	There may not even be an opportunity for participants to ask the meaning of a question.
Potential for fraud (people filling out multiple questionnaires)	Not a problem.	Not a problem.	Not a problem.	Potential for filling out multiple surveys.
Sampling Issues				
Geographical diversity		Can easily call people.		Easy to distribute to a broad sample.
Cheaply contacting large representative sample		Long distance calls are affordable.[b]		Very cheap because there is no need to have someone administer the survey.[c]
Getting a good response rate—Avoiding nonresponse bias	People respond to the personal approach.	If you precede your call with a letter and make multiple attempts, nonresponse rate can be reduced.		
Ethical Issues				
				May be unable to debrief participants.

[a]When administering a measure to a group, you should take steps to make participants feel that their responses cannot be seen by other participants. These steps may include providing a cover sheet, separating participants by at least one desk, allowing participants to put their completed questionnaire in an unmarked envelope, and having participants put their questionnaires into a box (rather than handing the questionnaire to another participant or to the researcher).

[b]If you use random digit dialing, you get a better sample than you would if you used most other methods; however, some groups will still be underrepresented (e.g., people who do not have phones and, because of the ethical problems involved in calling people's cell phones, people whose only phone is a cell phone).

[c]The quality of your initial sample will depend on the method you use. If you use a mail survey, you will probably have a pretty good sample, although you will underrepresent people who have recently moved and the homeless. If you use a web survey, you will underrepresent the poor and people over 50.

Your first step is to determine what population (what particular group) you wish to sample from and figure out a way to get all of their phone numbers. Often, your population is conveniently represented in a telephone book, membership directory, or campus directory. Once you obtain the telephone numbers, you are ready to draw a random sample from your population. (Later in this chapter, you will learn how to draw a random sample.)

When you draw your sample, pull more names than you actually plan to survey. You won't be able to reach everyone, so you'll need some alternate names. Usually, we draw 25% more names than we actually plan on interviewing.

Next, do what any good survey researcher would do. That is, as you'll see in the next section ("Planning a Survey"), (1) decide whether to ask your questions as essay questions, multiple-choice questions, or some other format; (2) edit your questions; and (3) put your questions in a logical order.

After editing your questions and putting them in the right order, further refine your survey. Start by having a friend read the survey to you. Often, you will find that some of your questions don't "sound" right. Edit them so they sound better. Then, conduct some practice telephone interviews. For example, interview a friend on the phone. As a result of the practice interviews, you may find that you need to refine your questions further to make them easier to understand. Much of this editing will involve shortening the questions.

Once you've made sure your questions are clear and concise, concentrate on keeping your voice clear and slow. Try not to let your tone of voice signal that you want participants to give certain answers. Tape yourself reading the questions, and play it back. Is your voice hinting at the answer you want participants to give? If not, you're ready to begin calling participants—provided you have (a) taken proper steps to preserve the anonymity of respondents and the confidentiality of their responses, (b) weighed the benefits of the survey against the costs to participants, and (c) received approval from your professor and either your school's Internal Review Board (IRB) or your department's ethics committee.

If you get a busy signal or a phone isn't answered, try again later. As a general rule, you should phone a person six to eight times at different times of the day before replacing that person with an alternate name or number.

When you do reach a person, identify yourself and ask for the person on the list—or, if you don't have a list, randomly select a member of the household who meets your criteria (e.g., "I would like to speak to the adult living in the house who most recently had a birthday."). Note that if you survey whoever happens to answer the phone, you will bias your sample (because women and more outgoing people are more likely to answer the phone).

Once you are talking with the appropriate person, briefly introduce the study. Tell the person:

- the general purpose of the study (but do not bias the respondents' answers by stating specific objectives or specific hypotheses)
- the topics that will be covered
- the sponsor of the survey
- the average amount of time it takes to complete the interview
- the steps that you are taking to safeguard the respondent's confidentiality
- that the respondent is free to skip any question
- that the respondent can quit the interview at any time

After providing this introduction, ask the person whether she or he is willing to participate. If the person agrees, ask each question slowly and clearly. Be prepared to repeat and clarify questions.

Once the survey is completed, thank your respondent. Then, offer to answer any questions. Usually, you should give participants the option of being mailed a summary of the survey results.

Planning a Survey

Before conducting a telephone survey—or any other type of survey—you need to do some careful planning. In this section, we will take you through the necessary steps in developing and executing your survey.

Deciding on a Research Question

As with all psychological research, the first step in designing a survey is to have a clear research question. You need a hypothesis to guide you if you are to develop a cohesive and useful set of survey questions. Writing a survey without a hypothesis to unify it is like writing a story without a plot: In the end, all you have is a set of disjointed facts that tell you nothing.

Part of developing a clear research question is specifying your target population: all the members of the group. Knowing your population will help you word your questions, pretest your questions, and obtain a representative sample of your population.

Not only do you want a clear research question but you also want an important one. Therefore, before you write your first survey question, justify why your research question is important. You should be able to answer at least one of these questions:

1. What information will the survey provide?
2. What practical implications could the survey results have?

Choosing the Format of Your Questions

You've decided that your research question is appropriate. In addition, you've also decided what kind of survey instrument (questionnaire or interview) will give you the best information. Now, you are ready to decide what types of questions to use.

Fixed-Alternative Questions

You might decide to use **fixed-alternative questions**: questions in which respondents have to choose between two or more answers. Your survey might include several types of fixed-alternative questions: true–false, multiple-choice, and rating scale.

Nominal-Dichotomous Items. Sometimes, fixed-alternative questions ask respondents to tell the researcher whether they belong to a certain category. For example, participants may be asked to categorize themselves according to gender, race, or religion. Because these questions do not tell us about how much of a quality a participant has but instead only whether the person has a given quality, these questions yield nominal data. (For more on nominal data, see Chapter 6.)

Dichotomous questions—questions that allow only two responses (usually "yes" or "no")—also give you nominal (qualitative) data because they ask whether a person has a given quality. Often, respondents are asked whether they are a member of a category (e.g., "Are you employed?" or "Are you married?").

Sometimes, several dichotomous questions are asked at once. Take the question: "Are you African American, Hispanic, Asian, or Caucasian (non-Hispanic)?" Note that this question could be rephrased as several dichotomous questions: "Are you African American?" ("yes" or "no"), "Are you Hispanic?" ("yes" or "no"), and so on. The information is still dichotomous—either participants claim to belong to a category or they don't. Consequently, the information you get from these questions is still categorical, qualitative information. If you code African American as a "1," Hispanic as "2," and so on, there is no logical order to your numbers. Higher numbers would not stand for having more of a quality. In other words, different numbers stand for different types (different qualities) rather than for different amounts (quantities).

The fact that **nominal-dichotomous items** present participants with only two—usually very different—options has at least two advantages. First, respondents often find it easier to decide between 2 choices (such as, "Are you for or against animal research?"), than between 13 (for example, "Rate how favorably you feel toward animal research on a 13-point scale."). Second, when there are only two very different options, respondents and investigators should have similar interpretations of the options. Therefore, a well-constructed dichotomous item can provide reliable and valid data.

Although there are advantages to offering only two choices, there are also disadvantages. One disadvantage of nominal-dichotomous items is that some respondents will think that their viewpoint is not represented by the two alternatives given. To illustrate this point, consider the following question:

> "Do you think abortion should continue to be legal in the United States?" ("yes" or "no").

How would people who are ambivalent toward abortion respond? How would people who are fervently opposed to legalized abortion feel about not being allowed to express the depth of their feelings?

If you have artificially limited your respondents to two alternatives, your respondents may not be the only ones irritated by the fact that your alternatives prevent them from accurately expressing their opinions. You should be annoyed, as well—because by depriving yourself of information about subtle differences among respondents, you deprive yourself of **power:** the ability to find relationships among variables.

Likert-Type and Interval Items. One way to give yourself power is to use **Likert-type items.** Likert-type items typically ask participants to respond to a statement by choosing "strongly disagree" (scored a "1"), "disagree" (scored a "2"), "undecided" ("3"), "agree" ("4"), or "strongly agree" ("5").

Traditionally, most psychologists have assumed that a participant who strongly agrees (a "5") and a participant who merely agrees (a "4") differ by as much, in terms of how they feel, as a participant who is undecided (a "3") differs from someone who disagrees (a "2"). Both participants differed by the same distance on the scale (1 point), and so both supposedly differed by the same amount psychologically. In other words, Likert-type scales are assumed to yield interval data (To learn more about interval data, see Chapter 6). Questions 4–11 in Box 8-1 are examples of Likert-type, interval scale items.

Likert-type items are extremely useful in questionnaire construction. Whereas dichotomous items allow respondents only to agree or disagree, Likert-type items give respondents the freedom to strongly agree, agree, be neutral, disagree, or strongly disagree. Thus, Likert-type items yield more information than nominal-dichotomous items. Furthermore, because Likert-type items yield interval data, responses to Likert-type items can be analyzed by more powerful statistical tests than nominal-dichotomous items.

The major disadvantage of Likert-type items is that respondents may resist the fixed-alternative nature of the question. One approach to this problem is to have a "Don't Know" option. That way, respondents won't feel forced into an answer that doesn't reflect their true position. In an interview, you can often get around the problem by reading the question (e.g., "On a 1, *strongly disagree*, to 5, *strongly agree*, scale, do you think college is stressful for students?") as if it were an open-ended question (e.g., "Do you think college is stressful for students?") and then recording the participant's answer under the appropriate alternative. As you can see, many of the questions in Box 8-1 could be read like open-ended items.

Using Likert-Type Items to Create Summated Scores. If you have several Likert-type items that are designed to measure the same variable (such as liking for students), you can sum (add up) each respondent's answers to all those questions to get a total score for each respondent on that variable. For example, consider Questions 6–11 in Box 8-1. For each of those questions, a "5" indicates a high degree of liking for students, whereas a "1" indicates a low level of liking for students. Therefore, you might add (sum) the answers (scores) for each of those questions to produce a **summated score** for student liking. Suppose you obtained the following pattern of responses from one professor:

Question 6 = 1 (strongly disagree)

Question 7 = 2 (disagree)

Question 8 = 1 (strongly disagree)

Question 9 = 3 (undecided)

Question 10 = 1 (strongly disagree)

Question 11 = 2 (disagree)

Then, the summated score (total score for liking students) would be 10 (because 1 + 2 + 1 + 3 + 1 + 2 = 10).

There are two statistical advantages to using summated scores. First, just as a 50-question multiple-choice test is more reliable (less influenced by random error) than a 1-question multiple-choice test, a score based on several questions is more reliable than a score based on a single question. Second, analyses are often simpler for summated scores. If we summed the responses for Questions 6–11 in Box 8-1, we could compare computer users and noncomputer users on "student liking" by doing one *t* test.[1] Without a summated score, you would have to perform six separate *t* tests, and then correct the *t* test for the effects of having done multiple analyses.[2]

Conclusions About Fixed-Alternative Items. Fixed-alternative questions are not limited to asking respondents whether they belong to a certain category, support a certain position, or do a certain behavior. Fixed-alternative questions can be used to ask respondents how strongly respondents believe in a certain position. For example, a question might ask, "How much do you agree or disagree with the following statement?" (The fixed alternatives could be strongly agree, agree, disagree, strongly disagree.) Similarly, fixed-alternative questions can ask how much of a certain behavior the person did. For instance, "How many days a week do you study?" (The fixed alternatives could be: a. 0, b. 1, c. 2, d. 3, e. 4, f. 5, g. 6, h. 7.) If asked the right way, these "how many" and "how much" questions can yield interval data (as

---

[1]To compute a *t*, you would subtract your two group means and then divide by the standard error of the differences. To calculate the standard error of the differences by hand, you can (a) use the formula: standard error of the mean = $\sqrt{s_1^2/N_1 + s_2^2/N_2}$, where s = standard deviation and N = number of participants, and where $_1$ refers to group 1 and $_2$ refers to group 2; or (b) follow the more detailed set of instructions in Appendix D.

[2]Alternatively, you could use a more complex statistical procedure such as multivariate analysis of variance (MANOVA).

discussed in Chapter 6, interval data allow you to compare participants in terms of how *much* of a quality they have).

Unfortunately, many of these "how much" and "how many" questions are *not* asked the right way, thus they do not yield interval data. For example, when asking respondents about their grade-point averages, some researchers make 1 = 0.00–0.99, 2 = 1.0–1.69, 3 = 1.7–2.29, 4 = 2.3–2.7, 5 = 2.8–4.0. Note that the response options do not cover equal intervals. The interval covered by option "4" is .4, whereas the range of GPAs covered by option "5" is 1.2. Because there aren't equal intervals between response options, averaging participants' responses is meaningless.

A better choice of options would be 1 = 0.00–0.99, 2 = 1.00–1.99, 3 = 2.00–2.99, and 4 = 3.00–4.00. Probably the best thing to do would be to abandon the fixed-response format and just ask participants the open-ended question, "What is your grade-point average?"

Open-Ended Questions

Before discussing other situations in which you might want to use **open-ended questions,** let's distinguish open-ended questions from fixed-alternative questions. Whereas fixed-response items may resemble multiple-choice questions, open-ended questions may resemble fill-in-the-blank, short-answer, or essay questions. Whereas fixed-response questions force participants to choose among several researcher-determined response options, open-ended questions allow participants to respond in their own words. There are two major advantages to letting participants respond in their own words.

First, you avoid putting words in participants' mouths. To illustrate how fixed alternatives may influence participants, consider the question "What is the most important thing for children to prepare them for life?" When the question was asked as a fixed-alternative question, almost two-thirds of respondents chose the alternative "To think for themselves." However, when the question was asked as an open-ended question, fewer than 1 in 20 respondents gave any response resembling "To think for themselves" (Schwarz, 1999).

Second, you can find out the beliefs behind the respondents' answers to the fixed-alternative questions. In some cases, open-ended questions may reveal that there are no beliefs behind a participant's answers to the fixed-alternative questions. That is, you might find that although the respondent is dutifully checking and circling responses, the respondent really doesn't know anything about the topic.

In other cases, asking open-ended questions allows you to discover that respondents making the same ratings have different opinions. For example, consider two professors who respond to Question 11 in Box 8-1, "I like college students" with "undecided." Open-ended questions may allow you to discover that one professor circles "undecided" because he is new to the college and doesn't know, whereas the other professor circles "undecided" because she has mixed feelings about students. Without asking open-ended questions, you would not have known that these two respondents have different reasons for giving the same response.

Although there are two major advantages to letting respondents answer in their own words, there are also two major disadvantages. First, open-ended questions are hard for participants to answer. Because of the difficulty of generating their own responses, participants will often skip open-ended questions. Second, answers to open-ended questions are hard to score. Answers may be so varied that you won't see an obvious way to code them. If you aren't careful, the coding strategy you finally adopt will be arbitrary.

To help you come up with a logical and systematic method of coding open-ended questions, try to come up with a content analysis scheme (see Chapter 7) *before* you start collecting data. Once you have done a content analysis, you may convert the information from your open-ended questions into numbers. If you rated answers to a question on a 1(*not at all aggressive*) to 5 (*extremely aggressive*) scale, you would analyze these quantitative ratings as interval data. If you coded responses in terms of whether ideas about loyalty were mentioned (not mentioned = 0, mentioned = 1), you would analyze these qualitative, categorical data as nominal data (to learn more about nominal data, see Chapter 6).

Choosing the Format of Your Survey

If you use an interview, in addition to deciding on the format of your questions, you also need to decide on the format of your interview. You have a choice between three interview formats: structured, semistructured, and unstructured.

Structured Interview

In psychological research, the most popular interview format is the **structured interview:** an interview in which all respondents are asked a standard list of questions in a standard order. The structured interview is popular because the structure reduces the risk of interviewer bias and increases reliability. To build on the strengths of the structured interview, consider asking only fixed-alternative questions: By using a standard list of questions, you reduce the risk of interviewer bias—and, by using fixed-alternative questions, you obtain easily interpretable responses.

Semistructured Interview

In psychological research, a less popular interview format is the **semistructured interview.** Like the structured interview, the semistructured interview is constructed around a core of standard questions. Unlike the structured interview, however, the interviewer may expand on any question in order to explore a given response in greater depth.

Like the structured interview, the semistructured interview tells you how respondents answered the standard questions. In addition, the semistructured interview allows the investigator to ask additional questions to follow up on any interesting or unexpected answers to the standard questions.

Unfortunately, the advantage of being able to follow up on questions is usually outweighed by two major disadvantages. First, data from the follow-up questions are hard to interpret because different participants are asked different questions. One can't compare how Participant 1 and Participant 2 answered follow-up Question 6c if Participant 1 was the only person asked that follow-up question.

Second, even the answers from the standard questions are also hard to interpret because the standard questions were not asked in the same standard way to all participants. Participant 1 might have answered Question 2 right after Question 1, whereas Participant 2 answered Question 2 after answering Question 1 and 10 minutes of follow-up questions. Those follow-up questions might shape the answers to Question 2 (Schwarz, 1999). Thus, in giving the interviewer more freedom to follow up answers, you may be giving the interviewer more freedom to bias the results. In other words, by deciding which answers to probe and how to probe them, the interviewer may affect what participants say in response to the standard questions.

Given the disadvantages of the semistructured interview, when should it be used? Perhaps the best time to use it is when you are conducting a pilot (preliminary) study so that you can better formulate your research question. For instance, you may know that there are a few questions you want to ask, but you also know that you "don't really know enough to know what to ask." The standard questions may give you some interpretable data, from which you may be able to get some tentative answers to the specific questions you do have. From the answers to the follow-up questions, you may get some ideas for other questions you could ask in your next survey.

In short, if you do not yet know enough about your respondents or a certain topic area to create a good structured interview, you may want to first conduct a semistructured interview. What you learn from the results of that interview may enable you to generate a good set of questions that you can then use in either a structured interview or a questionnaire.

Unstructured Interview

The **unstructured interview** is popular in the media, in the analyst's office, and with inexperienced researchers. In the unstructured interview, interviewers have objectives that they believe can be best met without an imposed structure. Therefore, there isn't a set of standard questions. The interviewer is free to ask what she wants, how she wants to, and the respondent is free to answer how he pleases. Without standardization, the information is extremely vulnerable to interviewer bias and is usually too disorganized for meaningful analysis.

Because of these problems, the unstructured interview is best used as an exploratory device. As a research tool for reaping meaningful and accurate information, the unstructured survey is limited. As a tool for a beginning researcher, the unstructured interview is virtually worthless.

Editing Questions: Nine Mistakes to Avoid

By now, you have probably decided that you will use either a structured interview or a questionnaire. It's time to focus on your questions. Although asking questions is a part of everyday life, asking good survey questions is not. Therefore, in this section, you will learn how to avoid nine mistakes people often make when writing questions.

1. Avoid Leading Questions

Remember, your aim is to get accurate information, not to get agreement with your beliefs. Therefore, don't ask **leading questions:** questions that clearly lead participants to the answer you want. For example, don't ask the question, "You disapprove of the biased, horrible way that television news covers the abortion issue, don't you?" Instead ask, "Do you approve or disapprove of the way television news shows cover the abortion issue?"

2. Avoid Questions That Are Loaded With Social Desirability

Don't ask questions that have a socially correct answer, such as, "Do you donate money to worthwhile causes?" Generally, the answers to such questions cannot be trusted because participants will respond with the socially desirable answer. Such questions may also contaminate participants' responses to subsequent questions because such questions may arouse respondents' suspicions. For instance, the respondent may think, "They said there were no right or wrong answers. They said they just wanted my opinion. But obviously, there are right and wrong answers to this survey." Or, the respondent may think, "They knew I would give that answer. Anyone would give that answer. This survey is starting to feel like one of those 'surveys' used by people who try to sell you something. What are they trying to sell?"

3. Avoid Double-Barreled Questions

You wouldn't think of asking a respondent more than one question at the same time. But that's exactly what happens when you ask a **double-barreled question:** more than one question packed into a single question (e.g., "How much do you agree with the following statement: 'Colleges need to spend more time on students' emotional *and* physical development'?"). The responses to this question are uninterpretable because you don't know whether participants were responding to the first statement, "Colleges need to spend more time on students' emotional development," the second statement, "Colleges need to spend more time on students' physical development," or both statements.

As you can see, the conjunction *and* allowed this question to be double-barreled. Almost all double-barreled questions are joined by *and* or some other conjunction. So when looking over your questions, look suspiciously at all *ands, ors, nors,* and *buts.*

4. Avoid Long Questions

Short questions are less likely to be double-barreled. Furthermore, short questions are easier to understand. A useful guideline is to keep most of your questions under 10 words and all your questions under 20 words.

5. Avoid Negations

The appearance of a negation, such as *no* or *not,* in a questionnaire item increases the possibility of misinterpretation. Furthermore, it takes more time to process and interpret a negation than a positively stated item. To illustrate, compare the next two questions: "Do you not like it when students don't study?" versus "Do you like it when students study?"

6. Avoid Irrelevant Questions

Make sure your questions seem relevant to your participants and that your questions are relevant to your research question. For example, "Do you eat fondue?" is irrelevant to the research question, "Are professors who use computers more sympathetic to students?"

Although there are many obvious reasons for not including irrelevant questions, the most important reason is that irrelevant questions annoy respondents. If you ask an irrelevant question, many respondents will conclude that you are either incompetent or disrespectful. Because they have lost respect for you, they will be less likely to give accurate answers to the rest of your questions. In fact, they may even refuse to continue with the survey.

7. Avoid Poorly Worded Response Options

From your experiences with multiple-choice tests, you are keenly aware that the response options are part of the question. The options you choose will affect the answers that participants give (Schwarz, 1999). Not only should you carefully consider the wording of each option but you should also carefully consider how many options you will include.

As a general rule, the more options, the greater your ability to detect subtle differences between participants' answers. According to this rule, if you use a 1-to-7 scale, you may find differences that you would have failed to find had you used a 1-to-3 scale.

However, like most rules, this one has exceptions. If you give participants too many options, participants may be overwhelmed. Likewise, if the options are too similar, participants may be confused. The easiest way to determine how many options are appropriate is to pretest your questions.

8. Avoid Big Words

Your task is not to impress respondents with your large vocabulary. Instead, your task is to make sure respondents understand you; therefore, use simple words and avoid jargon.

9. Avoid Words and Terms That May Be Misinterpreted

There are three steps you can take to make sure that participants know exactly what you are talking about.

First, avoid abbreviations and slang terms. Abbreviations that are meaningful to you may be meaningless to some respondents. Similarly, slang terms often have different meanings to different groups. Thus, if you want to know people's attitudes toward marijuana, use the word "marijuana" rather than a slang term like "dope." Dope may be interpreted as meaning marijuana, heroin, or all drugs.

Second, be specific. If you want to know whether your respondents like college students, don't ask, "How do you feel about students?" Instead, ask, "Do you like college students?"

Third, pretest the questions on members of your target population. Often, the only way to find out that a question or term will be misinterpreted is by asking members of your target group what they think the question means. For example, through extensive pretesting, you might find that a seemingly straightforward question such as, "Should Pittsburgh increase coke production?" may be interpreted in at least five different ways:

1. Should Pittsburgh increase cocaine production?
2. Should Pittsburgh increase coal production?
3. Should Pittsburgh increase steel production?
4. Should Pittsburgh increase soft drink production?
5. Should Pittsburgh increase Coca-Cola production?

Similarly, if you were asking about sex, your participants may or may not consider masturbation and oral sex as instances of sex. If pretesting shows that participants will not interpret the word the way you intend, you may need to use another word or you may need to define the term (e.g., "For the purpose of this survey, consider sex to include masturbation, oral sex, and sexual intercourse.").

In conclusion, even if you carefully evaluate and edit each question, there are some problems that you can discover only by having people try to answer your questions. Therefore, *pretesting questions is one of the most important steps in developing questions.*

Sequencing Questions

Once you have edited and pretested your questions, you need to decide in what order to ask them. Ordering questions is important because the sequence of questions can influence results (Krosnick & Schuman, 1988). To appropriately sequence questions, follow these five rules:

1. Put innocuous questions first, personal questions last.
2. Qualify early.
3. Be aware of response sets.
4. Keep similar questions together.
5. Put demographic questions last.

1. Put Innocuous Questions First, Personal Questions Last

Participants are often tense or anxious at the beginning of a survey. They don't know what to expect. They don't know whether they should continue the survey. Indeed, they may be looking for an excuse to quit the survey. Thus, if the first question is extremely personal, participants may decide to withdraw from the survey. Even if participants don't withdraw, starting them out with a personal question may put them on the defensive for the entire survey. If, on the other hand, your first questions are simple, interesting, innocuous, and nonthreatening, participants may relax and feel comfortable enough to respond frankly to personal questions.[3]

Putting the most sensitive questions at the end of your survey will not only give you more honest responses but also more responses. To illustrate, suppose that you have a 20-item survey in which all but one of the questions are relatively innocuous. If you put the sensitive item first, respondents may quit the survey immediately. Because this item was the first question you asked, you have gathered no information whatsoever. If, on the other hand, you put the sensitive item last, respondents may answer the question because they have a deeper involvement with both you and the survey than they did at the beginning. Furthermore, even if they quit, you still have their responses to 19 of the 20 questions.

2. Qualify Early

If people must meet certain qualifications to be asked certain questions, find out if your participant has those qualifications before asking her those questions. In other words, don't ask people questions that don't apply to them. There is no need to waste their time—and yours—by collecting useless information. Participants don't like having to repeatedly answer questions by saying, "Doesn't apply."

The survey in Box 8-1 begins with a simple qualifying question: "What is your position at Bromo Tech?" This question establishes the presence of two qualifications for the survey: (1) that the person is a professor, and (2) the person teaches at Bromo Tech. If a respondent doesn't meet these qualifications, the survey is terminated. By terminating the survey early in the interview, we save our time, the respondent's time, and our client's money.

3. Be Aware of Response Sets

If all your questions have the same response options, some participants may lock onto one of those options. For example, if each question has the alternatives, "Strongly Agree, Agree, Neutral, Disagree, Strongly Disagree," some respondents may circle the option "Neutral" for every question. By always checking the neutral option, they can get the questionnaire over with as soon as possible.

To avoid the neutral response set, you may want to eliminate the neutral option. However, you will still be vulnerable to response sets because the neutral response set isn't the only response bias. As we mentioned earlier, there are a variety of response sets, including the "yea-saying" (always agreeing) and the "nay-saying" (always disagreeing) biases.

One of the most common ways of dealing with response sets is to alternate the way you phrase the questions. You might ask respondents to strongly agree, agree, disagree, or strongly disagree to the statement, "Most students work hard on their studies." Then, later in the questionnaire, you could ask them to strongly agree, agree, disagree, or strongly disagree with the statement, "Most students are lazy when it comes to their studies."

4. Keep Similar Questions Together

There are three reasons why you get more accurate responses when you keep related questions together.

---

[3]Not everyone agrees with this rule. For example, Dillman (1978) suggests that surveys should start with questions that hook the respondents' interest. If you are having trouble getting people to participate in your survey, you might consider Dillman's advice. However, when we have carefully explained the purpose of the survey before administering it (in accordance with the principle of informed consent), participants who start the survey usually finish it.

First, your participants will perceive the survey to be organized and professional. Therefore, they will take the survey seriously.

Second, participants will be less likely to misunderstand your questions. You minimize the problem of participants thinking that you are asking about one thing when you are really asking about another topic.

Third, because you ask all the related questions together, participants are already thinking about the topic before you ask the question. They are already thinking about the topic, thus they can respond quickly and accurately. If respondents aren't thinking about the topic before you ask the question, it may take some respondents awhile to think of the answer to the question. At best, this makes for some long pauses. At worst, respondents will avoid long pauses by saying they don't know or by making up an answer.

5. Put Demographic Questions Last

In addition to writing items that directly address your research question, you should ask some questions that will reveal your sample's **demographics:** statistics relating to the age, sex, education level, and other characteristics of the group or its members. In our survey of college professors (see Box 8-1), we asked four demographic questions (Questions 12–15).

By comparing our sample's responses to these demographic questions with the population's demographics, we may be able to detect problems with our sample. For example, we can look in the college catalog or go to the personnel office to find out what percentage of the population we are interested in (all teachers at Bromo Tech) are men. Then, we can compare our sample demographics to these population demographics. If we found that 75% of the faculty are men, but that only 25% of our sample were men, we would know that our sample wasn't representative of the faculty.

Note that we, like most researchers, put the demographic questions last (Questions 12–15). We put them last for two reasons. First, respondents are initially suspicious of questions that do not clearly relate to the purpose of the survey. Second, people seem increasingly reluctant to provide demographic data. To reduce suspiciousness and increase openness, we try to put our respondents at ease before we ask demographic questions.

Putting the Final Touches on Your Survey Instrument

You've written your questions, carefully sequenced them, and pretested them. Now, you should carefully proofread and pretest your questionnaire to make sure that it is accurate, easy to read, and easy to score.

Obviously, participants are more likely to take your research seriously if your questionnaire looks professional. Therefore, your final copy of the questionnaire should be free of smudges and spelling errors. The spaces between questions should be uniform.

Even though the questionnaire is neatly typed, certain key words may have been scrambled and omitted. At best, these scrambled or missing words could cause embarrassment. At worst, they would cause you to lose data. Therefore, not only should you proofread the questionnaire to ensure that the form of the questionnaire looks professional, but you should also pretest the questionnaire to ensure that the content is professional.

Once you have thoroughly checked and rechecked both the form and the content of the questionnaire, you should fill out the questionnaire and then code your own responses. Then, you should consider three strategies for making coding easier.

1. Put the answer blocks in the left margin. This will allow you to score each page quickly because you can go straight down the page without shifting your gaze

from left to right and without having to filter out extraneous information (see Box 8-1).

2. Have respondents put their answers on a separate answer sheet. With an answer sheet, you don't have to look through and around questions to find the answers. The answer sheet is an especially good idea when your questionnaire is longer than one page because the answer sheet saves you the trouble of turning pages.

3. Have participants put their responses on a coding sheet that can be scored by computer. Computer scoring is less time consuming, less tedious, and more accurate than hand scoring.

Choosing a Sampling Strategy

You have decided what questions you will ask and how you will ask them. You know why you are asking the questions: Your questions will answer a question you have about your population. Your next step is to decide whom in your population you will ask. If your population is extremely small (all art history teachers at your school), you may decide to survey every member of your population. Usually, however, your population is so large that you can't easily survey everyone. Therefore, instead of surveying the entire population, you will survey a sample of people from that population. Whether you acquire your sample by a probability sampling method such as either pure random sampling or proportionate stratified random sampling, or whether you use a nonprobability sampling method such as either convenience sampling or quota sampling, your goal is to get a sample that is representative of your population.

Random Sampling

In **random sampling,** each member of the population has an equal chance of being selected. Furthermore, the selection of respondents is independent. In other words, the selection of a given person has no influence on the selection or exclusion of other members of the population from the sample: Having selected Sam doesn't have any effect on whether you will select Mary.

Obtaining a Random Sample. To select a random sample for a survey, you would first identify every member of your population. Next, you would go to a random numbers table and use that table to assign each member of the population a random number. Then, you would rank each member from lowest to highest based on the size of his or her random number. Thus, if a person were assigned the random number 00000, that person would be the first person on the list, whereas a person assigned the number 99999 would be the last person on the list. You would select your sample by selecting names from the beginning of this list until you got the sample size you needed. If you needed 100 respondents, you would select the first 100 names on the list.

As you can imagine, random sampling can be time consuming. First, you have to identify every member of the population—and have a way of contacting them. Identifying every member of the population can be a chore, depending on your population. Obtaining their contact information can be a real nightmare—especially if you are trying to get their e-mail addresses. If you are interested in a student sample, then a trip to the registrar's office might yield a list of all currently enrolled students and their phone numbers. In fact, most schools can generate a computerized random sample of students for you. If your population is your local community, the local telephone book may help you assess much of that population. However, realize that the phone book will leave out people too poor to have phones, people who use only their cell phones, people who have recently moved, and people with unlisted numbers. Thus, if you have the money, you may choose to buy census tapes from the government or from marketing research firms.

After you've identified the population and obtained the best list of that population you can get, you have to assign random numbers to your potential respondents. Just the first step—assigning random numbers to all members of a population—can be cumbersome and time consuming. Imagine assigning 1,000,000 random numbers to names! But after that's done, you still have to order the names based on these random numbers to determine whom you will sample. Fortunately, computers can eliminate many of the headaches of random sampling—especially if you can find a computer file or database that already has all the names of everybody in your population.

Despite the hassles involved with random sampling, researchers willingly use it because random sampling allows them to generalize the results of one study to a larger population. To be more specific, you can use inferential statistics to infer the characteristics of a population from a random sample of that population.

Determining an Appropriate Sample Size. As you know, your random sample may differ from the population by chance. For example, although 51% of the people in your population are women, perhaps only 49% of the people in your random sample will be women. You also know that you can reduce random sampling error by increasing your sample size. In other words, a random sample of 10,000 will tend to reflect the population more accurately than a random sample of 10. However, surveying 10,000 people may cost more time and energy than the added accuracy it buys. To determine how many people you will need to randomly sample, consult Table 8-4.

| Table 8-4 | Required Sample Size as a Function of Population Size and Desired Accuracy (Within 5%, 3%, or 1%) at the 95% Confidence Level |

	SAMPLING ERROR		
SIZE OF THE POPULATION	5%	3%	1%
50	44	48	50
100	79	92	99
200	132	169	196
500	217	343	476
1,000	278	521	907
2,000	322	705	1,661
5,000	357	894	3,311
10,000	370	982	4,950
20,000	377	1,033	6,578
50,000	381	1,066	8,195
100,000	383	1,077	8,926
1,000,000	384	1,088	9,706
100,000,000	384	1,089	9,800

Example of how this table works: If you are sampling from a population that consists of 50 people and you want to be 95% confident that your results will be within 5% of the true percentage in the population, you need to randomly sample 44 people.

Note: Table provided by David Van Amburg of MarketSource, Inc.

Proportionate Stratified Random Sampling

What if you can't afford to survey as many people as Table 8-4 says you need? Then, if you use pure random sampling, random sampling error may cause your sample to be less representative than you would like. With pure random sampling, the only defense you have against random sampling error is a large sample size. With **proportionate stratified random sampling,** on the other hand, you don't leave the representativeness of your sample entirely to chance. Instead, you make sure that the sample is similar to the population in certain respects. For example, if you know that the population is 75% male and 25% female, you make sure your sample is 75% male and 25% female.[4] You would accomplish this goal by dividing your population (stratum) into two subpopulations, or substrata. One substratum would consist of the population's men, the other substratum would consist of the population's women. Next, you would decide on how many respondents you would sample from each substratum (for example, you might sample 75 from the male stratum and 25 from the female stratum). Finally, you would draw random samples from each substratum. In this last step, the only difference between proportionate stratified random sampling and basic random sampling is that you are collecting two random samples from two substrata (e.g., male professors and female professors), rather than one sample from the main population (e.g., professors).

By using proportionate stratified random sampling, you have all the advantages of random sampling, but you don't need to sample nearly as many people. Thus, thanks to proportionate stratified sampling, the Gallup Poll can predict the outcome of U.S. presidential elections based on samples of only 300 people.[5] Furthermore, a proportionate stratified random sample ensures that your sample matches the population on certain key variables.

Convenience Sampling

In **convenience sampling** (also called accidental sampling, haphazard sampling, and nonprobability sampling), you simply sample people who are easy to survey. Convenience surveys are very common. Newspapers ask people to mail their responses to a survey question, and radio stations ask people to call in their reactions to a question. Even television stations sometimes ask viewers to express their reactions to a story by filling out a survey on the station's website.

---

[4]If you are going to do stratified random sampling, typically you will do proportionate random sampling. That is, if the first stratum comprises $3/4$ of the population and the second was $1/4$ of the population, $3/4$ of your total sample would be from the first population and $1/4$ would be from the second population. In other words, the size of your sample from the first stratum would be 3 times as big as your sample from the second stratum. However, there are cases in which you would not do proportionate random sampling. For example, suppose that you wanted a sample of at least 100 persons from a certain subgroup (stratum) so that you could make relatively precise statements about that subgroup, but that subgroup (stratum) made up a tiny percentage of the population (e.g., 1%). If you used proportionate sampling, to get 100 people from a subgroup that made up only 1% of the population, you would need a total sample of 10,000 $(10,000 \times .01 = 100)$ people (9,900 of which would be from the majority group). In such a case, you would probably use disproportionate random sampling. For example, you might sample 100 from your 1% group and 100 from your 99% group. To make estimates of the total population's behavior, you have to mathematically correct for oversampling from the 1% group. For example, if the average rating on a -50 (extremely dissatisfied) to $+50$ (extremely satisfied) scale was -20 for your 1% group and $+20$ for your 99% group, you should not estimate the population satisfaction at 0. Instead, you should give each response from a member of your 99% stratum 99 times more weight than you would give a response from the 1% group. Consequently, you would multiply the average of the 99% group by 99, multiply the average of the 1% group by 1, add those two results, and then divide by 100 to get your estimate of the population's satisfaction: $+19.6$ $([(99 \times 20) + (1 \times -20)]/100)$.

[5]The Gallup poll has successfully predicted the winner in the last 5 presidential elections and has been accurate in predicting the actual percentage candidates will get. For example, in the 2000 election, Gallup was within .1% of Bush's actual percentage.

Figure 8-3	Convenience Samples Are Biased Samples

"We need a bit more science in our market surveys."

Reprinted by permission of CartoonStock.

To see how you would get a convenience sample, suppose that you were given 1 week to get 1,000 responses to a questionnaire. What would you do? Provided you had approval from your school's internal review board (IRB), you might (a) go to areas where you would expect to find lots of people, such as a shopping mall, (b) ask your professors if you could do a survey in their classes, (c) put an ad in the newspaper, offering people money if they would respond to a questionnaire, or (d) put your survey on the Internet.

Although you can use convenience sampling techniques to get a relatively large sample quickly, you do not know whether the sample represents your population. Your best bet is that it does *not* (see Figure 8-3). In fact, if your respondents are actively volunteering to be in your survey, you can bet that your sample is biased. People who call in to radio shows, write letters in response to questions in the newspaper, or respond to ads asking for people to be in a survey do not represent a significant portion of the population: people without the time or desire to respond to such surveys.

Quota Sampling
Quota sampling is designed to make your convenience sample more representative of the population. Like proportionate stratified random sampling, quota sampling is designed to guarantee that your sample matched the population on certain characteristics. For instance, you might make sure that 25% of your sample was female, or that 20% of your sample was Hispanic.

Unlike proportionate stratified random sampling, however, quota sampling doesn't involve random sampling. So, even though you met your quotas, your sample may not reflect the population at all. For example, you may meet your 20% quota of Hispanics by hanging around a hotel where there is a convention of high school Spanish teachers; obviously, the Hispanics in your survey would not be representative of the Hispanics in your community.

Conclusions About Sampling Techniques

If we were to rank sampling techniques in terms of their ability to produce representative samples, the rankings would be:

1. Proportionate stratified random sampling
2. Random sampling
3. Quota sampling
4. Convenience sampling

To get samples that represent your population, we recommend that you use either simple random sampling or proportionate stratified random sampling. A sample of 400 people using either of these random sampling techniques will get you a more representative sample of a large population than a sample of a million people using nonrandom sampling. Unfortunately, Kinsey, a biologist turned sex researcher, did not appreciate this fact. As a result of stubbornly using nonrandom sampling, Kinsey collected much more data than he needed to and was able to draw far fewer legitimate conclusions than he should have.

Note, however, that random sampling will not be accurate unless you have an accurate list of your population—and you may not be able to get such a list. For example, if you wanted to randomly sample people who will vote in the next election, the list of such voters does not exist. You can get a list of registered voters, you can get a list of voters who have voted in the last few elections, but you cannot get a list of only those people who will vote in the next election.

Although most polling organizations do a decent job of maintaining a good list, some use poor lists. One of the most infamous cases of working from a poor list was the poll that led to the headline you may have seen in a history book: "Dewey beats Truman." The problem was that the list the polling company worked from was compiled from telephone books and automobile registrations. Back in 1936, the wealthy were much more likely to have phones, to have cars, and to be Republicans. Thus, the poll of Republicans yielded a strong preference for the Republican candidate (Dewey) rather than the actual winner (Truman).

However, even if you have a perfect list and draw a perfect sample from that list, you may not end up with a perfect sample because of nonresponse bias (see Figure 8-4). In other words, your sample will not represent members of the population who choose not to respond. Nonresponse bias is so powerful that it can even cause exit polls of voters to be inaccurate. For example, in the 2004 election, it appears that Bush voters were less likely to participate in exit polls than Kerry voters, thus making it appear that Kerry had defeated Bush.

There are two things you can do about the bias caused by nonresponse. First, you can get your response rate so high that nonresponse is not a big problem. For instance, by mailing out information to participants in advance, by keeping the survey short, and by calling people back repeatedly, some telephone interviewers have obtained response rates of 97% or better.

Figure 8-4   **The Challenge of Capturing the Population**

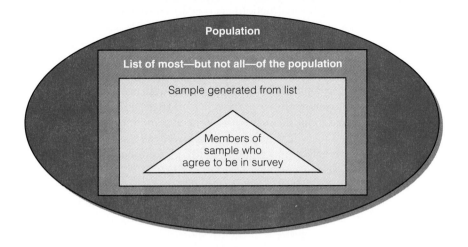

We would like to measure the population: all the members of a particular group. However, we usually do not start with the actual population. Instead, we start with a list of the population members—a list that is usually incomplete. Then, we usually take a sample from that list, a sample that is not a perfect sample of that list. Finally, we get people who agree to and actually do fill out the survey—a group that usually is a biased subgroup of our sample. Thus, our respondents are usually not a perfect reflection of the population.

Second, keep detailed records on the people who refused. If possible, unobtrusively record their sex, race, and estimated age. By knowing who is dropping out of your sample, you may know to whom your results don't apply.

Administering the Survey

You have your survey questions. You've carefully sequenced your questions, and you've determined your sampling technique. You have weighed the benefits and the risks of doing your survey and you have taken steps to maintain your participants' confidentiality. You have had your study approved by your professor and either your department's ethics committee or your school's Internal Review Board (IRB). Now it's time for you to actually administer your survey.

As with any research, you must follow APA's ethical guidelines (APA, 2002) and conduct yourself professionally (see Appendix C: "Practical Tips for Conducting and Ethical and Valid Study"). For example, participants should always be greeted. If participants can't be greeted in person (as with a mail questionnaire), the questionnaire should be accompanied by a written greeting: a cover letter. In this written greeting, you should introduce yourself, explain the nature of your study, and request the participant's help—just as you would if you were greeting the participant in person. In addition to being polite, you should inform participants about (a) anything that would affect their decision to participate, such as how long the survey will take, whether the questions deal with any sensitive issues, and whether participants will be compensated for their participation; (b) their right to skip questions they don't want to answer; (c) their right to quit the study at any point; and (d) steps you will take to keep their responses confidential.

Participants should always be given clear instructions. As with any other study, an important part of these instructions is making it clear that participation is entirely voluntary. In an interview, the instructions are oral. In a questionnaire, they are written. However, if an investigator is administering the questionnaire, any written instructions can be backed up with oral ones.

After participants complete the survey, they should be thanked and debriefed about the purpose of the survey. At the end of a mail questionnaire, you should thank your participants, give them any additional instructions, and give them the opportunity to be debriefed. For example, you might write, "Please mail your questionnaire in the enclosed envelope. To find out more about the survey, put a check mark in the upper left-hand corner of the questionnaire and we will send you a summary of the results once the data have been analyzed. If you wish to talk to me about the study, please call me at 1-800-555-5555. Thank you for your participation."

Finally, as in all studies, you should be careful to ensure your participants' confidentiality. Before the survey begins, you and any other people working on the survey should sign a statement that they will not discuss participants' responses. As the data are collected, you must ensure that their responses are kept private. If you are interviewing participants, for instance, you must interview them in a private place where their responses will not be overheard. If you are having them fill out a questionnaire in a group setting, you should use a cover page and spread out participants so that they do not see one another's responses. If possible, you should not have participants put their names on the survey.

After participants respond to your survey, you must store and dispose of data in a way that keeps their data private. For example, you must store the information in a secure place (e.g., a locked file cabinet). If participants' names or other identifying information are on the cover sheet, you should probably either destroy the cover sheet as soon as possible or store the cover sheet in one place and the rest of the survey data in another place.

Analyzing Survey Data

Once you have collected your survey data, you need to analyze them. In this section, we will show you how to summarize and make inferences from your data.

Summarizing Data

The first step in analyzing survey data is to determine what data are relevant to your hypotheses. Once you know what data you want, you need to summarize those data. How you summarize your data will depend on what kind of data (e.g., nominal, ordinal, interval, or ratio) you have.

The type of data you have will depend on the type of questions you ask. When you ask rating scale questions or when you ask people to quantify their behavior ("How many hours a week do you use a computer?"), you probably can assume that your data are interval scale data.

If, on the other hand, you ask questions that people have to answer either "yes" or "no" ("Do you use a computer?" "Do you like students?"), or questions that call on people to put themselves into qualitatively different categories ("Are you male or female?"), you have nominal data.

| Table 8-5 | **Table of Means and Interactions** |

Table of Means for Computer Usage on Question 11: "I Like College Students"

COMPUTER USAGE

Yes	No
4.0	3.0

Average score on a 1 (*strongly disagree*) to 5 (*strongly agree*) scale.

Table of Means for Gender on Question 11: "I Like College Students"

GENDER

Men	Women
3.25	3.75

Average score on a 1 (*strongly disagree*) to 5 (*strongly agree*) scale.

Interaction for Gender by Computer Usage on Question 11: "I Like College Students"

COMPUTER USAGE

Gender	Yes	No
Men	3.5	3.0
Women	4.5	3.0

Average score on a 1 (*strongly disagree*) to 5 (*strongly agree*) scale.

Summarizing Interval Data

If all you need to know is the typical response to an interval scale question (e.g., the average of respondents' answers to the question, "How many hours a week do you use computers?"), all you need to calculate is the mean and standard deviation for that question.[6]

Summarizing Relationships Between Pairs of Variables. Rather than being interested only in the average response to a question, you will probably also want to know about the relationship between the answer to one question with the answers to other questions—in other words, the relationship between two or more variables. To begin to explore such a relationship, you will usually want to construct tables of means. For example, because we expected that there would be a relationship between computer use and sympathy for students, we compared computer users' average sympathy for students with noncomputer users' average sympathy for students (see the top of Table 8-5). To supplement your tables of means, you

---

[6]If you need help computing these statistics, you can (a) use a web calculator to do so, (b) use the formula for the mean (total divided by number of scores) and the formula for the standard deviation (for each score, subtract it from the mean, square the result, add up all those squared terms, and then divide that total by one less than the number of scores), or (c) follow the more detailed instructions in Appendix D.

may want to compute a correlation coefficient[7] to get an idea of the strength of the relationship between your two variables.[8]

Describing Complex Relationships Among Three or More Variables. Once you have looked at relationships between pairs of variables (for example, computer use and sympathy; gender and sympathy; gender and computer use), you may want to see how three or more variables are related. The easiest way to compare three or more variables is to construct a table of means, as we have done at the bottom of Table 8-5. As you can see, this 2×2 table of means allows us to look at how both computer use and gender are related to sympathy.

Summarizing Ordinal and Nominal Data

If your data are not interval scale data, don't summarize your data by computing means. For example, if you code 1 = man, 2 = woman, do not say that "the mean gender in my study was 1.41."

Similarly, if you are having participants *rank* several choices, do not say that the mean rank for Option B was 2.2. To understand why not, imagine that five people were ranking three options (Semon, 1990). Option A was ranked as second best by all five people (the rankings were "2-2-2-2-2"). Option B, on the other hand, was ranked best by two people and ranked third best by three people (the rankings were "1-1-3-3-3"). The mean rank for Option A is 2.0; the mean rank for Option B is 2.2 (Semon, 1990). Thus, according to the mean, A is assumed to be better liked (because it is closest to the average rank of 1.0, which would mean first choice).

In this case, however, the mean is misleading (Semon, 1990). The mean gives the edge to A because the mean assumes that the difference between being a second choice and being a third choice is the same as the difference between being a first choice and being a second choice. As you know, this is not the case. There is usually a considerable drop-off between one's first (favorite, best) choice and the one's second choice (runner-up, second best), but not such a great difference between one's second and third choices (Semon, 1990). For example, you may find an enormous drop-off between your liking of your best friend and your second best friend or between your favorite football team and your second favorite football team.

To go back to our example of Options A and B, recall that A's average rank was better than B's. However, because two people ranked B best and nobody ranked A first, we could argue that Option B was better liked (Semon, 1990). The moral of this example is that if you do not have interval data, do not use means to summarize your data. Instead, use frequencies or percentages.

Summarizing Relationships Between Pairs of Variables. To look at relationships among nominal variables, use a table to compare the different groups' responses. You could use a table of percentages to display the percentage of people belonging to one category (e.g., those

---

[7]Technically, the name of the correlation you would compute would be called the point biserial correlation. There is a special formula you can use specifically for calculating the point biserial r. However, if you use the formula for the Pearson r or if you have a computer calculate the Pearson r, you will obtain the correct value for the correlation coefficient (Cohen & Cohen, 1983).

[8]To compute Pearson r by hand, you can use the formula

$$N \times \Sigma(X \times Y) - (\Sigma X) \times (\Sigma Y) / \sqrt{([N \times (\Sigma X^2) - (\Sigma X)^2] \times [N \times (\Sigma Y^2) - (\Sigma Y)^2])}$$

or, if you want more detailed instructions, you can follow the steps described in Appendix D. For more information about correlation coefficients, see Chapter 7.

Table 8-6 Tables of Nominal Data

Computer Use by Gender

	GENDER	
Computer Use	Men	Women
Yes	(A)	(B)
	20	15
No	(C)	(D)
	55	10

Computer Use, Gender, and Academic Department

COMPUTER USE BY GENDER				COMPUTER USE BY GENDER		
	Gender				Gender	
Computer Use	Men	Women		Computers Use	Men	Women
Yes	10	10		Yes	20	20
No	80	0		No	40	20
Physical science professors				Social science professors		

belonging to the category "women professors") who also belong to a second category (e.g., "computer users"). Alternatively, you could use a frequency table to display the number of people belonging to one category who also belong to a second category. As you can see from Table 8-6, a frequency table can help you visualize similarities and differences between groups.

If you want to compute a measure to quantify how closely two nominal variables are related, you can calculate a correlational coefficient called the *phi coefficient*.[9] Like most correlation coefficients, phi ranges from −1 (perfect negative correlation) to +1 (perfect positive correlation).

Describing Complex Relationships Among Three or More Variables. If you want to look at how three or more variables are related, do not use the phi coefficient. Instead, construct tables of frequencies, as we have done in Table 8-6. These two 2 × 2 tables of frequencies do for our ordinal data what the 2 × 2 table of means did for our interval data—allow us to look at three variables at once.

Using Inferential Statistics

In addition to using descriptive statistics to describe the characteristics of your sample, you may wish to use inferential statistics. Inferential statistics may allow you to generalize the results of your sample to the population it represents. There are two main reasons why you might want to use inferential statistics.

---

[9] If you code data as "0" does not belong to the category and "1" belongs to the category, you can calculate the phi coefficient using the Pearson *r* formula:

$$N \times \Sigma(X \times Y) - (\Sigma X) \times (\Sigma Y) / \sqrt{([N \times (\Sigma X^2) - (\Sigma X)^2] \times [N \times (\Sigma Y^2) - (\Sigma Y)^2])}.$$

For step-by-step instructions on how to compute phi, see Appendix D.

First, you might want to use inferential statistics to estimate certain **parameters** (characteristics of the population) such as the population mean for how much time professors spend using computers. For example, if you wanted to use the average amount of time professors in your sample said they used computers to estimate the average amount of time all Bromo Tech professors spend using computers, you would be using **parameter estimation.**

Second, you might want to determine whether the relationship you found between two or more variables would hold in the population. For instance, you might want to determine whether using computers and student sympathy are related in the population. Because you are deciding whether to reject the **null hypothesis** (that the variables are *not* related in the population), this use of inferential statistics is called **hypothesis testing.**

In hypothesis testing, the researcher determines how likely it is that the obtained results would occur if the null hypothesis is true. If the results are extremely unlikely given that the null hypothesis is true, the null hypothesis is rejected. Typically, "extremely unlikely" means that the *probability* of finding such a result given that the null hypothesis was true is less than 5 in 100 ($p < .05$). If the null hypothesis is rejected, the relationship between variables is declared **statistically significant:** probably not due to chance alone; reliable.

Parameter Estimation With Interval Data

As we just mentioned, one reason for using inferential statistics would be to estimate population parameters. From our survey of computer usage and student sympathy, we might want to estimate one parameter: the amount of sympathy the average professor at our school has for students.

Our best guess of the amount of sympathy the average professor at our school has for students is the average amount of sympathy the average professor in our sample has for students. This guess may be inaccurate because the average for our sample may differ from the average in the population. Therefore, it is often useful to establish a range in which the population mean is likely to fall. For example, you may want to establish a **95% confidence interval:** a range in which you can be 95% sure that the population mean falls.

You can establish 95% confidence intervals for any population mean from the sample mean, if you know the **standard error of the mean.**[10] You establish the lower limit of your confidence interval by subtracting approximately two standard errors from the sample mean. Then, you establish the upper limit of your confidence interval by adding approximately two standard errors[11] to the sample mean. Thus, if the average sympathy rating for all the professors in our sample was 3.0 and the standard error was .5, we could be 95% confident that the true population mean is somewhere between 2.0 and 4.0.[12]

---

[10]The standard error of the mean equals the standard deviation divided by the square root of the number of participants. Thus, if the *sd* is 8 and the sample size is 100, the standard error of the mean would be $8/\sqrt{100} = 8/10$. For more on the standard error, see either Chapter 7 or Appendix D.

[11]To determine precisely what you should multiply the standard error by, look at the .05 significance column of Table E-1 (in Appendix E) in the row corresponding to one less than your sample size. If your sample size is less than 61, you will have to multiply the standard error by a number larger than two. If your sample size is greater than 61, multiplying by two will give you a larger confidence interval than you need: You would be more than 95% confident that the true population mean is within that interval. Usually, the number of standard errors will vary from 1.96 to 2.776. To be more precise, the exact number will depend on your degrees of freedom (*df*)—and your *df* will be 1 less than your number of participants. (For example, if you have a mean based on 11 participants' scores, your *df* will be 10.) Once you have calculated your *df*, go to the *t* table (Table E-1) in Appendix E. In that table, you will look under the .05 column (it starts with 12.706) and find the entry corresponding to your *df*. Thus, if you have a *df* of 10, you would multiply your standard error by 2.228; if you had a *df* of 120, you would multiply your standard error by 1.98.

[12]If we had 61 participants (see the previous footnote).

Hypothesis Testing With Interval Data

You can also use statistics to see if there are significant differences between groups. That is, we might want to know if the differences between groups that we observe in our sample also apply to the population at large.

Testing Relationships Between Two Variables. By using a *t* test,[13] we could test whether the differences in sympathy we observed between computer users and noncomputer users were too large to be due to sampling error alone and thus probably represented a true difference.

The *t* test between means is not the only way to determine whether there is a relationship between computer usage and student sympathy. We could also see whether a relationship exists by determining whether the correlation coefficient between those two variables was significant.[14]

If you were comparing more than one pair of variables, you could do several *t* tests or test the significance of several correlations (for more about these analyses, see Chapter 7 or our website). In either case, you should correct for doing more than a single statistical test. One way to correct for doing more than one test is to use a more stringent significance level than the conventional .05 level, such as a .01 significance level. Note that the more tests you do, the more stringent your significance level should be. For example, if you looked at 5 comparisons, you might use the .01 level; if you looked at 50 comparisons, you might use the .001 level.

To understand why you should correct for doing multiple tests, imagine that you are betting on coin flips. You win if you get a heads. If you flip a coin once, it's fair to say that there's a 50% chance of getting a heads. However, if you flip a coin three times and declare victory if any of those flips come up heads, then it's not fair to claim that you only had a 50% chance of winning. Similarly, a .05 significance level implies that you only have a 5% chance of getting those results by chance alone. This false alarm rate (Type 1 error rate) of .05 applies only if you were doing one test. If you are doing 100 tests and none of your variables are related, then it would not be unusual for you to get 5 false alarms (because .05 + 100 = 5).

Testing Relationships Among More Than Two Variables. Suppose you wanted to look at more than two variables at once. For example, suppose you wanted to explore the relationship between computer usage, gender, and sympathy summarized in Table 8-5. You might especially be interested to see whether gender was a moderator variable—whether it qualified or modified the relationship between computer usage and sympathy. For example, you might ask, "Is computer usage a better predictor of student sympathy for women or for men?" To answer questions involving moderator variables, you might analyze your data using analysis of variance (ANOVA).[15]

If you are dealing with multiple predictors, ANOVA is probably the simplest analysis you can do. To learn about more sophisticated analyses that you might use or that you may encounter as you read research articles, see Box 8-2.

---

[13]To compute a *t*, you would subtract your two group means and then divide by the standard error of the differences. To calculate the standard error of the differences by hand, you can (a) use the formula: standard error of the mean = $\sqrt{s_1{}^2/N_1 + s_2{}^2/N_2}$, where s = standard deviation and N = number of participants, and where $_1$ refers to group 1 and $_2$ refers to group 2; or (b) follow the more detailed set of instructions in Appendix D. To learn more about *t*, see either Chapter 10 or Appendix D.

[14]The formula for this test is

$$t = \frac{r \times \sqrt{(N-2)}}{\sqrt{(1 - [r \times r])}}$$

To find out more about the test, see Appendix D.

[15]To learn more about ANOVA, see Chapter 11 or Appendix D.

BOX 8-2 Advanced Analyses

If your data include multiple measures or multiple predictors, you should consider using analyses designed to deal with multiple variables. For example, suppose that, rather than trying to determine whether a single predictor (computer usage) predicted the answers to a single variable (sympathy), you were trying to determine whether two predictors (computer usage and gender) predicted the answers to two dependent measures: (1) responses to Question 4 and (2) responses to Question 10.

Multiple ANOVAs and Multivariate Analysis of Variance

One approach to determining whether computer usage and gender predict the answers to these two questions would be to perform two ANOVAs (one on Question 4 and one on Question 10). If you perform multiple ANOVAs, you should correct your significance level for the number of ANOVAs you computed, just as you would if you computed multiple *t* tests (see this chapter's section "Testing Relationships Between Two Variables").[a]

Factor Analysis

In an earlier example, we avoided the problem of doing analyses on multiple measures (e.g., separate analyses for Questions 6, 7, 8, 9, and 10) by deciding that the sum of answers to Questions 6 through 10 would be our student sympathy measure. Although combining the answers to those five questions into one measure simplified our analyses, a critic might question whether those five questions actually measured the same underlying variable. In published research, most investigators would do a **factor analysis** to make the case that those five items were indeed measuring the same underlying factor (to learn more about factor analysis, see Appendix D).

Multiple Regression

Even if a survey researcher's sole goal is to predict responses to a single question (e.g., Question 11), analyzing the results may be complicated—if respondents' answers to several other questions might predict their answers to that particular question. To go back to our sample survey, suppose your sole goal was to predict respondents' answers to Question 11: "I like students." Although you are trying to predict responses to only one question, you have many potential predictors (e.g., professor rank, professor experience, computer usage, gender, answers to Questions 4–10, and answers to Questions 12–15). If you want to know (a) how best to use these predictors to come up with an accurate prediction of how people will respond to Question 11, (b) how accurate that prediction will be, or (c) how important each of these predictors are, you should probably use multiple regression to analyze your data (to learn more about multiple regression, see Appendix D).

Structural Equation Modeling

Structural equation modeling (SEM) often has two elements: (1) a measurement model that, like factor analysis, specifies how an observed measure (e.g., answers to some test questions) correlates with a hypothetical, unobserved factor (e.g., shyness), and (2) a cause–effect model that specifies which variables are causes and which are effects (Kline, 1998). However, not all SEMs involve both aspects.

Factor analysis, for example, is an SEM technique that does not look for cause–effect relationships between variables. Instead, it focuses exclusively on establishing a measurement model: a model that specifies how scores on a measure—called indicators, observed variables, or manifest variables–are related to some invisible, underlying factor. Therefore, in factor analysis, researchers collect scores on several indicators of each hypothetical variable and then create a measurement model that specifies how these observed measures (e.g., test items or test scores) are associated with an unobservable, hypothetical latent factor (e.g., creativity) that is not directly observed.

Thus, if we thought our survey was measuring two different things (e.g., creativity and assertiveness), we would hope that our factor analysis would support the idea that our questions were measuring two factors (in technical lingo, we would hope that "two factors were extracted and those factors accounted for over 60% of the variability in scores"). We would also hope that our

[a]Some believe the way to make sure that your *actual* significance level (your chance of making a Type 1 error: the error of declaring that a relationship between variables is statistically significant when, in reality, there is no relationship between the variables) is equal to your *stated* significance level when doing multiple ANOVAs is to do a multivariate analysis of variance (MANOVA) on your data first. If the overall MANOVA is significant, many believe you can then do your specific ANOVAs. However, as Huberty and Morris (1989) point out, such a strategy may not be an effective way to reduce Type 1 errors. In our example, there would be benefits to using MANOVA. A significant main effect for computer usage would suggest that the computer usage predicts the answers to at least one of the two questions. A significant interaction between computer usage and question would suggest that the correlation between computer usage and Question 4 is different from the correlation between computer usage and Question 10.

Figure 8-5 | Possible Results From a Factor Analysis

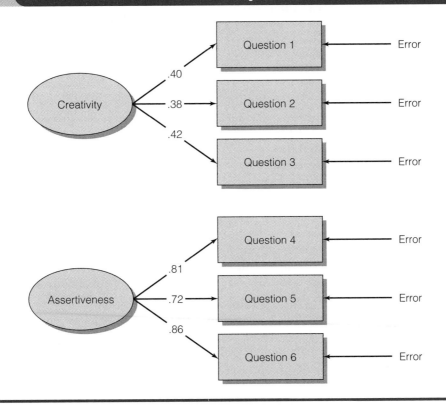

creativity questions all correlated with each other, so that we could infer that the creativity questions all correlated with (loaded on) the same factor (construct), and that our assertiveness questions correlated with each other and that they loaded on a different construct. Thus, Figure 8-5 would support the idea that we had two factors (the circles), one measured by Questions 1–3, another measured by Questions 4–6.

Path analysis, on the other hand, does not have a measurement model. It does not try to make connections between observed scores and some invisible construct. Instead, path analysis focuses exclusively on trying to establish cause–effect paths between the observed, measured variables. One use of path analysis is to test a hypothesis that one variable mediates the effect of another.

For example, suppose we measure A, an attitude (e.g., liking research methods), B, a behavior (e.g.,

studying research methods), and C, a consequence (e.g., grade in research methods). Rather than hypothesizing that liking research methods has a direct effect on grades (A → C), the investigator may hypothesize a model in which A's effect on C is an indirect effect, mediated by B (A → B → C). In path analysis, the researcher uses multiple regression (just described) to estimate the strength of the paths between the variables. (Path analysis relies so much on multiple regression that one expert calls path analysis "multiple regression with pictures" [B. M. Byrne, 2004].) If the direct path between A → C is strong and the indirect path (A → B → C)[b] is weak, the researcher would conclude that A's effect on C is direct. If, on the other hand, the indirect path (A → B → C) is strong and the direct A → C path is weak, the researcher might conclude that A's effect on C is mediated through B.

---

[b]If you aren't given the strength of the indirect path (A → B → C), you can calculate it by multiplying the A-B path coefficient by the B-C coefficient. So, if the A → B path was .4 and the B → C path was .2, the A → B → C path would be .08.

continued

BOX 8-1   *(continued)*

In short, most structural equation models are more complex than either path analysis or factor analysis. Most SEMs are more complicated than path analysis because, rather than confining themselves to observed variables, they test relationships between unobserved (latent) factors. In a sense, because most SEMs use multiple indicators of each hypothetical factor, most

SEMs incorporate a factor analysis. However, most SEMs are more complicated than factor analysis because most SEMs test not only a relationship between a hypothetical factor and measures of that factor but also try to determine how one hypothetical factor causes a change in another.

Using Inferential Statistics With Nominal Data

Just as inferential statistics can be applied to interval data, they can be applied to nominal data. Indeed, if you do research as part of your job, you may be more likely to do parameter estimation and hypothesis testing with nominal data than with interval data.

Parameter Estimation With Nominal Data. You might start by doing some basic parameter estimation such as estimating the percentage of people who have some characteristic. If you used random sampling and chose your sample size according to the first column of Table 8-4, you can be 95% confident that your sample percentages are within 5% of the population's percentages. Thus, if you find that 35% of your participants are women, you would be 95% confident that 30–40% of your population are women.

Hypothesis Testing With Nominal Data. After estimating the percentages of the population that had certain characteristics, you might go on to look for differences between groups. In that case, you would use significance tests to determine whether differences between sample percentages reflect differences in population percentages. For example, in your sample, you may find that more men than women use computers. Is that a relationship that holds in your population—or is that pattern due to random sampling error? To rule out the possibility that the pattern is an artifact of random sampling error, use a statistical test. But instead of using a t test, as you would with interval data, you would use a test that doesn't require you to have interval data: the **chi-square (χ^2) test.**[16]

If you are performing more than one chi-square test, you should correct for the number of analyses performed by raising your significance level to compensate for doing multiple analyses. For example, if you are comparing five chi-squares, you should use a .01 significance level rather than a .05 significance level.

Concluding Remarks

In this chapter, you learned the essence of good survey research. Early in the chapter, you were introduced to the applications and limitations of survey research. You saw the advantages and disadvantages of different survey formats, as well as the strengths and weaknesses of different kinds of questions. After learning how to write a survey, you learned how to administer, score, and analyze survey data. If you apply what you have learned in this chapter (see Figure 8-6), you will be a skilled survey researcher.

---

[16] To compute a chi square, you first calculate the expected number of observations that should be in each cell by taking the row total for that cell, multiplying it by the column total, and then dividing by the total number of observations. Then, for each cell, you take the actual total for the cell, subtract the expected score for that cell, square the difference, and then divide the difference by the expected score. Now that you have a result for each cell, add up all those results to get your chi square. To see whether your chi square is significant, go to Table E-2 in Appendix E. For more detailed instructions and an example of how to do a chi-square test, see Appendix D.

Figure 8-6 Guidelines for Survey Research

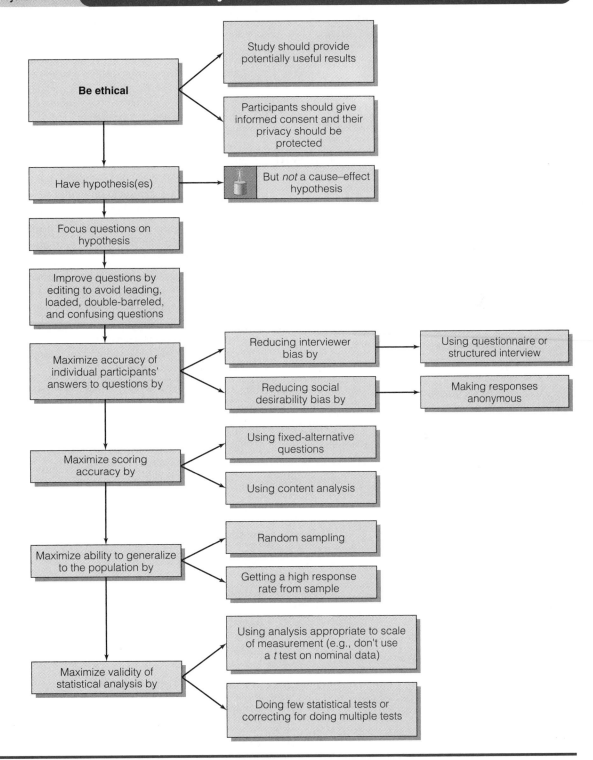

SUMMARY

1. Surveys can help you describe what people are thinking, feeling, or doing.

2. Surveys allow you to gather information from a large sample with less effort and expense than most other data-gathering techniques.

3. In a survey, it is important to ask only relevant questions.

4. Don't accept respondents' answers as truth. People don't always tell the truth or even know what the "truth" is.

5. Surveys yield only correlational data. You cannot draw cause–effect conclusions from correlational data.

6. There are two main drawbacks to self-administered questionnaires: (1) They have a low return rate, and (2) respondents may misinterpret questions.

7. Investigator-administered questionnaires have a higher response rate than self-administered questionnaires.

8. Interviews are especially useful for exploratory studies. However, interviews are expensive, and the interviewer may bias participants' responses.

9. Telephone surveys have higher response rates, are easier to administer, and offer greater anonymity than personal interviews.

10. Your first step in survey research is to have a hypothesis.

11. There are three basic question formats: nominal-dichotomous, Likert-type, and open-ended.

12. Structured surveys are more useful than unstructured.

13. In survey research, you want to ask the right people the right questions.

14. To ask the "right people," you need a representative sample. To get a representative sample, you must first know what your population (the group that you want to generalize to) is. Once you know your population, you can try to get a representative sample by using either random or proportionate stratified random sampling. Unfortunately, getting your random sample may be hampered by nonresponse bias.

15. To ask good questions, (1) make sure they relate to your hypotheses; (2) edit them so they are short, clear, and unbiased; and (3) pretest them.

16. Careful attention should be placed on sequencing questions. Keep similar questions together and put personal questions last.

17. Be aware of response biases, such as a tendency of participants to agree with statements or the tendency to answer questions in a way that puts the participant in a positive light.

18. Spending a little time deciding how to code your questionnaire before you administer it can save a great deal of time later on.

19. Both random and proportionate stratified random sampling allow you to make statistical inferences from your data.

20. Participants in survey research should be treated with the same respect as human participants in any other kind of study.

KEY TERMS

survey *(p. 208)*

population *(p. 208)*

descriptive hypothesis *(p. 209)*

retrospective self-report *(p. 214)*

social desirability bias *(p. 214)*

demand characteristics *(p. 215)*

response set *(p. 215)*

nonresponse bias *(p. 215)*

questionnaire *(p. 215)*

interview *(p. 215)*

self-administered questionnaire *(p. 216)*

interviewer bias *(p. 220)*

random digit dialing *(p. 221)*

fixed-alternative question *(p. 224)*

dichotomous question *(p. 224)*

nominal-dichotomous item *(p. 225)*

power *(p. 225)*

Likert-type item *(p. 225)*

summated score *(p. 226)*

open-ended question *(p. 227)*

structured interview *(p. 228)*

semistructured interview *(p. 228)*

unstructured interview *(p. 229)*

leading question *(p. 229)*

double-barreled question *(p. 229)*

demographics *(p. 233)*

random sampling *(p. 234)*

proportionate stratified random sampling *(p. 236)*

convenience sampling *(p. 236)*

quota sampling *(p. 237)*

parameters *(p. 244)*

parameter estimation *(p. 244)*

null hypothesis *(p. 244)*

hypothesis testing *(p. 244)*

statistically significant *(p. 244)*

95% confidence interval *(p. 244)*

standard error of the mean *(p. 244)*

factor analysis *(p. 246)*

chi-square test *(p. 248)*

EXERCISES

1. You probably have participated in many surveys. For one of those surveys, answer the following questions:
   a. What was the topic of the survey?
   b. What do you think the hypothesis was?
   c. Did they use an oral interview or a written questionnaire? Do you think they made the right choice? Why or why not?

2. State a hypothesis that can be tested by administering a survey. Why is a survey a good way to test your hypothesis?

3. Is an interview or a questionnaire the best way to test your hypothesis? Why?

4. For the three basic question formats, list their advantages and disadvantages in the grid below.

QUESTION FORMAT	NOMINAL-DICHOTOMOUS	LIKERT-TYPE	OPEN-ENDED
ADVANTAGES			
DISADVANTAGES			

5. Write three nominal-dichotomous questions that might help you test your hypothesis.

6. Write three Likert-type questions that might help you test your hypothesis.

7. Write three open-ended questions that might help you test your hypothesis.

8. Edit your questions using the points presented in this chapter.

9. Why can you make statistical inferences from data obtained from a random sample?

10. Why might having participants sign informed consent statements (a statement that they had been informed of the nature of the study, the risks and benefits of the study, the participants' right to refuse to be in the study, the participants' right to quit the survey at any point, and the participants' right to

confidentiality) make a survey research study less ethical? (Hints: Under what circumstances does the APA ethical code not require informed consent for surveys [see Appendix C]? Under what circumstances would requiring informed consent reduce the value of the survey without providing any benefits to participants?)

WEB RESOURCES

1. Go to the Chapter 8 section of the book's student website and
   a. Look over the concept map of the key terms.
   b. Test yourself on the key terms.
   c. Take the Chapter 8 Practice Quiz.

2. If you are ready to draft a method section, click on the "Method Section Tips" link.

3. If you want to have a better understanding of correlation coefficients, click on the "Correlator" link.

4. Use the sample data and the statistical calculators available from the "Evaluate a Questionnaire" link

to evaluate the reliability and construct validity of a questionnaire.

5. Use the sample data and the statistical calculators available from the "Analyzing Results" link to practice analyzing and interpreting data from a survey. If you wish, you can also use that link to find out how to use multiple regression to analyze survey responses.

INFOTRAC COLLEGE EDITION EXPLORATIONS

1. To read an interesting survey study on regrets, do an InfoTrac College Edition keyword search using the phrase "survey and regrets."

2. To get some insights into the challenges of survey research, do an InfoTrac College Edition keyword search using the phrase "conflicting surveys."

3. To look at how even simple surveys can get some interesting results, do an InfoTrac College Edition

keyword search using the phrase "students and surveys and cheating."

4. To see the challenges of trying to make a case for a cause–effect relationship, do an InfoTrac College Edition keyword search using the phrase "correlates of hair loss" to read Wells, Willmoth, and Russell's (1995) survey of balding men.

Internal Validity

9

Any person armed with an understanding of causation
has the power to change, alter, repair, and control.

—*Neal Roese*

Overview

This chapter is about **internal validity:** establishing that a factor causes an effect. If you need to determine whether a treatment, action, intervention, training program, lecture, or therapy works, you need to conduct a study that has internal validity. For example, you would need a study with internal validity to determine whether

- piano lessons increase IQ scores
- listeners will be more persuaded by hearing a weak argument when listeners are sitting down than by hearing the same argument when they are standing up
- students will do better on an exam if it is printed on blue rather than white paper
- a restaurant server's manner (e.g., squatting down next to a customer as opposed to standing up, smiling an open-mouthed smile as opposed to a closed-mouth smile) increases the amount of money the server gets in tips
- music will cause shoppers to go through the store faster
- sugar will make young children more active
- students will have higher test scores when taught in classrooms that have windows
- keeping a log of what one should be grateful for will make people score higher on a happiness test
- full-spectrum lighting will increase people's scores on a mood scale

Establishing internal validity involves meeting three challenges. Each challenge builds on, and is more difficult than, the one before it.

First, because changes in the cause must be accompanied by changes in the outcome variable, you must establish that variations in the alleged cause are related to variations in the outcome variable. For example, if you are going to show that sugar causes children to be more active, you first need to show that when children have more sugar, they are more active. Similarly, if you are going to show that writing about things one is thankful for increases happiness, you need to establish that people who write about things for which they are thankful are happier than people who do not write about things for which they are thankful. You should be able to determine whether differences in one factor are accompanied by differences in the outcome variable by measuring both variables and using the appropriate statistics. For example, you might be able to establish that the average (mean) score of the group asked to write about what they are grateful for is significantly (reliably) different from the mean score of the group not assigned that task.

Second, because the cause must come before its effects, you must establish that changes in the treatment came *before* changes in the outcome variable. By manipulating the treatment, you will usually be able to establish that changes in the treatment came before—and are followed by—changes in the outcome variable. For example, if you have the treatment group participants write about things they are thankful for and then measure mood, you will usually be able to make the case that participants writing about what they were grateful for came before—not after—increases in happiness. Note that if you did not manipulate a treatment—for example, if you just counted how many grateful entries people had in their diaries—it could be that happiness caused gratitude rather than gratitude causing happiness. In other words, if you don't manipulate the treatment, what you think is a cause may actually be an effect.

Third, because many nontreatment factors may have caused the changes in your outcome variable, you must establish that the treatment (writing about what they should be grateful for) is the only factor responsible for the effect (higher scores on the happiness measure). Put another way, your final challenge is to show that the difference in the outcome measure (higher happiness scores) is not due to anything other than the treatment (the gratitude manipulation). Because meeting this last challenge—ruling out **extraneous factors:** factors other than the treatment—is so tricky, ruling out extraneous factors is the focus of this chapter.

The most direct way to rule out extraneous factors is to eliminate them from your study, thus ensuring that they can't be responsible for your results. In the abstract, there are two ways you can get rid of extraneous factors:

1. *The idealized two-group design:* Create two identical groups; treat them the same, except give only one of the groups the treatment; then compare the treatment group to the no-treatment group.

2. *The idealized pretest-posttest design:* Find some participants; give them the outcome measure; make sure that nothing in their life changes, except that they get the treatment; then give them the outcome measure again.

In practice, however, neither of these approaches succeeds in eliminating extraneous variables. As a result—contrary to what many people believe—neither can prove that a treatment caused an effect.

In this chapter, you will learn why these two approaches fail to establish internal validity. Along the way, you will learn about Campbell and Stanley's (1963) eight threats to internal validity:

1. *Selection:* Treatment and no-treatment groups were different before the treatment was administered.

2. *Selection by maturation interaction:* Treatment and no-treatment groups were predisposed to grow apart.

3. *Regression effects:* If participants are chosen because their pretest scores were extreme, those extreme scores may be extremely affected by random measurement error. Their posttest scores will probably be affected by random error to a more normal—lesser—extent and thus will tend to be more normal.

4. *Mortality:* Differences between conditions are due to participants dropping out of the study.

5. *Maturation:* Apparent treatment effects are really due to natural, physiological changes, such as growth and development.

6. *History:* Things other than the treatment have changed in the participants' environments.

7. *Testing:* Changes resulted from the practice and experience participants got on the pretest.

8. *Instrumentation:* The way participants were measured changed from pretest to posttest.

Specifically, you will know enough about those eight threats to

1. detect their presence in research that erroneously claims to prove that a certain factor has an effect

2. avoid using a design that is vulnerable to these threats

3. take steps to prevent these threats from corrupting the internal validity of your research

Problems With Two-Group Designs

To begin our exploration of Campbell and Stanley's eight threats to validity, let's examine the first approach for ruling out extraneous variables: obtaining two identical groups. Specifically, suppose you obtain two groups of participants and treat them identically, except that only one of the groups receives the treatment (e.g., writing about events for which they should be grateful). Then, you give both groups a happiness scale and note that they have different levels of happiness.

Why We Never Have Identical Groups

What do you conclude? If the groups were identical before you introduced the treatment, you would correctly conclude that the treatment caused the groups to differ. However, if the groups were different before you introduced the treatment, the difference in scores could be due to **selection** (also called **selection bias**): having groups that were different from one another before the study began.

Self-Assignment to Group Produces Selection Bias

How can you avoid selection bias? A first step toward avoiding selection error is to prevent **self-selection:** participants choosing what condition they want to be in. You want to avoid self-selection because it leaves you with groups that differ on at least one dimension: One group chose the treatment, whereas the other chose to avoid the treatment. Furthermore, the groups probably also differ in ways that you do not know about.

Sometimes the effects of self-selection are obvious. For example, suppose you compare two groups—one group offers to stay after work to attend a seminar on "Helping Your Company"; the other does not. If you find that the seminar group is more loyal to the company than the no-seminar group, you can't conclude that the effect is due to the seminar: After all, the groups probably differed in loyalty before the study began.

Sometimes the effects of self-selection are not as obvious. For instance, what if you let participants choose whether they get to be in the gratitude condition or in the no-gratitude condition? If you find that the gratitude group is happier than the no-gratitude group, you can't conclude that the effect was due to the gratitude manipulation. People who prefer to write about what they are thankful for may be happier than people who prefer not to write about what they are thankful for. You may not know exactly how participants who choose one condition differ from those who choose another condition. But you do know that they differ—and those differences may cause the groups to differ at the end of the study.

Researcher Assignment to Group Produces Selection Bias

We've seen that letting participants assign themselves to a group creates unequal, nonequivalent groups. However, if you assign participants to groups, you might unintentionally bias your study. For example, you might put all the smiling participants in the gratitude condition and all the frowning participants in the no-treatment condition.

Arbitrary Assignment to Group Produces Selection Bias: Choosing Groups Based on Their Differences Results in Having Groups That Are Different

To avoid the bias of "stacking the deck," you might assign participants to groups on the basis of some arbitrary rule. For example, why not assign students on the right-hand side of the room to the no-treatment group and assign students on the left side of the room to the treatment group? The answer is simple: "Because the groups are not equal." At the very least, the groups differ in that one group prefers the right side, whereas the other group prefers the left side. The groups probably also differ in many other ways. For instance, if the left side of the room is near the windows and the right side is near the door, we can list at least four additional potential differences between "left-siders" and "right-siders":

1. People sitting on the left side of the room may be more energetic (they chose to walk the width of the room to find a seat).

2. People sitting on the left side of the room may be early-arrivers (students who came in late would tend to sit on the right side so they would not disrupt class by crossing the width of the room).

3. People sitting on the left side may be more interested in the outdoors (they chose to have access to the window).

4. People sitting on the left side may have chosen those seats to get a better view of the professor's performance (if the professor shows the typical right-hander's tendency of turning to the right, which would be the students' left).

You can probably come up with many other differences between left-siders and right-siders in a particular class. But the point is that the groups definitely differ in at least one respect (choice of side of room), and they almost certainly differ in numerous other respects (see Figure 9-1).

What's true for the arbitrary rule of assigning participants to groups on the basis of where they sit is true for any other arbitrary rule. Thus, any researchers who assign participants on the basis of an arbitrary rule (the first-arriving participants assigned to the treatment group, people whose last names begin with a letter between *A* and *L* in the treatment group, etc.) make their research vulnerable to selection bias.

One infamous example of how arbitrary assignment can produce misleading research was Brady's (1958) "executive monkey" study. In that study, Brady tested monkeys in pairs. Each pair consisted of an "executive monkey" and a "worker monkey." The executive monkey controlled a switch that, if pressed at the right time, would prevent both monkeys from getting a shock. Brady found that the executive monkeys were more likely to get ulcers than the worker monkeys.

Although the study seemed to suggest that human executives deserve their high salaries because their responsibilities give them stress and ulcers, later research showed that individuals who do not have control (like the worker monkeys) were more likely to be stressed and get ulcers than individuals who have control (Seligman, 1975). The problem with Brady's research was selection bias—he assigned the monkeys who learned how to use the switch the fastest to be the executive monkeys. This arbitrary assignment was a big mistake, probably because the monkeys who learned to use the switch the fastest were those who were most upset by the shocks.

Arbitrarily assigning participants to groups does not work because you are assigning participants to groups based on their differences. Your groups can't be equal when you are deliberately ensuring that they are different on some variable—even if that variable (e.g., how fast one learns to use a switch, preference for side of the room, etc.) doesn't seem important.

Problems With Matching on Multiple Variables

If you can assign participants in a way that guarantees they are different, why can't you assign participants in a way that guarantees they are identical? In other words, why not use **matching:** choosing your groups so that they have identical characteristics?

Figure 9-1   Arbitrary Assignment to Groups Produces Selection Bias

a. The rule of choosing "every other person" to get the treatment is not random. The problem with this rule is most obvious when applied to situations in which people are encouraged to line up "boy/girl."

b. The arbitrary rule of assigning the front of the class to one treatment and the back of the class to no treatment does not work. Ask any teacher! The two groups are definitely different.

Figure 9-1 **(Continued)**

c. Assigning by left side versus right side ruins an attention study's internal validity. Students on the window-side of the room are sitting there because they want to look out the window or at the clock. The students on the other side of the room may be sitting there to avoid distractions.

The Impossibility of Perfectly Matching Individual Participants: Identical Participants Do Not Exist. In the abstract, matching seems like an easy, foolproof way of making sure that your two groups are equal. In practice, however, matching is neither easy nor foolproof. Imagine the difficulty of finding two people who match on every characteristic and then assigning one to the no-treatment condition and the other to the treatment condition. It would be impossible. Even identical twins would not be exactly alike—they have different first names and different experiences.

The Difficulty of Matching Groups on Every Variable: There Are Too Many Variables. Obviously, you can't create the situation in which each member of the treatment group has an identical clone in the no-treatment group. Nor can you get two groups that, on the average, match on every variable. Try as you might, there would always be some variable on which you had not matched—and that variable might be important. Even if you created two groups that had the same average age, same average intelligence, same average income, same average height, and same average weight, there would still be thousands of variables on which the groups might differ. The groups might differ in how they felt on the day of the study, how they were getting along with their parents, how many books they had read, their overall health, and so forth.

Two Difficulties With Matching Groups on Every Relevant Variable. You know you can't match your no-treatment and treatment groups on every single characteristic, but do you need to make the groups identical in every respect? No, you need them to be identical only in respect to the variable you want to measure. For example, suppose you were studying happiness. Then, all you would need to do is match your groups on every characteristic that will influence their scores on your happiness measure.

Unfortunately, there are two problems with this "solution." First, matching only on those factors that influence the key variable may be impossible because there may be thousands of factors that influence happiness. Second, you probably do not know every single characteristic that influences happiness. After all, if you knew everything about happiness, you would not be doing a study to find out about happiness.

Problems With Matching on Pretest Scores

Instead of matching participants on every characteristic that affects the variable you want to measure, why not match participants on the variable you want to measure? In your case, why not match participants on the happiness scores? Before you assign participants to groups, test people on the happiness scale (what researchers call a pretest). Next, match your groups so that the treatment group and no-treatment group have the same average pretest score. Finally, at the end of the study, test the participants again, giving participants what researchers call a posttest. If you find a difference between your groups on the posttest, then you should be positive that the treatment worked, right? Wrong!

Even if the treatment had no effect whatsoever, two groups that scored the same on the pretest could differ on the posttest. As you will see in the next two sections, there are two reasons matching on pretest scores may not make your groups equivalent: (1) selection by maturation interactions and (2) regression.

Selection by Maturation Interactions: Participants Growing in Different Ways. The first reason matching on pretest scores doesn't work is because you may have a **selection by maturation interaction:** The groups started out the same on the pretest but afterward developed at different rates or in different directions. Selection by maturation interactions occur when participants who are similar in one respect grow apart because they differ in other respects.

To visualize the strong impact that selection by maturation interaction can have, imagine you studied some 4th-grade boys and girls. You put all the boys in one group. Then, you had them lift weights. You saw that the average weight they could lift was 40 lbs (18.14 kg). You then picked a group of 4th-grade girls who could also lift 40 lbs. Thus, your groups are equivalent on the pretest. Then, you introduced the treatment: strength pills. You gave the boys strength pills for 8 years. When both groups were in the 12th grade, you measured their strength. You found that the boys were much stronger than the girls. This difference might be due to the strength pills; however, the difference might instead be due to the boys naturally developing greater strength than the girls. In other words, the difference may be due to failing to match on a variable (gender) that influences muscular maturation.

In addition to growing apart because of different rates of physical maturation, groups may also grow apart because of different rates of social, emotional, or intellectual maturation. To illustrate this point, let's examine a situation in which the two groups are probably changing in different ways on virtually every aspect of development.

Suppose a researcher matched a group of 19-year-old employees with a group of 63-year-old employees on the basis of job performance. The researcher then enrolled the 19-year-olds in a training program. When the researcher compared the groups 2 years later, the researcher found that the 19-year-olds were performing better than the 63-year-olds. Why?

Although the difference could have been due to training, it also may have had nothing to do with the training. Instead, the difference may have been due to (1) the 19-year-olds' productivity increasing because they are just learning their jobs and (2) the 63-year-olds' productivity naturally declining as this group anticipates retirement. Therefore, the apparent treatment effect may really be a selection by maturation interaction.

You may be saying to yourself that you would never make the mistake of matching 19-year-olds and 63-year-olds on pretest scores. If so, we're glad. You intuitively know that you can't make groups equivalent by merely matching on pretest scores. We would caution you, however, to realize that age is not the only—or even the most important—variable that affects maturation.[1] Many factors, such as intelligence, motivation, and health, affect maturation. Thus, if you are going to match on pretest scores, you must also match on all of the variables that might affect maturation. Otherwise, you run the risk of a selection by maturation interaction.

To repeat, matching on pretest scores is incomplete. Pretest scores are good predictors of posttest scores but not perfect predictors. Many factors affect how a participant does on the posttest. If the groups are not matched on these other relevant variables, two groups that started out the same on the pretest may naturally grow apart. Thus, what looks like a treatment effect may really be a selection by maturation interaction.

If you were somehow able to match on pretest scores and all other relevant variables, you would be able to rule out selection by maturation. However, you would still have the problem that your matched groups might not be equal on the pretest variable.

The Regression Effect: Participants With Extreme Scores Tend to Have Less Extreme Scores on Retests. How could your groups not be equal if you measured them and made sure that they were equal? The problem is that because measurement is not perfect, measuring groups as equal does not mean they are equal.

Even though we tend to assume that measurement is perfect, it is not. For example, if a police officer stops you for speeding, the officer might say, "You were going 75." Or the officer might say, "I clocked you at 75." The officer's two statements are very different. You may have been going 40 and the radar mis-timed you (radars have clocked trees at over 100 mph), or you may have been going 95. In any event, you probably were not going at exactly the speed that the officer recorded. Even in this age of advanced technology, something as simple as measuring someone's height is not immune to measurement error. In fact, one of the authors fluctuates between 5 ft 5 in (165 cm) and 5 ft 8 in (172.7 cm), depending on which physician's office she is measured at. If measurements of variables as easy to measure as height are contaminated with random error, measurements of psychological variables—variables that are harder to measure than height—will also be victimized by random measurement error.

Because of random measurement error, a measure of an individual's height, weight, mood, free-throw shooting ability, or almost anything else might be inaccurate. Thus, two individuals having the same score on a measure might actually differ on the variable being measured. For example, if you tested free-throw shooting ability by having people shoot two free throws, a good and a poor free throw shooter might both score 50% on your measure.

Although random error might cause two individuals who differ to have the same scores, could random error cause two groups that differ to have the same average score? At first you

---

[1]Note that, contrary to ageist stereotypes, we might find that the older workers improved more than the younger workers. That is, older workers are much more productive and involved than many people assume. Indeed, this ageism is probably why our poor researcher was forced to do such a flawed study. The researcher was able to get management to invest in training for the younger workers but not for the older workers. In essence, the researcher used the older workers as a comparison group because management gave her no choice.

might think the answer would be "no." You might reason that because random error is, by definition, unsystematic and unbiased, it should affect each group to about the same extent. Because random error tends to balance out, it would seem unlikely, for example, that random measurement error would inflate the free-throw shooting percentage of individuals in the treatment group but deflate the free-throw percentage of the individuals in the no-treatment group. Yet, even though your first reaction is reasonable, it is mistaken: Random error may have one effect on the treatment group and another on the no-treatment group.

Given that random error tends to balance out, how could random error have one effect on the treatment group and another effect on the no-treatment group? To answer this question, imagine a group of extremely high scorers and a group of extremely low scorers. For the purpose of this example, let's imagine having hundreds of people each shoot five free throws. From those hundreds, we will select two groups of foul shooters: (1) a group in which all members hit all five free throws, and (2) a group in which all members missed all five free throws.

Why is the extremely high scoring group doing so well? It's unlikely that these scores reflect each individual's true score. Indeed, probably none of the people who hit all five foul shots really are 100% foul shooters. It's more likely that most of these foul shooters are good, but they are also benefiting from some good fortune. A few may be average or even poor foul shooters whose scores are being pushed up by random error (even Shaq has hit five free throws in a row). One thing we know for sure—nobody in this group had random error push down their free-throw percentage. In short, the average score of this group has been pushed up by random error.

Now, let's look at the group of extremely low scorers. Why are they scoring so low? Perhaps all of them are 0% foul shooters. It is more likely, however, that many are poor to average foul shooters experiencing a run of bad luck. One thing we know for sure—nobody in this group had random error inflate his or her free-throw percentage. In short, the average score of this group has probably been pushed down by random error.

What will happen if we retest both groups? The first group will tend to do a bit worse than before: Their average will not be 100%. On the pretest, random error pushed their scores in only one direction—up. That probably won't happen on the retest. Instead, random error will probably push some of their scores up and some of their scores down. As a result, their scores will revert to more normal levels on the retest. Similarly, the second group will tend to score at more normal levels on the retest: Their average will probably not be 0%. On the pretest, random error pushed their scores in only one direction—down. That probably won't happen two times in a row.

As we have seen, the 0% group will do better on the retest, but the 100% group will do worse. Put another way, both groups' average scores become less extreme on the retest.

Why does each group's average score become less extreme on the retest? In other words, why do their scores revert back to more normal levels? The short answer is that on the retest, each group's average score is less influenced by random error. The long answer is that (1) the groups were initially selected because of their extreme pretest scores; (2) their extreme pretest scores were due, in part, to random measurement error pushing their scores in one direction; and (3) random error, which by its very nature is inconsistent, probably won't push all the groups' scores in that same direction on the retest.

Thus far, we have considered the case in which two groups who score much differently on the pretest (0% versus 100% on a foul-shot test) might appear to grow more similar on a retest. But how could two groups (1) seem to be similar on a pretest and then (2) seem to grow apart on the retest? For example, how could two groups that appeared to be 60% shooters on the pretest end up scoring very differently on the retest? The key to seeing how this illusion would work is to realize that extreme scores are only extreme relative to their group's average.

To illustrate, suppose we have a large group of 90% career free-throw shooters and a large group of 30% career free-throw shooters. We then have people from each group shoot 10 free throws. We find that several from each group shoot 60% (6 out of 10) on our pretest. For the career 30% free-throw shooters, 60% is extremely good. For the career 90% free-throw shooters, 60% is extremely bad.

We now have two groups that each shot 60% on our pretest. The first group was taken from extreme scorers from the 90% group, whereas the second group was taken from extreme scorers from the 30% group. The two groups match on the pretest, but this matching is just a mirage due to random measurement error. On the posttest, this mirage will disappear because participants' scores will be affected by chance to a more usual (and lesser) degree. The first group will score closer to its average score of 90% and the second group will score closer to its average score of 30%. In technical terminology, both groups will exhibit what we call **regression toward the mean** (also called regression effect, regression artifact, statistical regression, reverting to average, and regression): the tendency for scores that are extremely unusual to revert back to more normal levels on the retest.

As you might imagine, regression toward the mean could mimic a treatment effect. If, in our free-throw shooting example, you administered a treatment between the pretest and the posttest, people might mistakenly believe that the treatment was responsible for the groups scoring differently on the posttest. For example, if you yelled at the first group after their poor (for them) pretest performance, people might think that your yelling is what caused them to do better on the posttest.

Regression toward the mean also explains why many parents believe that punishment is more effective than it is. After children have behaved unusually badly, their behavior will tend to revert to more normal (better) levels (regression to the mean). But those parents who have punished their children might note the punishment–better behavior relationship and attribute the improved behavior to the punishment. They have been tricked by regression toward the mean.

Although regression toward the mean is tricky enough by itself to fool most of the people most of the time, sometimes it has help. A deceiving swindler might intentionally use regression toward the mean to make it look like a worthless treatment had a positive effect. The key would be to intentionally take advantage of random measurement error to make it look like two dissimilar groups were really similar on the pretest.

Unfortunately, a researcher might unintentionally rely on measurement error to match two groups on a factor on which they actually differ. For instance, suppose a researcher who works for a continuing care retirement community (CCRC) wants to test a memory improvement program. The researcher decides she wants to provide an intervention for those residents who score between the 40th and 45th percentiles for older adults on the *Wechsler Memory Scale* because she believes this group will benefit most from her treatment. The researcher needs to find two groups whose scores fall within this range, give one group the memory training, and see whether the training group scores better on the posttest than the no-training group.

In this CCRC, there are three levels of care: independent living, assisted living, and nursing care. The researcher decides to focus on the assisted living residents because she believes that those residents will be most likely to contain individuals who are healthy and who score somewhat below average (50th percentile by definition is average) on the memory scale.

She administers the pretest, but finds only 8 assisted living residents who score between the 40th and 45th percentiles. She knows that she needs more participants. She decides to use these 8 residents as her treatment group and looks elsewhere for her no-treatment group. She rules out the nursing care residents because she wants the groups to be equivalent in terms of health and activity level. Instead, she tests independent living residents and finds 8 who score within the range.

At the end of the study, the researcher gives both groups the memory test again (the posttest). When she looks at the results, she is horrified: the no-treatment group (the 8 independent living residents) scores much higher on the posttest than the treatment group (the 8 assisted living residents). On closer examination, she finds that the scores of the independent living residents *increased* from pretest to posttest, whereas the scores of the assisted living residents *decreased* from pretest to posttest.

What happened? Did the true level of memory functioning improve for the independent living residents even though they received no memory training? No. Did the training program actually decrease the memory functioning of those residents in assisted living? No.

What happened was that the investigator selected scores that were likely to be heavily contaminated with random measurement error. To understand how this occurred, think about what would cause healthy older adults who are capable of independent living—a group that would average well above the 50th percentile—to score in the 40th–45th percentile on a memory test. These scores, which would be uncharacteristically low for them, might be due to some unusual event, such as the flu or to jet lag following a vacation abroad. If they scored in the 45th percentile on the pretest because of illness or jet lag, would it be likely that they would score this low again? No, chances are their posttest score will be higher because it will be a more accurate reflection of their true memory ability.

Just as the researcher selected participants from the independent living group based on scores that were likely to be loaded with random measurement error, the researcher selected participants from assisted living based on scores that were likely to be loaded with random measurement error. People requiring assisted living are much more likely to suffer from health problems that will directly (cardiovascular disease, mild dementia) or indirectly (medication side effects) decrease their memory ability below the 40th percentile.

Consider how a person in assisted living could score in the 45th percentile. What would cause them to score above their true score? Probably some form of luck would be involved. Just as you may occasionally get lucky guessing on a multiple-choice test, perhaps a few people in assisted living might get lucky on a memory test. That is, if you tested 200 people in assisted living, 8 might score near average on memory function just by chance. But would these same 8 be lucky a second time? It is a good bet that they would not. Instead, their second score should be a more accurate reflection of their true score. Consequently, when retested, they would get lower scores than they did the first time.

Conclusions About Matching on Pretest Scores. There are two reasons why matching on pretest scores does not make your groups equal. First, matching on pretest scores is incomplete because the pretest performance is not a perfect indicator of posttest performance. Many factors determine how participants will change from pretest to posttest. Therefore, to predict a participant's posttest score, you need to match not only on the pretest score but also on every other variable that might affect how participants will change. If you do not, you may have two groups that started out the same, but naturally grew apart—no thanks to the treatment. In other words, you may have what appears to be a treatment effect, but is really a selection by maturation effect.

Second, you match on scores, which are flawed indicators of characteristics, rather than on the characteristics themselves. Because of measurement error, it's possible to get two groups that match on pretest scores but that are very different on the variable the pretest was supposed to measure. In short, random error may create the illusion that two dissimilar groups are similar.

As convincing as the illusion of similarity may be, it is only a temporary mirage. The mirage is temporary because it is based on choosing those participants whose scores had been blown in a certain direction by random error, which by its nature is inconsistent and directionless. Thus, on retesting, the winds of chance will probably not blow those scores in the same direction.

Put another way, the illusion of similarity was built by choosing those participants whose scores were extremely influenced by random error. On retesting, random error will probably exert a less extreme influence on scores (just as lightning is unlikely to strike the same person twice). Consequently, the extremely deviant scores will revert back to more typical levels (regression toward the mean). As a result, the mirage that made the groups look similar on the pretest probably won't last until the posttest.

If the two groups that only appeared to be similar on the pretest reveal their true differences during the posttest, a naïve observer may believe that the groups "became different" because of the treatment. However, you should realize two facts:

1. The groups did not become different. They were different all along—they only seemed similar at the beginning because of an illusion created by random measurement error.

2. Given that the groups did not become different, there is no reason to say that the treatment made them become different.

Mortality. Even if our groups were identical to start with, they might not stay that way because of participant **mortality (attrition):** participants dropping out of the study. In the two-group study, selection and mortality, like two sides of the same coin, make the participants in one group systematically different from participants in the other. Selection makes the participants who are in one group differ from those in the other group by making those who *enter* the two groups differ in some systematic way; mortality makes two groups unequal by having the participants who *stay in* the two groups differ in some systematic way.

To understand the threat posed by mortality, suppose we have designed a program for high-risk youths. To test the program's effectiveness, we put 40 at-risk youths into our intense training program and compare them to a no-treatment group consisting of 40 other at-risk youths. We find that youths who complete our training program are much more likely to get a good job than the youth in the no-training group. However, 75% of the treatment group youths drop out of our rigorous program. Thus, we are comparing the 10 elite survivors of the treatment group against everyone in the no-treatment group. Consequently, our training program's apparent "success" may simply be due to comparing the best of one group against everyone in the other group.

Conclusions About Two-Group Designs

In the previous example, mortality seriously threatened the validity of our study. Even if the groups had been the same to start with, they were not the same at the end of the study. However, with two-group designs, we usually have a big problem even before mortality has a chance to be a problem: Our two groups are not identical at the start of the study (see Table 9-1). If we don't match, our groups are different. If we do match, our groups may still be different (see Figure 9-2). So, differences between our groups at the end of the study may be due to our groups being different to start with, rather than due to the treatment.

Table 9-1 **Why the Selection Problem Is Difficult to Eliminate**

1. Self-assignment causes selection bias.

2. Researcher assignment can cause selection bias.

3. Arbitrary assignment to a group causes selection error by making the groups differ in at least one respect.

4. We can't match participants on every variable.

5. We can't even match participants on all relevant variables. Therefore, "matched" groups may differ from each other in terms of "unmatched" variables. These unmatched variables may cause the groups to behave differently on the posttest.

6. We have to worry about the effects of unmatched variables even when we match on pretest scores. As cases of selection by maturation interactions demonstrate, just because participants scored the same at pretest, it does not mean they will score the same at posttest.

7. Even if there were no selection by maturation interactions, matching on pretest scores is imperfect because scores may be heavily influenced by random error. The groups may appear to be similar only because one or both groups' pretest scores are heavily influenced by random error.

Figure 9-2 **Making Two Groups Identical: A Game You Can't Win**

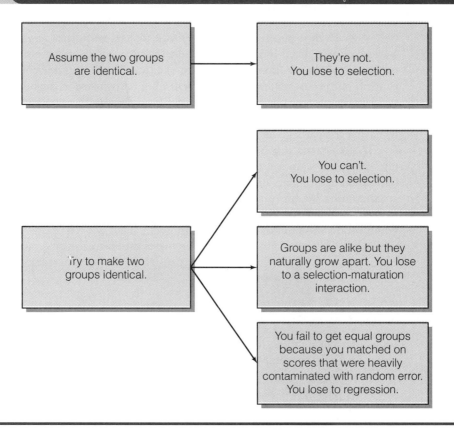

Problems With the Pretest–Posttest Design

The only way we could have two identical groups of participants would be to have the same participants in both groups. Each participant could be in both the no-treatment group and in the treatment group. For instance, we might use a **pretest–posttest design:** a design in which we give each participant the pretest, administer the treatment, then give each participant the posttest. By making sure that the participants in the treatment group are the same participants who were in the no-treatment group, we eliminate the threat of selection.

At first glance, the pretest–posttest design seems to be a perfect way to establish internal validity. However, the pretest–posttest design can have internal validity only if the treatment is the sole reason that posttest scores differ from pretest scores. Unfortunately, the treatment is not the only reason that participants' scores may change from pretest to posttest.

Three Reasons Participants May Change Between Pretest and Posttest

Even without the treatment, participants may change over time. For instance, a participant's mood may change by the minute. To be more specific, besides the treatment, there are at least three reasons that participants may change from pretest to posttest: (1) maturation, (2) history, and (3) testing.

Maturation: Participants Change on Their Own

A participant may change between the time of the pretest and the time of the posttest as a result of **maturation:** the natural biological or developmental changes that occur inside the participant (see Figure 9-3). People are constantly changing. From one moment to the next, they may become more hungry, more bored, or more fatigued. From one month to the next, they will grow older, and they may mature.

To see how maturation might masquerade as a treatment effect, suppose you institute a safe driving program for young adults. You start your study with a group of 20-year-olds, show them videos about the dangers of risky driving, and measure them again when they

Figure 9-3 **A Happy Case of Maturation**

Ugly Duckling   Swan

are 25. You find that when they are 25 they take fewer risks than when they were 20. Your problem is that you do not know whether the safe driving program or natural development is responsible for the change. Similarly, if you give a baby 10 years of memory training, you will find that her memory improves. However, this difference is probably due not to the training, but to maturation.

History: Environment Changes Participants

In addition to changing because of events that occur inside the participant, the participant may change because of events—other than the treatment—that occur in the outside world. Thus, even if the treatment has no effect, a participant may change between pretest and posttest because of **history**: any change in the participant's environment that has nothing to do with the treatment but has a systematic effect on a condition's average score (see Figure 9-4). History can involve events as important and far-reaching as a world war or as unimportant and limited as a campus rumor.

 Figure 9-4 **A Mythical Case of History**

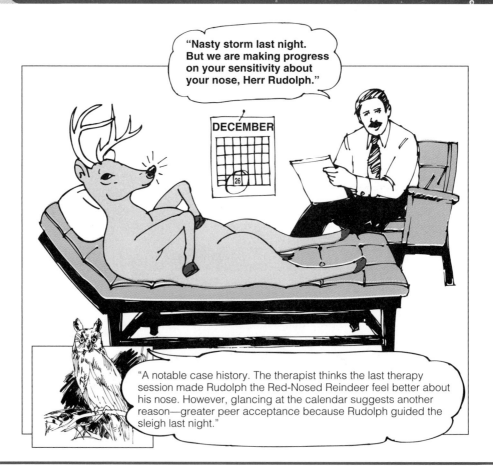

To understand the kinds of events that can be labeled "history" and how history can bias a study, suppose two social psychologists have a treatment (an ad) they think will change how Americans feel about space exploration. However, between pretest and posttest, a spacecraft explodes. The change in attitudes may be due to the explosion (history) rather than to their ad. Or, suppose an investigator was examining the effect of diet on maze-running speed. However, between pretest and posttest, the heat went off in the rat room, and the rats nearly froze to death. As you can see from these examples, events that happen in a participant's life (history) between the pretest and the posttest can cause changes that could be mistaken for treatment effects.

Testing: Measuring Participants Changes Participants

One event that always occurs between the start of the pretest and the start of the posttest is the pretest itself. If the pretest changes participants (e.g., it motivates them to learn what is on the test, or it makes them better at taking the test by giving them practice on the test), you have a **testing effect.** For example, if your instructor gave you the same test twice, you would score better the second time around. Your improvement would be due to finding out and remembering the answers to questions you missed. Because of the testing effect, people who have taken many intelligence tests (for example, children of clinical psychologists) may score very high on IQ tests regardless of their true intelligence.

The testing effect is not limited to knowledge tests. Rather, it can occur with virtually any measure. To illustrate, let's look at a pretest that has nothing to do with knowledge. Suppose we were to ask people their opinions about Greenland entering the World Bank. Would we get a different answer the second time we asked this question? Yes, because the very action of asking for their opinion may cause them to think about the issue more and to develop or change their opinion. In short, whether you are measuring a person's attitudes, cholesterol, exercise habits, or almost anything else, your measurements may stimulate the person to change.

Three Measurement Changes That May Cause Scores to Change Between Pretest and Posttest

Obviously, participants' scores may change because participants have changed. What is less obvious is that participants' scores may change because how participants are measured has changed. As you will soon see, even when the participants themselves have not changed, the way their scores are measured may change due to (1) instrumentation, (2) regression, and (3) mortality.

Instrumentation: Changes in How Participants Are Measured

One reason a participant's score may change from pretest to posttest is **instrumentation:** changes in the measuring instrument causing changes in scores. But why would the measuring instrument used for the posttest be different from the one used during the pretest?

Sometimes, changes in the measuring instrument are unintentional. Suppose you are measuring aggression using the most changeable measuring instrument possible: the human rater. As the study progresses, raters may broaden their definition of aggression. Consequently, raters may give participants higher posttest scores on aggression, even though participants' behavior has not changed. Unfortunately, there are many ways that raters could change between pretesting and posttesting. Raters could become more conscientious, less conscientious, more lenient, less lenient, and so forth. Any of these changes could cause an instrumentation effect.

Sometimes, changes in the instrument occur because the researcher is trying to make the posttest better than the pretest. For example, the researcher may retype the original questionnaire to make the scales look nicer, to fix typographical errors, or to eliminate bad questions. Unfortunately these changes, no matter how minor they may seem and no matter how logical they may be, may cause instrumentation effects. Thus, the time to refine your measure is before—not while—you conduct your study.

Regression Revisited: Changes in How Random Error Affects Measurements

Even if the measuring instrument is the same for both the pretest and posttest, the degree to which random measurement error affects scores may differ from pretest to posttest. You do not escape regression toward the mean by a pretest–posttest design rather than a two-group design.

To show that you do not get away from regression toward the mean by using the pretest–posttest design, think back to the researcher who was investigating the effects of a memory training program in older adults. Suppose that she had decided not to compare the 8 highest-scoring assisted-living residents with a group of independent-living residents. Instead, after having the 8 assisted-living residents who scored highest on the pretest complete the training program, she readministered the memory test as her posttest. What would she observe?

As before, she would have observed that the assisted living residents' memory scores dropped from pretest to posttest. This drop is not due to the training program robbing patients of memories. Rather, the posttest scores more accurately reflect the patients' poor memories. The posttest scores are lower than the pretest scores only because the pretest scores were inflated with random measurement error.

The pretest scores were destined to be inflated with measurement error because the investigators selected only those residents whose scores were extreme (for their group). Extreme scores tend to have extreme amounts of measurement error.

To understand why extreme scores tend to have extreme amounts of measurement error, realize that a participant's score is a function of two things: the participant's true characteristics and measurement error. Thus, an extreme score may be extreme because measurement error is making the score extreme. To take a concrete example, let's consider the three possibilites for a student getting a perfect score on an exam:

1. The student is a perfect student.
2. The student is a very good student and had some good luck.
3. The student is an average or below-average student but got incredibly lucky.

As you can see, if you study a group of people who got perfect scores on the last exam, you are probably studying a group of people whose scores were inflated by measurement error. If participants were measured again, random error would probably be less generous. (After all, random error could not be more generous. There's only one place for scores to go—down.) Therefore, if you were to give them a treatment (memory training) and then look at their scores on the next exam, you would be disappointed. The group that averaged 100% on the first test might average "only" 96% on the second test.

In the case we just described, regression's presence is relatively obvious because people recognize that test scores are influenced by random error. Note, however, that almost any measure is influenced by random error—and any measure that is influenced by random error is potentially vulnerable to regression toward the mean. For example, suppose you are trying to make inferences about a participant's typical behavior from a sample of that participant's behavior. If the behavior you observe is not typical of the participant's behavior, you have measurement error. Even if you measured the behavior you observed perfectly, you have measurement error because you have not measured the participant's typical behavior perfectly.

To see how a sample of behavior may not be typical of normal behavior, let's look at a coin's behavior. Suppose you find a coin that comes up heads 6 times in a row. Although you have accurately recorded that the coin came up heads 6 times in a row, you might be making a mistake if you concluded that the coin was biased toward heads. In fact, if you were to flip the coin 10 more times, you probably would not get 10 more heads. Instead, you would probably get something close to 5 heads and 5 tails.

Coins are not the only things to exhibit erratic behavior. Virtually every behavior is inconsistent and therefore prone to atypical streaks. For example, suppose you watch someone shoot baskets. You accurately observe that she made five out of five shots. Based on these observations, you may conclude that she is a great shooter. However, you may be wrong. Perhaps if you had observed her shooting on a different day, you would have seen her make only one of five shots.

To illustrate how this subtle form of measurement error can lead to regression toward the mean, suppose a person who had been happy virtually all of her life feels depressed. This depression is so unlike her that she seeks therapy. Before starting the therapy, the psychologist gives her a personality test. The test verifies that she is depressed. After a couple of sessions, she is feeling better. In fact, according to the personality test, she is no longer depressed. Who could blame the psychologist for feeling proud?

But has the psychologist changed the client's personality? No, the client is just behaving in a way consistent with her normal personality. The previous measurements were contaminated by events that had nothing to do with her personality. Perhaps her depressed manner reflected a string of bad fortune: getting food poisoning, her cat running away, and being audited by the IRS. As this string of bad luck ended and her luck returned to normal, her mood returned to normal.

Regression toward the mean is such a clever impersonator of a treatment effect that regression fools most of the people most of the time. Many people swear that something really helped them when they had "hit bottom." The baseball player who recovers from a terrible slump believes that hypnosis was the cure; the owner whose business was at an all-time low believes that a new manager turned the business around; and a man who was at an all-time emotional low feels that his new girlfriend turned him around. What these people fail to take into account is that things are simply reverting back to normal (regressing toward the mean). When listening to stories about how people bounced back due to some miracle treatment, remember comedian Woody Allen's line: "I always get well, even without the leeches."

Mortality (Attrition): Changes in How Many Participants Are Measured

The last reason that you could find differences between pretest and posttest scores would be that you were measuring fewer participants at posttest than you were at pretest. In other words, as was the case in the two-group study, a pretest-posttest study may fall victim to mortality.

To illustrate how much of an impact mortality can have on a pretest-posttest study, imagine that you are studying the effect of diet on memory in older adults. You pretest your participants, give them your new diet, and test them again. You find that the average posttest score is higher than the average pretest score. However, if the pretest average is based on

100 participants and the posttest average is based on 70 participants, your results may well be due to mortality. Specifically, the reason posttest scores are higher than pretest scores may be that the people who scored poorly on the pretest are no longer around for the posttest.

Although death is the most dramatic way to lose participants, it is not the most common way to lose participants. Usually, attrition results from participants quitting the study, failing to follow directions, or moving away.

Note that not all attrition is equal. For example, if you are losing participants due to their moving away, it is possible that you are losing just as many low scorers as high scorers and that this attrition has little systematic effect on posttest scores. If, on the other hand, you are losing participants who can't or won't stay on your treatment program, you are probably losing the low-scoring participants and this loss will have a large effect on posttest scores.

Conclusions About Trying to Keep Everything Except the Treatment Constant

We tried to create a situation in which we manipulated the treatment while keeping everything else constant. However, nothing we tried worked.

When we tried to compare a treatment group with a no-treatment group, we had to worry that our groups were not identical before the study started. Even when we matched our groups, we realized that the groups might not be identical because

1. we could not match groups on every characteristic
2. we could not match groups based on participants' actual characteristics, so we had to match them based on imperfect measures of those characteristics

Because we could not get equivalent groups at the start of the study, we did not dwell on the additional problems of keeping groups equivalent. That is, we did not stress the mortality problem that would result if, for example, more participants dropped out of the treatment group than out of the no-treatment group.

Because of the problems with comparing a treatment group against a no-treatment group (see Table 9-2), we tried to measure the same group before and after giving them the treatment. Although this pretest–posttest tactic got rid of some threats to validity, it introduced others (see Figure 9-5). As Table 9-3 shows, participants may change from pretest to posttest for a variety of reasons that have nothing to do with the treatment. Participants may change as a result of

1. natural development (maturation)
2. other things in their lives changing (history)
3. learning from the pretest (testing)

Furthermore, participants may appear to change from pretest to posttest because

1. the posttest measure was a different instrument than the pretest measure (instrumentation)
2. their pretest scores were unduly influenced by chance (setting up regression toward the mean)
3. participants dropped out of the study, so that the posttest group is not the same group of individuals as the pretest group (mortality)

Table 9-2	Questions to Ask When Examining a Two-Group (Treatment Versus No-Treatment) Study
Selection	Were groups equal before the study began?
Selection by maturation interaction	Would the groups have naturally grown apart, even without the treatment?
Regression effects	Even if the groups appeared equivalent before the study began, was this apparent equivalence merely a temporary illusion created by random measurement error?
Mortality	Did more participants drop out of one group than the other?

Figure 9-5 | **The Impossible Dream: Making Sure the Only Thing That Could Make Participants' Scores Change in a Pretest–Posttest Design Is the Treatment**

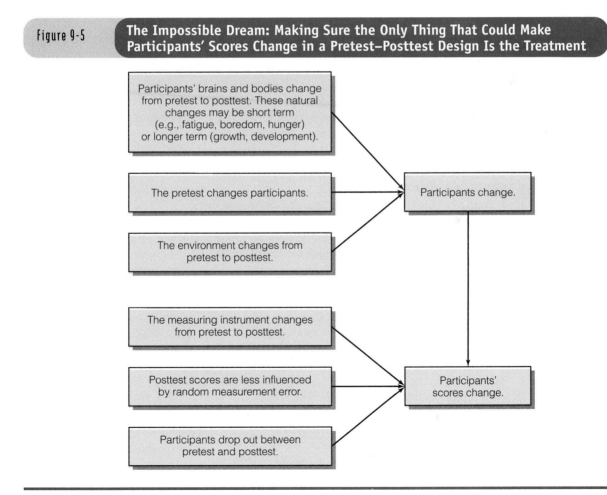

You would like to say that the treatment was the only factor that could cause the scores to change from pretest to posttest, but that's not easy to do.

Table 9-3	Questions to Ask When Examining a Pretest–Posttest (Before–After) Study
Maturation	Could the before–after (pretest–posttest) differences have been due to natural changes resulting from participants becoming older?
History	Could other events in the participants' lives have caused the pretest–posttest differences?
Testing	Could participants have scored differently on the posttest because of the practice and experience they got on the pretest?
Instrumentation	Were participants measured with the same instrument, in the same way, both times?
Regression	Were participants selected for their extreme pretest scores? Participants who get extreme scores have a tendency to get less extreme scores the second time around.
Mortality	Did everyone who took the pretest stick around for the posttest—or is the posttest group a more select group than the pretest group?

Ruling Out Extraneous Variables

Why couldn't we eliminate extraneous variables? Was it because we used improper research techniques? No; as you will see in later chapters, matching participants and testing participants before and after treatment are useful research techniques.

We couldn't eliminate extraneous variables because it can't be done. Keeping everything the same is impossible. Imagine, in our ever-changing world, trying to make sure that only one thing in a participant's life changed!

Accounting for Extraneous Variables

Fortunately, you do not have to eliminate extraneous variables to rule out their effects. As you will learn in Chapter 10, you can combine random assignment and statistics to rule out the effects of extraneous variables. (Random assignment involves using a random process, such as a coin flip, to determine which treatment a participant receives. In the simplest case, random assignment results in half the participants receiving the treatment and half receiving no treatment.)

Even without using random assignment (a technique discussed in the next chapter), you can still try to rule out the effects of extraneous variables. In a sense, tracking down a treatment's effect without using random assignment is much like a detective tracking down a murderer. Just as the detective is confronted with more than one suspect for a murder, you are confronted with more than one suspect for an effect. Just as the detective can't make the suspects disappear, you can't eliminate extraneous factors. However, like the detective, you can use logic to rule out some suspects.

Before you can begin to account for the actions of every suspicious extraneous variable, you have to know "who" each of these variables is. At first glance, identifying all of the thousands of variables that might account for the relationship between the treatment and the effect seems as impossible as eliminating all those variables.

Identifying Extraneous Variables

Fortunately, identifying the extraneous variables is not as difficult as it first appears because every one of these thousands of factors falls into eight categories: Campbell and

Stanley's (1963) eight threats to validity. Thus, you really have only eight suspects: selection, history, maturation, testing, regression, mortality, instrumentation, and selection by maturation. If you can show that they were not responsible for the effect, you can conclude that the treatment was responsible.

The Relationship Between Internal and External Validity

If you rule out all eight threats, you have established internal validity—you have demonstrated that a factor causes an effect in a particular study. But you have not demonstrated that you can generalize your results outside your particular study. Internal validity alone does not guarantee that an investigator repeating the study using different participants (patients hospitalized with depression instead of college students) or using a different setting (a library instead of a lab) would obtain the same results. If you want to generalize your results, you need external validity.

If internal validity does not guarantee external validity, why bother with establishing internal validity? One answer is that you may not care about external validity. Some researchers do not care about generalizing their results; they may only want to show that a certain treatment causes a certain effect in a certain setting. For example, therapists may want to show that with their patients, in their hospital, giving the patients an exercise program reduces patients' alcohol consumption. The therapists may not care whether the treatment would work with other kinds of patients at other hospitals (external validity). They only care that they have a method that works for them. However, few people are so single-minded that they are totally unconcerned with external validity.

Given that most researchers are concerned about external validity, you might think that most researchers would take many steps to maximize their study's external validity. However, for at least three reasons, researchers often take relatively few steps targeted specifically at boosting their study's external validity.

First, results from internally valid experiments tend to generalize (Anderson, Lindsay, & Bushman, 1999). That is, if an experiment showing that a factor has an effect is replicated (repeated) with a different group of participants or in a different setting, the replication will usually also find that the factor has an effect. As Anderson et al. wrote, "The psychological laboratory has generally produced psychological truths rather than trivialities" (p. 3).

Second, if other researchers using other types of participants and other settings all replicate the findings of the original study, these replications produce a strong case for the finding's external validity. Indeed, replications by other researchers usually produce stronger evidence that a finding has external validity than anything the original researcher can do.

Third, the things that the original researcher would do to improve a study's external validity may reduce its internal validity (see Table 9-4). Or, to look at it another way, the steps a researcher might take to improve internal validity may end up reducing the study's external validity. For instance, to reduce the problem of selection bias, you might use twins as your participants. Although using twins as participants could increase internal validity by reducing differences between your treatment and no-treatment groups, it might hurt the generalizability of your study. Your results might apply only to twins.

Similarly, you might reduce the threat of history by testing your participants in a situation such as a lab where they are isolated from nontreatment factors. This highly controlled situation may increase internal validity because the treatment was one of the only things to change during the study. However, you would have to wonder whether the treatment would

Table 9-4	Classic Conflicts Between the Goals of Internal and External Validity
TACTIC USED TO HELP ESTABLISH INTERNAL VALIDITY	**TACTIC'S IMPACT ON EXTERNAL VALIDITY**
Use participants who are very similar to each other to reduce the effects of selection. For example, study only twins or study only rats.	Studying such a narrowly defined group raises questions about the degree to which the results can be generalized to different participant populations. Do the results hold for people who are not twins? Animals that are not rats?
Study participants in a highly controlled laboratory setting to reduce the effects of extraneous factors such as history.	Studying participants in an isolated, controlled environment, such as a lab, raises questions about the extent to which the results might generalize to more complex, real-life settings.

have the same effect outside this artificial situation. Would the results generalize to real life, where the factors from which you isolated your participants would come into play?

Concluding Remarks

As you have seen, internal validity and external validity are sometimes in conflict. The same procedures that increase internal validity may decrease external validity. Fortunately, however, internal validity and external validity are not necessarily incompatible. As you will see in future chapters, you can do studies that have both.

If you want to establish both internal and external validity, many would argue that you should first establish internal validity. After all, before you can establish that a factor causes an effect in most situations, you must show that the factor causes an effect in at least one situation.

But how can you establish internal validity? In this chapter, we tried two basic approaches (the no-treatment/treatment group design and the pretest–posttest design), and both failed. In the next chapter, you will learn the easiest and most automatic way to establish internal validity: the simple experiment.

SUMMARY

1. If you observe an effect in a study that has internal validity, you know what caused that effect.

2. Campbell and Stanley (1963) described eight major threats to internal validity: selection, selection by maturation interaction, regression, maturation, history, testing, mortality, and instrumentation.

3. When you compare a treatment group to a no-treatment group, beware of selection: the groups being different even before you administer the treatment.

4. To reduce selection bias, participants should never get to choose what amount of treatment they get.

In addition, participants' characteristics, attitudes, or behaviors should have nothing to do with whether they are put in the treatment rather than in the no-treatment group.

5. It is impossible to match two groups of participants so that they are identical in every respect: Participants simply differ in too many ways.

6. Even matching participants on pretest scores is not perfect because of the problems of selection by maturation interactions and regression.

7. Selection by maturation occurs when your two groups mature (naturally change) at different rates or in different directions.

8. The fact that extreme scores tend to be a little less extreme the second time around is called regression toward the mean. It can cause two groups that appear to be matched on a pretest to score differently on the posttest.

9. In the pretest–posttest design, you measure a group, administer the treatment, and measure the group again.

10. Using the pretest–posttest method is not as perfect as it first appears. It is vulnerable to testing, history, regression, maturation, mortality, and instrumentation effects.

11. Regression can occur in the pretest–posttest design because the participant may have gotten the treatment when he or she had "hit bottom." Consequently, there was no place to go but up.

12. Maturation refers to inner, biological changes that occur in people merely as a result of time. In some cases, becoming more mature—not the treatment—accounts for people changing from pretest to posttest.

13. History refers to outside events—other than the treatment—that may influence participants' scores. Events that occur in the participants' world between pretest and posttest can cause participants to change from pretest to posttest.

14. Testing effect refers to the fact that taking a pretest may affect performance on a posttest.

15. Instrumentation occurs when the posttest measuring instrument is different from the pretest measuring instrument.

16. External validity is the degree to which the results from a study can be generalized to other types of participants and settings.

17. Internal and external validity are not necessarily incompatible.

KEY TERMS

internal validity *(p. 254)*

extraneous factor *(p. 255)*

selection (or selection bias) *(p. 256)*

matching *(p. 257)*

selection by maturation interaction *(p. 260)*

regression (toward the mean) *(p. 263)*

mortality (attrition) *(p. 265)*

pretest–posttest design *(p. 267)*

maturation *(p. 267)*

history *(p. 268)*

testing effect *(p. 269)*

instrumentation (bias) *(p. 269)*

EXERCISES

1. What questions would you ask a researcher who said that the no-treatment and treatment groups were identical before the start of the study?

2. In all of the following cases, the researcher wants to make cause–effect statements. What threats to internal validity is the researcher apparently overlooking?
   a. Employees are interviewed on job satisfaction. Bosses undergo a 3-week training program. When employees are reinterviewed, dissatisfaction seems to be even higher. Therefore, the researcher concludes that the training program caused further employee dissatisfaction.
   b. After completing a voluntary workshop on improving the company's image, workers are surveyed. Those who attended the workshop are now more committed than those in the no-treatment group who did not make the workshop. Therefore, the researcher concludes that the workshop made workers more committed.
   c. After a 6-month training program, employee productivity improves. Therefore, the researcher concludes that the training program caused increased productivity.
   d. Morale is at an all-time low. As a result, the company hires a "humor consultant." A month

later, workers are surveyed and morale has improved. Therefore, the researcher concludes that the consultant improved morale.

e. Two groups of workers are matched on commitment to the company. One group is asked to attend a 2-week workshop on improving the company's image; the other is the no-treatment group. Workers who complete the workshop are more committed than those in the no-treatment group. Therefore, the researcher concludes that the workshop made workers more committed.

3. A hypnotist claims that hypnosis can cause increases in strength. To "prove" this claim, the hypnotist has participants see how many times they can squeeze a hand-grip in 2 minutes. Then, he hypnotizes them and has them practice for 2 weeks. At the end of 2 weeks, they can squeeze the hand-grips together many more times than they could at the beginning. Other than hypnosis, what could have caused this effect?

4. How could a quack psychologist or "healthcare expert" take advantage of regression toward the mean to make it appear that certain phony treatments actually worked?

5. How could a participant's score on an ability test change even though the person's actual ability had not?

6. Suppose a memory researcher administers a memory test to a group of residents at a nursing home. He finds grade-school students who score the same as the older patients on the memory pretest. He then administers an experimental memory drug to the older patients. A year later, he gives both groups a posttest.
   a. If the researcher finds that the older patients now have a worse memory than the grade-school students, what can the researcher conclude? Why?
   b. If the researcher finds that the older patients now have a better memory than the grade-school students, what can the researcher conclude? Why?

7. What is the difference between history and maturation?

8. What is the difference between testing and instrumentation?

9. Suppose a researcher reports that a certain argument strategy has an effect, but only on those participants who hold extreme attitudes. Why might the researcher be mistaken about the effects of the persuasive strategy?

10. What is the difference between internal and external validity?

WEB RESOURCES

1. Go to the Chapter 9 section of the book's student website and do the following:
   a. Look over the concept map of the key terms.
   b. Test yourself on the key terms.
   c. Take the Chapter 9 Practice Quiz.
   d. Download the Chapter 9 tutorial.

INFOTRAC COLLEGE EDITION EXPLORATIONS

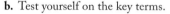

To read a simple explanation of the problems with non-experimental designs, do an InfoTrac College Edition keyword search using the phrase "diet and disease puzzle."

The Simple Experiment

What you have is an experience, not an experiment.

—*R. A. Fisher*

Overview

Why do people behave the way they do? How can we help people change? To answer these questions, we must be able to isolate the underlying causes of behavior, and to do so, we must design a study that has **internal validity:** the ability to determine whether a factor causes an effect.

This chapter introduces you to one of the easiest ways to establish that a factor causes an effect: the simple experiment. You will start by learning the basic logic behind the simple experiment. Then, you will learn how to weigh statistical, ethical, and validity issues in order to design a useful simple experiment. Finally, you will learn how to interpret the results of such an experiment.

Logic and Terminology

The **simple experiment** involves two groups of participants. At the start of the experiment, the two groups should not differ from each other in any systematic way, but during the experiment, the experimenter will treat one group differently from the other. For example, the experimenter may

- Assign the groups different *types* of activities (e.g., playing violent versus nonviolent videogames)
- Assign the groups different *amounts* of an activity (e.g., one group might meditate for 30 minutes whereas the other group meditates for 10 minutes)
- Appear one way (e.g., well dressed) to one group and another way (e.g., casually dressed) to the other group
- Have confederates (people who pretend to be participants but who are actually the researcher's assistants) behave one way (e.g., agreeing with the participant) when interacting with members of one group and another way (e.g., disagreeing with the participant) when interacting with the other group
- Have a certain object (e.g., a mirror or a gun) in the testing room when members of one group are tested but not when members of the other group are tested
- Make the testing room's environment more intense on a certain dimension (e.g., how hot it is, how loud it is, how it is lit, how it smells, or the concentration of negative ions in it) when members of one group are tested and less intense on that dimension when the other group is tested
- Give the groups different instructions ("memorize these words by repeating them over and over" versus "make a sentence out of these words," or "keep a log of what you have to be grateful for" versus "keep a log of hassles you encounter")
- Give the groups different printed stimuli (whether or not the sentences participants are asked to unscramble make participants think about older people, whether the words participants are to memorize are concrete and easy to visualize [e.g., "bell"] or abstract and hard to visualize [e.g., "liberty"], whether the exam is printed on blue or white paper, whether the people in the photograph are attractive or unattractive)
- Give the groups different contexts for interpreting stimuli (the researcher may vary the gender, age, attractiveness, or background of the person whose job application, school record, essay, or character is being judged)
- Give the groups different feedback ("the test suggests you are outgoing" versus "the test suggests you are shy," or "you did well on the task" versus "your performance on the task was average)

- Give the groups different chemicals (sugar-sweetened lemonade versus artificially sweetened lemonade, caffeinated versus decaffeinated colas)

Often, half the participants (the treatment group) receive a treatment, whereas the other half (the no-treatment group) receive no treatment. If, at the end of the experiment, the two groups differ significantly, we can conclude that the treatment—the only systematic difference between the groups—caused that significant difference.

But how do we set up a situation in which the only systematic difference between the no-treatment and the treatment groups is the treatment? The answer is **independent random assignment.** In random assignment, every participant—regardless of that participant's characteristics—has an equal chance of being assigned to either the treatment or no-treatment group. If we provide each participant an equal chance of being assigned to either group, there will still be unsystematic, chance differences between our groups before we introduce the treatment, but there should not be any systematic differences between them.

To review, random assignment, the key to the simple experiment, involves two processes. First, we *randomly* divide our participants into two similar halves. Second, we *assign* one of those halves to get a treatment different from the other.

We have given you a general idea of what random assignment is, but how would you actually randomly assign participants to either a no-treatment or a treatment group?[1] You might think that you could flip a coin for each participant: If the coin comes up heads, the participant gets the treatment; if the coin comes up tails, the participant does not get the treatment. However, coin-flipping does not work because "a tossed coin is slightly more likely to land on the face it started out on than on the opposite face" (Klarreich, 2004, p. 363). Even computers have trouble producing random sequences (Klarreich, 2004). So what should you do? (The "eenie meenie minie moe" method is not an option because it isn't random.) The solution is to use a random numbers table to assign participants to condition (Wilkinson & the Task Force on Statistical Inference, 1999). To learn how to use a random numbers table, see Box 10-1.

---

[1]Instead of using pure independent random assignment, researchers typically use independent random assignment with the restriction that an equal number of participants must be in each group.

BOX 10-1   Randomly Assigning Participants to Two Groups

There are many ways to randomly assign participants to groups. Your professor may prefer another method. However, following these steps guarantees random assignment and an equal number of participants in each group.

Step 1: On the top of a sheet of paper, make two columns. Title the first "Control Group." Title the second "Experimental Group." Under the group names, draw a line for each participant you will need. Thus, if you were planning to use eight participants (four in each group), you would draw four lines under each group name.

CONTROL GROUP	EXPERIMENTAL GROUP
_____	_____
_____	_____
_____	_____
_____	_____

Step 2: Turn to a random numbers table, like the one at the end of this box (or the one in Appendix E). Roll a die to determine which column in the table you will use. Make a note in that column so that others could check your methods (Wilkinson & the Task Force on Statistical Inference, 1999).

continued

BOX 10-1 *(continued)*

Step 3: Assign the first number in the column to the first space under Control Group, the second number to the second space, and so on. When you have filled all the spaces for the control group, place the next number under the first space under Experimental Group and continue until you have filled all the spaces. Thus, if you used the random numbers table at the end of this box and you rolled a "5," you would start at the top of the fifth column of that table (the column starts with the number 81647), and your sheet of paper would look like this:

CONTROL GROUP EXPERIMENTAL GROUP
81647   06121
30995   27756
76393   98872
07856   18876

Step 4: At the end of each control group score, write down a "C." At the end of each experimental group score, write down an "E." In this example, our sheet would now look like this:

CONTROL GROUP EXPERIMENTAL GROUP
81647C   06121E
30995C   27756E
76393C   98872E
07856C   18876E

Step 5: Rank these numbers from lowest to highest. Then, on a second piece of paper, put the lowest number on the top line, the second lowest number on the next line, and so on. In this example, your page would look like this:

06121E   30995C
07856C   76393C
18876E   81647C
27756E   98872E

Step 6: Label the top line "Participant 1," the second line "Participant 2," and so forth. The first participant who shows up will be in the condition specified on the top line, the second participant who shows up will be in

the condition specified by the second line, and so forth. In this example, the first participant will be in the experimental group, the second in the control group, the third and fourth in the experimental group, the fifth, sixth, and seventh in the control group, and the eighth in the experimental group. Thus, our sheet of paper would look like this:

Participant Number 1 = 06121E
Participant Number 2 = 07856C
Participant Number 3 = 18876E
Participant Number 4 = 27756E
Participant Number 5 = 30995C
Participant Number 6 = 76393C
Participant Number 7 = 81647C
Participant Number 8 = 98872E

Step 7: To avoid confusion, recopy your list, but make two changes. First, delete the random numbers. Second, write out "Experimental" and "Control." In this example, your recopied list would look like the following:

Participant Number 1 = Experimental
Participant Number 2 = Control
Participant Number 3 = Experimental
Participant Number 4 = Experimental
Participant Number 5 = Control
Participant Number 6 = Control
Participant Number 7 = Control
Participant Number 8 = Experimental

RANDOM NUMBERS TABLE

			COLUMN			
Row	1	2	3	4	5	6
1	10480	15011	01536	02011	81647	69179
2	22368	46573	25595	85393	30995	89198
3	24130	48360	22527	97265	76393	64809
4	42167	93093	06243	61680	07856	16376
5	37570	39975	81837	76656	06121	91782
6	77921	06907	11008	42751	27756	53498
7	99562	72905	56420	69994	98872	31016
8	96301	91977	05463	07972	18876	20922

Experimental Hypothesis: The Treatment Has an Effect

If you do not randomly assign your participants to two groups, you do not have a simple experiment. However, before you randomly assign participants, you must have an **experimental hypothesis:** a prediction that the treatment will cause an effect. To generate an experimental hypothesis, you must predict that the treatment and no-treatment groups will differ because of the treatment's effect. For example, you might hypothesize that people getting 3 hours of full-spectrum light will be happier than those getting no full-spectrum light because full-spectrum light causes increases in happiness.

Be aware that not all hypotheses are cause–effect hypotheses. Sometimes, hypotheses involve describing what happens rather than finding out what makes things happen. If you generate a hypothesis that is *not* a cause–effect statement, it is *not* an experimental hypothesis. Thus, if you hypothesize that men are more romantic than women, you do not have an experimental hypothesis. Similarly, if you predict that athletes will be more assertive than nonathletes, you do not have an experimental hypothesis. In short, to have an experimental hypothesis, you must predict that some treatment that you manipulate will cause an effect.

Null Hypothesis: The Treatment Does Not Have an Effect

Once you have an experimental (cause–effect) hypothesis, pit it against the **null hypothesis:** the hypothesis that the treatment has no effect. The null hypothesis essentially states that any difference you observe between the treatment and no-treatment group scores could be due to chance. Therefore, if our experimental hypothesis was that getting 3 hours of full-spectrum lighting will cause people to be happier, the null hypothesis would be getting 3 hours of full-spectrum lighting will have *no* demonstrated effect on happiness.

If your results show that the difference between groups is probably not due to chance, you can reject the null hypothesis. By rejecting the null hypothesis, you tentatively accept the experimental hypothesis: You conclude that the treatment has an effect.

But what happens if you fail to demonstrate conclusively that the treatment has an effect? Can you say that there is no effect for full-spectrum lighting? No, you can only say that you failed to prove beyond a reasonable doubt that full-spectrum lighting causes a change in happiness. In other words, you're back to where you were before you began the study: You do not know whether full-spectrum lighting causes a change in happiness.[2]

To reiterate a key point, *the failure to find a treatment effect doesn't mean that the treatment has no effect.* If you had looked more carefully, you might have found the effect.

To help yourself remember that you can't prove the null hypothesis, think of the null hypothesis as saying, "The difference between conditions *may* be due to chance." Even if you could prove that "The difference may be due to chance," what would you have you proved? Certainly, you would not have proved that the difference *is* due to chance.

Conclusions About Experimental and Null Hypotheses

In summary, you have learned four important points about experimental and null hypotheses:

1. The experimental hypothesis is that the treatment has an effect.
2. The null hypothesis is that the treatment has no effect.
3. If you reject the null hypothesis, you can tentatively accept the hypothesis that the treatment has an effect.
4. If you fail to reject the null hypothesis, you can't draw any conclusions.

---

[2]Those of you who are intimately familiar with confidence intervals may realize that null results do not necessarily send the researcher back to square one. Admittedly, we do not know whether the effect is greater than zero, but we could use confidence intervals to estimate a range in which the effect size probably lies. That is, before the study, we may have no idea of the potential size of the effect. We might think the effect would be anywhere between -100 units and $+100$ units. However, based on the data collected in the study, we could estimate, with 95% confidence, that the effect is between a certain range. For example, we might find, at the 95% level of confidence, that the effect is somewhere in the range between -1 units and $+3$ units.

To remember these four key points, think about these hypotheses in the context of a criminal trial. In a trial, the null hypothesis is that the defendant did not commit the crime. The experimental hypothesis is that the defendant did cause the crime. The prosecutor tries to disprove the null hypothesis so that the jury will accept the experimental hypothesis. In other words, the prosecutor tries to disprove, beyond a reasonable doubt, the hypothesis that the defendant is "not guilty." If the jury decides that the null hypothesis is highly unlikely, they reject it and find the defendant guilty. If, on the other hand, they still have reasonable doubt, they fail to reject the null hypothesis and vote "not guilty." Note that their "not guilty" verdict is not an "innocent" verdict. Instead, it is a verdict reflecting that they are not sure, beyond a reasonable doubt, that the null hypothesis is false.

Manipulating the Independent Variable

Once you have your hypotheses, your next step is to manipulate the treatment. In any experiment, "participants are presented with the same general scenario (for example, rating photographs of potential dating partners), but at least one aspect of this general scenario is manipulated" (Ickes, 2003, p. 22). In the simplest case of manipulating the treatment, you administer (assign) the treatment to some participants and withhold it from others. The goal is that the conditions will be the same except for the treatment manipulation, as in the following classic experiments:

- In the first study showing that leading questions could bias eyewitness testimony, Loftus (1975) had students watch a film of a car accident and then gave students a questionnaire. The manipulation was whether the first question on the questionnaire was "How fast was Car A going when it ran the stop sign?"—a misleading question because Car A did *not* run the stop sign—*or* "How fast was Car A going when it turned right?"—a question that was not misleading.
- In the first study showing that people's entire impressions of another person could be greatly influenced by a single trait, Asch (1946) had participants think about a person who was described as either (a) "intelligent, skillful, industrious, warm, determined, practical, cautious" *or* (b) "intelligent, skillful, industrious, cold, determined, practical, cautious."
- In the first study showing that sex role stereotypes affect how people perceive infants, Condry and Condry (1976) had all participants use a form to rate the same baby. The only difference between how participants were treated was whether the infant rating form listed the infant's name (a) as "David" and sex as "male" *or* (b) as "Dana" and sex as "female."
- In the first study showing that the pronouns people use when they describe their closest relationships affects how people see those relationships, Fitzsimons and Kay (2004) had all participants write five sentences about their closest same-sex friend and rate the relationship with this friend for its closeness, importance, and intimacy. The only difference between groups was that one group was told to begin each sentence with "We," and was given the example, "We have known each other for 2 years," whereas the other group was told to begin each sentence with "(Insert friend's name) and I," and given the example, "John and I have known each other for 2 years."

To understand how you would manipulate a treatment, let's go back to trying to test the hypothesis about the effect of full-spectrum lighting on mood. To do this, you must vary the amount of light people get—and the amount should be independent of (should not depend on or be affected by) the individual's personal characteristics. To be specific, the amount of full-spectrum light participants receive should be determined by independent random assignment. Because the amount *varies* between the treatment group and the no-treatment group; because it varies *independently* of each participant's characteristics; and because it is determined by *independent* random assignment, full-spectrum lighting is the **independent variable.**

In simple experiments, there are two values, or **levels of an independent variable.** The two levels can be types of treatment (e.g., lighting versus psychotherapy) or amounts (e.g., 1 hour of lighting versus 2 hours of lighting). In our lighting experiment, participants are randomly assigned to one of the following two levels of the independent variable: (1) 3 hours of full-spectrum lighting and (2) no full-spectrum lighting.

Experimental and Control Groups: Similar, but Treated Differently

The participants who are randomly assigned to get the higher level of the treatment (3 hours of full-spectrum light) are usually called the **experimental group.** The participants who are randomly assigned to get a lower level of the treatment (in this case, no treatment) are usually called the **control group.** Thus, in our example, the experimental group is the treatment group and the control group is the no-treatment group.

The control group is a comparison group. We compare the experimental (treatment) group to the control (no-treatment) group to see whether the treatment had an effect. Because comparing the experimental group to the control group makes sense only if the groups are roughly equivalent at the start of the experiment, there should not be any systematic difference between them until the experimenter gives them different levels of the independent variable.

As the terms *experimental group* and *control group* imply, you should have several participants (preferably more than 30) in each of your conditions. The more participants you have, the more likely it is that your two groups will be similar at the start of the experiment. Conversely, the fewer participants you have, the less likely it is that your groups will be similar before you administer the treatment. For example, if you are doing an experiment to evaluate the effect of a strength pill and have only two participants (a 6 ft 4 in., 280-lb [1.9 m, 127 kg] offensive tackle and a 5 ft 1 in., 88-lb [1.5 m, 40 kg] person recovering from a long illness), random assignment will not have the opportunity to make your "groups" equivalent. Consequently, your control group would not be a fair comparison group.

The Value of Independence: Why Control and Experimental Groups Shouldn't Be Called "Groups"

Although we have noted that the experimental and control groups are groups in the sense that there should be several participants in each "group," that is the only sense in which these "groups" are groups. To conduct an experiment, you do *not* find two groups of participants and then randomly assign one group to be the experimental group and the other to be the control group.

Why You Should Not Choose Two Preexisting Groups

To see why not, suppose you were doing a study involving 10,000 janitors at a Los Angeles company and 10,000 managers at a New York company. You have 20,000 people in your experiment: one of the largest experiments in history. Then, you flip a coin and—on the basis of that single coin flip—assign the LA janitors to no treatment and the New York managers to treatment. Even though you have 10,000 participants in each group, your treatment and no-treatment groups differ in at least two systematic ways (where they live and what they do) before the study begins. Your random assignment is no more successful in making your groups similar than it was when you had only two participants. Consequently, to get random assignment to equalize your groups, you need to assign each participant **independently:** individually, without regard to how previous participants were assigned.

Why You Should Not Let Your Groups Become "Groups"

Your concern with independence does not stop at assignment. After you have independently assigned participants to condition, you want each of your participants to remain independent. To maintain independence, do not test the control participants in one group session and the experimental participants in a separate group session. Having one testing session for the control group and a second session for the experimental group hurts independence in two ways.

First, when participants are tested in groups, they may become group members who influence each others' responses rather than independent individuals. For example, instead of giving their own individual, independent responses, participants might respond as a conforming mob.

As a concrete example of the perils of letting participants interact, imagine that you are doing an ESP experiment. In the control group, only 30 of the 60 participants correctly guessed that the coin would turn up heads. In the experimental group, on the other hand, all 60 participants correctly guessed that the coin would turn up heads. Had each experimental group participant made his or her decision independently, such results would rarely[3] happen by chance. Thus, we would conclude that the treatment had an effect. However, if all the experimental group members talked to one another and made a group decision, they were not acting as 60 individual participants but as one group. In that case, the results would not be so impressive: Because all 60 experimental participants acted as one, the chances of all of them correctly guessing the coin flip were the same as the chances of one person correctly guessing a coin flip: 1 in 2 (50%).

Although this example shows what can happen when participants are tested in groups and allowed to interact freely, interaction can disturb independence even when group discussion is prohibited. Participants may influence one another through inadvertent outcries (laughs, exclamations like, "Oh no!") or through subtle nonverbal cues. In our lighting–happiness experiment, if we tested all the participants in a single group session, one participant who is crying uncontrollably might cause the entire experimental group to be unhappy, thereby leading us to falsely conclude that the lighting caused unhappiness. If, on the other hand, we tested each participant individually, the unhappy participant's behavior would not affect anyone else's responses.

The second reason for not testing all the experimental participants in one session and all the control participants in another is that such group testing turns the inevitable, random differences between testing sessions into systematic effects. For instance, suppose that when the experimental group was tested, there was a distraction in the hall, but there was no such

---

[3]To be more precise, it should happen with a probability of $(1/2)^{60}$, which is less than .000000000000000009% of the time.

distraction while the control group was tested. Like the treatment, this distraction was presented to all the experimental group participants, but to none of the control group participants. Thus, if the distraction did have an effect, its effect might be mistaken for a treatment effect. If, on the other hand, participants were tested individually, it is unlikely that only the experimental participants would be exposed to distractions. Instead, distractions would have a chance to even out so that participants in both groups would be almost equally affected by distractions.

But what if you are sure you won't have distractions? Even then, the sessions will differ in ways unrelated to the treatment. If you manage to test the participants at the same time, you'll have to use different experimenters and different testing rooms. If you manage to use the same experimenter and testing room, you'll have to test the groups at different times. Consequently, if you find a significant difference between your groups, you will have trouble interpreting those results. Specifically, you have to ask, "Is the significant difference due to the groups getting different levels of the treatment or to the groups being tested under different conditions (e.g., having different experimenters or being tested at different times of day)?"

To avoid these problems in interpreting your results, make sure that the treatment is the only factor that systematically varies. In other words, use independent random assignment and then test your participants individually (or in small groups) so that random differences between testing sessions have a chance to even out. If you must run participants in large groups, do not run groups made up exclusively of *either* experimental or control participants. Instead, run groups made up of *both* control and experimental participants.

The Value of Assignment (Manipulating the Treatment)

We have focused on the importance of independence to independent random assignment. Independence helps us start the experiment with two "groups" of participants that do not differ in any systematic way. But assignment is also a very important aspect of independent random assignment.

Random Assignment Makes the Treatment the Only Systematic Difference Between Groups

Random assignment to treatment group helps ensure that the only systematic difference between the groups is the treatment. With random assignment, our groups will be equivalent on the nontreatment variables we know about as well as on the (many) nontreatment variables we don't know about.

In our experiment, random assignment makes it so that one random sample of participants (the experimental group) is assigned to receive a high level of the independent variable whereas the other random sample of participants (the control group) is assigned to receive a low level of the independent variable. If, at the end of the study, the groups differed by more than would be expected by chance, we could say that the difference was due to the only nonchance difference between them: the treatment.

Without Random Assignment You Do Not Have a Simple Experiment

If you cannot randomly assign participants to your different groups, you cannot do a simple experiment. Because you cannot randomly assign participants to have certain personal characteristics, simple experiments cannot be used to study the effects of participant characteristics such as gender, race, personality, and intelligence.[4] For example, it makes no sense to assign a man to be a woman, a 7 ft 2 in (218 cm) person to be short, or a shy person to be outgoing.

To see why we need to be able to assign participants, let's imagine that you try to look at the effects of lighting on mood without using random assignment. Suppose you get a group of people who use light therapy and compare them to a group of people who do not use light therapy. What would be wrong with that?

The problem is that you are selecting two groups of people who you know are different in at least one way, and then you are assuming that they don't differ in any other respect. The assumption that the groups are identical in every other respect is probably wrong. The light therapy group probably feels more depressed, lives in colder climates, is more receptive to new ideas, and is richer than the other group.

Because the groups differ in many ways other than in terms of the "treatment," it would be foolish to say that the treatment—rather than one of these many other differences between the groups—is what caused the groups to score differently on the happiness measure. For example, if the group of light users is more depressed than our sample of nonusers, we could not conclude that the lighting caused their depression. After all, the lighting might be a partial cure for—rather than a cause of—their depression.

But what if the group of lighting users is less depressed? Even then, we could not conclude that the lighting is causing an effect. Lighting users may be less depressed because they are richer, have more spare time, or differ in some other way from those who don't use lights. In short, if you do not randomly *assign* participants to groups, you cannot conclude anything about the effects of a treatment.

If, on the other hand, you start with one group of participants and then randomly assign half to full-spectrum lighting and half to normal lighting, interpreting differences between the groups would be much simpler. Because the groups probably were fairly similar before the treatment was introduced, large group differences in happiness are probably due to the only systematic difference between them—the lighting.

Collecting the Dependent Variable

Before you can determine whether the lighting caused the experimental group to be happier than the control group, you must measure each participant's happiness. You know that each person's happiness will be somewhat dependent on the individual's personality and you predict that their score on the happiness *variable* will also be *dependent* on the lighting. Therefore, scores on the happiness measure are your **dependent variable.** Because the dependent variable is what the participant does that you measure, the dependent variable is also called the **dependent measure.**

The Statistical Significance Decision: Deciding Whether to Declare That a Difference Is Not a Coincidence

After measuring the dependent variable, you will want to compare the experimental group's happiness scores to the control group's. One way to make this comparison is to subtract the

---

[4]You can, however, use experiments to investigate how participants react to people who vary in terms of these characteristics. For example, you can have an experiment in which participants read the same story except that one group is told that the story was written by a man, whereas the other group is told that the story was written by a woman. Similarly, you can randomly determine, for each participant, whether the participant interacts with a male or female experimenter.

average of the happiness scores for the control (comparison) group from the average of the experimental group's happiness scores.

Unfortunately, knowing how much the groups differ doesn't tell you how much of an effect the treatment had. After all, even if the treatment had no effect, nontreatment factors would probably still make the groups differ. In other words, even if the treatment had no effect, the groups may differ due to random error.

How can you determine that the difference between groups is due to something more than random error? To determine the probability that the difference is not exclusively due to chance, you need to use **inferential statistics:** the science of chance.

Statistically Significant Results: Declaring That the Treatment Has an Effect

If, by using statistics, you find that the difference between your groups is greater than could be expected if only chance were at work, your results are statistically significant. The term **statistical significance** means that you are sure, beyond a reasonable doubt, that the difference you observed is not a fluke.

What is a reasonable doubt? Usually, before researchers commit themselves to saying that the treatment has an effect, they want a 5% probability ($p = .05$) or less ($p < .05$) that they would get such a pattern of results when there really was no effect. Consequently, you may hear researchers say that their results were "significant at the point oh-five level" and, in journal articles, you will often see statements like, "the results were statistically significant ($p < .05$)."

To review, if you do a simple experiment, you will probably find that the treatment group mean is different than the control group mean. Such a difference is not, by itself, evidence of the treatment's effect. Indeed, because random assignment does not create identical groups, you would expect the two group means to differ to some extent. Therefore, the question is not "Is there a difference between the group means?" but rather "Is the difference between the group means bigger than would be expected if only random factors were at work?" To answer that question, you need to use statistics.

Using statistics, you might find that if only chance factors were at work (that is, if the independent variable had no effect), you would get that large a difference less than 5% of the time. If differences as big or bigger than what you found occur less than 5% of the time by chance alone ($p < .05$) when the null hypothesis is true, you would probably conclude that the null hypothesis is false. To state your conclusion more formally, you might say that "the results are statistically significant at the .05 level." By "statistically significant," you mean that because it's unlikely that the difference between your groups is due to chance alone, you conclude that some of the difference was due to the treatment. With statistically significant results, you would be relatively confident that if you repeated the study, you would get the same pattern of results—the independent variable would again cause a similar type of change in the scores on the dependent variable. In short, statistical significance suggests that the results are reliable and replicable.

Statistically Significant Effects May Be Small

Statistical significance does not, however, mean that the results are significant in the sense of being large. Just because a difference is statistically significant—reliably different from zero—doesn't mean the difference is large. Even a tiny difference can be statistically reliable. For example, if you flipped a coin 5,000 times and it came up heads 51% of the time, this 1% difference from what would be expected by chance (50% heads) would be statistically significant.

Table 10-1	**Limits of Statistical Significance**

Statistically significant differences are

1. probably not due to chance alone
2. not necessarily large
3. not necessarily in the direction you predicted
4. not necessarily important

Statistically Significant Results May Be Insignificant (Trivial)

Nor does statistical significance mean that the results are significant in the sense of being important. If you have a meaningless hypothesis, you may have results that are statistically significant but meaningless.

Statistically Significant Results May Refute Your Experimental Hypothesis

Finally, statistically significant results do not necessarily support your hypothesis. For example, suppose your hypothesis is that the treatment improves behavior. A statistically significant effect for the treatment would mean that the treatment had an effect. But did the treatment improve behavior or make it worse? To find out, you have to look at the means to see whether the treatment group or no-treatment group is behaving better.

Summary of the Limitations of Statistically Significant Results

In short, statistically significant results tell you nothing about the direction, size, or importance of the treatment effect (see Table 10-1). Because of the limitations of statistical significance, the American Psychological Association appointed a task force to determine whether significance testing should be eliminated. The task force did "not support any action that could be interpreted as banning the use of null significance testing or p values in psychological research and publication" (American Psychological Association, 1996b). However, the task force did recommend that, in addition to reporting whether the results were statistically significant, authors should provide information about the direction and size of effects.

Null Results: Why We Can't Draw Conclusions From Nonsignificant Results

You now know how to interpret statistically significant results. But what if your results are *not* statistically significant? That is, what if you can't reject the null hypothesis that the difference between your groups could be due to chance? Then, you have *failed* to reject the null hypothesis; therefore, your results would be described as "not significant."

As the phrase "not significant" suggests, you can't draw any conclusions from such findings. With **nonsignificant results** (also called **null results**), you do not know whether the treatment has an effect that you failed to find or whether the treatment really has no effect (see Figure 10-1).

Nonsignificant results are analogous to a "not guilty" verdict: Is the defendant innocent, or did the prosecutor present a poor case? Often, defendants get off, not because of overwhelming proof of their innocence, but because of lack of conclusive proof of their guilt.

Figure 10-1 | The Meaning of Statistical Significance

Before doing a statistical analysis, we know that the difference between groups could be due to *either* } **Treatment or chance**

After doing a statistical analysis that reveals a significant difference, we know that the difference between the groups is *probably* due to: } **Treatment ~~or chance~~**

If the statistical test fails to reach significance, then the difference could be due to *either:* } **Treatment or chance**

If the results are statistically significant, we can conclude that the difference between the groups is not due entirely to chance and therefore some of the difference must be due to the treatment. However, if the results are not statistically significant, the results could be due to chance or treatment. Put another way, we don't know any more than we did before we subjected the results to statistical analysis.

Table 10-2 | Common Errors in Discussing Null Results

STATEMENT	FLAW
"The results were not significant. Therefore, the independent variable had no effect."	"Not that I know of" is not the same as proving "there isn't any."
"The treatment had an effect, even though the results are not significant."	"Not significant" means that you failed to find an effect. Therefore, the statement could be translated as, "I didn't find an effect for the treatment, but I really did."

You have seen that nonsignificant results neither confirm nor deny that the treatment had an effect. Unfortunately, you will find some incompetents treating null results as proof that the treatment has an effect—whereas other bad researchers will treat null results as proof that the treatment has no effect (see Table 10-2).

Nonsignificant Results Are Not Significant

All too often, people act like nonsignificant results are really significant. They may say, "The difference between my groups shows that the treatment had an effect, even though the difference is not significant." Reread the previous quote because you're sure to see it again: It's one of the most common contradictory statements that researchers make. People making this statement are really saying, "The difference is due to the treatment, even though I've found no evidence that the difference isn't simply due to chance."

Null Results Do Not Prove the Null Hypothesis: "I Didn't Find It" Doesn't Mean It Doesn't Exist

As we have just discussed, some people act like null results secretly prove the experimental hypothesis. On the other hand, some people make the opposite mistake: They incorrectly assume that null results prove the null hypothesis. That is, they falsely conclude that null results prove that the treatment had no effect. Some individuals make this mistake because they think the term "null results" implies that the results prove the null hypothesis. Those people would be better off thinking of null results as "no results" than to think that null results support the null hypothesis.

Thinking that nonsignificant results support the null hypothesis is a mistake because it overlooks the difficulty of conclusively proving that a treatment has an effect. People should realize that not finding something is not the same as proving that the thing does not exist. After all, people often fail to find things that clearly exist, such as books that are in the library, items that are in the grocery store, and keys that are on the table in front of them.

Even in highly systematic investigations, failing to find something doesn't mean the thing does not exist. For example, in 70% of all murder investigations, investigators do not find a single identifiable print at the murder scene—not even the victim's. Thus, the failure to find the suspect's fingerprints at the scene is hardly proof that the suspect is innocent. For essentially the same reasons, the failure to find an effect is not proof that there is no effect.

Summary of the "Ideal" Simple Experiment

Thus far, we have said that the simple experiment gives you an easy way to determine whether a factor causes an effect. If you can randomly assign participants to either a treatment or no-treatment group, all you have to do is find out whether your results are statistically significant. If your results are statistically significant, your treatment probably had an effect. No method allows you to account for the effects of nontreatment variables with as little effort as random assignment.

Errors in Determining Whether Results Are Statistically Significant

There is one drawback to random assignment: Differences between groups may be due to chance rather than to the treatment. Admittedly, statistical tests—by allowing you to predict the extent to which chance may cause the groups to differ—minimize this drawback. Statistical tests, however, do not allow you to perfectly predict chance all of the time. Therefore, you may err by either underestimating or overestimating the extent to which chance is causing your groups to differ (see Table 10-3).

Table 10-3	**Possible Outcomes of Statistical Significance Decision**	
STATISTICAL SIGNIFICANCE DECISION	REAL STATE OF AFFAIRS	
	Treatment has an effect	**Treatment does not have an effect**
Significant: Reject the null hypothesis	Correct decision	Type 1 error
Not significant: Do not reject the null hypothesis	Type 2 error	Correct decision

Type 1 Errors: "Crying Wolf"

If you underestimate the role of chance, you may make a **Type 1 error:** mistaking a chance difference for a real difference. In the simple experiment, you would make a Type 1 error if you mistook a chance difference between your experimental and control groups for a treatment effect. More specifically, you would make a Type 1 error if you declared that a difference between your groups was statistically significant, when the treatment really didn't have an effect. In nonresearch settings, examples of Type 1 errors include:

- a jury convicting an innocent person because they mistake a series of coincidences as evidence of guilt
- a person responding to a false alarm, such as thinking that the phone is ringing when it's not or thinking that an alarm is going off when it's not
- a physician making a "false positive" medical diagnosis, such as telling a woman she is pregnant when she isn't

Reducing the Risk of a Type 1 Error

What can you do about Type 1 errors? *There is only one thing you can do: You can decide what risk of a Type 1 error you are willing to take.* Usually, experimenters decide that they are going to take less than a 5% risk of making a Type 1 error. In other words, they say their results must be significant at the .05 level ($p < .05$) before they declare that their results are significant. They are comfortable with the odds of their making a Type 1 error being less than 5 in 100. But why take even that risk? Why not take less than a 1% risk?

Accepting the Risk of a Type 1 Error

To understand why not, imagine you are betting with someone who is flipping a coin. For all 10 flips, she calls "heads." She wins most of the 10 flips.

Let's suppose that you will refuse to pay up if you have statistical proof that she is cheating. However, you do not want to make the Type 1 error of attributing her results to cheating (using a biased coin) when the results are due only to luck. How many of the 10 flips does she have to win before you "prove" that she is cheating?

To help you answer this question, we looked up the odds of getting 8, 9, or 10 heads in 10 flips of a fair coin.[5] Those odds are as follows:

EVENT	PROBABILITY EXPRESSED IN PERCENTAGES	PROBABILITY EXPRESSED IN DECIMAL FORM
Chances of 8 or more heads	5.47%	.0547
Chances of 9 or more heads	1.08%	.0108
Chances of 10 heads	0.1%	.001

From these odds, you can see that you can't have complete, absolute proof that she is cheating. Thus, if you insist on taking 0% risk of falsely accusing her (you want to be absolutely 100% sure), you would not call her a cheat—even if she got 10 heads in a row. As you can see from the odds we listed, it is very unlikely (.1% chance), but still possible, that she could get 10 heads in a row, purely by chance alone. Consequently, if you are going to accuse her of cheating, you are going to have to take some risk of making a false accusation.

---

[5]You do not need to know how to calculate these percentages.

If you were willing to take more than a 0% risk but were unwilling to take even a 1% risk of falsely accusing her (you wanted to be more than 99% sure), you would call her a cheat if all 10 flips turned up heads—but not if 9 of the flips were heads. If you were willing to take a 2% risk of falsely accusing her (you wanted to be 98% sure), you would call her a cheat if either 9 or 10 of the flips turned up heads. Finally, if you were willing to take a 6% risk of falsely accusing her (you would settle for being 94% sure), you could refuse to pay up if she got 8 or more heads.

This betting example gives you a clue about what happens when you set your risk of making a Type 1 error. When you determine your risk of making a Type 1 error, you are indirectly determining how much the groups must differ before you will declare that difference statistically significant. If you are willing to take a relatively large risk of mistaking a difference that is due only to chance for a treatment effect, you may declare a relatively small difference statistically significant. If, on the other hand, you are willing to take only a tiny risk of mistakenly declaring a chance difference statistically significant, you must require that the difference between groups be relatively large before you are willing to call it statistically significant. In other words, all other things being equal, the larger the difference must be before you declare it significant, the less likely it is that you will make a Type 1 error. To take an extreme example of this principle, if you would not declare even the biggest possible difference between your groups statistically significant, you would never make a Type 1 error.

Type 2 Errors: "Failing to Announce the Wolf"

The problem with not taking any risk of making a Type 1 error is that, if the treatment did have an effect, you would be unable to detect it. In trying to be very sure that a difference is due to treatment and not to chance, you may make a **Type 2 error:** overlooking a genuine treatment effect because you think the differences between conditions might be due to chance. Examples of Type 2 errors in nonresearch situations include:

- a jury letting a criminal go free because they wanted to be sure beyond any doubt and they realized that it was possible that the evidence against the defendant was due to numerous, unlikely coincidences
- a person failing to hear the phone ring
- a radar detector failing to detect a speed trap
- a physician making a "false negative" medical diagnosis, such as failing to detect that a woman was pregnant

In short, whereas Type 1 errors are errors of commission (yelling "fire" when there is no fire), Type 2 errors are errors of omission (failing to yell "fire" when there is a fire). In trying to avoid Type 1 errors, you may increase your risk of making Type 2 errors. In the exteme case, if you are never willing to risk making a Type 1 error, you will never detect real treatment effects. But because you want to detect real treatment effects, you want your study to have **power:** the ability to find real differences and declare those differences statistically significant; or, put another way, the ability to avoid making Type 2 errors.[6]

---

[6]In a sense, power (defined as 1.00 − the probability of making a Type 2 error) and Type 2 errors are opposites. *Power* refers to the chances (given that the treatment really does have a certain effect) of *finding* a significant treatment effect, whereas the probability of a *Type 2 error* refers to the chances (given that the treatment really does have a certain effect) of *failing to find* a significant treatment effect. If you use plug numbers into the formula "1.00 − power = chances of making a Type 2 error," you can see that power and Type 2 errors are inversely related. For example, if power is 1, you have a *0%* chance of making a Type 2 error (because 1.00 − *1.00* = 0%). Conversely, if the treatment has an effect and power is 0, you have a *100%* chance of making a Type 2 error (because 1.00 − *0* = 100%). Often, power is around .40, meaning that, if the treatment has an effect, the researcher has a 40% (.40) chance of finding that effect and a *60%* chance of not finding that effect (because 1.00 − .40 = 60%).

The Need to Prevent Type 2 Errors: Why You Want the Power to Find Significant Differences

You can have power without increasing your risk of making a Type 1 error. Unfortunately, many people don't do what it takes to have power.

If you don't do what it takes to have power, your study may be doomed: Even if your treatment has an effect, you will fail to find that effect statistically significant. In a way, looking for a significant difference between your groups with an underpowered experiment is like looking for differences between cells with an underpowered microscope.

As you might imagine, conducting a low-powered experiment often leads to frustration over not finding anything. Beginning researchers frequently frustrate themselves by conducting such low-powered experiments. (We know we did.) Why do beginning researchers often fail to design sufficiently powerful experiments?

Statistics and the Design of the Simple Experiment

One reason inexperienced researchers fail to design powerful experiments is they simply do not think about power—a "sin" that many professional researchers also commit (Cohen, 1990). But even when novice researchers do think about power, they often think that it is a statistical concept and therefore has nothing to do with design of experiments. Admittedly, power is a statistical concept. However, *statistical concepts should influence the design of research.* Just as a bridge builder should take engineering into account before building a bridge, a researcher should take statistics into account before conducting a study. Thus, if you take statistical power into account when designing your study, your study will have enough power to find the differences that you are looking for—if those differences really exist.

Power and the Design of the Simple Experiment

To have enough power, you must reduce the risk of chance differences hiding the treatment effect. As you can see from Figure 10-2, two ways to stop random error from overwhelming your treatment effect are (1) reduce the effects of random error and (2) increase the size of the treatment effect.

Reduce the Effect of Random Error

One of the most obvious ways to reduce the effects of random error is to reduce the potential sources of random error. The major sources of random error are random differences between testing situations, random measurement error, random differences between participants, and sloppy coding of data.

Standardize Procedures and Use Reliable Measures. Because a major source of random error is random variation in the testing situation, you can reduce random error by standardizing your experiment. Standardization consists of keeping the testing environment and the experimental procedures as constant as possible. Thus, to improve power, you might want the noise level, illumination level, temperature, and other conditions of testing to be the same for each participant. Furthermore, you would want to treat all your experimental group participants identically and treat all your control group participants identically. In addition to reducing random error by standardizing procedures, you should also reduce random error by using a reliable dependent measure (for more about how reliable measures boost power, see Chapter 6).

Figure 10-2	**Cutting Down on Random Error and Building Up the Treatment Effect: Two Ways to Avoid Losing Your Treatment Effect in a "Jungle" of Random Error**

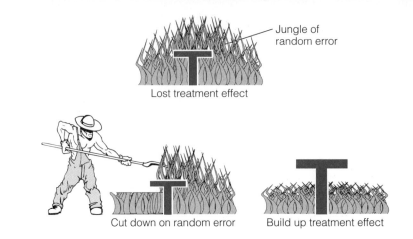

The desire for both reliable measures and strict standardization makes some psychologists love both instruments and the laboratory. Under the lab's carefully regulated conditions, experimenters can create powerful and sensitive experiments.

Other experimenters, however, reject the laboratory setting in favor of real-world settings. By using real-world settings, they can more easily make a case for their study's external validity. The price they pay for leaving the laboratory is that they are no longer able to keep many nontreatment variables (temperature, distractions, noise level, etc.) constant. These variables, free to vary wildly, create a jungle of random error that may hide the treatment's effect.

Because of the large variability in real-world settings and the difficulties of using sensitive measures in the field, even die-hard field experimenters may first look for a treatment's effect in the lab. Only after they have found that the treatment has an effect in the lab will they try to detect the treatment's effect in the field.

Use a Homogeneous Group of Participants. Like differences between testing sessions, differences between participants can hide treatment effects. Even if the treatment effect causes a large difference between your groups, you may overlook that effect, mistakenly believing that the difference between your groups is due to the fact that your participants are years apart in age and worlds apart in terms of their experiences.

To decrease the chances that between-subject differences will mask the treatment's effect, choose participants who are similar to one another. For instance, select participants who are the same gender, same age, and have the same IQ. Or, study rats instead of humans. With rats, you can select participants that have grown up in the same environment, have similar genes, and even have the same birthday. By studying homogeneous participants under standardized situations, rat researchers can detect very subtle treatment effects.

Code Data Carefully. Obviously, sloppy coding of the data can sabotage the most sensitively designed study. So, why do we mention this obvious fact?

We mention it because careful coding is a cheap way to increase power. If you increase power by using nonhuman animals as participants, you may lose the ability to generalize to humans. If you increase power by using a lab experiment rather than a field experiment, you may lose some of your ability to generalize to real-world settings. But careful coding costs you nothing—except for a little time spent rechecking the coding of your data.

Let Random Error Balance Out. Thus far, we have talked about reducing the effects of random error by reducing the amount of random error. But you can reduce the *effects* of random error on your data without reducing the *amount* of random error in your data.

The key is to give random error more chances to balance out. To remind yourself that chance does balance out in the long run, imagine flipping a fair coin. If you flipped it six times, you might get five tails and one head—five times as many tails as heads. However, if you flipped it 1,000 times, you would end up with almost as many heads as tails.

Similarly, if you use five participants in each group, your groups probably won't be equivalent before the experiment begins. Thus, even if you found large differences between the groups at the end of the study, you might have to say that the differences could be due to chance alone. However, if you use 60 participants in each group, your groups should be fairly equivalent before the study begins. Consequently, a treatment effect that would be un-detected if you used 5 participants per group might be statistically significant if you used 60 participants per group. In short, to take advantage of the fact that random error balances out, boost your study's power by studying more participants.

Create Larger Effects: Bigger Effects Are Easier to See

Until now, we have talked about increasing power by making our experiment more sensitive to small differences. Specifically, we have talked about two ways of preventing the "noise" caused by random error from making us unable to "hear" the treatment effect: (1) reducing the amount of random error and (2) giving random error a chance to balance out. However, we have left out one obvious way to increase our experiment's ability to detect the effect: making the effect louder (bigger) and thus easier to hear (detect).

As you might imagine, bigger effects are easier to find. But how do we create bigger effects? Your best bet for increasing the size of the effect is to give the control group participants a very low level of the independent variable while giving the experimental group a very high level of the independent variable. Hence, to have adequate power in the lighting experiment, rather than giving the control group 1 hour of full-spectrum light and the experimental group 2 hours, you might give the control group no full-spectrum light and the experimental group 4 hours of full-spectrum light.

To see how researchers can maximize the chances of finding an effect by giving the experimental and control groups widely different levels of treatment, let's consider an experiment by T. D. Wilson and Schooler (1991). Wilson and Schooler wanted to determine whether thinking about the advantages and disadvantages of a choice could hurt one's ability to make the right choice. In one experiment, they had participants rate their preference for the taste of several fruit-flavored jams. Half the participants rated their preferences after completing a "filler" questionnaire asking them to list reasons why they chose their major. The other half rated their preferences after completing a questionnaire asking them to "analyze why you feel the way you do about each jam in order to prepare yourself for your evaluations." As Wilson and Schooler predicted, the participants who thought about why they liked the jam made less accurate ratings (ratings that differed more from experts' ratings) than those who did not think about why they liked the jam.

Although the finding that one can think too much about a choice is intriguing, we want to emphasize another aspect of Wilson and Schooler's study: the difference between the amount of time experimental participants reflected on jams versus the amount of time that control participants reflected on jams. Note that the researchers did not ask the control group to do any reflection whatsoever about the jams. To reiterate, Wilson and Schooler did not have the control group do a moderate amount of reflection and the experimental group do slightly more reflection. If they had, Wilson and Schooler might have failed to find a statistically significant effect.

Conclusions About How Statistical Considerations Impact Design Decisions

By now, you can probably appreciate why R. A. Fisher said, "To consult a statistician after an experiment is finished is often merely to ask him to conduct a post mortem examination. He can perhaps say what the experiment died of." The reason you should think about statistics before you do an experiment is that statistical considerations influence virtually every aspect of the design process (see Table 10-4). For example, statistical considerations even dictate what kind of hypothesis you can test. Because you cannot accept the null hypothesis, the only hypotheses that you can hope to support are hypotheses that the groups will differ. Therefore, you cannot do a simple experiment to prove that two treatments have the same effect or that a certain treatment will be just as ineffective as no treatment.

Not only do statistical considerations dictate what types of hypotheses you can have, but they also mandate how you should assign your participants. Specifically, if you do not assign your participants to groups using independent random assignment, you do not have a valid experiment.

Statistical considerations also dictate how you should treat your participants. You will not have a valid experiment if you let participants influence one another's responses or if you do anything else that would violate the statistical requirement that individual participants' responses must be independent.

Table 10-4	Implications of Statistics for the Simple Experiment	
STATISTICAL CONCERN/REQUIREMENT	**IMPLICATIONS FOR DESIGNING THE SIMPLE EXPERIMENT**
Observations must be independent.	You must use independent random assignment and, ideally, you will test participants individually.
Groups must differ for only two reasons—random differences and the independent variable.	You must randomly assign participants to groups.
It is impossible to accept the null hypothesis.	You cannot use the experiment to prove that a treatment has no effect or to prove that two treatments have identical effects.
You need enough power to find a significant effect.	You should 1. Standardize procedures. 2. Use sensitive, reliable dependent variables. 3. Code data carefully. 4. Use homogeneous participants. 5. Use many participants. 6. Use extreme levels of the independent variable.

Even when statistics are not dictating what you must do, they are suggesting what you should do. To avoid making Type 2 errors, you should do the following:

1. Standardize your procedures.
2. Use sensitive and reliable dependent measures.
3. Carefully code your data.
4. Use homogeneous participants.
5. Use many participants.
6. Use extreme levels of the independent variable.

Nonstatistical Considerations and the Design of the Simple Experiment

Statistical issues are not the only issues that you should consider when designing a simple experiment. If you considered only statistical power, you could harm your participants, as well as your experiment's external and construct validity. Therefore, in addition to statistical issues such as power, you must also consider external validity, construct validity, and ethical issues.

External Validity Versus Power

Many of the things you can do to improve your study's power may hurt your study's external validity. For example, using a laboratory setting, homogeneous participants, and extreme levels of the independent variable all improve power, but all may reduce external validity.

By using a lab experiment to stop unwanted variables from varying, you may have more power to find an effect. However, by preventing unwanted variables from varying, you may hurt your ability to generalize your results to real life—where these unwanted variables *do* vary.

By using a homogeneous set of participants (18-year-old, White males with IQs between 120 and 125), you reduce between-subject differences, thereby enhancing your ability to find treatment effects. However, because you used such a restricted sample, you would not be as able to generalize your results to the average American as a researcher whose participants were a random sample of Americans.

Finally, by using extreme levels of the independent variable, you may be able to find a significant effect for your independent variable. If you use extreme levels, though, you may be like the person who used a sledgehammer to determine the effects of hammers—you don't know the effect of realistic, naturally occurring levels of the treatment variable.

Construct Validity Versus Power

Your efforts to improve power may hurt not only your experiment's external validity but also its construct validity. For example, suppose you had two choices for your measure. The first is a 100-point rating scale that is sensitive and reliable. However, the measure is vulnerable to subject bias: If participants guess your hypothesis, they can easily circle the rating they think you want them to. The second is a measure that is not very reliable or sensitive, but it is a measure that participants couldn't easily fake. If power was your only concern, you would pick the first measure despite its vulnerability to subject bias. With it, you are more likely to find a statistically significant effect. However, because construct validity should be an important concern, many researchers would suggest that you pick the second measure.

If you sought only statistical power, you might also compromise the construct validity of your independent variable manipulation. For instance, to maximize your chances of getting a significant effect for full-spectrum lighting, you would give the experimental group full-spectrum lighting and make the control group an **empty control group:** a group that gets no kind of treatment. Compared to the empty control group, the treatment group

1. receives a gift (the lights) from the experimenter

2. gets more interaction with, and attention from, the experimenter (as the experimenter checks participants to make sure they are using the lights)

3. adopts more of a routine than the controls (using the lights every morning from 6:00 A.M. to 8:00 A.M.)

4. has higher expectations of getting better (because they have more of a sense of being helped) than the controls

As a result of all these differences, there is a reasonable chance of finding a significant difference between the two groups. Unfortunately, if you find a significant effect, it's hard to say that the effect is due to the full-spectrum lighting and not due to any of these other side effects of your manipulation.[7]

To minimize these side effects of the treatment manipulation, you might give your control group a **placebo treatment:** a substance or treatment that has no effect. Thus, rather than using a no-light condition, you might expose the control group to light from an ordinary 75-watt incandescent light bulb. You would further reduce the chances of bias if you made both the experimenters and participants **blind (masked):** unaware of which kind of treatment the participant was getting. If you make the researcher who interacts with the participants blind, that researcher will not bias the results in favor of the experimental hypothesis. Similarly, by making participants blind, you make it less likely that participants will bias the results in favor of the hypothesis.

In short, the use of placebos, the use of **single blinds** (in which either the participant or the experimenter is blind), and the use of **double blinds** (in which both the participant and the experimenter are blind) all may reduce the chances that you will obtain a significant effect. If you use these procedures, however, and you still find a significant effect, you can be relatively confident that the treatment itself—rather than some side effect of the treatment manipulation—is causing the effect.

You have seen that what is good for power may harm construct validity, and vice versa. But what tradeoffs should you make? To make that decision, you might find it helpful to see what tradeoffs professional experimenters make between power and construct validity. Do experienced experimenters use empty control groups to get significant effects? Or, do they avoid empty control groups to improve their construct validity? Do they avoid blind procedures to improve power? Or, do they use blind procedures to improve construct validity?

Often, experimenters decide to sacrifice power for construct validity. For example, in their jam experiment, Wilson and Schooler did not have an empty control group. In other words, their control group did not simply sit around doing nothing while the experimental group filled out the questionnaire analyzing reasons for liking a jam. Instead, the control

---

[7]The problem of using an empty control group is even more apparent in research on the effect of surgery. For example, if a researcher finds that rats receiving brain surgery run a maze slower than a group of rats not receiving an operation, the researcher should not conclude that the surgery's effect was due to removing a part of the brain that plays a role in maze-running.

group also completed a questionnaire. The questionnaire was a "filler questionnaire" about their reasons for choosing a major. If Wilson and Schooler had used an empty control group, critics could have argued that it was the act of filling out a questionnaire—not the act of reflection—that caused the treatment group to make less accurate ratings than the controls. For example, critics could have argued that the controls' memory for the jams was fresher because they were not distracted by the task of filling out a questionnaire.

To prevent critics from arguing that the experimenters influenced participants' ratings, Wilson and Schooler made the experimenters blind. To implement the blind technique, Wilson and Schooler employed two experimenters. The first experimenter had participants (a) taste the jams and (b) fill out either the control group (filler) questionnaire or the experimental group (reasons) questionnaire. After introducing the participants to Experimenter 2, Experimenter 1 left the room. Then, Experimenter 2—who was unaware of (blind to) whether the participants had filled out the reasons or the filler questionnaire—had participants rate the quality of the jams.

Ethics Versus Power

As you have seen, increasing a study's power may conflict with both external and construct validity. In addition, increasing power may conflict with ethical considerations. For example, suppose you want to use extreme levels of the independent variable (food deprivation) to ensure large differences in the motivation of your animals. In that case, you need to weigh the benefits of having a powerful manipulation against ethical concerns, such as the comfort and health of your subjects (for more about ethical concerns, see Chapter 2 and Appendix C).

Ethical concerns determine not only how you treat the experimental group but also how you treat the control group. Just as it might be unethical to administer a potentially harmful stimulus to your experimental participants, it also might be unethical to completely withhold a potentially helpful treatment from your control participants. For instance, it might be ethically questionable to completely withhold a possible cure for depression from your controls. Therefore, rather than maximizing power by completely depriving the control group of a treatment, ethical concerns may dictate that you give the control group a moderate dose of the treatment. (For a summary of the conflicts between power and other goals, see Table 10-5.)

Analyzing Data From the Simple Experiment: Basic Logic

After carefully weighing both statistical and nonstatistical considerations, you should be able to design a simple experiment that would test your experimental hypothesis in an ethical and internally valid manner. If, after consulting with your professor, you conduct that experiment, you will have data to analyze.

To understand how you are going to analyze your data, remember why you did the simple experiment. You did it to find out whether the treatment would have an effect on a unique population—all the participants who took part in your experiment. More specifically, you wanted to know the answer to the hypothetical question: "If I had put all my participants in the experimental condition, would they have scored differently than if I had put all of them in the control condition?" To answer this question, you need to know the averages of two **populations:**

Average of Population #1—what the average score on the dependent measure would have been if all your participants had been in the control group.

| Table 10-5 | **Conflicts Between Power and Other Research Goals** |

ACTION TO HELP POWER	HOW ACTION MIGHT HARM OTHER GOALS
Use a homogeneous group of participants to reduce random error due to participants.	May hurt your ability to generalize to other groups.
Test participants under controlled laboratory conditions to reduce the effects of extraneous variables.	1. May hurt your ability to generalize to real-life situations where extraneous variables are present. 2. Artificiality *may* hurt construct validity. If the setting is so artificial that participants are constantly aware that what they are doing is not real and just an experiment, they may *act* to please the experimenter rather than expressing their "true" reactions to the treatment.
Use artificially high or low levels of the independent variables to get big differences between groups.	1. You may be unable to generalize to realistic levels of the independent variable. 2. May be unethical.
Use an empty control group to maximize the chance of getting a significant difference between the groups.	Construct validity is threatened because the significant difference may be due to the participants' expectations rather than to the independent variable.
Test many participants to balance out the effects of random error.	Expensive and time-consuming.

Average of Population #2—what the average score on the dependent measure would have been if all your participants had been in the experimental group.

Unfortunately, you cannot measure both of these populations. If you put all your participants in the control condition, then you won't know how they would have scored in the experimental condition. If, on the other hand, you put all your participants in the experimental condition, you won't know how they would have scored in the control condition.

Estimating What You Want to Know: Your Means Are Sample Means

You can't directly get the population averages you want, so you do the next best thing—you estimate them. You can estimate them because, thanks to independent random assignment, you split all your participants (your population of participants) into two random samples. That is, you started the experiment with two random samples from your original population of participants. These two "chips off the same block" were the control group and the experimental group (see Figure 10-3).

The average score of the random sample of your participants who received the treatment (the experimental group) is an estimate of what the average score would have been if all your participants received the treatment. The average score of the random sample of participants who received no treatment (the control group) is an estimate of what the average score would have been if all of your participants had been in the control condition.

Figure 10-3

The Control Group and the Experimental Group Are Two Samples Drawn From the Same Population

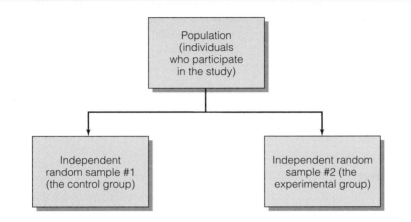

Problem: If the average score for the experimental group is different from the average score for the control group, is this difference due to the two groups receiving different treatments? To random error related to sampling? (Two random samples from the same population may differ.)

Calculating Sample Means: Getting Your Estimates

Even though only half your participants were in the experimental group, you will assume that the experimental group is a fair sample of your entire population of participants. Thus, the experimental group's average score should be a reasonably good estimate of what the average score would have been if all your participants had been in the experimental group. Similarly, you will assume that the control group's average score is a fairly good estimate of what the average score would have been if all your participants had been in the control group. Therefore, the first step in analyzing your data will be to calculate the average score for each group. Usually, the average you will calculate is the **mean:** the result of adding up all the scores and then dividing by the number of scores.

Comparing Sample Means: How to Compare Two Imperfect Estimates

Once you have your two sample means, you can compare them. Before talking about how to compare them, let's understand why we are comparing the means. We are comparing the sample means because we know that, before the treatment was administered, both groups represented a random sample of the population consisting of every participant who took part in the study. Thus, at the end of the experiment, if the treatment had no effect, the control and experimental groups would both still be random samples from that population.

As you know, two random samples from the same population will probably be similar to each other. For instance, two random samples of the entire population of New York City should be similar to each other, two random samples from the entire population of students at your school should be similar to each other, and two random samples from the entire group of participants who took part in your study should be similar to each other. Consequently, if the treatment has no effect, at the end of the experiment, the experimental and control groups should be similar to each other.

Why We Must Do More Than Subtract the Means From Each Other

Because two random samples from the same population should be similar to each other, you might think all we need to do is subtract the control group mean from the experimental group mean to find the effect. But such is not the case: Even if the treatment has no effect, the means for the control group and experimental group will rarely be identical. To illustrate, suppose that Dr. N. Ept made a serious mistake while trying to do a double-blind study. Specifically, Dr. N. Ept succeeded in not letting his assistants know whether the participants were getting the real treatment or a placebo, but failed in that all the participants got the placebo. In other words, both groups ended up being random samples of the same population—participants who did not get the treatment. Even in such a case, the two groups will probably have different means.

How Random Error Affects Data From the Simple Experiment

Dr. N. Ept's study illustrates an important point: Even if groups are random samples of the same population, they may still differ because of random error. You are probably aware of random error from reading about public opinion polls that admit to a certain degree of sampling error.

To help you see how random error could affect the results of a simple experiment, let's simulate conducting a small-scale experiment. Be warned that this simulation won't show us what would typically happen in an experiment. Instead, this simulation is rigged to demonstrate the worst random error can do. Nevertheless, the simulation does demonstrate a fundamental truth: Random error alone can create groups that differ substantially from each other.

To conduct this simulation, assume that you have the following four participants, who would tend to score as follows:

Abby	10
John	20
Mary	70
Paul	40

Now use Box 10-1 to randomly assign each participant to either the experimental or control group. Then, get an average for each group. Repeat this process several times. If you do this, you will simulate what happens when you do an experiment and the treatment has no effect.

As doing this simulation will reveal, which participants end up in which group varies greatly depending on where on the random numbers table you happen to start—and there are many different places you could start. Not all of these possible ways of splitting participants into control and experimental groups are going to produce identical groups. Indeed, you may even find that random assignment sometimes results in having all men in the experimental group and all women in the control group.

In summary, the control and experimental groups start off as random samples of your participants. At the start of the study, these groups are not identical. Instead, they will probably start off being fairly similar. Occasionally, however, they may start off being fairly different. If they start off as different, then they may score differently on the dependent measure task at the end of the experiment—even when the treatment has no effect. Thus, even if the treatment had no effect, random error might make the experimental group score differently (either higher or lower) than the control group.

Because random error can affect the results of a study, you need to understand random error to understand the results of a study. More specifically, to interpret the results of a simple experiment, you need to understand two important statistical principles:

1. Random error affects individual scores.
2. Random error may also cause group means to differ.

Fortunately, as you will soon see, you already intuitively understand both of these principles.

Random Error Makes Scores Within a Group Differ

To see that you intuitively grasp the first principle (random error affects individual scores), consider the following scores:

CONTROL	EXPERIMENTAL
70	80
70	80
70	80

Is there something strange about these data? Most students we show these data to correctly realize that these data are faked. Students are suspicious of these data because scores within each group do *not* vary: There is no within-groups variability in this experiment. The data make it look like the only thing that affects scores is the treatment. With real data, however, scores would be affected by nontreatment factors: There would be within-groups variability.

When asked to be more specific about why they think the data are faked, students point out that there are at least two reasons why scores within each group should differ. First, participants within each group differ from each other, so their scores would reflect those differences. That is, because participants in the control group aren't all clones of each other, their scores won't all be the same. Likewise, because participants in the experimental group aren't all identical, their scores shouldn't all be identical.

Second, even if a group's participants were all identical, random measurement errors alone would prevent participants from getting identical scores. For instance, even if the control group participants were clones, participants' scores would probably vary due to the measure's less-than-perfect reliability. Similarly, even if all the experimental group participants were identical, their scores would not be: Many random factors—from random variations in how the experimenter treated each participant to random errors in coding of the data—would inevitably cause scores within the experimental group to differ.

In summary, most students have an intuitive understanding that there will be differences within each group (within-groups variability), and these differences are due to factors completely unrelated to the treatment. To be more specific, these differences are due to random error caused by such factors as individual differences, random measurement error, and imperfect standardization.

Random Error Can Make Group Means Differ

To see whether you intuitively grasp the second principle (random error may cause group means to differ from each other), consider the following data:

CONTROL	EXPERIMENTAL
70	70
80	80
100	70

Do you think the experimental group is scoring significantly higher than the control group? Most students wisely say "no." They realize that if the participant who scored "100" had been randomly assigned to the control group rather than the experimental group, the results may have been completely different. Thus, even though the group means differ, the difference may not be due to the treatment. Instead, the difference between these two group means could be entirely due to random error.

As you have just seen, even if the treatment has no effect, random error may cause the experimental group mean to differ from the control group mean. Therefore, we cannot say that there is a treatment effect just because there is a difference between the experimental group's average score and the control group's. Instead, if we are going to find evidence for a treatment effect, we need a difference between our groups that is "too big" to be due to random error alone.

When Is a Difference Too Big to Be Due to Random Error?

What will help us determine whether the difference between group means is too big to be due to random error alone? In other words, what will help us determine that the treatment had a statistically significant effect?

To answer the question of how we determine whether the treatment had a statistically significant effect, we'll look at three sets of experiments. Let's begin with the two experiments tabled below. Which of the following two experiments do you think is more likely to reveal a significant treatment effect?

EXPERIMENT A		EXPERIMENT B	
Control	Experimental	Control	Experimental
70	70	70	80
71	73	71	81
72	72	72	82

Bigger Differences Are Less Likely to Be Due to Chance Alone

If you picked Experiment B, you're right! All other things being equal, bigger differences are more likely to be "too big to be due to chance alone" than smaller differences. Therefore, bigger differences are more likely to reflect a treatment effect. Smaller differences, on the other hand, provide less evidence of a treatment effect.

To appreciate the fact that small differences provide less evidence of a treatment effect, let's consider an extreme case. Specifically, let's think about the case where the difference between groups is as small as possible: zero. In that case, the control and experimental groups would have identical means. If the treatment group's mean is the same as the no-treatment group's mean, there is no evidence of a treatment effect.

"Too Big to Be Due to Chance" Partly Depends on How Big "Chance" Is

You have seen that the size of the difference is one factor that affects whether a result is statistically significant. All other things being equal, bigger differences are more likely to be significant.

But, the size of the difference isn't the only factor that determines whether a result is too big to be due to chance. To illustrate this fact, compare the two experiments below. Then, ask yourself, is Experiment A or Experiment B more likely to reveal a significant treatment effect? That is, in which experiment is the difference more likely to be too big to be due to chance?

EXPERIMENT A		EXPERIMENT B	
Control	Experimental	Control	Experimental
68	78	70	70
70	80	80	80
72	82	60	90

Differences Within Groups Tell You How Big Chance Is

In both experiments, the difference between the experimental and control group mean is 10. Therefore, you can't tell which difference is more likely to be too big to be due to chance just by seeing which experiment has a bigger difference between group means. Instead, to make the right choice, you have to figure out the answer to this question: "In which experiment is chance alone a less likely explanation for the 10-point difference?"

To help you answer this question, we'll give you a hint. The key to correctly answering this question is to look at the extent to which scores vary within each group. The more variability within a group, the more random error is influencing scores. All other things being equal, the more random error makes individual scores within a group differ from one another (the bigger within-groups variability), the more random error will tend to make group means differ from each other.

Now that you've had a hint, which experiment did you pick as being more likely to be significant? If you picked Experiment A, you're correct!

If you were asked why you picked A instead of B, you might say something like the following: "In Experiment B, the experimental group may be scoring higher than the control group merely because the participant who scored a 90 randomly ended up in the experimental group rather than in the control group. Consequently, in Experiment B, the difference between the groups could easily be due to random error."

Such an explanation is accurate, but it doesn't fully elaborate the complexity of your reasoning. Let's detail the four steps you went through:

1. You realized that there was more variability within each group in Experiment B than in Experiment A. That is, in Experiment B relative to Experiment A, (1) control group scores were further from the control group mean, and (2) experimental group scores were further from the experimental group mean.

2. You recognized that within-groups variability could not be due to the treatment. You realized that the differences among participants' scores within the control group could not be due to the treatment because none of those participants received the treatment. You also realized that the differences among scores within the experimental group could not be due to the treatment because every participant in the experimental group received the same treatment. Therefore, when scores within a group vary, these differences must be due to nontreatment factors such as individual differences.

3. You realized that random assignment turned the variability due to nontreatment factors (such as individual differences) into random error. Thus, you realized that the greater within-groups variability in Experiment B meant there was more random error in Experiment B than in Experiment A.

4. You realized that the more random error is spreading apart scores within each group, the more random error could be spreading the groups apart.

As you have seen, all other things being equal, the larger the differences between your group means, the more likely the results are to be significant. As you have also seen, the smaller your within groups variability (an index of the degree to which your individual scores are influenced by random error), the more likely your results are to be statistically significant. Thus, you have learned two of the three factors that determine whether a difference is significant. To find out what the third factor is, compare Experiments A and B below. Which is more likely to produce a significant result?

EXPERIMENT A			EXPERIMENT B	
Control	Experimental		Control	Experimental
68	70		68	70
70	72		70	72
72	74		72	74
			68	70
			70	72
			72	74
			68	70
			70	72
			72	74

In both experiments, the group means are equally far apart, so you can't look at group differences to figure out which experiment is more likely to be significant. In both experiments, the random variability within each group is the same; therefore, looking at within-groups variability will not help you figure out which experiment is more likely to be significant. Which one do you choose?

With Larger Samples, Random Error Tends to Balance Out

If you chose Experiment B, you're correct! Experiment B is the right choice because it had more participants. In Experiment B, it's less likely that random error alone would cause the groups to differ by much because *with large enough samples, random error tends to balance out to 0.* If you flip a coin 4 times, you are likely to get either 75% heads or 75% tails. That is, random error alone will probably cause a deviation of 25% or more from the true value of 50% heads. If, on the other hand, you flip a coin 4,000 times, you will almost never get more than 51% heads or fewer than 49% heads. Because 4,000 flips gives random error an opportunity to balance out, random error will almost never cause a deviation of even 1% from the true value.

Just as having more coin flips allows more opportunities for the effects of random error to balance out, having more participants allows more opportunities for random error to balance out. Thus, Experiment B, by having more participants, does a better job than Experiment A at allowing the effects of random error to balance out. Consequently, it's less likely that random error alone would cause Experiment B's groups to differ by a large amount. Therefore, a difference between the control group mean and the treatment group mean that would be big enough to be statistically significant (reliable) in Experiment B might *not* be significant in Experiment A.

Table 10-6	Basic Idea of the *t* Test

GENERAL IDEA

Observed difference (between two group means)

Difference expected by chance (measured by the standard error of the difference between means)

FORMULA

$$t = \frac{\text{Group 1 Mean} - \text{Group 2 Mean}}{\sqrt{\dfrac{S_1^2}{N_1} + \dfrac{S_2^2}{N_2}}}$$

where S_1 = standard deviation of Group 1, S_2 = standard deviation of Group 2, N_1 equals number of participants in Group 1, and N_2 equals number of participants in Group 2. The standard deviation can be calculated by the formula

$$S = \sqrt{(\Sigma X - M)^2 / N - 1}$$

where X stands for the individual scores, M is the sample mean, and N is the number of scores.

Notes:
1. A large *t* value is likely to be statistically significant. That is, large *t* (above 2.6) is likely to result in a *p* value smaller than .05.
2. *t* will tend to be large when
   a. The difference between experimental group mean and the control group mean is large.
   b. The standard error of the difference is small. The standard error of the difference will tend to be small when
      i. The standard deviations of the groups are small (scores in the control group tended to stay close to the control group mean, scores in the experimental group tended to stay close to the experimental group mean).
      ii. The groups are large.

Analyzing the Results of the Simple Experiment: The *t* Test

To determine whether a difference between two group means is significant, researchers often use either ANOVA[8] (analysis of variance, a technique we discuss in the next chapter) or the ***t* test** (to see how to do a *t* test, you can use the formula in Table 10-6 or consult Appendix D).[9] Although we have not yet talked about the *t* test, you already understand the basic logic behind it. The basic idea behind the *t* test is to see *whether the difference between two groups is larger than would be expected by random error alone.* Thus, you should not be surprised to find that the *t* ratio takes the difference between the sample means and divides that difference by an index of the extent to which random error might cause the groups to differ. To be more precise, *t* equals the difference between means divided by the standard error of the difference between means (see Table 10-6).

---

[8]The logic of ANOVA is similar to that of the *t* test. Indeed, for a simple experiment, the *p* value for the ANOVA test will be exactly the same as the *p* value from the *t* test. Thus, if the *t* test is statistically significant (*p* is less than .05), the ANOVA test will also be statistically significant (*p* will be less than .05). In addition, for the simple experiment, you can get the value of the ANOVA test statistic (called "F") by squaring your *t* value. Thus, if *t* is 2, *F* will be 4. To learn more about ANOVA, see the next chapter or see Appendix D.

[9]Although *t* test and ANOVA analyses are commonly used, they are criticized. The problem is that both *t* tests and ANOVA tell us only whether a result is statistically significant—and, as we discussed earlier, nonsignificant results don't tell you anything and significant results don't tell you anything about the size of your effect. Therefore, many argue that, rather than using significance tests, researchers should use confidence intervals. For more on the statistical significance controversy, see Box D-1 in Appendix D. For more about confidence intervals, see Appendix D.

Making Sense of the Results of a *t* Test

Once you have obtained your *t* value, you should calculate the degrees of freedom for that *t*. To calculate degrees of freedom, subtract 2 from the number of participants. Thus, if you had 32 participants, you should have 30 degrees of freedom.

If you calculate *t* by hand, you need to compare your calculated *t* to a value in a *t* table like the one in Appendix E to determine whether your *t* ratio is significant. To use the *t* table in Appendix E, you need to know how many degrees of freedom *(df)* you have. For example, if you had data from 32 participants, you would look at the *t* table in Appendix E under the row labeled "30 *df*." When comparing the *t* ratio you calculated to the value in the table, act like your *t* ratio is positive even if your *t* value is actually negative. In other words, take the absolute value of your *t* ratio.

If the absolute value of your *t* ratio is *not* bigger than the number in the table, your results are *not* statistically significant at the **$p < .05$ level.** If, on the other hand, the absolute value of your *t* ratio is bigger than the number in the table, your results are statistically significant at the $p < .05$ level.

If you had a computer calculate *t* for you, make sure that the degrees of freedom *(df)* for *t* are two fewer than the number of participants. For example, if you thought you entered scores for 32 participants but your *df* = 18, you know there is a problem because the computer is acting as though you entered only 20 scores.

If you had a computer calculate *t* for you, it might provide you with only the *t*, the degrees of freedom, and the *p* value, as in the following case:

$$df = 8, t = 4, \text{ and } p = .0039$$

From the *df* of 8, you know that the *t* test was calculated based on scores from 10 participants (10 − 2 = 8). From the *p* value of less than .05, you know the results are statistically significant at the .05 level. That is, you know that if the null hypothesis were true, the chances of your obtaining differences between groups that were as big as or bigger than what you observed were less than 5 in 100.

Many computer programs will provide you with more information than the *df*, *t*, and *p* values. Some will provide you with what might seem like an overwhelming amount of information, such as the following:

1. *df* = 8, *t* = 4, and Sig. (2-tailed) = .0039
2. Mean difference = 4.00
3. 95% CI of this difference: 1.69 to 6.31
4. Group 1 mean = 11.00; Group 1 *SD* = 1.58; *SEM* = 0.71
5. Group 2 mean = 7.00; Group 2 *SD* = 1.58; *SEM* = 0.71

The first line tells you that the *t* test was calculated based on scores from 10 participants (10 − 2 = 8, the *df*) and that the results were statistically significant. The second line tells you that the Group 1 mean was 4 units bigger than the Group 2 mean. The third line tells you that you can be 95% confident that the true difference between the means is between 1.69 units and 6.31 units. (To learn more about how the confidence interval [CI] was calculated, see Box 10-2.)

The fourth line describes Group 1's data, and the fifth line describes Group 2's data. Both of those lines start by providing the group's average score (the mean) followed by a measure of how spread out the group's scores are: the standard deviation (*SD*). Be concerned

BOX 10-2 Beyond Statistical Significance: Obtaining Information About Effect Size

Your study's *t* value gives you almost everything you need to know to determine whether your results are *statistically* significant. However, you may also want to know whether your results are *practically* significant. To know that, you may need to know how large your effect is.

Using *t* to Estimate the Treatment's Average Effect: Confidence Intervals

One way to estimate effect size is to take advantage of information you used when you computed your *t*. In calculating *t*, you divided the top of the *t* ratio by the standard error of the difference between means. The top of the *t* ratio is the difference between the mean of the no-treatment group and the mean of the treatment group. As such, it is an estimate of the treatment effect. Thus, if the treatment group scores 2 points higher than the no-treatment group, our best estimate is that the treatment improved scores by 2 points.

Unfortunately, our best estimate is almost certainly wrong: We have almost no confidence that the treatment effect is exactly 2.000. We would be more confident of being right if we said that the treatment effect was somewhere between 1 and 3 points. We would be even more confident of being right if we said that the real effect was somewhere between 0 and 4 points. What we would like to do is be more specific. We would like to say how confident we are that the real effect is within a certain range. For example, we would like to be able to say that we are "95% confident that the effect of the treatment is between 1 and 3 points."

Fortunately, we can specify that we are 95% confident that the real effect is between two values by using the information we used to execute the *t* test: the mean difference (the top of our *t* ratio), the standard error of the difference (the bottom of our *t* ratio), and the critical value of *t* at the .05 level. You can find the critical value by looking in the *t* table [Table E-1] at the intersection of the ".05" column and the row corresponding to your experiment's degrees of freedom. For example, if you had data from 42 participants, the value would be 2.021.

The middle of our confidence interval will be the difference between the means of the treatment group and the no-treatment group. That is, it will be the top of the *t* ratio. In this example, that difference is 2. To get our confidence interval's upper value, we start with the difference between our means (2). Then, we add the number we get by multiplying the standard error of the difference (the bottom of our *t* value) by the critical value of *t*. To illustrate, suppose that the difference between our means was 2, the standard error of the difference was 1, and the critical value of *t* was 2.021. To 2, we would add 2.021 (the standard error of the difference [1] × the critical value of *t* [2.021] = 2.021). Thus, the upper value of our confidence interval would be 4.021 (2 + 2.021).

To get the lower value, we reverse the process. We will again start with 2 (the difference between our means). This time, however, we will subtract, rather than add, 2.021 (the product of multiplying the standard error by the critical *t* value) from 2. Therefore, the lower value of our interval would be −0.021 [2 − (1 × 2.021) = 2 − 2.021 = −.021].

As the result of our calculations, we could say that we were 95% confident that the true effect was in the interval ranging from −0.021 to 4.021. By examining this interval, we can form two conclusions. First, we cannot confidently say that the treatment effect has any effect because 0 (zero effect, no effect) was within our interval. Second, we see that our confidence interval is large and so our study lacks power and precision. Therefore, we may want to repeat the study in a way that shrinks the interval (e.g., using more participants, using more reliable measures, using more homogeneous participants, using more standardized procedures) so that we can more precisely estimate the treatment's effect.

For example, in the original study, we studied 42 participants. If we repeated the study using 62 participants and again found a difference between our groups of 2, we would be 95% confident that the true effect was between .35 and 3.6.[a] Not only is this interval narrower than the original interval (which went from −0.021 to +4.021), but it also does not include zero. Therefore, we could confidently say that the treatment did have some

[a] When we calculated this confidence interval we assumed that the standard deviations (an index of the extent to which participants' scores differ from the mean; a 0 would mean that everyone had the same score—the mean score) within each of your groups would be the same as they were in the original study. If your procedures were more standardized when you repeated the study, the standard deviations might be smaller and so your intervals might be even smaller than what we projected.

(continued)

BOX 10-2 **(continued)**

effect. Note another lesson from this example: Even though the first study's results were not statistically significant (because we could not say that the treatment effect was significantly different from zero) and the second study's results were significant (because we could say that the treatment effect was significantly different from zero), the two studies do not contradict each other. The difference in the results is that the second study, by virtue of its greater power and precision, allows you to make a better case that the treatment effect is greater than zero.

Using *t* to Compute Other Measures of Effect Size: Cohen's *d* and *r²*

In the previous section, you learned how to provide a range that you were 95% confident contained the average effect of the treatment. However, even if you knew precisely what the average effect of the treatment was, you would not know all you should know about the treatment's effect size. For example, suppose you know that the average effect was 2. Is 2 a small effect? If your participants' scores range from 0 to 100, a difference between your control group and experimental group of 2 units might be a relatively small effect. If, on the other hand, scores in your control group vary from 0 to 1, and

scores in your treatment group vary from 2 to 3, a treatment effect of 2 units would be a relatively large effect. Therefore, to know the relative size of an effect, you need an effect size measure that takes into account the variability of the scores.

One popular effect size measure is Cohen's *d*. If you had the same number of participants in each group, you can calculate Cohen's *d* from your *t* value by using the following formula: Cohen's $d = 2t/\sqrt{df}$. Thus, if *t* is 3 and *df* is 9, Cohen's *d* will be $(2 \times 3)/\sqrt{9} = 6/3 = 2$. Usually, social scientists view a *d* of .2 as indicating a small effect, a *d* of .5 as indicating a medium effect, and a *d* of .8 as indicating a large effect.

Another way of measuring the relationship between the treatment and your dependent variable is to square the correlation *(r)* between the treatment and the dependent variable. The result will be a measure, called the **coefficient of determination,** that can range from 0 (no relationship) to 1.00 (perfect relationship). Usually, social scientists view a coefficient of determination of .01 as small, of .09 as moderate, and of .25 as large (for more about the coefficient of determination, see Chapter 7). If you have computed *d*, you can compute the coefficient of determination (*r²*) by using the following formula: $r^2 = d^2/(d^2 + 4)$. To see the relationships among these effect size measures, see Table 10-7.

Table 10-7 | **Relationship Among Different Effect Size Measures**

| | | INFORMATION FROM THE *t* TEST | | EFFECT SIZE MEASURES | | |
| | | | Mean Difference (example with low variability in scores) | Mean Difference (example with moderate variability in scores) | | |
t	Degrees of Freedom				*d*	*r²* (also called η²)
2	9		2	4.7	1.33	.31
2	16		1.4	3.7	1.0	.20
2	25		1.2	3.0	0.8	.14
2	36		1.0	2.5	0.67	.10
2	49		0.8	2.2	0.57	.08
2	64		0.7	1.9	0.50	.06
2	81		0.7	1.7	0.44	.05
2	100		0.6	1.5	0.40	.04

if the *SD* of either group is extremely high—a high *SD* may mean that you have entered a wrong value (e.g., when typing data from a 1-to-5 scale, you typed "55" instead of "5"). Both lines end with their group's standard error of the mean (*SEM*): an indicator of how far off the group's sample mean is likely to be from the actual population mean. If either group's *SEM* is large, your experiment has little power, and you probably failed to find a significant effect.

Suppose that your experiment was powerful enough to find an effect that is statistically significant at the $p < .05$ level. In that case, because there's less than a 5% chance that the difference between your groups is solely due to chance, you can be reasonably sure that some of the difference is due to your treatment.

To learn about the size of your treatment's effect, you might want to use Box 10-2 to compute an index of effect size such as Cohen's *d*. For example, suppose your computer analysis presented the following results:

1. $df = 30$, $t = 3.10$, and $p < .05$
2. Mean difference = 3.46
3. 95% CI of this difference: 1.57 to 5.35; $SED = 1.12$
4. Group 1 mean = 8.12; Group 1 $SD = 3.0$; $SEM = 0.75$
5. Group 2 mean = 4.66; Group 2 $SD = 3.32$; $SEM = 0.83$

Using that data and Box 10-2, you would be able to determine that Cohen's *d* was 1.13.

Then, you could write up your results as follows:[10] "As predicted, the experimental group recalled significantly more words ($M = 8.12$, $SD = 3.0$) than the control group ($M = 4.66$, $SD = 3.32$), $t(30) = 3.10$, $p < .05$, $d = 1.13$."

You could include even more information: APA strongly encourages researchers to supplement significance tests with means, standard deviations, and both confidence intervals and effect size measures. However, at the very least, you should say something like this: "As predicted, the experimental group recalled significantly more words ($M = 8.12$) than the control group ($M = 4.66$), $t(30) = 3.10$, $p < .05$." The key is that you must do more than report that your results are statistically significant. Indeed, largely because some researchers have focused only on whether their results are statistically significant, a few researchers have suggested that statistical significance testing be banned (for more on the statistical significance controversy, see Box D-1 in Appendix D). Although not everyone agrees that statistical significance testing should be banned, almost everyone agrees that researchers need to do more than report *p* values.

Assumptions of the *t* Test

The validity of any *p* values you obtain from any significance test will depend on how well you meet the assumptions of that statistical test. For the *t* test, two of these assumptions are especially important: (1) having at least interval scale data and (2) having independent observations.

---

[10]*M* stands for mean, *SD* stands for standard deviation (a measure of the variability of the scores; the bigger the SD, the more spread out the scores are and the less the scores cluster around the mean), and *d* stands for Cohen's *d* (a measure of effect size). *SD* will usually be calculated as part of computing *t* (for more about *SD*, see Appendix D). To learn how to compute *d*, see Box 10-2.

Two Critical Assumptions

Because the *t* test must determine whether one group's mean score is significantly larger than the other's, groups with higher means must have more of the quality you are measuring than groups with lower means. To be more specific, because only interval and ratio scale data allow you to compute such "meaningful means," you must be able to assume that you have either interval scale or ratio scale data (for a review of interval and ratio scale data, see Chapter 6).

Because you cannot compute meaningful means on either qualitative data or ranked data, you cannot do a *t* test on those data. You cannot compute meaningful means on qualitative (nominal, categorical) data because scores relate to categories rather than amounts. With qualitative (nominal) data, 1 might equal "nodded head," 2 might equal "gazed intently," and 3 might equal "blinked eyes." With such nominal data, computing a mean (e.g., the mean response was 1.8) would be meaningless.

With ranked and other ordinal data, the numbers have an order, but they still don't refer to specific amounts and so means can be meaningless and misleading. For example, although averaging the ranks of second- and third-place finishers in a race would result in the same mean rank (2.5) as averaging the ranks of the first- and fourth-place finishers, the mean times of the two groups might vary greatly. The average times of the first- and fourth-place finishers could be much faster or much slower than the average of the times of the second- and third-place finishers.

Although having either nominal or ordinal data prevents you from comparing group means with a *t* test, you can still compare two groups using tests, such as the Mann-Whitney U test (for ordinal data) and the chi-square test (for either nominal or ordinal data), that do not involve comparing means. (For more on these tests, see Appendix D.)

The second assumption you must meet to perform a legitimate *t* test is that your observations must be independent. Specifically, (a) participants must be assigned independently (e.g., individually so that the assignment of Mary to the experimental group has no effect on whether John is assigned to the experimental group); (b) participants must respond independently (e.g., no participant's response influences any other participant's response); and (c) participants must be tested independently so that other than the treatment, there is no systematic difference between how experimental and control group participants are treated.

If you followed our advice and independently and randomly assigned each participant to either the experimental or the control conditions, and then ran participants individually (or in small groups or in larger groups that mixed experimental and control participants), your observations are independent. If, however, your observations are not independent, you cannot legitimately do a conventional independent groups *t* test. Indeed, violating independence often means that the data from your study are unanalyzable and thus worthless.

To reiterate, to do a meaningful independent samples *t* test in a simple experiment, your data must meet two key assumptions: You must have at least interval scale data, and you must have used independently assigned participants to groups. In addition to these two pivotal assumptions, the *t* test makes two less vital assumptions (see Table 10-8).

Two Less Critical Assumptions

First, the *t* test assumes that the individual scores in the population from which your sample means were drawn are **normally distributed:** half the scores are below the average score; half are above; the average score is the most common score; about 2/3 of the scores are within one standard deviation of the mean; about 19/20 of the scores are within two standard deviations of the mean; and if you were to plot how often each score occurred, your plot would resemble a bell-shaped curve. The reason for this assumption is that if the individual scores

Table 10-8 — Effects of Violating the *t* Test's Assumptions

ASSUMPTION	CONSEQUENCES OF VIOLATING ASSUMPTION
Observations are independent (participants are independently assigned and participants do not influence one another's responses).	Serious violation; probably nothing can be done to salvage your study.
Data are interval or ratio scale (for example, numbers must not represent qualitative categories, nor may they represent ranks [first, second, third, etc.]).	Do not use a *t* test. However, you may be able to use another statistical test (e.g., Mann-Whitney U, Chi-square).
The population from which your sample means was drawn is normally distributed.	If the study used more than 30 participants per group, this is not a serious problem. If, however, fewer participants were used, you may decide to use a different statistical test.
Scores in both conditions have the same variance.	Usually not a serious problem.

in the population are normally distributed, the distribution of sample means based on those scores will also tend to be normally distributed.[11] The assumption that individual scores are normally distributed is usually nothing to worry about because most distributions are.

But what if the individual scores aren't normally distributed? Even then, your sample means probably will be normally distributed—provided you have more than 30 participants per group. That is, as the **central limit theorem** states, with large enough samples (and 30 per group is usually large enough), the distribution of sample means will be normally distributed, regardless of how individual scores are distributed.

To understand why the central limit theorem works, realize that if you take numerous large samples from the same population, your sample means will differ from one another for only one reason: random error. Because random error is normally distributed, the distributions of sample means will be normally distributed—regardless of the shape of the underlying population.

The second assumption is that the variability of scores within your experimental group will be about the same as the variability of scores within your control group. To be more precise, the assumption is that scores in both conditions will have the same variance.[12] Usually, the penalty for violating the assumption of equal variance is not severe. Specifically, if you have unequal variances, it won't seriously affect the results of your *t* test, as long as one variance isn't more than $2\frac{1}{2}$ times larger than the other.

---

[11]Why do we have to assume that the distribution of sample means is normally distributed? We need to know precisely how the sample means are distributed to establish how likely it is that the two sample means could differ by as much as they did by chance alone. In other words, if we are wrong about how the sample means are distributed, our *p* value—our estimate of the probability of the sample means differing by as much as they did if their population means were the same—would be wrong.

[12]To get the variance for a group, square that group's standard deviation *(SD)*. If you used a computer to get your *t*, the computer program probably displayed each group's *SD*. If you calculated the *t* by hand, you probably calculated each group's *SD* as part of those calculations. Some computer programs will do a statistical test such as Levene's Test for Equality of Variance to tell you how reasonable it is to assume that the groups have the same variance. If the *p* value for the Levene's Test for Equality of Variance is statistically significant, it means that the variances are probably different: It does *not* mean that the treatment has an effect. If the variances are significantly different, instead of a conventional t test, you may want to do Welch's test instead.

Questions Raised by Results

Obviously, if you violate key assumptions of the *t* test, people should question your results. But even if you don't violate any of the *t* test's assumptions, your results will raise questions—and this is true whether or not your results are statistically significant.

Questions Raised by Nonsignificant Results

Nonsignificant results raise questions because the null hypothesis cannot be proven. Therefore, null results inspire questions about the experiment's power such as the following:

1. Did you have enough participants?
2. Were the participants homogeneous enough?
3. Was the experiment sufficiently standardized?
4. Were the data coded carefully?
5. Was the dependent variable sensitive and reliable enough?
6. Would you have found an effect if you had chosen two different levels of the independent variable?

Questions Raised by Significant Results

If your results are statistically significant, it means you found an effect for your treatment. Hence, there's no need to question your study's power. However, a significant effect raises other questions. Sometimes, questions are raised because statistical significance doesn't tell us how big the effect is (see Box 10-2).

Sometimes, questions are raised because the experimenter sacrificed construct or external validity to obtain adequate power. For example, if you used an empty control group, you have questionable construct validity. Consequently, one question would be: "Does your significant treatment effect represent an effect for the construct you tried to manipulate or would a placebo treatment have had the same effect?" Or, if you used an extremely homogeneous group of participants, the external validity of your study might be questioned. For instance, skeptics might ask: "Do your results apply to other kinds of participants?" Thus, skeptics might want you to increase the external validity of your study by repeating it with a more representative sample. Specifically, they might want you to first use random sampling to obtain a representative group of participants and then randomly assign those participants to either the control or experimental group.

At other times, questions are raised because of a serious limitation of the simple experiment: It can study only two levels of a single independent variable. Because of this, there are two important questions you can ask of any simple experiment:

1. To what extent do the results apply to levels of the independent variable that were not tested?
2. To what extent could the presence of other variables modify (strengthen, weaken, or reverse) the treatment's effect?

Concluding Remarks

As you have seen, the results of a simple experiment always raise questions. Although results from any research study raise questions, some questions raised by the results of the simple experiment are due to the fact that the simple experiment is limited to studying only two levels of a single variable. If the logic of the simple experiment could be expanded to designs that would study several levels of several independent variables at the same time, such designs could answer several questions at once. Fortunately, as you will see in Chapters 11 and 12, the logic of the simple experiment can be extended to produce experimental designs that will allow you to answer several research questions with a single experiment.

SUMMARY

1. Psychologists want to know the causes of behavior so that they can understand people and help people change. Only experimental methods allow us to isolate the causes of an effect.

2. Studies that don't manipulate a treatment are not experiments.

3. Many variables, such as participant's age, participant's gender, and participant's personality, can't be manipulated. Therefore, many variables can't be studied using an experiment.

4. The simple experiment is the easiest way to establish that a treatment causes an effect.

5. The prediction that the treatment will cause an effect is called the experimental hypothesis.

6. The null hypothesis, on the other hand, states that the treatment will not cause an observable effect.

7. With the null hypothesis, you only have two options: You can reject it, or you can fail to reject it. You can never accept the null hypothesis.

8. Typically, in the simple experiment, you administer a low level of the independent (treatment) variable to some of your participants (the comparison or control group) and a higher level of the independent variable to the rest of your participants (the experimental group). Near the end of the experimental session, you observe how each participant scores on the dependent variable: a measure of the participant's behavior.

9. To establish causality with a simple experiment, participants' responses must be independent. Because of the need for independence, your experimental and control groups are not really groups. Instead, these "groups" are sets of individuals.

10. Because independent random assignment is the cornerstone of the simple experiment, without it you do not have a simple experiment.

11. Independent random assignment is necessary because it is the only way to make sure that the only differences between your groups are either due to chance or to the treatment.

12. Independent random assignment makes it likely that your control group is a fair comparison group. Therefore, if you use random assignment, the control and experimental groups should be fairly equivalent before the treatment is introduced.

13. Random assignment can be used only if you are manipulating a treatment. It involves assigning a level of a treatment to participants—and can help a study's internal validity.

14. Your goal in using independent random assignment is to create two samples that accurately represent your entire population of participants. You use the mean of the control group as an estimate of what would have happened if all your participants had been in the control group. You use the experimental group mean as an estimate of what the mean would have been if all your participants had been in the experimental group.

15. The t test tries to answer the question, "Does the treatment have an effect?" In other words, would participants have scored differently had they all been in the experimental group than if they had all been in the control group?

16. If the results of the t test are statistically significant, the difference between your groups is greater than would be expected by chance (random error) alone. Therefore, you reject the null hypothesis and conclude that your treatment has an effect. Note, however, that statistical significance does not tell you that your results are big, important, or of any practical significance.

17. There are two kinds of errors you might make when attempting to decide whether a result is statistically significant. Type 1 errors occur when you mistake a chance difference for a treatment effect. Before the study starts, you choose your "false alarm" risk (risk of making a Type 1 error). Most researchers decide to take a 5% risk. Type 2 errors occur when you fail to realize that the difference between your groups is not solely due to chance. In a sense, you overlook a genuine treatment effect.

18. By reducing your risk of making a Type 1 error, you increase your risk of making a Type 2 error. That is, by reducing your chances of falsely "crying wolf" when there is no treatment effect, you increase your chances of failing to correctly yell "wolf" when there really is a treatment effect.

19. Because Type 2 errors can easily occur, nonsignificant results are inconclusive results.

20. To prevent Type 2 errors, (a) reduce random error; (b) use many participants to balance out the effects of random error; and (c) try to increase the size of your treatment effect.

21. You can easily determine your risks of a Type 1 error, but there's no way you can design your experiment to reduce them. In contrast, it is hard to determine your risk of making a Type 2 error, but there are many ways you can design your study to reduce your risk of making such errors.

22. If your experiment minimizes the risk of making Type 2 errors, your experiment has power. In the simple experiment, *power* refers to the ability to obtain statistically significant results when your independent variable really does have an effect.

23. Sometimes, efforts to improve power may hurt the study's external validity. For example, to get power, researchers may use a highly controlled lab setting rather than a real-life setting. Similarly, power-hungry researchers may study participants who are very similar to each other rather than a wide range of participants.

24. Occasionally, efforts to improve power may hurt the study's construct validity.

25. Using placebo treatments, single blinds, and double blinds can improve your study's construct validity.

26. Ethical concerns may temper your search for power—or even cause you to decide not to conduct your experiment.

27. Because of random error, you cannot determine whether your treatment had an effect simply by subtracting your experimental group mean from your control group mean. Instead, you must determine whether the difference between your group means could be due to random error.

28. The t test involves dividing the difference between means by an estimate of the degree to which the groups would differ when the treatment had no effect. More specifically, the formula for the t test is: (Mean 1 − Mean 2)/standard error of the difference.

29. The degrees of freedom for a two-group between-subjects t test are 2 less than the total number of participants.

30. The t test is a common way to analyze data from a simple experiment.

31. If your data do not meet the assumptions of the t test, your statistical analysis may give you misleading results.

KEY TERMS

internal validity *(p. 280)*

simple experiment *(p. 280)*

independent random assignment *(p. 281)*

experimental hypothesis *(p. 282)*

null hypothesis *(p. 283)*

independent variable *(p. 285)*

levels of an independent variable *(p. 285)*

experimental group *(p. 285)*

control group *(p. 285)*

independently, independence *(p. 286)*

dependent variable (dependent measure) *(p. 288)*

inferential statistics *(p. 289)*

statistical significance *(p. 289)*

null results (nonsignificant results) *(p. 290)*

Type 1 error *(p. 293)*

Type 2 error *(p. 294)*

power *(p. 294)*

empty control group *(p. 300)*

placebo treatment *(p. 300)*

blind (masked) *(p. 300)*

single blind *(p. 300)*

double blind *(p. 300)*

population *(p. 302)*

mean *(p. 303)*

t test *(p. 309)*

p < .05 level *(p. 310)*

coefficient of determination *(p. 312)*

normally distributed, normal distribution *(p. 314)*

central limit theorem *(p. 315)*

EXERCISES

1. A professor has a class of 40 students. Half of the students chose to take a test after every chapter (chapter test condition) outside of class. The other half of the students chose to take in-class "unit tests." Unit tests covered four chapters. The professor finds no statistically significant differences between the groups on their scores on a comprehensive final exam. The professor then concludes that type of testing does not affect performance.
   a. Is this an experiment?
   b. Is the professor's conclusion reasonable? Why or why not?

2. Participants are randomly assigned to meditation or no-meditation condition. The meditation group meditates three times a week. The meditation group reports being significantly more energetic than the no-meditation group.
   a. Why might the results of this experiment be less clear-cut than they appear?
   b. How would you improve this experiment?

3. Theresa fails to find a significant difference between her control group and her experimental group $t(10) = 2.11$, not significant.
   a. Given that her results are not significant, what—if anything—would you advise her to conclude?
   b. What would you advise her to do? (Hint: You know that her t test, based on 10 degrees of freedom, was not significant. What does the fact that she has 10 degrees of freedom tell you about her study's sample size, and what does it suggest about her study's power?)

4. A training program significantly improves worker performance. What should you know before advising a company to invest in such a training program?

5. Jerry's control group is the football team; the experimental group is the baseball team. He assigned the groups to condition using random assignment. Is there a problem with Jerry's experiment? If so, what is it? Why is it a problem?

6. Students were randomly assigned to two different strategies of studying for an exam. One group used visual imagery; the other group was told to study the normal way. The visual imagery group scores 88% on the test as compared to 76% for the control group. This difference was not significant.
   a. What, if anything, can the experimenter conclude?
   b. If the difference had been significant, what would you have concluded?
   c. "To be sure that they are studying the way they should, why don't you have the imagery people form one study group and have the control group form another study group?" Is this good advice? Why or why not?
   d. "Just get a sample of students who typically use imagery and compare them to a sample of students who don't use imagery. That will do the same thing as random assignment." Is this good advice? Why or why not?

7. Bob and Judy are doing the same study, except that Bob has decided to put his risk of a Type 1 error at .05 whereas Judy has put her risk of a Type 1 error at .01. (Note that consulting Table E-1 in Appendix E will help you answer parts a and b.)
   a. If Judy has 22 participants in her study, what t value would she need to get significant results?
   b. If Bob has 22 participants in his study, what t value would he need to get significant results?
   c. Who is more likely to make a Type 1 error? Why?
   d. Who is more likely to make a Type 2 error? Why?

8. Gerald's dependent measure is the order in which people turned in their exam (first, second, third, etc.). Can Gerald use a t test on his data? Why or why not? What would you advise Gerald to do in future studies?

9. Are the results of Experiment A or Experiment B more likely to be significant? Why?

EXPERIMENT A	
Control Group	Experimental Group
3	4
4	5
5	6

EXPERIMENT B	
Control Group	Experimental Group
0	0
4	5
8	10

10. Are the results of Experiment A or Experiment B more likely to be significant? Why?

EXPERIMENT A	
Control Group	Experimental Group
3	4
4	5
5	6

EXPERIMENT B	
Control Group	Experimental Group
3	4
4	5
5	6
3	4
4	5
5	6
3	4
4	5
5	6

WEB RESOURCES

1. Go to the Chapter 10 section of the book's student website and do the following:
   a. Look over the concept map of the key terms.
   b. Test yourself on the key terms.
   c. Take the Chapter 10 Practice Quiz.
   d. Do the interactive end-of-chapter exercises.

2. Do a *t* test using a statistical calculator by going to the "Statistical Calculator" link.

3. Find out how to conduct a field experiment by reading "Web Appendix: Field Experiments."

4. If you want to write your method section, use the "Tips on Writing a Method Section" link.

5. If you want to write up the results of a simple experiment, click on the "Tips for Writing Results" link.

INFOTRAC COLLEGE EDITION EXPLORATIONS

1. Do an InfoTrac College Edition keyword search using the phrase "Stroop and violence" to find Williamson, Kosmitzki, and Kibler's (1995) simple experiment on the effects of viewing violence on women.

2. Get at least two ideas for simple experiments from Wadeley's (2001) easy-to-read *Psychology Review* article by doing an InfoTrac College Edition keyword search using the phrase "pets and stress and gender."

Expanding the Simple Experiment

The Multiple-Group Experiment

Perhaps too much of everything is as bad as too little.

—*Edna Ferber*

Overview

We devoted Chapter 10 to the simple experiment: the design that involves randomly assigning participants to two groups. The simple experiment is internally valid and easy to conduct. However, it is limited in that you can study only two values of a single independent variable.

In this chapter, you will see why you might want to go beyond studying two values of a single variable. Then, you will see how the principle that gives the simple experiment internal validity (random assignment of participants to two groups) can be extended to experiments that study the effects of three or more values of a single independent variable. Finally, you will learn how to analyze data from such experiments.

The Advantages of Using More Than Two Values of an Independent Variable

The simple experiment is ideal if an investigator wants to compare a single treatment group to a single no-treatment control group. However, as you will see, investigators often want to do more than compare two groups.

Comparing More Than Two Kinds of Treatments

We do not live in a world where there are only two flavors of ice cream, only two types of music, and only two opinions on how to solve any particular problem. Because people often choose between more than two options, investigators often compare more than two different kinds of treatments.

For instance, to decide how police should respond to a domestic dispute, investigators compared three different strategies: (1) arrest a member of the couple, (2) send one member away for a cooling off period, and (3) give advice and mediate the dispute (Sherman & Berk, 1984). Clearly, investigators could not compare three different treatments in one simple, two-group experiment. Therefore, instead of randomly assigning participants to two different groups, they randomly assigned participants to three different groups. (To learn how to randomly assign participants to more than two groups, see Box 11-1.)

In another case of attacking an applied problem, Cialdini (2005) saw a problem we all see—a well-intentioned, written request to do something good—and he wondered what most of us have wondered: Would wording the request differently make it more effective? Specifically, he questioned the effectiveness of hotel room signs that urge guests to conserve water by reusing towels because doing so will (1) preserve the environment and (2) help the hotel donate money to an environmental cause. Cialdini believed that approaches that used psychological principles would be more effective than the hotels' usual approach, and he could think of at least two principles that he could apply.

First, he could apply the principle that people tend to do what they believe others do. Thus, he created a sign stating that 75% of guests reuse their towels.

Second, he could apply the principle that people tend to repay a favor. Thus, he created a sign stating that the hotel had already donated money to protect the environment on behalf of the hotel guests and wanted to recover that expense.

To test his two solutions against conventional practice, Cialdini needed at least three groups: (1) a group that got the conventional treatment—a "preserve the environment plus

BOX 11-1 Randomly Assigning Participants to More Than Two Groups

Step 1 Across the top of a piece of paper write down your conditions. Under each condition draw a line for each participant you will need.

GROUP 1	GROUP 2	GROUP 3
_____	_____	_____
_____	_____	_____
_____	_____	_____
_____	_____	_____

Step 2 Turn to a random numbers table (there's one in Table E-6, Appendix E). Roll a die to determine which column in the table you will use.

Step 3 Assign the first number in the column to the first space under Group 1, the second number to the second space, and so forth. When you have filled the spaces for Group 1, put the next number under the first space under Group 2. Similarly, when you fill all the spaces under Group 2, place the next number in the first space under Group 3.

GROUP 1	GROUP 2	GROUP 3
12	20	63
39	**2**	64
53	37	95
29	**1**	18

Step 4 Assign the first person who participates in your study to the condition with the lowest random number (in this case, the lowest random number is "1" and it's in Group 2). The second participant will be in the condition with the second lowest random number, and so on. Thus, in this example, your first two participants would be in Group 2, and your third participant would be in Group 1.

hotel donation" group, (2) a "most other people are doing it" group, and (3) a "repay a favor" group. As Cialdini suspected, both the "repay a favor" and the "most other people are doing it" reused their towels much more than the group that saw the sign hotels typically used.

Clearly, Cialdini could not compare three groups in a single, two-group experiment. Thus, he used a multiple-group experiment. If, like Cialdini, you want to compare more than two treatments, you should use a multiple-group experiment.

Comparing Two Kinds of Treatments With No Treatment

Even when you are interested in comparing only two types of treatments, you may be better off using a multiple-group experiment. To understand why, let's consider the following research finding: For certain kinds of back problems, people going to a chiropractor end up better off than those going for back surgery. Although an interesting finding, it leaves many questions unanswered. For example, is either treatment better than nothing? We don't know because the researchers didn't compare either treatment to a no-treatment control condition. It could be that both treatments are worse than nothing and chiropractic treatment is merely the lesser of two evils. On the other hand, both treatments could be substantially better than no treatment and chiropractic could be the greater of two goods.

Similarly, if we compared two untested psychological treatments in a simple experiment, we would know only which is better than the other: We would not know whether the better one was the less harmful of two "bad" treatments or the more effective of two "good" treatments. Thus, we would not know whether the lesser of the two treatments was (1) moderately harmful, (2) neither harmful nor helpful, or (3) mildly helpful. However, by using a three-group experiment that has a no-treatment control group, we would be able to judge not only how effective the two treatments were relative to each other but also their overall, general effectiveness. Consider the following examples of how adding a no-treatment control group helps us know what effect the treatments had.

- In a classic experiment, Loftus (1975) found that leading questions distorted participants' memories of a filmed car accident. All participants watched a film of a car accident, completed a test booklet that contained questions about the film, and a week later, answered some more questions about the film. But participants were not treated identically because not all participants got the same test booklet. Instead, each participant was randomly assigned to receive one of the following three test booklets:

  1. The "presume" booklet contained 40 questions asked of all participants, plus 5 additional questions that asked whether certain objects—objects that were *not* seen in the film—were in the film. These 5 additional questions were leading questions: questions suggesting that the object was shown in the film (e.g., "Did you see **the** school bus in the film?").
  2. The "mention but don't presume" booklet contained 40 questions asked of all participants, plus 5 additional questions that asked whether certain objects— objects that were *not* seen in the film—were in the film. This booklet was the same as the "presume" booklet except that the 5 additional questions did *not* suggest that the item was shown in the film (e.g., "Did you see **a** school bus in the film?").
  3. A control booklet that contained 40 questions asked of all participants.

- Note that without a control group, Loftus would not have known whether the difference between the nonleading question and leading question group was due to (a) the nonleading question condition sharpening memory or (b) the leading question condition distorting memory.
- Anderson, Carnagey, and Eubanks (2003) looked at the effects of violent lyrics on aggressive thoughts. Had they used only nonviolent and violent songs, they would not have known whether nonviolent songs reduced aggressive thoughts or whether violent songs increased aggressive thoughts. Thanks to the no-song control condition, they learned that violent lyrics increased aggressive thoughts.

Comparing More Than Two Amounts of an Independent Variable to Increase External Validity

In the simple experiment, you are limited to two amounts of your independent variable. However, we do not live in a world where variables come in only two amounts. If we did, other people would be either friendly or unfriendly, attractive or unattractive, like us or unlike us, and we would be either rewarded or punished, included or excluded, and in complete control or have no control. Instead, we live in a world where situations vary not so much in terms of whether a quality (e.g., noise) is present but rather the degree to which that quality is present.

Not only that, but we live in a world where more is not always better. Sometimes, too little of some factor can be bad, too much can be bad, but (to paraphrase the littlest of the three bears) a medium amount is just right. In such cases, a simple, two-valued experiment can lead us astray.

To see how this happens, suppose that a low amount of exercise leads to a poor mood, a moderate amount of exercise leads to a good mood, and a high amount of exercise leads to

Figure 11-1 How a Multiple-Group Experiment Can Give You a More Accurate Picture of a Relationship Than a Simple Experiment

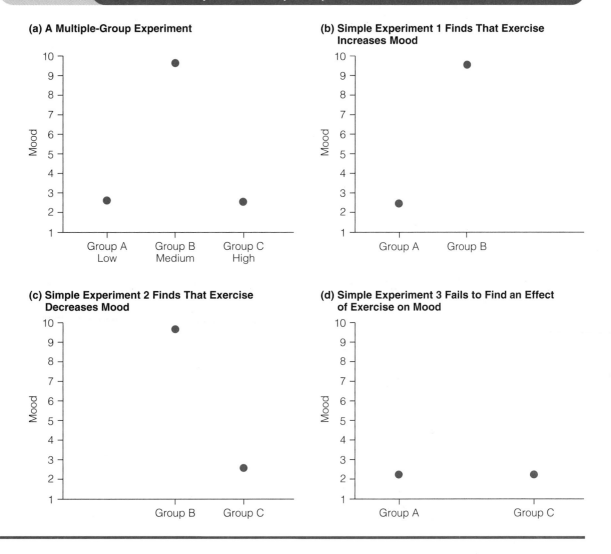

(a) A Multiple-Group Experiment

(b) Simple Experiment 1 Finds That Exercise Increases Mood

(c) Simple Experiment 2 Finds That Exercise Decreases Mood

(d) Simple Experiment 3 Fails to Find an Effect of Exercise on Mood

a poor mood. Such an upside-down "U"-shaped relationship is plotted in Figure 11-1a. As you can see, if we did a multiple-group experiment, we would uncover the true relationship between exercise and mood. However, if we did a simple experiment, our findings might be misleading. For example, if we did the simple experiment depicted in

- Figure 11-1b, we might conclude that exercise *increases* mood
- Figure 11-1c, we might conclude that exercise *decreases* mood
- Figure 11-1d, we might conclude that exercise does not affect mood

As this example illustrates, to make accurate statements about the effects of an independent variable, the researcher must know the independent and dependent variables' **functional relationship:** the shape of the relationship.

Figure 11-2 **Linear Relationship Between Two Points**

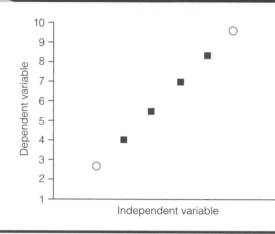

If you are going to accurately map the shape of a functional relationship, you need more than the two data points that a simple experiment provides. Simple experiments do not enable you to uncover the nature of a functional relationship because many different shaped lines can be drawn between two points. To appreciate this, consider Figure 11-2. From the two known data points (the empty circles), can you say what the relationship between the variables is?

No, you can't. Perhaps the relationship is a **linear relationship:** one that is graphically represented by a straight line. A straight line does fit your two points. However, maybe your relationship is *not* linear: As you can see from Figure 11-3, many other curved lines also fit your two points.

Because lines of many different shapes can be drawn between the two points representing a simple experiment's two group means, the simple experiment does not help you discover the functional relationship between the variables. Thus, if your simple experiment indicated that 100 minutes of exercise produced better mood than 0 minutes of exercise, you would not know the functional relationship between exercise and mood. Therefore, if we asked you about the effects of 70 minutes of exercise on mood, you could do little more than guess. If you assumed that the exercise-mood relationship is linear, you would guess that exercising 70 minutes a day would be (a) better than no exercise and (b) worse than exercising 100 minutes a day. But if your assumption of a linear relationship is wrong (and it well could be), your guess would be inaccurate.

To get a line on the functional relationship between variables, you need to know more than two points (means). Therefore, suppose you expanded the simple experiment into a multilevel experiment by adding a group that gets 50 minutes of exercise a day. Then, you would have a much clearer idea of the functional relationship between exercise and happiness. As you can see in Figure 11-4 on page 328, using three levels can help you identify the functional relationship among variables. If the relationship is linear, you should be able to draw a straight line through your three points. If the relationship is U-shaped, you'll be able to draw a "U" through your three points.

| Figure 11-3 | Some Possible Nonlinear Relationships |

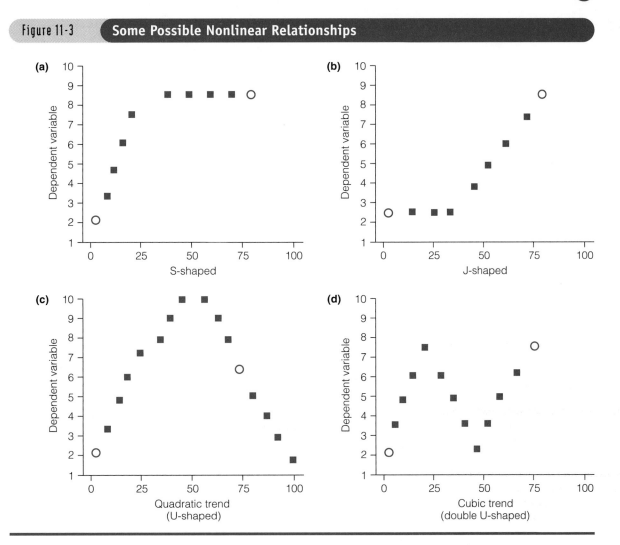

Note: The circles represent the known data points. The boxes between the circles are what might happen at a given level of the independent variable, depending on whether the relationship between the variables is characterized by (a) an S-shaped (negatively acclelerated) trend, (b) a J-shaped (positively accelerated) trend, (c) a U-shaped (quadratic) trend, or (d) a double U-shaped (cubic) trend.

Because you can get a good picture of the functional relationship when you use three levels of the independent variable, you can make accurate predictions about unexplored levels of the independent variable. For example, if the functional relationship between exercise and happiness were linear, you might obtain the following pattern of results:

Group 1	0 minutes of exercise per day	0.0 self-rating of happiness
Group 2	50 minutes of exercise per day	5.0 self-rating of happiness
Group 3	100 minutes of exercise per day	10.0 self-rating of happiness

Figure 11-4 **Having Three Levels of the Independent Variable (Three Data Points) Helps You Identify the Shape of the Functional Relationship**

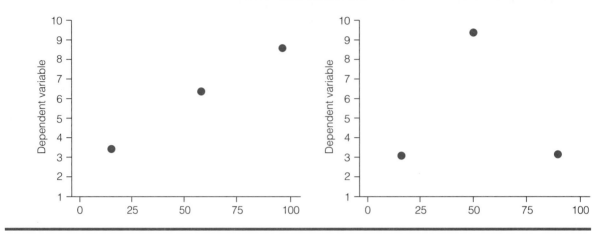

With these three points, we can be relatively confident that the relationship is linear (fits a straight line). Most nonlinear relationships (see Figure 11-3) would not produce data that would fit these three data points.

If we had these three data points, we could be relatively confident that the relationship is curvilinear (fits a curved line). Specifically, we would suspect that we had a quadratic relationship: a relationship shaped like a "U" or an upside-down "U."

In that case, you could confidently predict that 70 minutes of exercise would be less beneficial for increasing happiness than 100 minutes of exercise.

If, on the other hand, the relationship was S-shaped (as in Figure 11-3), you might get the following pattern of results:

Group 1	0 minutes of exercise per day	0.0 self-rating of happiness
Group 2	50 minutes of exercise per day	10.0 self-rating of happiness
Group 3	100 minutes of exercise per day	10.0 self-rating of happiness

In that case, you would predict that a person who exercised 70 minutes would do as well as someone exercising 100 minutes a day.

The more groups you use, the more accurately you can pin down the shape of the functional relationship. Yet, despite this fact, you do not have to use numerous levels of the independent variable. Why? Because nature prefers simple patterns. That is, most functional relationships are linear (straight lines), and few are more complex than U-shaped functions. Consequently, you will rarely need more than four levels of the independent variable to pin down a functional relationship. In fact, you will usually need no more than three carefully chosen levels.

Conclusions: Multilevel Experiments and External Validity

In summary, knowing the functional relationship between two variables is almost as important as knowing that a relationship exists. If you want to give practical advice, you should be able to say more than: "If you exercise 100 minutes a day, you will be happier than someone who exercises 0 minutes a day." Who exercises exactly 100 minutes a day? You want to be able to generalize your results so that you can tell people the effects of exercising

50 minutes, 56 minutes, 75 minutes, and so forth. Yet, you have no intention of testing the effects of every possible amount of exercise a person might do. Instead, you want to test only a handful of exercise levels. If you choose these levels carefully, you will be able to map the functional relationship between the variables. Mapping the functional relationship, in turn, will allow you to make educated predictions about the effects of treatment levels that you have not directly tested.

When mapping functional relationships, psychologists often manipulate independent variables that have names starting with "number of," such as number of others, number of milligrams of a drug, or number of seconds of exposure to a stimulus. You may be inspired by studies like the following classics.

- In Asch's (1955) line-judging experiments, he led participants to believe that they were in a visual perception study along with some other participants. The participant's job was to pick the line on the right that matched the line on the left. The experiment was really a social influence experiment, and the other participants were really confederates (assistants) of the experimenter. Asch wanted to know whether the size of group would affect people's conformity to the group. He found that as group size went from two to five, participants were more likely to conform. However, he found that increasing the group size beyond seven actually decreased the chances that participants would go along with the group.
- In Latané, Williams, and Harkins's (1979) social loafing experiments, investigators wanted to know how loafing would change as a function of group size. They found that adding two members to a group increased loafing, but that adding two members increased loafing more in smaller groups than in larger groups.
- In Milgram, Bickman, and Berkowitz's (1969) conformity experiment, confederates looked up at the sixth floor window of an office building. Because the researchers were interested in the effects of group size on conformity, the researchers had either 1, 2, 3, 5, 10, or 15 confederates look up at the office building. Then, they counted what percentage of people passing by also looked up. They found that the bigger their initial group, the stronger the group's influence.
- In Darley and Latané's (1968) study of helping behavior, participants thought they were talking via intercom to either one, two, or five other participants (actually, the participant was alone—the voices came from a tape-recording) when one of them had a seizure. They found that the *more* people participants thought were in the group, the *less* likely participants were to help.
- In Ambady and Rosenthal's (1993) "thin slices" experiments, participants watched—with the sound off—either three 2-second, three 5-second, or three 10-second clips video clips of a professor. The researchers found that participants in all three groups came up with same ratings of the professor as students who sat in the professor's class all term.
- In Basson, McInnes, Smith, Hodgson, and Koppiker's (2002) study of the effect of Viagra on women, neither the 10-mg, 50-mg, or 100-mg doses of Viagra were more effective in increasing sexual response than a placebo.

Although it is easy to map functional relationships when the name of your independent variable starts with "number of," realize that you can map functional relationships between most variables because—with a little work—most variables can be quantified. If you can manipulate a variable between two extreme levels (e.g., low and high), you can probably also manipulate it in between those extremes (e.g., medium). To illustrate, consider a variable that is not obviously quantitative: similarity. Byrne (1961) manipulated similarity from 0% to 100% by (a) making participants believe they were seeing an attitude scale from another student and then (b) manipulating the proportion of responses that matched the participant from 0% to 100%.

If your independent variable involves exposing participants to a stimulus, you can usually quantify your manipulation by doing some work before you start your study. Specifically, you could (a) produce several variations of the stimulus, (b) have volunteers rate each of those variations, and then (c) use the variations that have the values you want in your experiment. For example, suppose you wanted to manipulate physical attractiveness by showing participants photos of people who varied in attractiveness. You could take a photo of an attractive person, then (a) get some less attractive photos of the person by messing with the person's makeup or by messing with their picture using a computerized photo editing program, (b) have some volunteers rate the attractiveness of each photo on a 0-to-10 scale, and (c) use the photos that were consistently rated 4, 6, and 8 as the three stimuli for your experiment. Realize that this scaling strategy is not just for pictures: If your manipulation was "severity of a crime" or "legitimacy of an excuse" or almost anything else, you could still use this scaling strategy.

Using Multiple Groups to Improve Construct Validity

You have seen that multilevel experiments—because their results can generalize to a wider range of treatment levels—can have more external validity than simple experiments. In this section, you will learn that multilevel experiments can also have more construct validity than simple experiments.

Confounding Variables in the Simple Experiment

In Chapter 10, you saw that thanks to random assignment, simple experiments are able to rule out the effects of variables unrelated to the treatment manipulation. For example, because of random assignment, the effects of participant variables such as gender, race, and personality usually will not be confused for a treatment effect. In other words, a statistically significant difference between the control group and the experimental group at the end of the experiment will probably not be due to the groups being different before the treatment was introduced.

So, simple experiments effectively control for the effects of variables that have nothing to do with the treatment manipulation. But what if the treatment is manipulating more than the one variable it's supposed to be manipulating? For instance, what if an "exercise" manipulation is also manipulating social support? Simple experiments are not always effective in ruling out the effects of variables that are manipulated along with the treatment.

In an ideal world, this limitation of the simple experiment would not be a problem. Your treatment would be a pure manipulation that creates one—and only one—systematic difference between the experimental group and the control group. Unfortunately, it is rare to have a perfect manipulation. Instead, the treatment manipulation usually produces several differences between how the experimental and control groups are treated.

For example, suppose that a simple experiment apparently found that the "attractive" defendant was more likely to get a light sentence than the "unattractive" defendant. We would know that the "attractiveness" manipulation had an effect. However, it could be that in addition to manipulating attractiveness, the researchers also manipulated perceived wealth. Thus, wealth, rather than attractiveness, might account for the manipulation's effect. Specifically, people may be less likely to give wealthy defendants long sentences.

Because of impurities in manipulations, you often end up knowing that the treatment manipulation had an effect, but not knowing whether the treatment had an effect because it manipulated (a) the variable you wanted to manipulate or (b) some other variable that you did not want to manipulate (the impurity). In short, simple experiments may lack construct validity because the independent variable manipulation is contaminated by variables that are unintentionally manipulated along with the treatment. In technical terminology, the manipulation's construct validity is weakened by **confounding variables:** variables, other than the independent variable, that may be responsible for the differences between your conditions.

The following example[1] illustrates the general problem of confounded manipulations. Imagine being in a classroom that has five light switches, and you want to know what the middle light switch does. Assume that in the "control" condition, all the light switches are off. In the "experimental" condition, you want to flick the middle switch. However, because it is dark, you accidentally flick on the middle three switches. As the lights come on, the janitor bursts into the room, and your "experiment" is finished. What can you conclude?

You can conclude that your manipulation of the light switches had an effect. That is, your study has internal validity. But, because you manipulated more than just the middle light switch, you can't say that you know what the middle light switch did. Put another way, if you were to call your manipulation a "manipulation of the middle switch," your manipulation would lack construct validity.

Because of confounding variables, it is often hard to know what it is about the treatment that caused the effect. In real life, variables are often confounded. For example, your friend may know she got a hangover from drinking too much wine, but not know whether it was the alcohol in the wine, the preservatives in the wine, or something else about the wine that produced the awful sensations. A few years ago, a couple of our students joked that they could easily test the hypothesis that alcohol was responsible. All they needed us to do was donate enough money to buy mass quantities of a pure manipulation of alcohol—180 proof, totally devoid of impurities. These students understood how confounding variables can contaminate real-life manipulations—and how confounding variables can make it hard to know what it was about the manipulation that caused the effect.

Having a multiple-group experiment can allow you to know what it is about the source that causes a treatment's effect. For example, if you wanted to look at the effects of cell phones on driving behavior, you could have a no cell phone group, a cell phone group, and a cell phone with headset group. By comparing the regular cell phone group to the headset group, you might be able to see whether reaching for the phone was a source of the cell phone users' driving problems. To see how having more than two groups has helped researchers track down the source of a treatment's effect, consider the following examples.

- Gesn and Ickes (1999) found that participants who saw a video of another person did a passable job at knowing what that person was thinking. But why? Was it the person's words—or was it their nonverbal signals? To find out, Gesn and Ickes compared one group that heard only the words (audio only) to another group that got only the nonverbal signals. (The nonverbal group saw video of the person accompanied by a filtered sound track that allowed participants to hear the pitch, loudness, and rhythm of the person's speech, but not the actual words.) Gesn and

---

[1]We are indebted to an anonymous reviewer for this example and other advice about confounding variables.

Ickes found that the words, rather than nonverbal signals, were what helped participants figure out what the person was thinking. Specifically, whereas the audio-only group did nearly as well as the normal video group, the video with filtered audio group did very poorly.

- Langer, Blank, and Chanowitz (1978) had their assistant get into lines to use the copier and then ask one of three questions:

1. Can I cut in front of you?
2. Can I cut in front of you because I'm in a rush?
3. Can I cut in front of you because I want to make a copy?

- The researchers found that 60% of participants in the no-excuse condition let the assistants cut in front, 94% of the participants in the good-excuse condition let the assistants cut in, and 93% of the participants in the poor-excuse condition let the assistants cut in front of them. By having both a no-excuse control group and a good-excuse control group, the researchers were able to establish that it was (a) important to have an excuse but (b) the quality of the excuse was unimportant.
- In the false memory study we discussed earlier, Loftus (1975) included a control group who was asked about objects that weren't in the film without implying that those objects were in the film. The fact that this control group did not have false memories allowed Loftus to discover that the false memories in the leading question condition were caused by suggesting that the object was present—and not by the mere mention of the false object.

To understand how confounding variables can contaminate a simple experiment, let's go back to the simple experiment on the effects of exercise that we proposed earlier in this chapter. You will recall that the experimental group got 100 minutes of exercise class per day, whereas the control group got nothing. Clearly, the experimental group participants were treated differently from the control group participants. The groups didn't differ merely in terms of the independent variable (exercise). They also differed in terms of several other (confounding) variables: The exercise group received more attention and had more structured social activities than the control group.

Hypothesis-Guessing in Simple Experiments. Furthermore, participants in the experimental group knew they were getting a treatment, whereas participants in the control group knew they were not receiving any special treatment. If experimental group participants suspected that the exercise program should have an effect, the exercise program may appear to have an effect—even if exercise does not really improve mood. In other words, the construct validity of the study might be ruined because the experimental group participants guessed the hypothesis (**hypothesis-guessing**).

Because of the impurities (confounding variables) of this exercise manipulation, you cannot say that the difference between groups is due to exercise by itself. Although all manipulations have impurities, this study's most obvious—and avoidable—impurities stem from having an **empty control group:** a group that gets no treatment, not even a placebo (a placebo is a treatment that doesn't have an effect, other than possibly by changing a participants' expectations). Thus, if you chose to use a placebo control group instead of the empty control group, you could reduce the impact of confounding variables.

Increasing Validity Through Multiple Control Groups
Choosing the placebo control group over the empty control group does, however, often come at a cost. Often, it would be better to have both control groups.

To see how hard it can be to choose between an empty control group and a placebo group, consider the studies comparing the effect of antidepressant drugs to the effect of a placebo. If those simple experiments had compared groups getting antidepressants to empty control groups, those studies would have grossly overestimated the effectiveness of antidepressant drugs (Kirsch, Moore, Scoboria, & Nicholls, 2002). However, because those studies did not use empty control groups, they don't tell us the difference between getting the drug and receiving no treatment. Given that patients will be choosing between drug treatment and no drugs (Moerman, 2002), the lack of an empty control group is a problem. It would have been nice to have compared the antidepressant group to both an empty control group as well as to a placebo group.

The Value of a Placebo Group. To take another example of the difficulty of choosing between a placebo group and an empty control group, let's go back to the problem of examining the effects of exercise on mood. If you use an empty control group that has nothing done to them, interpreting your results may be difficult. More specifically, if the exercise group does better than this "left alone" group, the results could be due to hypothesis-guessing (e.g., participants in the exercise condition figuring out that exercise should boost their mood) or to any number of confounding variables (such as socializing with other students in the class, being put into a structured routine, etc.).

If, on the other hand, you use a placebo-treatment group (for example, meditation classes), you would be able to control for some confounding variables. For example, both your treatment and placebo groups would be assigned to a structured routine. Still, you won't know what the treatment's effect is.

The Value of an Empty Control Group: "Placebos" May Not Be Placebos. You won't know what the effect of your treatment is because you do not know what the effect of your placebo treatment is. Ideally, you would like to believe that your placebo treatment has no effect. In that case, if the treatment group does worse than the placebo group, the treatment is harmful; if the treatment group does better, the treatment is helpful.

If, however, what you hope is a placebo treatment turns out to be a treatment that really does have an effect, you are going to have trouble evaluating the effect of your treatment. For example, suppose you find that the exercise group is more depressed than the meditation group. Could you conclude that exercise increases depression? No, because it might be that although exercise reduces depression, meditation reduces it more. Conversely, if you found that the exercise group is less depressed than the meditation group, you could not automatically conclude that exercise decreases depression. It may be that meditation increases depression greatly, and exercise increases depression only moderately: Exercise may simply be the lesser of two evils.

To find out whether exercise increases or decreases depression, you need to compare the exercise group to a no-treatment group. Thus, if you were interested in the effects of exercise on depression, you have two options: (1) Use a simple experiment and make the hard choice between an empty control group and a placebo group, or (2) use a multiple-group experiment so that you can include both an empty and a placebo control group.

Using Multiple Imperfect Control Groups to Compensate for Not Having the Perfect Control Group. Even if you are sure you do not want to use an empty control group, you may still need more than one control group because you will probably not have the perfect control group. Instead, you may have several groups, each of which controls for some confounding variables but not for others. If you were to do a simple experiment, you may have to decide which of several control groups to use. Choosing one control group—when you realize you need more than one—is frustrating. It would be better to be able to use as many as you need.

But how often do you need more than one control group? More often than you might think. In fact, even professional psychologists sometimes underestimate the need for control groups. Indeed, many professional researchers get their research articles rejected because a reviewer concluded that they failed to include enough good control groups (Fiske & Fogg, 1990).

You often need more than one control group so that your study will have adequate construct validity. Even with a poor control group, your study has internal validity: You know that the treatment group scored differently than the control group. But what is it about the treatment that is causing the effect? Without good control group(s), you may think that one aspect of your treatment (the exercise) is causing the effect, when the difference is really due to some other aspect of your treatment (the socializing that occurs during exercise).

To illustrate how even a good control group may still differ from the experimental group in several ways having nothing to do with the independent variable, consider the meditation control group. The meditation control group has several advantages over the empty control group. For example, if the exercise group was less depressed than a meditation control group, we could be confident that this difference was not due to hypothesis-guessing, engaging in structured activities, or being distracted from worrisome thoughts for awhile. Both groups received a "treatment," both engaged in structured activities, and both were distracted for the same length of time.

The groups, however, may differ in that the exercise group did a more social type of activity, listened to louder and more upbeat music, and interacted with a more energetic and enthusiastic instructor. Therefore, the exercise group may be less depressed for several reasons having nothing to do with exercise: (1) liking their exercise partners; (2) feeling arousal and positive mood as a result of the music; and (3) being exposed to an upbeat leader.

To rule out all these possibilities, you might use several control groups. For instance, to control for the "social activity" and the "energetic model" explanations, you might add a group that went to a no-credit acting class taught by an enthusiastic professor. To control for the music explanation, you might add a control group that listened to music or perhaps even watched aerobic dance videos. By using all of these control groups, you may be able to rule out the effects of confounding variables.

Analyzing Data From Multiple-Group Experiments

You have just learned that multiple control groups may give you more construct validity than one control group. Earlier, you learned that multiple treatment groups allow you to more accurately map the functional relationship between the independent variable and the dependent variable than a two-group experiment. Before that, you learned that the multiple-group experiment allows you to compare more treatments at one time than a two-group experiment. In short, you have learned that there are at least three good reasons to conduct a multiple-group experiment instead of a simple experiment:

1. to improve construct validity
2. to map functional relationships
3. to compare several treatments at once

However, before you conduct a multiple-group experiment, you should understand how it will be analyzed because the way that it will be analyzed has implications for (a) what treatment groups you should use, (b) how many participants you should have, and even (c) what your hypothesis should be.

Even if you never conduct a multiple-group experiment, you will read articles that report results of such experiments. To understand those articles, you must understand the logic and vocabulary used in analyzing them.

Analyzing Results From the Multiple-Group Experiment: An Intuitive Overview

As a first step to understanding how to analyze the results of multiple-group experiments, let's look at data from three experiments that compared the effects of no-treatment, meditation, and aerobic exercise on happiness. All of these experiments had 12 participants rate their feelings of happiness on a 0-to-100 (not at all happy to very happy) scale. Here are the results of Experiment A:

	NO-TREATMENT	MEDITATION	EXERCISE
	50	51	53
	51	53	53
	52	52	54
	51	52	52
Group Means	51	52	53

Compare these results to the results of Experiment B:

	NO-TREATMENT	MEDITATION	EXERCISE
	40	60	78
	42	60	82
	38	58	80
	40	62	80
Group Means	40	60	80

Are you more confident that Experiment A or Experiment B found a significant effect for the treatment variable? If you say B, why do you give B as your answer? You answer B because there is a bigger difference between the groups in Experiment B than in Experiment A. That is, the group means for Experiment B are farther apart than the group means for Experiment A. Group B's means being farther apart—what statisticians call greater **variability between group means**—gives you two hints that Experiment B is more likely to be the study that obtained significant results.

First, you intuitively realize that to find a treatment effect, you need between-group variability. After all, if the between-group variability was zero (indicating that the means of the exercise group, the no-treatment group, and the meditation group were all the same), you couldn't argue that the treatment had an effect.

Second, you intuitively realize a small difference between group means might easily be due to chance (rather than to the treatment), but a larger difference is less likely to be due to chance.[2] Thus, you realize that the more variability there is between group means, the more likely it is that at least some of that variability is due to treatment.

---

[2]Similarly, if your favorite team lost by one point, you might blame luck. However, if your team lost by 30 points, you would be less likely to say that bad luck alone was responsible for the defeat.

Now, compare Experiment B with Experiment C. Here are the results of Experiment C:

	EXERCISE	NO-TREATMENT	MEDITATION
	10	10	100
	80	90	80
	60	60	60
	10	80	80
Group Means	40	60	80

Do you think the results from Experiment B or Experiment C are stronger evidence of a treatment effect? Both experiments have the same amount of variability between group means. Therefore, unlike in our first example, you cannot use the rule of choosing the experiment with the means that differ the most to choose Experiment B. Yet, once again, you will pick Experiment B. Why?

You will pick Experiment B because you are concerned about one aspect of Experiment C: the extreme amount of variability within each group. You realize the only reason scores within a group vary is random error. (If participants in the same treatment group get different scores, those different scores can't be due to the treatment. Instead, the differences in scores must be to nontreatment variables, such as individual differences. In a randomized experiment, such nontreatment variables become random error.) Thus, you see that Experiment C is more affected by random error than Experiment B.

The large amount of random error in Experiment C (as revealed by the *within-groups* variability) bothers you because you realize that this random error—rather than the treatment—might be the reason the groups differ from one another. That is, the same random variability that makes individual scores within a group differ from each other might also make the group means differ from each other.[3] In Experiment B, on the other hand, the small amount of within-group variability indicates that there is virtually no random variability in the data. Therefore, in Experiment B, you feel fairly confident that random error is not causing the group means to differ from one another. Instead, you believe that the means differ from one another because of the treatment.

Intuitively then, you understand the three most important principles behind analyzing the results of a multiple-group experiment. Specifically, you realize the following:

1. Within-groups variability is not due to the treatment, but instead is due to random error. That is, differences within a treatment group can't be due to the treatment because everyone in the group is getting the same treatment. Instead, differences among group members must be due to factors such as individual differences and random measurement error.

2. Between-groups variability is not a pure measure of treatment effects. Admittedly, treatment effects should cause the groups to differ from one another. However, random variability will also cause the groups to differ from one another. Consequently, even if no treatment was administered, the group means would

---

[3]To get a sense of how random sampling error might cause the group means to differ, randomly sample two scores from the no-treatment group. Compute the mean of this group. If you do this several times, you will get different means. These different means can't be due to a treatment effect because none of the participants in any of your samples are receiving the treatment. The reason you are getting different means even though you are sampling the same group is random sampling error. Fortunately, statistics can help us determine how likely it is that the differences among group means are entirely due to random error.

probably differ. In other words, between-group variability is not a pure index of variability due to treatment (treatment effects) because between groups variability is affected by random error.

3. If you compare between-group variability (the effects of random error plus any treatment effects) to within-group variability (the effects of random error alone), you may be able to determine whether the treatment had an effect.

Analyzing Results From the Multiple-Group Experiment: A Closer Look

You now have a general idea of how to analyze data from a multiple-group study. To better understand the logic and vocabulary used in these analyses—a must if you are to understand an author's or a computer's report of such an analysis—read the next few sections.

Within-Groups Variability: A Pure Measure of Error

As you already know, within-groups variability does not reflect the effects of treatment. Instead, it reflects the effects of random error. For example, because all the participants in the meditation group are getting the same treatment (meditation), any differences among those participants' scores can't be due to the treatment. Instead, the differences among scores of meditation group participants are due to such random factors as individual differences, unreliability of the measure, and lack of standardization. Similarly, differences among the scores of participants in the no-treatment group are due not to treatment, but to irrelevant random factors. The same is true for differences within the exercise group. Thus, calculating within-groups variability will tell us the extent to which chance causes individual scores to differ from each other.

To measure this within-groups variability, we first look at the variability of the scores within each group. To be more specific, we calculate an index of variability called the variance. If we have three groups, we could calculate a variance for each group, giving us three separate indexes of within-groups variability. We would then have three separate estimates of the extent to which the groups could differ due to random error alone. Because we want only one estimate of variability due to random error, we average all these within-group variances to come up with the best estimate of random variability—the within-groups variance. Fortunately, we can use this estimate of how much random error causes individual scores to differ from each other to estimate the extent to which random error is likely to cause group means to differ from each other.

Because the **within-groups variance** gives us an index of the degree to which *random error* alone may cause your group means to differ, within-groups variance is often referred to as **error variance.**

Between-Groups Variability: Error Plus (Possibly) Treatment

Once you have an index of the degree to which your groups could vary from each other due to chance alone (the within-groups variance), the next step is to get an index of the degree to which your groups actually vary from one another. It is at this step where it becomes clear that you cannot use a *t* test to analyze data from a multiple-group experiment. When using a *t* test, you determine the degree to which the groups differ from one another in a straightforward manner: You subtract the average score of Group 1 from the average score of Group 2. Subtraction works well when you want to compare two groups, but does not work well when you have more than two groups. You can subtract only two scores at a time. So, if you have three groups, which two groups do you compare? Group 1 with Group 2? Or, Group 2 with Group 3? Or, Group 1 with Group 3?

You might answer this question by saying "all of the above." Thus, with three groups, you would do three *t* tests: one comparing Group 1 against Group 2, a second comparing Group 1 against Group 3, and a third comparing Group 2 against Group 3. However, that's not allowed!

An analogy will help you understand why you cannot use multiple *t* tests. Suppose a stranger comes up to you with a proposition: "Let's bet on coin flips. If I get a 'head,' you give me a dollar. If I don't, I give you a dollar." You agree. He then proceeds to flip three coins at once and then makes you pay up if even one of the coins comes up heads. Why is this unfair? This is unfair because he misled you: You thought he was going to flip only one coin at a time, so you thought he had only a 50% chance of winning. But because he's flipping three coins at a time, his chances of getting at least one head are much better than 50%.[4]

When you do multiple *t* tests, you are doing basically the same thing as the coin hustler. You start by telling people the odds that a single *t* test will be significant due to chance alone. For example, if you use conventional significance levels, you would tell people that if the treatment has no effect, the odds of getting a statistically significant result for a particular *t* test are less than 5 in 100. In other words, you are claiming that your chance of making a Type 1 error is no more than 5%.

Then, just as the hustler gave himself more than a 50% chance of winning by flipping more than one coin, you give yourself a more than 5% chance of getting a statistically significant result by doing more than one *t* test. The 5% odds you quoted would hold only if you had done a single *t* test. If you are using *t* tests to compare three groups, you will do three *t* tests, which means the odds of at least one turning out significant by chance alone are much more than 5%.[5]

So far, we've talked about the problems of using a *t* test when you have a three-group experiment. What happens if your experiment has more than three groups? Then, the *t* test becomes even more deceptive (just as the coin hustler would be cheating even more if he flipped more than three coins at a time). The more groups you use in your experiment, the greater the difference between the significance level you report and the actual odds of at least one *t* test being significant by chance (Hays, 1981).

To give you an idea of how great the difference between your stated significance level and the actual odds can be, suppose you had six levels of the independent variable. To compare all six groups with one another, you would need to do 15 *t* tests. If you did that and used a .05 significance level, the probability of getting at least one significant effect by chance alone would be more than 50%: Your risk of making a Type 1 error would be 10 times greater than you were claiming it was!

As you have seen, the *t* test is not useful for analyzing data from the multiple-group experiment because it measures the degree to which groups differ (vary) by using subtraction—and you can only subtract two group averages at a time. To calculate the degree to which more than two group means vary, you need to calculate a variance between those means.

The between-groups variance indicates the extent to which the group means vary (differ). Thus, if all your groups have the same mean, between-groups variance would be zero because there would be no (zero) differences between your group means. If, on the other hand, there are large differences between the group means, between-group variance will be large.

---

[4] To be more precise, his chances of getting at least one head are 87.5%.

[5] To be more precise, your chances are 14.26%.

So, the size of the between-groups variance depends on the extent to which the group means differ. But what affects the extent to which the group means differ? As you saw earlier, there are two factors.

One factor is random error. Even if the treatment has no effect, random error alone will almost always cause differences between the group means. If the experiment uses an unreliable measure, few participants, and poorly standardized procedures, random error alone may cause large differences between the group means. If the experiment uses a reliable measure, many participants, and highly standardized procedures, random error alone would tend to cause smaller differences between the group means. In short, when there is no treatment effect, the groups will still differ from each other due to random error. To be more specific, when there is no treatment effect, between-groups variance should be roughly equivalent to a more direct measure of random error—within-groups variance.

The other factor that *may* affect the extent to which the groups differ from each other is the treatment effect. If the treatment has an effect, the differences between the group means should be greater than when the treatment doesn't have an effect. Because of the treatment effect's influence on the size of the between-groups variance, the between-groups variance is often called **treatment variance.**

To recap, when there is a treatment effect, the between-group variance is the sum of two quantities: an estimate of random error plus an estimate of treatment effects. Therefore, if the treatment has an effect, between-groups variance (which is affected by the treatment plus random error) will be larger than the within-groups variance (which is affected only by random error).

Comparing Between-Groups Variance to Within-Groups Variance: Are the Differences Between Groups Due to More Than Random Error?

Once you have the between-groups variance (an estimate of random error plus any treatment effects) and the within-groups variance (an estimate of random error), the next step is to compare the two variances. If the between-groups variance is larger than the within-groups variance, some of the between-groups variance may be due to a treatment effect. The statistical *analysis* that allows you to compare the between-groups *variance* to the within-groups variance and thereby determine whether the treatment had an effect is called **analysis of variance (ANOVA).**

When doing an ANOVA, you compare two variances by dividing the between-groups variance by the within-groups variance. That is, you set up the following ratio:

$$\frac{\text{Between-Groups Variance}}{\text{Within-Groups Variance}}$$

Instead of using the term *variance,* you are more likely to see the term *mean square.* Thus, you are more likely to read about authors setting up the following ratio:

$$\frac{\text{Mean Square Between Groups}}{\text{Mean Square Within Groups}}$$

Note that authors tend to leave off the word *groups.* As a result, you are likely to see the ratio described as

$$\frac{\text{Mean Square Between}}{\text{Mean Square Within}}$$

To shorten the expression even further, authors tend to abbreviate mean square between as *MSB* and mean square within as *MSW*. Therefore, you are likely to see the ratio of the variances described as

$$\frac{MSB}{MSW}$$

To complicate things further, recall that authors may not use the terms *between* or *within*. Rather than use a name that refers to how these variances were calculated, authors may instead use a name that refers to what these variances estimate. Thus, because between-groups variance is, in part, an estimate of treatment effects, authors may refer to *MS* between as mean square *treatment* (abbreviated *MST*). Similarly, because within-groups variance is an estimate of the degree to which random error is affecting estimates of the treatment group means, authors may refer to mean square *within* as mean square *error* (abbreviated *MSE*).

Regardless of what names or abbreviations they give the two variances, the ratio of the between-groups variance to the within-groups variance is called the **_F_ ratio.** Consequently, the following three ratios are all *F* ratios:

$$\frac{MSB}{MSW} = \frac{MS\,\text{Treatment}}{MS\,\text{Error}} = \frac{MST}{MSE}$$

In ANOVA summary tables, terms are shortened even more. Thus, when scanning computer printouts or when reading articles, you may see tables resembling the one below:

SOURCE	MEAN SQUARE	F
Treatment	10	2
Error	5	

Why an F *of 1 Does Not Show That the Treatment Had an Effect.* Conceptually, the *F* ratio can be portrayed as follows:

$$F = \frac{\text{Random Error} + \text{Possible Treatment Effect}}{\text{Random Error}}$$

By examining this conceptual formula, you can see that the *F* ratio will rarely be much less than 1. To illustrate, imagine that the null hypothesis is true: There is no (zero) treatment effect. In that case, the formula is (random error + 0)/random error, which reduces to random error/random error. As you know, if you divide a number by itself (e.g., 5/5, 8/8), you get 1.[6]

You now know that if the null hypothesis were true, the *F* ratio would be approximately 1.00.[7] That is,

$$F = \frac{\text{Random Error} + 0}{\text{Random Error}} = \frac{\text{Random Error}}{\text{Random Error}} = 1.00$$

But what would happen to the *F* ratio if the treatment had an effect? To answer this question, let's look at what a treatment effect would do to the top and the bottom half of the *F* ratio.

---

[6]The only exception is that 0/0 = 0.

[7]If you get an *F* below 1.00, it indicates that you have found no evidence of a treatment effect. Indeed, in the literature, you will often find statements such as, "There were no other significant results, all *F*'s < 1." If you get an *F* substantially below 1.00, you may want to check to be sure you did not make a computational error. If your *F* is negative, you have made a computational error: *F* can't be less than 0.

If the treatment has an effect, the top of the F ratio, the between-groups variance should get bigger. Not only is the between-groups variance affected by random error (as it was when the treatment did not have an effect), but now that the treatment is also making the group means differ, between-groups variance is also influenced by the treatment.

We explained that a treatment effect increases the *top* of the F ratio, but what does a treatment effect do to the *bottom* of the F ratio? Nothing. Whether or not there is a treatment effect, the bottom of the F ratio, the within-groups variance, always represents only random error. With or without a treatment effect, a group's scores differ from one another solely because of random error.

Let's now use our knowledge of how treatment effects influence the top and bottom parts of the F ratio to understand how treatment effects influence the entire F ratio. When there is a treatment effect, the differences between group means are due not only to random error (the only thing that affects within-groups variance) but also to the treatment's effect. Consequently, when there is a treatment effect, the between-groups variance (an index of random error plus treatment effect) should be larger than the within-groups variance (an index of random error). Put more mathematically, when there is a treatment effect, you would expect the ratio of between-groups variance to within-groups variance to be greater than 1. Specifically,

$$F = \frac{\text{Between-Groups Variance (Treatment + Random Error)}}{\text{Within-Groups Variance (Random Error)}} > 1,$$

when the treatment has an effect.

Using an F Table. Not all Fs above 1.00 are statistically significant, however. To determine whether an F ratio is enough above 1.00 to indicate that there is a significant difference between your groups, you need to consult an F table, like the one in Appendix E.

Calculating Degrees of Freedom. To use the F table, you need to know two degrees of freedom: one for the top of the F ratio (between-groups variance, MS treatment) and one for the bottom of the F ratio (within-groups variance, MS error).

Calculating the degrees of freedom for the top of the F ratio (between-groups variance) is simple. It's just one less than the number of values of the independent variable. So, if you have three values of the independent variable (no-treatment, meditation, and exercise), you have 2 (3 − 1) degrees of freedom. If you had four values of the independent variable (e.g., no-treatment, meditation, archery, aerobic exercise), you would have 3 (4 − 1) degrees of freedom. Thus, for the experiments we have discussed in this chapter, *the degrees of freedom for the between-groups variance equals the number of groups − 1.*

Computing the degrees of freedom for the bottom of the F ratio (within-groups variance) is also easy. The formula is N (number of participants) − G (groups). Thus, if there are 20 participants and 2 groups, the degrees of freedom = 18 (20 − 2 = 18).[8]

Let's now apply this formula to some multiple-group experiments. If we have 33 participants and 3 groups, the df for the error term = 30 (because 33 − 3 = 30). If we had 30 participants and 5 groups, the df error would = 25 (because 30 − 5 = 25). To repeat, the simplest way of computing the error df for the experiments we discussed in this chapter is to use the

[8] As you may recall, you could have used this $N - G$ formula to get the degrees of freedom for the t test described in Chapter 10. However, because the t test always compares 2 groups, people often memorize the formula $N - 2$ for the t test instead of the more general formula $N - G$.

Table 11-1	**Calculating Degrees of Freedom**

SOURCE OF VARIANCE (SV)	CALCULATION OF df
Treatment (between groups)	Number of Groups − 1 ($G-1$)
Within subjects (error variance)	Number of participants minus number of groups ($N-G$)
Total	$N-1$

formula $N-G$, where N = total number of participants and G = total number of groups (see Table 11-1).

Once you know the degrees of freedom, you can simply find the column in the F table that corresponds to those degrees of freedom. If your F ratio is larger than the value listed, the results are statistically significant at the $p < .05$ level.

Making Sense of an ANOVA Summary Table or Computer Printout. Usually, you will not have to look up F values in an F table. Instead, you will have a computer calculate F and look it up in a table for you. However, if you had a computer calculate F for you, you should make sure that the degrees of freedom on the printout are correct. If not, the computer has misunderstood your design or you have miscoded some data. If you had a computer calculate F for you, the computer might provide you with an analysis of variance (ANOVA) summary table like this one:

SOURCE OF VARIANCE	SUM OF SQUARES (SS)	df	MS	F	p
Treatment (between)	88	2	44	44	< .05
Error (within)	12	12	1		
Total	100	14			

The first column, the source of variance column, may sometimes have only the heading "Source." The two main sources of variance will be your treatment (which may be labeled as "Treatment," "Between groups," "BG," "Groups," "Between," "Model," or the actual name of your independent variable) and random error (which may be labeled as "Error," "Within groups," "WG," or "Within").

The second column, the sum of squares column, may be labeled "Sum of Squares," "SS," or "Type III Sum of Squares." Note that if you add the sum of squares treatment to the sum of squares error, you will get the sum of squares total.

The third column, the degrees of freedom column, is often abbreviated *df*. As we mentioned earlier, you should check the *df* column to make sure that the analysis is based on the right number of treatment groups and the right number of participants. From the *df* column in our ANOVA table, we know two things. First, because the formula for the treatment is $df = G -1$ and because the treatment *df* is 2, we know that a three-group ANOVA has been calculated (3 [groups] − 1 = 2 [*df*]). Second, because the formula for total *df* is N − 1 (number of participants − 1) and because the total *df* is 14, we know that the ANOVA is based on data from 15 participants (because 15 [participants] − 1 = 14 [*df*]).

The fourth column, the Mean Square column, is often abbreviated *MS*. The *MS* Treatment will be the *SS* Treatment divided by the *df* Treatment. Note that if *MS* Treatment is *not* bigger than *MS* Error, the results will *not* be statistically significant.

The fifth column contains the F ratio. The F ratio is the *MS* Treatment divided by *MS* Error. In the table above F is 44 because 44 (*MST*) divided by 1 (*MSE*) = 44.

The sixth column, the p value column, tells you how likely it would be to get differences between the groups this large or larger if the null hypothesis (the null hypothesis is that the treatment has no effect) were true. In this case, p is less than .05, suggesting that it is unlikely that you would obtain these results if the null hypothesis were true. Traditionally, such results would be called "statistically significant." An author might start to summarize the results of such an ANOVA by writing, "Consistent with the hypothesis, the treatment had an effect, $F(2, 12) = 44, p < .05$."

The Meaning of Statistical Significance in ANOVA

If your results are statistically significant, what does that mean? *Statistical significance means that you can reject the null hypothesis.* In the multiple-group experiment, the null hypothesis is that the differences among all your group means are due to chance. That is, all your groups are essentially the same. Rejecting this hypothesis means that, because of treatment effects, all your groups are *not* the same. In other words, you can conclude that at least two of your groups differ. However, such significant results raise two questions.

The first question is, "How large is the effect?" One way to get an estimate of the effect size is simply to look at the differences between the means. For example, looking at the effect of antidepressants on relieving depression suggests that the effect of such drugs is only to increase scores by 2 points on a 50-point scale (Kirsch, Moore, Scoboria, & Nicholls, 2002). Another strategy is to compute **eta squared (η^2)**: an estimate of effect size that ranges from 0 to 1 and is comparable to r squared.[9]

Computing eta squared from an ANOVA summary table is simple: Just divide the Sum of Squares Treatment by the Sum of Squares total. For example, in our ANOVA table, SS treatment was 88 and SS total was 100; therefore, eta squared was .88 (because $88/100 = .88$)—indicating an extremely large effect. Thus, an author might start to describe such results by writing, "Consistent with the hypothesis, the treatment had an effect, $F(2, 12) = 44, p < .05, \eta^2 = 0.88$." Note that you would normally not get such a large eta squared. Indeed, social scientists tend to view any eta squared (or r squared) of .25 or above to be large (.09 to .25 is considered moderate; less than .09 is considered small).

The second question is, "Which groups differ from each other?" Even in a three-group experiment, there are several possibilities: Group 1 might differ from Group 2, and/or Group 2 might differ from Group 3, and/or Group 1 might differ from Group 3. As we just said, a significant F does not tell you which groups differ. Therefore, once you have performed an F test to determine that at least some of your groups differ, you need to do additional tests to determine which of your groups differ from one another.

Beyond ANOVA: Pinpointing a Significant Effect

You might think that all you would have to do to determine which groups differ is compare group means. Some group means, however, may differ from others solely as a result of chance. To determine which group differences are due to treatment effects, you need to do additional tests. These additional, more specific tests are called post hoc t tests.

Post Hoc t Tests Among Group Means: Which Groups Differ? At this point, you may be saying that you wanted to do t tests all along. Before you complain to us, please hear our two-pronged defense.

---

[9]To learn about r squared, review our section titled "Coefficient of Determination" in Chapter 7, Box 10-2 in Chapter 10, or look at Appendix D.

First, you can go in and do **post hoc tests** only *after* you get a significant *F*. That is, you can't legitimately use follow-up tests to ask "which of the groups differ" until you first establish that at least some of the groups do indeed differ. To do post hoc tests without finding a significant *F* is considered statistical malpractice. Such behavior would be like a physician doing a specific test to find out which strain of hepatitis you had after doing a general test that was negative for hepatitis. At best, the test will not turn up anything, and your only problem will be the expense and pain of an unnecessary test. At worst, the test results will be misleading because the test is being used under the wrong circumstances. Consequently, you may end up being treated for a hepatitis you do not have. Analogously, a good researcher does not ask which groups differ from one another unless the more general, overall analysis of variance test has first established that at least some of the groups do indeed differ.[10]

Second, post hoc tests are not the same as conventional *t* tests. Unlike conventional *t* tests, post hoc *t* tests are designed to correct for the fact that you are doing more than two comparisons. As we mentioned earlier, doing more than one *t* test at the $p = .05$ level and claiming that you have only a 5% risk of making a *Type 1* error is like flipping more than one coin at a time and claiming that the odds of getting a "heads" are only 50%. In both cases, the odds of getting the result you hope for are much greater than the odds you are stating. Thus, we cannot simply do an ordinary *t* test. Instead, we must correct for the number of comparisons we are making. Post hoc *t* tests take into consideration how many tests are being done and make the necessary corrections.

At this point, we will not require you to know how to do post hoc tests. (If you want to know how to conduct a post hoc test, see Appendix E.) You should, however, be aware that if you choose to do a multiple-group experiment, you should be prepared to do post hoc analyses.

You should also be aware that if you read a journal article describing the results of a multiple-group experiment, you may read the results of post hoc tests. For example, you may read about a Bonferroni *t* test, Tukey test, Scheffe test, Dunnett test, Newman-Keuls test, Duncan, or an LSD test. When reading about the results of such tests, do not panic: The author is merely reporting the results of a post hoc test to determine which means differ from one another.

Post Hoc Trend Analysis: What Is the Shape of the Relationship? Rather than wanting to know which particular groups differ from one another, you may want to know the shape of the functional relationship between the independent and dependent variables so that you could either (a) better generalize to levels of the treatment that were not tested or (b) test a theory that predicts a certain functional relationship. If you want to know the shape of the functional relationship, instead of following up a significant main effect with post hoc tests between group means, follow up the significant effect with a **post hoc trend analysis.**

But why should you do a trend analysis to determine the shape of the functional relationship between your independent and dependent variables? Can't you see this relationship by simply graphing the group means? Yes and no. Yes, graphing your sample's means allows

---

[10]Although everyone agrees that you need to do an ANOVA before doing a post hoc *t* test not everyone agrees that you need to do an ANOVA before doing other tests. Indeed, Robert Rosenthal (1992) argued that researchers should almost never do the general, overall *F* test. Instead, he argued that if you have specific predictions about which groups differ, you should do normal *t* tests to compare those group means. Those *t* tests are often called "planned comparisons" because the researcher planned to make those comparisons before collecting data. Planned comparisons involving *t* tests are sometimes also called "*a priori t* tests" ("a priori" means in advance) to emphasize that the *t* tests were done before peeking at the data.

you to see the pattern in the data produced by your experiment. No, graphing does not tell you that the pattern you observe represents the true relationship between the variables because your pattern could be due to random error (e.g., if even one mean is thrown off by random error, that could make a linear relationship look nonlinear). Just as you needed statistics to tell you if the difference between two groups was significant (even though you could easily see whether one mean was higher than the other), you need statistics to know if the pattern you observe in your data (a straight line, a curved line, a combination of a curve and a straight line, etc.) would occur if you repeated the experiment. The statistical test you need to determine whether the pattern in your data reflects a reliable functional relationship is a post hoc trend analysis.

Computing a post hoc trend analysis is easy. You can either follow the simple directions in Appendix E or use a computer program that does the analysis for you. Although you might be tempted to forget about post hoc trend analysis until it comes time to analyze your data, don't make that mistake.

If you do not think about post hoc trend analysis when designing your experiment, you will probably be unable to do a valid post hoc trend analysis on your data. Therefore, if you think that you might want to know about the functional relationship between the variables in your experiment, you should keep three facts in mind *before* conducting that experiment (see Box 11-2).

First, to do a post hoc trend analysis, you should have selected levels of your independent variable that increase proportionally. For example, if you were using three levels of a drug, you would not use 5 mg, 6 mg, and 200 mg. Instead, you might use 10 mg, 20 mg, and 30 mg, or 10 mg, 100 mg, and 1000 mg.

Second, you must have at least an interval scale measure of your dependent variable. Your map of the functional relationship can't be accurate unless your measure of the dependent variable is to scale. If you tried to find the relationship between the loudness of the music playing on participants' personal stereos and distance walked, you would have to measure distance by number of meters walked rather than by blocks walked (unless all your blocks are the same length). In short, you can't do a trend analysis if you have ordinal or nominal data.

Third, the more levels of the independent variable you have, the more trends you can look for. Specifically, the number of trends you can examine is one less than the number of levels you have. If you had only two levels, you can test only for straight lines (linear component). If you have three groups, you can test for straight lines (linear component), and for a U-shaped curve (quadratic component). With four levels, you can test for straight lines, U-shaped curves, and double U-shaped lines (cubic component). Thus, if you are expecting a double U-shaped curve, you must use at least four levels of the independent variable.

BOX 11-2 Requirements for Conducting a Valid Post Hoc Trend Analysis

1. Your independent variable must have a statistically significant effect.

2. Your independent variable must be quantitative, and the levels used in the experiment should vary from one another by some constant proportion.

3. Your dependent variable must yield interval or ratio-scale data so that your map of the functional relationship will be to scale.

4. The number of trends you can look for is one less than the number of levels of your independent variable.

Concluding Remarks

By using a multiple-group experiment rather than a simple experiment, you can ask more refined questions. For example, you may go beyond asking, "Is there an effect?" to asking "What is the nature of the functional relationship?"

By using a multiple-group experiment rather than a simple experiment, you can get more valid answers to your questions. For example, by using appropriate control groups, you can learn not only that the treatment manipulation worked but also why it worked.

Although adding more levels of the treatment is a powerful way to expand the simple experiment, an even more powerful way to expand the simple experiment is to add independent variables. As you will see in the next chapter, adding independent variables not only increases construct and external validity but also opens up a whole new arena of research questions.

SUMMARY

1. The multiple-group experiment is more sensitive to nonlinear relationships than the simple experiment. Consequently, it is more likely to obtain significant treatment effects and to accurately map the functional relationship between your independent and dependent variables.

2. Knowing the functional relationship allows more accurate predictions about the effects of unexplored levels of the independent variable.

3. To use the multiple-group experiment to discover the functional relationship, you should select your levels of the independent variable carefully, and your dependent measure must provide at least interval scale data.

4. Multiple-group experiments may have more construct validity than a simple experiment because they can have multiple control groups and multiple treatment groups.

5. To analyze a multiple-group experiment, you first have to conduct an analysis of variance (ANOVA). An ANOVA will produce an F ratio.

6. An F ratio is a ratio of between-groups variance to within-groups variance.

7. Random error will make different treatment groups differ from each other. If the treatment has an effect, the treatment will also cause the groups to differ from each other. In other words, between-groups variance is due to random error and may also be due to treatment effects. Because it may be affected by treatment effects, between-groups variance is often called treatment variance.

8. Scores within a treatment group differ from each other for only one reason: random error. That is, the treatment cannot be responsible for variability within each treatment group. Therefore, within-groups variance is an estimate of the degree to which random error affects the data. Consequently, another term for within-groups variance is error variance.

9. The F test is designed to see whether the difference between the group means is greater than would be expected by chance. It involves dividing the between-groups variance (an estimate of random error plus possible treatment effects) by the within-groups variance (an estimate of random error). If the F is 1 or less, there is no evidence that the treatment has had an effect. If the F is larger than 1, you need to look in an F table (under the right degrees of freedom) to see whether the F is significant.

10. The first degrees of freedom (between groups/treatment) equals the number of groups minus one, abbreviated $G - 1$. The second degrees of freedom (within groups/error) equals the number of participants minus the number of groups, abbreviated $N - G$. Thus, if you had 5 groups and 40 participants, you would look at the F table under 4 $(5 - 1)$ and 35 $(40 - 5)$ degrees of freedom.

11. You are most likely to get a significant F if between-group variability is large (your groups differ from each other) and within-groups variability is small.

12. If you get a significant F, you know that the groups are not all the same. If you have more than two groups, you have to find out which groups differ. To find out which groups are different, do not just look at the means to see which differences are biggest.

Instead, do post hoc tests to find out which groups are reliably different.

13. The following table summarizes the mathematics of an ANOVA table.

SOURCE OF VARIANCE (SV)	SUM OF SQUARES (SS)	DEGREES OF FREEDOM (df)	MEAN SQUARE (MS)	F
Treatment (T)	SST	Levels of $T - 1$	$SST/df\,T$	$MST/MS\,E$
Error (E)	SSE	Participants – Groups	$SSE/df\,E$	
Total	SST + SSE	Participants – 1		

KEY TERMS

functional relationship *(p. 325)*

linear relationship *(p. 326)*

quadratic relationship *(p. 328)*

confounding variables *(p. 331)*

hypothesis-guessing *(p. 332)*

empty control group *(p. 332)*

variability between group means *(p. 335)*

within-groups variance (error variance) *(p. 337)*

treatment variance *(p. 339)*

analysis of variance (ANOVA) *(p. 339)*

F ratio *(p. 340)*

eta squared (η^2) *(p. 343)*

post hoc test *(p. 344)*

post hoc trend analysis *(p. 344)*

EXERCISES

1. A researcher randomly assigns each member of a statistics class to one of two groups. In one group, each student is assigned a tutor who is available to meet with the student 20 minutes before each class. The other group is a control group not assigned a tutor. Suppose the researcher finds that the tutored group scores significantly better on exams.
   a. Can the researcher conclude that the experimental group students learned statistical information from tutoring sessions that enabled them to perform better on the exam? Why or why not?
   b. What changes would you recommend in the study?

2. Suppose people living in homes for older adults were randomly assigned to two groups: a no-treatment

group and a transcendental meditation (TM) group. Transcendental meditation involves more than sitting with eyes closed. The technique involves both "a meaningless sound selected for its value in facilitating the transcending, or settling-down, process and a specific procedure for using it mentally without effort again to facilitate transcending" (Alexander, Langer, Newman, Chandler, & Davies, 1989, p. 953). Thus, the TM group was given instruction in how to perform the technique, then "they met with their instructors half an hour each week to verify that they were meditating correctly and regularly. They were to practice their program 20 minutes twice daily (morning and afternoon) sitting comfortably in their own room with eyes closed and using a timepiece to ensure correct length of practice" (Alexander et al., 1989, p. 953).

Suppose that the TM group performed significantly better than other groups on a mental health measure.[11]

a. Could the researcher conclude that it was the transcendental meditation that caused the effect?

b. What besides the specific aspects of TM could cause the difference between the two groups?

c. What control groups would you add?

d. Suppose you added these control groups and then got a significant F for the treatment variable? What could you conclude? Why?

3. Assume you want to test the effectiveness of a new kind of therapy. This therapy involves screaming and hugging people in group sessions followed by individual meetings with a therapist. What control group(s) would you use? Why?

4. Assume a researcher is looking at the relationship between caffeine consumption and sense of humor.

a. How many levels of caffeine should the researcher use? Why?

b. What levels would you choose? Why?

c. If a graph of the data suggests a curvilinear relationship, can the researcher assume that the functional relationship between the independent and dependent variables is curvilinear? Why or why not?

d. Suppose the researcher used the following four levels of caffeine: 0 mg, 20 mg, 25 mg, 26 mg. Can the researcher easily do a trend analysis? Why or why not?

e. Suppose the researcher ranked participants based on their sense of humor. That is, the person who

laughed least got a score of 1, the person who laughed second-least scored a 2, and so on. Can the researcher use these data to do a trend analysis? Why or why not?

f. If a researcher used four levels of caffeine, how many trends can the researcher look for? What are the treatment's degrees of freedom?

g. If the researcher used three levels of caffeine and 30 participants, what are the degrees of freedom for the treatment? What are the degrees of freedom for the error term?

h. Suppose the F is 3.34. Referring to the degrees of freedom you obtained in your answer to "g" (above) and to Table E-3 (Appendix E), are the results statistically significant? Can the researcher look for linear and quadratic trends?

5. A computer analysis reports that $F(6, 23) = 2.54$. The analysis is telling you that the F ratio was 2.54, and the degrees of freedom for the top part of the F ratio = 6 and the degrees of freedom for the bottom part = 23.

a. How many groups did the researcher use?

b. How many participants were in the experiment?

c. Is this result statistically significant at the .05 level? (Refer to Table E-3.)

6. A friend gives you the following Fs and significance levels. On what basis would you want these Fs (or significance levels) rechecked?

a. $F(2, 63) = .10$, not significant

b. $F(3, 85) = -1.70$, not significant

c. $F(1, 120) = 52.8$, not significant

d. $F(5, 70) = 1.00$, significant

7. Complete the following table.

SOURCE OF VARIANCE (SV)	SUM OF SQUARES (SS)	DEGREES OF FREEDOM (df)	MEAN SQUARE (MS)	F
Treatment (T) 3 levels of treatment	180	—	—	—
Error (E), also known as within-groups variance	80	8	—	

[11]A modification of this study was actually done. The study included appropriate control groups.

8. Complete the following table.

SOURCE OF VARIANCE (SV)	SUM OF SQUARES (SS)	DEGREES OF FREEDOM (df)	MEAN SQUARE (MS)	F
Treatment (T) (between-groups variance)	50	5	—	—
Error (E) (within-groups variance)	100	—	—	
Total	—	30		

9. A study compares the effect of having a snack, taking a 10-minute walk, or getting no treatment on energy levels. Sixty participants are randomly assigned to condition and then asked to rate their energy level on a 0 (not at all energetic) to 10 (very energetic) scale. The mean for the "do nothing" group is 6.0, for having a snack 7.0, and for walking 7.8. The F ratio is 6.27.

   a. Graph the means.
   b. Are the results statistically significant?

   c. If so, what conclusions can you draw? Why?
   d. What additional analyses would you do? Why?
   e. How would you extend this study?

WEB RESOURCES

1. Go to the Chapter 11 section of the book's student website and do the following
   a. Look over the concept map of the key terms.
   b. Test yourself on the key terms.
   c. Take the Chapter 11 Practice Quiz.
   d. Download the Chapter 11 tutorial.

2. Do an analysis of variance using a statistical calculator by going to the "Statistical Calculator" link.

3. If you want to write your method section, use the "Tips on Writing a Method Section" link.

4. If you want to write up the results of a one factor, between-participants experiment, click on the "Tips for Writing Results" link.

INFOTRAC COLLEGE EDITION EXPLORATIONS

Do an InfoTrac College Edition search for "arousal and misattribution" to find Savitsky, Medvec, Charlton, and Gilovich's fascinating 1998 article reporting the results of two 3-group experiments.

12

Expanding the Experiment

Factorial Designs

> I'm an earth sign, she was a water sign,
> together we made mud.
>
> —*Woody Allen*

Overview

To understand the relationship between the design we will discuss in this chapter and the experimental designs we discussed in previous chapters, let's look at three ways you might partially replicate Langer, Blank, and Chanowitz's (1978) classic experiment. In that experiment, research assistants tried to cut in front of participants who were in line to use a copier. Participants were randomly assigned to receive one of several requests.

If you were to replicate that study as a simple experiment, participants would be randomly assigned to one of two requests. For example, if you chose to vary quality of excuse, half your participants might be asked, "Can I cut in front of you?" (no excuse condition), whereas the other half might be asked, "Can I cut in front of you because I want to make a copy?" (nonsensical excuse condition). In the following table, we have diagrammed the design and results of such a simple experiment.

Proportion of Participants Who Agreed to Let the Researcher Cut in Front of Them to Use the Copier as Function of Researcher's Excuse

TYPE OF EXCUSE	
Group 1	**Group 2**
No excuse	**Senseless** excuse ("I need to make copies")
.60	.93

In Chapter 10, we showed how the simple experiment's logic makes it internally valid. However, we also pointed out that the simple experiment is limited because it can study only two levels of a single independent variable. For example, with a single simple experiment, you cannot compare three different excuse conditions (e.g., no excuse, senseless excuse, and reasonable excuse), three levels of temperature (e.g., cold, medium, hot), or three types of music (e.g., classical, rock, and rap).

In Chapter 11, we showed how to extend the simple experiment's logic to experiments that study three or more levels of a single independent variable. By randomly assigning participants to three or more levels of the treatment, you can look at the effects of varying three levels of excuses, temperature, music, or any other variable. For example, by adding a level to the excuse experiment diagrammed earlier, you can expand it into the three-group experiment diagrammed here:

Proportion of Participants Who Agreed to Let the Researcher Cut in Front of Them to Use the Copier as Function of Researcher's Excuse

TYPE OF EXCUSE		
Group 1	**Group 2**	**Group 3**
No excuse	**Senseless** excuse ("I need to make copies")	**Reasonable** excuse ("because I'm in a rush")
.60	.93	.94

As we discussed in Chapter 11, experiments that manipulate three or more levels of a factor can have impressive internal, external, and construct validity.

In this chapter, as in Chapter 11, we show how to extend the basic logic of the simple experiment. However, instead of showing you how to stretch the simple experiment by adding more *levels* of a factor, we show you how to expand the simple experiment by adding more *factors*. For example, rather than learning how to expand a simple experiment on excuses to include more than two levels of excuses, you will learn how to add another factor, such as size of request, so you can study the effects of both excuses and size of request in the same experiment (see the following diagram).

Proportion of Participants Who Agreed to Let Researcher Cut in Front of Them to Use the Copier as Function of Excuse

TYPE OF EXCUSE

Size of Request	No Excuse	Senseless Excuse ("I need to make copies")	Reasonable Excuse ("because I'm in a rush")
Small ("I have 5 pages")	.60	.93	.94
Large ("I have 20 pages")	.24	.24	.42

Note: Data are from Langer, Blank, and Chanowitz (1978).

In technical terms, you will learn about **factorial experiments:** experiments that study the effects of two or more independent variables (factors) in a single experiment. Specifically, you will learn (a) why you should want to study the effects of two independent variables in a single experiment, (b) how to design such experiments, and (c) how to analyze the results of such experiments.

The 2 × 2 Factorial Experiment

To understand why and how to design factorial experiments, we will focus on the simplest factorial experiment: the 2 × 2 ("2 by 2") between-subjects factorial experiment. Before discussing why you would want to do a 2 × 2 factorial experiment, let's be clear about what it is. Although all factorial experiments must include at least two levels of two factors, factorial experiments can differ in (a) how many levels of each factor they have and (b) how many factors they have.

To let people know how many levels each factor has, researchers use terminology similar to that used by builders. When a builder refers to a "2 by 4," the builder means a board for which the first dimension (thickness) is 2 inches and the second dimension (width) is 4 inches. Similarly, when a researcher refers to a "2 by 4," the researcher means that the first experimental factor has 2 levels and the second experimental factor has 4 levels.

Thus, in a 2 × 2 factorial experiment, there are two independent variables and both have two levels. To be more specific, the first "2" in "2 by 2" indicates that the first factor has two levels. For example, if excuse is the first factor, you might have two levels: (1) no excuse and (2) reasonable excuse. The second "2" in "2 × 2" indicates that the second factor (e.g., size of request) has 2 levels. The "×"—pronounced as "by"—indicates that the first variable is crossed (combined) with the second factor. That is, rather than conditions consisting of only a single manipulation (e.g., no excuse or reasonable excuse), each condition will consist of a manipulation of the first factor (e.g., no excuse or reasonable excuse) combined with a manipulation of the second factor (e.g., small request or large request). Thus, in a 2 (Excuse: none, reasonable) × 2 (Size of request: small, large) factorial, crossing 2 levels of 2 different independent variables would result in 4 (2 × 2) different treatment conditions: (1) a no excuse, small request condition; (2) a no excuse, large request condition; (3) a reasonable excuse, small request condition; and (4) a reasonable excuse, large request condition (see the next table).[1]

Size of Request	No Excuse	Reasonable Excuse ("because I'm in a rush")
Small ("I have 5 pages")	.60	.94
Large ("I have 20 pages")	.24	.42

In the 2 × 2 *between-subjects* factorial experiment, each participant is randomly assigned to experience one—and only one—of the four treatment combinations. Thus, in the example diagrammed previously, you would have four groups: (1) a no excuse, small request group; (2) a no excuse, large request group; (3) a reasonable excuse, small request group; and (4) a reasonable excuse, large request group.

To better understand how a 2 × 2 between-subjects factorial experiment works, consider the following 2 (no exclusion vs. exclusion) × 2 (individual credit vs. group credit) between-subjects factorial experiment done by Williams and Sommer (1997). To manipulate the first factor (exclusion), Williams and Sommer used some deception. While participants were in the waiting room, each participant waited with two confederates (research assistants who acted like they were participants). Based on random assignment, the confederates either (1) included the participant in a fun activity (not-excluded condition) or (2) left the participant out of the fun activity (excluded condition).

After the exclusion manipulation, the participant and the confederates left the waiting room. Before arriving at the room where they were to work on the task of writing down "as many uses for a knife as you possibly can in 12 minutes," participants were randomly assigned to the second factor: whether a person would get personal credit for each idea that person generated (individual credit) or whether only the group got credit for the ideas generated (collective credit). Thus, if you were to repeat the Williams and Sommer (1997) study, you would randomly assign participants so that one-fourth of your participants were in each of the four conditions diagrammed in the following table:

GROUP **1**	GROUP **2**
Not Excluded	**Not Excluded**
Individual Credit	**Collective Credit**
GROUP **3**	GROUP **4**
Excluded	**Excluded**
Individual Credit	**Collective Credit**

---

[1]If we had 3 levels of excuse instead of just 2, we would have a 3 × 2 design instead of a 2 × 2. With a 3 × 2, we would have 6 (3 × 2) different conditions. If we had three, 2-level factors (excuse type, request size, and gender of experimenter), we would have a 2 × 2 × 2 design. With a 2 × 2 × 2 experiment, we would have 8 (2 × 2 × 2) experimental conditions.

Each Column and Each Row of the 2 × 2 Factorial Is Like a Simple Experiment

You could view each *row* of the 2 × 2 factorial as a simple experiment. With that perspective, you would see the 2 × 2 factorial experiment as two simple experiments, both of which looked at whether participants work harder when working for themselves or when working for the group (see the following table).

SIMPLE EXPERIMENT **1** (Effect of individual versus group credit for participants in the not excluded conditions)	GROUP **1** *Not Excluded* ***Individual Credit***	GROUP **2** *Not Excluded* ***Collective Credit***
SIMPLE EXPERIMENT **2** (Effect of individual versus group credit for participants in the excluded conditions)	GROUP **3** Excluded <u>Individual Credit</u>	GROUP **4** Excluded <u>Collective Credit</u>

You could also view each *column* of the 2 × 2 factorial as a simple experiment. With that perspective, you would see the 2 × 2 factorial experiment as two different simple experiments, both of which looked at whether participants work harder when they have been included or when they have been excluded (see the following table).

SIMPLE EXPERIMENT **3** (EFFECT OF BEING EXCLUDED FOR PARTICIPANTS IN THE INDIVIDUAL CREDIT CONDITIONS)	SIMPLE EXPERIMENT **4** (EFFECT OF BEING EXCLUDED FOR PARTICIPANTS IN THE GROUP CREDIT CONDITIONS)
GROUP **1** **Not Excluded** **Individual Credit**	GROUP **2** *Not Excluded* Collective Credit
GROUP **3** **Excluded** **Individual Credit**	GROUP **4** *Excluded* Collective Credit

If you looked at both the rows and the columns, you would see that the factorial experiment contains four simple experiments (see the following table).

	COLUMN CONTAINING SIMPLE EXPERIMENT **3** (Effect of exclusion for participants in the individual credit conditions)	COLUMN CONTAINING SIMPLE EXPERIMENT **4** (Effect of exclusion for participants in the group credit conditions)
ROW CONTAINING SIMPLE EXPERIMENT **1** (Effect of individual versus group credit for not excluded participants)	GROUP **1** **Not Excluded** **Individual Credit**	GROUP **2** *Not Excluded* **Collective Credit**
ROW CONTAINING SIMPLE EXPERIMENT **2** (Effect of individual versus group credit for excluded participants)	GROUP **3** **Excluded** **Individual Credit**	GROUP **4** *Excluded* **Collective Credit**

How One Experiment Can Do More Than Two

To illustrate how similar each row of a 2 × 2 is to a simple experiment, suppose you had done a simple experiment involving the two groups listed in the first row of the 2 × 2 (the not excluded/individual credit group versus the not excluded/collective credit group). In that case, you would see the effect of working for oneself versus working for the group in a simple experiment in which none of the participants were excluded from the fun activity. In the same way, if you did the 2 × 2 experiment diagrammed above and compared the two groups in the first row of the 2 × 2 (the not excluded/individual credit group versus the not excluded/group credit group), you would get the **simple main effect** of working for oneself versus working for the group when none of the participants were excluded from the fun activity.

The 2 × 2 Yields Four Simple Main Effects

Because the 2 × 2 contains four simple experiments, if we used certain statistical techniques, we could use the 2 × 2 to find four simple main effects:

1. the simple main effect for *credit* in the not excluded conditions (by looking at the first row and comparing the *individual credit,* not excluded group with the *collective credit,* not excluded group)

2. the simple main effect for *credit* in the excluded conditions (by looking at the second row and comparing the *individual credit,* excluded group with the *collective credit,* excluded group)

3. the simple main effect for *exclusion* in the individual credit conditions (by looking at the first column and comparing the individual credit, *not excluded* group with the individual credit, *excluded* group)

4. the simple main effect for *exclusion* in the collective credit conditions (by looking at the second column and comparing the collective credit, *not excluded* group with the collective credit, *excluded* group)

The simplest way to *estimate* these simple main effects is to subtract the relevant group means from each other. To illustrate, suppose the cell means for our four groups were as follows:

GROUP **1**
Not Excluded
Individual
12

GROUP **2**
Not Excluded
Collective
10

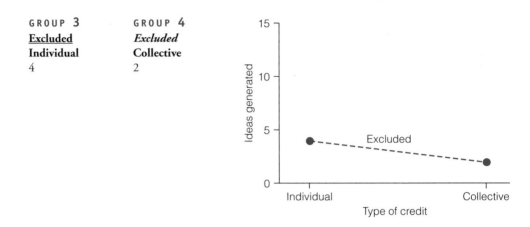

GROUP **3**
Excluded
Individual
4

GROUP **4**
Excluded
Collective
2

With these means, we could estimate four simple main effects: two individual credit/group credit simple main effects (by looking at the two rows) and two excluded simple main effects (by looking at two columns). Let's first look for the two credit simple main effects by comparing the groups that differ in terms of credit but are the same in terms of exclusion:

1. The simple main effect for *credit* in the not excluded conditions = −2 (10 − 12; see the first row).

2. The simple main effect for *credit* in the excluded conditions = −2 (2 − 4; see the second row).

Now, let's look for the two exclusion simple main effects by comparing the groups that are different in terms of exclusion but are the same in terms of credit:

3. The simple main effect for *exclusion* in the individual credit conditions = −8 (4 − 12); see the first column).

4. The simple main effect for *exclusion* in the collective credit conditions = −8 (2 − 10; see the second column).

The following table displays *estimates* of our four simple main effects.

	INDIVIDUAL CREDIT	COLLECTIVE CREDIT	CREDIT SIMPLE MAIN EFFECTS
Not Excluded	12	<u>10</u>	−2 (<u>10</u> − 12)
Excluded	**4**	**2**	−2 (**2** − **4**)
Exclusion simple main effects	−8 (**4** − 12)	−8 (**2** − <u>10</u>)	

The 2 × 2 Yields 2 Pairs of Simple Main Effects

We have shown you that the 2 × 2 can yield four simple main effects. However, the strength of the 2 × 2 is not that it produces four separate main effects. Instead, its strength is that it produces two *pairs* of simple main effects: (1) a pair of simple main effects relating to the first independent variable (e.g., two credit simple main effects) and (2) a pair of simple main effects relating to the second independent variable (e.g., two exclusion simple main effects).

To capitalize on the two pairs of simple main effects that the 2 × 2 produces, researchers' analyses focus on two things:

1. combining (*averaging*) each treatment's pair of simple main effects to estimate each treatment's overall, average effect

2. contrasting (*subtracting*) each treatment's pair of simple main effects to determine whether the treatment has one effect on one group of participants but a different effect on a different group of participants

Averaging a Treatment's Simple Main Effects Lets You Estimate the Overall Main Effect: The Average Effect of Varying a Factor

To combine a treatment's simple main effects, you average them. The *average* of a treatment's two simple main effects allows you to estimate the treatment's **overall main effect:** the average effect of varying that treatment.

In the exclusion-credit study, the researcher would average the two credit simple main effects to get an estimate of the overall main effect for credit. To illustrate, suppose the simple main effect of collective credit was −2 in the not excluded condition (the collective credit, not excluded participants generated an average of 2 fewer ideas than the individual credit, not excluded participants). Furthermore, suppose that the simple main effect of collective credit was −4 in the exclusion condition (the collective credit, excluded participants generated an average of 4 fewer ideas than the individual credit, excluded participants). In that case, the estimate for the overall main effect of collective credit would be −3 (because the average of −2 and −4 is −3).

To estimate the overall main effect for exclusion, the researcher would average the two exclusion simple main effects. If the overall exclusion effect was statistically significant, it would mean that, on the average, participants who were excluded generated a different number of ideas than the participants who were *not* excluded.

One reason researchers emphasize overall main effects is convenience. It is easier to talk about one overall main effect than about two simple main effects.

However, a more important reason for averaging the two simple main effects into an overall main effect is that it allows us to make more general statements about that variable's effects. Consider the advantage of averaging the two simple main effects of exclusion. Because we combined two simple main effects, we are not confined to saying that being excluded makes you work less if the group gets credit for your efforts. Instead, we can say that, on the average, across conditions that varied from participants getting personal credit for their efforts to participants getting only group credit for their efforts, participants who felt excluded worked less. Consequently, we can be more confident that the effect of exclusion generalizes across a variety of reward systems.

Subtracting a Treatment's Simple Main Effects Lets You Estimate the Interaction

But what if exclusion's simple main effect is different in the collective credit condition than in the individual credit condition? Then:

(a) You should *not* make a general statement about the effects of exclusion without mentioning that the exclusion effect changes depending on whether the person is working for individual credit or for collective credit

(b) You should be happy that you can compare exclusion's simple main effects with each other.

Table 12-1	Simple Main Effects, Overall Main Effects, and Interactions

Simple Main Effects

Definition	The effects of one independent variable at a specific level of a second independent variable. The simple main effect could have been obtained merely by doing a simple experiment.
How Estimated	By comparing the mean for one group with the mean for a second group (for instance, comparing the average for the excluded, individual credit group to the average for the not excluded, collective credit group).
Question Addressed	What is the effect of the exclusion in the individual credit condition?

Overall Main Effect

Definition	The average effect of a treatment.
How Estimated	By averaging a treatment's simple main effects. If the average of the two simple main effects is significantly different from zero, there is an overall main effect.
Question Addressed	What is the average effect of exclusion in this study?

Interaction

Definition	The effect of a treatment is different, depending on the level of a second independent variable. That is, the effect of a variable is uneven across conditions.
How Estimated	By looking at the *differences* between a treatment's simple main effects. If the treatment's simple main effects are the same, there is no interaction. If, however, the treatment's two simple main effects differ significantly, there is an interaction.
Question Addressed	Does exclusion have the same effect on idea generation for those who get individual credit for their ideas as it has on those who get group credit?

By comparing the two simple main effects of exclusion (the exclusion simple main effect for the individual credit condition and the exclusion simple main effect for the collective credit condition), you would be able to tell whether the effect of exclusion *depended on* whether participants are working for themselves or for the group.

If the simple main effects of exclusion differ *depending* on the type of credit, there is an **interaction** between exclusion and credit (see Table 12-1). If, on the other hand, exclusion's simple main effects do not differ from each other (exclusion has the same effect in the individual credit condition as it has in the collective credit condition), you do not have an interaction. If you do not have an interaction, the effect of combining those variables is what you would expect from adding up their individual effects.

Why You Want to Look for Interactions: The Importance of Moderating Variables

Interactions are important and common (see Table 12-2). Treatments will tend to have one effect on one group but another effect on another group. For example, eating grapefruit is

Table 12-2	Ways of Thinking About Interactions

VIEWPOINT	HOW VIEWPOINT RELATES TO INTERACTIONS
Chemical Reactions	Lighting a match, in itself, is not dangerous. Having gasoline around is not, in itself, dangerous. However, the *combination* of lighting a match in the presence of gasoline is explosive. Because the explosive effects of combining gas and lighting a match are different from simply adding their separate, individual effects, gasoline and matches interact.
Personal Relationships	John likes most people.
	Mary is liked by most people.
	But John dislikes Mary.
	Based only on their individual tendencies, we would expect John to like Mary. Apparently, however, like gasoline and matches, the combination of their personalities produces a negative outcome.
Sports	The whole is not the same as the sum of the parts. That is, a team is not the sum of its parts. The addition of a player may do more for the team than the player's abilities would suggest—or the addition may help the team much less than would be expected because the team "chemistry" is upset. In other words, the player's skills and personality may interact with those of the other players on the team or with the team's strategy. Sometimes, the result is that adding the player will help the team more than what would be expected by knowing only the team's characteristics and the player's characteristics. Sometimes, adding the player will help the team less than what would be expected if one knew only the team's characteristics and the player's characteristics. Knowing the interaction between the team and the player—how the two will mesh together—may be almost as important as knowing the player's abilities.
	Good pitchers get batters out.
	Poor hitters are easier to get out than good hitters are.
	However, sometimes a poor hitter may have a good pitcher's "number" because the pitcher's strengths match the hitter's strengths. Similarly, some "poor" pitchers are very effective against some of the league's best batters. Managers who can take advantage of these interactions can win more games than would be expected by knowing only the talents of the individual team members.
Prescription Drugs	Drug A may be a good, useful drug.
	Drug B may also be a good, useful drug.
	However, taking Drug A and B together may result in harm or death. Increasingly, doctors and pharmacists have to be aware of not only the effects of drugs in isolation but also of their combined effects. Ignorance of these interactions can result in deaths and in malpractice suits.

(continued)

Table 12-2	**Ways of Thinking About Interactions** (*continued*)
Making General Statements	Interactions indicate that you cannot make a general, simple statement that one variable always has a specific effect.
	You cannot talk about the effects of one variable without mentioning that the effect of that variable depends on a second variable. Therefore, if you have an interaction, when discussing a factor's effect, you need to say "but," "except when," "depending on," "only under certain conditions." Indeed, you will often see results sections say that the main effect was "qualified by a _____ interaction" or "the effect of the _____ variable was different depending on the level of (the other) variable."
Visually	If you graph an interaction, the lines will not be parallel. That is, the lines either already cross or if they were extended, they would eventually cross.
Mathematically	If you have an interaction, the effect of combining the variables is *not* the same as adding their two effects. Rather, the effect is better captured as the result of multiplying the two effects. That is, when you add 2 to a number, you know the number will increase by 2, regardless of what the number is. However, when you multiply a number by 2, the effect will depend on the other number. When doubling a number, the effect is quite different when the number to be doubled is 2 than when it is 1,000 or than when it is -40. To take another example of the effect of multiplication, consider the multiplicative effects of interest rates on your financial condition. If interest rates go up, that will have a big, positive effect on your financial situation if you have lots of money in the bank; a small, positive effect if you have little money in the bank; and a negative effect on your finances if you owe money to the bank (you will have to pay more interest on your debt).

good for most people, but not for people who are taking certain kinds of medications. For those people, eating grapefruit may kill them. For them, the positive main effect for eating grapefruit is unimportant relative to the dangerous grapefruit $\times$ drug interaction.[2]

Interactions do not have to be dangerous. The only requirement for an interaction is that the effect of combining treatments is different from the sum of their individual effects. For example, there is an interesting interaction involving caffeine and nicotine, both of which are stimulants. Consuming caffeine increases physiological arousal—unless people have nicotine in their system. For people who have a lot of nicotine in their system, caffeine actually reduces physiological arousal: The person who has smoked several cigarettes can wind down by drinking a caffeinated cola.[3]

Interactions do not have to involve reversing the treatment's original effect. To have an interaction, all that is required is that the effect of combining the treatments has an effect that is different from the sum of their individual effects. Thus, if two drugs each have a mild positive effect but taking both drugs together has an enormously positive effect, you have an

---

[2]A popular and effective allergy medicine was taken off the market because of this deadly interaction.
[3]We are indebted to an anonymous reviewer for this example.

interaction. Likewise, if one drug has a mild positive effect and another drug has no measurable effect, but taking both drugs together has an enormous effect, you have an interaction.

If neither drug has a measurable effect by itself but taking both drugs together has a strong effect, you have an interaction. If either drug by itself has a moderate positive effect but taking both drugs together still has no more than a moderate positive effect, you have an interaction. If either drug by itself has a moderate positive effect, but taking both drugs together has no effect, you have an interaction. In short, whether the relationship between the treatments could be characterized as "better apart" (two is less than one), "it takes two" (alone they are nothing), "better together" (two is more than one plus one), or "one is enough" (one plus one only equals one), *as long as the effect of combining treatments is different from the sum of their individual effects, you have an interaction.*

Interactions do not have to involve drugs. As most people believe that the effect of an action depends on (interacts with) other factors. For example:

- Most people know that telling someone "congratulations" will have a good effect if she has just been promoted but a bad effect if she has just been fired.
- Most people suspect that, under some conditions, it pays to accuse others of something, but under some conditions, accusing others may backfire.

As these examples illustrate, people often suspect that social variables interact.

Research supports the popular notion that some treatments will have one effect on one group of participants, but a different effect on another group. For example, Rucker and Petty (2003) found that, of the two groups of participants who read about an employee who had a *bad* work ethic, the group that learned that the employee had accused his coworkers of having a bad work ethic liked the employee *more* than did the group that did not learn of the employee making such accusations. On the other hand, of the two groups of participants who read about an employee who had a *good* work ethic, the participants who learned that the employee had accused his coworkers of having a bad work ethic liked the employee *less* than did the participants who were not told that the employee had made any accusations. Thus, there was an employee reputation × accusation interaction.

The previous example illustrates that interactions—the effects of a combination of treatments being different from the sum of those variables' individual effects—may involve social variables. Note, however, that interactions can involve any variables—even physical variables such as noise and lighting. For instance, consider the effects of two manipulated variables: (1) noise level and (2) perception of control. If you make a group of participants believe they have no control over the noise level in the room, increasing the noise level seriously harms performance. But for participants led to believe that they can control the noise level, on the other hand, increasing the noise level does not harm performance. Thus, noise level interacts with perceived control (Glass & Singer, 1972).

Because of this interaction between noise level and perceived control, you cannot simply say that noise hurts performance. You have to say that the effect of noise level on performance *depends* on (is moderated by) perceived control. In other words, rather than stating a simple rule about the effects of noise, you have to state a more complex rule. This complex rule puts qualifications on the statement that noise hurts performance. Specifically, the statement that noise hurts performance will be qualified by some phrase such as "depending on," "but only if," or "however, that holds only under certain conditions."

Because the concept of interaction is so important, let's consider one more example. As a general rule, we can say that getting within 12 inches (30 cm) of another person will make that person uncomfortable. Thus, the main effect of getting physically closer to someone is to produce a negative mood. However, what if the person who comes that close is extremely attractive? Then, getting closer may elicit positive feelings. Because the effect of interpersonal distance is moderated by attractiveness, we can say that there is an interaction between distance and attractiveness.

In short, you now know two facts about interactions. First, if there is an interaction involving your treatment, it means that the treatment has one effect under one set of conditions, but another effect under another set of conditions. Second, interactions play an important role in real life.

Interesting Questions in Modern Psychology Are Often Questions About Interactions

As psychology has progressed, psychologists have focused increasingly more attention on interactions. One reason psychologists focus on interactions is because psychologists have already discovered the main effects of many variables. We know how most individual variables act in isolation. Now, it is time to go to the next step—addressing the question, "What is the effect of combining these variables?" Put another way, once we learn what the general effect of a variable is, we want to find out what specific conditions may modify (moderate) this general, overall effect. Consequently, in Chapter 3, we encouraged you to generate research ideas that involved moderating variables. In other words, we encouraged you to do what many psychologists do—focus on interactions rather than main effects.

Another reason psychologists focus on interactions is that interactions are common. Consequently, psychologists now frame general problems and issues in terms of interactions. Rather than asking, "What is the (main) effect of personality and what is the (main) effect of the situation?" psychologists are now asking, "How do personality and the situation interact?" Asking this question has led to research indicating that some people are more influenced by situational influences than others (Snyder, 1984).

Similarly, rather than looking exclusively at the main effects of heredity and the main effects of environment, many scientists are looking at the interaction between heredity and environment. In other words, rather than asking, "What is the effect of a certain environment?" they are asking, "Are the effects of a certain environment different for some people than for others?"

Looking for these interactions sometimes produces remarkable findings. For example, psychologists have found that certain children may thrive in an environment that would harm children who had inherited a different genetic predisposition (Plomin, 1993). Eventually, such research may lead to new ways of educating parents. For instance, rather than telling parents the one right way to discipline children, parent education may involve teaching parents to identify their child's genetic predispositions and then alter their parenting strategies to fit that predisposition. In short, much of the recent research in psychology has involved asking questions that relate to interactions, such as "Under what conditions do rewards hurt motivation?"

External Validity Questions Are Questions About Interactions

We do not mean to imply that the interest in interactions is an entirely new phenomenon. Anyone interested in external validity is interested in interactions. If you are concerned that a treatment won't work on a certain type of person (women, minorities, retired adults), you are concerned about a treatment × type of person interaction. If you are concerned that a treatment that worked in one setting (a hospital) won't have the same effect in a different setting (a school), you are concerned about a treatment × setting interaction. If you are concerned that a treatment won't have the same effect in another culture, you are concerned about a treatment × culture interaction. If you are concerned that the superiority of one treatment over another will diminish over time, you are concerned about a treatment × time interaction. In summary, determining the external validity of your findings is often a matter of determining whether your treatment interacts with time, setting, culture, or type of participant.

Questions in Applied Psychology Are Often Questions About Interactions

Understandably, applied psychologists have always been interested in interactions. One of the founders of applied psychology, Walter Dill Scott, was fascinated by the fact that some people will like an advertisement that others will hate. Therefore, he investigated personality × type of ad interactions.

Most applied psychologists have shared Scott's interest in determining which treatments work on which type of people. For example, therapists know that a therapeutic approach (behavior therapy, drug therapy) that works well for some patients (e.g., individuals with phobias) may not work as well for others (e.g., individuals who are depressed). In other words, good therapists know about treatment × type of patient interactions.

In conclusion, the applied psychologist is keenly interested in interactions. When clients pay for advice, they do not want the expert to know only about main effects. That is, they do not want the expert to stop at saying, "My recommended course of action works in the average case, and so it may work for you." Instead, paying clients may quiz the expert about interactions involving the expert's proposed treatment. For example, they may ask, "Are there circumstances in which this treatment might make things worse—and does my case fit those circumstances?" To answer this question—that is, to know when a treatment will be helpful and when it will be harmful—the expert must know about the interactions involving that treatment.

Examples of Questions You Can Answer Using the 2 × 2 Factorial Experiment

Now that you have a general understanding of main effects and interactions, let's apply this knowledge to a specific experiment. If you were to replicate the Williams and Sommer's (1997) 2 (Exclusion: not excluded, excluded) × 2 (Credit: individual, group) experiment we described earlier, you would look for three different kinds of effects (see Table 12-3).

First, you could look at the main effect of exclusion: exclusion's *average* effect. You could estimate the overall main effect for exclusion by *averaging* the two exclusion simple main effects. For example, if, on the average, excluded participants generated significantly fewer ideas than participants who were not excluded did, you would have an exclusion main effect.

Second, you could look at the main effect of credit: credit's average effect. You could estimate the overall main effect for credit by *averaging* the two credit simple main effects. For

Table 12-3	Questions Addressed by a 2 × 2 Experiment
EFFECT	QUESTION ADDRESSED
Overall main effect for credit	"On the average, does varying type of credit have an effect?"
Overall main effect for exclusion	"On the average, does varying exclusion have an effect?"
Interaction between exclusion and credit	"Does the effect of exclusion *differ depending on* what type of credit participants get?"
	Put another way,
	"Does the effect of credit *differ depending on* whether participants are excluded?"

example, if, on the average, participants who got personal credit for their ideas generated significantly more ideas than participants in the group credit conditions did, you would have a credit main effect.

Third, you could look at the interaction between exclusion and credit: the extent to which exclusion's effect *differs* depending on what type of credit participants get. Thus, if exclusion *greatly* reduced the number of ideas that group credit participants generated but *slightly* reduced the number of ideas individual credit participants generated, you might have an interaction. You might also have an interaction if included participants generated *fewer* ideas in the collective credit condition than in the individual credit condition (perhaps because the included participants felt comfortable enough with their position in the group to loaf in the group-reward condition), whereas excluded participants generated *more* ideas in the group credit condition than in the individual condition (perhaps because the excluded participants were working hard in a desperate attempt to get accepted by the group). You can estimate the interaction by *subtracting* the two exclusion simple main effects from each other to get the *difference* between them.

If there is no difference between the two exclusion simple main effects, there is no interaction. That is, if exclusion's simple main effects are both the same, the effect of exclusion does not depend on type of credit.

To review, a significant main effect for exclusion would mean that, on the average, varying exclusion had an effect on ideas generated. A significant main effect for credit would mean that, on the average, varying credit had an effect on how many ideas participants generated. Finally, a significant interaction would mean that the combination of exclusion and credit produces an effect that is different (more, less, or opposite) from what you would expect from knowing only exclusion's and credit's individual overall main effects.

To illustrate that an interaction indicates that the combination of factors has an effect that is different from the sum of the factor's individual effects, imagine the following situation. The average effect of inclusion was to boost ideas generated by 2, and the average effect of individual credit was also to boost ideas generated by 2. If we asked you to guess how many more ideas the participants who had the advantages of both being included as well as receiving individual credit (the included/individual credit group) generated relative to the participants who had neither of these advantages (the excluded/collective credit participants), you might, after adding up the effects of inclusion (+2) and individual credit (+2), say "4." If there is no interaction, your guess should be fairly accurate.

But if there is an interaction, your guess would be wrong: The mean number of ideas generated by the inclusion/individual credit participants would *not* be 4 more than the mean for the exclusion/group credit participants. If the interaction magnified the effects of the two factors, the inclusion/individual credit participants might, on the average, generate 6 more ideas than the excluded/collective credit participants.

If, on the other hand, the interaction reversed the effect of the two factors, the inclusion/individual credit participants might, on the average, generate 2 *fewer* ideas than the excluded/collective credit participants. If the interaction was the result of one factor neutralizing the effect of another, the inclusion/individual credit participants might, on the average, generate no (0) more ideas than the excluded/collective credit participants. In short, if you had a exclusion × credit interaction, you couldn't predict how many ideas the the included/individual credit group would generate merely by adding up the exclusion's and credit's individual effects.

As you can imagine, significant interactions force scientists to answer such questions as, "Does working for group credit cause people to loaf?" by saying, "Yes, but it depends on . . ." or "It's a little more complicated than that." Psychologists do not give these kinds of responses to make the world seem more complicated than it is.

On the contrary, psychologists would love to give simple answers. Like all scientists, psychologists prefer parsimonious explanations (simple, elegant explanations that involve few principles) to more complex explanations. Therefore, psychologists would love to report main effects that are not qualified by interactions. Psychologists would like to say that giving individual credit always increases performance and that excluding people always decreases performance. However, if interactions occur, scientists have the obligation to report them— and in the real world, interactions abound. Only the person who says "Give me a match; I want to see if my gas tank is empty" is unaware of the pervasiveness of interactions. Time and time again, you learn that when variables combine, the effects are different than you would expect from knowing only their individual, independent effects.

Because we live in a world where we are exposed to more than one variable at a time and because the variables we are exposed to often interact, you may be compelled to do an experiment that captures some of this complexity. But how would you describe the results from such a factorial experiment?

Potential Results of a 2 × 2 Factorial Experiment

You would describe the results of a 2 × 2 factorial experiment in terms of (1) whether you had a main effect for your first independent variable, (2) whether you had a main effect for your second independent variable, and (3) whether you had an interaction. As you can see from Table 12-4, getting a main effect for your first independent variable does not mean that you will be more likely to get a main effect for your second independent variable or that you will be more likely to get an interaction. Instead, like the results of three separate coin flips, the three different results are independent. Also like the results of three coin flips, there are eight basic patterns of results you could obtain.

If you did a study, how would you know which of these patterns of results you obtained? At some point, you would need to do a statistical analysis, such as analysis of variance (ANOVA). Without such a statistical analysis, the patterns you observed in your data might be due to random error rather than to statistically reliable treatment effects. Either before or after doing such an analysis, however, you would probably like to see what patterns exist in your data. Therefore, you might calculate the mean response for each group and then make a table of those means. In the next section, we will show you how those tables of means can help you make sense of your results.

Table 12-4	Eight Potential Outcomes of a 2 × 2 Factorial Experiment		
1.	A Main Effect for Variable 1	No Main Effect for Variable 2	No Interaction
2.	No Main Effect for Variable 1	A Main Effect for Variable 2	No Interaction
3.	A Main Effect for Variable 1	A Main Effect for Variable 2	No Interaction
4.	A Main Effect for Variable 1	A Main Effect for Variable 2	An Interaction
5.	No Main Effect for Variable 1	No Main Effect for Variable 2	An Interaction
6.	A Main Effect for Variable 1	No Main Effect for Variable 2	An Interaction
7.	No Main Effect for Variable 1	A Main Effect for Variable 2	An Interaction
8.	No Main Effect for Variable 1	No Main Effect for Variable 2	No Interaction

Note that having (or not having) a main effect has no effect on whether you will have an interaction.

One Main Effect and No Interaction

Let's start by supposing you replicate the Williams and Sommer (1997) experiment we discussed earlier. Using a 2 (not excluded versus excluded) × 2 (individual credit versus group credit) factorial experiment, suppose you found results like the ones displayed in Table 12-5. To understand your results, you might start looking at the experiment as though it were four separate simple experiments. Thus, if you look only at the first row, it is just like you are looking at the effects of credit in a simple experiment in which all participants were included in the fun activity.

As you can see from the first row of Table 12-5, the individual credit group generated just as many ideas (8) as the collective credit group. Thus, varying credit had no noticeable effect in the no-exclusion condition.

To find out what happened in the excluded groups, look at the second row. Note that looking at the second row is just like looking at a simple experiment that varied credit (while making all the participants feel excluded). As you can see by the fact that both the individual credit and the collective-credit groups generated 6 ideas, varying credit had no noticeable effect in the exclusion condition.

Averaging the effect of credit over both the not excluded and the excluded conditions, you find that credit's average (overall) effect was zero. Put another way, the individual-credit groups' scores, on the average, were the same as the collective-credit groups'. Thus, there was no overall main effect for the credit manipulation.

Looking at the columns tells you about the effect of varying exclusion. For example, looking at the first column is like looking at a simple experiment that varied exclusion (while giving all participants individual credit). As you can see, the excluded group generates an average of 2 *fewer* ideas than the not excluded group. Thus, there may be a simple main effect for exclusion in the individual-credit condition.

Table 12-5	**Main Effect for Exclusion, No Interaction**		
	INDIVIDUAL CREDIT	COLLECTIVE CREDIT	CREDIT SIMPLE MAIN EFFECTS
Not Excluded	8	8	0 ($\underline{8} - 8 = 0$)
Excluded	6	6	0 ($\mathbf{6} - 6 = 0$)
Exclusion simple main effects	-2 ($\mathbf{6} - 8 = -2$)	-2 ($\mathbf{6} - \underline{\mathbf{8}} = -2$)	

Averaging a treatment's simple main effects gives us the treatment's overall main effect:

Simple main effect of **Exclusion** in the individual credit condition	-2
Simple main effect of **Exclusion** in the collective credit condition	$\underline{-2}$
Average effect (overall main effect) of **Exclusion**	$-4/2 = -2$
Simple main effect of **Credit** in the inclusion condition	0
Simple main effect of **Credit** in the exclusion condition	$\underline{0}$
Average effect (overall main effect) of **Credit**	$0/2 = 0$

Comparing a treatment's simple main effects tells us whether there is an interaction: Because there are no differences between exclusion's two simple main effects (both are -2), there is no interaction. In other words, because the effect of exclusion is not affected by what kind of credit participants get (individual versus collective), there is no interaction.

Figure 12-1 **Main Effect for Exclusion, No Interaction**

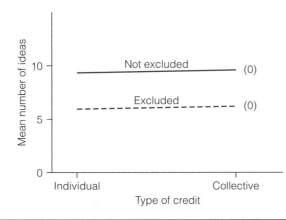

Note: **Numbers in parentheses represent the credit simple main effects. Thus, the simple main effect of credit was 0 in both the not excluded condition and the excluded condition.**

Looking at the second column shows you the effect of exclusion for the collective-credit participants. In a way, looking at the second column is like looking at a simple experiment that manipulated exclusion (while giving all participants collective credit). As you can see, the exclusion group generates an average of 2 *fewer* ideas than the inclusion group. Thus, there may be a simple main effect for exclusion in the collective-credit condition.

Because exclusion decreases idea generation for both the individual-credit and the collective-credit participants, there seems to be an overall main effect for exclusion. Our best estimate of this average effect of exclusion is that exclusion reduces the mean number of ideas generated by 2.[4]

Because exclusion's effect does not differ depending on credit condition, there is no interaction between exclusion and credit. Specifically, there is no interaction because exclusion reduces the mean number of ideas generated by the same amount (2) in the individual credit condition as it does in the collective credit condition.

Although making tables of means is a useful way to summarize data, perhaps the easiest way to interpret the results of a factorial experiment is to graph the means. To see how graphing can help you interpret your data, graph the data in Table 12-5. Before you plot your data, start by beginning to make a graph of a simple experiment that manipulates credit. Once you have a vertical *y*-axis labeled "Mean number of ideas," and a horizontal *x*-axis that has labels for both individual credit and collective credit, you are ready to plot your data. Start by plotting two points representing the two means from the top row. Next, draw a line between those points and label that line "Not excluded." Then, plot the bottom row's two means. Draw a line between those two points and label that line "Excluded." Your graph should look something like Figure 12-1. If it doesn't, please consult Box 12-1.

---

[4]Because of random error, you don't know what the effect actually is. Indeed, without using statistical tests, you can't claim that you have a significant main effect or an interaction. However, because our purpose in this section is to teach you how to interpret tables and graphs and because the tables and graphs you will see in journal articles will almost always be accompanied by a statistical analysis, we will pretend—in this section—that any differences between means are statistically significant and due entirely to treatment effects.

BOX 12-1 · Turning a 2 × 2 Table Into a Graph

If you have never graphed a 2 × 2 before, you may need some help. How can you graph three variables (the two factors and the dependent variable) on a two-dimensional piece of paper? The short answer is that you need to use two lines instead of one.

To see how to make such a graph, get a sheet of notebook paper and a ruler. Starting near the left edge of the sheet, draw a 4-inch line straight down the page. This vertical line is called the *y*-axis. The *y*-axis corresponds to scores on the dependent measure. In this case, your dependent measure is ideas generated. So, label the *y*-axis "Mean number of ideas."

Now that you have a yardstick (the *y*-axis) for recording ideas generated, your next step is to put marks on that yardstick. Having these marks will make it easier for you to plot the means accurately. Start marking the *y*-axis by putting a little hash mark on the very bottom of the *y*-axis. Label this mark "0." A half an inch above this mark, put another mark. Label the mark "5." Keep making marks until you get to "20."

Your next step is to draw a horizontal line that goes from the bottom of the *y*-axis to the right side of the page. (If you are using lined paper, you may be able to trace over one of the paper's lines.) The horizontal line is called the *x*-axis. On the *x*-axis, you should put one of your independent variables. It usually doesn't matter which independent variable you put on the *x*-axis. However, some people believe you should put the moderator variable on the x-axis. If you don't have a moderator variable, those same people believe you should put the factor you consider most important on the *x*-axis. For the sake of this example, put "Type of credit" about an inch below the middle of the *x*-axis. Then, put a mark on the left-hand side of the *x*-axis and label this mark "Individual." Next, put a mark on the right side of the *x*-axis and label it "Collective."

You are now ready to plot the means in the left column of Table 12-5. Once you have plotted those two means, draw a straight line between those two means. Label that line "Not excluded." Next, plot the two means in the right column of Table 12-5. Then, draw a line between those two points. Label this second line (which should be above your first line) "Excluded." Your graph should look something like Figure 12-1.

Figure 12-1 confirms what you saw in Table 12-5. Exclusion decreased idea production relative to inclusion, as shown by the excluded partipants' line being below the not excluded participants' line. Credit did *not* affect idea production, as shown by the fact that both lines stay perfectly level as they go from individual credit (left) side to collective credit (right) side of the graph.

Finally, there is no interaction between credit and exclusion on idea production, as shown by the fact that the lines are parallel.[5] The lines are parallel because credit is having the same effect on the not excluded group as it is on the excluded group. In this case, credit is having no (0) effect on either group.

Note that if you graph your data, you need to see only whether the lines are parallel to know whether you have an interaction. *If your lines are parallel, you do not have an interaction.* If, on the other hand, your lines have different slopes, you may have an interaction.[6]

---

[5]If you have a bar graph instead of a line graph, you can't simply look to see if the lines are parallel because there are no lines. Instead, the key is to see whether the relationship between the dark bar and the light bar on the left side of the graph is the same as the relationship between the dark bar and the light bar on the right side of the graph. For example, if, on the left side of the graph, the dark bar is taller than the light bar, but on the right side of the graph, the dark bar is shorter than the light bar, you may have an interaction. Alternatively, you may convert the bar graph into a line graph by (a) drawing one line from the top, right corner of the first dark bar to the top, left corner of the other dark bar, and (b) drawing a second line from the top, right corner of the first light bar to the top, left corner of the other light bar.

[6]Remember that because of random error, we don't know what the effect actually is. To know whether we had an interaction, we would need to do a statistical significance test.

Table 12-6	**Main Effect for Credit, No Interaction**		
	INDIVIDUAL CREDIT	COLLECTIVE CREDIT	CREDIT SIMPLE MAIN EFFECTS
Not Excluded	10	5	-5 ($\underline{5} - 10 = -5$)
Excluded	10	5	-5 ($\underline{5} - 10 = -5$)
Exclusion simple main effects	0 (**10** $-$ 10 = 0)	0 ($\underline{5} - \underline{5} = 0$)	

Averaging a treatment's simple main effects gives us the treatment's overall main effect:

Simple main effect of **Exclusion** in the individual credit condition	0
Simple main effect of **Exclusion** in the collective credit condition	$\underline{0}$
Average effect (overall main effect) of **Exclusion**	$0/2 = 0$
Simple main effect of **Credit** in the inclusion condition	-5
Simple main effect of **Credit** in the exclusion condition	$\underline{-5}$
Average effect (overall main effect) of **Credit**	$-10/2 = -5$

Comparing a treatment's simple main effects tells us whether there is an interaction: Because there are no differences between exclusion's two simple main effects (both are 0), there is no interaction. In other words, because the effect of exclusion is not affected by what kind of credit participants get (individual versus collective), there is no interaction.

Instead of having no interaction and a main effect for exclusion, you could have no interaction and a main effect for credit. This pattern of results is shown in Table 12-6. From the top row, you can see that in the not excluded groups, collective credit decreased the number of ideas generated by 5. Looking at the bottom row, you see that in the excluded groups, collective credit also decreased the number of ideas generated by 5. Averaging the effect of credit over both the excluded and the not excluded conditions, you estimate that credit's average effect, the overall main effect of credit, was -5.

Whereas looking at the rows tells you about the effects of credit, looking at the columns tells you about the effect of exclusion. Looking at the first column tells you about the effect of exclusion in the individual credit conditions. When you look at the first column (the individual credit column), you can see that in the individual credit conditions, the not excluded participants generated the same number of ideas (5) as the excluded participants. Thus, there was no simple main effect of exclusion in the individual credit conditions.

Looking at the second column (the collective credit column) tells you about the effect of exclusion in the collective-credit conditions. You can see that in the collective-credit condition, the not excluded participants generated the same number of ideas (10) as excluded participants. Thus, there was no simple main effect for exclusion in the collective-credit condition.

To determine the overall main effect of exclusion, average exclusion's two simple main effects. Because there was no (zero) observed effect for varying exclusion in both the individual credit condition (the first column) and the collective-credit condition (the second column), there is no (zero) overall main effect for varying exclusion.

To determine whether there is a exclusion by credit interaction, you could subtract the exclusion main effects from each other ($0 - 0 = 0$). Or, you could subtract the credit main effects from each other ($-5 - -5 = 0$). Either way, the result is zero, suggesting that you don't have a credit by exclusion interaction. You do not have an interaction because the effect of credit is not affected by the exclusion variable: Collective-credit decreases idea generation by 5 ideas, regardless of whether participants are excluded.

Two Main Effects and No Interaction

Table 12-7 reflects another pattern of effects you might obtain. From the first row, you can see that in the not excluded groups, collective credit decreased the number of ideas generated by 4 (10 − 6). Looking at the second row, you see that, in the excluded groups, group credit also decreased the number of ideas generated by 4 (8 − 4). Averaging the effect of group credit over all the exclusion conditions, you find that the average effect of credit (the overall main of credit) was to decrease the number of ideas generated by 4.

Looking at the columns tells you about the effect of varying exclusion. The first column tells you about what happens in the individual credit conditions. As you can see, in the individual credit conditions, the participants who were excluded generated 2 (10 − 8) fewer ideas than those who were not excluded. Looking at the second column, you see that, in the collective-credit conditions, excluded participants produce, on the average, 2 (6 − 4) fewer ideas than the not excluded participants. Because exclusion decreases the number of ideas generated in both the individual credit and the collective-credit groups, it appears that there is a exclusion main effect.

Comparing the two columns tells you that there is no interaction because the effect of exclusion is unaffected by credit. As Table 12-7 demonstrates, the effect of exclusion is independent of (does not depend on) the type of credit. In this case, exclusion decreases idea generation by 2 ideas, regardless of whether participants are in the individual credit condition or in the collective-credit conditions.

Table 12-7 | **Main Effect for Credit and Exclusion, No Interaction**

	INDIVIDUAL CREDIT	COLLECTIVE CREDIT	CREDIT SIMPLE MAIN EFFECTS
Not Excluded	10	6	−4 (6 − 10 = −4)
Excluded	8	4	−4 (4 − 8 = −4)
Exclusion simple main effects	−2 (8 − 10 = −2)	−2 (4 − 6 = −0)	

Averaging a treatment's simple main effects gives us the treatment's overall main effect:

Simple main effect of **Exclusion** in the individual credit condition	−2
Simple main effect of **Exclusion** in the collective credit condition	−2
Average effect (overall main effect) of **Exclusion**	−4/2 = −2

Simple main effect of **Credit** in the not excluded condition	−4
Simple main effect of **Credit** in the not excluded condition	−4
Average effect (overall main effect) of **Credit**	−8/2 = −4

Comparing a treatment's simple main effects tells us whether there is an interaction: Because there are no differences between exclusion's two simple main effects (both are −2), there is no interaction. In other words, because the effect of exclusion is not affected by what kind of credit participants get (individual versus collective), there is no interaction.

Figure 12-2   **Main Effect for Exclusion and Credit, No Interaction**

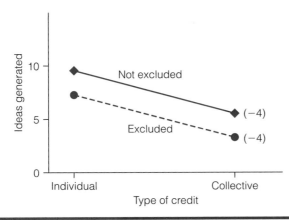

Note: **Numbers in parentheses represent the credit simple main effects. Thus, the simple main effect of credit was −4 in the not excluded condition and in the excluded condition.**

To look at this lack of exclusion × credit interaction from a different perspective (a credit × exclusion perspective), look at the rows. Comparing the rows shows you that the effect of credit is unaffected by the level of exclusion. Specifically, collective credit decreases idea generation by 4 ideas for both the excluded and the not excluded groups.

We have shown you two ways to use a table of means (like Table 12-7) to determine whether you have an interaction: (1) by comparing (subtracting) the simple main effects of the two rows, and (2) by comparing (subtracting) the simple main effects of the two columns. There is a third way. If either simple main effect for a factor is the same as that factor's overall main effect, you do not have an interaction. Thus, in the current example, we know there is no interaction because the simple main effect of collective credit in the not excluded conditions (−4) is the same as the overall main effect of collective credit (−4).

Although a table of means gives you valuable information, you may understand your data better if you graph the means. To appreciate this point, look at a graph of Table 12-7's means: Figure 12-2. As you can see from the excluded line being below the not excluded line, exclusion decreased idea production relative to inclusion. As you can see from both lines sloping downward as they go from the individual credit (left) side to collective credit (right) side of Figure 12-2, collective credit, relative to individual credit, decreased idea production. Finally, as you can see from the parallel lines, there is no interaction between credit and exclusion. The lines are parallel because credit affects the excluded groups the same (parallel) way that it affects the not excluded groups.

Two Main Effects and an Interaction

Now imagine that you got a very different set of results from your exclusion-credit study. For example, suppose you found the results in Table 12-8.

As the table shows, you have main effects for both credit and exclusion. The average effect of collective credit is to decrease the number of ideas generated by 3, and the average effect of exclusion is to decrease the number of ideas generated by 5.

Table 12-8	Main Effect for Credit and Exclusion, and a (Cross-over) Interaction		
	INDIVIDUAL CREDIT	COLLECTIVE CREDIT	CREDIT SIMPLE MAIN EFFECTS
Not Excluded	20	12	-8 ($\underline{12} - 20 = -8$)
Excluded	10	12	2 ($\underline{12} - 10 = 2$)
Exclusion simple main effects	-10 (**10** $- 20 = -10$)	($\underline{12} - \underline{12} = 0$)	

Averaging a treatment's simple main effects gives us the treatment's overall main effect:

Simple main effect of **Exclusion** in the individual credit condition	-8
Simple main effect of **Exclusion** in the collective credit condition	2
Average effect (overall main effect) of **Exclusion**	$-6/2 = -3$

Simple main effect of **Credit** in the not excluded condition	-10
Simple main effect of **Credit** in the excluded condition	0
Average effect (overall main effect) of **Credit**	$-10/2 = -5$

Comparing a treatment's simple main effects tells us whether there is an interaction: Because exclusion's two simple main effects are different, there is an interaction. In other words, because the effect of exclusion is affected by what kind of credit participants get (individual versus collective), there is an interaction.

However, the specific effect of collective credit varies depending on whether participants are excluded. In the *not* excluded condition, collective credit *decreases* the number of ideas generated by 8 (20 vs. 12). In the excluded condition, on the other hand, collective credit *increases* ideas generated by 2 (12 vs. 10). Because the effect of credit differs depending on exclusion, there is an interaction.

To see this interaction, look at Figure 12-3a. As you can see, the lines are not parallel because the slope of the excluded line is different from the slope of the not excluded line. This difference in slope indicates that the effect of credit is different in the excluded condition than in the not excluded condition. In this case, the excluded line slopes upward (indicating that excluded participants generate *more* ideas in the collective credit condition than in the individual credit condition), whereas the not excluded line slopes downward (indicating that not excluded participants generate *fewer* ideas in the collective credit condition than in the individual credit condition). When the lines slope in opposite directions—indicating that the effect a treatment has with one group of participants is opposite from that treatment's effect on the other group of participants—the interaction is often called a **crossover (disordinal) interaction** (because the lines often *cross*).

Crossover interactions are also called *disordinal interactions* because they can't be merely the result of having ordinal rather than interval data. That is, even if your measure can't tell you how much more of a quality one participant has than another, that problem with your measure won't make it look like the treatment is increasing the quality in one condition but decreasing it in the other condition.

Such a measurement problem could, however, cause other types of interactions. For example, consider Figure 12-3b, in which both lines slope downward but the not excluded line slopes downward more sharply than the excluded line. As you can see from Figure 12-3b, the lines are not parallel—and, therefore, there is an interaction. Such an interaction could

| Figure 12-3a | **Main Effects for Exclusion and Credit, and a Crossover (Disordinal) Interaction** |

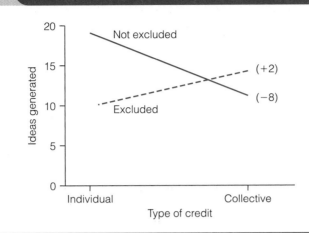

Note: Numbers in parentheses represent the credit simple main effects. Thus, the simple main effect of credit was −8 in the not excluded condition but +2 in the excluded condition.

| Figure 12-3b | **Main Effects for Exclusion and Credit and an Ordinal Interaction** |

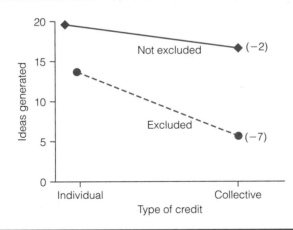

Note: Numbers in parentheses represent the credit simple main effects. Thus, the simple main effect of credit was only −2 in the not excluded condition but was −7 in the excluded condition.

be due to the not excluded participants being more affected by the collective credit manipulation than the excluded participants were. However, such an interaction could also be due to your ordinal measure making it look like the treatment has more of an effect in one condition than the other. In this case, if ideas generated is an ordinal measure of effort (e.g., it is easy to come up with the first few ideas but each additional idea is harder to get), it may be that going from 20 to 18 ideas is just as much of a reduction in effort as going from 12 to 7 ideas. Because interactions that appear to be due to a treatment having more of an effect in one condition than in another could be due to ordinal data, such interactions are called *ordinal interactions*.

An Interaction and No Main Effects

You have seen that you can have main effects with interactions, but can you have interactions without main effects? To answer this question, consider the data in Table 12-9 and Figure 12-4a.

From the graph (Figure 12-4a), you can see that the lines are not parallel. Instead, the lines actually cross. In this case, the crossover interaction is due to group credit having one kind of effect (decreasing idea production) in the not excluded condition, but having an opposite effect (increasing idea production) in the excluded condition. (In this case, "X" marks the crossover interaction. Sometimes, as you can see from Figure 12-4b, a graph of such a crossover interaction looks like a sideways "V" rather than an "X.")

Although you have an interaction between exclusion and credit, you do not have a main effect for either exclusion or credit. As you can tell by looking at Table 12-9, the individual credit groups average as many ideas as the collective-credit groups. Therefore, there isn't a credit main effect. Similarly, because the excluded groups produce, on the average, the same number of ideas as the not excluded groups, there isn't an exclusion main effect.

Thus, you would have to say that neither exclusion nor credit has a main effect. Yet, you would not want to say that neither exclusion nor credit has any effect. Instead, you would either say that (1) exclusion has an effect, but its effect depends on the type of credit participants receive, or (2) credit has an effect, but its effect depends on whether participants are excluded.

Table 12-9 **No Main Effects for Credit or Exclusion With a (Crossover) Interaction**

	INDIVIDUAL CREDIT	COLLECTIVE CREDIT	CREDIT SIMPLE MAIN EFFECTS
Not Excluded	15	<u>10</u>	-5 ($\underline{10} - 15 = -5$)
Excluded	10	<u>15</u>	$+5$ ($\underline{15} - 10 = +5$)
Exclusion simple main effects	-5 (**10** $- 15 = -5$)	($\underline{15} - \underline{10} = +5$)	

Averaging a treatment's simple main effects gives us the treatment's overall main effect:

Simple main effect of **Exclusion** in the individual credit condition	-5
Simple main effect of **Exclusion** in the collective credit condition	$+5$
Average effect (overall main effect) of **Exclusion**	$0/2 = 0$

Simple main effect of **Credit** in the not excluded condition	-5
Simple main effect of **Credit** in the excluded condition	$+5$
Average effect (overall main effect) of **Credit**	$0/2 = 0$

Comparing a treatment's simple main effects tells us whether there is an interaction: Because exclusion's two simple main effects are different, there is an interaction. In this case, because excluded participants have one kind of response to collective credit whereas not excluded participants have a different kind of response to collective credit, there is an interaction.

Figure 12-4a **No Main Effects and a Crossover Interaction: The Classic "X"-Shaped Pattern**

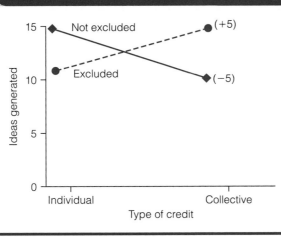

Note: **Numbers in parentheses represent the credit simple main effects. Thus, the simple main effect of credit was −5 in the not excluded condition but +5 in the excluded condition.**

Figure 12-4b **No Main Effects and a Crossover Interaction: The Classic "V"-Shaped Pattern**

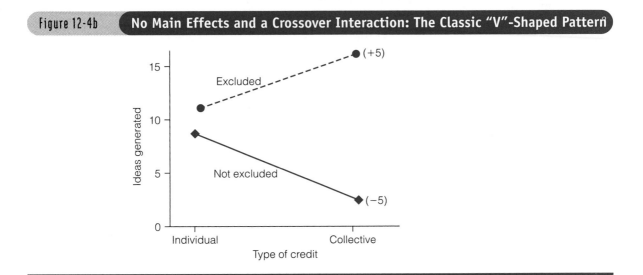

Note: **Numbers in parentheses represent the credit simple main effects. Thus, the simple main effect of credit was −5 in the not excluded condition but +5 in the excluded condition.**

Regardless of whether you emphasize the effect of exclusion (as in the first statement) or the effect of credit (as in the second statement), you cannot talk about the effect of one variable without talking about the other. In short, if you have an interaction, the effect of one variable depends on the other—even when you don't have any main effects.

An Interaction and One Main Effect

You have seen that you can have no main effects and an interaction. You have also seen that you can have two main effects and an interaction. Can you also have one main effect and an interaction? Yes—such a pattern of results is listed in Table 12-10 and graphed in Figure 12-5.

Table 12-10	Main Effect for Credit With an Interaction		
	INDIVIDUAL CREDIT	COLLECTIVE CREDIT	CREDIT SIMPLE MAIN EFFECTS
Not Excluded	8	<u>12</u>	4 (<u>12</u> − 8 = 4)
Excluded	**10**	**<u>10</u>**	0 (**<u>10</u>** −10 = 0)
Exclusion simple main effects	+2 (**10** − 8 = +2)	(**<u>10</u>** − <u>12</u> = −2)	

Averaging a treatment's simple main effects gives us the treatment's overall main effect:
Simple main effect of **Exclusion** in the individual credit condition   +2
Simple main effect of **Exclusion** in the collective credit condition   <u>−2</u>
     Average effect (overall main effect) of **Exclusion**   0/2 = 0

Simple main effect of **Credit** in the not excluded condition   4
Simple main effect of **Credit** in the excluded condition   <u>0</u>
     Average effect (overall main effect) of **Credit**   4/2 = 2

Comparing a treatment's simple main effects tells us whether there is an interaction: Because exclusion's two simple main effects are different, there is an interaction. In this case, because excluded participants have one kind of response to collective credit whereas not excluded participants have a different kind of response to collective credit, there is a crossover interaction.

Figure 12-5	Main Effect for Credit With an Interaction

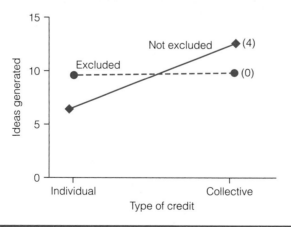

Note: Numbers in parentheses represent the credit simple main effects. Thus, the simple main effect of credit was 4 in the not excluded condition but 0 in the excluded condition. Because the simple main effect of credit differs depending on exclusion condition, there is an interaction.

As Table 12-10 reveals, the average effect of varying exclusion is zero. (The +2 effect of exclusion in the individual credit condition is cancelled out by the −2 effect of exclusion in the collective credit condition.) The average effect of varying credit, on the other hand, is to increase the average number of ideas generated by 2. Note, however, that credit's effect is uneven. In the not excluded condition, collective credit has a positive (12 − 8 = +4) effect on idea generation. But in the exclusion condition, credit has no observable effect (10 − 10 = 0). Because the effect of credit differs depending on exclusion condition, there is a credit × exclusion interaction.

Figure 12-5 tells the same story. By looking at that figure, you realize there may be an interaction because the lines are not parallel. They are not parallel because the effect of credit is dramatic in the not excluded conditions but undetectable in the excluded conditions.

Whereas you can glance at Figure 12-5 and instantly see the interaction, seeing the main effects requires more mental visualization. If there is a main effect for exclusion, one of the exclusion lines should, on the average, be higher than the other. When one line is always above the other, it is easy to tell whether there seems to be a main effect. In this case, however, the lines cross—making it hard to tell whether one line is, on the average, above the other. If you get a ruler and mark the midpoint of each line, you will see that the midpoint of both lines is at the same spot. Or, you may realize that the excluded line is below the not excluded line just as often and to the same extent as it is above the excluded line. In either case, you would conclude that there is no main effect for exclusion.

To determine whether there is a main effect for credit, you could mentally combine the two lines. If you do that, you would "see" that this combined line slopes upward, indicating a positive main effect for credit. (If you can't visualize such a line, you can create one in three steps. First, take a ruler and put a point halfway between the left ends of the two lines [i.e., a point halfway between the two individual credit points]. Second, put a point halfway between the right ends of the two lines [i.e., a point halfway between the two collective credit points]. Third, draw a line between the two points you just drew.) Alternatively, you could reason that because the not excluded line slopes upward and the excluded line stays level, the average of the two lines would have to slope upward.

If you prefer not to think about lines at all, convert the graph into a table of means. To practice, take Figure 12-5 and see if you can convert it into a table resembling Table 12-10. Once you have your table of means, you will be able to see that the average for the collective credit groups is higher than the average for the individual credit groups.

No Main Effects and No Interaction

The last pattern of results you could obtain is to get no statistically significant results. That is, you could fail to find an exclusion effect, fail to find a credit effect, and fail to obtain an interaction between inclusion and credit. An example of such a dull set of findings (possibly caused by a lack of power) is listed in Table 12-11.

Table 12-11	No Main Effects and No Interaction	
	INDIVIDUAL CREDIT	COLLECTIVE CREDIT
Not Excluded	12	12
Excluded	12	12

Analyzing Results From a Factorial Experiment

You can now graph and describe all the possible patterns of results from a 2×2 experiment. But how would you analyze your results to determine whether a main effect or an interaction is significant?

You would probably use analysis of variance (ANOVA) to analyze your data. Using ANOVA to analyze a factorial experiment is similar to using ANOVA to analyze data from a single factor experiment. The main difference is that instead of testing for one main effect, you will be testing for two main effects and an interaction. Thus, your ANOVA summary table might look like this:

SOURCE OF VARIANCE	SUM OF SQUARES (SS)	df	MEAN SQUARE (MS)	F
Credit Main Effect (A)	900	1	900	9.00
Exclusion Main Effect (B)	200	1	200	2.00
Interaction (A × B)	100	1	100	1.00
Error Term (within groups)	3,600	36	100	
Total	4,800	39		

What Degrees of Freedom Tell You

Despite the fact that this ANOVA table has two more sources of variance than the ANOVA for the multiple-group experiment described in Chapter 11, most of the rules that apply to the ANOVA table for that design also apply to the table for a factorial design (see Box 12-2). In terms of degrees of freedom, you can still use the two rules we discussed in Chapter 11:

1. The number of treatment levels is one more than the treatment's degrees of freedom. Because the ANOVA summary table above states that the degrees of freedom for credit is 1, we know that the study used two levels of credit. Likewise, because the degrees of freedom for exclusion is 1, we know the study used two levels of exclusion. Thus, the ANOVA summary table tells us that the study used a 2×2 design.

2. The total number of participants is one more than the total degrees of freedom. Therefore, because the ANOVA table states that the total degrees of freedom was 39, we know that there were 40 (39 + 1) participants in the experiment.

The only new rule is for the for the interaction's degrees of freedom. To calculate the interaction term's degrees of freedom, multiply the degrees of freedom for the main effects making up that interaction. For a 2×2 experiment, that would be 1 (df for first main effect) $\times$ 1 (df for second main effect) = 1. For a 2×3 experiment, that would be 1 (the df for the first main effect would be 1) $\times$ 2 (the df for the second main effect) = 2.

What F and p Values Tell You

To determine whether an effect was significant, you look at the p value for the effect. If the p value is less than .05, the effect is statistically significant. If you do not have the p values, compare the F for that effect to the value given in the F table (see Table E-3 in Appendix E) under the appropriate number of degrees of freedom. If your obtained F is larger than the value in the table, the effect is statistically significant.

BOX 12-2 | **The Mathematics of an ANOVA Summary Table for Between-Subjects Factorial Designs**

1. Degrees of freedom (*df*) for a main effect equal 1 less than the number of levels of that factor. If there are 3 levels of a factor (low, medium, high), that factor has 2 *df*.

2. Degrees of freedom for an interaction equal the product of the *df* of the factors making up that effect. If you have an interaction between a factor that has 1 *df* and a factor that has 2 *df*, that interaction has 2 *df* (because 1 × 2 = 2).

3. To get the total degrees of freedom, subtract 1 from the number of participants. Therefore, if you have 60 participants, the total degrees of freedom should be 59 (60 − 1).

4. To get the *df* for the error term, determine how many groups you had. Then, subtract the number of groups from the number of participants. In a 2 × 2, you have 4 (2 × 2) groups. Therefore, if you had 60 participants, your *df* error is 56 (60 − 4). If you had a 3 × 2, you would have 6 (3 × 2) groups. Therefore, the *df* error would be 54 (60 − 6). Another way to get the *df* error is to (a) add up the

df for all the main effects and interactions, and then (b) subtract that sum from the total degrees of freedom. Thus, if you had 1 *df* for the first main effect, 1 *df* for the second main effect, 1 *df* for the interaction, the sum of the *df* for your main effects and interactions would be **3** (1 + 1 +1). You would then subtract that sum (3) from the *df* total. Thus, if the *df* total was 59, your error term would be 56 (59 − 3).

5. To get the mean square for any effect, get the sum of squares for that effect, and then divide by that effect's *df*. If an effect's sum of squares was 300, and its *df* was 3, its mean square would be 100 (because 300/3 = 100). If the effect's sum of squares was 300, and its *df* was 1, its mean square would be 300 (because 300/1 = 300).

6. To get the *F* for any effect, get its mean square and divide it by the mean square error. If an effect's mean square was 100, and the mean square error was 50, the *F* for that effect would be 2.

What Main Effects Tell You: On the Average, the Factor Had an Effect

Generally, you will want to start your inspection of the *ANOVA* results by seeing whether any of your overall main effects are significant. If you have a significant effect for a factor, the overall effect of that factor is either to increase or to decrease scores on the dependent measure. If you have a significant main effect, your next step would be to find out whether this main effect was qualified by an interaction.

If the interaction was not significant, your conclusions are simple and straightforward. Having no interactions means there are no "ifs" or "buts" about your main effects. That is, you have not found anything that would lead you to say that the main effect occurs only under certain conditions. For instance, if you have a main effect for exclusion and no interactions, exclusion had the same kind of effect throughout your experiment—no matter what type of credit participants received. When you don't have interactions, you can just talk about the overall main effects. Thus, your Results section might resemble the following:

> A 2 (Exclusion: not excluded, excluded) × 2 (Credit: individual, collective) between-subjects *ANOVA* was conducted to assess the effects of exclusion and credit on idea production. Contrary to our hypothesis, this analysis did not find that the excluded group generated significantly fewer ideas ($M = 11.8$) than the not excluded group ($M = 12.2$), $F(1, 48) = 2.14$, *ns*. However, the analysis did reveal the expected main effect for credit, with individual credit participants generating more ideas ($M = 16$) than collective credit participants generated ($M = 8$), $F(1, 48) = 4.21$, $p = .04$, $r_{effect\ size} = .12$. The credit main effect was not qualified by an exclusion × credit interaction, $F(1, 48) = 1.42$, *ns*.

If, on the other hand, you had an interaction, you would replace the last sentence with something like the following:

> These findings are qualified, however, by a significant exclusion $\times$ credit interaction, $F(1, 48) = 4.60$, $p < .04$, $\eta^2 = .08$. In the individual credit conditions, participants generated as many ideas in the not excluded condition ($M = 16.1$, $SD = 3.33$) as in the excluded condition ($M = 16.3$, $SD = 3.46$). However, in the collective credit conditions, participants generated more ideas in the excluded condition ($M = 10.1$, $SD = 3.22$) than in the not excluded condition ($M = 6.1$, $SD = 3.11$).

What Interactions Usually Tell You: Combining Factors Leads to Effects That Differ From the Sum of the Individual Main Effects

As you just saw, when you have a significant interaction, describing the results is more complicated than when you don't have a significant interaction. You can't just talk about one variable's effect without also stating that the variable's effect depends on (is moderated by, is qualified by) a second variable.

At a more concrete level, having an interaction means that a treatment factor has a different effect on one group of participants than on another. In our exclusion–credit example, having an interaction means the simple main effect of exclusion in the individual credit condition is different from the simple main effect of exclusion in the collective credit condition. Because exclusion's simple main effects differ, rather than talking about exclusion's general, average, overall main effect, you should talk about the specific, individual, simple main effects that make up that overall main effect.

Before you can do this, however, you must understand them. The easiest way to understand the pattern of the simple main effects—and thus understand the interaction—is to graph them.[7] In addition to looking at the slope of each line, examine the relationship between your lines to see why they aren't parallel.

If the lines are sloping in different directions, you have a disordinal interaction and you know that the interaction is not merely an artifact of having ordinal data. Therefore, you know that the treatment has one effect in one condition and a different effect in another.

If, on the other hand, both lines are sloping in the same direction but one is steeper than the other, you have an ordinal interaction and you know that your interaction may merely be an artifact of having ordinal data. Therefore, you can't be confident that the interaction is due to the treatment's effect being stronger with one group than with another.

Putting the 2 × 2 Factorial Experiment to Work

You now understand the logic behind the 2 × 2 design. In the next sections, you will see how you can use the 2 × 2 to produce research that is more interesting, has greater construct validity, and has greater external validity than research produced by a simple experiment.

Adding a Replication Factor to Increase Generalizability

The generalizability of results from a single simple experiment can always be questioned. Critics ask questions such as, "Would the results have been different if a different experimenter

---

[7]Interactions suggest that, rather than looking at the overall main effects, you should look at the individual simple main effects. One way to understand an interaction is to do statistical analyses on the individual simple main effects. The computations for these tests are simple. However, there are some relatively subtle issues involved in deciding which test to use.

had performed the study?" and "Would the results have been different if a different manipulation had been used?" Often, the researcher's answer to these critics is to do a **systematic replication:** a study that varies from the original only in some minor aspect, such as using different experimenters or different stimulus materials.

For example, Morris (1986) found that students learned more from a lecture presented in a rock-video format than from a conventional lecture. However, Morris used only one lecture and one rock video. Obviously, we would have more confidence in his results if he had used more than one conventional lecture and one rock-video lecture.

Morris would have benefited from doing a 2 × 2 experiment. Because the 2 × 2 factorial design is like doing 2 simple experiments at once, Morris could have (1) obtained his original findings and (2) replicated them with a different set of stimulus materials. Specifically, in addition to manipulating the factor of presentation type (conventional lecture vs. rock-video lecture), he could also have manipulated the replication factor of **stimulus sets:** the particular stimulus materials shown to one or more groups of participants. For example, he could have done a 2 (presentation type [conventional lecture versus rock-video format]) × 2 (stimulus sets [material about Shakespeare versus material about economics]) study. Because psychologists often want to show that the manipulation's effect can occur with more than just one particular stimulus set, experimenters routinely include stimulus sets as a replication factor in their experiments.[8]

Stimulus sets are not the only replication factor that researchers use. Some researchers employ more than one experimenter to run the study and then use experimenter as a factor in the design.

Some of these researchers use experimenter as a factor to show the generality of their results. Specifically, they want to show that certain experimenter characteristics (gender, attractiveness, status) do not alter the treatment's effect.

Other researchers use experimenters as a factor to establish that the experimenters are not biasing the results. For instance, Ranieri and Zeiss (1984) were worried that experimenters might unintentionally influence participants' responses to their experiment's dependent measure: a self-report scale of mood. Therefore, they used three experimenters and randomly assigned participants to experimenter. If different experimenters had obtained different patterns of results, Ranieri and Zeiss would have suspected that the results might be due to experimenter effects rather than to the manipulation itself.

Thus far, we have discussed instances in which the investigator's goal in using the factorial design was to increase the generalizability of the experimental results. Thus, in a study that uses stimulus set as a replication factor, researchers hope that the treatment × stimulus set interaction will not be significant. Similarly, most researchers who use experimenter as a factor hope that there will not be a treatment × experimenter interaction.

Using an Interaction to Find an Exception to the Rule: Looking at a Potential Moderating Factor

You may often read a research report and say to yourself, "But I bet that would not happen under _____ conditions." In that case, you should do a study in which you essentially repeat the original experiment except that you add what you believe will be a moderating factor that will interact with the treatment.

[8]However, psychologists have not all agreed that the traditional, fixed-effects analysis of variance should be used to analyze such studies (see Clark, 1973; Cohen, 1976; Coleman, 1979; Kenny & Smith, 1980; Richter & Seay, 1987; Wickens & Keppel, 1983; Wike & Church, 1976).

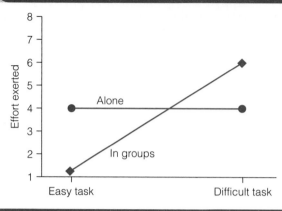

Figure 12-6 **Interaction Between Task Difficulty and Number of Coworkers on Effort**

Note: **Effort was scored on a 1-to-7 scale, with higher numbers indicating more effort.**

To see how a moderating factor experiment would work, let's look at a study by Jackson and Williams (1985). Although aware of the phenomenon of social loafing—individuals don't work as hard on tasks when they work in groups as when they work alone—Jackson and Williams felt that social loafing would not occur on extremely difficult tasks. Therefore, they did a study, which, like most social-loafing studies, manipulated whether participants worked alone or in groups. In addition, they added what they thought would be a moderating factor—whether the task was easy or difficult.

As expected, and as other studies had shown, social loafing occurred. But, social loafing occurred only when the task was easy. When the task was difficult, the reverse of social loafing occurred: Participants worked harder in groups than alone. This interaction between task difficulty and number of workers confirmed Jackson and Williams's hypothesis that task difficulty moderated social loafing (see Figure 12-6).

To see how you could take advantage of Jackson and Williams's research strategy, let's review what they did. With part of their study, they replicated an existing finding (the social-loafing main effect). With the other part, they tested whether another variable would moderate (interact with) the social-loafing main effect. If you like this strategy of proposing a study that tests both a safe prediction (e.g., a replication) and a risky prediction (e.g., an untested interaction), consider a moderating factor study. (For tips on designing a moderating factor study, see Chapter 3.)

Using Interactions to Create New Rules

Although we have discussed looking for an interaction to find an exception to an existing rule, some interactions do more than complicate existing rules. Some interactions reveal new rules. Consider Tversky's (1973) 2 × 2 factorial experiment. She randomly assigned students to one of four conditions:

1. Student expected a multiple-choice test and received a multiple-choice test.
2. Student expected a multiple-choice test and received an essay test.
3. Student expected an essay test and received a multiple-choice test.
4. Student expected an essay test and received an essay test.

Figure 12-7 **The Effect of Expectations and Type of Test on Performance**

She found an interaction between type of test expected and test received. Her interaction showed that participants did better when they got the *same* kind of test they expected (see Figure 12-7).

Similarly, a researcher might find an interaction between mood (happy, sad) at the time of learning and mood (happy, sad) at the time of recall. The interaction might reveal that recall was best when participants were in the *same* mood at the time of learning as they were at the time of recall. As you can see, the 2 × 2 experiment may be useful for you if you are interested in assessing the effects of *similarity*.

Conclusions About Putting the 2 × 2 Factorial Experiment to Work

As you have seen, expanding a simple experiment into a 2 × 2 experiment allows you to test more—and more interesting—hypotheses. You can look at the main effect of the factor you would have studied with the simple experiment, plus the main effect of an additional factor, plus the interaction between those two factors. In many cases, the hypothesis involving the interaction may be the most interesting.

Hybrid Designs: Factorial Designs That Allow You to Study Nonexperimental Variables

Rather than converting a simple experiment into a 2 × 2 experiment by adding a second experimental factor, you could convert a simple experiment into a 2 × 2 hybrid design by adding a nonexperimental factor. The nonexperimental factor could be any variable that you cannot randomly assign, such as age, gender, or personality type.

Hybrid Designs' Key Limitation: They Do Not Allow Cause–Effect Statements Regarding the Nonexperimental Factor

In such a hybrid 2 × 2 design, you could make cause–effect statements about the effects of the experimental factor, but *you could **not** make any cause–effect statements regarding the non-experimental factor.* Thus, although the study described in Table 12-12 includes gender of

Table 12-12	The Hybrid Design: A Cross Between an Experiment and a Nonexperiment

	MEN	WOMEN	GENDER SIMPLE MAIN "EFFECTS"
Not Excluded	10	12	2 (12 − 10 = 2)
Excluded	8	14	6 (14 − 8 = 6)
Exclusion simple main effects	−2 (8 − 10 = −2)	+2 (14 − 12 = +2)	

Averaging a factor's simple main effects gives us the factor's overall main effect:

Simple main effect of **Exclusion** for men	−2
Simple main effect of **Exclusion** for women	+2
Average effect (overall main effect) of **Exclusion**	0/2 = 0
Simple main "effect" of **Gender** in the not excluded condition	2
Simple main "effect" of **Gender** in the excluded condition	6
Average effect (overall main effect) of **Credit**	8/2 = 4

Comparing a treatment's simple main effects tells us whether there is an interaction: Because there are differences between exclusion's two simple main effects, there is no interaction. In other words, because the effect of exclusion is different for men than for women, there is an exclusion by gender interaction

Note that the hybrid 2 × 2 design answers two questions that the simple experiment does not:

1. Do male and female participants differ on the dependent variable? (Answered by the gender main effect.)

2. Is the effect of exclusion different in our sample of men than in our sample of women? (Answered by the gender by treatment interaction.)

participant as a variable, the study does not allow us to say anything about the effects of a participant's gender.

You can't make cause–effect (causal) statements regarding the effects of the participant's gender because your two groups may differ not only in terms of gender but also in hundreds of other ways. For example, they may differ in terms of college major, age, conscientiousness, self-esteem, loneliness, or experience working in teams. Any one of the hundreds of potential differences between the groups might be responsible for the difference in behavior between the two groups. Therefore, you cannot legitimately say that gender differences—rather than any of these other differences—caused your two groups to behave differently.

To help emphasize that you can make causal statements only about those independent variables that you randomly assign, randomly assigned variables are often called "true" independent variables or "strong" independent variables. In contrast, predictor variables that are not randomly assigned are called "weak" independent variables to highlight the fact that you can't determine whether they have an effect.

Reasons to Use Hybrid Designs

If you cannot make causal statements about the nonexperimental factor, why would you want to add a nonexperimental variable to your simple experiment? The most obvious and exciting reason is that you are interested in that nonexperimental variable.

Figure 12-8

The Effect of Being Angered on the Aggressiveness of Type A and Type B Personality Types

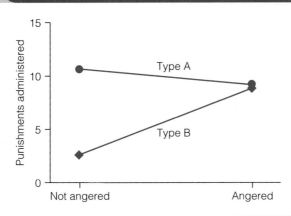

Source: From Holmes, D. S., & Will, M. J. (1985). Expression of interpersonal aggression by angered and nonangered persons with Type A and Type B behavior patterns, by D. S. Holmes and M. J. Will, 1985, *Journal of Personality and Social Psychology, 48,* 723–727.

To see how adding a nonexperimental variable (age of participant, introvert–extrovert, etc.) can spice up a simple experiment, consider the following simple experiment: Participants are either angered or not angered in a problem-solving task by a confederate who poses as another participant. Later, participants get an opportunity to punish or reward the confederate. Obviously, we would expect participants to punish the confederate more when they had been angered. This simple experiment, in itself, would not be very interesting.

Holmes and Will (1985) added a nonexperimental factor to this study—whether participants were Type A or Type B personalities. (People with Type A personalities are thought to be tense, hostile, and aggressive, whereas people with Type B personalities are thought to be more relaxed and less aggressive.) The results of this study were intriguing: If participants had *not* been angered, Type A participants were more likely to punish the confederate than Type B participants. However, if participants had been angered, Type A and Type B participants behaved similarly (see Figure 12-8).

Likewise, Hill (1991) could have done a relatively uninteresting simple experiment. He could have determined whether research participants are more likely to want to talk to a stranger if that stranger is supposed to be "warm" than if the stranger supposedly lacks warmth. The finding that people prefer to affiliate with nice people would not have been startling.

Fortunately, Hill conducted a more interesting study by adding another variable: need for affiliation. He found that participants who were high in need for affiliation were very likely to want to interact with an allegedly warm stranger, but very unlikely to want to interact with a stranger who allegedly lacked warmth. For low need for affiliation participants, on the other hand, the alleged warmth of the stranger made little difference.

As you have seen, adding a nonexperimental factor can make a study more interesting. As you will see in the next sections, you can add a nonexperimental variable to a simple experiment for most of the same reasons you would add an experimental variable: to increase the generalizability of the findings, to look for a similarity effect, and to look for a moderating factor. In addition, you may add a nonexperimental factor to increase your chances of finding a significant effect for your experimental factor.

Increasing Generalizability

You could increase the generalizability of a simple experiment that used only men as participants by (a) using both men and women as participants and then (b) making gender of the participant a factor in your design. This design would allow you to determine whether the effect held for both men and women.

Studying Effects of Similarity: The Matched Factors Design

If you were interested in similarity, you might include some participant characteristic (gender, status, etc.) as a factor in your design, while manipulating the comparable (matching) experimenter or confederate factor. For example, if you were studying helping behavior, you could use style of dress of the participant (well-dressed/casual) and style of dress of the confederate as factors in your design. You might find this interaction: Well-dressed participants were more likely to help confederates who were well-dressed, but casually dressed participants were more likely to help confederates who were dressed casually. This interaction would suggest that similarity of dress influences helping behavior (see Figure 12-9).

Finding an Exception to the Rule: The Moderating Factors Design

Looking for the effects of similarity is not the only reason you would want to examine interactions involving participant characteristics. As we mentioned earlier, you might look at interactions involving participants to see whether a treatment that works with one type of person is as effective with another type of person. The treatment could be any intervention—from a therapy technique to a teaching style.

For instance, if you thought that intelligence would be a moderating variable for the effectiveness of computerized instruction, you might use intelligence as a factor in your

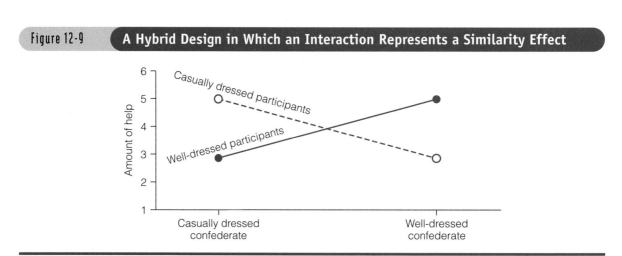

Figure 12-9 **A Hybrid Design in Which an Interaction Represents a Similarity Effect**

design. To do this, you would first give your participants an IQ test and then divide them into two groups (above-average intelligence and below-average intelligence). Next, you would randomly assign the high-intelligence group to condition so that half of them were in computerized instruction and half were in lecture instruction. You would do the same for the low-intelligence group.

This hybrid study might reveal some interesting findings. Suppose you found that computerized instruction substantially increases learning for low-IQ children but slightly decreases learning for high-IQ children. If you had done only a simple experiment, you might have found a significant positive effect for the new teaching technique. On that basis, you might have made the terrible mistake of recommending that computerized instruction be used to teach all children.

Boosting Power: The Blocked Design

Suppose you were solely interested in seeing whether instructional technique had an effect and you had no interest in either IQ or the interaction between IQ and instructional technique. Even then, you might still include IQ as a factor in your experiment. Specifically, before the study begins, you might divide your participants into two *blocks* (groups): the low-IQ block and the high-IQ block. Then, you would randomly assign each member of the high-IQ group to instruction condition, thereby ensuring that half of the high-IQ participants are assigned to the computerized instruction condition and half are assigned to the lecture condition. Next, you would randomly assign each member of the low-IQ block to instruction condition.

In other words, you would do exactly the same study that we just recommended you do if you were looking at IQ as a moderating factor. However, this study would be a **blocked design:** a factorial design in which, to boost power, participants are first divided into groups (blocks) on a participant variable (e.g., low-IQ block and high-IQ block) that is highly correlated with the dependent measure, and then participants from each block are randomly assigned to experimental condition.

The difference between doing this blocked design and doing the moderating factors study we just described is not *what* you are doing, but *why* you are doing it. If you are using a blocked design, you do not care about your blocking variable and you do not care about the interaction between your blocking variable and your treatment. You are using the blocking variable solely to boost your chances of finding a statistically significant effect for your treatment.

To understand how the blocking variable will increase your chances of finding the treatment's effect, you first have to understand that just like decreasing the amount of dust on a microscope's lens increases your chances of seeing differences between cells, decreasing error variance increases your chances of seeing differences between treatment conditions. Then, you have to understand that blocked designs reduce error variance.

To understand how blocked designs reduce error variance, realize what error variance is—variability that is not accounted for in your study. If you use a simple experiment, individual differences in IQ are not accounted for; consequently, any variations in scores due to individual differences in IQ contribute to error variance. If, on the other hand, you use a blocked design that blocks on IQ, you account for some of the variance due to individual differences in IQ, thereby reducing your error variance. In a sense, you use your blocking variable to soak up variance that would otherwise be error variance. By shrinking the error variance, you make your treatment's effect easier to spot.

Concluding Remarks

We hope that you understand how factorial designs can help you refine your existing research ideas and generate new research ideas. We know that understanding factorial designs, one of the most common research methods in psychology, will increase your ability to read, understand, and evaluate other people's research.

SUMMARY

1. Factorial experiments allow you to look at the effects of more than one independent variable at a time.

2. The simplest factorial experiment is the one that looks at the effects of only two levels of two independent variables: the 2 × 2 ("two by two") experiment.

3. In addition to allowing you to see the individual effects of two factors in one experiment, the 2 × 2 experiment allows you to see whether the factors' combined effects are different from the sum of their individual effects.

4. Whenever the effect of combining two independent variables is different from the sum of their individual effects, you have an interaction. In other words, an interaction occurs when one independent variable's effect depends on the level of a second (moderating) variable. For example, the independent variable may have one effect when the second factor is absent and a different effect when the second factor is present.

5. Interactions often indicate that a general rule does not always apply. For instance, a treatment × distraction interaction indicates that the treatment does not have the same effect on people who are being distracted as on people who are not being distracted.

6. Interactions can most easily be observed by graphing your data. If your two lines aren't parallel, you may have an interaction.

7. A significant interaction usually qualifies main effects. Thus, if you find a significant interaction, you can't talk about your main effects without referring to the interaction.

8. Sometimes, an interaction represents similarity. For instance, in a 2 (place of learning: basement or top floor) × 2 (place of testing: basement or top floor) factorial experiment, an interaction may reveal that it is best to be tested in the *same* place you learned the information.

9. The following summarizes the mathematics of an ANOVA summary table for a factorial design:

SOURCE OF VARIANCE (SV)	SUM OF SQUARES (SS)	DEGREES OF FREEDOM (df)	MEAN SQUARE (MS)	F
A	SS A	Levels of A − 1	SSA/df A	MSA/MSE
B	SS B	Levels of B − 1	SSB/df B	MSB/MSE
$A \times B$ Interaction	SS $(A \times B)$	df $A \times$ df B	SS/df	MS $(A \times B)$/MSE
Error	SSE	Participants − Groups	SSE/df E	
Total	SS A + SS B + SS(AXB) + SSE	Participants − 1		

10. With the hybrid factorial design, you can look at an experimental factor and a factor that you do not manipulate (personality, gender, age) in the same study. However, because you did not manipulate the nonexperimental factor, you cannot say that you know anything about the effects of your nonexperimental factor.

11. Once you have an idea for a simple experiment, you can easily expand that idea into an idea for a factorial experiment. For example, you could add a replication factor (such as stimulus set) to try to establish the generalizability of your treatment's effect. In that case, you would not be expecting a significant interaction. Alternatively, if you wanted

to show that the treatment didn't have the same effect under all circumstances, you could add a potential moderating variable. In that case, you would be expecting a significant interaction between the treatment and the factor that you believe will moderate its effect.

12. If you have a nonmanipulated factor (e.g., participant's age), you can look at differences between groups on this factor. However, even though these differences are called main effects of the factor, do not make the mistake of thinking that these differences represent effects of the factor.

KEY TERMS

factorial experiment *(p. 352)*

simple main effect *(p. 355)*

overall main effect *(p. 357)*

interaction *(p. 358)*

crossover (disordinal) interaction *(p. 372)*

systematic replication *(p. 381)*

stimulus set *(p. 381)*

blocked design *(p. 387)*

EXERCISES

1. What is the difference between
   a. a simple main effect and an overall main effect?
   b. an overall main effect and an interaction?

2. Can you have an interaction without a main effect?

3. Suppose an experimenter looked at the status of speaker and rate of speech on attitude change and summarized the experiment's results in the following table. Describe the pattern of those results in terms of main effects and interactions. Assume that all differences are statistically significant.

	STATUS OF SPEAKER	
Rate of Speech	**Low Status**	**High Status**
Slow	10	15
Fast	20	25

Attitude Change

4. Describe the pattern of results in the following table in terms of main effects and interactions. Assume that all differences are statistically significant.

	STATUS OF SPEAKER	
Rate of Speech	**Low Status**	**High Status**
Slow	10	15
Fast	20	30

Attitude Change

5. Half the participants receive a placebo. The other half receive a drug that blocks the effect of endorphins (pain-relieving substances, similar to morphine, that are produced by the brain). Half the placebo group and half the drug group get acupuncture. Then, all participants are asked to rate the pain of various shocks on a 1-to-10 (*not at all painful* to *very painful*) scale. The results are as follows: placebo, no acupuncture group, 7.2; placebo, acupuncture group, 3.3; drug, no acupuncture group, 7.2; drug and acupuncture group, 3.3.
   a. Graph the results.
   b. Describe the results in terms of main effects and interactions (making a table of the data may help).
   c. What conclusions would you draw?

6. The following table is an incomplete ANOVA summary table of a study looking at the effects of similarity and attractiveness on liking. Complete

the table. (Hint: If you are having trouble, consult Box 12-2 or the sample ANOVA summary table in Summary point 9.) Then, answer these three questions.

a. How many participants were used in the study?

b. How many levels of similarity were used?

c. How many levels of attractiveness were used?

SV	SS	df	MS	F
Similarity (S)	10	1	—	—
Attractiveness (A)	—	2	20	—
S × A interaction	400	—	200	—
Error	540	54	—	
Total	990	59		

7. A professor does a simple experiment. In that experiment, the professor finds that students who are given lecture notes do better than students who are not given lecture notes. Imagine that you are asked to replicate the professor's simple experiment as a 2 × 2 factorial.

a. What variable would you add to change the simple experiment into a 2 × 2?

b. Graph your predictions.

c. Describe your predictions in terms of main effects and interactions.

8. A lab experiment on motivation yielded the following results:

GROUP	PRODUCTIVITY
No financial bonus, no encouragement	25%
No financial bonus, encouragement	90%
Financial bonus, no encouragement	90%
Financial bonus, encouragement	90%

a. Make a 2 × 2 table of these data.

b. Graph these data (for help with graphing, see Box 12-1).

c. Describe the results in terms of main effects and interactions. Assume that all differences are statistically significant.

d. Interpret the results.

9. A memory researcher looks at the effects of processing time and rehearsal strategy on memory.

GROUP	PERCENT CORRECT
Short exposure, simple strategy	20%
Short exposure, complex strategy	15%
Long exposure, simple strategy	25%
Long exposure, complex strategy	80%

a. Graph these data.

b. Describe the results in terms of main effects and interactions. Assume that all differences are statistically significant.

c. Interpret the results.

10. Suppose a researcher wanted to know whether lecturing was more effective than group discussion for teaching basic facts. Therefore, the researcher did a study and obtained the following results:

SOURCE OF VARIANCE	SS	df	MS	F
Teaching (T)	10	1	10	5
Introversion/ Extroversion (I)	20	1	20	10
T × I interaction	50	1	50	25
Error	100	50	2	

a. What does the interaction seem to indicate?

b. Even if there had been no interaction between teaching and extroversion, would there be any value in including the introversion–extroversion variable? Explain.

c. What, if anything, can you conclude about the effects of introversion on learning?

WEB RESOURCES

1. Go to the Chapter 12 section of the book's student website and do the following:

a. Look over the concept map of the key terms.

b. Test yourself on the key terms.

c. Take the Chapter 12 Practice Quiz.

2. Download the Chapter 12 tutorial to practice the following:

a. interpreting ANOVA tables

b. interpreting graphs of results of factorial experiments

3. Do an ANOVA using a statistical calculator by going to the "Statistical Calculator" link.

INFOTRAC COLLEGE EDITION EXPLORATIONS

1. Do an InfoTrac College Edition keyword search using the phrase "factorial experiments and psychology" to read Turnbull and Wolfson's (2002) interesting study on exercise, feedback, and mood.

2. Do an InfoTrac College Edition keyword search using the phrase "factorial experiments and advertising" to read Goldberg and Hartwick's factorial experiment (1990) on variables that affect advertising's effectiveness and Shepherd's (1997) article on how and why direct mail marketers should use factorial experiments.

3. Do an InfoTrac College Edition keyword search using the phrase "hand gestures and recall" to find Frick-Horbury and Guttentag's (1998) hybrid factorial study of the effects of limiting hand gestures on recall for both low- and high-SAT students.

13

Matched Pairs, Within-Subjects, and Mixed Designs

The art of being wise is the art of knowing what to overlook.

—*WILLIAM JAMES*

Overview

In Chapters 10, 11, and 12, you learned that you could perform an internally valid experiment by independently and randomly assigning participants to groups. Although you understand the logic of randomly assigning participants to groups, you may still have two basic reservations about between-subjects designs.

First, you may believe that these designs are wasteful in terms of the number of participants they require. For example, in the simple experiment, each participant is either in the control group *or* in the experimental group. If each participant was in both the control group *and* the experimental group, one participant could do the job of two.

Second, you may be concerned that between-subject designs are not powerful enough. You may believe that between-subject differences may hide treatment effects that would be detected if each participant acted as his or her own control. For example, suppose you use a simple experiment to examine the effect of a video game "The Sims" on cooperation. If playing "The Sims" makes the video game group slightly more cooperative than the comparison group, this effect may be overlooked because the small difference may be dismissed as just being due to random differences between the two groups. If, on the other hand, we use each participant as his or her own control, the difference that the treatment created between the two conditions could not be dismissed as being due to random differences between the two groups. Consequently, the treatment's effect might be detected and found to be statistically significant.

You are rightfully concerned about the twin weaknesses of between-subjects experiments: They require many participants and have relatively little power. In this chapter, you will learn about designs that address these twin weaknesses: the matched-pairs design (a special type of between-subjects design), and two types of within-subjects designs (sometimes called a "repeated measures design"): the randomized within-subject design and the counterbalanced within-subjects design.

In the matched-pairs design, you first reduce between-subject differences by matching pairs of participants on a key characteristic. Then, you let random assignment and statistics take care of the effects of the remaining differences between subjects.

In the randomized within-subjects design, you avoid the problem of between-subject differences by using participants as their own controls. Then, you let randomization take care of the effects of the remaining uncontrolled variables. By limiting the variables that randomization has to account for, the pure within-subjects design—like the matched-pairs design—often has impressive power. For all its power, however, the randomized within-subjects design has some serious weaknesses. To build on its power but avoid those weaknesses, many researchers use what they consider a refinement of the randomized within-subjects design—the counterbalanced within-subjects design.

After learning about the two main types of pure within-subjects designs, you will learn about **mixed designs:** designs in which at least one factor is a within-subjects factor, and at least one factor is a between-subjects factor. Thus, in mixed designs, all participants get all levels of the within-subjects factor(s), but different participants get different levels of the between-subject factor(s). Mixed designs are popular because they can have both the power of a within-subjects and the strengths of a between-subjects design.

Finally, you will learn how to weigh the tradeoffs involved in choosing among various experimental designs. Thus, by the end of this chapter, you will be better able to choose the best experimental design for your research problem.

The Matched-Pairs Design

If you do not have enough participants to do a powerful simple experiment, you might use a design, such as a matched-pairs design, that requires fewer participants. As you will see, the **matched-pairs design** combines the best aspects of matching and random assignment: It uses matching to reduce the effects of irrelevant variables, and it uses random assignment to establish internal validity.

Procedure

In the matched-pairs design, you first measure your participants on a variable that correlates with the dependent measure. For example, if you were measuring memory, your matching variable could be education, IQ, or scores on a memory test. After getting scores from all your participants on a measure of the matching variable, you would consider the two lowest scorers to be a matched pair, the next lowest scorers to be another matched pair, and so on until you had matched up all the participants. Thus, if you were doing a memory experiment using a matched-pairs design, you might first give all your participants a memory test. Next, you would rank their scores on this memory test from lowest to highest. Then, you would pair the two highest scorers, the next two highest scorers, and so on. This would give you pairs of participants with similar scores on the memory pretest. Finally, you would randomly assign one member of each pair to the control group and the other member to the experimental group (e.g., you might assign random numbers to all the participants and then put the member of the pair with the higher random number in the experimental condition and the lower-scoring member in the control condition).

Considerations in Using Matched-Pairs Designs

You now have a general idea of how to conduct a matched-pairs experiment. You also know how it compares to a simple experiment: Unlike a simple experiment, it uses matching; like a simple experiment, it uses random assignment (see Table 13-1). But should you use a matched-pairs experiment instead of a simple experiment? When considering a matched-pairs design, you should consider four questions:

1. Can you find an effective matching variable?
2. Will matching give you more power?
3. Will matching harm external validity?
4. Will matching harm construct validity?

Table 13-1   **Comparing the Matched Design with the Simple Experiment**

MATCHED DESIGN	SIMPLE EXPERIMENT
First, *match* participants on key characteristics.	*No matching.*
Then, *randomly assign* each member of the pair to condition.	*Randomly assign* participants to condition.

Finding an Effective Matching Variable

As we suggested earlier, you can make effective use of the matched-pairs design only if you can create pairs that are very similar to each other in terms of the dependent measure. The most direct way to get such pairs is to start your study by giving all the participants the dependent measure as a pretest and then matching participants based on their pretest scores. Thus, in a memory experiment, participants could be matched based on scores on an earlier memory test; in a maze-running experiment, participants could be matched based on scores on an earlier maze-running trial.

If you cannot match on pretest scores, you may have to search the research literature (see Web Appendix B) to find a matching variable. If you are lucky, you will find matching variables that other researchers have used. More likely, however, you will find out what variables correlate with your dependent measure. Unfortunately, after doing your library research, you may find that (a) there are no variables that have a strong, documented relationship with performance on the dependent measure, or that (b) there are good matching variables, but for ethical or practical reasons you cannot use them.

Power

You want to find an appropriate matching variable so that your study will have adequate **power:** the ability to find differences between conditions. Indeed, the reason you may choose a matched-pairs design is to avoid the power problems that plague researchers who use other types of between-subject designs.

As we discussed in Chapter 10, researchers who rely exclusively on random assignment to make groups similar lose power because individual differences between participants hide treatment effects. Specifically, because participants differ from each other, between-subjects researchers can't assume that the treatment group and the no-treatment group are extremely similar before the start of the experiment—especially if the groups are small. Consequently, if the groups differ at the end of the experiment, these researchers may not know whether this difference is due to the treatment or to the groups being different before the experiment began. Indeed, if a simple experiment has fewer than 30 participants, even a large difference between the treatment and no-treatment groups could be entirely due to random error.

If matching makes your groups extremely similar to each other before the experiment begins, then there isn't much random error due to individual differences to hide your treatment effects. Therefore, the same, small difference that would not be statistically significant with a simple experiment may be significant with a matched-pairs design.

How can a matched-pairs design give you more power than a simple experiment? The key, as we mentioned before, is that the matched-pairs design reduces random error, allowing the treatment effect to be seen as statistically significant. Mathematically, the matched pairs design is more likely to find a statistically significant treatment effect because (a) the reduced random error results in larger t values and (b) larger t values are more likely to be statistically significant.

Why would the t value be larger in a matched-pairs design? The answer lies in the fact that the t value equals the difference between the means of the two conditions divided by an estimate of random error (the standard error of the difference). So, *with less random error, the t value becomes larger* (and thus more likely to be statistically significant). For example, if the standard error of the difference for a simple experiment is 6 seconds, then a difference of 6 seconds between conditions would yield a t value of 1.0 (because 6/6 = 1.0)—a t value too low to be statistically significant. However, if a matched-pairs design reduced random error so much that the standard error of the difference was only 1.0, then that same difference of

6 seconds would yield a *t* value of 6.0 (because 6/1 = 6.0)—a *t* value that would probably be statistically significant. In other words, if matching limits the effects of individual differences, you may be able to find relatively small treatment effects.

But what if matching fails to reduce random error? For example, suppose a researcher matched participants on shoe size. In that case, the *t* value will be roughly the same as it would have been in the simple experiment because matching hasn't reduced the amount of random error in the study. In that case, the matched-pairs design would then be *less powerful* than the simple experiment.

To understand why poor matching leads to a matched-pairs design that is less powerful than a simple experiment, you need to know two facts: (1) Matched-pairs designs have half the degrees of freedom of a same-sized simple experiment, and (2) all other things being equal, fewer degrees of freedom means less power. We'll now take a closer look at these two facts.

By using a matched-pairs design instead of a simple experiment, you lose half your degrees of freedom because, whereas degrees of freedom for a simple experiment equals number of *participants* − 2, the degrees of freedom for a matched-pairs study equals number of *pairs* − 1. Thus, if you used 20 participants in a simple experiment, you would have 18 degrees of freedom (two fewer than the number of participants). But if you used 20 participants (10 pairs) in a matched-pairs design, you would have only 9 degrees of freedom (one fewer than the number of pairs).

Critical Values of *t*

LEVEL OF SIGNIFICANCE FOR TWO-TAILED *t* TEST

df	.05
1	12.706
9	2.262
18	2.101
60	2.000
120	1.980

Losing degrees of freedom can cause you to lose power. As you can see by looking at this mini *t* table, the fewer degrees of freedom you have, the larger your *t* value must be to reach significance. For example, with 18 degrees of freedom (what you'd have if you tested 20 participants in a simple experiment), you would need only a *t* value of 2.101 for your results to be statistically significant at the .05 level. On the other hand, with 9 degrees of freedom (what you'd have if you tested 20 participants [10 pairs of participants] in a matched-pairs experiment), your *t* value would have to be at least 2.262 to be statistically significant at the .05 level. That is, a difference between your treatment conditions that would have been big enough to be statistically significant if you had used a simple experiment might not be statistically significant with a matched-pairs design in which you matched on a variable that did not correlate with your measure. Thus, if you obtained the same t value with the matched-pairs design as you would have obtained with a simple experiment, then the matched-pairs design cost you power.

If your matching is any good, however, you should not get the same *t* value with a matched-pairs design as with a simple experiment. Instead, you will get a larger *t* value with a matched-pairs design because you have reduced a factor that shrinks *t* values—random error due to differences between participants. Usually, the increase in the size of the *t* value will more than compensate for the degrees of freedom you will lose. Thus, as long as you can match participants on a relevant variable, you will get more power by switching from a simple experiment to a matched-pairs design.

External Validity

Power is not the only consideration in deciding to use a matched-pairs design. You may use—or avoid—matching for reasons of external validity.

Matched-Pairs Designs May Have Good External Validity. A matched-pairs design may have more external validity than an equally powerful simple experiment. Why? Because unlike the simple experiment, the matched-pairs design can have power without limiting who can be in the experiment.

To obtain adequate power, a researcher using a simple experiment may have to severely restrict the kind of individual who can be in the study. That is, to reduce the degree to which differences between participants create random differences between treatment and no-treatment groups, the experimenter may be forced to use participants who are all very similar. For example, to create a simple experiment that would be as powerful as a matched-pairs design, an experimenter might need to limit participants to male, albino rats between 180 and 185 days of age. Another researcher might attempt to reduce random error due to individual differences by allowing only middle-class women with IQs between 115 and 120 to be in the experiment.

With a matched-pairs design, however, you can reduce random differences between the treatment and no-treatment groups without choosing participants who are all alike. Because you can reduce random error by matching up the participants you do have rather than by limiting the kinds of participants you can have, the matched-pairs design may allow you to generalize your results to a broader population.

Matched-Pairs Designs May Have Poor External Validity. Matched-pairs designs, however, do not always have better external validity than simple experiments. For example, if participants drop out of the study between the time they are tested on the matching variable and the time they are to perform the experiment, matching will reduce the generalizability of your results. For instance, suppose you start off with 16 matched pairs, but end up with only 10 pairs. In that case, your experiment's external validity is compromised because your results may not apply to individuals resembling the participants who dropped out of your experiment.

Even if participants do not drop out, matching may still harm external validity because your results generalize only to situations in which individuals perform the matching task before getting the treatment. To illustrate, imagine that an experimenter uses a matched-pairs design to examine the effect of caffeine on anxiety. In that experiment, participants take an anxiety test, then either consume caffeine (the experimental group) or do not (the control group), and then take the anxiety test again. Suppose that the participants receiving caffeine become more anxious than those not receiving caffeine.

Can the investigator generalize her results to people who have not taken an anxiety test before consuming caffeine? No, it may be that caffeine increases anxiety only when it is consumed after taking an anxiety test. For example, taking the anxiety test may make participants so concerned about their level of anxiety that they interpret any increase in arousal as an increase in anxiety. Because of the anxiety test, the arousal produced by caffeine—which might ordinarily be interpreted as invigorating—is interpreted as anxiety.

Construct Validity

In the caffeine study we just discussed, taking the anxiety test before and after the treatment might make participants aware that the experimenter is looking at the effects of a drug on anxiety. The participants' awareness of the hypothesis may harm the study's construct validity. For example, if participants believe that the hypothesis is that the drug will increase anxiety, they may act more anxious to help the researcher prove the hypothesis.

However, the fact that participants guess the hypothesis does not, by itself, ruin the experiment's construct validity. For instance, if you used a treatment condition and a placebo condition, it does not matter whether participants think that taking a pill is supposed to increase anxiety. Because both groups have the same hypothesis ("The pill I took will increase my anxiety"), knowing the hypothesis would not cause the treatment group to differ from the placebo group. Therefore, a significant difference between groups would have to be due to the treatment (the drug in the treatment group's pill).

If, on the other hand, your independent variable manipulation has poor construct validity, matching will make your manipulation's weaknesses more damaging. To see how matching can magnify a manipulation's weaknesses, imagine that the caffeine study used an empty control group (nothing was given to the participants who did not receive the treatment). The experimental group participants fill out an anxiety measure, take a pill, and then fill out another anxiety measure. The experimental group participants might think that the pill is supposed to increase their anxiety level, thereby causing them to be more anxious—or at least, to report being more anxious. The control group participants, not having been given a pill, would not expect to become more anxious. Consequently, a significant difference between the groups might be due to the two groups acting on different beliefs about what the researchers expected, rather than to any ingredient in the pill.

Analysis of Data

We have talked about how matching, by making your study powerful, can help you obtain a significant difference. We have also warned you about external validity and construct validity problems that should make you cautious when interpreting such significant differences. But how do you know whether you have a significant difference?

As we have already suggested, you cannot use a regular, between-subjects t test. That test compares the overall, average score of the treatment group with the overall, average score of the no-treatment group.

With a matched-pairs design, you need a test that will allow you to compare the score of one member of a matched pair directly with the score of the other member—and to make that comparison for each of your pairs. If you have ratio or interval scale data,[1] you can make those comparisons using the **dependent groups t test.**[2] If you plan to do a dependent groups t test by hand, see Appendix D. If you plan to have a computer do a dependent groups t test for you, see Box 13-1.

---

[1] If you have only ordinal data, you should use the sign test. If you don't know what type of data you have, consult Chapter 5.
[2] You can also analyze such data using a within-subjects ANOVA (see Box 13-2).

BOX 13-1   Using the Computer to Conduct a Dependent Groups *t* Test

When looking for a computer program to do an analysis on a matched pairs design or on a two-condition within-subjects design, realize that the test you are using may go by at least five names: (a) *t* test for correlated samples, (b) *t* test for dependent samples, (d) *t* test for paired samples, (d) repeated measures *t* test, and (d) within-subjects *t*. Realize also that you are not limited to using a t test. For example, you could compute a within-subjects analysis of variance (see Box 13-2).

  If you use a *t* test, the computer should provide you with at least three sets of information. First, it should tell you the number of observations you had in each condition. Thus, if you had four scores for condition 1, it should tell you that "*n*" for condition 1 was 4. Second, it should give you the mean (*M*) and the standard deviation (*SD*) for each condition. Third, it should give you the *t* value, the degrees of freedom (*df*) for the test, and the two-tailed probability (*p*) of obtaining a difference that great or greater between your two means if the null hypothesis were true. For

example, a printout might look like the following two tables.

	CONDITION **1**	CONDITION **2**
n	4	4
M	6.25	2.5
SD	0.957	1.291
t	*df*	two-tailed *p*
15	3	.0006

  You might report such results as follows.[a] "As predicted, significantly more words were recalled in the treatment condition ($M = 6.25$, $SD = 0.95$) than in the control condition ($M = 2.5$, $SD = 1.29$), $t(3) = 15.0$, $p < .05$."

[a]*M* stands for mean, *SD* stands for standard deviation (a measure of the variability of the scores), and *p* stands for the probability of obtaining a difference between conditions at least that large if the treatment had no effect. *SD* will usually be calculated as part of computing *t* (for more about *SD*, see Appendix D).

BOX 13-2   Using the Computer to Conduct a Within-Subjects Analysis of Variance

If you had conducted a matched pairs study or a two-condition within-subjects study, you could analyze your data using a dependent groups *t* test (see Box 13-1) or a within-subjects ANOVA. If, instead of using the dependent groups *t* test as we did in Box 13-1, we used a within-subjects ANOVA, we would get similar results. For example, our printout might look like the following one.

DESCRIPTIVE STATISTICS

	CONDITION **1**	CONDITION **2**
n	4	4
M	6.25	2.5
SD	0.957	1.291

WITHIN SUBJECTS ANOVA TABLE

SOURCE	SS	df	MS	F	p
Treatment	27.68	1	27.68	225	.0006
Error	0.37	3	0.123		

  If you compare this ANOVA printout with the within-subjects printout in Box 13-1, you will note three similarities. First, the table listing the descriptive

statistics in the within-subjects ANOVA printout is identical to the table listing the descriptive statistics in the within-subjects *t*-test printout. The computer reports the same number of observations per condition, the same average for each condition, and the same variability of scores within each condition, regardless of whether you use a within-subjects *t* test or a within-subjects ANOVA.

  Second, the *p* value for the treatment (.0006) is identical to the within-subjects ANOVA table as it is in the within-subjects *t* test. Both tests are equally likely to find a significant result.

  Third, the *df* error (3) is the same as the *df* for the *t*. In both cases, *df* equals number of participants minus two.

  Even the differences between the printouts reveal similarities. For example, the *F* value (225) is the *t* value (15) squared.

  Given the similarities between the two types of analyses, you probably will not be surprised to learn that they would be written up similarly. Thus, you might report the above-described results as follows. "As predicted, significantly more words were recalled in

continued

the treatment condition ($M = 6.25$, $SD = 0.95$) than in the control condition ($M = 2.5$, $SD = 1.29$), $F(1,3) = 225.0$, $p < .05$."

If you had more than two levels of your independent variable, you could not use a within-subjects t test to analyze your data. You could, however, analyze such data with a multiple level within-subjects ANOVA.

If you were to analyze such data with a multiple-level within-subjects ANOVA, your printout might resemble the printout of a two-level within-subjects ANOVA. Indeed, the most noticeable difference would be that your degrees of freedom will be different. For example, If you have 3 levels of the treatment, your treatment df will be 2.

As we have suggested, if you switch from looking at the printout of a two-level within-subjects design to looking at the printout of a three-level within-subjects design, you probably will not see a big difference. However, if you switch from looking at the printout from one computer program to another, you may notice a big difference. For example, in one program, a three-level, within-subjects ANOVA printout might look like the following printout.

WITHIN SUBJECTS **ANOVA** TABLE

SOURCE	SS	df	MS	F	p
Treatment	12.133	2	6.067	26	.0001
Error	1.867	8	0.233		

GENERAL LINEAR MODELS PROCEDURE

REPEATED MEASURES ANALYSIS OF VARIANCE

UNIVARIATE TESTS OF HYPOTHESES FOR WITHIN-SUBJECTS EFFECTS

SOURCE: TREATMENT

df	TYPE III SUM OF SQUARES (ss)	MEAN SQUARE	F VALUE	PR > F[a]	GEISSER GREENHOUSE EPSILON PROB LEVEL[b] (G-T)	HUYNH FELDT EPSILON PROB LEVEL (H-F)
2	12.33	6.067	26	0.0001	0.0001	0.0001

[a] The value in this column corresponds to the p value or significance level that most programs give you.
[b] The probability value in this column or in the next column should be used if certain assumptions of the within-subjects ANOVA have been violated.

However, the same analysis in another program might look like the table below—minus the footnotes. We added the footnotes to help you decipher the table.

TESTS OF WITHIN-SUBJECTS EFFECTS

MEASURE

SOURCE	TYPE III SUM OF SQUARES (ss)[a]	df	MEAN SQUARE[b]	F[c]	SIG.[d]
Treatment	12.133	2[e]	6.067	26	.000
Error (Treatment)	1.867	8	.233		

[a] Treat this column like the previous table's sum of squares (SS) column.
[b] Mean Square is calculated by dividing the Sum of Squares (12.133) by the df (2).
[c] $F = MS$ for the effect divided by MS error. The bigger F is, the more likely the results are to be statistically significant.
[d] This column represents how likely it is that one would obtain a result this large or larger if the null hypothesis were true. Traditionally, when the value in this column is less than .05, the results are considered "statistically significant."
[e] If there are 2 degrees of freedom (df), then there must be three levels of the "treatment" variable.

In yet another program, the printout might look like the following table—minus the footnotes. (We added the footnotes to help you decipher the table.)

Table 13-2	Advantages and Disadvantages of Matching

ADVANTAGES	DISADVANTAGES
More power because matching reduces the effects of differences between participants.	Matching makes more work for the researcher.
Power is not bought at the cost of restricting the subject population. Thus, results may, in some cases, be generalized to a wide variety of participants.	Matching may alert participants to the experimental hypothesis.
	Results cannot be generalized to participants who drop out after the matching task.
	The results may not apply to individuals who have not been exposed to the matching task prior to getting the treatment.

Conclusions About the Matched-Pairs Design

In summary, the matched-pairs design's weaknesses stem from matching (see Table 13-2). If you can't find an effective matching variable, matching may actually hurt power. If matching alerts participants to the purpose of your experiment, matching may hurt your construct validity. If participants drop out of the experiment between the time they are measured on the matching variable and the time they are to be given the treatment, matching costs you the ability to generalize your results to the participants who dropped out. Finally, even if participants do not get suspicious and do not drop out, matching still costs you time and energy.

Although matching has its costs, matching usually offers one big advantage—power without restricting your subject population. Because the matched pairs design combines the power of matching with the internal validity promoting properties of random assignment, the matched pairs design is hard to beat when you can study only a few participants.

Within-Subjects (Repeated Measures) Designs

One set of designs that can beat the matched-pairs design, at least in terms of power, are the **within-subjects designs** (also called **repeated-measures designs**). In all within-subjects designs, each participant receives all the levels or types of the treatment that the experimenter administers, and the participant is measured after receiving each level or type of treatment. In the simplest case, each subject would receive only two levels of treatment: no treatment and the treatment. For example, a participant might get no treatment, complete the dependent-measure task, get a treatment, and repeat the dependent-measure task again. The experimenter would estimate the effect of the treatment by comparing how each participant scored when receiving the treatment with how that same participant scored when not receiving the treatment.

Considerations in Using Within-Subjects Designs

You now have a general idea of how a within-subjects (repeated measures) experiment differs from a between-subjects design (for a review, see Table 13-3). But what do you have to gain—or lose—by using a within-subjects design instead of a between-subjects design? As you'll soon see, by using a within-subjects design instead of a between subjects design, you will gain power; however, you may lose internal validity.

Table 13-3	**Comparing Three Designs**		
	BETWEEN SUBJECTS	MATCHED-PAIRS DESIGN	WITHIN-SUBJECTS
Role of random assignment	Randomly assign participants to treatment condition.	Randomly assign members of each pair to condition.	Randomly assign to sequence of treatment conditions.
Approach to dealing with the problem that differences between participants may cause differences between the treatment and no-treatment conditions.	Allow random assignment and statistics to account for any differences between conditions that could be due to individual differences.	Use matching to reduce the extent to which differences between conditions could be due to individual differences. Then, use random assignment and statistics to deal with the effects of individual differences that were not eliminated by matching.	Avoid the problem of individual differences causing differences between conditions by comparing each participant's performance in one condition with his or her performance in the other condition(s).

Increased Power

Despite potential problems with the within-subjects design's internal validity, the within-subjects design is extremely popular because it increases power in two ways.

The first way is similar to how the matched-pairs design increases power—by reducing random error. As you may recall, the matched-pairs experimenter tries to reduce random error by reducing individual differences by comparing similar participants with one another. Within-subjects experimenters are even more ambitious: They want to eliminate random error due to individual differences. Therefore, they do not compare one participant with another participant; instead, they compare each participant's score under one condition with that same participant's score under another condition.

The second way the within-subjects design increases power is by increasing the number of observations you get from each participant. The more observations you have, the more random error will tend to balance out; the more random error balances out, the more power you will have. With between-subjects designs, the only way you can get more observations is to get more participants because you can only get one observation per participant. But in a within-subjects experiment, you get at least two scores out of each participant. In the simplest case, your participants serve double duty by being in both the control and experimental conditions. In more complex within-subjects experiments, your participants might do triple, quadruple, or even octuple duty. In short, in within-subjects experiments, you can get more data with fewer participants.

Order Effects May Harm Internal Validity

As you intuitively realize, the main advantage of within-subjects designs is their impressive power. By comparing each participant with him or herself, even subtle treatment effects may be statistically significant.

However, as you may also intuitively realize, the problem with comparing participants with themselves is that, even without the treatment, participants may change over time.

Table 13-4	In A Within-Subjects Design, the Treatment May Not Be the Only Factor Being Manipulated	
	EVENTS THAT OCCUR BEFORE BEING TESTED	
	Drug 1 Condition	**Drug 2 Condition**
Between-Subjects Experiment	Get Drug 1	Get Drug 2
Within-Subjects Design	Get Drug 1	Get Drug 1
		Play Video Game
		Get Drug 2

Consequently, the **order** (first or last) in which an event occurs within a sequence of events can be very important. For example, the lecture that might have been fascinating had it been the first lecture you heard that day might be only tolerable if it is your fourth class of the day. Because order affects responses, if a participant reacts differently to the first treatment than to the last, we have a dilemma: Do we have a treatment effect or an order effect?

To get a better idea of how **order (trial) effects** can complicate within-subjects experiments, let's examine a within-subjects experiment. Imagine being a participant in a within-subjects experiment where you take a drug (e.g., caffeine), play a video game, take a second drug (e.g., aspirin), and play the video game again.

If you perform differently on the video game the second time around, can the experimenters say that the second drug has a different effect than the first drug? No. The experimenters can't safely make conclusions about the difference between the two drugs because they are comparing your performance on trial 1, when you had been exposed to only one treatment (drug 1), to your performance on trial 2, by which time you had been exposed to three "treatments": (1) drug 1, (2) playing the game, and (3) drug 2 (see Table 13-4).

Four Sources of Order Effects

In the next few sections, you will see how being exposed to "treatments" other than the second drug can hurt the study's internal validity. We will start by showing you how the variable of *order* (first trial versus second trial) may affect your performance. Specifically, we will look at four nontreatment reasons why you may perform differently on the task after the second treatment:

1. You may do better after the second treatment because you are performing the dependent-measure task a second time. For example, the practice you got playing the game after the first drug may help you when you play the game again.

2. You may do worse after the second treatment because you are bored or tired with the dependent-measure task.

3. You may score differently because you are experiencing some delayed or lingering effects of the first treatment.

4. You may have figured out the experimental hypothesis right after you received the second treatment.

In summary, you need to be aware that the order in which participants get a treatment may affect the results. Thus, Treatment A may appear to have one kind of effect when it comes first, but may appear to have a different kind of effect when it comes second.

Practice Effects

If you perform better after the second treatment than you did after the first treatment, your improvement may merely reflect **practice effects:** You may have learned from the first trial. The first trial, in effect, trained you how to play the video game—although that wasn't the researcher's plan. Not surprisingly, practice effects are common: Participants often perform better as they warm up to the experimental environment and get accustomed to the experimental task. Unfortunately, rather than seeing that you improved because of practice, the researcher may mistakenly believe that you improved due to the treatment.

Fatigue Effects

If your performance is not enhanced by practice, it may decline due to **fatigue effects.**[3] You may do worse on later trials merely because you are becoming tired or less enthusiastic as the experiment goes on. Unfortunately, a researcher might interpret your fatigue as a treatment effect.

Treatment Carryover Effects

Practice and fatigue effects have nothing to do with any of the treatments participants receive. Often, practice and fatigue effects are simply due to getting more exposure to the dependent-measure task. Thus, in the video game example, performance may improve as you learn the game or worsen as you get bored with the game. However, exposure to the dependent measure is not the only thing that can affect performance in later trials. The effects of a treatment received before the first trial may affect responses in later trials. The effects of an earlier treatment on responses in later trials are called **carryover (treatment carryover) effects.**

To imagine treatment carryover effects, suppose that on Trial 1, the researcher gave you a tranquilizer and then measured your video game performance. On Trial 2, the researcher gave you an antidepressant and measured your video game performance. On Trial 3, the researcher gave you a placebo and measured your video game performance. If your performance was worst in the placebo (no-drug) condition, the researcher might think that your better performance on earlier trials was due to the drugs improving your performance. The researcher, however, could be wrong. Your poor performance in the placebo condition may be due to carryover effects from the previous treatments: You may just be starting to feel certain effects of the drugs that you consumed during the earlier trials. Depending on the time between the trials, you may be feeling either "high" or hungover.

Sensitization Effects

A fourth factor that might cause you to perform differently after the second treatment is **sensitization.** Sensitization occurs when, after getting several different treatments and performing the dependent variable task several times, participants realize (become sensitive to) what the independent and dependent variables are, and thus, during the latter parts of the

---

[3]Fatigue effects could be viewed as cases in which performance is hurt by practice, whereas practice effects could be viewed as cases in which performance is improved by practice.

experiment, guess the experimental hypothesis and play along with it. For example, by the third trial of the video game experiment, you should realize that the experiment had something to do with the effects of drugs on video game performance.

Note that sensitization has two effects. First, it threatens construct validity because participants figure out what the hypothesis is and thus may be acting to support the hypothesis rather than reacting to the treatment. Second, it threatens internal validity because it makes participants behave differently during the last trial (when they know the hypothesis) than they did during the first trial (when they did not know the hypothesis).

Review of the Four Sources of Order Effects

You have seen that because of practice, fatigue, carryover, and sensitization, the sequence in which participants receive the treatments could affect the results. For example, suppose participants all received the treatments in this sequence: Treatment A first, Treatment B second, and Treatment C last. Even if none of the treatments had an effect, the effect of order (first versus second versus last) might make it look like the treatments had different effects.

If practice effects caused participants to do better on the last trial, participants would do best on the trial where they received Treatment C. Thus, even if none of the treatments had an effect, the investigator might mistakenly believe that Treatment C improves performance.

If fatigue effects caused participants to perform the worst on the last treatment condition, participants would do worst on the trial where they received Treatment C. Thus, even if none of the treatments had an effect, the investigator might mistakenly believe that Treatment C decreases performance.

Treatment carryover effects might also affect performance on the last trial. For example, if the effect of Treatment B is helpful but delayed, it might help performance on the last trial. If, on the other hand, the effect of Treatment B is harmful but delayed, it might harm performance on the last trial. Thus, even if Treatment C has no effect, the investigator might mistakenly believe that Treatment C is harmful (if Treatment B's delayed effect is harmful) or that Treatment C is helpful (if Treatment B's delayed effect is helpful).

Sensitization might also create the illusion that Treatment C has an effect. The participants were most naïve about the experimental hypothesis when receiving the first treatment (Treatment A), least naïve when receiving the last treatment (Treatment C). Thus, the ability of the participant to play along with the hypothesis increased as the study went on. Changes in the ability to play along with the hypothesis may create order effects that could masquerade as treatment effects.

Dealing With Order Effects

You have seen that (a) the sources of order effects are practice, fatigue, carryover, and sensitization; and that (b) order effects threaten the internal validity of a within-subjects design. How can you use this knowledge to prevent order effects from threatening your experiment's internal validity?

Minimizing Each of the Individual Sources of Order Effects

Perhaps the best place to start to reduce the effect of order is to attack the four root causes of order effects: practice, fatigue, carryover, and sensitization.

Minimizing Practice Effects. To minimize the effects of practice, you can give participants extensive practice before the experiment begins. For example, if you are studying maze running and you have the rats run the maze 100 times before you start administering treatments, they've probably learned as much from practice as they can. Therefore, it's unlikely that the rats will benefit greatly from the limited practice they get during the experiment.

Minimizing Fatigue Effects. You can reduce fatigue effects by making the experiment interesting, brief, and undemanding.

Minimizing Treatment Carryover Effects. You can reduce carryover effects by lengthening the time between treatments to allow adequate time for the effect of earlier treatments to wear off before the participant receives the next treatment. For instance, if you were looking at the effects of drugs on how well rats run a maze, you might reduce treatment carryover effects by spacing your treatments a week apart (for example, antidepressant pill, wait a week, anti-anxiety pill, wait a week, placebo).

Minimizing Sensitization Effects. You can reduce sensitization by preventing participants from noticing that you are varying anything (Greenwald, 1976). For example, suppose you were studying the effects of different levels of full-spectrum light on typing performance. In that case, there would be three ways that you could prevent sensitization.

First, you could use very similar levels of the treatment in all your conditions. By using slightly different amounts of full-spectrum light, participants may not realize that you are actually varying amount of light.

Second, you could change the level of the treatment so gradually that participants do not notice. For example, while you gave participants a short break in between trials, you could change the lighting level watt by watt until it reached the desired level.

Third, you might be able to reduce sensitization effects by using good placebo treatments. In this example, rather than using darkness as the control condition, you could use light from a normal bulb as the control condition.

A General Strategy for Reducing Order Effects

To this point, we have given you some strategies to reduce practice effects, to reduce fatigue effects, to reduce carryover effects, and to reduce sensitization (see Table 13-5 for a review). However, by reducing the number of experimental conditions, you can reduce all four causes of order effects at once because there will be fewer opportunities for them to affect your study.

Table 13-5	Order Effects and How to Minimize Their Impact	
EFFECT	**EXAMPLE**	**WAYS TO REDUCE IMPACT**
Practice Effects	Getting better on the task due to becoming more familiar with the task or with the research situation.	Give extensive practice and warm-up before introducing the treatment.
Fatigue Effects	Getting tired as the study wears on.	Keep study brief, interesting.
Carryover Effects	Effects of one treatment lingering and affecting responses on later trials.	Use few levels of treatment. Allow sufficient time between treatments for treatment effects to wear off.
Sensitization	As a result of getting many different levels of the independent variable, the participant—during the latter part of the study—becomes aware of what the treatment is and what the hypothesis is.	Use subtly different levels of the treatment. Gradually change treatment levels. Use few treatment levels.

To see how fewer conditions leads to fewer order-effect problems, compare a within-subjects experiment that has 11 conditions with one that has only 2 conditions. In the 11-condition experiment, participants have 10 opportunities to practice on the dependent-measure task before they get the last treatment; in the 2-condition experiment, participants only have one opportunity for practice. The 11-condition participants have 11 conditions to fatigue them; 2-condition participants only have 2. In the 11-condition experiment, there are 10 treatments that could carry over to the last trial; in the 2-condition experiment there is only 1. Finally, in the 11-condition experiment, participants have 11 chances to figure out the hypothesis; in the 2-condition experiment, they only have 2 chances.

Mixing Up Sequences to Try to Balance Out Order Effects: Randomizing and Counterbalancing

Although you can take steps to reduce the impact of order, you can never be sure that you have eliminated its impact. Therefore, if you gave all your participants Treatment A first and Treatment B second, you could not be sure that the difference between the average of the Treatment A scores and the average of the Treatment B scores was due to a treatment effect. Instead, the difference could simply be due to an order (trials: first versus second) effect.

To avoid confusing an order (trials) effect for a treatment effect, you should not give all your participants the same sequence of treatments. For example, in a two-condition study, you should not give all of your participants the treatments in this sequence: Treatment A first, Treatment B second. Instead, some participants should get the treatment sequence: Treatment B first and then Treatment A.

There are two basic approaches you could use to make sure that not all participants get the treatments in the same sequence: (1) Randomize the sequence of treatments for each participant, or (2) counterbalance the sequence of treatments.

Randomized Within-Subjects Designs

You can mix up the sequences by randomly determining, for each participant, which treatment they get first, which treatment they get second, and so on. If you use this randomization strategy to sequence each participant's series of treatments, you have a randomized within-subjects design.

Procedure

The **randomized within-subjects design** is very similar to the matched-pairs design. For example, the procedural differences between the two-condition, randomized, within-subjects experiment and matched-pairs experiment stem from a single difference: In the within-subjects experiment, you get a pair of scores from a single participant, whereas in the matched-pairs design, you get a pair of scores from a matched pair of participants. Thus, in the matched-pairs case, each participant only gets one treatment, but in the within-subjects experiment, each participant gets two treatments.

Other than each participant receiving more than one treatment, the two designs are remarkably similar. The matched-pairs researcher randomly determines, for each pair, who will get what treatment. In some pairs, the first member will get Treatment A, whereas the second member will get Treatment B; in other pairs, the first member will get Treatment B, whereas the second member will get Treatment A.

The within-subjects researcher randomly determines, for each individual, the sequence of the treatments. For some individuals, the first treatment will be Treatment A (and the second treatment will be Treatment B); for other individuals, the first treatment will be Treatment B (and the second treatment will be Treatment A). In short, whereas the matched-pairs experimenter randomly assigns members of pairs to different treatments, the within-subjects experimenter randomly assigns individual participants to different sequences of treatments.

To see the similarities and differences between the matched-pairs and within-subjects designs, imagine that we are interested in whether observers' judgments about other people are influenced by irrelevant information. Specifically, we want to see whether pseudorelevant information (information that seems relevant but really isn't relevant) affects whether observers see others as passive or assertive. Therefore, we produce pseudorelevant descriptions ("Bill has a 3.2 GPA and is thinking about majoring in psychology") and "clearly irrelevant" descriptions ("Bob found 20 cents in a pay phone in the student union when he went to make a phone call").

In a matched-pairs design, you would match participants—probably based on how assertively they tend to rate people. Then, one member of the pair would read a "pseudorelevant" description while the other read a "clearly irrelevant" description. After reading the information, each participant would rate the assertiveness of the student he read about on a 9-point scale ranging from "very passive" to "very assertive."

In a randomized within-subjects design, on the other hand, each participant would read both "pseudorelevant" and "clearly irrelevant" descriptions. After reading the information, they would rate the assertiveness of each of these students on a 9-point scale ranging from "very passive" to "very assertive." Thus, each participant would provide data for both the "pseudorelevant" condition and the "clearly irrelevant" condition. The sequence of the descriptions would be randomized, with some sequences having the pseudorelevant description first and others having the clearly irrelevant description first.

Hilton and Fein (1989) conducted such a randomized within-subjects experiment and found that participants judged the students described by pseudorelevant information as more assertive than students described by clearly irrelevant information. Consequently, Hilton and Fein concluded that even irrelevant information affects our judgments about people.

Analysis of Data

To analyze data from the two-condition within-subjects design, you can use the same dependent-groups *t* test that you used to analyze matched-pairs designs.[4] The only difference is that instead of comparing each member of the pair with the other member of that pair, you compare each participant with him- or herself. Because the dependent-groups *t* test can be used to analyze data from a within-subjects design, it can also be called the *within-subjects t test*. Instead of using a within-subjects *t* test (see Box 13-1), you could use a within-subjects analysis of variance (see Box 13-2).

Conclusions About Randomized Within-Subjects Designs

As you might expect from two designs that can be analyzed with the same technique, the randomized within-subjects design and the matched-pairs design are very similar. In terms

---

[4] If you have more than two conditions, you cannot use a *t* test. Instead, you must use either within-subjects analysis of variance (ANOVA) or multivariate analysis of variance (MANOVA).

Table 13-6	Comparing the Matched-Pairs Design With the Within-Subjects Design

MATCHED-PAIRS DESIGN	WITHIN-SUBJECTS DESIGN
Powerful.	More powerful.
Order effects are *not* a problem.	Order effects are a serious problem.
Uses random assignment to balance out differences between participants.	Uses randomization to balance out order effects.
Useful for assessing variables that vary between subjects in real life.	Useful for assessing variables that vary within subjects in real life.

of procedures, the only real difference is that the matched-pairs experimenter randomly assigns members of pairs to treatments, whereas the randomized within-subjects experimenter randomly assigns individual participants to sequences of treatments. Because both designs have impressive power, both should be seriously considered if participants are scarce.

The randomized within-subjects design, however, has some unique strengths and weaknesses stemming from the fact that it collects more than one observation per participant (see Table 13-6). Because it uses individual participants (rather than matched pairs) as their own controls, the randomized within-subjects design is more powerful than the matched-pairs design—and more useful when you want to generalize your results to real-life situations in which individuals get more than one "treatment." Thus, if you were studying the effects of political ads, you might use a within-subjects design because, in real life, a person is likely to be exposed to more than one political ad about a candidate (Greenwald, 1976).

Although there are benefits to collecting more than one observation per participant, having to contend with order effects (practice, fatigue, carryover, and sensitization) is a major drawback. As we have suggested, you can try to minimize order effects, and you can *hope* that randomization will balance out the sequence of your treatments so that each condition comes first about the same number of times as it comes last.

Counterbalanced Within-Subjects Designs

Instead of merely hoping that chance might balance out the sequence of your treatments, why not make sure by using a **counterbalanced within-subjects design.** In this design, as in all within-subjects designs, each participant gets more than one treatment. Unlike other within-subjects designs, however, participants are randomly assigned to systematically varying sequences of conditions in a way that ensures that *routine order effects* are balanced out.[5] Thus, if you were studying two levels (A and B) of a factor, the counterbalanced design would ensure that half your participants got Treatment A first and that half got Treatment B first. Now that you understand the main objective of counterbalancing, let's look at an example to see how counterbalancing achieves this goal.

---

[5]In football, for example, teams change sides every quarter and this usually balances out the effects of wind. However, if the wind shifts in the fourth quarter, counterbalancing fails to balance out the effects of wind. Similarly, if basketball teams change sides at the end of every half (as in international rules), but a rim gets bent (or fixed) during halftime, counterbalancing has failed to balance out the effects of different baskets.

Procedure

If you were to use a counterbalanced design to study a two-level factor, you would randomly assign half of your participants to receive Treatment A first and Treatment B second, whereas the other half would receive Treatment B first and Treatment A second. By randomly assigning your participants to these counterbalanced sequences, most order effects will be neutralized. For example, if participants tend to do better on the second trial, this will not help Treatment A more than Treatment B because both occur in the second position equally often.

Advantages and Disadvantages of Counterbalancing

By using a counterbalanced design, you have not merely balanced out routine order effects, but you have also added another factor to your design—the between-subjects factor of counterbalancing sequence. Adding the factor of counterbalancing sequence has two disadvantages and several advantages.

Disadvantages of Adding a Counterbalancing Factor

A minor disadvantage is that your statistical analysis is now more complex. Rather than using the dependent (within-groups) *t* test, you now have to use a mixed analysis of variance. This would be a major disadvantage if you had to compute statistics by hand. However, because computers can do these analyses for you, this disadvantage really is minor.

The major disadvantage of adding the two-level between-subjects factor of counterbalancing sequence is that you now need more participants than you did when you were planning to use a pure within-subjects design. You need two groups of participants to determine whether the two-level between-subjects factor of counterbalanced sequence has an effect. One of those groups will receive the A–B sequence, the other will receive the B–A sequence. To have enough power to see whether the A–B sequence leads to higher average scores than the B–A sequence, you will need at least 30 participants in each group.[6] In the pure within-subjects design, on the other hand, we were not comparing one group against another. Thus, in a sense, by going from a pure within-subjects design to a counterbalanced design, you are going from having zero levels of a between-subjects factor to having two levels of a between-subjects factor. As you may recall from our discussion of multiple-group experiments (Chapter 11), the more levels of a between-subjects factor you have, the more participants you need.

As you go beyond two levels of the independent variable, the number of different possible sequences—and thus the levels of the between subjects factor of counterbalancing—explodes. For example, if you have 3 levels, there are 6 possible sequences (ABC, BCA, CAB, ACB, BAC, CBA), and thus counterbalancing would be a 6-level factor; if you have 4 levels, counterbalancing will be a 24-level factor, and if you have 5 levels, counterbalancing will be a 120-level factor.

To avoid the problem of having too many levels of the between-subjects factor of counterbalancing, you have two options. First, if you can administer the same treatment more than once to the same participant, you can get by with a single sequence. Ideally, this sequence would involve all possible orders (e.g., ABC, BCA, CAB, ACB, BAC, CBA).

---

[6]In most cases, 30 participants per group is too few. Usually, researchers should have at least 60 participants per group (Cohen, 1990).

However, if you could present each treatment only twice, a sequence in which you first presented the treatments in one order (e.g., ABC) and then present them in the reverse order (e.g., CBA) offers some protection from order effects. Thus, if you had five treatments, you might present them in this sequence: ABCDEEDCBA.

Second, rather than randomly assigning participants to every possible sequence (as you would in complete counterbalancing), you randomly assign participants to as many sequences as you have levels of your independent variable. Thus, if you have four treatments (A, B, C, and D), you would randomly assign participants to four sequences.

The first key to this partial counterbalancing is to select a set of sequences that, like complete counterbalancing, has every condition occur in every position equally often (e.g., Treatment A occurs first just as often as it occurs second, third, and fourth). The simplest way to do this is to have each condition appear once in each position. Thus, if you had four treatments, treatment A would appear first in one sequence, second in one sequence, third in one sequence, and fourth in one sequence—and the same would be true of treatments B, C, and D.

The second key to this partial counterbalancing is to have each condition come before every other condition just as many times as it comes after that condition (e.g., Treatment A comes before Treatment B twice and after Treatment B twice). To get such a set of sequences, you would use a Latin Square (see Box 13-3). Note, however, that even with partial counterbalancing, you need more participants than you would with a pure, randomized within-subjects design.

Advantages of Adding a Counterbalancing Factor

The disadvantage of needing more participants is sometimes offset by being able to discover more effects. With the two-condition within-subjects experiment, you can obtain only one main effect (the treatment main effect). By adding the two-level factor of counterbalancing sequence, you converted the two-condition experiment into a 2 (the within-subjects factor of treatment) × 2 (the between-subjects factor of counterbalancing sequence) experiment, thus giving you more information. Specifically, you can look for two main effects and an interaction (see Table 13-7). By looking at these three effects, you can find out three things.

First, as was the case with the pure within-subjects design, you can find out whether the treatment had an effect by looking at the treatment main effect. In the experiment described in Table 13-7, you can look at the treatment main effect to find out whether forming images of words is a more effective memory strategy than making sentences out of the words.

Second, by looking at the counterbalancing sequence main effect, you find out whether the group of participants getting one sequence of treatments (A–B) did better than the participants getting the other (B–A) sequence. In the experiment described in Table 13-7, the question is, "Did Group 1 (who formed images first and then formed sentences) recall more words than Group 2 (who formed sentences first and then formed images)?"

Third, by looking at the treatment × counterbalancing interaction, you find out whether participants score higher on the first trial or on the second. Looking at the treatment × counterbalancing interaction allows you to detect what some people call a "trials effect" and what others call an "order effect."

But how can looking at an interaction tell you that participants score differently on the first trial than the second? After all, significant interactions usually indicate exceptions to general rules rather than indicating a general rule such as, "participants do better on the first trial."

BOX 13-3   Latin Square Designs: The ABCs of Counterbalancing Complex Designs

You have seen an example of the simplest form of counterbalancing in which one group of subjects gets Treatment A followed by Treatment B (AB) and a second group gets Treatment B followed by Treatment A (BA). This simple form of counterbalancing is called AB, BA counterbalancing. Note that even this simple form of counterbalancing accomplishes two goals.

First, it guarantees every condition occurs in every position, equally often. Thus, in AB, BA counterbalancing, A occurs in both the first and last position. The same is true for B.

Second, each condition precedes every other condition just as many times as it follows that condition. That is, in AB, BA counterbalancing, A precedes B once and follows B once. This symmetry is called *balance*.

Although achieving these two objectives of counterbalancing is easy with only two conditions, with more conditions, counterbalancing becomes more complex. For example, with four conditions (A, B, C, D) you would have four groups. To determine what order the groups will go through the conditions, you would consult the following 4 × 4 Latin Square:

POSITION

	1	2	3	4
Group 1	A	B	D	C
Group 2	B	C	A	D
Group 3	C	D	B	A
Group 4	D	A	C	B

In this 4 × 4 complete Latin Square, Treatment A occurs in all four positions (first, second, third, and fourth), as do Treatments, B, C, and D. In addition, the square has balance. As you can see from looking at the square, every letter precedes every other letter twice and follows every other letter twice. For example, if you just

look at Treatments A and D, you see that A comes before D twice (in Groups 1 and 2) and follows D twice (in Groups 3 and 4).

Balance is relatively easy to achieve for 2, 4, 6, 8, or even 16 conditions. But, what if you have 3 conditions? Immediately you recognize that with a 3 × 3 Latin Square, A cannot precede B the same number of times as it follows B. Condition A can either precede B twice and follow it once or precede it once and follow it twice. Thus, with an uneven number of conditions, you cannot create a balanced Latin Square.

One approach to achieving balance when you have an uneven number of treatment levels is to add or subtract a level so you have an even number of levels. However, adding a level may greatly increase the number of sequences and groups you need. Subtracting a level, on the other hand, may cause you to lose vital information. Therefore, you may not wish to alter your study to obtain an even number of levels. Fortunately, you can achieve balance with an uneven number of treatment levels by using two Latin Squares.* For instance, consider the 3 × 3 squares below.

If you randomly assign subjects to six groups, as outlined above, you ensure balance. See for yourself that if you take any two conditions, one condition will precede the other three times and will be preceded by the other condition three times.

SQUARE **1** POSITION					SQUARE **2** POSITION		
	1	2	3			1	2	3
Group 1	A	B	C		Group 4	C	B	A
Group 2	B	C	A		Group 5	A	C	B
Group 3	C	A	B		Group 6	B	A	C

*Another option is to use incomplete Latin Square designs. However, the discussion of incomplete Latin Square designs is beyond the scope of this book.

The first step to seeing why a significant treatment × counterbalancing interaction tells you that participants score differently on the first trial than on the second is to imagine such an interaction. Suppose that participants who get Treatment A *first* score highest after receiving Treatment A, *but* participants who get Treatment B *first* score highest after receiving Treatment B. At one level, this is an interaction: The rule that participants score highest when receiving Treatment A only holds when they receive Treatment A first. However, the cause of this interaction is an order (trials) effect: Participants score highest on the first trial.

| Table 13-7 | **A 2 × 2 Counterbalanced Design** |

The first group gets a list of words, is asked to form images of these words, and is asked to recall these words. Then, they get a second list of words, are asked to form a sentence with these words, and are asked to recall the words.

The second group gets a list of words, is asked to form a sentence with these words, and is asked to recall these words. Then, they get a second list of words, are asked to form images of those words, and are asked to recall those words.

GROUP **1**

First Task	**Second Task**
Form Images	Form Sentences

GROUP **2**

First Task	**Second Task**
Form Sentences	Form Images

Questions this study can address include the following:

1. Do people recall more when asked to form sentences than when asked to form images?
2. Do Group 1 participants recall more words than Group 2 participants? In other words, is one sequence of learning the two different memory strategies better than the other?
3. Do people do better on the first list of words they see than on the second? That is, does practice help or hurt?

To get a clearer idea of what a counterbalanced study can tell us, let's look at data from the memory experiment we mentioned earlier. In that experiment, each participant learned one list of words by making a sentence out of the list and learned one list of words by forming mental images. Thus, as would be expected from a within-subjects design, each subject's performance under one treatment condition (sentences) was compared with that same subject's performance under another treatment condition (images).

As would be expected from a two-group between-subjects design, participants were randomly assigned to one of two groups. As would be expected from a counterbalanced design, the groups differed in terms of the counterbalanced sequence in which they received the treatments. Half the participants (the group getting the sentence–image sequence) formed sentences for the first list, then formed images to recall the second list. The other half (the group getting the image–sentence sequence) formed images to recall the first list, then formed sentences to recall the second list.

Now that you have a basic understanding of the study's design, let's examine the study's results. To do so, look at both the table of means for that study (Table 13-8) and the analysis of variance summary table (Table 13-9).

By looking at Table 13-9, we see that the main effect for the between-subjects factor of counterbalanced sequence is not significant. As Table 13-8 shows, members of both groups recalled, on the average, 14 words in the course of the experiment. Participants getting the treatment sequence A–B did not, on the average, recall more words than participants getting the sequence B–A.

Next, we see that the within-subjects factor of the memory strategy factor was also not significant. Because participants recalled the same number of words in the imagery

Table 13-8 **Table of Means for a Counterbalanced Memory Experiment**

	MEMORY STRATEGY		
GROUP'S SEQUENCE	IMAGES	SENTENCES	IMAGES–SENTENCES DIFFERENCE
Group 1 (images 1st, sentences 2nd)	8	6	+2
Group 2 (sentences 1st, images 2nd)	6	8	–2
	14/2 = 7	14/2 = 7	Strategy Main Effect = 0

Counterbalancing Main Effect = 0

On the average, participants in both groups remembered a total of 14 words (8 in one condition, 6 in another)

Strategy Effect = 0
   Average recalled in image condition was 7 ([8 + 6]/2).
   Average recalled in sentence condition was 7([6 + 8]/2).

Order Effect = +2
   Participants remember the first list best.
   They averaged 8 words on the first list, 6 on the second.

The order (first vs. second) effect is revealed by an *interaction* involving counterbalancing *group* and rehearsal *strategy*.

That is, Group 1 did better in the image condition (8 to 6), but Group 2 did better in the sentence condition (8 to 6).

Table 13-9 **ANOVA Summary Table for a Counterbalanced Design**

ANALYSIS OF VARIANCE TABLE

SOURCE	SS	df	MS	F	p
Group Sequence (counterbalancing)	0	1	0	0	n.s.*
Error Term for Between-Subjects	44	22	2		
Factor Memory Strategy	0	1	0	0	n.s.
Interaction Between Memory Strategy and Group Sequence	10	1	10	10	$p < .01$
(effect of order—1st versus 2nd list) Within-Subjects Error Term	23	23	1.0		

*n.s. is abbreviation for not statistically significant.

Note: "*p*" values in an ANOVA summary table indicate the probability that the researchers could get differences between their conditions that were this big even if the variables were not related. That is, the *p* values tell you the probability that the difference between the groups could occur due to chance alone. Thus, the smaller the *p* value, the less likely the results are due only to chance—and the more likely that the variables really are related.

| Table 13-10 | Effects Revealed by a 2 × 2 Counterbalanced Design |

GROUP **1**

First Ad	Second Ad
Emotional Ad	Rational Ad

GROUP **2**

First Ad	Second Ad
Rational Ad	Emotional Ad

Questions Addressed by the Design:

1. Is the rational ad more effective than the emotional ad? (Main effect of the within-subjects factor of type of ad)
2. Is it better to show the emotional ad and then the rational ad or the rational ad and then the emotional ad? (Main effect of the between-subjects factor of counterbalancing sequence)
3. Are attitudes more favorable to the candidate after seeing the second ad than after seeing the first? (Ad by counterbalancing interaction)

condition (7) as they did in the sentence condition (7), we have no evidence that one strategy is superior to the other. Thus, there is no treatment effect.

Finally, we have a significant interaction of memory strategy and group sequence. By looking at Table 13-8, we see that this interaction is caused by the fact that Group 1 (which gets images first) recalled more words in the imagery condition whereas Group 2 (which gets sentences first) recalled more words in the sentences condition. In other words, participants do better on the first list than on the second.

What does this order (trials) effect mean? If the researchers were not careful in their selection of lists, the order effect could merely reflect the first list being made up of words that were easier to recall than the second list. The researchers, however, should not have made that mistake.[7] Therefore, if the experiment were properly conducted, the order effect must reflect either the effects of practice, fatigue, treatment carryover, or sensitization. In this case, it probably reflects the fact that the practice participants get on the first list hurts their memory for the second list. Psychologists do not consider this negative practice effect a nuisance. On the contrary, this negative practice effect is one of the most important and most widely investigated facts of memory—proactive interference.

Now that you understand the three effects (two main effects and the treatment × counterbalancing interaction) that you can find with a 2 × 2 counterbalanced design, let's look at an experiment where the researcher is interested in all three effects. Suppose that Mary Jones, a politician, produces two commercials: an emotional commercial and a rational commercial. She hires a psychologist to find out which commercial is most effective so she'll know which one to give more airtime. The researcher uses a counterbalanced design to address the question (see Table 13-10).

---

[7]There are at least three ways to avoid this mistake: (a) extensively pretest the lists to make sure that both are equally memorable, (b) consult the literature to find lists that are equally memorable, and (c) counterbalance lists so that, across participants, each list occurred equally often under each instructional condition. The third approach is probably the best.

By looking at the treatment main effect, the researcher is able to answer the original question, "Which ad is more effective?" By looking at the counterbalancing sequence main effect, the researcher is able to find out whether one sequence of showing the ads is better than another, thus enabling him to answer the question, "Should we show the emotional ad first and then the rational ad or should we show the ads in the opposite sequence?" Finally, by looking at the ad by counterbalancing interaction, the researcher is able to determine if there is an order (trials) effect, leading him to be able to answer the question, "Are participants more favorable toward the candidate after they've seen the second ad?" Obviously, he would expect that voters would rate the candidate higher after seeing the second ad than they did after seeing the first ad.

Let's suppose that all three effects were statistically significant and the means were as follows:

	TYPE OF AD	
	Emotional Ad	**Rational Ad**
Group 1: (Emotional–Rational sequence)	<u>4</u>	6
Group 2: (Rational–Emotional sequence)	8	<u>7</u>

Note: Scores are rating of the candidate on a 1 (strongly disapprove of) to 9 (strongly approve of) scale.

As you can see from comparing the emotional ad column with the rational ad column, the treatment main effect is due to the rational ad, on the average, being more effective than the emotional ad. As you can see from comparing the Group 1 row with the Group 2 row, Group 2 likes the candidate more than Group 1. Thus, the between-groups counterbalancing sequence main effect suggests that it would be better to present the ads in the Rational–Emotional sequence (Group 2's sequence) than in the Emotional–Rational sequence (Group 1's sequence).

The table doesn't make it as easy to see the order effect. To see whether participants liked the candidate better after the second trial than after the first, this table makes you interpret the treatment × counterbalancing interaction. To help you find the order effect in this table, we have underlined the mean for the ad that each group saw first. Thus, we underlined 4 because Group 1 saw the emotional ad first, and we underlined 7 because Group 2 saw the rational ad first. By recognizing that 4 + 7 is less than 8 + 6, you could determine that scores were lower on the first trial than on the second. To better see the order effect, you should rearrange the table so that the columns represent "Order of Ads" rather than "Type of Ad." Your new table would look like this:

	ORDER OF ADS	
	First Ad	**Second Ad**
Group 1: (Emotional–Rational sequence)	<u>4</u>	6
Group 2: (Rational–Emotional sequence)	<u>7</u>	8

As you can see from this table, the order effect reveals that people like the candidate more after the second ad. The ads *do* build on each other.

It's possible, however, that the consultant may not have obtained an order effect. For example, suppose the consultant obtained the following pattern of results:

	TYPE OF AD	
	Emotional Ad	**Rational Ad**
Group 1: (Emotional–Rational sequence)	<u>5</u>	6
Group 2: (Rational–Emotional sequence)	5	<u>6</u>

In this case, Group 1 participants (who get the rational ad last) and Group 2 participants (who get the rational ad first) both rate the candidate one point higher after seeing the rational ad than they do after seeing the emotional ad. Thus, there is no treatment by counterbalancing interaction. Because there is no treatment × counterbalancing interaction, there is no order effect. However, an easier way to see that there was no order effect would be to create the following table.

	ORDER OF ADS	
	First Ad	**Second Ad**
Group 1: (Emotional–Rational sequence)	<u>5</u>	6
Group 2: (Rational–Emotional sequence)	<u>6</u>	5

With these data, the consultant would probably decide to just use the rational ad.

Instead of obtaining no order effect, the consultant could have obtained an order effect such that people always rated the candidate worse after the second ad. For example, suppose the consultant obtained the following results:

	ORDER OF ADS	
	First Ad	**Second Ad**
Group 1: (Emotional–Rational sequence)	<u>5</u>	4
Group 2: (Rational–Emotional sequence)	<u>6</u>	4

If the consultant obtained these results, he would take a long, hard look at the ads. It may be that both ads are making people dislike the candidate, or it may be that the combination of these two ads does not work. Seeing both ads may reduce liking for the candidate by making her seem inconsistent. For example, one ad may suggest that she supports increased military spending while the other may suggest that she opposes increased military spending.

Conclusions About Counterbalanced Within-Subjects Designs

As you can see from this last example, the counterbalanced design does more than balance out routine order effects. It also tells you about the impact of both trials (order: first versus second) and sequence (e.g., rational then emotional ad versus emotional ad then rational ad). Therefore, you should use counterbalanced designs when

1. you want to make sure that routine order effects are balanced out
2. you are interested in sequence effects
3. you are interested in order (trials) effects

You will usually want to balance out order effects because you don't want order effects to destroy your study's internal validity. That is, you want a significant treatment main effect to be due to the treatment, rather than to order effects.

You will often be interested in **sequence effects** because real life is often a sequence of treatments (Greenwald, 1976). That is, most of us are not assigned to receive either praise or criticism; to see either ads for a candidate or against a candidate; to experience only success or failure, pleasure or pain, and so on. Instead, we usually receive both praise and criticism, see ads for and against a candidate, and experience both success and failure. Counterbalanced designs allow us to understand the effects of receiving different sequences of these "treatments." In counterbalanced designs, the main effect for the between-subjects factor of counterbalancing sequence can help you answer questions like the following:

- Would it be better to eat and then exercise—or to exercise and then eat?
- Would it be better to meditate and then study—or to study and then meditate?
- If you are going to compliment and criticize a friend, would you be better off to criticize, then praise—or to praise, then criticize?

Order (trials) effects, on the other hand, will probably interest you if you can control whether a particular event will be first or last in a series of events. Thus, you might be interested in using a counterbalanced design to find out whether it's best to be the first or the last person interviewed for a job. Or, if you want to do well in one particular course (research methods, of course), should you study the material for that course first or last? To find out about these order effects, you'd use a counterbalanced design and look at the treatment $\times$ counterbalancing interaction.

Choosing the Right Design

If you want to compare two levels of an independent variable, you have several designs you can use: matched pairs, within-subjects designs, counterbalanced designs, and the simple between-subjects design. To help you choose among these designs, we will briefly summarize the ideal situation for using each design.

Choosing a Design When You Have One Independent Variable

The matched-groups design is ideal when

1. you can readily obtain participants' scores on the matching variable without arousing their suspicions about the purpose of the experiment
2. the matching variable correlates highly with the dependent measure
3. participants are scarce

The pure within-subjects design is ideal when

1. sensitization, practice, fatigue, or carryover effects are not problems
2. you want a powerful design
3. participants are scarce
4. you want to generalize your results to real-life situations, and in real life, individuals tend to be exposed to both levels of the treatment

The 2 × 2 counterbalanced design is ideal when

1. you want to balance out the effects of order, or you are interested in learning the nature of any order or sequence effects
2. you have enough participants to meet the requirement of a counterbalanced design
3. you are not concerned that being exposed to both treatment levels will alert participants to the purpose of the experiment

The pure between-subjects design is ideal when

1. you think fatigue, practice, sensitization, or carryover effects could affect the results
2. you have access to a relatively large number of participants
3. you want to generalize your results to real-life situations, and in real life, individuals tend to receive either one treatment or the other, but not both

Choosing a Design When You Have More Than One Independent Variable

Thus far, we have discussed how to choose a design when you are studying the effects of a single variable (see Table 13-11). Often, however, you may want to investigate the effects of two or more variables.

In that case, you would appear to have three choices: a between-subjects factorial design, a within-subjects factorial design, and a counterbalanced design. However, counterbalancing becomes less attractive—especially for the beginning researcher—as the design becomes more complicated. Thus, as a general rule, beginning researchers who plan on manipulating two independent variables usually are choosing between a two-factor within-subjects design and a two-factor between-subjects design.

Using a Within-Subjects Factorial Design

You should use a pure within-subjects design when

1. you can handle the statistics (you will have to use within-subjects analysis of variance or multivariate analysis of variance)
2. sensitization, practice, fatigue, and carryover effects are not problems
3. you are concerned about power
4. in real-life situations, people are exposed to all your different combinations of treatments

Using a Between-Subjects Factorial Design

On the other hand, you should use a between-subjects design when

1. you are worried about the statistics of a complex within-subjects design
2. you are worried that order effects would destroy the internal validity of a within-subjects design
3. you are not worried about power
4. in real-life situations, people are exposed to either one combination of treatments or another

Table 13-11	Ideal Situations for Different Designs		
SIMPLE EXPERIMENT	**MATCHED GROUPS**	**WITHIN-SUBJECTS**	**COUNTERBALANCED DESIGN**
Participants are plentiful.	Participants are very scarce.	Participants are very scarce.	Participants are somewhat scarce.
Order effects could be a problem.	Order effects could be a problem.	Order effects are not a problem.	Want to assess order effects or order effects can be balanced out.
Power isn't vital.	Power is vital.	Power is vital.	Power is vital.
In real life, people usually only get one or the other treatment, rarely get both.	In real life, people usually only get one or the other treatment, rarely get both.	In real life, people usually get both treatments, rarely get only one or the other.	In real life, people usually get both treatments, rarely get only one or the other.
Multiple exposure to dependent measure will tip participants off about hypothesis.	Exposure to matching variable will *not* tip participants off about hypothesis.	Multiple exposure to dependent measure will *not* tip participants off about hypothesis.	Multiple exposure to dependent measure will *not* tip participants off about hypothesis.
Exposure to different levels of the independent variable will tip participants off about hypothesis.	Exposure to different levels of the independent variable will tip participants off about hypothesis. Matching variable is easy to collect and correlates highly with the dependent measure.	Exposure to different levels of the independent variable will *not* tip participants off about hypothesis.	Exposure to different levels of the independent variable will *not* tip participants off about hypothesis.

Using a Mixed Design

Sometimes, however, you will find it difficult to choose between a completely within-subjects design and a completely between-subjects design. For example, consider the following two cases.

Case 1: You are studying the effects of brain lesions and practice on how well rats run mazes. On the one hand, you do not want to use a completely within-subjects design because you consider brain damage to occur "between subjects" in real life (because some individuals suffer brain damage, and others do not). On the other hand, you do not want to use a completely between-subjects design because you think that practice occurs "within subjects" in real life (because all individuals get practice and, over time, the amount of practice an individual gets increases).

Table 13-12	Ideal Situations for Making a Factor Between or Within

Should a Factor Be a Between-Subjects Factor or a Within-Subjects Factor?

MAKE FACTOR BETWEEN SUBJECTS	MAKE FACTOR WITHIN SUBJECTS
Order effects pose problems.	Order effects are not a problem.
Lack of power is *not* a concern.	Lack of power is a serious concern.
You want to generalize the results to situations in which participants receive either one treatment or another.	You want to generalize the results to situations in which participants receive all levels of the treatment.

Case 2: You are studying the effects of subliminal messages and electroconvulsive therapy on depression. You expect that if subliminal messages have any effect, it will be so small that only a within-subjects design could detect it. However, you feel that electroconvulsive shock should not be studied in a within-subjects design because of huge carryover effects (see Table 13-12).

Fortunately, in these cases, you are not forced to choose between a totally within-subjects factorial and a totally between-subjects factorial. As you know from our discussion of counterbalanced designs, you can do a study in which one factor is varied between subjects and the other is varied within subjects. Such designs, called **mixed designs,** are analyzed using a mixed analysis of variance. (To learn how to interpret the results of a mixed analysis of variance, see Box 13-4.)

BOX 13-4	Not Getting Mixed Up About Mixed Designs

If you use a mixed design, you will probably have a computer analyze your data for you. Often, both entering the data and interpreting the printout are straightforward. For example, suppose you had two groups (one received Treatment X, the other Treatment Y), had each participant go through three trials, and collected the following data.

Participant	Group	Trial 1	Trial 2	Trial 3
Steve	X	1	3	7
Mary	X	2	4	6
Todd	X	3	6	7
Melissa	X	4	5	7
Tom	Y	4	5	7
Amy	Y	5	4	7
Rob	Y	4	5	6
Kara	Y	4	4	7

You might input the data as follows.

Group	Trial 1	Trial 2	Trial 3
1	1	3	7
1	2	4	6
1	3	6	7
1	4	5	7
2	4	5	7
2	5	4	7
2	4	5	6
2	4	4	7

Your printout might be relatively straightforward and resemble the following.

MEANS FOR CELLS, ROWS, AND COLUMNS

2.5	4.5	6.75
4.25	4.5	6.75
3.375	4.5	6.75

BETWEEN SUBJECTS

Source	SS	df	MS	F	p

BETWEEN SUBJECTS

	SS	df	MS	F	p
A	2.04	1	2.04	1.69	.24
Error term	7.25	6	1.21		

continued

WITHIN SUBJECTS

B	47.25	2	23.63	47.26	< .001
A × B	4.08	2	2.04	4.08	.044
Error term	6	12	.5		

However, in some programs, entering your data and interpreting the printout can be more complicated. To make sure that the computer has done the analysis you expected, check your printout carefully.

If your printout contains only one error term, the computer is analyzing your data as if you have a completely between-subjects design. If you take the *MS* for any treatment or interaction and divide it by your one and only *MSE,* you will get the *F* for that effect.

If, on the other hand, every main effect and every interaction has its own error term, the computer is analyzing your data as if you have a completely within-subjects design. In that case, if you have three effects (two main effects and an interaction effect), you will have three error terms.

Even if the computer seems to be analyzing your study as a mixed design, check the computer printout to be sure that it has correctly identified which factors are within and which are between. Start by looking at the degrees of freedom for all your main effects. If your between-subjects factor(s) have more levels than your within-subjects factor(s), then the degrees of freedom for your between-subjects main effect should be larger than the degrees of freedom for your within-subjects main effect. In any event, make sure that the *df* for each of your variable's main effects is one fewer than the number of levels of that variable. For example, if you have 4 levels of the between variable and 2 levels of the within variable, be sure that the degrees of freedom for the between variable is 3 and that the degrees of freedom for the within variable is 1.

Next, focus on your between-subjects factor(s). All between-subjects main effects—and all interactions that involve only between-subjects factors—should be tested against a single error term. To guarantee this, divide the *MS* for each between factors main effect and each exclusively between factors interaction by the *MS* for the between-subjects error term. In every case, you should get the same *F* that is reported in the printout.

To double-check that the computer correctly identified all the between-subjects variables, add up the degrees of freedom for all the between-subjects main effects, the df for the interactions that involved only between-subjects factors, and the *df* for the between-subjects error term. The total of these degrees of freedom should be one fewer than the number of participants.

Next, check the within factors. Each within-subjects main effect and each interaction that involves only within subjects factors should be tested against a different error term.

Finally, look at interactions in which at least one variable is a between factor and at least one variable is a within factor. To find the appropriate error term for these interactions, attend only to the within-subjects factors: Ignore the between-subjects factors. If A is a within factor and B is a between factor and you see an A × B interaction, this interaction should be tested against the same error term that A is tested against. If A is a within factor and B and C are between factors, the error term for the A × B × C interaction should still be the same error term that was used for testing A. If it is not, there is a mix up about which of your factors are within and which are between.

In both Case 1 and Case 2, the mixed design allows us to have both internal validity and power. In Case 1, we could make lesions a between-subjects variable by randomly assigning half the participants to get lesions and half not. That way we do not have to worry about carryover effects from the brain lesions. We could make *practice* a within-subjects variable by having each participant run the maze three times. Consequently, we have the power to detect subtle differences due to practice (see Table 13-13 and Figure 13-1).

In Case 2, we could make ECS therapy a between-subjects variable by randomly assigning half the participants to get electroconvulsive (ECS) therapy and half not. That way, we do not have to worry about carryover effects from the ECS. Then, we would expose all participants to a variety of subliminal messages, some designed to boost mood, and some to be neutral. By comparing the average overall depression scores from the ECS therapy group to that of the no-ECS group, we could assess the effect of ECS. By comparing participants'

Table 13-13	**Analysis of Variance Summary Table for a Mixed Design**				
SOURCE OF VARIANCE	*df*	*SS*	*MS*	*F*	*p*
Brain Lesion	1	51.0	*51.0*	*10.0*	.0068
Between-Subjects Error	14	72.4	*5.1*		
Trials	2	26.6	13.3	11.1	.0003
Lesions × Trials	2	13.7	6.8	5.7	.0083
Within-Subjects Error	28	33.6	*1.2*		

Note: The mean square error for the within-subjects term is much smaller than the between-subjects error term (1.2 to 5.1), giving the design tremendous power for detecting within-subjects effects. This table corresponds to the graph in Figure 13-1.

Figure 13-1	**An Interaction in a Mixed Design**

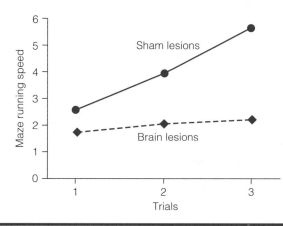

scores following the "positive" subliminal messages to their scores following "neutral" subliminal messages, we could detect even rather subtle effects of subliminal messages.

In a mixed design, you are able to test not only the main effects of two treatments but also the interaction of those treatments. In Case 1, the interesting statistical effects will probably involve the interaction rather than the two main effects. That is, we would not be terribly surprised to find a main effect for lesion, telling us that the brain-lesioned rats performed worse.[8] Nor would we be surprised to find a main effect for practice, telling us that participants improve with practice. However, we would be interested in knowing about the practice × lesion interaction. A significant practice × lesion interaction would tell us that one group of rats was benefiting from practice more than another. In this case, as you can see from Figure 13-1, the nonlesion group benefits most from practice. In Case 2, although we would be interested in both the ECS and subliminal message main effects, we might be most interested in the interaction between ECS and subliminal messages: Such an interaction would tell us whether the ECS group was more influenced by the subliminal messages than the no-ECS group.

[8]The lesion main effect would be especially unsurprising if our control group didn't get any surgery. However, such empty control groups are rare. Typically, the control group would be a "sham lesion" control group that got brain surgery and was treated the same as the treatment group except that, instead of being injected with a chemical that would destroy (lesion) part of the brain, they would be injected with a harmless saline solution.

In many mixed designs, both a main effect and the interaction will be of interest. For example, Hebl and Mannix (2003) found a between-subjects main effect indicating that participants who saw a picture of a male job applicant sitting next to an overweight woman rated the job applicant more harshly than participants who saw a picture of the same man sitting next to an average-weight woman. This between-subjects main effect was of interest. The interaction between this main effect and the within-subjects variable of rating dimension (willingness to hire applicant, applicant's professional qualities, applicant's interpersonal skills) was also of interest because Hebl and Mannix wanted to see whether being seen with an overweight woman influenced hiring judgments more than it affected judgments about the applicant's interpersonal skills.

Note the problems Hebl and Mannix would have had in interpreting their results if they had used either a completely within-subjects or a completely between-subjects design. If they had used a completely within-subjects design, each participant would rate the applicant both (1) after seeing the applicant in the presence of an overweight woman and (2) after seeing the applicant in the presence of an average-weight woman. Participants would have found the study strange and would probably have figured out the hypothesis, thereby making the weight of woman main effect hard to interpret.

If Hebl and Mannix had used a completely between-subjects design, one group of participants would make hiring judgments, another group would make interpersonal skills judgments, and yet another group would make judgments about the applicant's professional qualities. Because each participant would be providing one set of ratings rather than the three sets that Hebl and Mannix's participants did, each participant in a between-subjects design would be providing only 1/3 as much data as the participants in Hebl and Mannix's actual study. Because participants would be providing less data, the study would have been less powerful than Hebl and Mannix's actual study. Thus, if Hebl and Mannix had used a completely between-subjects design and failed to find an effect for the interaction, a scientist reading their work would wonder whether they would have succeeded in finding an interaction had they used a more powerful design.

As you can see from Hebl and Mannix's study and from our two hypothetical cases (Case 1 and Case 2), the mixed design has two major strengths. First, it allows you to examine the effects of two independent variables and their interaction. Second, instead of trading off the needs of one variable for the needs of another, you are able to give both variables the design they need. Because of its versatility, the mixed design is one of the most popular experimental designs.

Concluding Remarks

This chapter has expanded your ability to read about and conduct research. When reading reports of either within-subjects or mixed designs, you now know to ask

1. whether the multiple measures and manipulations may have led participants to figure out the hypothesis

2. what steps (e.g., counterbalancing) were taken to reduce order effects (practice, fatigue, carryover, and sensitization)—and whether those steps were sufficient to ensure the study's internal validity

3. whether a between-subjects design might have been more internally valid

When planning, conducting, or analyzing research, you now can

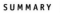

1. do experiments to determine the effect of a treatment and have a reasonable chance of finding the treatment effect even if the effect is small and you have access to only a few participants

2. replicate between-groups experiments that failed to find an effect with a more powerful design that is more likely to find an effect

3. use counterbalancing to control for order effects

4. take steps to minimize practice, fatigue, carryover, and sensitization, thus minimizing order effects

5. do research assessing the effects of order (e.g., trials) and the effect of interactions involving trials (e.g., does the effect of one treatment get stronger when it is repeatedly presented whereas the effect of another treatment weakens with repeated exposures?)

6. do research to determine the effect of different treatment sequences (e.g., is it more effective to have cognitive therapy followed by antidepressants or to have antidepressants followed by cognitive therapy?)

7. determine whether you should use a pure between-subjects experiment, a matched-pairs experiment, a within-subjects design, or a mixed design

8. interpret computer printouts of analysis of variance (ANOVA) analyses of both within-subjects as well as of mixed designs

SUMMARY

1. The matched-pairs design uses matching to reduce the effects of random differences between participants and uses random assignment and statistics to account for the remaining effects of random error. Because of random assignment, the matched-pairs design has internal validity. Because of matching, the matched-pairs design has power.

2. Because the matched-pairs design gives you power without limiting the kind of participant you can use, you may be able to generalize your results to a broader population than if you had used a simple experiment.

3. The matched-pairs design's weaknesses stem from matching: Matching may sensitize participants to your hypothesis and participants may drop out of the study between the time of the matching and the time the experiment is performed.

4. Within-subjects designs are also known as repeated-measures designs.

5. The two-condition within-subjects design gives you two scores per participant.

6. The within-subjects design increases power by eliminating random error due to individual differences and by increasing the number of observations that you obtain from each participant.

7. Both the matched-pairs design and the two-condition pure within-subjects design can be analyzed by the dependent groups t test. Complex within-subjects designs require more complex analyses. Specifically, they should be analyzed by within-subjects analysis of variance (ANOVA) or by multivariate analysis of variance (MANOVA).

8. Because of practice, fatigue, carryover, and sensitization effects, the participant may respond one way if receiving a treatment first and a different way if receiving the treatment last. These order effects may make it difficult to assess a treatment's real effect.

9. To reduce the effects of order, you should randomly determine the sequence in which each participant will get the treatments or use a counterbalanced design.

10. In the counterbalanced design, participants are randomly assigned to systematically varying sequences of conditions to ensure that routine order effects are balanced out.

11. Order effects are different from sequence effects. *Order effects* refer to whether participants respond differently on one trial (e.g., the first) than on some other trial (e.g., the last). Order is a within-subjects factor in a counterbalanced design.

12. Order effects can be detected by looking at the treatment × counterbalancing sequence interaction.

13. *Sequence effects* refer to whether participants respond differently to getting a series of treatments in one sequence than getting the treatments in a different sequence. For example, the group of participants who get the treatments arranged in the sequence Treatment A, then Treatment B may have higher overall average scores than the group of participants who get the treatments arranged in the sequence Treatment B, then Treatment A. Sequence is a between-subjects factor.

14. A counterbalanced design allows you to assess the effect of (a) the treatment, (b) receiving different counterbalanced sequences of treatments, and (c) order (whether participants respond differently on the first trial than on the last).

15. Because you must include the between-subjects factor of counterbalancing in your analyses, counterbalanced designs require more participants than pure within-subjects designs.

16. If you want to compare two levels of an independent variable, you can use a matched-pairs design, a within-subjects design, a counterbalanced design, or a simple between-subjects design.

17. Mixed designs have both a within- and a between-subjects factor. Counterbalanced designs are one form of a mixed design.

18. Mixed designs should be analyzed with a mixed analysis of variance or a multivariate analysis of variance.

KEY TERMS

mixed design *(p. 393)*

matched-pairs design *(p. 394)*

power *(p. 395)*

dependent groups *t* test *(p. 398)*

within-subjects design (repeated-measures design) *(p. 401)*

order *(p. 403)*

order (trial) effect *(p. 403)*

practice effect *(p. 404)*

fatigue effect *(p. 404)*

carryover (treatment carryover) effect *(p. 404)*

sensitization *(p. 404)*

randomized within-subjects design *(p. 407)*

counterbalanced within-subjects design *(p. 409)*

sequence effect *(p. 418)*

EXERCISES

1. What feature of the matched-pairs design makes it
   a. an internally valid design?
   b. a powerful design?

2. A researcher uses a simple between-subjects experiment involving 10 participants to examine the effects of memory strategy (repetition versus imagery) on memory.
   a. Do you think the researcher will find a significant effect? Why or why not?
   b. What design would you recommend?
   c. If the researcher had used a matched-pairs study involving 10 participants, would the study have

more power? Why? How many degrees of freedom would the researcher have? What type of matching task would you suggest? Why?

3. An investigator wants to find out whether hearing jokes will allow a person to persevere longer on a frustrating task. The researcher matches participants based on their reaction to a frustrating task. Of the 30 original participants, 5 quit the study after going through the "frustration pretest." Beyond the ethical problems, what problems are there in using a matched-pairs design in this situation?

4. What problems would there be in using a within-subjects design to study the "humor-perseverance" study (discussed in question 3)? Would a counterbalanced design solve these problems? Why or why not?

5. Why are within-subjects designs more powerful than matched-pairs designs?

6. Two researchers hypothesize that spatial problems will be solved more quickly when the problems are presented to participants' left visual fields than when stimuli are presented to participants' right visual fields. (They reason that messages seen in the left visual field go directly to the right brain, which is often assumed to be better at processing spatial information.) Conversely, they believe verbal tasks will be performed more quickly when stimuli are presented to participants' right visual fields than when the tasks are presented to participants' left visual fields. What design would you recommend? Why?

7. A student hypothesizes that alcohol level will affect sense of humor. Specifically, the student has two hypotheses. First, the more people drink, the more they will laugh at slapstick humor. Second, the more people drink, the less they will laugh at other forms of humor. What design would you recommend the student use? Why?

8. You want to determine whether caffeine, a snack, or a brief walk has a more beneficial effect on mood. What design would you use? Why?

9. Using a driving simulator and a within-subjects design, you want to compare the differences between driving unimpaired, driving while talking on a cell phone, and driving while legally intoxicated.
   a. Which order effects do you have to worry about? Why?
   b. To what degree would counterbalancing solve the problems caused by order effects?
   c. How would you try to prevent order effects from harming the validity of your study?

10. A researcher wants to know whether music lessons increase scores on IQ subtests and whether music lessons have more of an effect on some subtests (e.g., more of an effect on math than on vocabulary) than others.
   a. Would you make music lessons a between- or within-subjects factor? Why?
   b. Would you make subtests a between- or within-subjects factor? Why?
   c. If the researcher did an analysis of variance (ANOVA) on the data, the researcher would obtain three effects. Name those three effects.
   d. What effect would the researcher look for to determine whether music lessons increase scores on IQ subtests?
   e. What effect would the researcher look for to determine whether music lessons have more of an effect on math subtests than on vocabulary subtests?

WEB RESOURCES

Go to the Chapter 13 section of the book's student website and do the following:

1. Look over the concept map of the key terms.
2. Test your self on the key terms.
3. Take the Chapter 13 Practice Quiz.
4. Download the Chapter 13 tutorial to practice

   a. distinguishing between order and sequence effects
   b. interpreting printouts from within-subjects designs
   c. choosing among designs

5. Do an analysis on data from a within-subjects design using a statistical calculator by going to the "Statistical Calculator" link.

INFOTRAC COLLEGE EDITION EXPLORATIONS

1. To read about a study that illustrates the pros and cons of between- versus within-subjects, do an InfoTrac College Edition keyword search using the phrase "within-subjects designs" to find and read Terry's (1994) article examining the problems people have with remembering other people's names.

2. To read a short but informative discussion of within-subject designs, do an InfoTrac College Edition keyword search using the phrase "repeated measures and clinicians," and read Gliner, Morgan, and Harmon's (2002) article.

3. To read an interesting article that looks for an interaction involving odor in a mixed design, do an InfoTrac College Edition keyword search using the phrase "Stroop and odor."

14

Single-*n* Designs
and Quasi-Experiments

Real life is messy.

—*Anonymous*

Overview

To solve real-world problems, applied psychologists must identify the problem's causes. One powerful tool applied psychologists use to identify causes is the randomized experiment. However, as is often the case, when applied psychologists cannot randomly assign participants to treatment, they turn to two other types of studies: single-*n* designs and quasi-experiments. In this chapter, you will learn about these two types of studies and about how they compare to the randomized experiment. After reading this chapter, you will be able to design a study to determine the effect of a real-life treatment.

Inferring Causality in Randomized Experiments

Whether you use a randomized experiment or any other design, you must satisfy three criteria if you are to infer that one variable (e.g., smiling at others) causes a change in another variable (others helping you). Specifically, you must establish

1. covariation (that changes in the treatment are associated with changes in behavior)
2. temporal precedence (that changes in the treatment occur before changes in behavior)
3. that the change in behavior is not due to something other than the treatment

Establishing Covariation: Finding a Relationship Between Changes in the Suspected Cause and Changes in the Outcome Measure

Before you can show that the treatment causes a change in behavior, you must first establish **covariation:** that changes in the treatment are accompanied by changes in the behavior. Therefore, to show that smiling causes people to help you, you must show that people are more helpful to you when you smile than when you do not.

In the randomized experiment, you would establish covariation by seeing whether the amount of help you received when you smiled was greater than when you did not smile. If the average amount of helping was the same in both groups, you would not have covariation. Because you would not have covariation (variations in smiling would not correspond with variations in helping), you would not conclude that the treatment had an effect. If, on the other hand, you received more help in the smiling condition than in the no-smile condition, you would have covariation.

Establishing Temporal Precedence: Showing That Changes in the Suspected Cause Come Before Changes in the Outcome Measure

Establishing covariation, by itself, does not establish causality. You must also establish **temporal precedence:** that the treatment comes before the change in behavior. In other words, you must show that you smile at others before they help you. Otherwise, it may be that you react with a smile after people help you. Without temporal precedence, you can't determine which variable is the cause and which is the effect. Thus, one reason correlational designs fail to establish that changes in the "first" variable caused changes in the "second" variable is that such designs often don't allow you to know which variable changed first.

In a randomized experiment, you automatically establish that the treatment comes before the change in behavior (temporal precedence) by manipulating the treatment. You always present the independent variable (smiling) before you present the dependent measure task (giving participants an opportunity to help).

Battling Spuriousness: Showing That Changes in the Outcome Measure Are Not Due to Something Other Than the Suspected Cause

In addition to establishing temporal precedence, you must show that the covariation you observed could be due only to the treatment. Ideally, you would do this by showing that the treatment is the only thing that varies. Therefore, to show that your smiling causes others to help you, you must show that everything—except for your smiling—is the same during the times that you smile and the times that you do not smile.

The Value of Battling Spuriousness

It's difficult to prove that the only difference between the times when you get help and times when you don't is your smile. But without such proof, you can't say that your smiling causes people to be more helpful. Why not? Because you might be smiling more when the weather is nice or when you are with your friends. These same conditions (being with friends, nice weather) may be the reason you are getting help—your smile may have nothing to do with it. If you cannot be sure that everything else was the same, the relationship between smiling and helpfulness may be **spurious:** due to other variables. Because correlational designs do not rule out spuriousness, you can't use those designs to make cause-and-effect statements.

Battling Spuriousness Without Keeping All Nontreatment Variables Constant

In the randomized experiment, you do not keep everything—except for the treatment variable—constant. There are some nontreatment variables, such as individual differences, that you can't control. There may be other nontreatment variables that you choose not to control. For example, you may decide to do your experiment in a real-world setting where you can't keep temperature, noise, and other factors constant.

How do you deal with these nontreatment variables that aren't being controlled? You use random assignment so that these uncontrolled variables are now random variables. As you will see in the next two sections, there are two advantages of converting nontreatment variables into random variables: (1) Random variables should not influence one group significantly more than another, and (2) statistics can be used to subtract out the effects of random variables.

Random Variables Affect All Groups (Almost) Equally. One advantage of random assignment is that the nontreatment variables should not substantially affect one group more than the other. Random assignment should spread those variables more or less equally into each of your groups, just as an electric mixer should distribute ingredients fairly equally to both sides of the bowl. With random assignment, your conditions will be equivalent except for the effects of the independent variable and the chance impact of random variables. Therefore, as a result of random assignment, only random variables stand in the way of keeping irrelevant variables constant.

Statistics Can Help You Estimate the Effects of Random Variables. If you could remove those random variables, you would be able to keep everything constant, thereby isolating the treatment as the cause of the change in behavior. Unfortunately, in the randomized experiment, you cannot keep nontreatment variables constant, and you cannot remove them. However, you can use statistics to estimate their effects: If the difference between groups is greater than the estimated effects of random variables, the results are declared "statistically significant."

If you find a statistically significant effect for your treatment variable, you can argue that your treatment variable causes a change in scores on the dependent measure. However, you may be wrong. Even with statistics, you can't perfectly estimate the effects of random variables 100% of the time. If you underestimate the effects of random variables in your study, then you may falsely label a chance difference as a treatment effect. In technical terminology, you may make a Type 1 error.

Fortunately, before you do the study, you establish what your chances are of making a Type 1 error. Usually, most investigators make the chances of committing a Type 1 error fairly remote. Specifically, most investigators set the probability of mistaking chance variation as a genuine treatment effect at less than 5 in 100 ($p < .05$).

Single-*n* Designs

Can we make reasonable inferences about the causes of an effect without random assignment? Psychological pioneers such as Wundt, Helmholtz, Ebbinghaus, Fechner, and Skinner often attempted to do so by conducting studies that involved intensively studying a single participant.

Although these researchers were intensively studying individual participants, their research did not involve clinical case histories. They did not look back at events that happened in an individual's life, try to determine that a particular event came before the individual started acting in a certain way, and then trust that no other event could be responsible for the participant acting that way. Instead, these pioneers isolated the cause of the key behavior by controlling the events that occurred in the participant's life.

To get a general sense of how their approach differs from the case study approach (a detailed description of an individual), consider Skinner's experimental study of superstitious behavior. Skinner did not find a person who already engaged in superstitious behavior and then try to identify which of the person's thousands of genes, millions of life experiences, or billions of combinations among events and genes was responsible for the superstitious behavior. Nor did he look for people who claimed to have become less superstitious after an event (e.g., after going through primal scream therapy) and then assume that no other event within the person (becoming more mature) or outside the person (experiencing success) could be responsible for the change.

Instead, in a highly controlled environment (a Skinner box), Skinner induced and then eliminated superstitious behavior. Skinner arranged for a hungry pigeon to receive food "at regular intervals with no reference whatsoever to the bird's behavior" (Skinner, 1948, p. 168). Skinner was able to induce behavior that could be called superstitious, extinguish such behavior, and recondition it. He also demonstrated that behavior that could be described as superstitious was most likely when there was a 15-second interval between reinforcements. By systematically introducing and withdrawing the treatment, by observing changes in the behavior following changes in the treatment, and by not allowing other changes in the pigeon's environment, Skinner was able to make a convincing case that the treatment was the cause of the pigeon's superstitious behavior.

Note that the approach of a single-*n* researcher such as Skinner is like that of physicist performing an experiment whereas the approach of a case study researcher is like that of a naturalist observing a rare specimen. Specifically, Skinner and other researchers who use the

| Table 14-1 | **Designs and Causality** |

	ESTABLISH COVARIATION	MANIPULATE TREATMENT TO ESTABLISH TREATMENT COMES BEFORE EFFECT	RULE OUT OTHER EXPLANATIONS FOR RELATIONSHIP
Case studies			
Correlational study	√		
Quasi-experimental study	√	√	?
Randomized experiment	√	√	√
Single-*n* studies	√	√	√

single-*n* approach are able to do three things researchers who use case studies cannot (see Table 14-1).

First, Skinner was able to establish covariation because he was able to see how behavior changed as he repeatedly introduced and removed the treatment. Thus, he was able to establish a reliable, coincidence-free connection between the treatment and the superstitious behavior. The case study researcher, on the other hand, does not establish covariation. For example, suppose such a researcher studied the case of a Russian minister's brother who allegedly recovered from a mental illness after being thrown into an icy river (Henderson, 1985). Even if the story is true, the researcher has not established a reliable connection between being thrown into a cold river and mental health improvement (just as a reporter who finds a lottery winner has not established a reliable connection between playing Lotto and making money).

Second, Skinner was able to establish that the connection between rewards and superstitious behavior was a cause–effect connection because he was able to rule out nontreatment factors. By showing that before he introduced the rewards, the pigeon's rarely produced the behavior at a low and steady rate, he established that he had kept relevant nontreatment factors relatively constant. The case study researcher, on the other hand, cannot rule out the effects of other factors.

Third, Skinner and others can easily replicate (repeat) the study to verify the findings. If skeptical others obtain similar results, we can be more confident of the reliability of the original study's findings.

Like researchers using experimental designs, researchers using single-*n* designs establish that the cause comes before the effect (temporal precedence) by introducing the treatment variable before presenting the dependent measure task. Thus, both researchers would smile at the participant before giving the participant an opportunity to help. Like researchers using experimental designs, researchers using single-*n* designs establish covariation by comparing the different treatment conditions (comparing the amount of help received in the smiling versus no-smiling conditions). However, unlike researchers using experimental designs, researchers using single-*n* designs do not rely on randomization and statistical tests to rule out spuriousness (the effects of nontreatment factors).

Instead, the single-*n* researcher strives to keep nontreatment factors constant. That is, rather than letting nontreatment factors vary and then statistically accounting for the effects

Table 14-2	How Different Designs Infer Causality	
REQUIREMENT	**RANDOMIZED EXPERIMENTS**	**A–B SINGLE-*n* DESIGN**
Temporal Precedence (treatment came before changes in scores)	Introduce treatment before there is a change in the dependent variable.	Introduce treatment before there is a change in the dependent variable.
Covariation (different treatment conditions score differently on measure)	Observe difference between treatment and control conditions.	Observe difference between conditions A (baseline) and B (posttreatment behavior).
Accounting for Irrelevant Variables (determining that the change in behavior is not due to nontreatment factors)	1. Use independent random assignment to make sure all irrelevant factors vary randomly rather than systematically. 2. Then, use statistics to account for effects of these random factors. If the difference between groups is greater than would be expected as a result of these random factors, the difference is assumed to be the effect of the one non-random, systematically varied factor: the treatment.	1. Eliminate between-subject variables by using only one participant. 2. Control relevant environmental factors. Demonstrate that those factors have been controlled by establishing a stable baseline. Then, introduce treatment. If change occurs, that change is assumed to be due to the treatment.

of those variables, single-*n* researchers try to stop nontreatment factors from varying, thereby isolating the treatment's effect (see Table 14-2).

Battling Spuriousness by Keeping Nontreatment Factors Constant: The A–B Design

To understand how single-*n* researchers keep nontreatment factors constant, let's examine the simplest **single-*n* design,** the A–B design. In the **A–B design,** as in all single-*n* designs, the researcher studies a single participant and tries to make sure that the participant's behavior on the dependent-measure task occurs at a consistent rate. If we were studying the effects of rewards on how often a chicken pecked at a bar, we would first make sure the chicken was pecking at a constant rate. The process of ensuring that the behavior occurs at a steady, consistent rate is called establishing a **stable baseline.** This first step, the baseline behavior, is designated as A. Next, the researcher introduces the treatment and then compares posttreatment behavior (B) with baseline behavior (A).

As with all single-*n* designs, the A–B design strives to keep everything but the treatment constant. Specifically, the A–B design tries to make sure that differences between the conditions are not due to either of the two basic types of nontreatment variability: (a) between-subjects variability unrelated to the treatment and (b) within-subjects variability unrelated to the treatment.

As with all single-*n* designs, the A–B design makes sure that between-subjects variability can't cause the difference between treatment conditions. The difference between scores in the A condition and the B condition can't possibly be due to differences between participants because the participant in A was the same individual who was in the B condition.

Within-subjects variability, however, is a problem. An individual's moods and behaviors may naturally vary from moment to moment. Thus, in a sense, the same participant could be a different participant during the A phase of the study than during the B phase. So, how does the single-*n* researcher know that the treatment, rather than natural within-subjects variability, is responsible for the change in the participant's behavior?

The single-*n* researcher is confident that the difference between no-treatment and treatment conditions is not due to random within-subject variability because she has established a stable baseline. The **baseline** shows that the subject's behavior is not varying.

But how does a single-*n* researcher obtain a stable baseline? To obtain a stable baseline, the single-*n* researcher must hold constant all those variables that might affect the participant's responses.

If the researcher does not know what the relevant variables are, the participant's environment must be kept as constant as possible. Consequently, the researcher might perform the study under highly controlled conditions in a soundproof laboratory.

If the researcher knows what the relevant variables are, then only those variables need to be kept constant. Thus, if a researcher knew that parental praise was the only relevant variable in increasing studying behavior, the researcher would need to control only that one variable. However, the researcher usually does not know which variables can be safely ignored. Psychology has not advanced to the state where we can catalog what variables affect and don't affect every possible response.

After attempting to control variables, the researcher checks whether she has succeeded by looking at the baseline. If the baseline is not stable, the researcher continues to control variables until the behavior becomes stable.

But what if a researcher cannot achieve a stable baseline? Then, the researcher planning to use an A–B design has a problem: Changes in behavior that occur after the treatment is introduced may be due to something other than the treatment. Consequently, the researcher might not know whether the change in behavior is due to (a) normal fluctuations in the participant's behavior or (b) treatment effects.

There is still hope for the researcher who can't achieve a stable baseline. As you can see from Figure 14-1, if the participants' behavior changes dramatically after the treatment is introduced, A–B researchers can make a convincing case that the results are not due to normal baseline fluctuations.

Although it is difficult to achieve a stable baseline, we should point out that single-*n* researchers often do achieve a stable baseline. They are especially successful when they put a simple organism (e.g., a pigeon) in a simple environment (e.g., a Skinner box) and have it perform a simple behavior (e.g., peck a disk).

To this point, you have seen how the single-*n* researcher using an A–B design can hold individual difference variables and relevant environmental variables constant. But how does the researcher know that the difference between conditions is not due to **maturation:** natural biological changes in the organism, such as those due to development or fatigue?

The single-*n* researcher may limit maturation by choosing an organism that she knows won't mature substantially during the course of the study. She might use a pigeon or a rat because the extent of their maturation as it relates to certain tasks (bar pressing and pecking) is well documented.

Or, as you will soon see, the researcher may use a design that will allow her to account for maturation. But before looking at a design that accounts for maturation, let's look at an example of the A–B design.

In an early study of the effects of psychoactive drugs, Blough (1957) wanted to study the impact of LSD on a pigeon's visual perception. His first step was to place the pigeon in

Figure 14-1 — One Behavior Modification Program Appears to Reduce a Client's Cigarette Smoking

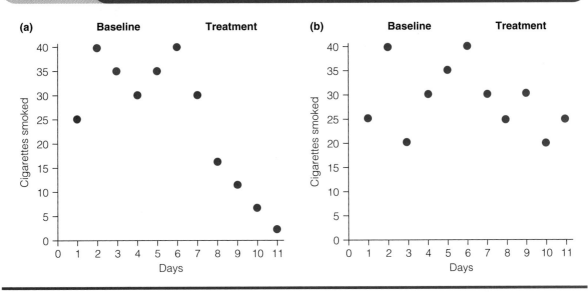

Note: In Figure 14-1a, the decrease in cigarettes smoked after the treatment was introduced on Day 7 seems to be due to the treatment. In Figure 14-1b, on the other hand, it is unclear whether the decrease in cigarettes smoked after Day 7 is due to anything more than normal fluctuations in the participant's behavior.

a highly controlled environment—a Skinner box—equipped with a light that illuminated a spot on the stimulus panel.

By varying the intensity of the light, Blough could make the spot easier—or more difficult—to see. On the wall of the Skinner box were two disks: "1" and "2." As an index of visual threshold, the pigeon was conditioned to peck at disk "1" when the spot was visible and to peck at disk "2" when the spot was not visible.

Before Blough administered his independent variable (LSD), he had to make sure that no other variables were influencing the pigeon's behavior. To do this, he had to keep all the relevant variables in the pigeon's environment constant. Therefore, he placed the pigeon in the Skinner box and carefully observed the pigeon's behavior. If he had succeeded in eliminating all nontreatment variables, the pigeon's behavior would be relatively stable—the relationship between pecking and illumination would be constant. If he had failed, he would have observed erratic fluctuations in the pigeon's pecking.

Once the pigeon's behavior was stable, Blough was ready to introduce the independent variable, LSD. After administering the LSD, Blough compared the pigeon's behavior after the treatment (B), to its behavior before the treatment (A). Blough found that after taking the LSD, the pigeon experienced decreased visual ability. Specifically, the pigeons pecked at disk 2 (cannot see spot) under a level of illumination that—prior to treatment—always led to a peck at disk 1. Because Blough had ensured that nontreatment variables were not influencing the pigeon's behavior, he concluded that the LSD was the sole cause of the decrease in visual ability.

Blough's study was exceptional because he knew that the pigeon's behavior on this task normally wouldn't change much over time. In studies with other kinds of participants or tasks, the researcher would not know whether participants would change, develop, or learn over time. Therefore, most researchers are not so confident that they have controlled all the important variables. In fact, as you will soon see, researchers know that two potentially important nontreatment variables have changed from measurement at baseline (A) to measurement after administering the treatment (B).

First, because the posttest occurs after the pretest, participants have had more practice on the posttest task. In technical terminology, their improved performance may be due to testing: the effects of doing the dependent measure task on subsequent performance on that task. For example, the practice a participant gets doing the task during the A phase may help the participant do better during the B phase.

Second, because the posttest occurs after the pretest, changes from pretest to posttest may be due to maturation. For instance, the participant's behavior may have changed over time due to fatigue, boredom, or development.

Variations on the A–B Design

Because psychologists want to know that their results are due to the treatment rather than to testing or maturation, single-*n* researchers rarely use the A–B design. Instead, they use variations on the A–B design such as the reversal design, psychophysical designs, and the multiple-baseline design.

The Reversal Design: Giving and Taking Away

In the **reversal design,** also known as the **A–B–A design** and the **A–B–A reversal design,** the researcher measures behavior (A), then administers the treatment and measures behavior (B), and then withdraws the treatment and measures behavior again (A).

To see why the A–B–A design is superior to the A–B design, consider one in a series of classic single-*n* designs demonstrating that behavior modification was an effective therapy for patients in mental hospitals (Ayllon & Azrin, 1968). In a mental hospital, Ayllon and Azrin worked with individuals who had been diagnosed as psychotic to see if a token economy was an effective way of increasing socially appropriate behavior. In a typical study, Ayllon and Azrin first identified an appropriate behavior (e.g., feeding oneself). Next, the researchers observed how often a certain patient performed that behavior. This phase of collecting baseline data for a patient could be labeled A. They then attempted to reinforce that behavior with a "token." Like money, the token could be exchanged for desirable outcomes such as candy, movies, social interaction, or privacy. During the treatment phase (labeled B), Ayllon and Azrin gave the patient tokens for each instance of the socially appropriate behavior and measured the behavior. They found that the patient performed more socially appropriate behaviors after the tokens were introduced. Therefore, a token economy increases socially appropriate behavior, right?

If Ayllon and Azrin's study had ended here, you could not be confident about that conclusion. Remember, with an A–B design, you don't know whether a change in behavior is due to maturation, testing, or the treatment.

Fortunately, Ayllon and Azrin expanded the A–B design to an A–B–A design by stopping the treatment while continuing to observe their patient's behavior. After removing the treatment, the incidence of socially appropriate behavior decreased. Consequently, they were able to determine that the treatment (tokens) increased socially appropriate behavior.

If, after withdrawing the treatment, socially appropriate behavior had continued to increase, they would not have concluded that the increase in socially appropriate behavior was due to the treatment. Instead, they would have concluded that the increase could be due to maturation or testing.

We should point out that the results were not quite as neat as we described. Admittedly, they found that socially appropriate behavior increased when they introduced the tokens and decreased when they stopped giving out tokens. Removing the tokens, however, did not cause the behavior to fall back all the way to baseline levels. Instead, the behavior fell back to near-baseline levels.

If tokens caused the effect, shouldn't their withdrawal cause the behavior to fall to baseline rather than near baseline? Admittedly, if the dependent measure (the rate of socially appropriate behavior) returned to baseline level, it would help make the case that the treatment had an effect. However, most behaviors won't return to baseline after you withdraw the treatment because of

1. maturation effects
2. testing effects
3. **carryover effects:** the treatment's effects persisting even after the treatment has been removed

Because of these three effects, you might be willing to say that the treatment had an effect, even if the behavior did not return to baseline. For example, you might be willing to say that the treatment had an effect if the participant's behavior was substantially different during treatment phase (B) than during either the pretreatment (A) and posttreatment (A) conditions (see Figure 14-2).

Unfortunately, even if posttreatment behavior returns to baseline, if the effects of practice or maturation are cyclical, your claim that the treatment caused an effect could be wrong.

Figure 14-2

Results From A–B–A Design: Number of Violent Acts Performed by Jim During the No-Punishment and "Time-Out" Punishment Phases

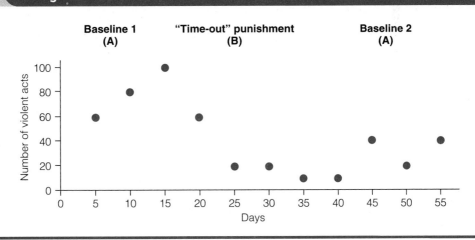

Note: Even though posttreatment violence did not revert back to pretreatment levels, a strong case can still be made that the time-out punishment reduced Jim's violent behavior.

For instance, suppose performance was affected by menstrual cycles. Performance might be good during the pretreatment phase (before menstruation), poor during the treatment phase (during menstruation), and good during the posttreatment phase (after menstruation). Although such an unsteady effect of maturation or testing would be unlikely, it is possible.[1]

To rule out the possibility that apparent treatment effects are due to some simple cyclical pattern involving either maturation or practice, you might extend the A–B–A design. For example, you might make it an A–B–A–B design. Ayllon and Azrin expanded their design to an A–B–A–B design and found that reintroduction of the token rewards led to an increase in the socially appropriate behavior.

Expanding beyond even the A–B–A–B design allows you to rule out the possibility of an even more complicated maturational or practice cycle. The more you expand the design, the less likely that maturation or practice would increase performance every time the treatment is introduced, but never increase performance when the treatment is removed. Thus, it would be very hard to describe a cycle of maturation and practice effects that could mimic treatment effects in an A–B–A–B–A–B–A–B–A–B–A–B–A–B design.

Psychophysical Designs

Psychophysical designs extend the A–B–A–B–A design. In psychophysical designs, participants are asked to judge stimuli. For instance, they may be asked to rate whether one light is brighter than another, one weight is heavier than another, or one picture is more attractive than another. The idea is to see how variations in the stimulus relate to variations in judgments. Because the dependent variable is psychological judgment and the independent variable is often some variation of a stimulus's physical characteristic (loudness, intensity, etc.), the name psychophysics is appropriate.

Because a participant can make psychophysical judgments quickly, a participant in a psychophysical experiment will be asked to make many judgments. Indeed, in a few exceptional cases, participants have been asked to make 67,000 judgments!

With so many judgments, you might worry about maturation effects. Participants might get tired as the research session goes on—and on.

In addition, you might be concerned about treatment carryover effects. Specifically, you might worry that earlier stimuli may affect ratings of later stimuli. Suppose you were rating how heavy you thought a 50-pound weight was. If the last 10 weights you had judged were all about 100 pounds, you might tend to rate 50 pounds as light. However, if the last 10 weights had all been around 10 pounds, you might tend to rate 50 pounds as heavy. Similarly, if you were judging how wealthy a person making $50,000 was, your rating would be affected by whether the previous people you had judged had been multimillionaires or poverty stricken (Wedell & Parducci, 1988).

Because of treatment carryover and maturation, the order of the treatments may affect the results. To deal with potential order effects, researchers often follow the advice of Gustav Fechner—psychophysics' inventor—by presenting each stimulus more than once and counterbalancing the order in which they present the stimuli. For example, if the researcher were interested in ratings of two stimuli (A and B), the researcher would present Stimulus A before Stimulus B half the time; the other half of the time, Stimulus B comes before Stimulus A. If Stimulus A receives different ratings when it is presented first than when it

---

[1]A similar problem could result if the individual you studied regularly went through periods of depression followed by periods of normal mood followed by depression (cyclical depression).

is presented last, the researchers know there are order effects. However, thanks to counterbalancing, these order effects should not make the average of Stimulus A's ratings different from the average of Stimulus B's.

In summary, maturation, testing, and carryover may cause order effects. To deal with these order effects, psychophysical designs often use three techniques:

1. multiple ratings
2. averaging
3. counterbalancing

The Multiple-Baseline Design

Another single-*n* design that rules out the effects of maturation, testing, and carryover is the multiple-baseline design. In a typical **multiple-baseline design,** you collect baselines for several key behaviors. For example, you might collect baselines for a child making her bed, putting away her toys, washing her hands, and vacuuming her room. Then, you would reinforce one of those key behaviors. If the behavior being reinforced (putting away her toys) increases, you might suspect that reinforcement is causing the behavior to increase.

Unfortunately, the increase in the desired behavior might be due to the child becoming more mature or due to some other nontreatment effect. To see whether the child's improvement in behavior is due to maturation or some other nontreatment factor, you would look at her performance on the other tasks. If those tasks are still being performed at baseline level, then nontreatment factors such as maturation and testing are not improving performance on those tasks and probably are not increasing the particular behavior you decided to reinforce. Therefore, you would be relatively confident that the improvement in putting away toys was due to reinforcement.

To be even more confident that the reinforcement is causing the change in behavior, you would reinforce a second behavior (washing hands) and compare it against the other nonreinforced behaviors. You would continue the process until you had reinforced all the behaviors, hoping to find that when you reinforced hand washing, hand washing increased—but that no other behavior increased. Similarly, when you reinforced tooth brushing, you would hope tooth brushing—and only tooth brushing—increased. If increases in behavior coincided perfectly with reinforcement, you would be confident that reinforcement was responsible for the increases in behavior (see Figure 14-3).

Evaluation of Single-*n* Designs

You have now examined some of the more popular single-*n* designs. Before leaving these designs, let's see how they stand up on three important criteria: internal, construct, and external validity.

Internal Validity

One strategy the single-*n* researcher uses to achieve internal validity is to keep many relevant variables constant. The single-*n* researcher holds individual difference variables constant by studying a single participant and may hold environmental variables constant by placing that participant in a highly controlled environment. For example, the single-*n* researcher may study a single rat pressing a bar inside a soundproof Skinner box.

Like the within-subjects researcher (see Chapter 13), the single-*n* researcher must worry that the changes in the participant's behavior could be due to the participant

| Figure 14-3 | **Hypothetical Data From a Multiple-Baseline Design** |

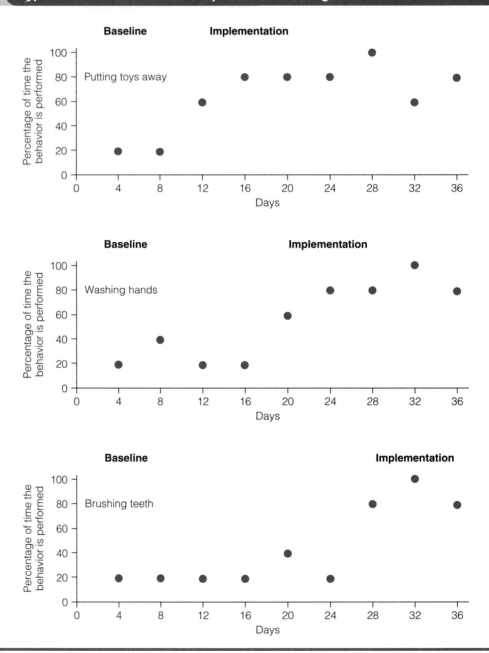

naturally changing over time (maturation) or due to the participant getting practice on the dependent-measure task (testing). Not surprisingly, within-subjects and single-*n* researchers may adapt similar strategies to deal with the threats of maturation and testing.

Both within-subjects and single-*n* researchers may try to rule out maturation by keeping their study so short that there is not enough time for maturation to occur. Both may try to reduce the effects of testing by giving participants extensive practice on the task before introducing the treatment, thereby reducing the chances that participants will benefit from any additional practice they get during the research study.

You don't have to take the single-*n* researchers' word that participants got enough practice. By showing that the response rate is stable before the treatment is introduced (the stable baseline), single-*n* researchers show that neither the practice nor anything else is causing the participant to improve during the latter part of the pretreatment phase.

Like the within-subjects experimenter, the single-*n* experimenter must be concerned about treatment carryover effects. Because of carryover, investigators using an A–B–A design frequently find that participants do not return to the original baseline. These carryover problems multiply when you use more levels of the independent variable and/or when you use more than one independent variable. Because carryover effects are a serious concern, most single-*n* researchers minimize carryover's complications by doing studies that have only two levels of a single independent variable. That is, rather than use an A–B–C–D–E–F–G–G–F–E–D–C–B–A design, most single-*n* researchers only use A–B–A–B designs. However, as you will soon see, internal validity concerns are not the only reason for simpler designs. Construct validity concerns also lead to choosing simpler designs.

Construct Validity

Although there are similarities between the single-*n* researcher and the within-subjects researcher in how they deal with internal validity concerns, the two researchers have even more in common when they attack threats to construct validity (see Table 14-3). For both researchers *sensitization* (participants figuring out the hypothesis because they have been exposed to several levels of the treatment) poses a serious problem, and both researchers use the same solutions. Specifically, both try to reduce the effects of sensitization by

1. using placebo treatments
2. using very few levels of treatment

Table 14-3	Similarities Between Within-Subjects Experiments and Single-*n* Designs		
PROBLEM	**SINGLE-*n* EXPERIMENT**	**WITHIN-SUBJECTS DESIGN**
Practice effects may harm internal validity.	Provide extensive practice before introducing treatment.	Provide extensive practice before introducing treatment.
Fatigue or maturation may harm internal validity.	Keep study brief.	Keep study brief.
Assorted order effects may harm internal validity.	Counterbalance sequence of treatments.	Counterbalance sequence and randomly assign participants to different sequences.
Carryover effects may harm internal validity.	Use few levels and few variables. Wait a long time between treatments.	Use few levels and few variables. Wait a long time between treatments.
Participants may learn what the study is about (sensitization), thus harming construct validity.	1. Use placebo treatments. 2. Use few levels of treatment. 3. Gradually increase or decrease intensity of treatment or use very similar levels.	1. Use placebo treatments. 2. Use few levels of treatment. 3. Gradually increase or decrease intensity of treatment or use very similar levels.

3. making the difference between the treatment conditions so subtle that participants don't realize that anything has changed (such as gradually varying the loudness of a stimulus)

External Validity

You may be satisfied with both the single-*n* designs internal validity and its construct validity. However, you probably question its external validity because you are concerned about (a) generalizing from a sample of one to most people and (b) generalizing from research conducted in highly controlled circumstances to real life.

To reduce your concerns about generalizing from a single participant, the single-*n* researcher would make four points. First, although it is risky to generalize from the sample of one that the single-*n* researcher uses, it is also risky to generalize from the nonrepresentative sample that most other experimenters use. If the participants who volunteer for a multiple-participant study are not a representative sample of any recognizable group, it is difficult to argue that such a study has more generalizability than a single-*n* study (Dermer & Hoch, 1999).

Second, even if a multiple-participant (multiple-*n*) experiment used a representative sample, the results may apply to groups but not to individuals. Just as a study may find that the average American family has 2.2 children even though no individual American family has 2.2 children, multiple-*n* experiments may find general truths that do not apply to any individual. For example, suppose that your treatment helps half the people but hurts the other half. Your multiple-*n* experiment might find no effect for the treatment (Dermer & Hoch, 1999).

Third, single-*n* researchers establish the external validity of their findings by replicating their studies. By demonstrating that the treatment has the same effect on each individual studied, they provide some evidence that the effect generalizes across individuals (Dermer & Hoch, 1999). In contrast, note that replicating a multiple-*n* experiment numerous times might fail to establish that the results apply to most people. For example, one could use multiple large random samples to replicate a multiple-*n* experiment numerous times, consistently obtain an average treatment effect, and fail to realize that the effect occurred only for certain types of participants.

Fourth, when single-*n* researchers investigate universal, fundamental processes, the results obtained from one individual can be generalized to the entire species. For example, the results of classical conditioning experiments performed on a single individual can be generalized to other members of that species.

To reduce your concerns about generalizing from research conducted in highly controlled circumstances, the single-*n* researcher would make three points. First, lab studies tend to have excellent external validity (Anderson, Lindsay, & Bushman, 1999).

Second, the setting to which you want to generalize may be just as highly controlled as the lab setting. For instance, you may want to generalize the results to clients in a biofeedback lab.

Third, not all single-*n* studies are conducted in lab settings. Many times, the setting is the real world. Single-*n* studies have been done in homes, schools, and businesses.

In short, the single-*n* design does not get high marks for external validity. However, under some circumstances, the results from a study using a single-*n* design may have a high degree of generalizability.

Conclusions About Single-*n* Designs

We have evaluated the single-*n* designs in terms of internal, construct, and external validity. Overall, single-*n* designs, although not possessing the internal validity of a true, randomized experiment, have some internal validity. Generally, single-*n* designs can have adequate construct validity. Thus, often the decision about whether to use a single-*n* design comes down to whether the researcher is worried about external validity. Consequently, single-*n* designs are most useful under two circumstances: (a) when external validity is not a goal and (b) when external validity is not a problem.

Establishing external validity is not a goal in those applied situations in which the investigator is interested in the causes of one individual's behavior. Suppose you were trying to change your own behavior or the behavior of a family pet. Or, suppose a therapist is treating a client and wants to see if the treatment is having a measurable effect on that particular patient. In all these cases, the single-*n* design would be the best way to evaluate the effect of the treatment.

Establishing external validity does not always require studying multiple participants. In some situations, generalizing the results from one participant to a larger group may be acceptable. For example, suppose that you want to make statements about fundamental, universal processes that we understand fairly well. Then, according to single-*n* researchers, you should use a single-*n* design. After all, it would be wasteful to study many participants if the treatment has the same effect on everyone. Because all people tend to respond similarly to reinforcements, the single-*n* design is commonly used in behavior modification research. Likewise, because everyone seems to respond similarly to psychophysical manipulations, the single-*n* design is also a popular alternative to the randomized experiment in psychophysical research.

Quasi-Experiments

Another popular alternative to the randomized experiment is the **quasi-experiment.** Like true experiments, quasi-experiments involve administering a treatment. Unlike true experiments, though, participants are not randomly assigned to treatment (Cook & Campbell, 1979).[2]

Ideally, researchers could determine a treatment's effect because they could always make sure that participants were randomly assigned to condition. Researchers, however, do not run the world.

People who do run the world usually won't relinquish their power to researchers. Those in control want to decide who gets which treatment, rather than letting researchers use random assignment to determine who gets which treatment. Judges usually like to decide what sentence to give, rather than leaving it up to random assignment. Parents may not allow their children to be randomly assigned to watch violent television. Bosses often want to choose who gets training. Cable companies may want to decide who to serve based on geography and income rather than on random assignment.

Even when money and power aren't issues, some people object that random assignment is not fair. On one hand, this argument seems absurd. What could be fairer than allowing

---

[2]According to this definition, single-*n* designs are quasi-experiments. However, people usually think of single-*n* designs as being different from quasi-experiments because, relative to other quasi-experiments, single-*n* experiments study fewer participants under more controlled conditions.

everyone who wants a treatment an equal chance at it? On the other hand, a good case can be made that the treatment should be given to the people who are the most needy or the most qualified.

For a variety of reasons, researchers are often unable to randomly assign participants to condition. Even when researchers can randomly assign, the internal validity of those studies may be weak because the random assignment does not stick (Ehrenberg, Brewer, Gamoran, & Willms, 2001). The random assignment may not stick because

1. participants assigned to receive one condition may get themselves re-assigned so they can receive what they consider the better treatment (e.g., the drug rather than the placebo, the enrichment program rather than the ordinary program)

2. participants drop out of one group much more than another (Ehrenberg et al., 2001)

Even if a researcher finds a situation in which the researcher can (a) randomly assign participants and (b) get the assignment to stick, that situation is probably not typical. Consequently, there may be questions about that field experiment's external validity (Ehrenberg et al., 2001).

As you have seen, researchers wishing to use random assignment to evaluate the effects of real-world treatments face three problems: (1) the powers-that-be may prohibit the study; (2) participants may reassign themselves to condition, thereby ruining the study's internal validity; and (3) studying participants who fully cooperate with random assignment may involve studying a nonrepresentative group of participants, thereby harming the study's external validity. Consequently, when evaluating the effects of many real-world treatments—from therapy, to training programs, to introducing new technology to social programs—using quasi-experimental designs is often the researcher's best option.

Because quasi-experimental designs are so useful for assessing the effects of real-life treatments, we will devote the rest of this chapter to these designs. We will begin by discussing the general logic behind quasi-experimental designs. Then, we will take a more detailed look at some popular quasi-experimental designs.

Battling Spuriousness by Accounting for—Rather Than Controlling—Nontreatment Factors

Like experimenters, quasi-experimenters can show that the change in behavior occurred after they introduced the treatment, establishing temporal precedence. Also like experimenters, quasi-experimenters assess covariation by comparing treatment versus nontreatment conditions. However, unlike experimenters, quasi-experimenters do not randomize the effects of nontreatment factors and then statistically control for those random effects. Furthermore, unlike single-*n* researchers, quasi-experimenters cannot control for nontreatment factors by keeping those factors constant.

Identifying Nontreatment Factors: The Value of Campbell and Stanley's Spurious Eight

The challenge in quasi-experiments is to rule out the effects of nontreatment variables without either the aid of random assignment or the ability to control nontreatment variables. The first step in meeting this challenge is to identify all the variables other than your treatment that might account for the change in participants' scores. After you have identified those nontreatment factors, you will try to demonstrate that those nontreatment factors did not account for the change in participants' scores. After you have ruled out all those nontreatment factors, you can argue that your treatment caused the effect.

To identify every possible nontreatment factor that could threaten your study's internal validity might seem like an unmanageable task. However, Campbell and Stanley (1963) made the task manageable by discovering that all these potential threats to internal validity fall into eight general categories. Thus, rather than dealing with an almost infinite number of specific threats to internal validity, researchers can focus on the following eight general threats to internal validity:

1. **Testing:** apparent treatment effects that are really due to participants having learned from the pretest. For example, practice on the pretest may improve performance on the posttest.

2. **Maturation:** apparent treatment effects that are really due to natural biological changes—from changes due to growing and developing to changes due to becoming more tired or more hungry.

3. **History:** apparent treatment effects that are really due to events in the outside world that are unrelated to the treatment.

4. **Instrumentation:** apparent treatment effects that are really due to changes in the measuring instrument. For example, the researcher may use a revised version of the measure on the retest.

5. **Regression (regression toward the mean, statistical regression):** apparent treatment effects that are really due to the tendency for participants who receive extreme scores on the pretest to receive less extreme scores on the posttest.

6. **Mortality (attrition):** apparent treatment effects that are really due to participants dropping out of the study. For instance, suppose that participants who would score poorly drop out of the treatment condition, but not out of the no-treatment condition. In that case, the treatment group would score higher than the no-treatment group, even if the treatment had no effect.

7. **Selection:** apparent treatment effects that are really due to the different treatment groups being different from each other before the study started.

8. **Selection-maturation interaction:** apparent treatment effects that are really due to groups that scored similarly on the pretest naturally growing apart and scoring differently on the posttest.

As you will soon see, the eight threats to validity fall into three general categories. First, there are those environmental and physiological events—other than the treatment—that cause individuals to change. Second, there are errors in measurement that cause changes in individuals' scores. Third, there are problems related to the fact that treatment and no-treatment groups—because different individuals are in the two groups—may differ from each other even when the treatment has no effect.

Three Reasons Individuals Change Even Without Treatment. The first three threats to validity—testing, maturation, and history—include all the nontreatment factors that can cause individual participants to change. The first two—testing and maturation—are threats we talked about in terms of the single-*n* design. As you may recall, we were concerned that testing (the participant learning from performing the dependent measure task several times) might cause the participant's behavior to change between the A and B phases of an A–B design. We were also concerned that maturation (any changes in the participant's internal, physiological environment, such as changes due to growing old or becoming hungry) might cause the participant's behavior to change. However, because we could keep the outside environment constant, we were not concerned about history (any nontreatment changes in the external environment).

How Measurement Errors Can Look Like a Treatment Effect. The next two threats, instrumentation and statistical regression, can cause participants in the treatment conditions to have different scores than they did in the no-treatment condition even though the participants themselves have not changed. With instrumentation, participants are tested with one measuring instrument in one condition and a different measuring instrument in another condition. No wonder their scores are different.

Statistical regression is harder to spot. To understand statistical regression (also called regression and regression toward the mean), remember that most scores contain some random error. Usually, however, random error's net effect on the overall average score is zero because the scores that random error pushes upward are balanced out by the scores that random error pulls downward.

But what if we select only those participants whose scores have been pushed way up by random error? When we retest them, their scores will go down. Their scores going down might fool us into thinking they had really changed. In fact, all that has happened is that random error isn't going to push up all these scores again (just as lightning is unlikely to strike the same place twice). Instead, this second time, random error will push some scores up, some scores down, and have almost no effect on the remaining scores.

You might wonder how we could select scores that have been pushed up by random error. One way is to select extreme scores. For example, if we select only those people who got 100% on an exam, we know that random error did not decrease their scores. However, random error (lucky guesses, scorer failing to see a question that was missed) could have increased those scores. Thus, if we give these people a test again, their scores are likely to go down. This tendency for extreme scorers to score less extremely when they are retested is called regression toward the mean.

Regression toward the mean is a powerful effect. Whether watching a baseball player on a hitting streak (or in a hitting slump), watching the economy, or observing a patient, you will find that extreme events tend to revert back to more normal levels.

To this point, we have talked about factors that could change an individual's scores. We explained that a participant in the treatment condition may change for reasons having nothing to do with the treatment (maturation, testing, history). We have also talked about how an individual's score can change, even though the individual doesn't really change (instrumentation, regression). In some cases, these changes in individual participants' scores could cause a treatment group to score differently from a no-treatment group.

Three Differences Between Treatment and No-Treatment Groups That Have Nothing to Do With the Treatment. Even when the individual scores are accurate and unaffected by treatment-irrelevant influences, the treatment group may differ from the no-treatment group simply because the participants in the treatment group have different characteristics than those in the no-treatment group. Basically, there are three treatment-irrelevant factors that could cause participants in the treatment condition to systematically differ from participants in the no-treatment condition: mortality, selection, and selection-maturation.

With mortality (attrition), for example, your poor performers may have dropped out of the treatment condition. As a result, your treatment condition scores would be higher than your no-treatment condition scores—even if your treatment had no effect.

With selection, you are comparing groups that were different before the study began. As the saying goes, "that's not fair—you're comparing apples and oranges." If your treatment group started out being very different from your no-treatment group, the differences between your group's scores at the end of the study may not be due to the treatment. Therefore, you shouldn't conclude that the difference in scores between your two groups is due to the treatment. Even if you selected two groups who scored similarly on your measure before you introduced the treatment, you can't conclude that they would have scored similarly at the end of the study because of selection-maturation interactions: Groups that scored similarly in the pretest may naturally mature at different rates.

Using Logic to Combat the Spurious Eight

Once you have identified the threats to internal validity, you must determine which threats are automatically ruled out by the design and which threats you can eliminate through logic (see Table 14-4). Quasi-experimental designs differ in their ability to automatically rule out the eight threats to internal validity. Some designs rule out most of these threats; some rule

Table 14-4 Steps Quasi-Experimenters May Take to Minimize Threats to Internal Validity

THREATS	PRECAUTIONS
History	Isolate participants from external events during the course of the study.
Maturation	Conduct the study in a short period of time to minimize the opportunities for maturation.
	Use participants who are maturing at slow rates.
Testing	Only test participants once.
	Give participants extensive practice on task prior to collecting data so that they won't benefit substantially from practice they obtain during the study.
	Know what testing effects are (from past data) and subtract out those effects.
	Use different versions of same test to decrease the testing effect.
Instrumentation	Administer same measure, the same way, every time.
Mortality	Use rewards, innocuous treatments, and brief treatments to keep participants from dropping out of the study.
	Use placebo treatments or subtly different levels of the treatment so that participants won't be more likely to drop out of the treatment condition.
	Make sure participants understand instructions so that participants aren't thrown out for failing to follow directions.
Regression	Don't choose participants on basis of extreme scores.
	Use reliable measures.
Selection	Match on all relevant variables.
	Don't use designs that involve comparing one group of participants with another.
Selection Interactions	Match on all relevant variables, not just on pretest scores. In addition, use tips from earlier in this table to reduce the effects of variables—such as history and maturation—that might interact with selection. In other words, reducing the role of maturation will also tend to reduce selection by maturation interactions.

out only a few. Yet, even with a quasi-experimental design that automatically rules out only a few of these threats, you may occasionally be able to infer causality.

To illustrate the potential usefulness of quasi-experimental designs, we will start by looking at a design that most people would not even consider to be in the same class as a quasi-experimental design: the **pretest–posttest design.** As the name suggests, you test one group of participants, administer a treatment, and then retest them.

This design does not rule out many threats automatically; hence, its low status as a design. However, because you are comparing individuals against themselves, it does automatically rule out selection and selection-maturation interactions.

Although the pretest–posttest design does not automatically rule out mortality, instrumentation, regression, maturation, history, and testing, you may still be able to rule out these threats. If nobody dropped out of your study, mortality (attrition) is not a problem. If you were careful enough to use the same measure and administer it in the same way, instrumentation is not a problem. If there were only a few minutes between the pretest and posttest, then history is unlikely.

If there were only a few minutes between pretest and posttest, maturation is also unlikely. About the only maturation that could occur in a short period would be boredom or fatigue. If performance was better on the posttest than on the pretest, then you could rule out boredom and fatigue—and thus maturation.

You might even be able to rule out regression. The key to ruling out regression is to realize that regression occurs when extreme pretest scores that were inflated (or deflated) by random error revert back to more average scores on the retest. Therefore, to rule out regression, you need to make the case that random error had not inflated (or deflated) pretest scores by establishing either that

1. your measure was so reliable (so free of random error) that random error would have little impact on pretest scores
2. participants in the study did not have pretest scores that were extreme

Thus far, in this particular study, you have been able to rule out every threat except testing—and you might even be able to rule out testing. For instance, if participants did not know they had been observed (e.g., you unobtrusively recorded how long they gazed into each other's eyes), testing should not be a problem. Or, if you used a standardized test, you might know how much people tend to improve when they take the test the second time. If your participants improved substantially more than people typically improve upon retesting, you could rule out the testing effect as the explanation for your results.

As you have seen, the pretest–posttest design, by itself, has poor internal validity because it automatically eliminates only a few threats to internal validity. But, as you have seen, you may be able to use your wits to rule out the remaining threats and thereby infer causality (see Table 14-5 for a review). Furthermore, as you will soon see, by extending the pretest–posttest design, you can create a quasi-experimental design that eliminates most threats to internal validity—the time-series design.

Time-Series Designs

Like the pretest–posttest design, the **time-series design** tests and retests the same participants. However, rather than use a single pretest and a single posttest, the time-series design uses several pretests and posttests. Thus, you could call time-series designs "pre–pre–pre–pre–post–post–post–post" designs.

Table 14-5	How to Deal With the Threats to Internal Validity If You Must Use a Pretest–Posttest Design

THREAT	HOW TO DEAL WITH IT
Selection	Automatically eliminated because participants are tested against themselves.
Selection by Maturation	Automatically eliminated because participants are tested against themselves.
Mortality	Not a problem if participants don't drop out. Conduct study over short period of time and use an undemanding treatment.
Instrumentation	Standardize the way you administer the measure.
Regression	Do not select participants based on extreme scores. Use a reliable measure.
Maturation	Minimize the time between pretest and posttest.
History	Minimize the time between pretest and posttest.
Testing	Use an unobtrusive measure. Have data from previous studies about how much participants' scores tend to change from test to retest.

To illustrate the differences between the pretest–posttest design and the time-series design, suppose you are interested in seeing whether a professor's disclosures about her struggles to learn course material affects how students evaluate her. Let's start by examining how you would use a pretest–posttest design to find the effect of such disclosures.

With a pretest–posttest design, you would have a class evaluate the professor before she tells them about her struggles to learn course material. Then, you would have them rate her after she discloses her problems. If you observed a difference between pretest and posttest ratings, you would be tempted to say that the difference was due to the disclosure. However, the difference in ratings might really be due to history, maturation, testing, mortality, instrumentation, or regression. Because you have no idea of how much of an effect history, maturation, testing, mortality, and instrumentation may have had, you cannot tell if you had a treatment effect.

Estimating the Effects of Threats to Validity With a Time-Series Design

What if you extended the pretest–posttest design? That is, what if you had students rate the professor after every lecture for the entire term, even though the professor would not disclose her problems with learning material until the fifth week? Then, you would have a time-series design.

What do you gain by all these pretests? From plotting the average ratings for each lecture, you know how much of an effect maturation, testing, instrumentation, and mortality tend to have (see Table 14-6). In other words, when you observe changes from pretest to pretest, you know those changes are not due to the treatment. Instead, those differences must be due to maturation, testing, history, instrumentation, or mortality.

For example, suppose ratings steadily improve at a rate of .2 points per week during the 5-week, predisclosure period. If you then found an increase of .2 points from Week 5 (when the professor made the disclosures about her problems) to Week 6, you would not attribute that increase to the disclosures. Instead, you would view such a difference as

Table 14-6	How Pretest–Posttest Designs and Time-Series Designs Stack Up in Terms of Dealing With Campbell and Stanley's Threats to Internal Validity

	TYPE OF DESIGN	
THREAT TO VALIDITY	PRETEST–POSTTEST	TIME-SERIES
Selection	Automatically eliminated.	Automatically eliminated.
Selection × Maturation Interactions	Automatically eliminated.	Automatically eliminated.
Mortality	Through logic and careful planning, this threat can be eliminated.	Through logic and careful planning, this threat can be eliminated.
Instrumentation	Through logic and careful planning, this threat can be eliminated.	Through logic and careful planning, this threat can be eliminated.
Maturation	Problem!	Often, you will be able to estimate the extent to which differences between your groups could be due to maturation.
History	Problem!	Problem!
Regression	Problem!	You should be able to determine whether regression is a plausible explanation for the difference between conditions.

being due to the effects of history, maturation, mortality, testing, or instrumentation. If, on the other hand, you found a much greater increase in ratings from Week 5 to Week 6 than you found between any other 2 consecutive weeks, you might conclude that the professor's disclosures about her struggles to learn course material improved her student evaluations (see Figure 14-4).

Problems in Estimating Effects of Nontreatment Factors

Unfortunately, that conclusion could be wrong. Your conclusion is valid only if you can correctly estimate the effects of history, maturation, mortality, testing, and instrumentation during the time that the treatment was administered. On the surface, it seems safe to assume that you can estimate the effects of those variables. After all, for the pretest period, you know what the effects of those variables were. Thus, you may feel safe assuming that the effects of those variables were the same during the treatment period as they were during the pretest period. But this assumption is correct only if the effects of history, maturation, mortality, instrumentation, and testing are relatively consistent over time. In other words, your conclusions about the treatment's effect could be wrong if there is a sudden change in any one of these nontreatment factors (see Table 14-7).

Sudden changes in these nontreatment factors are possible. As you will see, history and regression tend to produce sudden changes, and the effects of testing, instrumentation, mortality, and maturation are not always slow and consistent across time.

History. To see how history could produce a sudden change, imagine just some of the many specific events that could affect performance on the posttest. For instance, ratings of the professor might change as a result of students getting the midterm back, the professor becoming ill, the professor reading a book on teaching, and so on. Unlike the single-*n* design, the

Figure 14-4 | **Two Very Different Patterns of Results in a Time-Series Design in Which the Treatment Was Introduced After the Fifth Week**

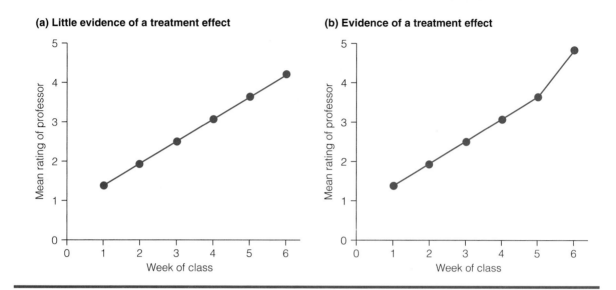

(a) Little evidence of a treatment effect

(b) Evidence of a treatment effect

Table 14-7 | **Threats to Time-Series Designs**

- History: By far the most serious threat
- Regression (although you should be able to tell whether regression could be a problem)
- Any other inconsistent effect. Usually, the only inconsistent effects will be history and regression. Usually, maturation, mortality, testing, and maturation will have consistent effects that you can estimate. However, if their effect is inconsistent, it could imitate a treatment effect. Thus, the following are possible, but unlikely, threats to a time-series study's validity
- Inconsistent maturation effects
- Inconsistent testing effects
- Inconsistent mortality effects (if you don't have any dropouts or if the number of dropouts is consistent throughout the study, you probably don't have a mortality problem)
- Inconsistent instrumentation effects (if you do your study properly, you shouldn't have instrumentation effects)

time-series design does not control all these history effects. Indeed, you could argue that the time-series design's lack of control over history, and thus its vulnerability to history, prevents it from reaching experimental-design status.

Although *history is the one threat to which the time-series is extremely vulnerable*, you can try to reduce its effects. One strategy is to have a very short interval between testing sessions, thus giving history fewer opportunities to have an effect.

In addition to reducing the effects of history, you can also try to do a better job of estimating its effects. Because the better you know the past, the better you should be able to estimate history's effects, you might collect an extensive baseline. Ideally, you would collect baseline data for several years to help you identify any patterns that might otherwise be mistaken for a treatment effect. For instance, your baseline would alert you to cyclical patterns in student evaluations, such as students being very positive toward the professor during the first 2 weeks of the term, more negative toward the professor after the midterm examination, then becoming more favorable during the last week of the term. Thus, consulting your baseline data would prevent you from mistaking these cyclical fluctuations for a treatment effect.

Regression. Like the effects of history, regression effects will not change steadily from week to week. After all, regression is due to chance measurement error, and chance measurement error will not change steadily and predictably from week to week. Although you cannot use a time-series design to measure regression's effect, you can use time-series designs to determine if regression is a likely explanation for your results. Specifically, you should suspect regression if

1. the ratings immediately before the treatment are extremely high or extremely low relative to the previous ratings
2. the posttreatment ratings, although very different from the most immediate pretreatment ratings, are not substantially different from earlier pretreatment ratings

Inconsistent Effects From Threats That Are Often Consistent. The effects of history and regression are difficult to estimate because they are likely to be inconsistent. Although the effects of instrumentation, mortality, testing, and maturation are less likely to be inconsistent, they sometimes are inconsistent.

Inconsistent Instrumentation Effects. If you administered the same rating scale in the same way for the first 5 weeks, your measurements from Weeks 1 through 5 would not be affected by instrumentation. As a result, your estimate for the amount of change to expect between Week 5 and Week 6 would not include any effect for instrumentation. However, suppose that you ran out of copies of the original rating scale during Week 6 and decided, while you were going to the trouble to run off more copies, that you would make some minor corrections to the form. Consequently, you handed out a refined version of your rating scale during Week 6—the same week the professor started telling her class about her struggles to learn course material. In that case, you might have an instrumentation effect that could not have been estimated based upon the previous weeks' data. Therefore, you might mistake an instrumentation effect for a treatment effect.

Inconsistent Mortality Effects. Similarly, if mortality does not follow a consistent pattern, you might mistake mortality's effects for treatment effects. For example, suppose that the last week to drop the course was the same week the professor started to tell the class about her problems. In that case, a disproportionate number of students who did not like the professor might drop out during that week. Consequently, the professor's ratings might improve because of attrition rather than because of her disclosures.

Inconsistent Testing Effects. In the study we've been discussing, the effect of testing should be gradual and consistent. However, the effect of testing will not be consistent in every study. In some studies, for example, participants will, in a flash of insight, discover the rule behind the task, and, as soon as they discover the rule, their performance increases dramatically.

Inconsistent testing effects are not limited to situations in which participants are aware of having an insight. That is, practice does not always produce steady, continuous improvement. As you know from experience, after weeks of work with little to show for it, you may suddenly improve.

Inconsistent Maturation Effects. Similarly, maturation's effect may sometimes be discontinuous. For instance, suppose you measure young children every 3 months on a motor abilities test. Then, you expose them to an enriched environment and measure them again. Certainly, you will see a dramatic change, but is this change due to the treatment? Or, is it due to the children jumping to a more advanced developmental stage (for example, learning to walk)?

You cannot escape sudden, sporadic maturation by studying adults. Even in our teacher evaluation study, participants might mature at an inconsistent rate. That is, first-year students might grow up quickly after getting their first exams back, or students might suddenly develop insight into the professor's lecturing style. If this sudden development occurred the same week the professor started to disclose her struggles to learn course material, maturation could masquerade as a treatment effect.

Eliminating, Rather Than Estimating, Threats to Internal Validity

In short, although the time-series design can rule out certain threats to validity by estimating the effects of those threats (see Table 14-8), there are certain effects that it cannot accurately estimate. Therefore, when using a time-series design, do not focus so much on estimating the impact of the eight threats to validity that you don't try to eliminate those eight threats.

Table 14-8	How the Time-Series Design Deals With Threats to Internal Validity
THREAT	**APPROACH**
Selection	Automatically eliminated because testing and retesting the same participants.
Selection × Maturation	Automatically eliminated because testing and retesting the same participants.
Instrumentation	If effects are constant, effects can be estimated. In addition, try to use the same instrument in the same way every time.
Mortality	If effects are constant, effects can be estimated. In addition, if no participants drop out, mortality is not a problem.
Testing	If effects are constant, effects can be estimated.
Maturation	If effects are constant, effects can be estimated. In addition, study slowly maturing participants or make sure that time between the last pretest and the posttest is very brief.
Regression	Regression is unlikely if ratings prior to introducing the treatment were not extreme and did not differ greatly from previous ratings. Because regression capitalizes on random error, regression is less likely if you use a measure that is relatively free of random error: a reliable measure.
History	Try to collect extensive pretest data to predict history's effects. In addition, you may try to make sure that 1. time between the last pretest and the posttest is brief. 2. participants are isolated from outside events.

Try to eliminate the threat of instrumentation by using the same measuring instrument each time and administering it the same way. In our student evaluation study, we would give students the same rating scales and the same instructions each time.

Likewise, try to eliminate mortality. If you had students sign their rating sheets, you could eliminate mortality by analyzing data from only those students who had perfect attendance.

If you can't eliminate a threat, at least try to reduce its effects. Try to reduce the effects of both maturation and history by keeping the interval between pretest and posttest short. Minimize the likelihood of regression effects by choosing the time that you will administer the treatment well in advance—don't administer the treatment as an immediate reaction to extremely low ratings.

Variations on the Traditional Time-Series Design

Now that you are familiar with the basic logic behind the time-series design, you are ready to see how it can be extended. One simple way of extending a time-series design is to increase the number of pretest and posttest measurements you take. There are two advantages to increasing the number of pretest and posttest measurements you take.

First, the more measurements you take, the better you should be at estimating the combined effects of maturation, history, mortality, testing, and instrumentation. Thus, you are less likely to mistake these effects for a treatment effect.

Second, the more measurements you have, the less likely it is that an unusual history, maturation, mortality, testing, or instrumentation effect would influence only the one, posttreatment measurement. To illustrate the advantages of having more measurements, suppose you measure student reactions on only the 5th, 6th, and 7th weeks. You administer the treatment between the 6th and 7th weeks. Would it be an unusual coincidence if history, maturation, mortality, or testing had more of an effect between the 6th and 7th weeks than between the 5th and 6th weeks? No—consequently, any of these threats to validity might easily imitate a treatment effect. However, what if you had students evaluate the teacher from Week 1 to Week 12? Then, it would be quite a coincidence for a threat to have an extraordinarily large effect between the 6th (the same week you gave the treatment) and 7th weeks, but not have such an effect between any of the other weeks.

Reversal Time-Series Designs. In addition to taking more measurements, you can extend your time-series design by administering and withdrawing the treatment. That is, you can imitate the single-*n* researcher's reversal design.

For example, you might test (pretest), administer the treatment, test again (posttest), withdraw the treatment, and test again. You might even withdraw and introduce the treatment several times.

To see the beauty of this reversal time-series design, imagine that you were able to get increases each time the professor tells her class about her struggles to learn course material, then decreases when she stops talking about her problems, followed by increases when the professor again tells her class about her studying woes. With that pattern of results, you would be confident that the disclosures made a difference.

Despite the elegance of the reversal design, ethical and construct validity problems may prevent you from using it. The ethical problems are the most serious: In some situations, you cannot ethically withdraw the treatment after you have administered it (for example, psychotherapy, reinforcement for wearing seatbelts).

The construct validity problems can also be serious. Specifically, withdrawing and re-administering the treatment may alert participants to your hypothesis. Consequently, your results may be due to participants guessing the hypothesis and playing along.

To prevent participants from guessing the hypothesis or becoming resentful when you withdraw the treatment, use placebo treatments or multiple levels of the treatment. If you were to use this design for your student evaluations study, you might have a placebo condition in which the professor discloses innocuous facts about studying experiences. Alternatively, you might use several levels of disclosure ranging from innocuous to intimate.

Two-Group Time-Series Design. A final way of extending the time-series design is to collect time-series data on two groups. One group, the comparison group, would not get the treatment. The advantage of using a comparison group is that it allows you to rule out certain history effects. In your disclosure study, the comparison group might be another section of the same professor's class. If, after the treatment was administered, the ratings went down only in the treatment group, you could rule out general history effects (midterm blues, spring fever) as an explanation of the results.

However, you can't rule out every history effect because the two classes may have different histories. For example, the afternoon class may be subjected to an overheated classroom whereas the morning class was not.

The Nonequivalent Control-Group Design

You do not have to use a time-series design. For example, rather than using a two-group time-series design, you could simply (a) give one group the treatment, then (b) measure both groups. Such a study would be called a nonequivalent control-group design. Essentially, the **nonequivalent control-group design** is the simple experiment without random assignment.

Because of the nonequivalent control-group design's similarity to the simple experiment, it has many of the simple experiment's strengths. For example, because every participant is tested only once, the nonequivalent control-group design, like the simple experiment, is not vulnerable to maturation, testing, or instrumentation. Furthermore, because of the control group, the nonequivalent group design, like the simple experiment, can usually deal with the effects of history, maturation, and mortality.

The Nonequivalent Control-Group Design Is Extremely Vulnerable to Selection

Because this design does not use random assignment, the control and treatment groups are not equivalent. Indeed, to make it clear that the control group is not equivalent to the treatment group, some have argued that using the term *control group* to describe the no-treatment group is inappropriate and should be replaced with the term *contrast group* (Wilkinson & the Task Force on Statistical Inference, 1999). Because the no-treatment and treatment groups are not equivalent, selection is a serious threat in this design.

Why Matching Doesn't Make Groups Equivalent

To address the selection threat, investigators often attempt either to ensure that each participant in the control group is identical in several key respects to a participant in the treatment group or to ensure that groups have the same average scores on key variables. These key variables may be background variables (age, gender, IQ) that are expected to correlate with scores on the dependent measure or they may be actual scores on the dependent measure (pretest scores).

Although you might think that matching would succeed at making the nonequivalent control group equivalent to the treatment group, realize two important points about matched participants:

1. Matched participants or groups are matched only on a few variables rather than on every variable.
2. Matched participants or groups are not matched on characteristics directly, but on imperfect measures of those characteristics.

You Can't Match on Everything. Just because two groups are matched on a few variables, you shouldn't think that they are matched on all variables. They aren't. The unmatched variables may cause the two groups to score differently on the dependent measure (see Table 14-9).

For instance, suppose you decide to use a nonequivalent group design to test your hypothesis about the effect of self-disclosing problems with learning material. To make the two classes similar, you match the classes on IQ scores, grade point averages, proportion of psychology majors, proportion of females and males, and proportion of sophomores, juniors, and seniors. However, you have not matched them in terms of interest in going on to graduate school, number of times they had taken classes from this professor before, and a few hundred other variables that might affect their ratings of the professor. These unmatched variables, rather than the treatment, may be responsible for the difference between your treatment and control groups.

Because investigators realize that they cannot match participants on every factor that may influence task performance, some investigators try to match participants on task performance (pretest scores). Yet, even when groups are matched on pretest scores, unmatched variables can cause the groups to score differently on the posttest. Just because two groups

Table 14-9	How Two Nonequivalent Control-Group Designs Stack Up in Terms of Dealing With Threats to Internal Validity

	TYPE OF NONEQUIVALENT CONTROL GROUP	
THREAT TO VALIDITY	**UNMATCHED**	**MATCHED**
Selection	Big problem!	Problem
Selection × *Maturation*	Problem	Problem
Regression	Not a problem	Big problem!
Mortality	Should not be a problem	Should not be a problem
Instrumentation	Should not be a problem	Should not be a problem
Maturation	Automatically eliminated by the design	Automatically eliminated by the design
Testing	Automatically eliminated by the design	Automatically eliminated by the design
History	Automatically eliminated by the design	Automatically eliminated by the design

of students start out with the same enthusiasm for a course, you cannot be sure that they will end the term with the same enthusiasm. For example, one group may end the term with more enthusiasm because that group began the course with a clearer understanding of what the course would be like, what the tests would be like, and how much work was involved. Consequently, although both groups might rate the professor the same at first, the groups may differ after they get the first exam back. For instance, because the naïve group had misconceptions about what the professor's exams would be like, they may rate the professor more harshly than the experienced group.

Although this change in student attitudes toward the professor might appear to be a treatment effect, it is not. Instead, the difference between the two groups is due to the groups differing on variables that they were not matched on—and those differences causing the groups to grow apart. Technically, there was a selection by maturation interaction. Because of interactions between selection and other variables, even matching on pretest scores does not free you from selection problems.

What can be done about interactions between selection and other variables? One approach is to assume that nature prefers simple, direct main effects to complex interactions. Thus, if an effect could be due to either a treatment main effect or an interaction between selection and maturation, assume that the effect is a simple treatment main effect. Be aware, of course, that your assumption could be wrong.

If you want to go beyond merely assuming that selection-maturation interactions are unlikely, you can make them less likely by making the groups similar on as many selection variables as possible. You can match the groups not only on pretest scores but also on other variables. With such extensive matching, there would be fewer variables on which the groups differed and, therefore, fewer selection variables to interact with maturation. Hence, you would reduce the chance of selection-maturation interactions occurring.

You have seen that one way to reduce interactions between selection variables and maturation is to reduce differences between groups that might contribute to selection. The other way to reduce interactions between selection and maturation is to reduce opportunities for maturation. After all, if neither group can mature, then you won't have a selection-maturation interaction. To reduce the potential for a selection by maturation interaction, you may decide to present the posttest as soon after the pretest as possible.

You Match on Measures of Variables—Not on Variables. As you have seen, failing to match on every relevant variable sets you up for selection-maturation interactions. Another problem with matching is that participants must be matched on observed scores, rather than on true scores.

Observed scores are not the same as true scores because observed scores are contaminated by measurement error. As a result of this measurement error, two groups might appear to be similar on certain variables, although they are actually very different on those variables.

How can participants score the same on a measure of a variable, but actually be different in terms of that variable? To see how, suppose a researcher wanted to examine the effect of a drug on treating clinical depression. The researcher has received approval and patients' permissions to give the drug to the 10 individuals at her small psychiatric facility who have been diagnosed with severe depression. However, she realizes that if the participants improve after getting the drug, it proves nothing. Maybe the patients would get better anyway. She wants to have a comparison group that does not get the drug. After getting a phone call asking her to give a guest lecture at a nearby college, she gets an idea. She could use some college students as her comparison group. After testing hundreds of students, she obtains a group of 10 college students who score the same on the depression scale as her group of 10 individuals who are hospitalized for depression.

But are the two groups equal in terms of depression? Probably not. The college student participants' scores are extremely depressed relative to the average college student. The fact that the participants' scores are extremely different from the mean (average) sets up regression toward the mean.

Regression toward the mean occurs because extreme scores tend to have an extreme amount of random error. Thus, when the students are tested again, their scores will be less extreme because their scores will not be as dramatically swayed by random error. On the posttest, the college student participants will probably score more like average college students—less depressed. In this case, because of regression toward the mean, a drug that has no effect may appear to hurt recovery from depression.

How can you stop from mistaking such a regression effect for a treatment effect? One approach is to reduce regression. As we mentioned earlier, there are two ways to reduce the potential for regression effects. First, because regression takes advantage of random measurement error, you can reduce regression by using a measure that is relatively free of random measurement error: a reliable measure. Second, because extreme scores tend to be more influenced by random error than less extreme scores, don't select participants who have extreme pretest scores.

A trickier approach to combat regression is to obtain results that regression cannot account for. In our depression example, regression would tend to make it look like the college students had improved more than the individuals who were hospitalized for depression. However, if you found the opposite results—the individuals who were hospitalized for depression improving in mood more than college students—regression would not be an explanation for your results. Thus, one approach to eliminating regression is to get results exactly opposite from what regression would predict.

There is no way to guarantee that your treatment's effect will push scores in exactly the opposite direction of where regression would push scores. Furthermore, even if the treatment effect goes against the regression effect, regression effect may cancel or even overwhelm the treatment effect. That is, even though your treatment had a positive effect, the treatment group's scores—because of regression—may still decline. When regression and selection by maturation are both pushing scores in the opposite direction of the treatment's effect, they may overwhelm the effects of even moderately effective treatments.

To illustrate how regression and selection by maturation can hide a treatment's effect, consider research attempting to determine the effects of social programs. Sometimes researchers try to find the effect of a social program by matching a group of individuals who participate in the program with individuals who are not eligible. For example, researchers compared children who participated in Head Start with an upper-income group of children who had the same test scores. Unfortunately, this often meant selecting a group of upper-income children whose test scores were extremely low compared to their upper-income peers. Consequently, on retesting, these scores regressed back up toward the mean of upper-income children. Because of this regression toward the mean effect, scores in the no-treatment group increased more than scores in the Head Start group.

Not only was regression a problem, but there was also the potential for a selection by maturation interaction—especially for studies that looked for long-term effects of Head Start. Even if the groups started out the same, the upper-income group, because of superior health, nutrition, and schools, might mature academically at a faster rate than the

Table 14-10	**Problems With Trying to Make Groups Equivalent by Matching**

PROBLEM	IMPLICATION
You cannot match on all variables.	Selection by maturation interactions possible.
You cannot match on true scores.	Regression effects possible.
Instead, you have to match on observed scores—and observed scores are affected by random error.	

disadvantaged group. Thus, not surprisingly, some early studies of Head Start that failed to take regression and selection by maturation into account made it look like Head Start harmed, rather than helped, children.

In conclusion, matching is not the perfect solution that it first appears to be (see Table 14-10). Therefore, the nonequivalent control-group design is a flawed way of establishing that a treatment has an effect.

Conclusions About Quasi-Experimental Designs

Unfortunately, all quasi-experimental designs are flawed methods of establishing that a treatment caused an effect. Although quasi-experiments ensure temporal precedence and assess covariation, quasi-experiments do not automatically rule out the effects of nontreatment factors. To compensate for the inability of their designs to automatically rule out the effects of nontreatment factors, quasi-experimenters use a variety of tactics.

Quasi-experimenters may combine two quasi-experimental designs, using one design to cover for another's weaknesses. For example, they may use a time-series design to rule out selection biases and then use a nonequivalent control-group design to rule out history effects.

Quasi-experimenters may also identify a specific threat to their study's internal validity and then take specific steps to minimize that threat (for a review, see Table 14-4). For instance, they may eliminate instrumentation biases by administering the same measure, the same way, every time.

Finally, they may eliminate some threats by arguing that the particular threat is not a likely explanation for the effect. For example, they may argue that mortality was low and therefore not a threat or that pretest scores were not extreme and so regression was not a problem.

When arguing that nontreatment factors are unlikely explanations for their results, quasi-experimenters often cite the **law of parsimony:** the assumption that the explanation that is simplest, most straightforward, and makes the fewest assumptions is the most likely. Thus, the time-series researcher argues that the simplest assumption to make is that the effects of maturation, instrumentation, testing, and mortality are consistent over time. Therefore, a dramatic change after introducing the treatment should not be viewed as a complex, unexpected maturation effect, but as a simple, straightforward treatment effect.

Clearly, the quasi-experimenter's job is a difficult one, requiring much creativity and effort. But there are rewards. Quasi-experimenters can often study the effects of treatments that couldn't be studied with conventional experimental designs. For example, quasi-experimenters can study treatments that could not—or should not—be randomly assigned, such as the effects of disasters, new laws, new technology, and new social programs. Furthermore, because quasi-experimenters often study real-world treatments, their studies sometimes have more external validity than traditional experimental designs.

Concluding Remarks

Quasi-experiments and single-*n* designs are extremely useful—if you want to infer that a treatment causes an effect and you cannot use random assignment. If you want to infer causality and you can use random assignment, you should probably use one of the designs described in Chapters 10–13. If you do not want to infer causality, you should use one of the methods discussed in Chapters 7 and 8.

SUMMARY

1. To infer that a treatment causes an effect, you must show that changes in the amount of the treatment are accompanied by changes in participants' behavior (covariation), that changes in the treatment come before changes in the behavior (temporal precedence), and that nothing other than the treatment is responsible for the change in behavior (the change is not due to spuriousness).

2. By comparing treatment and nontreatment conditions, you can determine whether the cause and the effect covary.

3. When you introduce the treatment, you make sure that the treatment comes before the change in behavior, thereby establishing temporal precedence.

4. Randomization is an effective way of ruling out the likelihood that nontreatment factors may be responsible for the change in behavior.

5. Like randomized experiments, single-*n* designs introduce the treatment to ensure temporal precedence and compare conditions to assess covariation.

6. Single-*n* researchers try to identify the important, nontreatment variables, and then they try to stop those variables from varying within their study.

7. Single-*n* researchers prevent individual difference variables from varying within their study by limiting their study to examining a single participant. That is, differences between subjects (between-subjects variability) cannot make the treatment condition score higher than the control condition because the subject in the treatment condition is the same subject that is in the control condition.

8. Single-*n* researchers may keep many environmental variables constant by keeping the participant in a highly controlled environment.

9. The A–B–A reversal design and the multiple-baseline design are used by single-*n* researchers to rule out the effects of maturation and testing.

10. When it comes to construct validity, the single-*n* researcher and the within-subjects researcher use very similar approaches. To prevent participants from figuring out the hypothesis, both researchers may use (a) few levels of the independent variable, (b) placebo treatments, and/or (c) gradual variations in the levels of the independent variable.

11. Unlike single-*n* researchers, quasi-experimenters cannot keep relevant nontreatment factors from varying.

12. Quasi-experimenters must explicitly rule out the eight threats to internal validity: history, maturation, testing, instrumentation, mortality (attrition), regression, selection, and selection by maturation interactions.

13. Instrumentation can be ruled out by using the same measure, the same way, every time.

14. By definition, mortality (attrition) will not be a threat to your study's internal validity if you can keep participants from dropping out of your study.

15. You can probably rule out regression if participants were not chosen on the basis of their extreme scores or if your measuring instrument is extremely reliable.

16. The time-series design is very similar to the A–B single-*n* design. The main differences are that the time-series design (a) studies more participants, (b) does not control the variables necessary to establish a stable baseline, and (c) doesn't isolate participants from history the way the single-*n* design does. Because the time-series design cannot control nontreatment, environmental events (history), the time-series' Achilles' heel is history.

17. The nonequivalent control-group design resembles the simple experiment. However, because participants are not randomly assigned to groups, selection is a serious problem in the nonequivalent control-group design.

18. Although quasi-experimental designs are not as good as experimental designs for inferring causality, they are more versatile.

KEY TERMS

covariation *(p. 429)*

temporal precedence *(p. 429)*

spurious *(p. 430)*

single-*n* designs *(p. 433)*

A–B design *(p. 433)*

stable baseline *(p. 433)*

baseline *(p. 434)*

maturation *(p. 434)*

reversal design (A–B–A design, A–B–A reversal design) *(p. 436)*

carryover effects *(p. 437)*

multiple-baseline design *(p. 439)*

quasi-experiment *(p. 443)*

testing *(p. 445)*

maturation *(p. 445)*

history *(p. 445)*

instrumentation *(p. 445)*

regression (also known as regression toward the mean and statistical regression) *(p. 445)*

mortality (attrition) *(p. 445)*

selection *(p. 445)*

selection-maturation interaction *(p. 445)*

pretest–posttest design *(p. 448)*

time-series design *(p. 448)*

nonequivalent control-group design *(p. 455)*

law of parsimony *(p. 459)*

EXERCISES

1. Suppose that the means for the treatment and no-treatment conditions are the same. If so, which requirement of establishing causality has not been met?

2. If the study does not manipulate the treatment, which requirement of establishing causality will be difficult to meet?

3. If participants are not randomly assigned to condition, which requirement for establishing causality will be almost impossible to meet?

4. Compare and contrast how single-*n* designs and randomized experiments account for nontreatment factors.

5. What arguments can you make for generalizing results from the single-*n* design?

6. How do the A–B design and the pretest–posttest design differ in terms of
   a. procedure?
   b. internal validity?

7. How does the single-*n* researcher's A–B–A design differ from the quasi-experimenter's reversal time-series design in terms of
   a. procedure?
   b. internal validity?

8. Design a quasi-experiment that looks at the effects of a course on simulating parenthood, including an assignment that involves taking care of an egg, on changing the expectations of junior-high school students about parenting. What kind of design would you use? Why?

9. An ad depicts a student who has improved his grade-point average from 2.0 to 3.2 after a stint in the military. Consider Campbell and Stanley's "spurious eight." Is the military the only possible explanation for the improvement?

10. One study found that students who had been held back a grade did worse in school than students who had not been held back. Based on this evidence, some people concluded holding students back a grade harmed students.

    a. Does this evidence prove that holding students back harms their performance? Why or why not?

    b. If you were a researcher hired by the Department of Education to test the assertion that holding students back harms them, what design would you use? Why?

WEB RESOURCES

1. Go to the Chapter 14 section of the book's student website and do the following:
   a. Look over the concept map of the key terms.
   b. Test yourself on the key terms.
   c. Take the Chapter 14 Practice Quiz.

2. Reading the interactive story that reviews different threats to internal validity.

3. Consider an alternative to using quasi-experiments by reading "Web Appendix: Field Experiments."

INFOTRAC COLLEGE EDITION EXPLORATIONS

1. Do an InfoTrac College Edition search for the phrase "research methods and clinical practice" to find a short article advising professionals to use single-*n* research with their clients.

2. Do an InfoTrac College Edition search for the phrase "single-subject design" to find (a) a clever application of the multiple baseline design to seeing how goal setting affects performance of basketball players (Swain & Jones, 1995), and (b) a brief description of Gliner, Morgan, and Harris's (2000) views of the strengths and weaknesses of single-*n* designs.

3. Do an InfoTrac College Edition search for the phrase "six designs" to find Strayhorn's (1996) short and entertaining article in which he ranks the relative value of several experimental and quasi-experimental designs—and explains the reasons for his rankings.

Putting It All Together

Writing Research Proposals and Reports

> It takes less time to do a thing right than it does
> to explain why you did it wrong.
>
> —*Henry Wadsworth Longfellow*

> If you fail to plan, you plan to fail.
>
> —*W. Clement Stone*

Overview

Your research should be carefully planned before you test your first participant. Without such planning, you may fail to have a clear hypothesis, or you may fail to test your hypothesis properly. In short, poor planning leads to poor execution.

Poor execution can lead to unethical research. At best, it wastes participants' time; at worst, it harms participants. Therefore, the purpose of this chapter is to help you avoid unethical research by showing you how to plan and report the results of your study. If you follow our advice, your research should be humane, valid, and meaningful.

Aids to Developing Your Idea

In this section, you will learn about two major research tools: the research journal and the research proposal. Many scientists regard the research journal and the research proposal as essential to the development and implementation of sound, ethical research.

The Research Journal

We recommend that you keep a **research journal:** a diary of your research ideas and your research experiences. Keeping a journal will help you in at least three ways: (1) You'll have a record of why and how you did what you did; (2) writing to yourself helps you think through decisions; and (3) a research journal can help you prepare your research proposal.

Because the journal is for your eyes only, it does not have to be neatly typed and free of grammatical errors. What is in the journal is much more important than how it is written.

What should you put in your journal? You should jot down every idea you have about your research project. At the beginning of the research process, when you are trying to develop a research hypothesis, use your research journal for brainstorming. Write down any research ideas that you think of and indicate what stimulated each idea. When you decide on a given idea, explain why you decided on that particular research idea. When reading related research, summarize and critique it in your journal. If you do quote any material, be sure to put that material in quotation marks. Otherwise, you will not be able to remember whether you have paraphrased or quoted that material when it comes time to write your paper. Whether you quote, paraphrase, summarize, or critique a source, write down the authors, year, title, and publisher for that source. This source information will come in handy when you write your research proposal. In short, whenever you have an insight, find a relevant piece of information, or make a design decision, record it in your journal.

To use the information in your journal, you will have to organize it. One key to effective organization is to write down only one idea per page. Another key is to rewrite or rearrange your entries every couple of days. Your goal in rearranging entries should be to put them in an order that makes sense to you. For example, your first section may deal with potential hypotheses, your second section may deal with ideas related to the introduction section of your paper, and your third section may deal with methods and procedures.

The Research Proposal

Like the research journal, the purpose of the research proposal is to help you think through each step of your research project. In addition, the research proposal will let others, such as your professor, think through your research plan so that they can give advice that will improve your study. By writing the proposal, you will have the opportunity to try out ideas and explore alternatives without harming a single participant. In other words, the process of writing the proposal will help you make intelligent and ethical research decisions.

Although the research proposal builds on the research journal, it is much more formal than the journal. When you write the proposal, you will have to go through several drafts. The result of this writing and rewriting will be a proposal that is not only clear, but also conforms in content, style, and organization to the guidelines given in the *Publication Manual of the American Psychological Association* (2001).

We want to emphasize that it is not enough to have good ideas. You must present them in a way that people will receive them. History is full of examples of people who had good ideas but got little credit because they expressed them poorly. Conversely, some people have become famous more for how well they expressed their ideas than for the originality of their ideas.

If you write using American Psychological Association (APA) style, you will have a better chance of expressing your ideas well. Think of APA style as a kind of language that makes it easier for professionals in the psychology field to communicate with one another.

If, on the other hand, you fail to write a research proposal or article that conforms to APA style, most professors will judge the content of your proposal more harshly. They will feel that if you cannot follow that style, you are incapable of doing good research.

To reiterate, following APA format is important. Indeed, one of the best-known professors of research design, Dr. Charles Brewer, cites learning APA style as one of the most important things students learn from his design class (Brewer, 1990).

As we have stressed, following APA style will help you communicate the content of your proposal. However, before you worry about how to communicate your content clearly, you need to have content: Style without substance is worthless. The substance of your proposal will be your statements regarding

1. why your general topic is important
2. what your hypothesis is
3. how your hypothesis is consistent with theory or past research
4. how your study fits in with existing research
5. how you define your variables
6. who your participants will be
7. what procedures you will follow
8. how you will analyze your data
9. what implications you hope your results will have for theory, future research, or real life

The research proposal's substance makes it the foundation for your study, and its substance and style make it the foundation of the final research report. To be more specific, the introduction and the method sections you write for your research proposal should be highly polished drafts of the introduction and method sections of your final report, whereas other parts of the research proposal will serve as rough drafts of the abstract, results, and discussion sections of your final report.

Writing the Research Proposal

Now that you know what a research proposal is, it is time for you to begin writing one. We will first show you how to write the introduction.

General Strategies for Writing the Introduction

The purpose of the **introduction** is to demonstrate to your readers that you have read the relevant research and thoroughly understand your research question. Once you have articulated the reasoning behind your hypothesis, you will explain your general strategy for testing the hypothesis. After reading the introduction, your reader should know

1. why your research area is important
2. what your hypothesis is
3. why your prediction makes sense
4. why your study is the best way to test the hypothesis

Establishing the Importance of Your Study

Before you can persuade people that your study is important and interesting, you must let them know exactly what concepts you are studying, and then explain why those concepts are important. To establish that your concepts are important, you will probably want to use one of the following three strategies:

1. *prevalence:* presenting statistical or other evidence of how often people encounter the basic principle or topic
2. *relevance:* presenting a case study or other arguments to illustrate how the concept has important implications for real life or for testing a theory
3. *precedence:* demonstrating that the concept has captured the interest of other researchers

Demonstrate the Concept's Prevalence. One strategy for showing that your study is important is to show that your general topic area is a common part of real life. Sometimes, authors boldly assert that the phenomenon they are studying is common. For example, authors may write "____ is a part of everyday life" or "People are bombarded with ____."

Rather than asserting "Most people have experienced ____," you might document the prevalence of the concept by presenting statistical evidence. Thus, if you were studying widowhood, you might present statistics on the percentage of people who are widowed. In the absence of statistics, you could use quotations from influential people or organizations (for example, the American Psychological Association) to stress the prevalence of your concept.

Demonstrate the Concept's Relevance to Real Life. Rather than emphasizing the concept's prevalence, you might emphasize its relevance. For example, you might stress the practical problems that might be solved by understanding the concept. Alternatively, you might demonstrate the problem's relevance by presenting a real-life example of your concept in action. Giving an example of the concept is a very good way to both define the concept and provide a vivid picture of its importance at the same time.

Demonstrate Historical Precedence. Finally, you might show that there is a historical precedence for your study. You could emphasize the great minds that have pondered the concept you will study, the number of people through the ages who have tried to understand the behavior, or the length of time that people have pondered the concept. Normally, you will also want to show that the research topic has—or should have—been important to both researchers and theorists.

Writing the Literature Review

One way of establishing historical precedence is to summarize research done on the topic. In addition to helping the reader understand your research question, citing research shows the reader that the field considers your general research area important. That is, if the field did not consider these concepts important, investigators would not be researching these areas, and their findings would not be published. Thus, it is not uncommon for introductions to include statements such as, "The focus of research for the past 20 years . . ." or "Historically, research has emphasized. . . ."

However, even if you do not use the literature review to establish the importance of the general concepts, you will still want to write it to show how your particular study fits in with existing work. In other words, although you can select one of many ways to show that your general concepts are important, the only way to show that your particular research study is important is to write a literature review. Hence, *all introductions should contain a literature review.*

Goals of the Literature Review. Because the literature review is designed to sell your particular study, you need to do more than merely summarize previous work. You must also use the summary to set the stage for your study. You will do so by showing that your study (a) corrects a weakness in previous research or (b) builds on and extends previous research. In short, you need to make the reader feel that there is a need for your research.

Deciding Which Research to Review. We have addressed the goals of the literature review. You know why you should review the literature. Now, let's talk about what you will review. Instead of reviewing informal sources such as magazine articles and people's personal websites, you will review either printed or online versions of journal articles (see Web Appendix B to learn how to find articles to review). When citing research reported in scholarly journal articles, your focus will usually be on reviewing recent research. However, you may also review one or two older, classic works as well as recent research. Critiquing—rather than merely summarizing—the articles you cite will show that you have thought about what you have read. By analyzing the strengths and weaknesses of a number of articles, you will establish that you have done your homework.

Although critiquing these journal articles may establish you as a scholar, realize that your goal is not simply to establish your credibility. Instead, your primary goal is to show how your study follows from existing research.

You may feel that these two goals (establishing your expertise versus showing that your study follows from existing research) conflict. On the one hand, you want to establish that you know what you are talking about. Therefore, you may feel that you should cite all research ever done in the field. On the other hand, you want to use the literature review to set up your research study. Consequently, you want to cite and analyze only those studies that bear directly on your study. To help you resolve the apparent conflict between these two goals, we offer two tips.

First, realize that your main goal is to set up your study. Thus, you will be offering in-depth critiques of only those studies that directly apply to your study.

Second, realize that introductions begin by talking about the general area and then focus on the specific research question. Thus, you should cite classic research that establishes the importance of your general topic. However, if those classic findings are only indirectly related to your work, you should probably cite them only in your first paragraph.

Not knowing what to include in a literature review is one of the two main problems students have in writing the literature review. The other problem is that their literature review often seems disorganized.

If you are going to write an organized literature review, you must start organizing before you start writing. Begin by grouping together the studies that seem to have something in common. If you have summaries of all your studies on large index cards, you might find that you have the following four piles of cards:

1. a pile that emphasizes the importance of the general concept
2. a pile that deals with problems with previous research
3. a pile that deals with reasons to believe that your hypothesis will not be supported
4. a pile that deals with reasons to believe that your hypothesis will be supported

Alternatively, you may find that you have three piles:

1. a pile that deals with how to measure your outcome variable
2. a pile that deals with studies that obtained a certain finding
3. a pile that deals with studies that obtained the opposite finding

Regardless of the specific content of your piles, the fact that you have piles shows that you have some way of organizing the studies. Now, you have to convert those organized piles into an organized literature review. Your first step is to turn each pile into a paragraph.

To help convert these piles into meaningful paragraphs, write a sentence summarizing what all the cards have in common. Each pile's sentence could be the topic sentence for a paragraph, with the rest of the pile providing evidence and citations for the statements made in that sentence (Kuehn, 1989).

Once you have finished a draft of your literature review, read it aloud. After fixing problems you find as you read the literature review aloud, outline it. Then, rate your literature review on the following 5-point scale:

1. Very few recent journal articles are cited.
2. Enough reports of original research are cited, but the articles are not clearly summarized.
3. Enough articles are cited and articles are clearly summarized, but a reader might not understand either (a) why those articles are being cited or (b) why they are being cited in that order.
4. Enough recent articles are cited, and articles are either (a) integrated with other summaries or (b) critiqued.
5. Enough recent articles are cited and articles are both (a) integrated with other summaries and (b) critiqued.

Note that your literature review should do more than evaluate other people's work: It should also set the stage for your study. For example, the measure you praise will be in your study; the manipulation you attack will not. Your literature review should do such a good job of setting the stage for your study that just from reading your literature review, a clever reader could guess what your hypothesis is and how you plan to test it.

However, you won't make readers guess the rationale for your hypothesis and for your study. After summarizing the relevant research, spell out the reasoning that led to your hypothesis so clearly that your readers will know what your hypothesis is before you actually state it.

Stating Your Hypothesis

Even though your readers may have guessed your hypothesis, leave nothing to chance: *State your hypothesis!* To emphasize a point that can't be emphasized enough, state your hypothesis boldly and clearly so that readers can't miss it. Let them know what your study is about by writing, "The hypothesis is. . . ."

When you state your hypothesis, be sensitive to whether you'll be testing it with an experiment or with a correlational study. Because only experiments allow you to test cause–effect hypotheses, your hypothesis should include the word *causes* (or synonyms for *causes*, such as *affects, impacts, influences, leads to,* and *makes*) only if you plan to conduct an experiment. If you don't plan on directly manipulating your predictor variable, you have a correlational study and therefore can test only whether two or more variables are related. Thus, if you were surveying people about their lifestyles and moods, your hypothesis should not be "A sedentary lifestyle causes depression" but rather "A sedentary lifestyle is related to depression."

Review of the Basic Elements of an Introduction

We have given you some general advice about how to write an introduction—an important section that will probably be between one fourth and one third the length of your final paper. You have seen the importance of clearly defining your concepts, critically summarizing research, carefully explaining the reasoning behind your hypothesis, and stating your hypothesis. Because of the importance of summarizing research, explaining the reasoning behind hypotheses, and stating hypotheses, you are probably not surprised to find that some authors include subheadings such as "Overview of Past Research," "Theoretical Background," and "Hypotheses" (sometimes labeled "Predictions") in their introductions. Although you do not need to include such subheadings, you should outline your introduction, and your outline should incorporate headings such as "Overview of Past Research," and "Hypotheses."

Specific Strategies for Writing Introduction Sections for Different Types of Studies

Although most introductions follow the same general outline, the specific way you justify your study will depend on the kind of study you are doing. In the next section, you will learn how to justify six common types of studies:

1. exploratory
2. direct replication
3. systematic replication
4. conceptual replication
5. replication and extension
6. theory testing

The Exploratory Study

In introducing an **exploratory study**—a study investigating a new area of research—you must take special care to justify your study, your hypothesis, and your procedures. You must compensate for the fact that your reader will not have any background knowledge about this new research area.

New Is Not Enough. Because of the lack of research in the area, you will not be able to use the common strategy of having your literature review show that your topic is important because it has inspired a lot of research. Although you will be able to show that your research area has been ignored, that will not be enough to justify your study: Many research areas (e.g., the psychology of tiddlywinks) have been ignored for good reasons. To justify your study, you must convince your readers that it is a tragedy that your research question has been overlooked. Make them believe this wrong must be righted to help psychology advance as a science.

One approach you can use to justify your exploratory study is to discuss hypothetical or real-life cases that could be solved or understood by answering your research question. For example, consider how Latané and Darley (1968) opened their pioneering work on helping behavior. Not only did they state that there was a lack of research on helping behavior, but they also bolstered their research justification by referring to the case of murder victim Kitty Genovese. Ms. Genovese was brutally attacked for more than 30 minutes in the presence of more than 30 witnesses—none of whom intervened. Thus, Latané and Darley effectively convinced readers that understanding why people fail to help is an important research area.

To reiterate, your first step in justifying an exploratory study is to show that the area is important. Once you have convinced your readers, you can further excite them by emphasizing that you are exploring new frontiers.

Spell Out Your Reasoning. In an exploratory study, as in all studies, you must spell out the rationale for your hypothesis. Because you are studying an unexplored dimension, you must give your readers the background to understand your predictions. Therefore, be extremely thorough in explaining the logic behind your predictions—even if you think your predictions are just common sense. Not everyone will share your opinion.

Beyond spelling out the common sense logic of your prediction, try to explain how your prediction is consistent with (a) theory and (b) research on related variables. For example, suppose you are interested in seeing how low-sensation seekers and high-sensation seekers differ in their reactions to stress. You might argue that your hypothesis is consistent with arousal theory—the theory that we all have an ideal level of arousal (Berlyne, 1971). That is, you might argue that high-sensation seekers like stress because it raises their arousal up to the optimal level, whereas low-sensation seekers hate stress because it raises their arousal beyond the optimal level.

In addition to—or instead of—using theory to support your hypothesis, you could use research on related concepts. Thus, in our example, you might start by arguing that introversion–extroversion and sensation-seeking are related concepts. Then, you might argue that because introversion and sensation-seeking are related, and because stress has different effects on introverts and extroverts, stress should also have different effects on low-sensation seekers versus high-sensation seekers.

Defend Your Procedures. In addition to explaining your predictions, you may have to take special care in explaining your procedures. If you are studying variables that have never been studied before, you can't tell the reader that you are using familiar, well-accepted measures and manipulations. Instead, you may have to invent—and justify—your own measures and manipulations. Therefore, you will need to explain, either in the introduction or in the method section, why your manipulations and measures are valid.

The Direct Replication

Rather than doing a completely original exploratory study, you may decide to do the opposite. That is, you may decide to do a **direct (exact) replication:** a repetition of an original study. Before doing a direct replication, you must be very clear about why you are repeating the study. If you are not careful, the reader may think you performed the study before you realized that someone else had already done the study. Even if you do spell out why you repeated the study, some journal reviewers will find the fact that you did a direct replication a legitimate reason to reject the paper for publication (Fiske & Fogg, 1990). However, you can use a two-pronged strategy to persuade people that your study is worth doing.

Document the Original Study's Importance. First, to justify a direct replication, you should show that the original study was important. To do this, discuss its impact on psychology. To get some objective statistics about the number of times the study has been cited, you can use the *Social Science Citation Index* described in Web Appendix B.

Explain Why the Results Might Not Replicate. After establishing the study's importance, try to convince your readers that the study's results might not replicate. There are basically four arguments you can make in support of the idea that the findings won't replicate.

1. The findings appear to contradict other published work.
2. The original study's statistically significant results may be a Type 1 error (mistaking a coincidence for a reliable relationship; declaring a chance difference statistically significant).
3. The original study's null results (failure to find significant results) may be a Type 2 error (a failure to find a real relationship).
4. People or times have changed so much from when the original study was performed that a replication would produce different results.

Perhaps the strongest argument you can make for replicating the study is to show that the findings appear to contradict other published work. The more you can make the case that other findings directly contradict the findings of the study you wish to replicate, the stronger the case for a replication.

One reason that the original study may be inconsistent with other published work is that the statistically significant result in the original study could be the result of a Type 1 error. Thus, if you showed that the original study's results would not have been significant at the conventional $p = .05$ level or that the authors used an unconventional statistical technique that inflated their chances of making a Type 1 error, you would have a strong case for replicating the study.

But what if the original study reported nonsignificant (null) results? Then you could argue that random error or poor execution of the study may have hidden real differences. That is, you could argue that the null results were due to a Type 2 error. If the original study's findings seem to conflict with several other published papers that *did* find a significant relationship between those variables, you have a compelling rationale for replicating the study.

If you can't reasonably argue that the original results are due to either a Type 1 or Type 2 error, you still might be able to justify a direct replication on the grounds that the study would come out differently today. For example, you might want to replicate a conformity study because you believe that as a result of cohort differences in parenting style, teenagers today are less conforming than teenagers were when the original study was conducted.

Regardless of what approach you take, you must present a compelling rationale for any study that is merely a rerun of another study.

The Systematic Replication

Rather than repeating the study, you might conduct a **systematic replication:** a study that makes a minor modification of the original study. As such, the systematic replication accomplishes everything the direct replication does and more. Therefore, every reason for doing a direct replication is also a reason for doing a systematic replication. In addition, you can justify a systematic replication by showing that modifying the procedures would improve the original study's power (ability to find relationships), construct validity, or external validity.

Improved Power. As we mentioned earlier, if you thought the original study's null results were due to Type 2 error, you could just redo the original study. However, if you just repeat the study, you may just repeat its Type 2 error. Therefore, instead of repeating the original study, you might make a minor change in procedure to improve power. For example, you might use more participants, more extreme levels of the predictor/independent variable, or a more sensitive measure (for instance, replacing *yes/no* questions with *strongly agree, agree, neutral, disagree,* and *strongly disagree* questions) than the original study used.

Improved Construct Validity. You might also want to modify the original study if you thought that the original study's results were biased by demand characteristics (clues that suggest to the participant how the researcher wants the participant to behave). Thus, you might repeat the study using a double-blind procedure (making sure that neither the participant nor the person who has direct contact with the participant knows what type of treatment the participant has received) to reduce subject and researcher bias.

Improved External Validity. If you are replicating a study to improve external validity, you should explain why you suspect that the results may not generalize to different stimulus materials, levels of the treatment variable, or participants. For example, even if it seems obvious to you why a study done on rats might not apply to humans, spell out your reasons for suspecting that the results wouldn't generalize.

The Conceptual Replication

Most of the reasons for conducting a systematic replication are also relevant for introducing and justifying a **conceptual replication:** a study that is based on the original, but uses different methods to better assess the true relationships between the variables being studied. In addition to having the same advantages as the systematic replication, the conceptual replication has several other unique selling points, depending on how you changed the original study.

Using a Different Measure. Your conceptual replication might differ because you used a different way of measuring the dependent measure than the original authors did. In that case, you should show that your measure is more reliable, sensitive, or valid than the original measure. To make the case for your measure, you may want to cite other studies that used your measure. As in the legal arena, precedent carries weight in psychology. If someone else published a study using a given measure, the measure automatically gains some credibility.

Using a Different Manipulation. Instead of trying to use a different measure of a construct, you might want to use a different manipulation of a construct. For example, if one researcher induced stress in participants by suggesting that they would get painful electric shocks, you might decide to replicate the study, but induce stress by giving participants a very short period of time to do certain mathematical problems. If you use a different manipulation, you should start by defining the variable you are trying to manipulate. Next, you should discuss weaknesses of previous manipulations. Then, show how your manipulation avoids those weaknesses. Conclude by showing that your manipulation is consistent with definitions of the concept you are trying to manipulate.

Using a Different Design. If you are changing the original study's design, let your readers know why you are making the change. For example, suppose you believe that the original study failed to find a significant effect because it used a relatively low powered design: a between-subjects experiment that compared a treatment group to a no-treatment group. If you are repeating the study using a more powerful design—a within-subjects (repeated measures) experiment that compares each participant's response in the treatment condition to that participant's response in the no-treatment condition—tell your readers that you switched to a within-subjects design to boost your chances of finding a significant effect.

The Replication and Extension

Your study may go beyond a conceptual replication to looking at additional factors or measures. In that event, your introduction would not only contain everything a conceptual replication would, but also a rationale for the additional factors or measures.

Rationale for Additional Factors. For example, suppose the original author found that people loaf when working in groups. You might think of a situation (for example, a group in which all members were good friends) in which social loafing wouldn't occur. Thus, you might include friendship as a factor in your design. Be sure to state (a) your reasons for including the factor and (b) your predictions regarding the factor.

Rationale for Additional Dependent Measures. Instead of adding a predictor/independent variable to a study, you might add an outcome/dependent measure. Your purpose would be to discover how the treatment produces the effect. In other words, you are trying to show that a certain mental or physiological reaction is both (a) triggered by the treatment and (b) the mediating mechanism by which the treatment has its effect on behavior.

How would you go about finding out the invisible processes underlying an observable effect? In a social-loafing experiment, you might collect measures of participants' perceptions of others to find out the cognitive processes responsible for social loafing (such as perceptions that their efforts are not being noticed). Or, you might monitor arousal levels in an attempt to discover the physiological reasons for social loafing (for example, lower physiological arousal in a group setting). However, even if you found that working in a group reduced arousal or changed perceptions, you could not say that these changes, in turn, caused the loafing.

Not surprisingly, then, the tricky part about writing an introduction to a *process* study is to persuade your readers that you really are going to be able to pin down the underlying causes of a phenomenon. You must do more than merely show that these processes occur before the phenomenon because these processes could be incidental side effects of the treatment. For instance, a fever may appear before you get ill—and may intensify as you get ill—but a fever doesn't cause you to be ill. It's a side effect of your illness. In the same way, a mental or physiological event may accompany a change in behavior, but not be the cause of that behavioral change.

Critics usually will not accept evidence that the treatment had certain effects on a physiological or mental process as proof that the treatment works by altering that process.

Instead, the proof some want is more direct: Show that the treatment doesn't work the same way when you mess with the mechanism (Sigall & Mills, 1998).

To show how clever some of these process-testing experiments can be, pretend that you and a friend are participants in the following experiment (Steele, Southwick, & Critchlow, 1981). Participants in your condition are asked to write an essay favoring a big tuition increase. According to dissonance theory, you will

1. feel unpleasant tension after writing this essay
2. reduce this tension by being less opposed to tuition increases

As dissonance theory would predict, you now are less opposed to tuition increases. But did you feel that unpleasant tension, and did you change your attitudes as a way to reduce that unpleasant tension? In other words, was dissonance the mediating mechanism for your attitude change?

To find out, let's look at participants in your friend's condition. Those participants also received the treatment. That is, like you, they wrote an essay favoring a big tuition increase. Unlike you, however, the experimenter set it up so that your friend and people in your friend's condition did not experience prolonged unpleasant tension after writing the essay. Specifically, the researcher set it up so that right after writing the essay, participants in your friend's group thought they had finished the dissonance study and were now participating in an unrelated study that involved judging beverages. Actually, that "study" was just a way of getting your friend and the other participants in that condition to drink alcohol without realizing that the researchers were using alcohol to reduce any unpleasant arousal (dissonance) caused by writing an essay that disagreed with their attitudes.

Consistent with the researchers' predictions, the effect of preventing that group from feeling dissonance was to prevent attitude change: People in the alcohol condition did not change their views about tuition increases. This study provides strong evidence that having people write counterattitudinal essays has its effect by creating unpleasant tension that people try to reduce. (For more about how to test hypotheses involving mediating variables, see Chapter 3.)

In summary, you can extend an existing study by adding measures or manipulations. Such extensions may provide insights into how a treatment has its effect. When proposing such a study, remember that you must (a) justify why you are adding the measure or manipulation and (b) explain your predictions regarding the additional measure or manipulation.

The Theory-Testing Study

If you are testing a prediction from a theory, there's good news and bad news. The good news is that you won't have to spend much effort justifying your study's importance. Almost everyone assumes that testing a theory is important.

The bad news is that not everyone will agree that your predictions follow from the theory. To convince them, you must clearly spell out how your predictions follow from the theory. By being clear, everyone will follow your logic, and some may even agree with it.

Writing the Method Section

You have reviewed the literature, developed a hypothesis, decided how to measure your variables, and stated your reasons for testing your hypothesis. Your preliminary work, however, is still not done. You must now decide exactly what specific actions you will take. In other words, although you probably have decided on the general design (for example, a simple experiment), your plan is not complete until each detail of your study has been thought through and written down.

In your journal, specify exactly what procedures you will follow. For example, what instructions will participants be given? Who will administer the treatment? Where? Will participants be run in groups or individually? How should the researcher interact with participants? Although your answers must be accountable to issues of validity, your paramount concern must always be ethics. You do not have the right to harm another.

Once you have thoroughly thought out each step of your study, you are ready to write the **method section**[1] of your proposal. This is the "how" section—here you will explain exactly how you plan to conduct your study. However, keep in mind that—just like the introduction—the method section is written on two levels. As you will recall, at one level, the introduction summarizes existing research; at another level, it sells the need for your study by pointing out deficiencies in existing research. Similarly, at one level, the method section tells the reader what you are going to do; at another level, it sells the reader on the idea that what you plan to do is the correct thing.

To sell the reader on what you plan to do, tell your reader about the wise design choices you have made. Thus, in the method section, point out that your measure is valid, that your manipulation is widely accepted, or that you are doing something a certain way to reduce demand characteristics, researcher biases, random error, or some other problem.

In short, selling the value of a research strategy is a never-ending job. If possible, you should sell your strategy in each of the method section's subsections.

The method must include two subsections: a participants section and a procedure section. However, it may include overview, design, apparatus, materials, manipulations, and dependent measures subsections.

Participants

In the participants section, you will describe the general characteristics of your participants. State how many participants you plan to have, how many will be men, how many will be women, their ages, and how you plan to obtain or recruit them. You should also indicate whether they will be tested individually or in groups. If they will be tested in groups, you should state the size of the groups. If you plan to exclude data from some participants, state the rule that you will use to exclude participants (such as excluding all participants who score above 16 on the Beck Depression Inventory).

The participants section is written in a straightforward and somewhat mechanical fashion. In fact, it is so mechanical that you can often model yours after a participants section you find in an article or after the following sample participants section.

> *Participants*
> The participants will be 80 introductory psychology students (52 men and 28 women) from Clarion University who will be given extra credit for their participation. Participants will be run individually and will be randomly assigned to experimental condition.

However, you should be aware of two serious problems with copying or paraphrasing parts of articles that convey approximately what you want to say.[2]

First, you may end up committing **plagiarism:** using someone else's words, thoughts, or work without giving proper credit. Plagiarism is considered a serious act of academic

---

[1]When writing your paper, please label this section "method" rather than "methods."

[2]We thank an anonymous reviewer for noting these problems.

dishonesty. Indeed, at some institutions, students convicted of plagiarism are expelled. Furthermore, concerns about plagiarism are no longer limited to colleges and universities. More and more, the world economy is based on information. Thus, more and more, businesses and individuals are concerned about the theft of ideas (now called "intellectual property"). Therefore, if you quote someone's work, use quotation marks; and if you paraphrase or in any sense borrow an idea from a source, cite that source.

Second, you will rarely find a section that says exactly what you want to say. So, rarely copy things word for word. For example, do not copy our sample participants section verbatim. Instead, create one that best describes how participants will be recruited and assigned in your study.

Design or Design Summary (Optional)

Like the participants section, the design section is easy to write. Merely describe the design of your study. For an experiment, state the number of levels (values) of each independent (treatment) variable and whether the independent variable is a between-subjects variable (each participant gets only one level of the variable) or a within-subjects variable (each participant gets all the levels of the variable that are used in the experiment). Then, tell the reader what the dependent variable (measure) is. For example, you might write, "The design is a 2 (source expertise: nonexpert vs. expert) $\times$ 2 (information type: unimportant vs. important) between-subjects design. The dependent measure is the number of items recalled."

Apparatus and Materials (Optional)

Apparatus refers to laboratory equipment—not computers you will use to type up instructions or copiers you will use to duplicate materials. If you are not using equipment to present stimuli or to collect responses from participants, then you do not need an apparatus section.

You can describe laboratory equipment in an apparatus section or in the procedure section. If you plan to use equipment made by a company, list the product's brand name and the model name and/or number. If you designed your equipment, briefly describe it. You need to give enough detail so that readers will have a general idea of what it looks like. If your apparatus is unusual, include a photo or diagram of it in the appendix.

If you are showing participants photographs, having them listen to a tape, or giving them a booklet of tests, you may need a materials section. If all your materials are measures, you may label your materials section "Measures"; if they are all tests, you may label your materials section "Tests." If your tests and questionnaires are straightforward or well-known, you may decide to embed your description of them in the procedure section rather than in a separate section.

If you used a test or questionnaire, provide at least one example of a typical item. This gives readers a feel for what the participants will see. In addition, if the measure has been published, reference the source of the measure. Finally, include a copy of your test or questionnaire in the appendix.

Procedure

As the name suggests, your procedure section will be a summary of what you actually are going to do. However, contrary to what the name suggests, the focus is on what happens to participants. Readers should be able to visualize what it would be like to be a participant in your study. Note how the sample paper (Appendix B) does a good job of showing what *happens from the participants' perspective.*

Like the authors of the sample paper, you can make it easy for readers to make a movie in their head of what happened to participants. Just use these two tactics:

1. Start with the first thing that happened to the participants, then discuss the second thing that happened to participants, and continue in chronological order, so that the last part of the procedure deals with the last thing that happened to participants.

2. Keep the focus on participants by making the word "participants" the subject of most sentences. That is, most sentences should deal with what participants do or see.

In addition to having trouble figuring out how to sequence and present information about procedures, beginning authors have trouble with what to put in and what to leave out of the procedure section. They know they are supposed to provide enough information so that a reader could replicate (repeat) the study, but they still ask, "How much detail should I include?" To help you answer this question, we offer five suggestions.

First, be sure to include enough information so that the reader will understand how you operationalized your independent and dependent variables. To help the reader understand your independent variable manipulation, include key elements of instructions to participants, especially when the experimental group receives different instructions from the control group. To help the reader understand the dependent measure, introduce it in a simple and straightforward manner (e.g., "The dependent measure was . . .").

Second, include any methodological wrinkles that you believe are critical to the study's internal, external, or construct validity. For example, if you used a placebo treatment or double-blind procedures, tell the reader.

Third, read the procedure sections of several related studies and mimic their style—but avoid plagiarism. Reading these sections will show you how to provide your readers with the right level of detail—enough so they could replicate the study, but not so much that they feel overwhelmed.

Fourth, leave out most of the "behind the scenes" details about events that participants don't see. Don't write, "We made the booklets by cutting sheets of paper in half, typing them up on a computer, and then using a copier"—or compound the error by also acknowledging the people who took care of those details. Statements such as "Tom randomly assigned participants to groups" or "Our nice secretary copied the booklets" do not belong in the method section. Send those people a card, thank them when you win an Academy Award, or acknowledge their contribution in the Author Notes section of your paper—just keep their names out of the method section.

Fifth, don't worry if your procedure section seems too brief. You can include your complete protocol (detailed list of what the researchers said and did) in the appendix of your proposal.

Writing the Results Section

In a proposal, you may not have a results section. After all, because the study hasn't been done, there are no results to report. Thus, your professor may advise you to replace the results section with a "Design and Data Analysis" section or even skip the section entirely.

If you do have a results, data analysis, or related section, the main goal is to show that you would know how to code and analyze participants' responses. As was the case with the method section, your goal is not only to tell the reader what you are going to do, but also to sell the reader on the idea that you are doing the right thing. Thus, it is important to be clear about not only what analysis you are going to do, but why. Ideally, your proposal should answer four questions:

1. What data will be analyzed? That is, how will a participant's response be converted into a score?
2. What statistical test will be used on those scores?
3. Why can that statistical test be used? Thus, you might show that the data meet the assumptions of the statistical test or you might cite a text or article that supports the use of the test under these conditions.
4. Why should the analysis be done? Usually, you will remind the reader of the hypothesis you want to test. To emphasize the value of the analysis, you may want to describe what results of that analysis would support your hypothesis and what outcomes would not. You might even—with your professor's permission—plug in imaginary outcomes of your study to give the reader a concrete example of how your proposed analyses will help test your hypotheses.

To illustrate how a results section might accomplish these goals, study the following sample results section:

> *Results*
> I will sum participants' responses to the two 5-point altruism items to come up with an altruism score for each participant that will range from 2 (*very low*) to 10 (*very high*). Those scores will be subjected to a 2 × 2 between-subjects analysis of variance.
> I hypothesize that mood will affect altruism. If the results turn out as I predict, positive-mood participants will score significantly higher on my altruism scale than negative-mood participants. This significant main effect would indicate support for the hypothesis that mood influences altruism. Furthermore, I also predict a significant mood by arousal interaction. Analyses of simple main effects will show that negative-mood participants who are in the high-arousal condition will score lower on altruism than negative-mood participants in the low-arousal condition. In contrast, positive-mood participants in the high-arousal condition will score higher on altruism than positive-mood participants in the low-arousal condition.

As you can see, the results section clearly shows the reader what data will be put into the analysis, what analyses will be done, and what results from the analyses will support the hypotheses.

Writing the Discussion Section

Once you have decided how you will analyze your data, you are ready to discuss how you will interpret them. By referring back to both the literature you discussed in the introduction and the arguments you made there, you should be able to address two key questions:

1. What would be the implications for interpreting existing theory and research if your hypothesis is supported?
2. What would be the implications if the results don't support your hypothesis?

In addition to addressing these two key questions, the **discussion** is the place to present the limitations of your study, to speculate about what research should be done to follow up on your study, and to discuss the practical implications of your study.

Writing this section is difficult because you do not know how the study will turn out. Probably the easiest thing to do is to imagine that your study turned out as you expected. In that case, your discussion can be primarily a rehash of the introduction.

To be more specific, your discussion should probably devote a paragraph to at least four of the following six points:

1. relating the predicted results to the hypothesis ("Consistent with my predictions, . . .")
2. relating the predicted results to previous research and theory discussed in the introduction ("This study joins others in showing . . ." or "The findings are consistent with ___ theory.")
3. discussing the limitations of the study ("However, because the current research is only correlational, one cannot say that the variables are causally related" or "The results may not generalize to noncollege students.")
4. discussing future research that would build on the present study ("Future research might consider testing the generality of this effect.")
5. discussing practical or theoretical implications of the research findings
6. summarizing the importance of remembering or building on the study's major findings ("To summarize, I found that the effectiveness of rewards depended on the participant's personality. This finding suggests that teachers should not use salient rewards on intrinsically motivated students. Furthermore, in light of these findings, learned industriousness theory must be revised. In short, this research takes a step toward better understanding creativity.")

Almost all authors devote the first paragraph of the discussion to the first of these six points (relating the results to the hypothesis). In fact, you will often see the first sentence of the discussion has both the words *support* and *hypothesis* in it. Similarly, almost all authors devote the second paragraph to the second of these points (relating the predicted results to previous research and theory discussed in the introduction). However, authors vary in how much they discuss the remaining four points.

Sometimes, authors use subheadings to signal which of the remaining four points they will highlight. Thus, if you browse discussion sections, you will see subheadings such as "Comparisons With Previous Research," "Limitations of the Current Study," "Suggestions for Future Research," "Implications," and "Concluding Remarks."

Do you need to have a separate paragraph for all six of these paragraphs? No. Usually, the content and organization of your discussion will be fine as long as you

1. connect your discussion to your introduction
2. explain how your study will contribute to existing knowledge
3. outline it

Putting on the Front and Back

You've written the introduction, method, results, and discussion sections. Now it's time to return to the beginning of your proposal. Specifically, it's time to type the title page and the abstract.

Title and Title Page

The title is the first thing readers will see; therefore, it should be simple, direct, and informative. Ideally, your title should be a brief statement about the relationship between your predictor/independent and criterion/dependent variables.

Avoid being too cute or obscure. If there is some catchy saying that you must include, use a colon and add a subtitle (e.g., "The Effect of Eating Sugar on Anxiety: A Bittersweet Dilemma").

The title should appear centered on a separate piece of paper. One double-spaced line below the title, center your name. For more information about typing and formatting the title page, see Appendix A.

The title should also appear, centered, at the top of the first page of your introduction. Thus, for the introduction, the title takes the place of the heading "Introduction."

Abstract

Once readers have read your title, they will continue to the next section—the **abstract:** a short, one-paragraph summary of your research proposal.

According to Jolley, Murray, and Keller (1992), most abstracts are organized around six sentences:

1. the general research topic (for example, "Love is a common topic in popular music.")
2. the number of participants and their treatment
3. how the dependent measure will be collected ("Participants will fill out the Reuben Love–Like Scale 10 min after receiving the treatment.")
4. the hypothesis ("The hypothesis is that listening to love ballads will raise scores on the Love–Like Scale.")
5. the main results—those that relate to your hypothesis (include this in your final research report, not in the proposal)
6. the implications of your results (a sentence or two at the end; this miniature version of your discussion section might read something like, "The findings call into question ___ theory's assumption that _____" or "The results suggest that future research needs to address whether __ interacts with ____.")

References

Now that you have the title and abstract written, it's time to compile your reference list. To help you organize your references, we suggest you write each reference on an index card and alphabetize the cards. If you have more than one reference for an author, put the cards for that author in chronological order (from oldest to most recent). By writing references on cards before you type them, you reduce the chances of making two common errors: (a) not including all your references (which can lead to charges of plagiarism), and (b) not typing all your references in alphabetical order. However, if you have all your references in one electronic file, you can compile and alphabetize your references without index cards.

Once you have your references organized, you need to format them in APA style. The easiest way to do that is to use the reference section of the sample paper (Appendix B) as a model. Thus, if you need to write the reference for a journal article with two authors, follow the example of the sample paper's first reference.

One problem with using any model is that you may think you are doing what the model is doing, but you really aren't. To make sure that you are following the model in the sample paper, check your references page against the reference checklist in Appendix A.

Author Note

The Author Note starts on the page after the references. It begins with the centered heading: Author Note. In the first paragraph, put your name followed by a comma, then your school's name followed by a period. In the next paragraph, thank anyone who helped you with the study or with the paper. In the final paragraph, tell readers where to write you. To write an Author Note, follow the example in the sample paper and check your Author Note against the Author Note checklist in Appendix A.

Writing the Research Report

If you wrote a research proposal, much of the work on your research report already has been done. Essentially, your research proposal was the first draft of your research report. The next few pages will help you convert that first draft into a polished, complete research report.

What Stays the Same or Changes Very Little

The title page and references from your proposal can be transferred to your research report without any changes. However, you will need to make minor changes to the introduction, method, and abstract.

You need to revise your introduction so that you describe what you did (past tense) rather than what you plan to do (future tense). For example, you no longer plan to test the hypothesis that X causes Y; instead, you tested the hypothesis that X caused Y.

Whereas you had to make only one change to the introduction, you will need to make three changes in the method section. First, you will need to change the method section to reflect any changes you made in how you conducted the study. Generally, the procedures you initially proposed are not the ones you end up following. Sometimes, after reading your proposal, your professor will ask you to make some modifications. Sometimes an ethics committee may mandate some changes. Often, after testing out your procedures on a few participants, you will make some changes so that the actual study will run more smoothly.

Second, you probably will have to make some minor changes in the participants section. Prior to running the study, you can rarely anticipate who your participants will be and how many you will have to exclude.

Third, you need to rewrite the method section in the past tense. In the proposal, you told readers what you were going to do; in the report, you tell them what you did.

Like your method section, your abstract needs only minor modifications. Specifically, you need to add a sentence to describe the main results, a sentence to discuss the implications of those results, and you need to check that the participant and procedure information are still accurate.

In contrast to the other sections, you will have to revise the results and discussion sections extensively before you can include them in your final report. Because these two sections change the most from proposal to final report, the rest of this chapter will be devoted to them.

Writing the Results Section

There are two main purposes of the **results section:** (a) to show the reader that you competently analyzed the data, and (b) to tell the reader what you found. To accomplish these goals, you will report from one to five kinds of results:

1. results describing the distribution of participants' scores
2. results supporting the validity of your measure
3. results of the manipulation check
4. results relating to your hypothesis
5. other statistically significant results

Results Describing the Distribution of Scores

At the beginning of your results section, you might include a subsection that describes the distribution of scores on your dependent variable. Thus, you might give the mean and the standard deviation (or range) of scores.[3] For example, you might report, "The scores on the measure were normally distributed ($M = 75$, range $= 50$–100)."

Most authors do not include a section that describes the distribution of scores. If you do include such a section, it probably will be for one of the following five reasons:

1. to make a case that the sample is representative of some population by showing either that the scores are very similar to the population's distribution of scores or that the scores were not unusually extreme
2. to argue that your data meet the assumptions of the statistical tests by showing that the scores were normally distributed or that the different groups had the same variances
3. to show that your data had to be transformed or that the data could not be analyzed by a certain statistical test because the data were not normally distributed
4. to argue that there should be no problems due to ceiling effects, floor effects, or restriction of range because there was a wide range of scores and those scores were normally distributed
5. to emphasize descriptive statistics that are of interest in their own right, as would be the case if reporting the percentage of the sample who had married before the age of 20

Results Supporting the Measure's Validity

Like the section describing the distribution of scores, the section supporting the measure's validity often is omitted. If you are using an accepted, validated measure, you probably will omit this section. If you choose to include this section, you probably will stress the results that emphasize the measure's

1. test–retest or alternate-forms reliability, indicating that the measure is not unduly influenced by random error, as shown by participants getting the same score from one day to the next (for more on test–retest reliability, see Chapter 5)

---

[3]If the data are *not* normally distributed, you may want to provide a graph of the raw scores.

2. interobserver reliability, indicating that the measure is objectively scored, as shown by different observers giving the participants the same scores (for more on interobserver reliability, see Chapter 5)

3. internal consistency, indicating that the items of a test or subscale are all measuring the same thing, as shown by people who score high on a characteristic according to one question on the test also scoring high on that characteristic according to other questions on the test (for more on internal consistency, see Chapter 5)

Results of the Manipulation Check

If you used a manipulation check, you should put these findings near the beginning of the results section. Although these results usually will be statistically significant and unsurprising, it is important to demonstrate that you manipulated what you said you would manipulate. Thus, reporting the outcome of your manipulation check is a good lead into discussing results relating to your hypothesis: Once you have shown the reader that you manipulated the variable you planned to manipulate, the reader is ready to know whether that variable produced the effects you expected.

Results Relating to Your Hypothesis

Your results section does not have to describe the distribution of scores, provide evidence for the validity of the measure, or describe the results of a manipulation check. However, it must describe the results relating to the hypothesis. In writing the results section, your main goal should always be to make it very easy for your readers to know how the hypothesis did.

To make it easy for readers to know how the hypothesis fared, tell your readers what the hypothesis was and whether it was supported. Then, use descriptive statistics (usually averages like means) and the results of the statistical test to link the results to the hypothesis. For example, if your hypothesis was that people who own cats are more likely to hug their children, report what the data said about this hypothesis: "The hypothesis that people who own cats would be significantly more likely to hug their children was supported. Cat owners hugged their children on the average 4.6 ($SD = 1.6$) times a day per child, whereas people who did not own cats hugged their children on the average 2.3 ($SD = 1.5$) times a day, $F(1,64) = 18.2, p < .05$."

Other Significant Results

After reporting results relating to your hypothesis (whether or not the results were significant), you should report any other statistically significant results. Even if the results are unwanted and make no sense to you, significant results must be reported. Therefore you might report: "There was an unanticipated relationship between gender of the child and cat ownership. Parents of girls owned more cats ($M = 2.0$, $SD = 1.0$) than parents of boys ($M = 1.0$, $SD = 1.8$), $F(1,64) = 20.1, p < .05$."

Tips on Writing the Results Section

Although you now know what a results section is, you may not believe that you know enough to write a decent one. To write a good results section, you need to realize that the goal of the results section is to help the reader understand what you found. To help your reader understand what you found, we offer four tips: (1) start off simply, (2) explain what you are doing,

(3) use means or other summary statistics to make the pattern of your results more concrete, and (4) focus on your hypothesis.

Tip 1: Start Off Simply. Sometimes, beginning writers lose their audience at the very beginning of the results section. To avoid that problem, start out simply and slowly. You might begin the section by just explaining what the scores meant. Your goal would be to give the reader some sense as to what a participant who had a low score did differently than a person getting a high score.

What if the meaning of the scores is too obvious? Or, what if you explained how scores were computed in the method section? Then, you might start the results section with a simple analysis. For example, you might discuss results relating to the degree to which the different coders coded the data similarly (e.g., "Raters agreed 98% of the time"). Or, you might discuss other results that should be predictable and easy to understand, such as the results of the manipulation check (e.g., "As predicted, the attractive ($M = 7.2$) pictures were rated as more attractive than the unattractive ($M = 2.1$) pictures, $t(28) = 81.2, p < .05$").

When discussing a set of analyses, one strategy is to start off by discussing simple findings and then moving to more complex findings. For example, report relationships between a treatment and the outcome variable (e.g., main effects) before discussing how that relationship is moderated by another variable (e.g., interactions involving that main effect). Another strategy is to discuss general findings before moving to more specific findings. Thus, you might first report that the treatment had an effect (e.g., by reporting the results of the overall F test) before talking about which particular groups differed from each other (e.g., by reporting the results of more specific follow-up tests).

Tip 2: Don't Report Results—Analyze Them. Do not, however, merely report results. That is, do not, in effect, shove the results of the computer printout in the reader's face and say "Here, see if you can make sense of this!" Instead, follow our second tip, which is to give the reader your *analysis* of the results.

Your analysis will not include every statistic the computer generated. Instead, you will give the reader only those statistics that make a point.

In addition to giving the reader an analysis only if the analysis makes a point, you will tell the reader what the point is. The reader should not be left wondering, "Why is she telling me this?" For example, if you are doing an analysis to see whether your manipulation check worked, you will let the reader know by writing something like, "As a check on the attractiveness manipulation, I conducted a t test on participants' ratings of the pictures. As predicted, the attractive ($M = 7.2$) pictures were rated as more attractive than the unattractive ($M = 2.1$) pictures, $t(28) = 81.2, p < .05$." To further help the reader realize the purpose of the analysis, you might even label that subsection "Attractiveness Manipulation Check."

Tip 3: Use Summary Statistics to Make the Findings More Concrete. Note that as we focused on telling the reader the general purpose and outcome of the analysis, we also presented the specific means for each group. By supplementing the general, abstract information (e.g., one group scored significantly higher than the other group) with specific, concrete information (the actual means), we went beyond giving the reader a general idea of what we found to letting the reader actually see what we found. Therefore, make your results section easier to understand by supplementing the results of statistical tests with the relevant means, frequencies, correlations, or other summary statistics.

Tip 4: Focus on the Hypothesis. The fourth, and most important tip, is to ask the question, "After reading the results section, will the reader know whether the results supported the hypothesis?" One way to determine whether you have achieved this goal is to ask a friend to read your results section. See whether your friend can answer these five questions:

1. What was the hypothesis?

2. Was the hypothesis supported?

3. What statistical test was used to find this out?

4. What were the results of that test (value of the statistic and the **probability value, or p value:** the chances of obtaining this pattern of results if only chance were at work)?

5. Did the averages (or some other summary statistic, such as percentages) for the different conditions help you understand whether the prediction was supported? If not, would a table or graph make things clearer?

By focusing on helping the reader understand whether the results supported the hypothesis, you will end up doing many of the things that we just suggested. You will leave out information that is irrelevant and distracting. You will include all information that helps the reader understand the results section such as what the scores represent, why the analysis is being done, and what the analysis shows.

Conclusions About Writing the Results Section

In short, you should try to make your results section as clear and understandable as possible. If you focus your results section on your hypothesis and have empathy for your reader, you should be able to write an understandable and useful results section.

Writing the Discussion Section

If the results matched your predictions, the discussion section you wrote for your proposal might work as the discussion section for the final report. However, there are two reasons why it will probably have to be substantially modified. First, it is unlikely that you will get exactly the results you expected. Second, during the course of conducting the research or writing the paper, you probably will think of problems or implications that you did not think of when you wrote your proposal.

As you revise the discussion section, realize that although you are making a case, you should argue like an impartial judge who has come to certain conclusions after carefully weighing all the evidence rather than like a crusading attorney who is trying to prove a point. In presenting your arguments, be sure to take the following seven steps:

1. Briefly review the research question or hypothesis.

2. Briefly summarize the results, relating them to the hypothesis.

3. Interpret the results in light of the arguments made in your introduction.

4. Acknowledge alternative explanations for your results, trying to dismiss these alternatives, if possible.

5. Discuss unexpected findings, and speculate on possible reasons for them.

6. Discuss, in general terms, future research. What would you do if you were to follow up on this research (assume an unlimited budget)? Follow-up research might focus on improving the methodology of your study, exploring unexpected findings, trying to rule out alternative explanations for your findings, testing the

generality of your findings, looking for practical implications of the findings, looking for variables that might have similar effects, or looking for mental or physiological factors that mediate the observed relationship.

7. Discuss the practical or theoretical implications of your findings.

Once you have written your discussion section, you are nearly finished. However, you will need to write several drafts before you have a paper that meets APA's requirements for style and format. To meet APA standards, your paper must be clear and well organized. It must be free of grammatical errors, spelling errors, biased language, wordiness, and informal language. Fortunately, your computer's spelling and grammar checker can help you catch and fix spelling errors, typographical errors, and grammatical errors, as well as problems due to using sexist or overly informal language (for specific advice on how to use your computer to edit your paper, see the Chapter 15 section of this text's student website). To edit your paper so that it conforms to APA format, check your "next-to-final draft" against the checklist in Appendix A. In addition, *make sure that your paper matches the format of the model paper in Appendix B.*

Concluding Remarks

Well, you've done it! If you carefully followed the advice in this book, you should have just completed a carefully planned, meaningful, and ethical research project. Congratulations and best wishes for your continued success as a researcher!

SUMMARY

1. The research journal and proposal will help you plan and conduct ethical and valid research.

2. The research proposal is more formal than the research journal and should conform to the *Publication Manual of the American Psychological Association* (2001).

3. In the introduction of your proposal, you need to summarize and critique relevant research. This critique should set up the reasons you think that your hypothesis (a) will be supported, (b) should be tested, and (c) should be tested the way you are going to test it.

4. In the introduction, state your hypothesis, explain why your predictions make sense, and explain why your study will provide a valid test of your hypothesis.

5. Before writing the method section, you should carefully plan out each step of your study.

6. Once you have planned out every detail of your study, you should formalize your plan in the method, results, and discussion sections in your proposal.

7. The method section is the "how" section in which you explain how you plan to conduct your study and why you are going to do it that way.

8. In the proposal's results section, you will discuss how you plan to analyze your results.

9. In the discussion section, you will explore the implications of your anticipated research findings for theory, future research, or real life.

10. Once you finish the body of the proposal, write the abstract (a brief summary of the proposal), the title page, and the reference section. Much of your final report will be based on your proposal—provided you wrote a good proposal.

11. The title page and reference sections of your proposal can be transferred directly to your final report. After you change the appropriate parts of the introduction to the past tense, it can be transferred to your final report. After you change the appropriate parts of the method section to the past tense, it may also be transferred (with only minor modifications) to the final report.

12. Try to make the results section as understandable as possible. Tell the reader what you are trying to find out by doing the analysis, and then explain what you actually did find out from doing the analysis.

13. In the results section, be sure to stress whether the results supported or failed to support your hypothesis.

14. In the discussion section, summarize the main findings of your study and relate these to the points you made in the introduction.

15. Writing involves a great deal of rewriting.

16. Do not plagiarize! Keep notes about what you read so that you can cite it. Realize that even if you didn't quote a source, you still have to cite it if you borrowed from it or got some ideas from it.

KEY TERMS

research journal *(p. 464)*

introduction *(p. 466)*

exploratory study *(p. 469)*

direct (exact) replication *(p. 471)*

systematic replication *(p. 472)*

conceptual replication *(p. 472)*

method section *(p. 475)*

plagiarism *(p. 475)*

discussion *(p. 478)*

abstract *(p. 480)*

results section *(p. 482)*

probability value *(p value)* *(p. 485)*

WEB RESOURCES

1. Go to the Chapter 15 section of the book's student website and do the following:
   a. Look over the concept map of the key terms.
   b. Test yourself on the key terms.
   c. Take the Chapter 15 Practice Quiz.
   d. Download the Chapter 15 tutorial.

2. Use the "Fast Start" link to download software that will help you make sure that your title page adheres to APA format.

3. Get some help in putting your reference page in APA format by clicking on the "Referencer" link.

4. Get more tips on finding articles to cite in your paper by clicking on the "Literature Search" link.

INFOTRAC COLLEGE EDITION EXPLORATIONS

Do an InfoTrac College Edition search for the phrase "unrealistic optimism and illusion of control" and find McKenna's 1993 article. The article is a good example of (a) how to write up the results of a study attempting to distinguish between two competing explanations for an event, and (b) how to incorporate suggestions for further research into a discussion section.

A

APA Format Checklist

Title Page

1. I have a separate title page.

2. At the top right-hand corner, I have
   a. a short, two- or three-word "mini-title" of my paper. This "mini-title" is the first two or three words of my title
   b. the number "1," indicating that it is page 1. The "1" is on the same line as the mini-title, just five spaces to the right of it (flush right)

3. I have put the "mini-title" of my paper and the page number into the "header" of my document, so that the "mini-title" and page number appear on the top right-hand corner of each page.

4. One double-spaced line below the mini-title and the page number, I have a line that
   a. starts at the left margin (about an inch from the left edge of the page)
   b. begins with the words "Running head:" followed by a two- to six-word phrase that describes my paper's topic (Note that the running head is *not* the same as the mini-title.)

5. My two-to-six-word running head is in all-capital letters and is fewer than 50 characters (including spaces) long.

6. I centered the title and capitalized the first letters of each word in the title (except for words like "and" and "of").

7. My title is simple and to the point. It contains the names of the key variables (in an experiment, the independent and dependent variables; in a correlational study, the predictor and criterion variables).

8. My name (first name, *middle initial,* and last name) is
   a. one double-spaced line below the title
   b. centered
   c. not accompanied by the word "by"

9. My school's name is
   a. one double-spaced line below my name
   b. centered

10. The rest of the page is blank.

Abstract

1. My Abstract is on its own separate page.

2. I have the number "2," indicating that the Abstract is page 2, at the top right-hand corner. The "2" is five spaces to the right of the mini-title.

3. The heading "Abstract" is centered at the top of page 2.

4. The text of my Abstract starts one double-spaced line below the heading ("Abstract").

5. My Abstract is a single, un-indented paragraph, and it contains fewer than 121 words.

6. To keep my Abstract as brief as possible, I used digits rather than writing out numbers.

7. I avoided starting any of my sentences with a number.

8. I avoided using the first person (e.g., "I," "my," "our," or "we").

9. I included a brief summary of the following sections of my paper:
   a. the introduction: my hypothesis (what I studied and why)
   b. the participants section: who the participants were
   c. the procedure: what the participants did
   d. the results: whether the data supported the hypothesis
   e. the discussion: the meaning of the results

Citing Sources

1. I gave credit where credit was due.
   a. I cited any source from which I got ideas—even if I did not quote that source. When I summarized or paraphrased from a source, I cited that source. To minimize the chances that I plagiarized, I did the following:
      i. If I had any paragraph without a citation in the Introduction or Discussion sections of my paper, I went back to my notes to make sure that I had not left out a citation.
      ii. If I had any doubt about whether to cite a source, I cited it.
   b. If I obtained information from a secondary source, I cited and referenced the secondary source.

2. I quoted appropriately.
   a. I listed the page number of the source from which I got the quote (something I would not do for a paraphrased citation).
   b. I put quotation marks around quotes shorter than 40 words.
   c. For quotes of 40 or more words, I separated the quote from the rest of my paper by indenting the whole quotation five spaces from the left margin.

3. My citations are free of common content errors.
   a. When citing authors, I limited myself to stating authors' last names. I did not mention authors' first names, professional titles (e.g., "Dr."), or professional affiliations.
   b. When citing sources, I used parentheses. I did not use footnotes to cite sources.
   c. I did not mention any article titles in the text of my paper.

4. I followed the rules regarding parentheses.
   a. When I mentioned the authors in the sentence, I put only the date in parentheses (e.g., "Jolley and Mitchell (2006) argued that . . .").
   b. If the authors' names are not part of the sentence, I put their names and the date in parentheses. I separated the last author's name from the date with a comma: "Some have argued that . . . (Jolley & Mitchell, 2006)."
   c. If the multiple-author citation was part of the sentence, I used "and" to connect authors' last names; however, if the multiple-author citation was in parentheses, I used "&" to connect authors' last names.
   d. When I cited several articles within one set of parentheses, I did the following:
      i. I listed the articles in alphabetical order. I did not put them in order by date.
      ii. I separated the articles from each other with semicolons: "(Brickner, 1980; Jolley, 2003; Mitchell, 2005; Ostrom, 1965; Pusateri, 1995; Williams, 1992)."

5. I correctly cited multiple-author papers.
   a. If the paper has more than six authors, I listed only the first author's last name followed immediately (with no comma) by "et al." (e.g., Glick et al., 2002).
   b. If I discussed a paper with three to five authors, I mentioned all the authors' last names the first time I cited that paper.
   c. If I discussed a paper with three to five authors and had already cited the paper, I used the first author's last name, followed immediately (with no comma) by et al. (e.g., First et al., 1996).
   d. I checked all my citations that used the phrase "et al." to make sure that I had (a) correctly used such citations and (b) correctly punctuated such citations.
      i. I did not overuse "et al." citations.
         1. I never used "et al." the first time I introduced a paper with fewer than six authors.
         2. I never use "et al." with a two-author paper.
      ii. I correctly punctuated my "et al." citations.
         1. I never put a period after "et" (e.g., "et. al.").
         2. I never put a comma between the first author's last name and "et al" (e.g., "First, et al.").

6. I cited the appropriate literature.
   a. It is clear what the articles cited have to do with my study.
   b. Most of my citations are to recent journal articles describing actual research studies. Few, if any, of my citations are to secondhand sources such as textbooks, magazines, and newspapers.

Introduction

1. My Introduction begins on a separate page (page 3).
2. My article's title is centered at the top of the first page of the Introduction.
3. To be sure that my Introduction was organized, I outlined it before writing it.
4. It is clear why my topic area is important.

5. It is clear why testing my hypothesis is important: I showed how my study builds on previous work or fills a gap in previous work.

6. It is clear why I believe that the hypothesis might be true. To make the logic behind my hypothesis clear, I explained relevant concepts and theories.

7. My hypothesis is clearly stated.

8. A reader should be able to foresee much of the rest of the paper (especially the essence of the Method section) after reading my Introduction.

9. I checked my Introduction against the "Citing Sources" checklist.

Method Section

1. I wrote the Method section of my research report in the past tense.

2. I put the heading "Method" (not "Methods") one double-spaced line below the last line of the Introduction, and I centered that heading.

3. I divided the Method section into at least two subsections (Participants and Procedure).

4. I put the heading "Participants" flush against the left margin, and I put that heading one double-spaced line below the heading "Method." (Do not use the word "subjects" if you studied humans.)

5. I italicized that heading (e.g., *Participants*).

6. I indented the text for the Participants section, and I began that text on the next double-spaced line after the "Participants" heading.

7. If I started a sentence with a number (such as, "Twenty undergraduates were participants"), I spelled out the number. (Note: You can write: "Participants were 20 undergraduates," but you cannot write: "20 undergraduates were participants.")

8. I have been specific about
   a. how I selected or recruited my sample of participants or nonhuman animal subjects
   b. how participants were compensated (if they were compensated)
   c. major demographic characteristics
      i. number of participants of each gender
      ii. age of participants (average age and either standard deviation or range of ages)
      iii. other demographic characteristics, if appropriate
   d. the number of participants who dropped out of the study
   e. the number of participants whose data were not analyzed and the reasons for not analyzing those data
   f. how participants were assigned to condition

9. I made it clear that participants were treated ethically.

10. I put the heading "Procedure" (a) in italics, (b) one double-spaced line after the last line of the previous subsection, and (c) flush against the left margin.

11. I indented the text for the Procedure section five spaces, and I started it one double-spaced line after the "Procedure" heading.

12. If I used standard laboratory equipment, I identified the manufacturer and model name and/or number.

13. I used complete sentences. For example, I did not merely provide a bulleted list of my materials or an outline of my operational definitions.

14. I focused on what happened to participants and what participants did—and presented the information in order from the first thing that happened to the last thing that happened.

15. Someone reading my report could replicate (repeat) my study.
    a. It is clear how (under what conditions) I tested each participant.
    b. It is clear how I turned each participant's response into a score.

16. I made a case for the study's validity.
    a. It is clear what I did to reduce the effects of researcher bias.
    b. It is clear how a control or comparison group ruled out an alternative explanation for a difference between groups.
    c. It is clear that the measure being used is reliable and valid.
        i. I cited evidence of the measure's reliability and validity.
        ii. I reported any data that I, as part of conducting the study, collected that related to the measure's validity. For example, if I had data related to the extent to which two different observers' scores agreed when scoring the same response, I reported those data.
    d. I gave my measure(s) and manipulation(s) names that are closely tied to my operational definitions (e.g., "Introversion Test Score") rather than using a general name that may not be valid (e.g., "shyness").
    e. I made it clear why my study is a good way to test my hypothesis.

Results

1. I centered the title "Results" one double-spaced line after the last line of the Method section. (I did not skip to a new page to begin the Results section.)

2. I wrote the Results section of my research report in the past tense.

3. I italicized all the letters that represent statistical symbols and abbreviations for statistical variables (e.g., "p" as the abbreviation for probability value), except Greek letters (α, β).

    Wrong: . . . t = 9.08, p < .05.

    Right: . . . t = 9.08, p < .05.

4. When I reported the result of a statistical test, I put the statistic, the degrees of freedom for the test, the value of the statistic, and the level of significance (the p value). The format, *except for the spacing,* conforms to what is shown below:

Statistic	*df*	Numerical Value of the Test	Probability
F	(2,46) =	3.85,	p < .05
t	(24) =	3.0,	p < .001
r	(24) =	.71,	p < .01

5. I included enough information about descriptive statistics to help readers know more than just the outcome of the statistical significance test. For example, if I used a *t* test or analysis of variance, I presented the means and standard deviations.

6. I determined my professor's views about reporting analyses beyond that of significance tests. Thus, I know whether my professor required me to follow the *Publication Manual of the American Psychological Association*'s suggestions that I
    a. include a confidence interval
    b. report an estimate of effect size, such as Cohen's *d* (e.g., "$F(2,46) = 3.85$, $p < .05, d = .27$")[1]

7. I made it clear to the reader
    a. what data I used in the analyses (how behaviors were turned into scores)—unless (a) I had already made the scoring clear in the Method section or (b) the scoring system was obvious
    b. what analyses I used on those data
    c. what significance level I used (if I used a significance test)
    d. why I did that analysis
    e. which groups scored significantly higher (I usually did this by including, in the text, average scores for my different groups. The summary statistics I included in text [averages] were usually sufficient to help the reader see the pattern in my data. However, I used a table or a graph if [a] I had more than four conditions, or [b] my professor required one.)
    f. whether the results support my hypothesis

8. If I used tables, I made sure that
    a. each table added meaningful information beyond that which was presented in the text of my Results section
    b. each table was referred to in the text of my paper (e.g., "As Table 1 indicates . . .")
    c. each table's number corresponded to when I referred to it in text (e.g., the first table I mentioned in text was Table 1)
    d. I double-spaced everything in each table
    e. I put each table on a separate page
    f. I put all my tables located near the end of my report—after the References
    g. My tables comply with the format illustrated by the following two tables

Table 1

Pearson Product Moment Correlation for Self-Esteem

	Body Concept	
Group	Attractiveness	Fitness
Female	.65***	.50**
Male	.35*	.70***

*$p < .05$, **$p < .01$, ***$p < .001$

Table 2

Analysis of Variance for Self-Esteem

Source	df	F
Exercise (E)	2	9.75**
Within-Group Error	57	(2.56)

Note. Value enclosed in parentheses represents mean square error.
**$p < .01$.

9. I referred to all graphs as figures ("Figure" 1, not "Graph" 1).

10. I gave each figure an informative heading.

11. I put each figure on a separate page.

12. I labeled both the x and y axes of each graph.

13. In pencil, on the back of each figure, I
    a. made it clear where the top of the figure was by writing the word "top" on the top of the page
    b. made it clear what manuscript the figure belonged to by writing my manuscript's short title (the first two to three words of the title)
    c. made it clear what the figure was by writing the figure number

14. I put all my figures at the end of my report.

Discussion

1. I centered the title "Discussion" and put it one double-spaced line after the last line of the Results section.

2. My first sentence describes whether the results support, fail to support, or refute my hypothesis, and my first paragraph summarizes my main findings.

3. I used the present tense when discussing my conclusions.

4. I compared my Discussion against the citing sources checklist.

5. I interpreted my results in the context of the theory, past research, and practical issues that I introduced in my Introduction. For example, I compared my results to what other researchers found.

6. I tried to explain results that were not predicted, and I admitted when my explanations were speculations.

7. I addressed alternative explanations for my results. I tried to rule out these alternative explanations, but when I could not, I admitted that I could not.

8. I pointed out the weaknesses and limitations of my study. I even sketched out future research that could be done to correct these weaknesses or overcome these limitations.

9. If I believed I could make a case for generalizing my results (I had a representative sample, the results were similar to what others had found, etc.), I made such a case.

10. I treated nonsignificant results as inconclusive.
    a. I did not use nonsignificant results as proof that a treatment had no effect.
    b. I did not use nonsignificant results that were almost significant as evidence that the treatment had an effect.

References

1. I started my References section on a separate page. I indicated the start of that page by centering the word "References" at the top of the page.

2. Everything is double-spaced.

3. My references are listed in alphabetical order (according to the last name of the first author).

4. The first line of each reference is not indented. Instead, it is flush against the left margin.

5. When a reference takes up more than one line, those additional lines are indented.

6. I started each reference with the authors' last names and initials, followed by the year of publication (in parentheses), and then a period.

7. I did not use the authors' first or middle names.

8. For all journal articles, I wrote down the volume number. (The volume number [e.g., 30] is different from the year [e.g., 2007]. The volume number can usually be found on the journal's cover, the journal's table of contents, and at the bottom of the first page of each article.)

9. Every reference—unless it ends with a URL—ends with a period.

10. If there is more than one author for a source, I separated authors' names with commas. (There is a comma after every author's name—except for the last author's name.)

11. I used italics correctly.
    a. I italicized the titles of all books.
    b. I italicized the titles of all journals.
    c. I italicized the volume numbers of every journal article cited.
    d. I put the titles of journal articles in normal, non-italicized type.

12. I correctly capitalized the names of books and titles of articles. That is, I capitalized only
    a. proper nouns (e.g., Asia, Skinner)
    b. the first word of titles of articles and books
    c. the first word following a colon in the title of an article or book

13. I used abbreviations appropriately.
    a. When citing journal articles, I avoided both the word "pages" and the abbreviation "pp."
    b. When mentioning where a book was published, I abbreviated, rather than wrote out, the name of the state. I used the two-letter state abbreviations (e.g., PA for Pennsylvania) that the U.S. Postal Service uses. I remembered that these abbreviations are capitalized and do not contain periods.

14. All the references in this section are also cited in my paper. If a reference was not cited, I either added that citation to the body of my paper or I deleted the reference.

15. All the sources cited in my paper are also listed in this section except for
    a. "personal communication" citations
    b. original works that I did not read but instead learned about through a secondary source
    c. classical works such as the Bible

Author Note

1. My Author Note begins on the page following the appendixes (if I do not have appendixes, it begins on the page following the References) with the centered heading "Author Note."

2. My Author Note makes disclosures about who, if anyone, helped me with my paper.

3. My Author Note includes my name, the name of my school, and information about how to contact me.

4. The first paragraph of my Author Note is not a sentence. Instead, it contains my name, a comma, my department (e.g., "Department of Psychology), a comma, and the name of my school.

5. The next to the last paragraph of my Author Note acknowledges people who helped me with my study or my paper.

6. The final paragraph begins with "Correspondence concerning this article should be addressed to" and is followed by an appropriate mailing address.

General Format

1. I double-spaced everything.

2. I put the first two or three words of the title, then five spaces, and then the page number at the top, right-hand corner of every page—except for those pages containing figures.

3. I started every paragraph by indenting five spaces with only two exceptions:
    a. I did not indent the Abstract.
    b. I did not indent Notes at the bottom of tables.

4. I did not use terms or labels that devalue, stereotype, exclude, or offend people belonging to groups other than my own (e.g., people older than I am, people with mental illnesses, people who have a different racial or ethnic background than I have). Instead, I used terms that were emotionally neutral or respectful.

5. I did not use sexist language (e.g., referring to males as "men" but referring to females as "girls," referring to the typical participant as "he" when most of your participants were women).

6. I spell-checked my document.

7. I used complete sentences (all of my sentences have subjects and verbs).

8. I was careful about not making statements that went beyond the evidence. Specifically, I
    a. reported what I observed (e.g., "took 10 seconds before pressing the button") rather than what I inferred (e.g., "they hesitated and worried about potential embarrassment before pressing the button")

    b. did not use the word "prove"

    c. did not claim something was a fact when it was an opinion

    d. did not make cause–effect statements without having evidence from an experiment

9. To help my paper sound professional, I
    a. outlined my paper to make sure it was organized
    b. read my paper aloud
    c. split up, shortened, or eliminated long sentences
    d. eliminated unnecessary words and redundant sentences
    e. used a grammar checker to weed out wordy phrases, sexist language, and other unprofessional language

10. My paper's appearance is professional. It
    a. is neatly typed
    b. is free of typographical errors
    c. has at least 1-in (2.54 cm) margins

11. I did not hyphenate words at the end of a line.

12. I put all my first-level headings (e.g., Abstract, Method, Results, Discussion, References, etc.) in a plain (not italicized, not boldfaced) font and centered them. I capitalized only the first letters of words of these headings. (Note that "Introduction" is not one of the first-level headings. Instead of "Introduction," the title is centered on the top of page 3.)

13. I italicized all my second-level headings (major subheadings such as Participants, Procedure, etc.) and put them flush against the left margin (I did not indent them). I capitalized only the first letters of words of these subheadings.

14. I did not include anyone's first name or affiliation in my paper (except for the title page).

15. The order of the sections in my paper is as follows: title page, Abstract, Introduction, Method, Results, Discussion, References, Appendixes, Author Note, tables, list of figure captions, and figures.

16. I used white, 8.5×11 in (22×28 cm), 20-pound, bond, nonerasable paper.

17. I typed my paper using
    a. 12-point type
    b. Times Roman, Times New Roman, or Courier font
    c. black print
    d. dark, easy-to-read print
    e. only one side of the paper

18. I avoided using
    a. contractions
    b. exclamation points
    c. hyphens at the end of lines
    d. boldfacing
    e. underlining
    f. one-sentence paragraphs

Sample APA-Style Paper

Adapted from Frank, M. G., & Gilovich, T. (1988). The dark side of self- and social-perception: Black uniforms and aggression in professional sports. *Journal of Personality and Social Psychology, 54,* 74–85. Used with the kind permission of Mark Frank, Thomas Gilovich, and the American Psychological Association.

Running head: BLACK UNIFORMS AND AGGRESSION

The Dark Side of Self-Perception:

Black Uniforms and Aggression

Mark G. Frank and Thomas Gilovich

Cornell University

Abstract

Black is viewed as the color of evil and death in virtually all cultures. With this association in mind, we were interested in whether a cue as subtle as the color of a person's clothing might have a significant impact on the wearer's behavior. To test this possibility, we performed a laboratory experiment to determine whether wearing a black uniform can increase a person's inclination to engage in aggressive behavior. We found that participants who wore black uniforms showed a marked increase in intended aggression relative to those wearing white uniforms. Our discussion focuses on the theoretical implications of these data for an understanding of the variable, or "situated," nature of the self.

The Dark Side of Self-Perception:

Black Uniforms and Aggression

A convenient feature of the traditional American Western film was the ease of which the viewer could distinguish the good guys from the bad guys: The bad guys wore the black hats. Of course, film directors did not invent this connection between black and evil, but built upon an existing association that extends deep into American culture and language. Americans can be hurt by others by being "blacklisted," or "blackballed," or "blackmailed" (Williams, 1964). When the Chicago White Sox deliberately lost the 1919 World Series as part of a betting scheme, they became known as the Chicago Black Sox, and to this day the "dark" chapter in American sports history is known as the Black Sox Scandal. In a similar vein, Muhammad Ali has observed that Americans refer to white cake as "angel food cake" and dark cake as "devil's food cake."

These anecdotes concerning people's negative associations to the color black are reinforced by the research literature on color meanings. In one representative experiment, groups of college students and seventh graders who were asked to make semantic differential rating of colors were found to associate black with evil, death, and badness (Williams & McMurty, 1970). Moreover, this association between black and evil is not strictly an American or Western phenomenon because college students in Germany, Denmark, Hong Kong, and India (Williams, Moreland, & Underwood, 1970) and Ndembu tribesmen in Central Africa (Turner, 1967) all report that the color black connoted evil and death. Thus, Adams and Osgood (1973) concluded that black is seen, in virtually all cultures, as the color of evil and death.

The intriguing question is whether these associations influence people's behavior in important ways. For example, does wearing black clothing lead the wearer to actually act more aggressively?

This possibility is suggested by studies on anonymity and "deindividuation" which show that a person's clothing can affect the amount of aggression he or she expresses. In one study, female participants in a "learning" experiment were asked to deliver shocks to another participant whenever she made a mistake. Under the pretense of minimizing individual identities, one half of the participants wore nurses' uniforms (a prosocial cue), and the other half wore outfits resembling Ku Klux Klan uniforms (an antisocial cue). As predicted, participants who wore nurses uniforms delivered less shock to the "learner" than did participants who wore the Ku Klux Klan uniforms, which demonstrates that the cues inherent in certain clothes can influence the wearer's aggressive behavior (Johnson & Downing, 1979).

Although such studies are suggestive, they involve rather contrived situations that raise troubling questions of experimental demand. Accordingly, we decided to seek parallel evidence for a link between clothing cues and aggressiveness by examining the effect of a much more subtle cue, the color of a person's uniform.

There are a couple of difficulties that confront any attempt to test whether wearing a black uniform tends to make a person more aggressive. First, any such test is fraught with the usual ethical problems involved in all research on human aggression. Second, because black is associated with violence, observers may be biased when judging the behavior of participants wearing black. The usual solution to these twin problems is to use some version of the bogus shock paradigm (Buss, 1961). However, we chose not to use this procedure because of the difficulty in finding participants who—given the publicity of Milgram's (1965, 1974) work—would not view the proceedings with extreme suspicion.

Our solution to these problems was to collect "behavioroid" data (Carlsmith, Ellsworth, & Aronson, 1976) in the form of the participants' intended aggressive behavior. Volunteers for an experiment on competition were led to believe that they would be vying against other participants in several competitive events. They were also led to believe that they could exercise some control over which events they were to participate in by selecting their 5 most preferred events from a list of 12. The 12 events varied in the amount of aggressiveness they called for, allowing us to use participants' choices as a measure of their reading to engage in aggressive action. By means of a suitable cover story, we elicited participants' choices twice: once individually when wearing their usual clothes, and later as a team of 3 wearing black or white jerseys. We hypothesized that wearing black jerseys would induce participants to view themselves as more mean and aggressive and thus would produce more of a "group shift" toward aggressive choices by participants wearing black jerseys than by those wearing white (Drabman & Thomas, 1977; Jaffe, Shapir, & Yinon, 1981).

Method

Overview

Participants participated in groups of 3 in an experiment ostensibly on the "psychology of competition." Each group was told that they would be competing against another team of 3 on a series of five games of everyone's choosing. To find out their preferences, they were asked to individually rank order 5 activities from a group of 12. After making their choices, the participants were outfitted in either white or black uniforms in the guise of facilitating team identity. Then, while the experimenter was supposedly administering instructions to the other team, the 3 participants were told to discuss their individual choices and to decide as a group on the rank ordering of the 5 activities they would like to include in the competition. This second ranking allowed us to assess whether the participants would choose more aggressive games as a group after donning black uniforms than after putting on white uniforms. Finally, as an auxiliary measure of aggression, participants were administered a brief version of Murray's (1943) Thematic Apperception Test (TAT) to assess their level of aggressive ideation.

Participants

The participants were 72 male students from Cornell University who were paid $3 for their participation. They were run in groups of 3, with the members of each group unacquainted with one another.

Procedure

As the participants reported for the experiment they were brought together in one room and led to believe that another group of participants was assembling in a different room. Participants were told

> You will be competing, as a team, on a series of five games against another group of 3 participants who are waiting in the next room. I matched the two teams for size as you came in, so the contests should be fair. This study is designed to mimic real-life competition as closely as possible . . . [and so] . . . we want you to choose the games you want to play.

Participants were then given a list of descriptions of 12 games and were asked to indicate, individually, which games they would like to play. They were asked to choose 5 of the 12 games and to rank order those 5. After reminding the participants not to discuss their choices with one another, the experimenter left the room, ostensibly to elicit the choices of the other team.

Upon his return, the experimenter collected the participants' individual choices and stated that "now I would like you to make a group decision as to which games you will play, because many times people's preferences are so divergent that we need to use a group choice to serve as a tie-breaker when deciding on which games to play." The experimenter further explained, "to make the experiment more like real-world competition and to build team cohesion, I would like you to put these uniforms on over your shirts. From now on you will be referred to as the black [white] team." The participants were then given black or white uniforms with silver duct-tape numerals (7, 8, and 11) on the backs.

The experimenter once again left the room to allow the participants to make their group choices and then returned after 5 min. He then explained,

> Now that I have everyone's individual and team selections, I will go and set up the five games that received the most votes. While I am doing this, I want you to complete a standard psychological task to get all of you in the same state of mind before we start.

Participants were asked to write a brief story about a scene depicted in a TAT card (Card 18 BM from Murray's, 1943, original series). Participants were given 4 min to write a story based on the following questions: (a) What is happening in the picture? (b) What is being thought by the characters in the picture? (c) What has led up to this picture? and (d) What will happen to the characters in the picture?

After 4 min the experimenter returned, collected the TAT protocols, and thoroughly debriefed the participants. All participants seemed surprised (and many disappointed) to learn that the experiment was over. The debriefing interview also made it clear that none of the participants had entertained the possibility that the color of the uniforms might have been the focus of the experiment.

Dependent Measures

The primary measure in this experiment was the level of aggressiveness involved in the games participants wanted to include in the competition. A group of 30 participants had earlier rated a set of descriptions of 20 games in terms of how much aggressiveness they involved. The 12 games that had received the most consistent ratings and that represented a wide spectrum of aggressiveness were then used as the stimulus set in this experiment. These 12 games were ranked in terms of these aggressiveness ratings and assigned point values consistent with their ranks, from the most aggressive (12, 11, and 10 points for "chicken fights," "dart gun duel," and "burnout," respectively) to the least aggressive (1, 2, and 3 points for "basket shooting," "block stacking," and "putting contest," respectively). Participants were asked to choose the 5 games that they wanted to include in the competition and to rank order their choices in terms of preference. To get an overall measure of the aggressiveness of each participant's preferences, we multiplied the point value of his first choice by 5, his second choice by 4, and so forth, and then added these five products. When comparing the choices made by the participants individually (without uniforms), we compared the average individual choices of the 3 participants with their group choice.

The second dependent measure in this experiment was participants' responses to the TAT card. Participants' TAT stories were scored on a 5-point aggressiveness scale (Feshbach, 1955). Stories devoid of aggression received a score of 1, those with a little indirect aggression a score of 2, those with considerable indirect or a little direct aggression a 3, those with direct physical aggression a 4, and those with graphic violence a 5. These ratings were made by two judges who were unaware of the participants' condition. The judges' ratings were in perfect agreement on 47% of the stories and were within one point on another 48%.

Results

The mean levels of aggressiveness in participants' individual and group choices are presented in Table 1. As expected, there was no difference in participants' individual choices across the two groups (Ms = 113.4 vs. 113.5) because they were not wearing different-colored uniforms at the time these choices were made. However, the participants who donned black uniforms subsequently chose more aggressive games (mean change in aggressiveness = 16.8), whereas those who put on white uniforms showed no such shift (mean change = 2.4). A 2 × 2 mixed ANOVA of participants' choices yielded a significant interaction between uniform color and individual-group choice $F(1,22)$ = 6.14, $p < .05$, indicating that the pattern of choices made by participants in black uniforms was different from that of those wearing white. Wearing black uniforms induced participants to seek out more aggressive activities, matched-pairs $t(11)$ = 3.21, $p < .01$; wearing white uniforms did not, matched-pairs $t(11)$ = 1.00, ns.

The participants who wore black uniforms also tended to express more aggressive ideation (M = 3.20) in their TAT stories than did participants wearing white uniforms (M = 2.89), although this difference was not significant, $t(70) < 1$.

Discussion

The results of this experiment support the hypothesis that wearing a black uniform can increase a person's inclination to engage in aggressive behavior. Participants who wore black uniforms showed a marked increase in intended aggression relative to those wearing white uniforms.

It should be noted, however, that our demonstration involved only intended aggression. It did not involve actual aggression. It would have been interesting to have allowed our participants to compete against one another in their chosen activities and seen whether those in black jerseys performed more aggressively. We refrained from doing so because of ethical and methodological difficulties (i.e., the difficulty of objectively measuring aggression, especially given that observers tend to be biased toward viewing people wearing black uniforms as being more aggressive). Nevertheless, the results of this experiment make the important point that in a competitive setting at least, merely donning a black uniform can increase a person's willingness to seek out opportunities for aggression. If the wearing of a black uniform can have such an effect in the laboratory, there is every reason to believe that it would have even stronger effects on the playing field (or rink), where many forms of aggression are considered acceptable behavior.

One question raised by this research concerns the generality of the effect of uniform color on aggression. It is very unlikely that donning any black uniform in any situation would make a person more inclined to act aggressively. We do not believe, for example, that the black garments worn by Catholic clergymen or Hassidic Jews do not make them any more aggressive than their secular peers. Rather, it would seem to be the case that the semantic link between the color black and evil and aggressiveness would be particularly salient in domains that already possess overtones of competition, confrontation, and physical aggression.

Perhaps the most important question raised by this research concerns the exact mechanisms by which the color of a uniform might affect the behavior of the wearer. Our own explanation for this phenomenon centers upon the implicit demands on one's behavior generated by wearing a particular kind of uniform. To wear a certain uniform is to assume a particular identity, an identity that not only elicits a certain response from others but also compels a particular pattern of behavior from the wearer (Stone, 1962). Wearing an athletic uniform, for example, thrusts one into the role of athlete, and leads one to "try on" the image that such a role conveys. When the uniform is that of a football or hockey player, part of that image—and therefore part of what one "becomes"—involves toughness, aggressiveness, and "machismo." These elements are particularly salient when the color of one's uniform is black. Just as observers see those in black uniforms as tough, mean, and aggressive, so too does the person wearing that uniform (Bem, 1972). Having inferred such an identity, the person then remains true to the image by acting more aggressively in certain prescribed contexts.

More broadly construed, then, our results serve as a reminder of the flexible or "situated" nature of the self (Alexander & Knight, 1971; Goffman, 1959; Mead, 1934; Stone, 1962). Different situations, different roles, and even different uniforms can induce people to try on different identities. Around those who are socially subdued or shy, an individual may become a vivacious extrovert; around true socialites, that same individual may retreat into a more reserved role. Some of the identities that people try to adopt are unsuitable, and those identities are abandoned. Abandoning such identities reassures people that at their core lies a "true" self. To a surprising degree, however, the identities people are led to adopt do indeed fit, and people continue to play them out in the appropriate circumstances. Perhaps the best evidence for this claim is the existence of identity conflict, such as that experienced by college students who bring their roommates home to meet their parents. This is often a disconcerting experience for many students because they cannot figure out how they should behave or "who they should be"—with their parents they are one person and with their friends they are someone else entirely.

The present investigation demonstrates how a seemingly trivial environmental variable, the color of one's uniform, can induce such a shift in a person's identity. This is not to suggest, however, that in other contexts the direction of causality might not be reversed. The black uniforms worn by gangs like the Hell's Angels, for example, are no doubt deliberately chosen precisely because they convey the desired malevolent image. Thus, as in the world portrayed in the typical American Western, it may be that many inherently evil characters choose to wear black. However, the present investigation makes it clear that in certain contexts at least, some people become the bad guys because they wear black.

References

Adams, F. M., & Osgood, C. E. (1973). A cross-cultural study of the affective meanings of color. *Journal of Cross-Cultural Psychology, 4,* 135–156.

Alexander, C. N., & Knight, G. (1971). Situated identities and social psychological experimentation. *Sociometry, 34,* 65–82.

Bem, D. J. (1972). Self-perception theory. In L. Berkowitz (Ed.), *Advances in experimental social psychology* (Vol. 6, pp. 1–62). New York: Academic Press.

Buss, A. M. (1961). *The psychology of aggression.* New York: Wiley.

Carlsmith, J. M., Ellsworth, P. C., & Aronson, E. (1976). *Methods of research in social psychology.* Reading, MA: Addison-Wesley.

Drabman, R. S., & Thomas, M. H. (1977). Children's imitation of aggressive and prosocial behavior when viewing alone and in pairs. *Journal of Communication, 27,* 199–205.

Feshbach, S. (1955). The drive-reducing function of fantasy behaviour, *Journal of Abnormal and Social Psychology, 50,* 3-11.

Goffman, E. (1959). *The presentation of self in everyday life.* New York: Doubleday.

Jaffe, Y., Shapir, N., & Yinon, Y. (1981). Aggression and its escalation. *Journal of Cross-Cultural Psychology, 12,* 21–36.

Johnson, R. D., & Downing, L. L. (1979). Deindividuation and valence of cues: Effects of prosocial and antisocial behavior. *Journal of Personality and Social Psychology, 37,* 1532–1538.

Mead, G. H. (1934). *Mind, self, and society.* Chicago: University of Chicago Press.

Milgram, S. (1965). Some conditions of obedience and disobedience to authority. *Human Relations, 18,* 57–76.

Milgram, S. (1974). *Obedience to authority.* New York: Harper.

Murray, H. A. (1943). *Thematic Apperception Test manual.* Cambridge, MA: Harvard University Press.

Stone, G. P. (1962). Appearance and the self. In A. M. Rose (Ed.), *Human behavior and social process* (pp. 86–118). Boston: Houghton Mifflin.

Turner, V. (1967). *The forest of symbols: Aspects of Ndembu ritual.* Ithaca, NY: Cornell University Press.

Williams, J. E. (1964). Connotations of color names among Negroes and Caucasians. *Perceptual and Motor Skills, 18,* 721–731.

Williams, J. E., & McMurty, C. A. (1970). Color connotations among Caucasian 7th graders and college students. *Perceptual and Motor Skills, 30,* 701–713.

Williams, J. E., Moreland, J. K., & Underwood, W. I. (1970). Connotations of color names in the U.S., Europe, and Asia. *Journal of Social Psychology, 82,* 3–14.

Author Note

Mark G. Frank, Department of Psychology, Cornell University; Thomas Gilovich, Department of Psychology, Cornell University.

We are grateful to Lauren Ostergren and Mark Schmuckler for their assistance in collecting our data and to Daryl Bem for commenting on an earlier version of the manuscript.

Correspondence concerning this article should be addressed to Mark Frank, Department of Psychology, Cornell University, Ithaca, New York 14850.

Table 1

Mean Level of Aggressiveness Contained in Participants' Chosen Activities as a Function of Uniform Condition

	Mean individual choice (without uniforms)		Group choice (with uniforms)		Change in aggression	
Uniform color	*M*	*SD*	*M*	*SD*	*M*	*SD*
White	113.4	23.9	115.8	25.4	+2.4	8.5
Black	113.5	18.4	130.3	22.9	+16.8	18.1

Practical Tips for Conducting an Ethical and Valid Study

Planning Your Procedures

You have reviewed the literature, developed a hypothesis, operationalized your variables, and given sound reasons for testing your hypothesis. However, your preliminary work is still not done. You must go from having a general idea of what you are going to do (e.g., "I am going to test my hypothesis using a simple experiment") to having a specific plan.

Writing out your plan helps you meet two APA guidelines designed to stop you from doing an unethical study. First, APA guidelines state that you should seek out the advice of experienced researchers to determine whether the study should be done. Based on your detailed proposal, those researchers can give you informed advice. Second, the guidelines state that you should obtain, if your school requires it, prior approval from your school to conduct research (see Institutional Approval, section 8.01, in Box C-1). To get your school's approval, you will need to submit a written proposal.

If your study is ethical, writing the proposal will help you do two things to make the study more ethical. First, it will help you anticipate and reduce any risks to the people who would participate in the study—a key APA ethical guideline (see Avoiding Harm, section 3.04 of the APA ethical code, in Box C-1). Second, you can share your written plan so that others can tell you about safeguards and alternatives you did not consider.

Ethical Considerations: Human Research

Because having a good written plan is so important, you will probably have to submit such a plan to your professor before doing any research.

However, your professor's approval may not be enough. For example, your professor may tell you that you must submit your research to the department's ethics committee or that you must submit your research to your school's Internal Review Board (IRB).

Dealing with the IRB

What will determine whether you have to submit your research to your school's IRB? If you are doing research that you want to present at a conference or publish in a journal, you will need to submit your study to your school's IRB.

But what if you are doing a study for a class assignment and have no intention of presenting or publishing your results? We can't give you a simple answer to this question

BOX C-1 **The American Psychological Association's Principles Covering the Treatment of Human Participants**

2.05 Delegation of Work to Others

Psychologists who delegate work to employees, supervisees, or research or teaching assistants or who use the services of others, such as interpreters, take reasonable steps to (1) avoid delegating such work to persons who have a multiple relationship with those being served that would likely lead to exploitation or loss of objectivity; (2) authorize only those responsibilities that such persons can be expected to perform competently on the basis of their education, training, or experience, either independently or with the level of supervision being provided; and (3) see that such persons perform these services competently. (See also Standards 2.02, Providing Services in Emergencies; 3.05, Multiple Relationships; 4.01, Maintaining Confidentiality; 9.01, Bases for Assessments; 9.02, Development and Use of Assessments; 9.03, Informed Consent in Assessments; and 9.07, Assessment by Unqualified Persons.)

3.04 Avoiding Harm

Psychologists take reasonable steps to avoid harming their clients/patients, students, supervisees, research participants, organizational clients, and others with whom they work, and to minimize harm where it is foreseeable and unavoidable.

3.10 Informed Consent

a. When psychologists conduct research or provide assessment, therapy, counseling, or consulting services in person or via electronic transmission or other forms of communication, they obtain the informed consent of the individual or individuals using language that is reasonably understandable to that person or persons except when conducting such activities without consent is mandated by law or governmental regulation or as otherwise provided in this Ethics Code. (See also Standards 8.02, Informed Consent to Research; 9.03, Informed Consent in Assessments; and 10.01, Informed Consent to Therapy.)

b. For persons who are legally incapable of giving informed consent, psychologists nevertheless (1) provide an appropriate explanation, (2) seek the individual's assent, (3) consider such persons' preferences and best interests, and (4) obtain appropriate permission from a legally authorized person, if such substitute consent is permitted or required by law. When consent by a legally authorized person is not permitted or required by law, psychologists take reasonable steps to protect the individual's rights and welfare.

d. Psychologists appropriately document written or oral consent, permission, and assent. (See also Standards 8.02, Informed Consent to Research; 9.03, Informed Consent in Assessments; and 10.01, Informed Consent to Therapy.)

4. Privacy and Confidentiality

4.01 Maintaining Confidentiality

Psychologists have a primary obligation and take reasonable precautions to protect confidential information obtained through or stored in any medium, recognizing that the extent and limits of confidentiality may be regulated by law or established by institutional rules or professional or scientific relationship. (See also Standard 2.05, Delegation of Work to Others.)

4.02 Discussing the Limits of Confidentiality

a. Psychologists discuss with persons (including, to the extent feasible, persons who are legally incapable of giving informed consent and their legal representatives) and organizations with whom they establish a scientific or professional relationship (1) the relevant limits of confidentiality and (2) the foreseeable uses of the information generated through their psychological activities. (See also Standard 3.10, Informed Consent.)

b. Unless it is not feasible or is contraindicated, the discussion of confidentiality occurs at the outset of the relationship and thereafter as new circumstances may warrant.

4.04 Minimizing Intrusions on Privacy

b. Psychologists discuss confidential information obtained in their work only for appropriate scientific or professional purposes and only with persons clearly concerned with such matters.

5.01 Avoidance of False or Deceptive Statements

a. Public statements include but are not limited to paid or unpaid advertising, product endorsements, grant applications, licensing applications, other credentialing applications, brochures, printed matter, directory listings, personal resumes or curricula vitae, or comments for use in media such as print or electronic transmission, statements in legal proceedings, lectures and public oral presentations, and published materials. Psychologists do not knowingly make public statements that are false, deceptive, or fraudulent concerning their research, practice, or other work activities or those of persons or organizations with which they are affiliated.

b. Psychologists do not make false, deceptive, or fraudulent statements concerning (1) their training, experience, or competence; (2) their academic degrees; (3) their credentials; (4) their institutional or association affiliations; (5) their services; (6) the scientific or clinical basis for, or results or degree of success of, their services; (7) their fees; or (8) their publications or research findings.

6. Record Keeping and Fees

6.01 Documentation of Professional and Scientific Work and Maintenance of Records

Psychologists create, and to the extent the records are under their control, maintain, disseminate, store, retain, and dispose of records and data relating to their professional and scientific work in order to (1) facilitate provision of services later by them or by other professionals, (2) allow for replication of research design and analyses, (3) meet institutional requirements, (4) ensure accuracy of billing and payments, and (5) ensure compliance with law. (See also Standard 4.01, Maintaining Confidentiality.)

6.02 Maintenance, Dissemination, and Disposal of Confidential Records of Professional and Scientific Work

a. Psychologists maintain confidentiality in creating, storing, accessing, transferring, and disposing of records under their control, whether these are written, automated, or in any other medium. (See also Standards 4.01, Maintaining Confidentiality; and 6.01, Documentation of Professional and Scientific Work and Maintenance of Records.)

8. Research and Publication

8.01 Institutional Approval

When institutional approval is required, psychologists provide accurate information about their research proposals and obtain approval prior to conducting the research. They conduct the research in accordance with the approved research protocol.

8.02 Informed Consent to Research

a. When obtaining informed consent as required in Standard 3.10, Informed Consent, psychologists inform participants about (1) the purpose of the research, expected duration, and procedures; (2) their right to decline to participate and to withdraw from the research once participation has begun; (3) the foreseeable consequences of declining or withdrawing; (4) reasonably foreseeable factors that may be expected to influence their willingness to participate such as potential risks, discomfort, or adverse effects; (5) any prospective research benefits; (6) limits of confidentiality; (7) incentives for participation; and (8) whom to contact for questions about the research and research participants' rights. They provide opportunity for the prospective participants to ask questions and receive answers. (See also Standards 8.03, Informed Consent for Recording Voices and Images in Research; 8.05, Dispensing with Informed Consent for Research; and 8.07, Deception in Research.)

b. Psychologists conducting intervention research involving the use of experimental treatments, clarify to participants at the outset of the research (1) the experimental nature of the treatment; (2) the services that will or will not be available to the control group(s) if appropriate; (3) the means by which assignment to treatment and control groups will be made; (4) available treatment alternatives if an individual does not wish to participate in the research or wishes to withdraw once a study has begun; and (5) compensation for or monetary costs of participating including, if appropriate, whether reimbursement from the participant or a third-party payor will be sought. (See also Standard 8.02a, Informed Consent to Research.)

8.03 Informed Consent for Recording Voices and Images in Research

Psychologists obtain informed consent from research participants prior to recording their voices or images for data collection unless (1) the research consists solely of naturalistic observations in public places, and it is not

continued

BOX C-1 **(continued)**

anticipated that the recording will be used in a manner that could cause personal identification or harm or (2) the research design includes deception, and consent for the use of the recording is obtained during debriefing. (See also Standard 8.07, Deception in Research.)

8.04 Client/Patient, Student, and Subordinate Research Participants

a. When psychologists conduct research with clients/patients, students, or subordinates as participants, psychologists take steps to protect the prospective participants from adverse consequences of declining or withdrawing from participation.

b. When research participation is a course requirement or opportunity for extra credit, the prospective participant is given the choice of equitable alternative activities.

8.05 Dispensing With Informed Consent for Research

Psychologists may dispense with informed consent only (1) where research would not reasonably be assumed to create distress or harm and involves (a) the study of normal educational practices, curricula, or classroom management methods conducted in educational settings; (b) only anonymous questionnaires, naturalistic observations, or archival research for which disclosure of responses would not place participants at risk of criminal or civil liability or damage their financial standing, employability, or reputation, and confidentiality is protected; or (c) the study of factors related to job or organization effectiveness conducted in organizational settings for which there is no risk to participants' employability and confidentiality is protected or (2) where otherwise permitted by law or federal or institutional regulations.

8.06 Offering Inducements for Research Participation

a. Psychologists make reasonable efforts to avoid offering excessive or inappropriate financial or other inducements for research participation when such inducements are likely to coerce participation.

b. When offering professional services as an inducement for research participation, psychologists clarify the nature of the services, as well as the risks, obligations, and limitations. (See also Standard 6.05, Barter With Clients/Patients.)

8.07 Deception in Research

a. Psychologists do not conduct a study involving deception unless they have determined that the use of deceptive techniques is justified by the study's significant prospective scientific, educational, or applied value and that effective nondeceptive alternative procedures are not feasible.

b. Psychologists do not deceive prospective participants about research that is reasonably expected to cause physical pain or severe emotional distress.

c. Psychologists explain any deception that is an integral feature of the design and conduct of an experiment to participants as early as is feasible, preferably at the conclusion of their participation, but no later than at the conclusion of the data collection, and permit participants to withdraw their data. (See also Standard 8.08, Debriefing.)

8.08 Debriefing

a. Psychologists provide a prompt opportunity for participants to obtain appropriate information about the nature, results, and conclusions of the research, and they take reasonable steps to correct any misconceptions that participants may have of which the psychologists are aware.

b. If scientific or humane values justify delaying or withholding this information, psychologists take reasonable measures to reduce the risk of harm.

c. When psychologists become aware that research procedures have harmed a participant, they take reasonable steps to minimize the harm.

8.10 Reporting Research Results

a. Psychologists do not fabricate data. (See also Standard 5.01a, Avoidance of False or Deceptive Statements.)

b. If psychologists discover significant errors in their published data, they take reasonable steps to correct such errors in a correction, retraction, erratum, or other appropriate publication means.

8.11 Plagiarism

Psychologists do not present portions of another's work or data as their own, even if the other work or data source is cited occasionally.

8.14 Sharing Research Data for Verification

a. After research results are published, psychologists do not withhold the data on which their conclusions are based from other competent professionals who seek to verify the substantive claims through reanalysis and who intend to use such data only for that purpose, provided that the confidentiality of the participants can be

protected and unless legal rights concerning proprietary data preclude their release. This does not preclude psychologists from requiring that such individuals or groups be responsible for costs associated with the provision of such information.

Source: Ethical Principles of Psychologists and Code of Conduct. (2002). *American Psychologist, 57,* 1597–1611. Reprinted with the kind permission of the American Psychological Association.

because, although all IRBs are governed by the same laws, they do not interpret the laws in the same ways. By law, IRBs are supposed to evaluate research and, by law, research is defined as a "a systematic investigation, including research development, testing and evaluation, designed to develop or contribute to generalizable knowledge" (45 C.F.R. Part 46, Section 46.102). Given the law, it seems clear that your study would not have to be reviewed by the IRB. In practice, however, about half of all IRBs believe that such class projects need to be reviewed.

If you have to submit your research to an IRB, you will probably need to fill out a form like the one in Box C-2. As you can tell from that form, if your study does need to be reviewed by an IRB, you will have to do much more than say that you want to do some research. You must have a specific hypothesis to be tested, and you must have your procedures clearly spelled out—including what you will say to participants before they agree to be in the study, and what you will say to them after they have participated in the study.

Levels of Review

If your study must go through the IRB process, it will go through one of three levels of review. The levels differ primarily in terms of how many people will evaluate your proposal. In the least rigorous review, "exempt from full board review," the IRB chairperson may be the only one to review your proposal. In the "expedited review," the IRB chairperson and one other person may be the only ones to review your proposal. In the most rigorous review, called "full board review," the entire IRB—a committee which must consist of at least one nonscientist and at least one person not affiliated with your school—may read and debate your proposal.

The level of review you get does not affect the kind of proposal you submit. In every case, you should submit a detailed, polished proposal. However, the level of review you get does affect how far in advance you must submit your proposal. If your proposal is classified as exempt from full board review, after you submit your proposal, you may get approval to start your study in less than a week. If, on the other hand, your proposal must undergo full board review, after you submit your proposal, you will probably not get approval to start your study for at least three weeks.

The level of review you get will depend on your study and the IRB chair. If your research involves minimal risk, the chair might agree to exempting your research from full board review. Usually, to get an exempt rating, you would have to answer "no" to questions 2–11 in the sample review form. You may be surprised to find that offering extra credit (question 2) could get your research negative attention from the IRB. One reason that giving participants extra credit can get you into trouble is that some students may feel they need extra credit to pass the course. Those students may feel they have no choice but to participate. In such a case, you would be in danger of violating APA principle 8.06a: "offering

---

BOX C-2 **Sample Ethical Review Form**

TITLE:

RESEARCHER:

1. State either the main hypothesis to be tested or the problem to be investigated:

2. Will extra credit be given to students who participate in the project?

        Yes   **No**

3. Will students who participate in the project be paid?

        Yes   **No**

4. Will participants include anyone other than students from our school?

        Yes   **No**

5. Will participants include children under 18, adults who are not legally competent, individuals with mental or physical disabilities, prisoners, or pregnant women?

        Yes   **No**

    If yes, circle group or groups.

6. Will participants be video/audiotaped?

        Yes   **No**

7. Will anyone other than the researchers be able to find out how an individual participant responded (are participants' responses coded in such a way that others could identify a particular participant's responses)?

        Yes   **No**

8. Does the research deal with sensitive aspects of participants' behavior such as illegal conduct, drug use (including alcohol), or sexual behavior?

        Yes   **No**

9. Are there any deceptive elements to the study?

        Yes   **No**

10. Will participants be exposed to any psychological stress such as fatigue, assault on values, or threats to self-esteem?

        Yes   **No**

11. Will participants be exposed to physical stress (electric shock, cold temperatures, etc.)?

        Yes   **No**

12. Are participants free to withdraw at any time without penalty?

        Yes   **No**

ATTACH THE FOLLOWING:

1. Draft of the method section: Describe, in detail, the methodology of your study (essentially, how will the study be conducted from start to finish, as far as human participants are concerned?). Be specific about any manipulations used and any measurement instruments involved.

2. Copies of questionnaires, surveys, tests, or other paper-and-pencil measures to be used in the study.

3. Informed consent form.

4. Debriefing form.

5. Confidentiality statement.

---

excessive . . . inducements for research participation when such inducements are likely to coerce participation."

If you are going to offer extra credit, you need to reassure the committee that students will not feel forced to participate. One way to reassure the committee is to make it clear that you will provide an alternative extra credit assignment (such as having students read and summarize a research article) for those who cannot or do not want to participate in your study.

Now that you realize how IRBs react to giving extra credit as an incentive, you can probably guess how they react to giving money as an incentive: They are not enthusiastic. Their concern, shared by APA, is that people may get an offer they do not feel they can refuse. Thus, as APA's guidelines suggest (see 8.06 in Box C-1), you should probably avoid paying participants. If you must pay them, the pay should usually be low—about minimum wage.

Note that questions 4 and 5 require you to think about who will be in your sample. To get approval for your project before you graduate, you usually will have to limit your participants to students at your school. Thus, you should probably answer "no" to question 4. Answering question 5 (about vulnerable and special populations) is trickier. For example, what are you going to do about the 17-year-old freshman who wants to be in your study? If you would include that person, many IRBs will still consider your research exempt (even though you are testing a minor)—but not all. Similarly, although most IRBs would encourage you to exclude participants who are not legally competent, some may consider excluding those people discrimination.

Questions 6 and 7 show that the more anonymous the participant will be, the more likely the research will be rated exempt. Question 8 shows that the less sensitive the information you are collecting, the more likely the research will be reviewed at the exempt level. Finally, answering "yes" to questions 9–11 or "no" to question 12 would probably mean that your research will receive full-board review.

In short, it is hard to predict how a particular IRB chair will classify your research. However, if you are not studying a vulnerable population, you are not collecting sensitive information, and you are carefully safeguarding the data, your research might be exempt. Your chances of getting an exempt status are better if you are not manipulating a treatment to see whether it has effect. Thus, if you are observing, surveying, interviewing people, or using any of the methods described in Chapter 7, you are more likely to get an exempt review than if you do an experiment.

Avoiding IRB Problems

Regardless of what level of review your research receives, you should write a proposal that makes the IRB more likely to trust that you will act in a professional and ethical manner (Forsyth, 2004). Specifically, according to Forsyth (2004), to maximize the chances that your IRB approves your proposal, you should make sure your proposal

1. is free of typos
2. includes an informed consent form (a form describing the study and that the participant signs, thereby indicating that the participant agrees to participate in the research), like the one in Box C-3 that
   - uses simple, nontechnical language
   - uses the word "research" in it
   - states any foreseeable risks or discomforts that might cause the participant to decide not to participate
   - states whom to contact if participants have a concern
   - states that the participant's participation is totally voluntary
   - states that the participant can quit the study at any time, without giving a reason, and without any penalty
   - states that the participant's responses will be confidential (if responses won't be confidential, this should be explained)
   - describes the steps you will take to protect confidentiality of data, including such details as where you will keep the data, who will have access to the data, and a statement that the computer files will be password protected

BOX C-3 **Sample Informed Consent Form**

TITLE: Personnel Decision Making

IRB APPROVAL NUMBER: 2007_018

PRINCIPAL INVESTIGATOR: Dr. Mitchell, (555) 555-5555; mitchell@clarion.edu, Psychology Department, Clarion University, Clarion, PA 16214

CO-INVESTIGATOR: Freda L. Student, (555) 393-5556, student@clarion.edu, 212 Givens Hall, Clarion University, Clarion, PA 16214

DESCRIPTION: The research study that I have been asked to participate in is investigating personnel decision-making. I will be asked to read personnel files of two job applicants and then asked to decide which of the two individuals I would be more likely to hire. I will be asked to justify my decision. The study will take about 30 minutes of my time.

PAYMENTS AND COSTS: To compensate me for my time, I will be paid $5.00. Other than my time, there will be no costs to me.

BENEFITS AND RISKS: The main benefit I will receive is that of gaining firsthand experience about how a research study is conducted and what I learn during debriefing. There are no reasonably foreseeable risks to me.

CONFIDENTIALITY: The responses I give will be kept confidential. Although the researchers may write up the results of this study, my name will never be used. Therefore, I consent to publication for scientific purposes.

RIGHT TO REFUSE OR END PARTICIPATION: I can withdraw from the study at any time without any problems. That is, if I choose to withdraw, I will receive full credit for participating. Furthermore, if participating becomes too stressful, I should withdraw from the study. Finally, I have the right to skip any questions that I do not wish to answer.

DEBRIEFING: After I have finished the study, the researcher will explain the study and gladly answer any questions I might have. If I have any questions about the research after that, I should feel free to call Dr. Mark Mitchell at (814) 555-5555 or e-mail Dr. Mitchell at mitchell@Clarion.edu.

CONCERNS ABOUT THE STUDY: If I have concerns about whether my rights as a research participant have been violated or if I have suffered any research-related harm (be it physical, psychological, social, or financial), I can contact Dr. Ramirez, the chair of Clarion University's IRB, phone: (814) 393-2389, e-mail: ramirez@clarian.edu; address: 157 Harvey Hall, Clarion University, Clarion, PA 16214.

NAME (PRINTED) _____.

I have read both pages of this statement and have had all my questions answered. Therefore, I give my written consent to participate in this investigation.

Signature _____ Date _____

Signature of person obtaining consent

_____ Date _____

3. contains a confidentiality form—a written pledge to keep the data confidential, and not to talk about the participants to anyone other than the investigators—signed by everyone who will work on the research

4. states the steps you have taken to make participants anonymous, such as not having them put their names on the answer sheet

5. states the steps you have taken to keep participants' responses confidential such as assigning each participant a code number and storing the code numbers and the participants' names in one place and the data in a different place

6. includes a debriefing form (a summary or a script of what the researcher will tell the participant about the study after the participant has finished the study) that
   - uses simple, nontechnical language
   - is about one full page typed
   - describes the hypotheses, why the procedures were used, and why the study was important

Weighing and Reducing Risks

Even if your research is approved by a review board, you must be extremely careful not to harm your participants. Ideally, your participants should feel just as well when they leave the study as they did when they began. Unfortunately, even in the most innocuous studies, protecting your participants from discomfort is much easier said than done.

Realize that any experience may be traumatic to some participants. Trauma can occur from things you would never think of as being traumatic. Because any study has risks and because you will not know all of the risks, *do not begin any study without your professor's permission.*

To begin to sensitize yourself to the risks involved in your proposed study, list the 10 worst things that could possibly happen to participants. If you are using human participants, be aware that not everyone will react in the same way. Some may experience trauma because the study triggers some painful memory, or they may feel badly because they think they did poorly or because they think their behavior ruined your study. Realize that because some of your participants may be under a lot of stress, some may be grieving, and some may have a mental illness, some of your participants may be unsettled by manipulations or stimuli that you might not consider upsetting. Because participants are often fragile, you should list some serious consequences in your worst-case scenario.

How to Recruit Participants in a Way That Reduces Risk

Because any study has the potential for harm, the possibility of severe consequences does not mean that your professor will not allow you to do the study. However, you and your professor should think about ways to minimize the risks.

Screening Participants. One method of minimizing risks is to screen out "vulnerable participants." For instance, if there is any reason to believe that your study may increase heart rate or blood pressure, you may want to make sure that only people in good health participate. If your study might harm people with low self-esteem, you may want to use only well-adjusted participants who have high levels of self-esteem. Therefore, you might give a measure of self-esteem to potential participants to eliminate those with low self-esteem.

Informed Consent. Not only should you screen participants, but you should also let participants screen themselves. That is, participants should be volunteers who give their **informed consent:** They should know what the study is about before volunteering for it.

How informed is informed consent? Very informed, when it comes to telling participants about any unpleasant aspect of the study. If participants are going to get shocked or exposed to loud noise or extreme cold, they should be informed of this beforehand. Consequently, if your study does involve unpleasantness, you may have difficulty getting participants to volunteer.

Informed consent is considerably less informed when it comes to more innocuous aspects of the study. After all, the study would be ruined if participants knew everything that would happen (and why it happened) before it happened. So, although participants are usually told the truth, they are not always told the whole truth. For example, a memory experiment's description would mention that participants have to memorize words, but might omit the fact that the researcher is looking at the order in which facts are recalled or that there is a surprise recall of all the lists at the end of the study.

Because participants are not fully informed about your study, there may be some things about it that they dislike. For example, suppose a participant finds the task too difficult or finds it upsetting to try the surprise recall task. What can you do?

One protection against these unexpected problems is to make sure participants understand that they can quit the study at any time. So, before the participants begin your study, tell them that if they find any aspect of the study uncomfortable, they can *and should* escape this discomfort by quitting the study. Assure them that it is their duty to quit if they experience discomfort and that they will still get full credit.

How to Modify the Study to Reduce Risk

You have seen that you can minimize ethical problems by letting participants know what they are in for and by letting them gracefully withdraw from the study. You should also minimize harm by making your study as humane as possible. You can make your study more ethical by reducing the strength of your treatment manipulation, carefully selecting stimulus materials, and by being a conscientious researcher.

Reducing the Treatment Strength. Although using extreme levels of your predictor variable may help you get a significant change in the criterion variable, extreme levels may harm your participants. For example, 24 hours of food deprivation is more likely to cause hunger than 12 hours. However, 24 hours of deprivation is more stressful to the participant. If you plan an unpleasant manipulation, remember your participants' welfare and minimize the unpleasant consequences as much as possible. Consider using levels of the predictor variable that are less severe than you originally intended.

Modifying Stimulus Materials. By modifying your stimulus materials, you may be able to prevent them from triggering unpleasant memories. For instance, if you were interested in the effects of caffeine on memory for prose, you would not want the prose passage to cover some topic like death, divorce, alcoholic parents, or rape. Instead, you would want to use a passage covering a less traumatic topic such as sports. If the sports article referred to someone's death or hospitalization, you might want to delete that section of the article.

How to Conduct the Study in a Way That Reduces Risk

Often, it is not the study that causes ethical problems, but the researcher's arrogance. For example, an arrogant researcher may rush through research sessions providing only superficial explanations and almost no time for questions and feedback. Although we know of a few participants who were hurt as a direct result of a research manipulation, we know of many more who were hurt because the researcher failed to treat them with respect. To ensure that you are sensitive, courteous, and respectful to all of your human participants, you should give your participants three things: time, power, and a thorough debriefing.

Give Participants Time. First, when scheduling your research sessions, make sure you leave a 10-minute gap between the end of one session and the beginning of the next. Some investigators feel that, like a physician, they should efficiently schedule people one after another. Their attempt at efficiency results in participants having to wait for the investigator, the investigator having to rush through the formalities of greeting participants, or—even worse—the investigator rushing through debriefing. Thus, the overly efficient investigator, like the overly efficient physician, is seen as unconcerned. Although this conduct does not become physicians, it is intolerable for psychological researchers.

After a research participant has given an hour of his or her time, you should be more than willing to answer any questions the participant has. Furthermore, if you rush through greeting or debriefing each participant, the participants will see you as uncaring. Consequently, they will be less likely to tell you about any psychological discomfort they felt and less likely to accept any aid you might offer. Thus, the first step is to walk, rather than to run, participants through your study.

Table C-1	Sample Debriefing Rating Scale

Being a participant in psychology studies should provide you with a firsthand look at research. On the scale below, please indicate how valuable or worthless you found being in today's study by circling a number from +3 to −3.

WORTHLESS −3 −2 −1 +1 +2 +3 VALUABLE

If you wish to explain your rating or to make comments on this study, either positive or negative, please do so below.

Note: This scale is a slightly modified version of a scale that has been used at The Ohio State University.

Give Participants Power. Second, give the participants power. That is, allow participants to rate your study on a scale such as the one in Table C-1. Give each participant's rating sheet to your instructor. Following this simple procedure helps you to be a conscientious and courteous researcher.

Debrief Participants. Third, thoroughly debrief your participants. Although you should try to anticipate and prevent every possible bad reaction a participant may have to being in your study, you will fail. Inevitably, your procedures will still cause some unpleasantness. After the study is over, you should try to address this unpleasantness by informing participants about the study, reassuring them that their reactions were normal, and expressing your appreciation for their participation.

You should also listen to participants and be sensitive to any unexpected, unpleasant reactions to your study. By being a good listener, you will often be able to undo any damage you have unwittingly done.

Occasionally, however, ordinary debriefing will not undo the harm caused to the research participant. In those cases, there are several steps you may take to alleviate distress. For participants who are upset with their responses, you should ask them whether they want you to destroy their data. For participants whom you cannot calm down, you should take them to talk to a professor, counselor, or friend—even if this means canceling a research session you had scheduled.

In addition to detecting and removing any harm that may have been produced by your study, during debriefing you should do the following:

1. Correct any misconceptions that were planted by the researchers.
2. Give a summary of the study in nontechnical terms (many departments believe this summary should be both written and oral, the written part being about one full page typed, describing the hypotheses, why the procedures were used, and why the study was important).
3. Provide participants an opportunity to ask whatever questions they may have (some departments want you to provide a number for participants to call so research participants can ask follow-up questions).
4. Thank the participant for participating.
5. Explain why deception was necessary (if deception was used).

Debriefing is a good time to assess the degree to which you and your co-investigators are conducting the study in an ethical manner. To do so, ask participants to complete an anonymous questionnaire that assesses their perceptions of the study. Such a questionnaire might include the following questions:

1. Could you quit the study at any time?
2. Were you given enough information to decide whether you wanted to participate? If not, what should have been told before you took part in the study?
3. What was the purpose of this research?
4. Were you treated with respect?
5. Was the researcher polite?
6. Did you have all your questions answered?
7. Were you deceived in any way? If so, did the researcher provide justification for the deception? Are you satisfied with that justification? Why or why not?
8. Did you experience more discomfort than you would in your day-to-day activities? If so, did the researcher provide sufficient justification for discomfort? What caused this discomfort?
9. Do you think your responses will be kept confidential?

In summary, you should be very concerned about ethics. Because ethics involves weighing the costs of the study against the potential benefits, you should do everything you can to minimize the risk of participants becoming uncomfortable. If, despite your efforts, a participant experiences discomfort, you should use the debriefing to reduce that discomfort.

Ethical Considerations: Animal Research

As in human research, conducting research with nonhuman animals in an ethical manner is vital. Unethical treatment of animals is inhumane and, in many cases, illegal. However, we have not spent much time on ethics in animal research for two reasons.

First, the basic concepts that govern human research also govern animal research. For example, pain and discomfort should be minimized. Likewise, any study that inflicts stress must be justifiable on the basis that (a) the study is likely to produce some benefit that outweighs the risks, and (b) there is no other way to get that potential benefit.

Second, because humane treatment of animals is so important, APA has taken the following three steps to almost guarantee that you cannot do animal research without knowing APA's ethical standards:

1. If you conduct research with animal participants, you must be trained in the humane care, handling, and maintenance of animals.
2. As a student, you cannot conduct research with animals unless you are supervised by someone who is well trained in both animal research and in how to handle, care for, and maintain animals.
3. A copy of the ethical guidelines relating to animal research must be posted in the animal lab. (See Box C-4.)

Because you will be shown how to take care of the animals, you will be supervised, and the guidelines will be right in the lab, you probably will not violate ethical principles out of ignorance. However, because violating ethical procedures in animal research may violate federal law, you should be very careful.

BOX C-4   Guidelines for Ethical Conduct in the Care and Use of Animals

I. Justification of the Research

    A. Research should be undertaken with a clear scientific purpose. There should be a reasonable expectation that the research will (a) increase knowledge of the processes underlying the evolution, development, maintenance, alteration, control, or biological significance of behavior; (b) determine the replicability and generality of prior research; (c) increase understanding of the species under study; or (d) provide results that benefit the health or welfare of humans or other animals.

    B. The scientific purpose of the research should be of sufficient potential significance to justify the use of animals. Psychologists should act on the assumption that procedures that would produce pain in humans will also do so in other animals.

    C. The species chosen for study should be best suited to answer the question(s) posed. The psychologist should always consider the possibility of using other species, nonanimal alternatives, or procedures that minimize the number of animals in research, and should be familiar with the appropriate literature.

    D. Research on animals may not be conducted until the protocol has been reviewed by an appropriate animal care committee, for example, an institutional animal care and use committee (IACUC), to ensure that the procedures are appropriate and humane.

    E. The psychologist should monitor the research and the animals' welfare throughout the course of an investigation to ensure continued justification for the research.

II. Personnel

    A. Psychologists should ensure that personnel involved in their research with animals be familiar with these guidelines.

    B. Animal use procedures must conform with federal regulations regarding personnel, supervision, record keeping, and veterinary care.*

    C. Behavior is both the focus of study of many experiments as well as a primary source of information about an animal's health and well-being. It is therefore necessary that

psychologists and their assistants be informed about the behavioral characteristics of their animal subjects so as to be aware of normal, species-specific behaviors and unusual behaviors that could forewarn of health problems.

    D. Psychologists should ensure that all individuals who use animals under their supervision receive explicit instruction in experimental methods and in the care, maintenance, and handling of the species being studied. Responsibilities and activities of all individuals dealing with animals should be consistent with their respective competencies, training, and experience in either the laboratory or the field setting.

III. Care and Housing of Animals

The concept of psychological well-being of animals is of current concern and debate and is included in Federal Regulations (United States Department of Agriculture [USDA], 1991). As a scientific and professional organization, APA recognizes the complexities of defining psychological well-being.

    Procedures appropriate for a particular species may be inappropriate for others. Hence, APA does not presently stipulate specific guidelines regarding the maintenance of psychological well-being of research animals. Psychologists familiar with the species should be best qualified professionally to judge measures such as enrichment to maintain or improve psychological well-being of those species.

    A. The facilities housing animals should meet or exceed current regulations and guidelines (USDA, 1990, 1991) and are required to be inspected twice a year (USDA, 1989).

    B. All procedures carried out on animals are to be reviewed by a local animal-care committee to ensure that the procedures are appropriate and humane.

    The committee should have representation from within the institution and from the local community. In the event that it is not possible to constitute an appropriate local animal-care committee, psychologists are encouraged to seek advice from a corresponding committee of a cooperative institution.

*U.S. Department of Agriculture. (1989, August 21). Animal welfare; Final rules. *Federal Register.* U.S. Department of Agriculture. (1990, July 16). Animal welfare; Guinea pigs, hamsters, and rabbits. *Federal Register.* U.S. Department of Agriculture. (1991, February 15). Animal welfare; Standards; Final rule. *Federal Register.*

continued

BOX C-4 *(continued)*

C. Responsibilities for the conditions under which animals are kept, both within and outside of the context of active experimentation or teaching, rests with the psychologist under the supervision of the animal-care committee (where required by federal regulations) and with individuals appointed by the institution to oversee animal care. Animals are to be provided with humane care and healthful conditions during their stay in the facility. In addition to the federal requirements to provide for the psychological well-being of nonhuman primates used in research, psychologists are encouraged to consider enriching the environments of their laboratory animals and should keep abreast of literature on well-being and enrichment for the species with which they work.

IV. Acquisition of Animals

A. Animals not bred in the psychologist's facility are to be acquired lawfully. The USDA and local ordinances should be consulted for information regarding regulations and approved suppliers.

B. Psychologists should make every effort to ensure that those responsible for transporting the animals to the facility provide adequate food, water, ventilation, space, and impose no unnecessary stress on the animals.

C. Animals taken from the wild should be trapped in a humane manner and in accordance with applicable federal, state, and local regulations.

D. Endangered species or taxa should be used only with full attention to required permits and ethical concerns. Information and permit applications can be obtained from:

Fish and Wildlife Service
Office of Management Authority
U.S. Dept. of the Interior
4401 N. Fairfax Dr., Rm. 432
Arlington, VA 22043
703-358-2104

Similar caution should be used in work with threatened species or taxa.

V. Experimental Procedures

Humane consideration for the well-being of the animal should be incorporated into the design and conduct of all procedures involving animals, while keeping in mind the primary goal of experimental procedures—the acquisition of sound, replicable data. The conduct of all procedures is governed by Guideline I.

A. Behavioral studies that involve no aversive stimulation to, or overt sign of distress from, the animal are acceptable. These include observational and other noninvasive forms of data collection.

B. When alternative behavioral procedures are available, those that minimize discomfort to the animal should be used. When using aversive conditions, psychologists should adjust the parameters of stimulation to levels that appear minimal, though compatible with the aims of the research. Psychologists are encouraged to test painful stimuli on themselves, whenever reasonable. Whenever consistent with the goals of the research, consideration should be given to providing the animals with control of the potentially aversive stimulation.

C. Procedures in which the animal is anesthetized and insensitive to pain throughout the procedure and is euthanized before regaining consciousness are generally acceptable.

D. Procedures involving more than momentary or slight aversive stimulation, which is not relieved by medication or other acceptable methods, should be undertaken only when the objectives of the research cannot be achieved by other methods.

E. Experimental procedures that require prolonged aversive conditions or produce tissue damage or metabolic disturbances require greater justification and surveillance. These include prolonged exposure to extreme environmental conditions, experimentally induced prey killing, or infliction of physical trauma or tissue damage. An animal observed to be in a state of severe distress or chronic pain that cannot be alleviated and is not essential to the purposes of the research should be euthanized immediately.

F. Procedures that use restraint must conform to federal regulations and guidelines.

G. Procedures involving the use of paralytic agents without reduction in pain sensation require particular prudence and humane concern. Use of muscle relaxants or paralytics alone during surgery, without general anesthesia, is unacceptable and should be avoided.

H. Surgical procedures, because of their invasive nature, require close supervision and attention to humane considerations by the psychologist. Aseptic (methods that minimize risks of infection) techniques must be used on laboratory animals whenever possible.

1. All surgical procedures and anesthetization should be conducted under the direct supervision of a person who is competent in the use of the procedures.

2. If the surgical procedure is likely to cause greater discomfort than that attending anesthetization, and unless there is specific justification for acting otherwise, animals should be maintained under anesthesia until the procedure is ended.

3. Sound postoperative monitoring and care, which may include the use of analgesics and antibiotics, should be provided to minimize discomfort and to prevent infection and other untoward consequences of the procedure.

4. Animals cannot be subjected to successive surgical procedures unless these are required by the nature of the research, the nature of the surgery, or for the well-being of the animal. Multiple surgeries on the same animal must receive special approval from the animal-care committee.

I. When the use of an animal is no longer required by an experimental protocol or procedure, in order to minimize the number of animals used in research, alternative uses of the animals should be considered. Such uses should be compatible with the goals of research and the welfare of the animal. Care should be taken that such an action does not expose the animal to multiple surgeries.

J. The return of wild-caught animals to the field can carry substantial risks, both to the formerly captive animals and to the ecosystem. Animals reared in the laboratory should not be released because, in most cases, they cannot survive, or they may survive by disrupting the natural ecology.

K. When euthanasia appears to be the appropriate alternative, either as a requirement of the research or because it constitutes the most humane form of disposition of an animal at the conclusion of the research:

1. Euthanasia shall be accomplished in a humane manner, appropriate for the species, and in such a way as to ensure immediate death, and in accordance with procedures outlined in the latest version of the American Veterinary Medical Association (AVMA) Panel on Euthanasia.**

2. Disposal of euthanized animals should be accomplished in a manner that is in accord with all relevant legislation, consistent with health, environmental, and aesthetic concerns, and approved by the animal-care committee. No animal shall be discarded until its death is verified.

VI. Field Research

Field research, because of its potential to damage sensitive ecosystems and ethologies, should be subject to animal-care committee approval. Field research, if strictly observational, may not require animal-care committee approval (USDA, 1989, p. 36126).

A. Psychologists conducting field research should disturb their populations as little as possible—consistent with the goals of the research. Every effort should be made to minimize potential harmful effects of the study on the population and on other plant and animal species in the area.

B. Research conducted in populated areas should be done with respect for the property and privacy of the inhabitants of the area.

C. Particular justification is required for the study of endangered species. Such research on endangered species should not be conducted unless animal-care committee approval has been obtained and all requisite permits are obtained (see IVD).

**Write to: AVMA, 1931 N. Meacham Road, Suite 100, Schaumburg, IL 60173, or call (708) 925-8070.

Source: Guidelines for Ethical Conduct in the Care and Use of Animals (1996). Reprinted with the kind permission of the American Psychological Association.

If you are conducting research with animals, you should consult APA's ethical guidelines for animal research (see Box C-4). In addition, you should work closely with your research supervisor. Finally, figure out some strategy so that you do not forget to take care of your animals. Unless you have a system, it is easy to forget to check on your animals during the weekend. Animals need food, water, gentle handling, and a clean living environment *every single day.*

Maximize the Benefits: The Other Side of the Ethics Coin

We have discussed ways of minimizing harm to animal subjects and human participants. However, minimizing harm is not enough to ensure that your study is ethical. You must also ensure that the potential benefits will be greater than the potential harm. Thus, an extremely harmless study can be unethical if the study has no potential benefits. In other words, just as you owe it to your participants to reduce potential harm, you owe it to your participants to maximize the potential benefits of your study. You maximize that potential by making sure your study provides accurate information. To provide accurate information, your study needs to have power and validity.

Having Adequate Power

One of the most serious obstacles to obtaining accurate information is lack of power (recall that power is the ability to find statistically significant differences or relationships when such differences or relationships truly exist). Remember, null results do not prove the null hypothesis. They only make people wonder about the study's power. There is no point in doing a study that is so powerless that it will lead to inconclusive, null (nonsignificant) results.

To have power, you should use a strong manipulation, a sensitive dependent measure, well-standardized procedures, a sensitive design, and enough participants. Often, your biggest obstacle to finding a significant effect will be a lack of participants.

As a general rule, you should have at least 16 participants in each group.[1] However, the number of participants you need in each group will be affected by the sensitivity of your design, the heterogeneity of your participants, the number of observations you get from each participant, the size of the difference you expect to find between conditions, and the sensitivity of your dependent measure.

If you have a within-subjects design, a reliable and sensitive dependent variable, and expect a rather large difference between your conditions, you may be able to use fewer than 16 participants per group. If, on the other hand, you are using a simple, between-subjects design, heterogeneous participants, a manipulation that may have little effect, and a relatively insensitive dependent measure, you may want at least 100 participants per condition.

Having Adequate Construct Validity

After ensuring that your study has adequate power, we would like to be able to tell you that you can take it easy and relax. Unfortunately, however, you cannot relax. Power is not your

---

[1]Having more participants will give you more power. Indeed, some (Cohen, 1990) would consider 64 participants per group to be a reasonable minimum. We have talked about minimums. Are there maximums? Could you have a design that was too powerful? Some would argue that in some cases, researchers use so many participants that even the smallest of effects, no matter how practically and theoretically insignificant, would be statistically significant. However, having an overpowered design is rarely a problem for novice researchers.

only concern when conducting psychological research. You must also ensure that the construct validity of your results is not destroyed by

1. researchers failing to conduct your study in an objective, standardized way
2. participants reacting to how they think you want them to react to the treatment, rather than reacting to the treatment itself

Minimizing Researcher Bias

If you use more than one investigator, you may be able to detect **researcher effects** by including the researcher as a factor in your design. In other words, randomly assign participants to both a condition and to a researcher. For example, if you have two treatment conditions (A and B) and two researchers (1 and 2), you would have four conditions: (1) A1, (2) B1, (3) A2, and (4) B2. After having Research 1 run conditions 1 and 2 and Researcher 2 run conditions 3 and 4, you could do an analysis of variance (ANOVA) using researcher as a factor to see whether different researchers got different results.[2]

Using ANOVA to detect researcher effects can be useful. However, there are at least two reasons why using it may not eliminate researcher effects.

First, this statistical approach will tell you only whether one researcher is getting different results than other researchers. If all your researchers are biased, you may not get a significant researcher effect. (Besides, if you are the only researcher, you cannot use researcher as a factor in an ANOVA.)

Second, and more importantly, detecting researcher effects is not the same as preventing researcher effects. To prevent researcher effects, you must address the three major causes of failing to conduct studies in an objective and standardized manner: (1) the loose-protocol effect, (2) the failure-to-follow-protocol effect, and (3) the researcher-expectancy effect.

Avoiding the Loose-Protocol Effect. Some studies fall victim to the loose-protocol effect: The instructions are not detailed enough to enable the researchers to behave in a standardized way. Fortunately, the loose-protocol effect can be avoided.

Before you start your study, carefully plan everything. As a first step, you should write a set of instructions that chronicles the exact procedure for each participant. These procedures should be so specific that by reading and following your instructions, another person could run your participants the same way you do.

To make your instructions specific, you might want to write a computer program based on these instructions. Because computers do not assume anything, writing such a program forces you to spell out everything down to the last detail. If you cannot program, just write the script as though a robot were to administer the study. Write each step, including the actual words that researchers will say to the participants. The use of such a script will help standardize your procedures, thus reducing threats to validity.

Once you have a detailed draft of your protocol, give it a test run. For example, to ensure that you are as specific as you think you are, pretend to be a participant and have several different people run you through the study using only your instructions. See how each individual behaves. This may give you clues as to how to tighten up your procedures. In addition, you should run several practice participants. Notice whether you change procedures in some subtle way across participants. If so, adjust your instructions to get rid of this variability.

---

[2] You may want to consult with your professor as to the type of ANOVA you should use. Experts argue about whether one should use a conventional ANOVA model or a "random effects" ANOVA model.

Table C-2	**Protocol Checklist for Research With Human Participants**

❏ I have my professor's permission to conduct the study.
❏ I have operational definitions of any variables that I will manipulate or measure.
❏ I have a suitable place to run my participants.
❏ I know how many participants I will need.
❏ I know how I will recruit and select my participants.
❏ I know how I will make the sign-up sheets available to potential participants.
❏ I have included a description of the study (including how long it takes and whether participants will get money or extra credit) on the sign-up sheet.
❏ If I am offering extra credit, I know how I will notify professors about which students participated.
❏ I have developed a consent form.
❏ If I am conducting an experiment, I know how I will assign participants to condition.
❏ I have written a detailed research protocol.
❏ I have written out the oral instructions I will give the participants.
❏ I have written out what I will say during debriefing.
❏ I now consistently follow the protocol.

At the end of your test runs, you should have a detailed set of instructions that you and any co-investigator can follow to the letter. To double-check your protocol, be sure it addresses all the questions listed in Table C-2.

Avoiding the Failure-to-Follow-Protocol Effect. Unfortunately, even if you write your protocol (procedures) in detail, you or your co-investigators may still fail to follow it. To avoid the researcher failure-to-follow-protocol effect, you need to make sure that (a) all investigators know the procedures, and (b) that everyone is motivated to follow them.

To make sure investigators learn the procedures, you should hold training sessions. Supervise investigators while they practice the procedures on each other and on practice participants.

Once researchers know the right way to run the study, the key is to make sure that they are motivated to run the study the same way every time. To do this, you might have them work in pairs. While one researcher runs the participants, the other will listen in through an intercom or watch through a one-way mirror. You may even wish to record research sessions.

If your researchers still have trouble following procedures, you may need to automate your study. For instance, you might use a computer to present instructions, administer the treatment, or collect the dependent measure. Because computers can follow instructions to the letter, they can help standardize your procedures. Of course, computers are not the only machines that can help. Other machines that could help you give instructions and present stimuli include automated slide projectors, tape recorders, and DVD players. Countless other devices could help you record data accurately, from electronic timers and counters to noise-level meters.

Avoiding the Researcher-Expectancy Effect. The final source of researcher bias is the **researcher-expectancy effect:** researchers' expectations are affecting the results. You can take three steps to prevent the researcher-expectancy effect:

1. Be very specific about how investigators are to conduct themselves. Remember, researcher expectancies probably affect the results by changing the investigator's behavior rather than by causing the investigator to send a telepathic message to the participants.

2. Do not let the investigators know the hypothesis.

3. Do not let investigators know what condition the participant is in—making the investigator "blind." Although making investigators blind is easiest in drug experiments where participants take either a placebo or the real drug, you can make investigators blind in nondrug experiments.

For example, if you present stimuli in booklets, you can make the booklets for different conditions look very similar. In that way, an investigator running a group of participants might not know whether the participant was in the experimental or control condition. For some studies, you may be able to use a second investigator who does nothing except collect the dependent measure. You could easily keep this second investigator in the dark about what treatment the participant received.

Avoiding Researcher Bias: A Summary. Whether you are the only investigator or one of a team of investigators, researcher effects may bias your results. Therefore, you should always try to prevent the loose-protocol effect, the failure-to-follow-protocol effect, and the researcher-expectancy effect.

Minimizing Participant Bias

Unfortunately, in psychological research, you must be aware not only of researcher effects, but also of **participant bias:** participants trying to behave in a way that they believe will support the researcher's hypothesis. Fortunately, there are various ways to prevent participants' expectancies from biasing your results.

For starters, you might make your researcher blind to reduce the chance that the participant will get any ideas from the researcher. Thus, the techniques for reducing researcher expectancies that we just discussed may also reduce the effects of participants' expectancies.

In addition, you may also be able to prevent participants from guessing your hypothesis by skillfully choosing your research design. In experimental investigations, for example, you might use a between-subject design rather than a within-subject design because participants who are exposed to only one treatment condition are less likely to guess the hypothesis than participants who are exposed to all treatment conditions.

Use Placebo Treatments So Participants Don't Know What You Are Manipulating. Another design trick you can use to reduce the impact of participants' expectancies is to use placebo treatments. Placebo treatments prevent participants from knowing that they are in the "no-treatment" condition. Therefore, if you have comparison condition(s), use placebo treatment(s) rather than no-treatment condition(s). That way, all groups think they are receiving the treatment. Thus, any treatment effect you find will not be due to participants changing their behavior because they expect the treatment to have an effect.

Use Unobtrusive Measurement Strategies So Participants Don't Know What You Are Measuring. Participants are less likely to know the hypothesis if they do not know what you are measuring. Obviously, if participants do not even know you are observing them, as in some field experiments, they will not know what you are measuring. Thus, if your hypothesis is an obvious one, you might consider doing either (a) a field study or (b) a lab study in which you put participants in one room and secretly monitor them from another room.

Even if the participant knows you are watching, the participant does not have to know what you are watching. That is, you can use unobtrusive measures. For example, you might put the participant in front of a computer and ask the participant to type an essay. Although the participant thinks you are measuring the essay's quality, you could have the computer programmed to monitor speed of typing, time between paragraphs, number of errors made, and number of times a section was rewritten. In addition, you might also tape-record and videotape the participant, monitoring his or her facial expressions, number of vocalizations, and loudness of vocalizations.

Create Experimental Realism So Participants Don't Focus on the Hypothesis. Rather than trying to obscure or confuse participants as to the purpose of the study, you might try to prevent participants from thinking about the purpose of the study. One way to do this is to design a study that has a high degree of **experimental realism:** a study that involves participants in the task. This means that participants are not constantly saying to themselves: "What does the researcher really want me to do?" or "If I were a typical person, how would I behave in this situation?" Note that experimental realism does not mean the study is like real life; it means that participants are engrossed in the task. As you know from video games, even an artificial task can be very high in experimental realism.

Maximizing Benefits: A Summary

Before now, you might have been surprised to see experimental realism and other strategies for reducing participant effects in a section on ethics. However, you now know that planning an ethical study involves taking into account many factors. Not only must you ensure the safety of your participants, but you must also demonstrate the validity of your methods. To avoid overlooking an important ethical consideration, consult Box C-1 and your professor.

Beyond the Proposal: The Pilot Study

Even after you have carefully designed your study, modified it based on comments from your instructor, and been given your professor's go-ahead to run it, you may still want to run several participants (friends, family members, other members of the class) just for practice. By running practice participants, you will get some of the "bugs" out of your study. Specifically, by running and debriefing practice participants, you will discover

1. whether participants perceived your manipulation the way you intended
2. whether you can perform the study the same way every time or whether you need to spell out your procedures in more detail
3. whether you are providing the right amount of time for each of the research tasks and whether you are allowing enough time in between tasks
4. whether your instructions were clear
5. whether your cover story was believable
6. whether you need to revise your stimulus materials
7. how participants like the study
8. how long it takes you to run and debrief a participant

In short, running practice participants helps you to fine-tune your study. Because it is so useful, many professional investigators run enough practice participants to constitute a small study—what researchers call a *pilot study.*

Conducting the Actual Study

The dress rehearsal is over. You have made the final changes in your procedures and your proposal. Now you are ready for the real thing—to conduct your study. This section will show you how.

Establishing Rapport

As you may imagine, some of your prospective participants may be apprehensive about the study. Participants often are not sure whether they are in the right place, or even whether the researcher is a Dr. Frankenstein.

To put your participants at ease, let them know they are in the right place, and be courteous. You should be both friendly and businesslike. The expert investigator greets the participant warmly, pays close attention to the participant, and seems concerned that the participant knows what will happen in the study. The expert investigator is obviously concerned that each participant is treated humanely and that the study is done professionally.

Being professional does not hurt how participants view you. Why? First, most participants like knowing that they are involved in something important. Second, some will view your professionalism as a way of showing that you value their time—which you should.

So, how can you exude a professional manner? Some novice investigators think that they appear professional when they act aloof and unconcerned. Nothing could be less professional. Participants are turned off by an indifferent, apathetic attitude. They feel that you do not care about the study and that you do not care about them.

To appear professional, you should be neatly dressed, enthusiastic, well-organized, and prompt. "Prompt" may be an understatement. You should be ready and waiting for your participants at least 10 minutes before the study is scheduled to begin. Once your participants arrive, concentrate exclusively on the job at hand. Never ask a participant to wait a few minutes while you socialize with friends.

What do you lose by being a "professional" investigator? Problem participants. If you seem enthusiastic and professional, your participants will also become involved in doing your study—even if the tasks are relatively boring. Thus, if you are professional in your manner and attitude, you will probably not even have to ask the participants to refrain from chatting throughout the study. Similarly, participants will stop asking questions about the study if you say, "I will explain the purpose at the end of the study."

Getting Participants to Follow Instructions

After you have established rapport, you need to give your participants instructions. To get participants to follow instructions to the letter, you might

1. repeat the instructions
2. orally paraphrase the instructions
3. have participants read the instructions
4. run participants individually
5. invite participants to ask questions
6. have participants demonstrate that they understand the instructions by quizzing them or by giving them a practice trial before beginning the study

Sticking to the Protocol

Once the study has begun, try to follow the procedure to the letter. Consistently following the same procedures improves power and reduces the possibility of bias. Therefore, do not let participants change your behavior by reinforcing or punishing you. For instance, imagine you are investigating long-term memory. You want to expose participants to information and then see what they can write down. However, if you do this, participants may be writing down information that is in short-term memory. Thus, you would not be assessing long-term memory. Therefore, you add a counting backward task that should virtually eliminate all of the information from short-term memory. Specifically, in your memory study, participants are exposed to information, are supposed to count backward from a number like 781 by 3s for 20 seconds, and then are asked to recall the information. Ideally, their recall will represent only what they have in long-term memory.

Unfortunately, many participants will find the counting task unpleasant, embarrassing, or simply an unwanted nuisance. Consequently, some participants will thank you for telling them they can stop; others will plead nonverbally for you to stop. Clearly, you cannot let any of these strategies stop you from making them count backward for the full 20 seconds. If you vary your procedures from participant to participant based on each participant's whims, your study will have questionable validity.

Debriefing

Once the study is over, you should debrief your participants. In debriefing, you should first try to find out whether the participants suspected the hypothesis. Simply ask participants what they thought the study was about. Then, explain the purpose of your study.

If you deceived your participants, you need to make sure they are not upset about it. You also need to make sure that they understand why deception was necessary. Participants should leave the study appreciating the fact that there was one and only one reason you employed deception: It was the only way to get good information about an important issue.

Making sure participants accept your rationale for deception is crucial for three reasons. First, you do not want your participants to feel humiliated or angry. Second, if they get mad, they may not only be mad at you, but also at psychologists in general. Perhaps that anger or humiliation will stop them from visiting a psychologist when they need help. Third, the unhappy participant may spread the word about your deception, ruining your chances of deceiving other participants.

After explaining the purpose of the study, you should answer any questions the participants have. Although this may sometimes seem like a waste of time, you owe it to your participants. They gave you their time, and now it is your turn.

After you have dealt with participants' questions and doubts, give them an opportunity to rate how valuable they felt the study was. This encourages you to be courteous to your participants, lets you know whether your study is more traumatic than you originally thought, and makes participants feel that you respect them because you value their opinions.

After participants rate your study, you should assure them that their responses during the study will be kept confidential. Tell them that no one but you will know their responses. Then, ask the participants not to talk about the study because it is still in progress. For example, you might ask them not to talk about the study until next week. Finally, you should thank your participants, escort them back to the waiting area, and say goodbye.

Ethical Concerns After the Study Is Over: The Need to Protect Confidentiality

You might think that once a participant leaves the study, your responsibilities to that participant end. Wrong! You are still responsible for guaranteeing the participant's privacy. Knowledge about a given participant is between you (the investigator) and the participant—*no one else*. Never violate this confidentiality. To ensure confidentiality, you should take the following precautions:

1. Assign each participant a number. When you refer to a given participant, always use the assigned number—never that participant's name.

2. Never store a participant's name and data in a computer—this could be a computer hacker's delight.

3. If you have participants write their names on booklets, tear off and destroy the cover of the booklet after you have analyzed the data.

4. Store a list of participants and their numbers in one place and the data with the participants' numbers on it in another place.

5. Don't gossip! There is rarely a reason to talk casually about a participant's behavior. Even if you do not mention any names, other people may guess or think they have guessed the identity of your participant. We realize that it is hard to keep a secret. However, to talk freely about someone who participated in your study is to betray a trust. Furthermore, keeping secrets will, for many of you, be an important part of your professional role: Therapists, researchers, consultants, lawyers, and physicians all must keep their clients' behaviors confidential.

D

Introduction to Statistics

Choosing the Correct Analysis

To analyze statistical data correctly, you must choose the correct statistical test. The test you should use when you have interval data is not the same test you should use when you have nominal data. The test you should use when you are comparing each participant with himself or herself is not the same test you should use when you are comparing one group to another group. The test that would work when you only had two conditions may not work when you are comparing more than two conditions. In other words, there are at least three factors you should take into consideration when choosing a statistical test: (a) the scale of measurement that your measure provides (see Chapter 6); (b) the type of comparison you are making (one group of participants compared to one or more other groups [between-subjects] or each participants compared to himself or herself [within-subjects]); and (c) the number of conditions you have. In the next three sections, we will show you how to take each of these three factors into account so that you can choose the right analysis for your study.

Scales of Measurement

Often, the type of test depends on what type of data you have. That is, you will do one kind of test if you have nominal data, but another kind of test if you have interval data. This fact is summarized in the following table.

SCALE OF MEASUREMENT	EXAMPLE	AVERAGE	MEASURE OF CORRELATION	TYPICAL STATISTICAL ANALYSIS
Nominal	When numbers represent categories, such as 1 = Democrat, 2 = Republican, 3 = Independent	Mode (most common score) or simply describe the percentage of participants in each category	Phi coefficient	Chi-square
Ordinal	Ranks (e.g., 1st, 2nd, 3rd)	Median (middle score)	Spearman's rho	Mann-Whitney (if testing two groups), Kruskal-Wallis (if testing more than two groups), Friedman test (if using within-subjects design)
Interval	Rating scales	Mean	Pearson r	t test, ANOVA
Ratio	Height, magnitude estimation	Mean	Pearson r	t test, ANOVA

Within-Subjects Versus Between-Subjects Designs

Another factor that determines which statistics you should use is whether you are using a within-subjects design (comparing each participant with himself or herself) or a between-subjects design. For example, if you were using a two-condition within-subjects design, rather than using a between-subjects ANOVA or an independent groups t test, you should use either a dependent groups t test or a within-subjects ANOVA.

Number of Conditions

Finally, you must also consider the number of conditions you are comparing. For example, if you have interval data and are comparing only two conditions, you can use a *t* test. If, however, you are comparing more than two conditions, you must use ANOVA instead.

These facts are summarized in the following table

	NUMBER OF CONDITIONS	
Type of Data	**Two**	**More Than Two**
Nominal, between-subjects	Chi-square	Chi-square
Nominal, within-subjects or matched pairs	McNemar test	Cochran Q test
Ordinal, between-subjects	Mann-Whitney test	Kruskal-Wallis test
Ordinal, within-subjects or matched pairs	Wilcoxon matched-pairs	Friedman test
Interval/ratio, between-subjects	Independent groups *t* test or between subjects ANOVA	Between-subjects ANOVA
Interval/ratio, within-subjects or matched subjects	Dependent *t* test or within-subjects ANOVA	Within-subjects ANOVA

Performing the Correct Analysis: An Overview of the Rest of This Appendix

If you refer to the information we just discussed, you will choose the right statistical test (see Figure D-1). But should you conduct a statistical significance test on your data? Not everyone agrees that you should (see Box D-1). Despite the controversy surrounding significance testing, most experts agree that statistical significance provides good evidence that a finding is reliable. Largely because statistically significant tests are helpful in preventing us from mistaking a coincidence for a genuine relationship, almost all articles you read will report the result of a significance test. Therefore, the rest of this appendix will be devoted to discussing the logic and computations behind the most commonly used statistical tests.

We will begin by discussing the independent groups *t* test. Learning about the *t* test will not only teach you about one of the most commonly used statistical techniques, but it will also give you the foundation for understanding other statistical techniques. We will then discuss the most common technique for analyzing the results of an experiment that has more than two groups: ANOVA. We will finish our discussion of techniques typically used by students to analyze data from experiments with a description of the dependent *t* test.

After talking about techniques commonly used in experiments, we will discuss techniques commonly used with correlational data. We will begin by talking about how to compute the Pearson *r*. Then, we will show you how to calculate and interpret the coefficient of determination. Next, we will show you how to find out if a Pearson *r* in your sample indicates that the two variables are really related in the population. Following this discussion of techniques that are commonly used when you have interval data, we show you how to do comparable analyses when you have nominal data. Finally, we will discuss more sophisticated ways of analyzing correlational data, including multiple regression, mediational analyses, and factor analysis.

Figure D-1   **Choosing the Right Statistical Test**

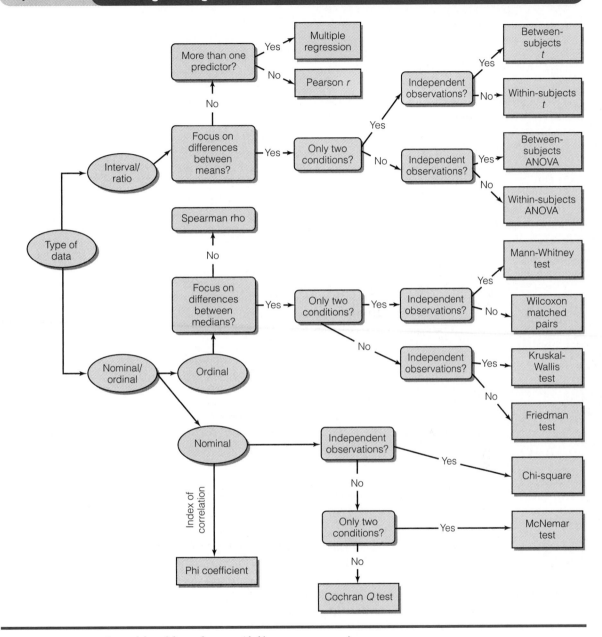

Source: Adapted from a figure provided by an anonymous reviewer.

BOX D-1 Ban Statistical Significance Testing?

Although many have criticized the use of statistical significance tests, psychologists—even most of the critics of such tests—still use them (Greenwald, Gonzalez, Harris, & Guthrie, 1996). To understand why, we will consider the major objections to statistical significance and how defenders of the statistical significance tests would respond to those objections. As you can see, the responses to the attacks on statistical significance fall into three general categories: (a) the attack reflects a problem not with statistical significance tests themselves but with how people use or think about statistical significance tests, (b) the attack would still be made if people used alternatives to significance tests, or (c) the attack is misguided.

OBJECTION TO STATISTICAL SIGNIFICANCE TESTING	REPLY TO OBJECTION	DEFENDER'S GENERAL COMMENT ABOUT THE ATTACK
The significance test doesn't tell you anything because the null is always false. Everything is connected to everything else. That is, two variables will always be related.	1. The evidence for the view that the null is always false is less than overwhelming. Scientists who have really wanted to believe that a treatment had an effect have used strong treatments and large sample sizes, and still failed to find significant effects. Indeed, most psychologists know that their work will not be published unless their results are statistically significant and yet they often fail to obtain significant effects for the variables of interest. 2. As Hagan (1998) points out, if opponents mean that every treatment has some effect on the measured dependent variable, then that means that (a) there are no Type 1 errors, (b) all null results are Type 2 errors, and (c) quack therapies really work. 3. Even if the null was always false, we would still want to know the direction of the effect (does it help or hurt). Significance testing is good at detecting the direction of an effect (Harris, 1997).	The attack is misguided.
The $p < .05$ level is arbitrary. Why would a p of .051 fail to be significant, whereas a p of .049 would be significant?	1. Before significance testing, people could just decide that their results "felt real and reliable." Currently, with the .05 criterion, they have to meet some objective standard. 2. In the situation described, any reasonable investigator would follow up on any interesting hypothesis that had a p value of .051. Usually, the investigator would replicate the study using more participants so that the study would have more power.	The problem is not as serious as critics allege—and alternative methods have similar problems.

OBJECTION TO STATISTICAL SIGNIFICANCE TESTING

REPLY TO OBJECTION

DEFENDER'S GENERAL COMMENT ABOUT THE ATTACK

3. Generally, if we are going to err, we should error on the side of caution. By sticking to the $p < .05$ level, we are unlikely to report that a treatment has one kind of effect when the treatment actually has the opposite effect.

4. As Greenwald, Gonzalez, Harris, and Guthrie (1996, p. 178) point out, people need "yes versus no" answers to many questions, such as "Is this treatment superior to a placebo?" When we must decide whether to act or not to act, we must use an arbitrary cutoff. For example, how sure do you have to be that going to a doctor would be the best thing to do before you actually go? If we used the same tactics as those who argue that the .05 significance level is arbitrary, we could make any cutoff seem arbitrary. For example, if you said "60%," we could reply, "so you would not go if you were 59.99% sure?" Note, however, that you are not being irrational: You have to have some cutoff or you would never act.

5. An alternative approach, using confidence intervals instead of significance tests has the same problem. (To learn more about confidence intervals, see Box 9-2 or Appendix D.)

The logic behind statistical significance is not—according to the rules of formal deductive logic—valid (Cohen, 1994). Statistical significance does not tell us how likely it is that the null is false. Instead, it gives us the probability of getting a set of results given that the null is true (Cohen, 1994).

1. The fact that significance testing is not valid according to the rules of formal logic does not mean it is illogical (Hagan, 1998). Most of what physical scientists do is not valid in terms of formal, deductive logic (T. A. Lavin, personal communication, July 18, 2002).

2. Philosophers would say that the arguments behind significance testing are logically valid abductive arguments (J. Phillips, personal communication, September 4, 2005).

3. Hagan (1998) argues that DNA testing uses a similar logic.

4. With simulated data, Type 1 error rates are what significance tests would predict (Estes, 1997).

5. In practice, significance tests (a) are very good at telling us the direction of an effect and (b) provide information about the probability that a replication of the study would obtain a significant effect (Greenwald et al., 1996).

The problem is not as serious as critics allege.

continued

BOX D-1 *(continued)*

OBJECTION TO STATISTICAL SIGNIFICANCE TESTING	REPLY TO OBJECTION	DEFENDER'S GENERAL COMMENT ABOUT THE ATTACK
Statistical significance is misunderstood. 1. Many think null results mean accepting the null (Shrout, 1997). 2. Many think statistical significance means the same as important (Shrout, 1997).	Would physics researchers change their methodology because the average person did not understand their methods? If there is a concern about significant results being misunderstood, there are alternatives to eliminating significance testing. For example, the public or the media could be educated about what "statistical significance" means or the term could be changed so that people did not confuse its meaning with the meaning of the word "significant." Similarly, Scarr (1997) suggests that the term "reliable" replace "significance."	The problem is due to people misunderstanding the term "statistical significance," not with statistical significance itself.
Statistical significance is not a measure of effect size. It is a measure of sample size and effect size. Therefore, we should measure effect size instead.	1. "Effect size" does not give you a pure measure of a variable's effect because "effect size" depends on (a) the power of the original manipulation, (b) how homogenous the sample is, and (c) the reliability and sensitivity of the dependent measure. Thus, with a different treament manipulation, measure, or sample, you will obtain a different effect size. In addition, an effect that would be large in a well-controlled laboratory study might be tiny in a real-world setting. Even when we (a) study variables in real world settings and (b) use measures that give us estimates of effect size, we still are unable to establish the relative strength of variables (e.g., the nature/nurture debate on IQ). 2. Estimates of effect size can be obtained from significance tests (see Box 9-2). 3. As Prentice and Miller (1992) point out, the fact that a weak manipulation of a variable has any effect at all can be convincing evidence for the importance of that variable. 4. A large effect size on a trivial variable (ratings on a scale) may be unimportant, whereas a small effect size on an important variable (health) may be important. 5. A large effect that does not persist may be less important than a small, lasting effect that accumulates over time.	The problem is not as serious as critics allege.

OBJECTION TO STATISTICAL SIGNIFICANCE TESTING	REPLY TO OBJECTION	DEFENDER'S GENERAL COMMENT ABOUT THE ATTACK
Significant effects may be small.	1. Small effects may be very important (a) when evaluating the relative validity of two theories, (b) when looking at an important variable (e.g., the effect size for aspirin on preventing heart attacks is tiny, but has enormous practical implications), and (c) when looking at variables that have effects that accumulate over time (e.g., if we produce even a tiny effect for a single commercial we present in the lab, the implications may be enormous because the person will probably see more than a million ads in the course of a lifetime). 2. Any informed person could determine whether the effect was small.	The problem is with people misunderstanding the meaning of statistical significance rather than with statistical significance tests.
Significance testing made our science unreliable, unlike physical sciences.	1. Our findings are as replicable as those in physics (Hedges, 1987). 2. Health research's abandonment of statistical significance seems to have made their research more conflicting rather than less. 3. Significance reduces our risk of mistaking a chance difference for a genuine effect. It also prevents us from believing that our data support whatever pattern we desire. Thus, significance testing has made our findings more—not less—reliable (Scarr, 1997). 4. Impressions that studies conflict often reflect a misunderstanding of significance tests. If one study is significant and the other is not, then one study refutes the null and the other *fails* to refute the null. The two studies are not in conflict because the second study does not support the null. 5. Other social scientists tend to want to model our approach because it has been so successful in producing reliable, objective findings.	The attack is misguided.
Significance tests are misused.	Everything can and will be misused (Abelson, 1997).	The attack is misguided.

continued

OBJECTION TO STATISTICAL SIGNIFICANCE TESTING	REPLY TO OBJECTION	DEFENDER'S GENERAL COMMENT ABOUT THE ATTACK
The p value doesn't tell you the probability that you would get similar results if you repeated the study. For example, if your results are significant at the $p = .05$ level, there is only about a 50% chance that if you repeated the study, you would again get significant results in the predicted direction.	There is a relationship between the p value and the chance of obtaining the same results in an exact replication (Greenwald et al., 1996).	This is a problem with people misunderstanding statistical significance rather than with significance testing.
Significance tests don't tell us anything because observed differences that are not significant would have been significant with a larger sample size.	As Hagen (1997) points out, with larger sample sizes, the observed differences will tend to get smaller. That is, with a small sample, the standard error of the difference is large. However, with many participants, the standard error of the difference shrinks, and large differences will be less likely to occur by chance.	The attack is misguided.
People doing statistical significance tests ignore power and thus make many Type 2 errors (Shrout, 1997).	Researchers should use studies that have more power. If they fail to do so, the problem is not with statistical significance testing, but with the researcher.	This is a problem with researchers rather than with significance testing.
A confidence interval (CI), in which the researcher would be 95% confident that the effect was more than ___ but less than ——, would be more informative than significance tests.	1. CI has many of the same problems as significance testing (Abelson, 1997). 2. An informed reader could construct confidence intervals from the reports of a significance test.	CIs should supplement, rather than replace, statistical significance testing.

Analyzing Data From the Simple, Two-Group Experiment: The Independent-Groups *t* Test

To use the independent-groups *t* test, you must meet the following criteria:

1. You must have two groups.
2. Your observations must be independent.
3. Each of your groups should have approximately the same variance.
4. Your scores should be normally distributed.
5. You must be able to assume that your data are either interval or ratio.

As long as your data meet these assumptions, then you can use the *t* test to analyze your data. Thus, the *t* test can be used to look at differences on any measure, such as between men and women, computer users versus nonusers, or any two independent groups. However, the most common use of the *t* test is to analyze the results of a simple (two-group, between-subjects) experiment.

To understand why you can use the *t* test to analyze the results of a simple experiment, remember why you did the simple experiment. You did it to find out whether the treatment would have an effect on a unique population—all the individuals who participated in your experiment. More specifically, you wanted to know the answer to the hypothetical question, "If I had put all my participants in the experimental condition, would they have scored differently than if I had put all of them in the control condition?" To answer this question, you need to know the averages of two populations:

Average of Population 1: what the average score on the dependent measure would have been if all your participants had been in the control group

Average of Population 2: what the average score on the dependent measure would have been if all your participants had been in the experimental group

Unfortunately, you cannot measure both of these populations. If you put all your participants in the control condition, then you won't know how they would have scored in the experimental condition. If, on the other hand, you put all your participants in the experimental condition, you won't know how they would have scored in the control condition.

Estimating What You Want to Know

Because you cannot directly get the population averages you want, you do the next best thing—you estimate them. You can do this because—thanks to independent random assignment—you divided all your participants (your population of participants) into two random samples. In other words, you started the experiment with two random samples from your original population of participants: the control group and the experimental group.

The average score of the random sample of your participants who received the treatment (the experimental group) is an estimate of what the average score would have been if all your participants received the treatment. The average score of the random sample of participants who received no treatment (the control group) is an estimate of what the average score would have been if all of your participants had been in the control condition.

Calculating Sample Means

Even though only half your participants were in the experimental group, you will assume that the experimental group is a fair sample of your entire population of participants. Thus, the experimental group's average score should be a reasonably good estimate of what the average score would have been if all your participants had been in the experimental group. Similarly, you will assume that the control group's average score is a fairly good estimate of what the average score would have been if all your participants had been in the control group. Therefore, the first step in analyzing your data will be to calculate the average score for each group. Usually, the average you will calculate is the *mean:* the result of adding up all the scores and then dividing by the number of scores.

Comparing Sample Means

Once you have your two sample means, you can compare them. We do this because we know that, before the treatment was administered, both groups represented a random sample of the population consisting of every participant who was in the study. Thus, if the treatment had no effect, at the end of the experiment, the control and experimental groups would both still be random samples from that population.

As you know, two random samples from the same population will be similar to each other. For example, two random samples of the entire population of New York City should be similar to each other, two random samples from the entire population of students at your school should be similar to each other, and two random samples from the entire group of participants who were in your study should be similar to each other. Thus, if the treatment has no effect, at the end of the experiment, the experimental and control groups should be similar to each other.

Because random samples of the same population should be similar, you might think all we need to do is subtract the control group mean from the experimental group mean to find the effect. But such is not the case: Even if the treatment has no effect, the means for the control group and experimental group will rarely be identical. To illustrate, suppose that Dr. N. Ept made a serious mistake while trying to do a double-blind study. Specifically, although he succeeded in not letting his assistants know whether the participants were getting the real treatment or a placebo, his study was ruined because all the participants got the placebo. In other words, both groups ended up being random samples of the same population—participants who did not get the treatment. Even in such a case, the two groups may have very different means.

Dr. N. Ept's study illustrates an important point: Even when groups are random samples of the same population, they may still differ because of random sampling error. You are aware of random sampling error from reading about public opinion polls that admit to a certain degree of sampling error or from reading about two polls of the same population that produced slightly different results.

In summary, some random samples will not be representative of their parent population. Because of the possibility that a sample may be strongly affected by random sampling error, your sample means may differ even if the real, parent population means do not.

Inferential Statistics: Judging the Accuracy of Your Estimates

We have told you that random error can throw off your estimates of population means. Because of random error, the treatment group mean is an imperfect estimate of what would have happened if all the participants had received the treatment and the control group mean is an imperfect estimate of what would have happened if none of the participants had received the treatment. Thus, the difference between your experimental group mean and control group mean could be due to random error. Consequently, finding a difference between the treatment group mean and the no-treatment group mean doesn't prove that you have a treatment effect.

If the difference between your group means could be due to random error, how can you determine whether a difference between the sample means is due to the treatment? You need to know how much of a difference random error could make. If the actual difference between your group means was much bigger than the difference that chance could make, then you could conclude that the treatment had an effect.

Estimating the Accuracy of Individual Sample Means

How can you determine whether the difference between your sample means is too large to be due to random error? Knowing the accuracy of each of your individual sample means should help. For example, suppose you knew the control group mean was within one point of its true population mean. Furthermore, suppose you knew that the experimental group mean was also within one point of its real population mean. In other words, you knew that (a) the estimate for what the mean would be if everybody had been in the control group was not off by more than one point, and that (b) the estimate for what the mean would be if everyone had been in the experimental group was also not off by more than one point.

If you knew all that, and if your control group mean differed from your experimental group mean by 20 points, then you would know that your two sample means represent different population means. In other words, you could assume that if all your participants had been given the treatment, they would have scored differently than if they had all been deprived of the treatment.

If, on the other hand, the two group means had differed by less than one point, the difference between the groups could easily be due to random error. In that case, you would not be able to conclude that the treatment had an effect.

Consider Population Variability: The Value of the Standard Deviation. You have seen that a key to determining whether your treatment had an effect is to determine how accurately your two sample means reflect their population means. But how can you do that? One factor that affects how well a mean based on a random sample of the population reflects the population mean is the amount of variability in the population. If there is no variability in the population, then all scores in the population will be the same as the mean. Consequently, there would be no sampling error. For example, if everyone in the population scored a 5, the population mean would be 5, and the mean of every random sample would also be 5. Thus, because all Roman Catholic cardinals hold very similar positions on the morality of abortion, almost any sample of Roman Catholic cardinals you took would accurately reflect the views of Roman Catholic cardinals on that issue.

If, on the other hand, scores in a population vary considerably (for example, ranging anywhere from 0 to 1,000), then independent random samples from that population could be extremely inaccurate. For instance, even if the population mean was 500, you might get sample means ranging from 0 to 1,000. Thus, two sample means from such a heterogeneous population could be very different.

To recap, you have seen that the variability of scores in a population affects how accurately individual samples will reflect that population. Because the extent of the variability of scores in the population influences the extent to which we have random sampling error, it would be nice to have an index of the variability of scores within a population.

The ideal index of the population's variability is the population's **standard deviation**: a measure of the extent to which individual scores deviate from the population mean. Unfortunately, to get that index, you have to know the population mean (for the control condition, the average of the scores if all the participants had been in the control condition; for the experimental condition, the average of the scores if all the participants had been in the experimental condition). Obviously, you don't know the population mean for either the control or experimental condition—that's what you are trying to find out!

Although you cannot calculate the population standard deviation, you can estimate it by looking at the variability of scores within your samples. In fact, by following the steps in Box D-2, you can estimate what the standard deviation would have been if everyone had been in the control group (by looking at variability within the control group) and what the standard deviation would have been if all your participants had been in the experimental group (by looking at variability within the experimental group).

One reason the standard deviation is a particularly valuable index of variability is that many populations can be completely described simply by knowing the standard deviation

BOX D-2 How to Compute a Standard Deviation

Assume we have four scores (108, 104, 104, 104) from a population. We could estimate the population's standard deviation by going through the following steps.

STEP 1: Calculate the mean (M).	STEP 2: Subtract scores from mean (105) to get differences.	STEP 3: Square differences.
108	— 105 = +3	$(+3)^2 = +9$
104	— 105 = −1	$(−1)^2 = +1$
104	— 105 = −1	$(−1)^2 = +1$
<u>104</u>	— 105 = −1	$(−1)^2 = +\underline{1}$
420 = Total		$SS = 12$

Mean = 420/4 = 105

STEP 4: Add (sum) the squared differences obtained in step 3 to get sum of squared differences, otherwise known as sum of squares. Sum of squares is often abbreviated as (SS). Sum of squares (SS) = 12.

STEP 5: Get variance by dividing SS (which was 12) by one less than the number of scores ($4 − 1 = 3$). This division yields a variance of 4 (because $12/3 = 4$).

STEP 6: Get the standard deviation by taking the square root of variance. Because the variance is 4, the standard deviation is 2 (because the square root of 4 is 2).

For those preferring formulas,

$S = \sqrt{(\Sigma X − M)^2 / N − 1}$ where X stands for the individual scores, M is the sample mean, S is the estimate of the population's standard deviation, and N is the number of scores.

and the mean. You probably already know that the mean is valuable for describing many populations. You know that for many populations, most scores will be near the mean and that as many scores will be above the mean as will be below the mean.

What you may not know is that for many populations, you can specify precisely what percentage of scores will be within a certain number of standard deviations of the mean. For instance, you can say that 68% of the scores will be within one standard deviation of the mean, 95% will be within two standard deviations of the mean, and 99% of the scores will be within three standard deviations of the mean. If a population's scores are spread out (distributed) in this manner, the population is said to be *normally distributed*.

As the term "normally distributed" suggests, many populations are normally distributed—from test scores to the heights of American women. Because normally distributed populations are common, graphing the distribution of scores in a population will often produce a **normal curve:** a bell-shaped, symmetrical curve that has its center at the mean (see Figure D-2).

It's convenient to summarize an entire distribution of scores with just two numbers: the mean, which gives you the center of a normal distribution; and the standard deviation, which gives you an index of the width of the distribution. It's comforting to know that 68% of the scores will be within one standard deviation of the mean, that 95% of the scores will be within two standard deviations of the mean, and that virtually all the scores will be within three standard deviations of the mean.

But the standard deviation has more uses than merely describing a population. You could use the standard deviation to make inferences about the population mean. For example, suppose you don't know the population's mean, but you know that the distribution is normally distributed and that its standard deviation is three. Then, you don't need much data to make certain inferences about that population. Specifically, you know that if you randomly selected a single score from that population, there would be a 68% chance that the population mean would be within 3 points (one standard deviation) of that score and a 95% chance that the population mean would be within 6 points (two standard deviations) of that score.

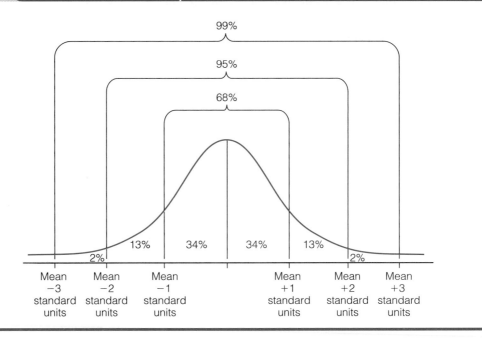

Consider Sample Size: The Role of the Standard Error. Of course, to estimate your control group's population mean, you would not use just one score. Instead, you would use the control group mean. Intuitively, you realize that using a sample mean based on several scores will give you a better estimate of the population mean than using a single score.

You also intuitively realize that using a sample mean based on many scores is better than using a sample mean based on a few scores. In other words, the bigger your independent random sample, the better your random sample will tend to reflect the population. Consequently, the bigger your sample, the closer its mean should be to the population mean.

To reiterate, the accuracy of your sample mean depends, in part, on how many scores you use to calculate that mean. However, the standard deviation does not take into account how many scores the sample mean is based on. The standard deviation will be the same whether the sample mean is based on 2 scores or 2,000. Because the standard deviation does not take into account sample size, the standard deviation is not a good index of your sample mean's accuracy.

A good index of the degree to which a sample mean may differ from its population mean must include both factors that influence the accuracy of a sample mean, namely:

1. population variability (the less population variability, the more accurate the sample mean will tend to be)

2. sample size (the larger the sample, the more accurate the sample mean will tend to be)

Not surprisingly, both of these factors are included in the formula for the **standard error of the estimate of the mean:** an index of the degree to which random error may cause a sample mean to be an inaccurate estimate of its population mean.

The standard error (of the estimate of the population mean) equals the standard deviation (a measure of population variability) divided by the square root of the number of participants (an index of sample size). Thus, if the standard deviation were 40 and you had 4 people in your sample, the standard error would be

$$\frac{40}{\sqrt{4}} = \frac{40}{2} - 20$$

Note that dividing by the square root of the sample size means that the bigger the sample size, the smaller the standard error. Thus, the formula reflects the fact that you have less random sampling error with larger samples. Consequently, in the example above, if you had used 100 participants instead of 4, your standard error would have shrunk from 20 $(40/\sqrt{4})$ to 4 $(40/\sqrt{100})$.

What does the standard error tell you? Clearly, the larger the standard error, the more likely a sample mean will misrepresent the population mean. But does this random error contaminate all samples equally or does it heavily infest some samples while leaving others untouched? Ideally, you would like to know precisely how random error is distributed across various samples. You want to know what percentage of samples will be substantially tainted by random error so that you know what chance your sample mean has of being accurate.

Using the Standard Error. Fortunately, you can know how sample means are distributed. As a result of drawing numerous independent random samples from a normally distributed population and plotting the means of each sample, statisticians have shown that the distribution of sample means is normally distributed. Most (68%) of the sample means will be within one standard error of the population mean, 95% will be within two standard errors of the population mean, and 99% will be within three standard errors of the population mean. Therefore, if your standard error is 1.0, you know that there's a 68% chance that the true population mean is within 1.0 points of your sample mean, a 95% chance that the population mean is within 2.0 points of your sample mean, and a 99% chance that the population mean is within 3.0 points of your sample mean.

When you can assume that the population is normally distributed, you can estimate how close your sample mean is to the true population mean. You do this by taking advantage of the fact that sample means from normally distributed populations will follow a very well defined distribution: the normal distribution. But what if the underlying population isn't normally distributed?

Even then, as the *central limit theorem* states, the distribution of sample means will be normally distributed—if your samples are large enough (30 or more participants). To understand why the central limit theorem works, realize that if you take numerous large random samples from the same population, your sample means will differ from one another for only one reason—random error. Because random error is normally distributed, your distribution of sample means will be normally distributed—regardless of the shape of the underlying population. Consequently, if you take a large random sample from any population, you can use the normal curve to estimate how closely your sample mean reflects the population mean.

Estimating Accuracy of Your Estimate of the Difference
Between Population Means

Because you know that sample means are normally distributed, you can determine how likely it is that a sample mean is within a certain distance of its population mean. But in the simple experiment, you are not trying to find a certain population mean. Instead, you are trying to find out whether two population means differ. As we mentioned earlier, you want to know whether there was a difference between two hypothetical population means: (a) what the mean score would have been if all your participants had been in the control group, and (b) what the mean score would have been if all your participants had been in the experimental group. Put another way, you are asking the question: "If all the participants had received the treatment, would they have scored differently than if they had all been in the control group?"

Because you want to know whether the treatment made a difference, your focus is not on the individual sample means, but on the difference between the two means. Therefore, you would like to know how differences between sample means (drawn from the same population) are distributed.

How the Differences Between Means Are Distributed: The Large Sample Case. Statisticians know how differences between sample means drawn from the same population are distributed because they have repeated the following steps thousands of times:

1. Take two random samples from the same population.
2. Calculate the means of the two samples (Group 1 and Group 2).
3. Subtract the Group 1 mean from the Group 2 mean to get the difference between Group 1 and Group 2.

From this work, statisticians have established three basic facts about the distribution of differences between sample means drawn from the same population.

First, if you subtracted the Group 1 mean from the Group 2 mean an infinite number of times, the average of all these differences would equal zero. This is because, in the long run, random error averages out to zero. Because random error averages out to zero, the mean of all the Group 1 means would be the true population mean—as would the mean of all the Group 2 means. Because the Group 1 means and the Group 2 means both average out to the same number, the average difference between the Group 1 and Group 2 means would be zero.

Second, the distribution of differences would be normally distributed. This makes sense because (a) the only way random samples from the same population can differ is because of random error, and (b) random error is normally distributed.

Third, the standard unit of variability for the distribution of differences between means is neither the standard deviation nor the standard error. Instead, it is the standard error of the difference between means.

The standard error of the difference *between* means is larger than the standard error *of* the mean. This fact shouldn't surprise you. After all, the difference between sample means is influenced by the random error that affects the control group mean *and* by the random error that affects the experimental group mean. In other words, sample means from the same population could differ because the first sample mean was inaccurate, because the second sample mean was inaccurate, or because both were inaccurate.

The formula for the standard error of the difference between means reflects the fact that this standard error is the result of measuring two unstable estimates. Specifically, the formula is

$$\sqrt{\frac{s_1^2}{N_1} + \frac{s_2^2}{N_2}}$$

where s_1 is the estimate of the population standard deviation for Group 1, and s_2 is the estimate of the population standard deviation for Group 2, N_1 is the number of participants in Group 1, and N_2 is the number of participants in Group 2.

We know that with large enough samples, the distribution of differences between means would be normally distributed. Thus, if the standard error of the difference was 1.0, we would know that (a) 68% of the time, the true difference would be within one point of the difference we observed; (b) 95% of the time, the true difference would be within two points of the difference we observed; and (c) 99% of the time, the true difference would be within three points of the difference we observed. Therefore, if our two sample means (the control group mean and the experimental group mean) differed by more than three points, we would be confident that the treatment had an effect. In other words, we would be confident that the groups were samples from populations that had different means. Therefore, we would conclude that if all the participants had received the treatment, their mean score would be different than if they had all been in the control condition.

If, however, we observed a difference of 1.0, we realize that such a difference might well reflect random error, rather than the groups coming from different populations. That is, with a difference of 1.0 and a standard error of the difference of 1.0, we could not disprove the null hypothesis. In other words, we would not be able to conclude that the treatment had an effect.

How Differences Are Distributed: The Small Sample Case. Although the distribution of differences would be normally distributed if you used large enough samples, your particular experiment probably will not use enough participants. Therefore, you must rely on a more conservative distribution, especially designed for small samples: the *t* distribution.

Actually, the *t* distribution is a family of distributions. The member of the *t* distribution family that you use depends on the sample size. That is, with a sample size of 10, you will use a different *t* distribution than with a sample size of 11.

The larger your sample size, the more the *t* distribution will be shaped like the normal distribution. The smaller your sample size, the more spread out your *t* distribution will be (see Figure D-3). Thus, with small samples, a difference between means of more than two standard errors of the difference might not be statistically significant (whereas such a difference would be significant with a large sample).

Figure D-3 **With Larger Samples, *t* Distributions Approximate the Normal Curve**

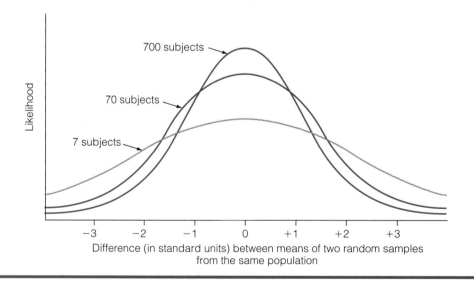

Difference (in standard units) between means of two random samples from the same population

Although the particular *t* distribution you use depends on sample size, you do not determine which particular *t* distribution to use by counting how many participants you have. Instead, you determine how many degrees of freedom (*df*) you have.

To calculate your degrees of freedom, simply subtract 2 from the number of participants in your experiment. For example, if you had 32 participants, your *df* would be 30 (because $32 - 2 = 30$).

Executing the *t* Test

You now understand that the difference between your experimental group mean and control group mean could be due to random error. You also realize that to estimate the chances that a difference between means could be due to random error, you need to do two things.

First, you need to compare the difference between the means to the standard error of the difference. In other words, you need to find out how far apart—*in terms of standard errors of the difference*—the two group means are.

Second, you need to use a *t* distribution to figure out how likely it is that two means could differ by that many standard errors of the difference. The particular *t* distribution you will use depends on your degrees of freedom.

Now that you understand the basic logic behind the *t* test, you're ready to do one. Start by subtracting the means of your two groups. Then, divide this difference by the standard error of the difference (see Box D-3). The number you will get is called a *t* ratio. Thus, *t* = difference between means/standard error of the difference. Less technically, the *t* ratio is simply the difference between your sample means divided by an index of random error.

Once you have your *t* ratio and your degrees of freedom, refer to a *t* table to see whether your *t* ratio is significant. Specifically, you would look under the row corresponding to your degrees of freedom. As we mentioned before, the degrees of freedom are two fewer than the number of participants. Thus, if you studied 32 participants, you would look at the *t* table in Appendix E under the row labeled 30 *df*.

When comparing the *t* ratio you calculated to the value in the table, act like your *t* ratio is positive. That is, even if you have a negative *t* ratio, treat it as if it is a positive *t* ratio. In other words, take the absolute value of your *t* ratio.

If the absolute value of your *t* ratio is not bigger than the number in the table, then your results are not statistically significant at the $p < .05$ level. If, on the other hand, the absolute

---

BOX D-3 Calculating the Between-Subjects *t* Test for Equal-Sized Groups

$$t = \frac{\text{Group 1 Mean} - \text{Group 2 Mean}}{\text{Standard Error of the Difference}}$$

And where the standard error of the difference can be calculated in either of the following 2 ways:

1.

$$\sqrt{\frac{S_1^2}{N_1} + \frac{S_2^2}{N_2}}$$

Where S_1 = standard deviation of Group 1 (see Box D-1), S_2 = standard deviation of Group 2, N_1

equals number of participants in Group 1, and N_2 equals number of participants in Group 2.

2.

$$\sqrt{\frac{SS \text{ Group 1} + SS \text{ Group 2}}{N - 2} \times (1/N_1 + 1/N_2)}$$

Where *SS* equals the sum of squares (see Box D-1), N_1 equals the number of participants in Group 1, N_2 equals the number of participants in Group 2, and *N* equals the total number of participants.

value of your t ratio is bigger than the number in the table, then your results are statistically significant at the $p < .05$ level.

If your results are statistically significant at the $p < .05$ level, there's less than a 5% chance that the difference between your groups is solely due to chance. Consequently, you can be reasonably sure that your treatment had an effect. You might report your results as follows: "As predicted, the experimental group's mean recall (8.12) was significantly higher than the control group's (4.66), $t(30) = 3.10, p < .05$."

ANOVA: Analyzing Data From a Multiple-Group Experiment

To analyze data from a multiple-group experiment, most researchers use analysis of variance. To use analysis of variance, as was the case with the t test, you must meet the following criteria.

1. Your observations must be independent.
2. Each of your groups should have approximately the same variance.
3. Your scores should be normally distributed.
4. You must be able to assume that your data are either interval or ratio.

In analysis of variance, you set up the **F-ratio:** a ratio of the between-groups variance to the within-groups variance. Or, to use proper terminology, you set up a ratio of mean square between (MSB) to mean square within (MSW).

To calculate mean square within groups, you must first calculate the sum of squares for each group. You must subtract each score from its group mean, square each of those differences, and then add up all those squared differences. If you had the following three groups, your first calculations would be as follows.

	GROUP 1	GROUP 2	GROUP 3
	5	6	14
	4	5	12
	3	4	10
Group Mean:	4	5	12

Sum of Squares Within for Group 1:

$$(5 - 4)^2 + (4 - 4)^2 + (3 - 4)^2 = (1)^2 + (0)^2 + (-1)^2 = 1 + 0 + 1 = 2$$

Sum of squares within for Group 2:

$$(6 - 5)^2 + (5 - 5)^2 + (4 - 5)^2 = (1)^2 + (0)^2 + (-1)^2 = 1 + 0 + 1 = 2$$

Sum of squares within for Group 3:

$$(14 - 12)^2 + (12 - 12)^2 + (10 - 12)^2 = (2)^2 + (0)^2 + (-2)^2 = 4 + 0 + 4 = 8$$

To get the sum of squares within groups, you add (sum) all of these sums of squares together $(2 + 2 + 8 = \mathbf{12})$.

To get the mean square within groups, you divide the sum of squares within groups (SSW) by the within-groups' degrees of freedom. In a multiple-group experiment, the within-groups' degrees of freedom equals the number of participants − number of groups.

You had 9 participants and 3 groups. Therefore, your within-groups' degrees of freedom is 6 (because $9 - 3 = 6$). In this case, because your sum of squares within is 12 and your within-groups degrees of freedom is 6, your *MSW* is 2 (12/6).

To get the mean square between groups, calculate the variance of the group means as follows:

Calculate the mean of the group means $(4 + 5 + 12)/3 = 21/3 = 7$.

Subtract each group mean from the overall mean and square each difference:

$$4 - 7 = -3; -3 \text{ squared} = 9$$
$$5 - 7 = -2; -2 \text{ squared} = 4$$
$$12 - 7 = 5; 5 \text{ squared} = 25$$

Add up all these squared differences $(25 + 9 + 4 = 38)$.

Divide this term by one less than the number of groups. Since you have three groups, divide by two.

So, your variance among groups is 19 ($38/2 = 19$).

To transform your variance among groups to a mean square between, multiply it by the number of participants in each group. In this case, you have three participants per group, so you multiply 19×3 and get 57.

Your *F* ratio is the ratio of mean square between (*MSB*) to mean square within (*MSW*). In this case, your *MSB* is 57 and your *MSW* is 2. Therefore, your *F* ratio is 57/2, or 28.5.

Thus, at this point, your ANOVA summary table would look like this:

SOURCE OF VARIANCE	SUM OF SQUARES	DEGREES OF FREEDOM	MEAN SQUARE	F RATIO
Treatment	?	?	57	28.5
Error	12	6	2	

To fill in the rest of the table, you need to know the sum of squares treatment and the degrees of freedom for the treatment. The degrees of freedom for the treatment are one less than the number of groups. Because you have 3 groups, your *df* for the treatment is 2. To get the sum of squares for the treatment, simply multiply the *df* for the treatment by the mean square for the treatment ($2 \times 57 = 114$).

Thus, your completed ANOVA summary table would look like this:

SOURCE OF VARIANCE	SUM OF SQUARES	DEGREES OF FREEDOM	MEAN SQUARE	F RATIO
Treatment	114	2	57	28.5
Error	12	6	2	

To determine whether the *F* of 28.5 is significant at the $p < .05$ level, you would look in the *F* table (Appendix E, Table E-3) for the critical *F* value for 2 degrees of freedom in the numerator and 6 degrees of freedom in the denominator. If 28.5 is larger than that value, the results would be statistically significant.

Analyzing Data From the Two-Condition Within-Subjects Experiment (or the Matched-Pairs Design): The Dependent *t* Test

If you are comparing two conditions (treatment and no treatment), but your observations are not independent, you cannot use the independent groups *t* test. Your treatment and no-treatment scores would not be independent if they both came from the same subject (as in a within-subjects design). Nor would they be independent if you used a matched-pairs design.

If you are using a two-condition within-subjects design (or a matched-pairs design) and you have interval data, you could analyze your data with a dependent groups (within-subjects) t test. The formula for the dependent t boils down to dividing the average difference between the conditions by the standard error of the difference. However, to calculate the t by hand, you need to execute the following seven steps.

STEP 1: For each matched pair (in the matched-pairs design) or for each participant (in the two-condition, within-subjects design), subtract the Condition 2 score from the Condition 1 score.

PAIR OR PARTICIPANT	CONDITION 1 SCORE	CONDITION 2 SCORE	DIFFERENCE
1	3	2	1
2	4	3	1
3	5	4	1
4	2	1	1
5	3	2	1
6	5	2	3
7	5	2	3
8	4	3	1
9	3	4	−1
10	5	6	−1

SUM OF DIFFERENCES = 10

AVERAGE DIFFERENCE = 10/10 = 1

STEP 2: Sum up the differences between each pair of scores, then divide by the number of pairs of scores to get the average difference.

STEP 3: Calculate the variance for the differences by subtracting each difference from the average difference. Square each of those differences, sum them up, and divide by one less than the number of pairs of scores.

PAIR OR PARTICIPANT	AVERAGE DIFFERENCE (AD)	OBSERVED DIFFERENCE (D)	AD − D	AD − D SQUARED
1	1	1	0	0
2	1	1	0	0
3	1	1	0	0
4	1	1	0	0
5	1	1	0	0
6	1	3	−2	4
7	1	3	−2	4
8	1	1	0	0
9	1	−1	2	4
10	1	−1	2	4

TOTAL SUM OF SQUARES = 16

VARIANCE OF DIFFERENCES = SUM OF SQUARES/$N-1$ = 16/9 = 1.77

STEP 4: Take the square root of the variance of the differences to get the standard deviation of the differences.

$$\text{Standard deviation of the differences} = \sqrt{\text{variance of the differences}} = \sqrt{1.77} = 1.33$$

STEP 5: Get the standard error of the difference by dividing the standard deviation of the differences by the square root of the number of pairs of scores.

$$\frac{\text{Standard deviation of the differences}}{\sqrt{N}} = \frac{1.33}{\sqrt{10}} = .42$$

STEP 6: Set up the t ratio by dividing the average difference by the standard error of the difference.

$$t = \frac{AD}{SED} = \frac{1}{.42} = 2.38$$

STEP 7: Calculate the degrees of freedom by subtracting 1 from the number of pairs of scores. In this example, because we have 10 pairs of scores, we have 9 degrees of freedom. Then, compare your obtained t value to the t value needed to be statistically significant. That value is listed in Table E-1 of Appendix E. In this case, the t value needed to be significant at the .05 level with 9 degrees of freedom is 2.262. Because our value (2.380) is higher than that, our results are statistically significant at the $p < .05$ level.

Correlational Analyses

If you are examining the relationship between scores on two or more variables, you may decide to use a correlational analysis. The type of analysis you use will depend not only on your goals, but also on whether your data are at least interval scale.

If you want to describe your data—and you have interval data—you would probably compute a Pearson r. If, on the other hand, your data are ordinal, you may choose to describe the relationship between your variables using a phi coefficient.

If you want to make inferences about whether a relationship exists in the population, the type of test you should use depends on your data. If you have interval data, you should determine whether the Pearson r between the variables is significantly different from zero. If, on the other hand, you have nominal data, you should do a chi-square test. In the next few sections, we will show you how to perform these tests.

Computing the Pearson r

If two variables are related, you can describe that relationship with a scatterplot. However, if both variables are interval-scale variables, you will probably also want to know what the Pearson r correlation coefficient is between the two variables.

The formula for the Pearson r is

$$\frac{\Sigma XY - [(\Sigma X \times \Sigma Y)/N]}{N \times sd\,x \times sd\,y}$$

where ΣX = the sum of all the scores on the first variable, ΣY = the sum of all the scores on the second variable, $\Sigma X \times Y$ = multiplying each pair of scores together and then adding up all those products, N = number of participants, $sd\,x$ = standard deviation of the x scores (the first set of scores), and $sd\,y$ = standard deviation of the y scores (the second set of scores).

This formula for the Pearson r makes sense once you realize three important facts.

1. The formula must produce an index of the degree to which two variables (which we will denote as X and Y) vary together.

2. The formula must produce positive numbers when the variables are positively correlated, negative numbers when the variables are inversely related, and the number zero when the variables are unrelated.

3. The formula must produce numbers between -1 and $+1$. That is, the formula can't produce numbers above $+1$ (or below -1), no matter how many scores there are and no matter how large those scores may be.

Because the Pearson r is an index of the degree to which two variables vary together, each pair of scores is multiplied together. Specifically, the X member of each pair is multiplied by the Y member of the pair. We then add up all these $X \times Y$ products.

However, correlation coefficients may be negative. Indeed, if X and Y are inversely related, Pearson r should indicate that by being negative. But if X and Y are both always positive (height and salary), how can we obtain a negative number? If both variables are always positive, we would obviously never get a negative number if all we did was multiply X times Y for each pair of scores and then added up those products. Thus, there must be more to the formula for correlation coefficients than just adding up all the $X \times Y$ products.

How can we obtain a negative number if X and Y are both always positive? To allow ourselves to get negative numbers when the variables are negatively (inversely) related, we subtract a number from the sum of the $X \times Y$ products. That number is an estimate of what the sum of all the $X \times Y$ products would have been if the two sets of scores were completely unrelated. Thus, if the variables are positively related, subtracting this estimate will still leave us with a positive number. If the variables are not related, subtracting this estimate will leave us with zero. If the variables are inversely related, subtracting this estimate from the actual product of $X \times Y$ will result in a negative number.

To this point, we have a formula that can produce positive and negative numbers. The formula does not, however, meet our final criterion for the correlation coefficient: Coefficients must always be between -1 and $+1$. The numbers produced by our incomplete version of the correlation formula might be far outside of the -1 to $+1$ range, especially if

1. we have many pairs of scores

2. the scores are extremely spread out

The more XY pairs there are, the more scores there will be to add up and the larger the total will tend to be. Similarly, the more spread out the scores, the more extreme the products of the scores can be. For example, if scores range from 1 to 5 on both variables, the individual $X \times Y$ products cannot be greater than 25 (because $5 \times 5 = 25$). However, if the scores on both variables can range from 1 to 10, the $X \times Y$ products can be as large as 100 (10×10).

You have seen that our incomplete formula would produce "correlation coefficients" that would be far outside the -1 to $+1$ boundaries of conventional correlation coefficients. More importantly, the correlation coefficients would be influenced by two factors that have nothing to do with the extent to which two variables are related to each other: (a) the number of pairs and (b) the variability (spread) of the distributions. Therefore, we need to add one more step to our formula. Specifically, we need to take the number we have obtained so far and divide it by an index composed of (a) the number of XY pairs, (b) a measure of the variability of the X scores (the first set of scores), and (c) a measure of the variability of the Y scores (the second set of scores).

By adding this final step, you now have a formula that will produce a correlation coefficient that will range between −1 and +1, regardless of whether you compute a correlation based on 5 pairs or 5,000 pairs and regardless of whether participants' raw scores range from 1.5 to 1.6 or from 200 to 200,000.

Thus, as we stated before, one formula for the Pearson r is:

$$\frac{\Sigma XY - [(\Sigma X \times \Sigma Y)/N]}{N \times sd\,x \times sd\,y}$$

where N = number of participants, $sd\,x$ = standard deviation of the x scores (the first set of scores), and $sd\,y$ = standard deviation of the y scores (the second set of scores).

To see this formula in action, imagine that you collected data from five students at your school on self-esteem (X) and grade-point average (Y). Furthermore, assume that self-esteem and grade-point average are interval-scale variables. To see if the variables were related, you would use the following steps to compute a Pearson r.

STEP 1: List each pair of scores in the following manner:

	SCORE FOR X	SCORE FOR Y	X TIMES Y
First pair of scores	1	1	1
Second pair of scores	2	2	4
Third pair of scores	3	2	6
Fourth pair of scores	4	4	16
Fifth pair of scores	5	3	15
	15	12	**42**

STEP 2: Sum the scores in each column.

STEP 3: Calculate the means for variables X and Y.

$$15/5 = 3 \qquad 12/5 = 2.4$$
$$\text{(Mean of } X) \qquad \text{(Mean of } Y)$$

STEP 4: Calculate the sum of squares (SS) for variables X and Y.

$(X - \overline{X})^2$	$(Y - \overline{Y})2$
$(1 - 3)^2$	$(1 - 2.4)^2$
$(2 - 3)^2$	$(2 - 2.4)^2$
$(3 - 3)^2$	$(2 - 2.4)^2$
$(4 - 3)^2$	$(4 - 2.4)2^2$
$(5 - 3)^2$	$(3 - 2.4)^2$
10	**5.2**

STEP 5: Calculate the variance for X and Y (Variance = SS/N).

$$10/5 = 2.0 \qquad 5.2/5 = 1.04$$

STEP 6: Calculate the standard deviations for X and Y (sd = square root of the variance).

$$\sqrt{2.0} = 1.41 \qquad \sqrt{1.04} = 1.02$$

STEP 7: Multiply the sum of X by the sum of Y. Then, divide by the number of pairs.

$$(15 \times 12)/5 = 180/5 = \mathbf{36}$$

STEP 8: Subtract the result that we calculated in Step 7 (36) from the sum of $X \times Y$ that we calculated in Step 1 (42).

$$42 - \mathbf{36} = 6$$

STEP 9: Divide the result (6) by the number of pairs times the standard deviation of X times the standard deviation of Y.

$$6/(5 \times 1.41 \times 1.02) = .83$$

Calculating the Coefficient of Determination

One problem with correlation coefficients is that they give you only a rough idea of the strength of the relationship between two variables. For example, if you compared a relationship described by a correlation of .1 with a relationship described by a correlation of .5, you would probably not immediately realize that the .5 relationship was 25 times stronger than the .1 relationship. Squaring the correlation coefficient gives you a better index of the strength of the relationship: the **coefficient of determination.**

The coefficient of determination represents the degree to which knowing a participant's score on one variable helps you know (determine) the participant's score on the other variable. The coefficient of determination can range from 0 (knowing participants' scores on one variable is absolutely no help in guessing what their scores will be on the other variable) to $+1.00$ (knowing participants' scores on one variable allows you to know exactly what their scores will be on the other variable).

If you had a correlation of $+1$, you would have a coefficient of determination of 1 (because $+1 \times +1 = 1.00$). Similarly, if you had a correlation coefficient of -1, you would have a coefficient of determination of 1 (because $-1 \times -1 = 1.00$). Thus, with either a $+1$ or -1 correlation coefficient, if you know a participant's score on one variable, you can predict that person's score on the other variable with 100% (1.00) accuracy.

Essentially, the coefficient of determination tells you the amount of scatter in your scatterplot. If the coefficient of determination is near 1, there is little scatter in your scatterplot. If you draw a straight line through your scatterplot, most of the points would be on or near that line. If, on the other hand, the coefficient of determination is near zero, there is a lot of scatter in your scatterplot. If you draw a straight line through the scatterplot of that data, very few of the points will be close to your straight line.[1]

To get a better idea of what the coefficient of determination indicates, imagine the following scenario. Participants take a test. The average score for those participants is 30. For each participant, the researcher has recorded the participant number ("1" for the first participant, "2" for the second, etc.) and the participant's score on the test. The researcher plots these data. As you can see from Figure D-4 (and the researcher confirms by computing a correlation coefficient), there is no relationship between participant number and participant test score.

---

[1]There are two cases in which you can have a zero correlation and yet draw a line through all the points: (1) when the line goes straight up and (2) when the line goes straight across the graph. However, you could draw such lines only when there was no variability in scores for one of the variables. In our self-esteem and grade-point average example, you would have a zero correlation if all your participants scored a 5 on the self-esteem measure (producing a vertical line). You would also get a zero correlation if all your participants had a 3.0 grade-point average (producing a horizontal line).

Plot Indicating No Relationship Between Participant Number and Scores

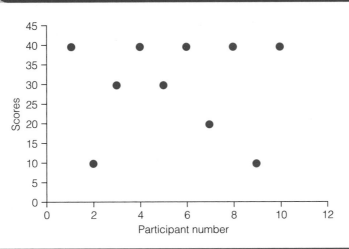

As Shown by This Best Fitting Prediction (Regression) Line, Predicting the Mean Is the Best Strategy When the Predictor Is Not Correlated With the Outcome Variable

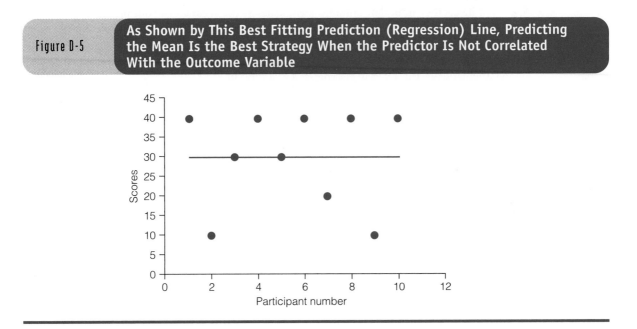

The researcher then asks you to predict people's scores on the test knowing only the average score (30). For every participant, you should guess "30." The researcher could represent your predictions as a line that went across the graph (see Figure D-5).

To see how far off your guesses were, the researcher could look at the distance between each of the data points and your prediction line. To assign you a score that would provide a rough index of how far off your estimates were, the researcher could (a) measure the difference between each participant's point and the prediction line, (b) square each of those differences, and then (c) add (sum) up all those squared differences. If your guesses had been perfectly accurate, the researcher would have obtained a score of 0 on this crude index.

However, your guesses were not perfect: You obtained a score of 1,000 on the researcher's makeshift index of inaccuracy.

Next, the researcher asks you to predict the scores again, but this time gives you a piece of worthless information (the participant's number). If you had to guess what a certain person's score was, you would not base your guess on the worthless information. Instead, you would again guess the mean: "30." For every participant, you should guess "30." Your prediction line would be the same as before and your score on her unsophisticated index of inaccuracy would still be 1,000.

What you are doing now is **regression:** you are using your knowledge of how two variables are associated to predict one from the other. Your prediction line is a regression line. Your goal in regression is for your predicted scores to match the actual scores. In other words, your predicted scores should match the actual scores on two key characteristics: (1) the mean of your predicted scores should be the same as the mean of the actual scores, and (2) your predicted scores should vary around the mean to the same extent that the actual scores vary around the mean. In this case, you accomplished the first goal: the mean of your predicted scores is the same as the mean of the actual scores. However, you failed miserably at the second goal: Your predicted scores are all the same as the mean (30) so they do not vary around the mean at all.

The coefficient of determination would assess the accuracy of your predictions by looking at *the percent of variance accounted for by the relationship between the predictor and the scores to be predicted.* What this means is that the coefficient of determination assesses the accuracy of predictions by looking at the overlap between the predicted scores and the actual scores. Mathematically, this overlap is expressed as a ratio of

$$\frac{\text{how much your predicted scores vary around the mean}}{\text{how much the actual scores vary around the mean}}$$

In this case, your accuracy, as measured by the coefficient of determination, is

$$\frac{0 \text{ (none of your predicted scores vary from the mean)}}{\text{how much the actual scores vary around the mean}} = 0$$

Ideally, you would like perfect accuracy: You would like your predicted scores to perfectly match up with the actual scores in terms of both mean and variation around the mean. If the variability of the predicted scores was the same as the variability of the actual scores, your ratio of predicted variance to actual variance—and your coefficient of determination—would be 1. For example, if the actual variance was 6, and the variance of your predicted scores was also 6,

$$\frac{6}{6} = 1$$

Although it may be unrealistic to expect perfect predictions that account for all the variance in scores, you would like to make predictions that account for some of the variance in the scores and are thus better than just guessing the mean. To make better predictions, you need a predictor that correlates with test scores. The more that predictor is correlated with test scores, the more your estimates will improve. As you can see from Table D-1, if the r between your predictor and the test is .1 or even .2, knowing the person's scores on the predictor reduces the error in your guesses only slightly. Even with an r of .2, your score on her particular index of inaccuracy would still be practically 1,000—what it was when you guessed "30" (the mean) for everybody's score.

| Table D-1 | Pearson *r*, the Coefficient of Determination, and Errors in Prediction |

r[a]	r^2 (ALSO CALLED η^2)	INDEX OF INACCURACY[b]
0	.00	1000
.1	.01	990
.2	.04	960
.3	.09	910
.4	.16	840
.5	.25	750
.6	.36	640
.7	.49	510
.8	.64	360
.9	.81	190
1.0	1.00	0

[a]Note two indications that accuracy of prediction increases as *r* increases: (a) r^2 increases and (b) an index of inaccuracy decreases.

[b]The numbers in this column are the total of the squared errors in prediction you would make if you (a) based all your predictions of participants' scores entirely on a best-fitting prediction line that used one predictor, (b) that one predictor correlated with participants' scores to the degree stated in the leftmost ("*r*") column, and (c) you were predicting all the participants' scores for the one particular sample we used for this example. Lower scores indicate more accuracy (less inaccuracy), whereas higher scores indicate less accuracy (more inaccuracy). Thus, 0 on the index reflects perfect accuracy (no errors in prediction).

Put another way, correlations between −.2 and +.2 do little to improve the accuracy of predictions. As you can see from Table D-1, an *r* of even .2 produces a coefficient of determination (r^2) that is very close to zero.

Determining Whether a Pearson *r* Is Statistically Significant

In addition to determining whether the relationship between your variables in the sample data is substantially above zero, you may want to determine whether the relationship between the variables is different from zero in the population. To illustrate why you might want to determine whether the Pearson *r* in the sample data indicates that the two variables are related in the population, suppose you collected self-esteem and grade-point average data from a random sample of students at your school. In that case, you could use your sample data to determine whether there is a relationship between self-esteem and grade-point average for the entire school. All you would have to do is determine whether the observed Pearson *r* is significantly different from zero by following the following steps . In this case, let's suppose that $r = +.58$ and there were five participants.

STEP 1: Compute a *t* value, using the formula

$$t = \frac{r \times \sqrt{(N-2)}}{\sqrt{1 - (r \times r)}}$$

where $r =$ the Pearson *r* and $N =$ number of participants.

Note that, all other things being equal, the bigger *N* is, the bigger *t* will be. Also, note that the bigger *r* is, the bigger *t* will tend to be. Not only does a larger *r* increase the size of the numerator, but it shrinks the size of the denominator. In other words, the larger the relationship and the more participants you have, the greater the chance of finding a statistically significant result.

$$t = \frac{.58 \times \sqrt{(5 - 2)}}{\sqrt{1 - (.58 \times .58)}}$$

$$= \frac{.58 \times 1.73}{\sqrt{1 - .34}}$$

$$= \frac{1.00}{.81} = 1.23$$

STEP 2: After computing the t value, look the value up in the t table (Table E-1 in Appendix E) under 3 degrees of freedom ($N - 2$) for the .05 level of significance. That value is 3.182. Because 1.23 does not reach that value, you would conclude that the correlation coefficient was not significantly greater than zero.

Computing a 2 × 2 Chi-Square and the Phi Coefficient

Calculating the Pearson r is a good way to describe the relationship between two interval-scale variables in your sample. Similarly, testing whether a Pearson r is statistically significant is a good way to determine whether the results in the sample would hold for the population.

But what if you do not have interval data? Even if you only have nominal data, you can conduct similar types of analyses using the chi-square and the phi coefficient.

Suppose you asked men and women whether they believed gay men deserved the same employment opportunities as heterosexual men. If you wanted to know whether there was a gender difference in their responses, you could find out by calculating a chi-square using the following steps.

STEP 1: Set up a table like the following one.

	WOMEN	MEN	TOTAL
Yes		A	B
No		C	D

(N) = Total **N**umber of participants

STEP 2: Replace the letter A with the number of women who said "yes."

Replace the letter B with the number of men who said "yes."

Replace the letter C with the number of women who said "no."

Replace the letter D with the number of men who said "no."

Replace N with the total number of participants.

By the end of this process, your table might look like the following one.

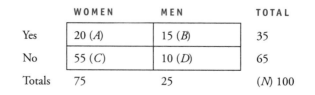

	WOMEN	MEN	TOTAL
Yes	20 (A)	15 (B)	35
No	55 (C)	10 (D)	65
Totals	75	25	(N) 100

STEP 3: Multiply the number in the (B) square by the number in the (C) square. Then, multiply the number in the (A) square by the number in the (D) square. For our data, that would be

$$B \times C = 15 \times 55 = 825$$
$$A \times D = 20 \times 10 = 200$$

STEP 4: Plug in the appropriate numbers in the following formula:

$$X^2 = \frac{N(B \times C - A \times D)^2}{(A + B) \times (C + D) \times (A + C) \times (B + D)}$$

$$= \frac{100(825 - 200)^2}{35 \times 65 \times 75 \times 25}$$

$$= \frac{100 \times 390{,}625}{4{,}265{,}625} = \frac{39{,}062{,}500}{4{,}265{,}625}$$

STEP 5: Turn to the Chi-Square Table (Table E-2 in Appendix E), and find the row corresponding to 1 degree of freedom. (For a 2 × 2 chi-square, your degrees of freedom will always be 1 because df equals the number of rows minus 1, times the number of columns minus 1.)

STEP 6: Determine whether your chi-square is one-tailed or two-tailed. If you predicted only that the groups would differ, then you have a two-tailed test. For example, if you predicted only that there would be a difference between the genders in views toward gay men's employment rights, you have a two-tailed test. If, on the other hand, you predicted which group would score higher than the other, then you have a one-tailed test. Thus, if you predicted that men were less likely to think that gay men should have equal employment opportunities, then you have a one-tailed test.

STEP 7: If you have a two-tailed test with a value of 3.84 or more, your test is significant at the .05 level. Our value of 7.937 exceeds that value, so our test would be significant at the .05 level.

To compute the phi coefficient, use the following formula:

$$\frac{B \times C - A \times D}{\sqrt{(A + B) \times (C + D) \times (A + C) \times (B + D)}}$$

In this case,

$$\frac{825 - 200}{\sqrt{4{,}265{,}625}} = 30$$

Introduction to Multiple Regression

Thus far, we have used correlational analyses to look at the relationship between two variables. However, some correlational analyses, such as multiple regression, can be used to look at the relationships among several variables. With most standard regression analyses, you end up with an equation that uses one or more predictors to predict scores on a question or measure. For example, suppose that you conducted a survey composed exclusively of 5-point questions and you want to find a set of predictors that will help you predict the answer to question 6. If only one of the predictors is useful, your regression equation might be *the answer to question 5 = the predicted score on question 6*. By substituting the possible values of question 5 into the equation, we could make use of that equation to construct the following table:

PARTICIPANT'S SCORE ON QUESTION 5	PARTICIPANT'S PREDICTED SCORE ON QUESTION 6 (Y)	PARTICIPANT'S ACTUAL SCORE ON QUESTION 6 (Y)	DIFFERENCE (RESIDUALS)
1	1	1	0
2	2	2	0
3	3	3	0
4	4	4	0
5	5	5	0

If we wanted to compare predicted scores (column 3 of our table) to the actual scores (column 4 of our table), we could subtract those two sets of scores. The differences between the predicted and actual scores are called residuals.

We could also compare the predicted scores to the actual scores with a graph. If we plotted a line based on the scores predicted by the equation (the numbers in the third column of our table), and then plotted the actual scores (the numbers in the fourth column of our table), we would construct the following graph:

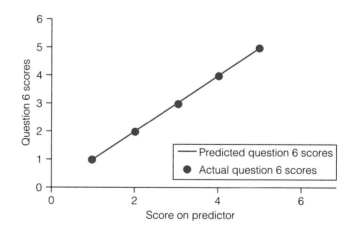

If two of your predictors were useful, your equation might be *2/3 × the answer to question 5 + 1/3 × the predicted answer to question 10 = the predicted score on question 6*. By substituting the possible values for questions 5 and 10 into the equation, we could use that equation to create the following table:

PARTICIPANT'S SCORE ON QUESTION 5	PARTICIPANT'S SCORE ON QUESTION 10	PARTICIPANT'S PREDICTED SCORE ON QUESTION 6	PARTICIPANT'S ACTUAL SCORE ON QUESTION 6
1	1	1.00	1.00
1	2	1.33	1.33
1	3	1.67	1.67
1	4	2.00	2.00
1	5	2.33	2.33
2	1	1.67	1.67
2	2	2.00	2.00
2	3	2.33	2.33
2	4	2.67	2.67
2	5	3.00	3.00
3	1	2.33	2.33
3	2	2.67	2.67
3	3	3.00	3.00
3	4	3.33	3.33
3	5	3.67	3.67
4	1	3.00	3.00
4	2	3.33	3.33
4	3	3.67	3.67
4	4	4.00	4.00
4	5	4.33	4.33
5	1	3.67	3.67
5	2	4.00	4.00
5	3	4.33	4.33
5	4	4.67	4.67
5	5	5.00	5.00

Alternatively, we could use the equation and the actual scores (the last two columns of the table) to construct the following graph:

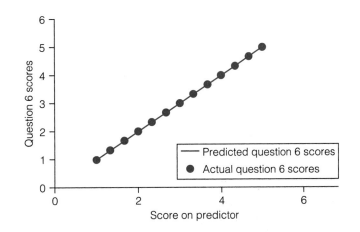

The line that we have drawn through the points is called a regression line. If you have the computer draw a regression line for your data, the line should appear to fit those data: The line's predicted scores should be close to the actual scores. If you could perfectly predict scores, every data point would be on your regression line (as in the two previous examples). If your equation was fairly accurate, then most of the points would be close to your regression line. If your equation was not very accurate, then the line would not fit the points.

You will not need to eyeball your data to determine how accurate your regression equation is. Almost all computerized statistics programs will provide an indicator of how accurate your equation is. This estimate of how well your predictors, as a group, predict your outcome measure is called "multiple R-squared." Multiple R-squared can range from 0 (using the regression equation to predict each participant's score would be no more accurate than predicting that each participant's score was the mean score) to 1 (your prediction equation can predict scores in your sample with 100% accuracy). (Note that most statistics programs will refer to multiple R-squared as either "R^2" or "R square.")

Most statistics programs will also provide you with an indication of which predictors are least important for predicting your outcome variable and which are most important. The least important predictors will tend to be left out of the final regression equation. The most important ones tend to be those that, when added to the equation, increase R-squared the most.[2]

How to Avoid Being Tricked by Multiple Regression

As we have said, computer programs can provide you with important information. However, that information may be misleading.

The equation that the computer generates may be greatly affected by an extreme score from a single research participant. Consequently, the regression equation that you get in one sample may be very different from the one that you would get if you were to repeat your study. To determine whether a few extreme scores are dramatically affecting the equation, you should scan the data for extreme scores and re-run your analysis without those extreme scores.[3] If you obtain essentially the same results on this second analysis, you can be relatively confident that your results are not being thrown off by an extreme score.

The multiple r-squared can be deceiving because it will tend to give you an inflated impression of how well the predictors correlate with the outcome variable. Keep in mind that the equation did not really predict your outcome variable. Instead, it was built, after looking at your outcome variable, to fit the data from your particular sample. Thus, just as you would not be surprised if someone was able to draw a line to fit your plotted data, you should not be surprised if a computer could fit a line to your existing data. Given a large number of predictor variables and a small number of scores, a formula can be made to fit almost any set of scores.

It's like "the Texan who shoots holes in the side of the barn and then draws a bull's-eye around the bullet holes" (Carroll, 2003, p. 375). Consequently, you may find that a multiple r-squared that seems large (e.g., .50) is not statistically different from chance. Therefore, before deciding whether a regression equation can predict scores on your outcome variable, you should determine whether the multiple r-squared is statistically significant. To do this, look for an

---

[2]Another way to determine the relative contributions of your predictors is to look at their beta weights in the final, standardized regression formula. The larger the beta weight is (often referred to as unstandardized coefficients and often abbreviated as β), the bigger the predictor's contribution.

[3]You may be able to spot an extreme score in a graph of your data by just looking for scores that seem to be almost off the graph. Another tactic is to look for scores that are more than 3 standard deviations from the mean. If your computer program lists the h values or D values of data points, consider extreme scores to be those with h values above .5 or D values greater than 1.

F test (ANOVA) testing either "Model," "Regression," or "R^2." To be statistically significant, the p value of the test (often abbreviated as either "Sig." or "Prob $> F$") should be less than .05.

A significant multiple r-squared tells you that your equation does more than just capitalize on chance. It produces an equation that fits the data better than an equation that used variables that were uncorrelated with your outcome variable. In other words, if you were to use the same equation on a new sample of data, your multiple r^2 would be greater than 0. However, you probably want to know more than that your equation's r-squared, after adjusting for chance, is greater than zero. You want to know how much greater than zero. To find out, look at the adjusted r-squared. The adjusted r-squared subtracts a value from the multiple r-squared to take into the account that even an equation full of variables that were uncorrelated with the outcome variable could be made to produce values that would correlate with the outcome variable. In short, if you look at the multiple r-squared instead of the adjusted r-squared, you can be fooled about how well your regression equation predicts participants' scores.

In addition, you may be fooled about the relative importance of an individual predictor variable. The amount that a predictor increases r-squared often depends on (a) when it was entered into the equation and (b) whether related variables were already entered into the equation. For example, suppose we were doing a survey and trying to predict responses to item 11 (whether people strongly disagree, disagree, neither agree nor disagree, agree, or strongly agree with the statement: "I like college students"). Suppose agreement with item 6 ("College is stressful for students") significantly correlates with item 11. If item 6 was the first variable we entered into the equation, item 6 would significantly increase r-squared: It would make r-squared significantly greater than zero. Any variance accounted for by item 6 is unique variance because question 6 is the only variable in the equation.

If, on the other hand, we added item 6 to the equation only after entering all the other items as predictors, adding item 6 might not significantly improve our equation's ability to predict item 11 responses because (a) we already have a large r-squared so improving it significantly would be difficult and (b) some of the variability that item 6 could account for has already been eaten up by related, competing variables (especially if we had the following items: "Colleges need to spend more time on students' emotional development" and "College students work hard on their studies" that, like item 6, tap into concerns about college being stressful). Thus, if we looked at the "Model Summary" section of an SPSS printout, we might find that the "R Square Change" for our model with question 6 added was not significantly different from our model without question 6 (e.g., "Sig. F Change" was greater than .05). Similarly, if we looked under the "Coefficients" table in the printout, we might find that the variable we labeled "Question 6" was not significant (e.g., the "t" associated with question 6 was less than 2 and the "Sig." in the Question 6 column was greater than .05).

To better understand how a regression equation may mislead you about the relative importance of a predictor, realize that the regression equation is sensitive to the unique contribution of each predictor. In a way, the same things that would allow you to make a large and unique contribution to an electronic discussion list are the same things that allow a predictor to make a large and unique contribution to the equation. It is easier to make a large and unique contribution if you are one of the first to enter the discussion, just as it is easier for a predictor to have a large and significant effect if it is the first entered into the equation. It is also easier to make a large and unique contribution if your viewpoint is different from that of the people who have already entered the discussion. Thus, a comment that you make in one list might be unique and contribute much, whereas the same comment might seem redundant in another list. Similarly, whether a predictor appears to be relevant may depend on the other variables in the equation. In more technical terminology, intercorrelations among predictors (sometimes called collinearity or multicollinearity) can cause the regression equation to underestimate the strength of a particular predictor variable.

Therefore, before deciding that a variable is unimportant for predicting your outcome variable, there are two things you should do. First, look at the Pearson r between the potential predictor and (a) the outcome variable and (b) the predictors that did make it into the regression equation. You may find that the potential predictor correlates well with the outcome variable but was left out of the equation because it correlates highly with a predictor that is already in the equation. In such a case, you might see what happens when you enter your potential predictor variable into the regression equation while leaving out predictors that correlate highly with that variable. Second, see whether your computer program provides the variance-inflation factor (VIF) statistic. If the VIF is greater than 5, do not trust the equation's estimates about the relative importance of your predictors.

Using Regression to Test for Moderator Variables

Although the results from multiple regression can be misleading, multiple regression is a flexible technique that has many uses: It can even help you find a moderator variable. To understand how this works, you have to understand that a moderator variable means that the combination of two variables is related to the outcome measure in a way that could not be predicted from knowing only their individual relationships with the outcome measure.

To illustrate, suppose that (a) newly married couples who had positive expectations tended to be happier with the marriage than those who entered with negative expectations, and (b) couples who tended to be skilled at interacting with each other in a positive constructive manner were happier with the marriage than those who were not skilled. From these findings, we might create a crude regression-type equation in which we would say that a (expectations) + b (skills) = c (predicted marital happiness). To plug numbers into our equation, we could give couples a +1 for positive expectations but a −1 for negative expectations and a +1 for good skills but a −1 for poor skills. Thus, a couple with positive expectations (+1) and good skills (+1) would have a predicted score a +2 (1 + 1 = 2), whereas a couple with low expectations (−1) and poor skills (−1) would have a predictor score of −2 (−1 + −1 = −2). In this model, our prediction is just a function of adding the values of our individual variables. Thus, a couple with good skills (+1) and low (−1) expectations would get a 0. Let's say that this additive model predicted actual marital happiness with some degree of accuracy.

To see whether we had a moderator variable, we would need to see whether certain combinations of expectations and skills (e.g., positive expectations combined with positive skills) had effects that were beyond what we would get from just adding the values of the individual variables together. For example, suppose couples with positive expectations (+1) and positive skills (+1) did not score a 2 but instead scored a 3 on our marital happiness scale. Or, suppose that couples with negative expectations (−1) and negative skills (−1) did not score a −2 but instead scored a 0 on our marital happiness scale. In both cases, adding the individual, average values of the predictors does not give us the right predicted value. Put another way, both cases suggest that skills moderate expectations.

How could we get multiple regression to tell us that the combination of our predictors has a relationship with marital happiness that is more than—and different from—the sum of the predictors' individual relationships with marital happiness? The basic strategy would be to see whether adding a variable that represents the combination of the two variables can improve the equation. In this case, the goal would be to better predict marital satisfaction by changing the formula "expectation + skills = satisfaction" to "expectation + skills + combination of expectations and skills = satisfaction."

| Table D-2 | Two Regression Equations Predicting Marital Satisfaction on a –3 to +3 Scale | | | | |

COUPLE'S CHARACTERISTICS	A	B	A × B	FORMULA 1 PREDICTION (A + B)	FORMULA 2 PREDICTION (A + B + A × B)
Positive expectations Positive skills	1	1	+1	2	3
Positive expectations Negative skills	1	−1	−1	0	−1
Negative expectations Positive skills	−1	1	−1	0	−1
Negative expectations Negative skills	−1	−1	+1	−2	−1

Note: Column A refers to expectations (positive = +1, negative = −1) and that Column B refers to skills (positive = +1, negative = −1).

To get the term expressing the combination (interaction) of the two variables, we could multiply the scores of the individual variables together. Multiplying those values gives us a positive number when there is a match between expectations and skills (the combination of positive expectations with positive skills produces +1, as does the combination of negative expectations with negative skills) and a negative number when there is a mismatch between expectations and skills (positive expectations combined with negative skills produces a −1, as does negative expectations combined with positive skills). Thus, our new formula is not

$$a \text{ (expectations)} + b \text{ (skills)} = c, \text{ but rather}$$
$$a \text{ (expectations)} + b \text{ (skills)} + a \times b \text{ (combination of expectations and skills)} = c.$$

As you can see from Table D-2, the two equations make different predictions. If the formula including a term expressing the combination (interaction) of the two variables does a significantly better job of predicting actual marital happiness, you have solid evidence that skill is a moderator variable. As it turns out, McNulty and Karney (2004) found that an equation including the interaction (combination) term does do a better job of predicting actual marital happiness. Thus, skill does moderate the effect of expectations: Couples with positive skills are better off having high expectations, but couples with poor skills are better off having low expectations.

To help yourself understand how skill—or any other moderator variable—modifies the relationship between two other variables, you could go back and compute two correlation coefficients between those two other variables: (1) a correlation between the two other variables for those cases that are above the mean on the moderator variable and (2) a correlation between the two other variables for those cases that are below the mean on the moderator variable. For example, you might find that the correlation between expectations and marital happiness is +.30 for couples who have above average skills, but that the correlation between expectations and marital happiness is −.20 for couples who have below average skills.[4]

---

[4]To make the difference between the two correlations bigger, you could compare participants who were one standard deviation above the mean on the moderator variable. If you want to see whether the correlation coefficients are significantly different, go to this book's website to do the appropriate statistical test.

Using Multiple Regression to Look for Mediator Variables: Answering "How" Questions

Suppose that, instead of showing that you have found a moderator variable, you want to show that you have found a mediating variable: an inner mental or physiological process variable that is the mechanism for the relationship between two other variables. That is, you may want to show that your predictor variable (Variable 1) does not have a direct effect on your outcome variable (Variable 3), but instead affects a mediating variable (Variable 2) and that mediating variable, in turn, affects your outcome variable (Variable 3). How can you make the case for this chain of events?

To make the case that, like a chain reaction involving three dominoes, the first affects the second, which in turn, affects the third, you can use multiple regression. For example, take the finding that people who most believe in punishing criminals tend to score low on the need for cognition scale, a measure of how much people enjoy thinking (Sargent, 2004). You might suspect that the reason for this relationship is that people who (1) don't like to think (2) may not think of the cultural, environmental, and situational reasons for a person's behavior and therefore would have a (3) greater desire to punish the person for the person's behavior.

To see whether thinking about situational causes for behavior mediates the relationship between, need for cognition and punishment, you would measure all three variables. Then, you would go through Baron and Kenney's (1986) four steps (see Figure D-6):

1. You would establish that need for cognition was related to punishment by finding a significant correlation between those two variables. (If you were going to argue that knocking over the first domino causes the second domino to fall, which, in

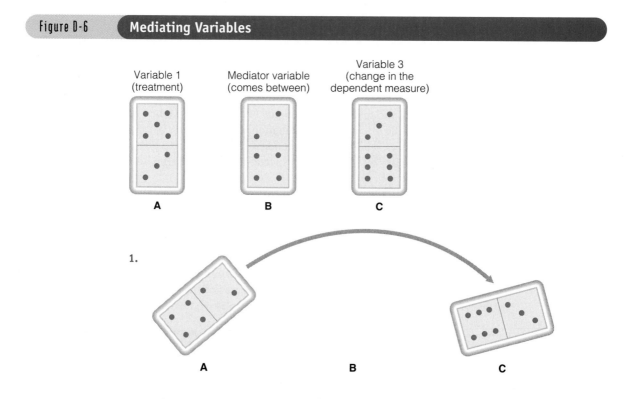

Figure D-6   **Mediating Variables**

Variable 1
(treatment)

Mediator variable
(comes between)

Variable 3
(change in the
dependent measure)

A   B   C

1.

A   B   C

Figure D-6 Mediating Variables (*continued*)

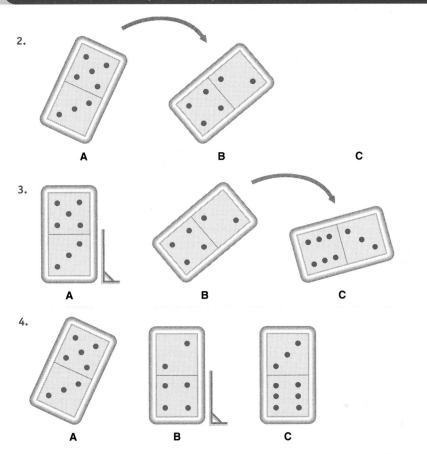

turn causes the third domino to fall, you would first have to show that knocking over the first domino correlates with the third domino falling. Similarly, if your predictor is going to influence the outcome variable, your predictor should correlate with the outcome variable.)

2. You would establish that need for cognition was related to your measure of thinking about situational, rather than personal, causes for behavior by finding a significant correlation between the two variables. (If you were going to argue that knocking over the first domino causes the second domino to fall, which, in turn causes the third domino to fall, you would have to show that knocking over the first domino correlates with the second domino falling. Similarly, if your predictor influences the outcome variable by influencing the mediator variable, your predictor should correlate with the mediating variable.)

3. You would show that your mediating variable has an effect beyond that of your predictor by showing that when you add your mediating variable (thinking about situational causes) to a regression equation that has already used your predictor (need for cognition), your mediating variable improves the equation's ability to

predict the amount of punishment a person gives. (If you were going to argue that knocking over the first domino causes the second domino to fall, which, in turn, causes the third domino to fall, you would have to show that, regardless of what happens to the first domino, knocking over the second domino causes the third domino to fall. Similarly, if your mediating variable causes changes in the outcome variable, it should be able to do independently of your predictor variable.)

4. You could argue that your predictor's effect is entirely through your mediating variable by showing that when you add your predictor (need for cognition) to an equation that has already used your mediator (thinking about situational causes), the predictor does not improve the equation's ability to predict the amount of punishment a person gives. (If you were going to argue that knocking over the first domino causes the second domino to fall, which, in turn causes the third domino to fall, you would have to show that, when you have already knocked down the second domino, there is no relationship between knocking down the first domino and the third domino falling. Similarly, if your predictor's effect is entirely through the mediating variable, the predictor variable will not have an effect that is independent of your mediating variable.)

Making the Case for Cause–Effect Relationships: Attempts to Answer "Why" Questions With Correlational Data

When we were discussing mediators, we were asking how a predictor variable had an effect. But first, we should first establish that the predictor variable had an effect. You might wonder how we knew that the predictor variable had an effect. Sometimes, we know because an experiment allowed us to establish it. But if we had only correlational data, how can researchers argue that the predictor had an effect on the outcome variable? After all, correlational techniques cannot establish cause–effect relationships because (1) with correlation, you do not know which variable came first so you can mistake causes for effects and (2) because both your variables may be effects of some other (third) variable, this third variable may be responsible for the relationship between your two variables. However, some researchers try to overcome these two problems with correlational data.

Researchers are sometimes able to establish which of their variables came first by using longitudinal and prospective methods—in which they measure a variable one time and then measure a second variable later. For example, if you collected individuals' scores on a mental health measure when they were 7 and then, 20 years later, you collected their college grade-point average, you know their college grade-point average could not have caused them to score poorly on a mental health measure when they were 7.

In terms of ruling out third variables, researchers may be able to rule out some third variables by statistically controlling for them. Usually, researchers would measure the suspected third variable and then try to rule out its effects using either a simple technique such as a partial correlation or ANCOVA or using a sophisticated technique such as structural equation modeling.

A partial correlation between two variables attempts to calculate the association between two variables when the effects of a third variable are accounted for. Thus, if the relationship between two variables (e.g., mother's skill at reading her child's mind and child's self-esteem) was due to a third variable (divorce leading to mothers being worse at reading their child's mind and divorce hurting a child's self-esteem), the partial correlation between mother's mind reading and child's self-esteem (controlling for divorce) would be zero.

In analysis of covariance (ANCOVA), a researcher might create two groups (children whose mothers were accurate mind readers and children whose mothers were poor mind readers) and use moms' self-esteem as a variable (a covariate) in the analysis. If, even after statistically controlling for moms' self-esteem, children of accurate mind readers had higher self-esteem than the children of poor mind readers, you could be confident that mom's self-esteem wasn't the third variable causing both poor mind reading and poor self-esteem. The problem is that you don't know whether there is some *other* third variable causing both poor mind reading and poor self-esteem.

Structural equation modeling (SEM) is better than ANCOVA or partial correlations at ruling out the effects of third variables. However, like ANCOVA and partial correlations, SEM can account for only third variables that the researcher knew about and measured. Furthermore, SEM, like ANCOVA and partial correlations, can confuse cause and effect. For example, if the child's high self-esteem causes the mother's accurate mind reading, all three methods might incorrectly conclude that the mother's accurate mind reading causes the child's high self-esteem.

In short, researchers cannot use correlational methods to make cause–effect statements. However, they can often make a better case that one variable has an effect on another by using logic and sophisticated statistical techniques than by using only correlation coefficients.

Introduction to Factor Analysis

We have shown you how researchers can use correlational analyses (a) to describe the relationship between two variables (with the Pearson r, the coefficient of determination, and the phi coefficient), (b) to determine whether two variables that were related in a sample are also related in the population (testing to see whether the Pearson r is statistically different from 0 or using the chi-square test), (c) to determine which combination of predictors allows you to best estimate scores on a measure, (d) to identify moderator variable, (e) to identify mediating variables, and (f) to make a case that one variable causes changes in another. However, we have not shown you a very common use of correlational analyses: to help assess the validity of a measure.

To see how this works, suppose you want to measure love, and you think that love has two different dimensions (sexual attraction and willingness to sacrifice for the other). Furthermore, you believe that these dimensions are relatively independent. For example, you believe that a person could be high on sexual attraction, but low on willingness to sacrifice—and vice versa.

One approach would be to make up a love scale that had two different subscales. If the subscales are really measuring two different things, then the following should apply:

1. A participant's answers to each question in the first subscale should correlate (correspond, agree) with each other.
2. A participant's answers to each question in the second subscale should correlate with each other.
3. A participant's score on the first subscale should not correlate highly with that participant's scores on the second subscale.

In our case, all the responses to items related to sexual attraction should correlate with one another, and all the responses to items related to sacrifice should correlate with one another. However, the sexual attraction items should not correlate highly with the sacrifice items.

A more sophisticated and extremely common approach to determining whether the items on a test correlate with each other is to do a factor analysis (Reis & Stiller, 1992). We can define *factor analysis* as a statistical technique designed to divide the many questions on a test into as few coherent groups as possible. Put another way, rather than explaining how participants answer the test by talking about how participants answer each individual question, factor analysis tries to explain participants' patterns of answers in terms of a smaller number of underlying hypothetical factors.

The logic behind factor analysis is straightforward: We assume that when participants' answers to one group of questions correlate with each other, then those questions all measure the same factor. For example, imagine that we have a 10-item test. In that test, participants answered the first six questions similarly: If we know how they answered one of those questions, we can make a reasonable prediction about how they answered the other five. Similarly, their responses to the last four items were highly correlated. However, their responses to the first six questions did not correlate very well with their answers to the last four questions. In such a case, factor analysis would say that because the test seems to be composed of two groups of items, the test measures two factors. In technical terminology, the first six items of the test would load on one factor, the last four items would load on another factor. Each question's *factor loading* tells us the degree to which it appears to be measuring a given factor.

Factor loadings, like correlation coefficients, can range from −1 to +1. Ideally, questions designed to measure a certain factor would have a factor loading of 1.0. However, because of unreliability and other measurement error, a question's factor loadings will usually be well below 1.0. Indeed, a factor loading of +.7 is considered very high and some researchers are happy when a question has a factor loading above +.3.

You have seen that factor analysis tries to find out how many factors are being measured by a test and how well individual questions measure those factors. But what results would you want to obtain from a factor analysis of your love scale? In this case, you would hope for two outcomes.

First, you would hope that the factor analysis supported the view that there were two different factors being measured by the test. You would be disappointed if the factor analysis reported that, based on participants' responses, your test seemed to be composed of three types of items. If the factor analysis supports the view that there are two factors, you might be able to report something like, "The two-factor solution accounts for a large amount (at least 60%) of the variability in participants' responses."

Second, you would hope that the factor analysis found that the items that you thought made up the sexual attraction subscale all corresponded to one factor and the items that made up the sacrifice subscale all corresponded to another factor. In technical terminology, you would hope that all the sexual attraction items loaded on one factor, and all the sacrifice items loaded on a different factor. Specifically, because factor loadings are like a correlation between the test question and the factor, you would want all your sexual attraction items to have high loadings (above .5) on the factor you want to label sexual attraction and near zero loadings on the factor that you want to label sacrifice. Conversely, you would want all your sacrifice items to have very low factor loadings on the factor that you want to label sexual attraction and high loadings on the factor you want to label sacrifice.

Statistics and Random Numbers Tables

Directions for Using Table E-1

Find the row labeled with the number of degrees of freedom that your study had (for the simple experiment, that number equals number of participants minus two). Then, unless you have a one-tailed test, read across until you find the column corresponding to your level of significance. The number in that cell will be the critical value of *t* for your study. To be statistically significant, the absolute value of *t* that you obtain from your study must be greater than the value you found in the table. For example, suppose $df = 40$ and $p < .05$ (two-tailed test). In that case, to be statistically significant, the absolute value of the *t* you calculated must be greater than 2.021.

Directions for Using Table E-2

Find the row that has the same number of degrees of freedom that your study had. (To calculate your *df*, subtract one from the number of columns in your chi-square, then subtract one from the number of rows, and then multiply those results together. Thus, with a 2×2 chi-square, you would have 1 *df* [because $1 \times 1 = 1$], and with a 3×2 chi-square, you would have 2 *df* [because $2 \times 1 = 2$]). Then, unless you have a one-tailed test, look across until you find the column corresponding to your level of significance. The number in that cell will be the critical value of chi-square for your study. To be statistically significant, your chi-square value must be greater than the value you found in the table. For example, if $df = 1$ and your significance level is $p < .05$, then your chi-square value must be greater than 3.84146.

Directions for Using Table E-3

Look up the degrees of freedom for the effect (the first *df*) and the error term (the second *df*). Thus, if you had 1 *df* for the effect and 25 for the error term, you would look under the column labeled "1" for the row labeled "25." There, you would find the critical value: 4.24. To be statistically significant at the $p < .05$ level, your obtained *F* would have to be greater than 4.24.

Table E-1 Critical Values of *T*

Level of Significance for Two-Tailed *t* Test

DF	.10	.05	.02	.01
1	6.314	12.706	31.821	63.657
2	2.920	4.303	6.965	9.925
3	2.353	3.182	4.541	5.841
4	2.132	2.776	3.747	4.604
5	2.015	2.571	3.365	4.032
6	1.943	2.447	3.143	3.707
7	1.895	2.365	2.998	3.499
8	1.860	2.306	2.896	3.355
9	1.833	2.262	2.821	3.250
10	1.812	2.228	2.764	3.169
11	1.796	2.201	2.718	3.106
12	1.782	2.179	2.681	3.055
13	1.771	2.160	2.650	3.012
14	1.761	2.145	2.624	2.977
15	1.753	2.131	2.602	2.947
16	1.746	2.120	2.583	2.921
17	1.740	2.110	2.567	2.898
18	1.734	2.101	2.552	2.878
19	1.729	2.093	2.539	2.861
20	1.725	2.086	2.528	2.845
21	1.721	2.080	2.518	2.831
22	1.717	2.074	2.508	2.819
23	1.714	2.069	2.500	2.807
24	1.711	2.064	2.492	2.797
25	1.708	2.060	2.485	2.787
26	1.706	2.056	2.479	2.779
27	1.703	2.052	2.473	2.771
28	1.701	2.048	2.467	2.763
29	1.699	2.045	2.462	2.756
30	1.697	2.042	2.457	2.750
40	1.684	2.021	2.423	2.704
60	1.671	2.000	2.390	2.660
120	1.658	1.980	2.358	2.617
∞	1.645	1.960	2.326	2.576

Source: This table is abridged from Table 12 of the *Biometrika Tables for Statisticians* (Vol. 1, 3rd ed.) by E. S. Pearson and H. O. Hartley (Eds.), 1970, New York: Cambridge University Press. Used with the kind permission of the Biometrika trustees.

Table E-2 Critical Values for Chi-Square Tests

Level of Significance

DF	.10	.05	.01	.001
1	2.70554	3.84146	6.63490	10.828
2	4.60517	5.99147	9.21034	13.816
3	6.25139	7.81473	11.3449	16.266
4	7.77944	9.48773	13.2767	18.467
5	9.23635	11.0705	15.0863	20.515
6	10.6446	12.5916	18.5476	22.458
7	12.0170	14.0671	18.4753	24.322
8	13.3616	15.5073	20.0902	26.125
9	14.6837	16.9190	21.6660	27.877
10	15.9871	18.3070	23.2093	29.588
11	17.2750	19.6751	24.7250	31.264
12	18.5494	21.0261	26.2170	32.909
13	19.8119	22.3621	27.6883	34.528
14	21.0642	23.6848	29.1413	36.123
15	22.3072	24.9958	30.5779	37.697
16	23.5418	26.2962	31.9999	39.252
17	24.7690	27.5871	33.4087	40.790
18	25.9894	28.8693	34.8053	42.312
19	27.2036	30.1435	36.1908	43.820
20	28.4120	31.4104	37.5662	45.315
21	29.6151	32.6705	38.9321	46.797
22	30.8133	33.9244	40.2894	48.268
23	32.0069	35.1725	41.6384	49.728
24	33.1963	36.4151	42.9798	51.179
25	34.3816	37.6525	44.3141	52.620
26	35.5631	38.8852	45.6417	54.052
27	36.7412	40.1133	46.9630	55.476
28	37.9159	41.3372	48.2782	56.892
29	39.0875	42.5569	49.5879	58.302
30	40.2560	43.7729	50.8922	59.703
40	51.8050	55.7585	63.6907	73.402
50	63.1671	67.5048	76.1539	86.661
60	74.3970	79.0819	88.3794	99.607
70	85.5271	90.5312	100.425	112.317
80	96.5782	101.879	112.329	124.839
90	107.565	113.145	124.116	137.208
100	118.498	124.342	135.807	149.449

Table E-3	Critical Values of F for $p < .05$

	1ST DF									
2ND DF	1	2	3	4	5	6	7	8	9	10
1	161.4	199.5	215.7	224.6	230.2	234.0	236.8	238.9	240.5	241.9
2	18.51	19.00	19.16	19.25	19.30	19.33	19.35	19.37	19.38	19.40
3	10.13	9.55	9.28	9.12	9.01	8.94	8.89	8.85	8.81	8.79
4	7.71	6.94	6.59	6.39	6.26	6.16	6.09	6.04	6.00	5.96
5	6.61	5.79	5.41	5.19	5.05	4.95	4.88	4.82	4.77	4.74
6	5.99	5.14	4.76	4.53	4.39	4.28	4.21	4.15	4.10	4.06
7	5.59	4.74	4.35	4.12	3.97	3.87	3.79	3.73	3.68	3.64
8	5.32	4.46	4.07	3.84	3.69	3.58	3.50	3.44	3.39	3.35
9	5.12	4.26	3.86	3.63	3.48	3.37	3.29	3.23	3.18	3.14
10	4.96	4.10	3.71	3.48	3.33	3.22	3.14	3.07	3.02	2.98
11	4.84	3.98	3.59	3.36	3.20	3.09	3.01	2.95	2.90	2.85
12	4.75	3.89	3.49	3.26	3.11	3.00	2.91	2.85	2.80	2.75
13	4.67	3.81	3.41	3.18	3.03	2.92	2.83	2.77	2.71	2.67
14	4.60	3.74	3.34	3.11	2.96	2.85	2.76	2.70	2.65	2.60
15	4.54	3.68	3.29	3.06	2.90	2.79	2.71	2.64	2.59	2.54
16	4.49	3.63	3.24	3.01	2.85	2.74	2.66	2.59	2.54	2.49
17	4.45	3.59	3.20	2.96	2.81	2.70	2.61	2.55	2.49	2.45
18	4.41	3.55	3.16	2.93	2.77	2.66	2.58	2.51	2.46	2.41
19	4.38	3.52	3.13	2.90	2.74	2.63	2.54	2.48	2.42	2.38
20	4.35	3.49	3.10	2.87	2.71	2.60	2.51	2.45	2.39	2.35
21	4.32	3.47	3.07	2.84	2.68	2.57	2.49	2.42	2.37	2.32
22	4.30	3.44	3.05	2.82	2.66	2.55	2.46	2.40	2.34	2.30
23	4.28	3.42	3.03	2.80	2.64	2.53	2.44	2.37	2.32	2.27
24	4.26	3.40	3.01	2.78	2.62	2.51	2.42	2.36	2.30	2.25
25	4.24	3.39	2.99	2.76	2.60	2.49	2.40	2.34	2.28	2.24
26	4.23	3.37	2.98	2.74	2.59	2.47	2.39	2.32	2.27	2.22
27	4.21	3.35	2.96	2.73	2.57	2.46	2.37	2.31	2.25	2.20
28	4.20	3.34	2.95	2.71	2.56	2.45	2.36	2.29	2.24	2.19
29	4.18	3.33	2.93	2.70	2.55	2.43	2.35	2.28	2.22	2.18
30	4.17	3.32	2.92	2.69	2.53	2.42	2.33	2.27	2.21	2.16
40	4.08	3.23	2.84	2.61	2.45	2.34	2.25	2.18	2.12	2.08
60	4.00	3.15	2.76	2.53	2.37	2.25	2.17	2.10	2.04	1.99
120	3.92	3.07	2.68	2.45	2.29	2.17	2.09	2.02	1.96	1.91
∞	3.84	3.00	2.60	2.37	2.21	2.10	2.01	1.94	1.88	1.83

Table E-3 · Critical Values of F for $p < .025$

	1ST DF														
2ND DF	1	2	3	4	5	6	7	8	9	10	12	15	20	24	30
1	647.8	799.5	864.2	899.6	921.8	937.1	948.2	956.7	963.3	968.6	976.7	984.9	993.19	97.2	1001
2	38.51	39.00	39.17	39.25	39.30	39.33	39.36	39.37	39.39	39.40	39.41	39.43	39.45	39.46	39.46
3	17.44	16.04	15.44	15.10	14.88	14.73	14.62	14.54	14.47	14.42	14.34	14.25	14.17	14.12	14.08
4	12.22	10.65	9.98	9.60	9.36	9.20	9.07	8.98	8.90	8.84	8.75	8.66	8.56	8.51	8.46
5	10.01	8.43	7.76	7.39	7.15	6.98	6.85	6.76	6.68	6.62	6.52	6.43	6.33	6.28	6.23
6	8.81	7.26	6.60	6.23	5.99	5.82	5.70	5.60	5.52	5.46	5.37	5.27	5.17	5.12	5.07
7	8.07	6.54	5.89	5.52	5.29	5.12	4.99	4.90	4.82	4.76	4.67	4.57	4.47	4.42	4.36
8	7.57	6.06	5.42	5.05	4.82	4.65	4.53	4.43	4.36	4.30	4.20	4.10	4.00	3.95	3.89
9	7.21	5.71	5.08	4.72	4.48	4.32	4.20	4.10	4.03	3.96	3.87	3.77	3.67	3.61	3.56
10	6.94	5.46	4.83	4.47	4.24	4.07	3.95	3.85	3.78	3.72	3.62	3.52	3.42	3.37	3.31
11	6.72	5.26	4.63	4.28	4.04	3.88	3.76	3.66	3.59	3.53	3.43	3.33	3.23	3.17	3.12
12	6.55	5.10	4.47	4.12	3.89	3.73	3.61	3.51	3.44	3.37	3.28	3.18	3.07	3.02	2.96
13	6.41	4.97	4.35	4.00	3.77	3.60	3.48	3.39	3.31	3.25	3.15	3.05	2.95	2.89	2.84
14	6.30	4.86	4.24	3.89	3.66	3.50	3.38	3.29	3.21	3.15	3.05	2.95	2.84	2.79	2.73
15	6.20	4.77	4.15	3.80	3.58	3.41	3.29	3.20	3.12	3.06	2.96	2.86	2.76	2.70	2.64
16	6.12	4.69	4.08	3.73	3.50	3.34	3.22	3.12	3.05	2.99	2.89	2.79	2.68	2.63	2.57
17	6.04	4.62	4.01	3.66	3.44	3.28	3.16	3.06	2.98	2.92	2.82	2.72	2.62	2.56	2.50
18	5.98	4.56	3.95	3.61	3.38	3.22	3.10	3.01	2.93	2.87	2.77	2.67	2.56	2.50	2.44
19	5.92	4.51	3.90	3.56	3.33	3.17	3.05	2.96	2.88	2.82	2.72	2.62	2.51	2.45	2.39
20	5.87	4.46	3.86	3.51	3.29	3.13	3.01	2.91	2.84	2.77	2.68	2.57	2.46	2.41	2.35
21	5.83	4.42	3.82	3.48	3.25	3.09	2.97	2.87	2.80	2.73	2.64	2.53	2.42	2.37	2.31
22	5.79	4.38	3.78	3.44	3.22	3.05	2.93	2.84	2.76	2.70	2.60	2.50	2.39	2.33	2.27
23	5.75	4.35	3.75	3.41	3.18	3.02	2.90	2.81	2.73	2.67	2.57	2.47	2.36	2.30	2.24
24	5.72	4.32	3.72	3.38	3.15	2.99	2.87	2.78	2.70	2.64	2.54	2.44	2.33	2.27	2.21
25	5.69	4.29	3.69	3.35	3.13	2.97	2.85	2.75	2.68	2.61	2.51	2.41	2.36	2.24	2.18
26	5.66	4.27	3.67	3.33	3.10	2.94	2.82	2.73	2.65	2.59	2.49	2.39	2.28	2.22	2.16
27	5.63	4.24	3.65	3.31	3.08	2.92	2.80	2.71	2.63	2.57	2.47	2.36	2.25	2.19	2.13
28	5.61	4.22	3.63	3.29	3.06	2.90	2.78	2.69	2.61	2.55	2.45	2.34	2.23	2.17	2.11
29	5.59	4.20	3.61	3.27	3.04	2.88	2.76	2.67	2.59	2.53	2.43	2.32	2.21	2.15	2.09
30	5.57	4.18	3.59	3.25	3.03	2.87	2.75	2.65	2.57	2.51	2.41	2.31	2.20	2.14	2.07
40	5.42	4.05	3.46	3.13	2.90	2.74	2.62	2.53	2.45	2.39	2.29	2.18	2.07	2.01	1.94
60	5.29	3.93	3.34	3.01	2.79	2.63	2.51	2.41	2.33	2.27	2.17	2.06	1.94	1.88	1.82
120	5.15	3.80	3.23	2.89	2.67	2.52	2.39	2.30	2.22	2.16	2.05	1.94	1.82	1.76	1.69
∞	5.02	3.69	3.12	2.79	2.57	2.41	2.29	2.19	2.11	2.05	1.94	1.83	1.71	1.64	1.57

continued

Table E-3 Critical Values of F for p < .01 (continued)

2ND DF	\multicolumn{15}{c}{1ST DF}													
	1	2	3	4	5	6	7	8	9	10	12	15	20	24	30
1	4052	4999.5	5403	5625	5764	5859	5928	5982	6022	6056	6106	6157	6209	6235	6261
2	98.50	99.00	99.17	99.25	99.30	99.33	99.36	99.37	99.39	99.40	99.42	99.43	99.45	99.46	99.47
3	34.12	30.82	29.46	28.71	28.24	27.91	27.67	27.49	27.35	27.23	27.05	26.87	26.69	26.60	26.50
4	21.20	18.00	16.69	15.98	15.52	15.21	14.98	14.80	14.66	14.55	14.37	14.20	14.02	13.93	13.84
5	16.26	13.27	12.06	11.39	10.97	10.67	10.46	10.29	10.16	10.05	9.89	9.72	9.55	9.47	9.38
6	13.75	10.92	9.78	9.15	8.75	8.47	8.26	8.10	7.98	7.87	7.72	7.56	7.40	7.31	7.23
7	12.25	9.55	8.45	7.85	7.46	7.19	6.99	6.84	6.72	6.62	6.47	6.31	6.16	6.07	5.99
8	11.26	8.65	7.59	7.01	6.63	6.37	6.18	6.03	5.91	5.81	5.67	5.52	5.36	5.28	5.20
9	10.56	8.02	6.99	6.42	6.06	5.80	5.61	5.47	5.35	5.26	5.11	4.96	4.81	4.73	4.65
10	10.04	7.56	6.55	5.99	5.64	5.39	5.20	5.06	4.94	4.85	4.71	4.56	4.41	4.33	4.25
11	9.65	7.21	6.22	5.67	5.32	5.07	4.89	4.74	4.63	4.54	4.40	4.25	4.10	4.02	3.94
12	9.33	6.93	5.95	5.41	5.06	4.82	4.64	4.50	4.39	4.30	4.16	4.01	3.86	3.78	3.70
13	9.07	6.70	5.74	5.21	4.86	4.62	4.44	4.30	4.19	4.10	3.96	3.82	3.66	3.59	3.51
14	8.86	6.51	5.56	5.04	4.69	4.46	4.28	4.14	4.03	3.94	3.80	3.66	3.51	3.43	3.35
15	8.68	6.36	5.42	4.89	4.56	4.32	4.14	4.00	3.89	3.80	3.67	3.52	3.37	3.29	3.21
16	8.53	6.23	5.29	4.77	4.44	4.20	4.03	3.89	3.78	3.69	3.55	3.41	3.26	3.18	3.10
17	8.40	6.11	5.18	4.67	4.34	4.10	3.93	3.79	3.68	3.59	3.46	3.31	3.16	3.08	3.00
18	8.29	6.01	5.09	4.58	4.25	4.01	3.84	3.71	3.60	3.51	3.37	3.23	3.08	3.00	2.92
19	8.18	5.93	5.01	4.50	4.17	3.94	3.77	3.63	3.52	3.43	3.30	3.15	3.00	2.92	2.84
20	8.10	5.85	4.94	4.43	4.10	3.87	3.70	3.56	3.46	3.37	3.23	3.09	2.94	2.86	2.78
21	8.02	5.78	4.87	4.37	4.04	3.81	3.64	3.51	3.40	3.31	3.17	3.03	2.88	2.80	2.72
22	7.95	5.72	4.82	4.31	3.99	3.76	3.59	3.45	3.35	3.26	3.12	2.98	2.83	2.75	2.67
23	7.88	5.66	4.76	4.26	3.94	3.71	3.54	3.41	3.30	3.21	3.07	2.93	2.78	2.70	2.62
24	7.82	5.61	4.72	4.22	3.90	3.67	3.50	3.36	3.26	3.17	3.03	2.89	2.74	2.66	2.58
25	7.77	5.57	4.68	4.18	3.85	3.63	3.46	3.32	3.22	3.13	2.99	2.85	2.70	2.62	2.54
26	7.72	5.53	4.64	4.14	3.82	3.59	3.42	3.29	3.18	3.09	2.96	2.81	2.66	2.58	2.50
27	7.68	5.49	4.60	4.11	3.78	3.56	3.39	3.26	3.15	3.06	2.93	2.78	2.63	2.55	2.47
28	7.64	5.45	4.57	4.07	3.75	3.53	3.36	3.23	3.12	3.03	2.90	2.75	2.60	2.52	2.44
29	7.60	5.42	4.54	4.04	3.73	3.50	3.33	3.20	3.09	3.00	2.87	2.73	2.57	2.49	2.41
30	7.56	5.39	4.51	4.02	3.70	3.47	3.30	3.17	3.07	2.98	2.84	2.70	2.55	2.47	2.39
40	7.31	5.18	4.31	3.83	3.51	3.29	3.12	2.99	2.89	2.80	2.66	2.52	2.37	2.29	2.20
60	7.08	4.98	4.13	3.65	3.34	3.12	2.95	2.82	2.72	2.63	2.50	2.35	2.20	2.12	2.03
120	6.85	4.79	3.95	3.48	3.17	2.96	2.79	2.66	2.56	2.47	2.34	2.19	2.03	1.95	1.86
∞	6.63	4.61	3.78	3.32	3.02	2.80	2.64	2.51	2.41	2.32	2.18	2.04	1.88	1.79	1.70

Using Table E-4 to Compute Trend Analyses

Suppose you had the following significant effect for sugar on aggression.

	DF	SS	MS	F
Sugar Main Effect	2	126.95	63.47	6.35
Error Term	21	210.00	10.00	

How would you compute a trend analysis for this data? You would start by calculating an F-ratio for the linear and quadratic effects so that you could complete the following ANOVA table.

	DF	SS	MS	F
Sugar Main Effect	2	126.95	63.47	6.35
Linear Trend	1			
Quadratic Trend	1			
Error Term	21	210.00	10.00	

Before you generate an F ratio, you must have a sum of squares. To compute the sum of squares for a trend, you must first get the sum of the scores for each condition/group. In this case, you will need the sum (total) of the scores for each of three groups: (a) the no sugar group, (b) the 50 mg of sugar group, and (c) the 100 mg of sugar group. One way to get the sum of scores for a condition is to add up (sum) all the scores for that condition. Another way to get the sum of scores for each condition is to multiply each condition's average by the number of scores making up each average. Thus, if one condition's mean was 10 and there were 8 scores making up that mean, the sum for that condition would be 10×8, which is 80.

Next, arrange these totals by placing the sum for the condition connected with the lowest level of the independent variable (e.g., no sugar condition) first, the sum for the condition with the next highest level of the independent variable next, and so on. In our example, you would order your sums like the following:

Total Number of Violent Instances per Condition

AMOUNT OF SUGAR	TOTAL NUMBER OF VIOLENT INSTANCES
0 mg	10.0
50 mg	50.0
100 mg	12.0

Now you are ready to consult the tables of orthogonal polynomials in Table E-4. Because this example involves three conditions, you would look for the three-condition table. The table reads as follows:

Three-Condition Case

	TREND	
	1 (Linear)	2 (Quadratic)
Condition 1	-1	1
Condition 2	0	-2
Condition 3	1	1
Weighting Factor	2	6

| Table E-4 | Coefficients of Orthogonal Polynomials |

		3-CONDITION CASE TREND		4-CONDITION CASE TREND			5-CONDITION CASE TREND			
		1	2	1	2	3	1	2	3	4
Condition		(Lin)	(Quad)	(Lin)	(Quad)	(Cubic)	(Lin)		(Quad)	(Cubic)
1		−1	1	−3	1	−1	−2	2	−1	1
2		0	−2	−1	−1	3	−1	−1	2	−4
3		1	1	1	−1	−3	0	−2	0	6
4				3	1	1	1	−1	−2	−4
5							2	2	1	1
Weighting Factor		2	6	20	4	20	10	14	10	70

		6-CONDITION CASE TREND					7-CONDITION CASE TREND					
		1	2	3	4	5	1	2	3	4	5	6
Condition		(Lin)	(Quad)	(Cubic)				(Lin)	(Quad)	(Cubic)		
1		−5	5	−5	1	−1	−3	5	−1	3	−1	1
2		−3	−1	7	−3	5	−2	0	1	−7	4	−6
3		−1	−4	4	2	−10	−1	−3	1	1	−5	15
4		1	−4	−4	2	10	0	−4	0	6	0	−20
5		3	−1	−7	−3	−5	1	−3	−1	1	5	15
6		5	5	5	1	1	2	0	−1	−7	−4	−6
7							3	5	1	3	1	1
Weighting Factor		70	84	180	28	252	28	84	6	154	84	924

Source: This table is adapted from Table VII of *Statistics* (pp. 662–664) by W. L. Hays, 1981, New York: Holt, Rinehart and Winston. Copyright © 1982 by Holt, Rinehart and Winston, Inc. Adapted by permission.

To get the numerator for the sum of squares for the linear trend, multiply the sum for the lowest level of the independent variable by the first value in the "Linear" column of the table for the three-condition case (−1), the second sum by the second value in the "Linear" column of the table (0), and the third sum by the third value in the "Linear" column of the table (+1). Next, get a sum by adding these three products together. Then, square that sum. So, for the sugar example we just described, you would do the following calculations:

$$[(-1 \times 10) + (0 \times 50) + (1 \times 12)]^2$$

or

$$(-10 + 0 + 12)^2$$

or

$$(2)^2$$

or

To get the denominator for the sum of squares, multiply the weighting factor for the linear trend (2) by the number of observations in each condition. Because there were eight observations in each condition, the denominator would be 16 (2 × 8). The sum of squares linear would be the numerator (4) divided by the denominator (16), which equals .25.

Once you have computed the sum of squares for the linear trend, the rest is easy. All you have to do is compute F ratio by dividing the mean square linear by the mean square error and then see if that result is significant.

Calculating the mean square linear involves dividing the sum of squares linear by the degrees of freedom linear. Because the degrees of freedom for any trend is always 1.00, you could divide your sum of squares (.25) by 1.00 and get .25. Or, you could simply remember that a trend's mean square is always the same as its sum of squares.

Getting the mean square error is also easy: Just find the mean square error in the printout that was used to test the overall main effect. In this example, the MSE is 10.

So, to get the F value for this linear comparison, you would divide the mean square for the comparison (.25) by the mean square error used on the overall main effect (10.0). Thus, the F would be .25/10, or .025. Because the F is below 1.00, this result is obviously not significant.

But how large would the F have had to be to be significant? That depends on how many trends you were analyzing. If you had decided to look only at the linear trend, the significant F at the .05 level would have to exceed the value in the F table for 1 degree of freedom (the df for any trend) and 21 degrees of freedom, the df for the error term. That value is 4.32.

However, if you are going to analyze more than one trend, you must correct for the number of Fs you are going to compute. The correction is simple: You divide the significance level you want (say .05), by the number of trends you will test. In this example, you are computing two Fs. Therefore, you should use the critical value of F for the significance level of .05/2 which is .025. So, rather than look in an F table listing the critical values of F for $p < .05$, you would look in an F table listing the critical values of F for $p < .025$. In this example, you would only declare a trend significant at the .05 level if the F for that trend exceeds the critical value for $F(1,21)$ at the .025 level: 5.83.

Obviously, the F for the linear component, $F(1,21) = .025$, falls far short of the critical value of 5.83. But what about the quadratic component? To determine whether the quadratic component is significant, you would follow the same steps as before. The only difference is that you would look at the "Quadratic" column of the table for the three-condition case instead of the "Linear" column.

Thus, you would first multiply the treatment sums by the constants listed in the "Quadratic" column, add them together, and square that sum. In other words,

$$[(1 \times 10) + (-2 \times 50) + (1 \times 12)]^2$$

or

$$[10 + (-100) + 12]^2$$

or

$$(-78)^2$$

or

$$6084$$

Then, you would divide 6084 by 8 (the number of observations in each condition) × 6 (the weighting factor for the quadratic effect). The result—6084/(8 × 6) = 6084/48 = 126.7—would be your SS quadratic. Note that 126.7, your SS quadratic, is also your MS

quadratic because MS quadratic is always the same as SS quadratic. The reason MS quadratic is always the same as SS quadratic is because (a) MS quadratic always equals SS quadratic $/df$ quadratic, (b) df quadratic always equals 1, and (c) $SS/1$ always equals SS.

To get the F for the quadratic trend, you would divide the MS quadratic (126.7) by MS error (10). Therefore, the F for the quadratic trend is $126.7/10 = 12.67$. As before, the critical value for the comparison is the F value for the .025 significance level with 1 and 21 degrees of freedom: 5.83. Because our F of 12.67 exceeds the critical value of 5.83, we have a statistically significant quadratic trend.

So, our complete ANOVA table, including the linear and quadratic components, is the following table:

	DF	SS	MS	F
Sugar Main Effect	2	126.95	63.47	6.35*
Linear	1	0.25	0.25	0.02
Quadratic	1	126.70	126.70	12.67*
Error Term	21	210.00	10.00	

*Significant at .05 level.

From looking at the table, you see that if you add up the degrees of freedom for all the trends involved in the sugar main effect $(1 + 1)$, you get the total df for the sugar main effect (2). More importantly, note that if you add up the sum of squares for the quadratic and linear trends $(126.70 + .25)$, you get the sum of squares for the overall effect (126.95). This fact gives you a way to check your work. Specifically, if the total of the sums of squares for all the components does not add up to the sum of squares for the overall effect, you have made a mistake.

Using Table E-5 to Compute Post Hoc Tests

Post hoc tests, such as the Tukey test, can be used after finding a significant main effect for a multilevel factor. These tests help determine which conditions are significantly different from one another.

To see how you could use Table E-5 to compute post hoc tests, suppose that an investigator studies 24 participants (8 in each group) to examine the effect of color (blue, green, or yellow) on mood. As you can see from the following table, the investigator's ANOVA table reveals a significant effect of color.

SOURCE	SUM OF SQUARES	DEGREES OF FREEDOM	MEAN SQUARE	F
Color	64	2	32.0	4.0*
Error	168	21	8.0	

*Significant at .05 level.

The means for the three color conditions are

BLUE	GREEN	YELLOW
10.0	5.0	8.0

The question is, "Which conditions differ from one another?" Does yellow cause a different mood than green? Does blue cause a different mood than yellow? To find out, we need to do a post hoc test. For this example, we will do the Tukey test.

Table E-5 — Critical Values for the Tukey Test at the .05 Level of Significance

Number of Means

DF ERROR	2	3	4	5	6	7	8	9
10	3.15	3.88	4.33	4.65	4.91	5.12	5.30	5.46
11	3.11	3.82	4.26	4.57	4.82	5.03	5.20	5.35
12	3.08	3.77	4.20	4.51	4.75	4.95	5.12	5.27
13	3.06	3.73	4.15	4.45	4.69	4.88	5.05	5.19
14	3.03	3.70	4.11	4.41	4.64	4.83	4.99	5.13
15	3.01	3.67	4.08	4.37	4.59	4.78	4.94	5.08
16	3.00	3.65	4.05	4.33	4.56	4.74	4.90	5.03
17	2.98	3.63	4.02	4.30	4.52	4.70	4.86	4.99
18	2.97	3.61	4.00	4.28	4.49	4.67	4.82	4.96
19	2.96	3.59	3.98	4.25	4.47	4.65	4.79	4.92
20	2.95	3.58	3.96	4.23	4.45	4.62	4.77	4.90
21	2.95	**3.57**	3.95	4.22	4.43	4.60	4.75	4.88
30	2.89	3.49	3.85	4.10	4.30	4.46	4.60	4.72
40	2.86	3.44	3.79	4.04	4.23	4.39	4.52	4.63
60	2.83	3.40	3.74	3.98	4.16	4.31	4.44	4.55
120	2.80	3.36	3.68	3.92	4.10	4.24	4.36	4.47
∞	2.77	3.31	3.63	3.86	4.03	4.17	4.29	4.39

Source: This table is abridged from Table 29 of the *Biometrika Tables for Statisticians* (Vol. 1, 3rd ed.) by E. S. Pearson and H. O. Hartley (Eds.), 1970, New York: Cambridge University Press. Used with the kind permission of the Biometrika Trustees.

The formula for the Tukey test is

$$\frac{\text{Mean 1} - \text{Mean 2}}{\sqrt{(MSE \times / \text{number of observations per condition})}}$$

Because the mean square error is 8 (see original ANOVA table) and there are 8 participants in each group, the denominator in this example will always be

$$\sqrt{(8 \times 1/8)}$$

or

$$\sqrt{8/8}$$

or

$$\sqrt{1}$$

or

$$1$$

The numerator will change, depending on what means you are comparing. Thus, if you are comparing blue and green, the numerator would be $10 - 5$, or 5. So, to see whether the blue and green conditions differ significantly, you would do the following calculations.

$$\frac{10.0 \text{ (blue mean)} - 5.0 \text{ (green mean)}}{\sqrt{(8 \times 1/8)}} = \frac{5.0}{\sqrt{1}} = \frac{5.0}{1.0} = 5.0$$

To find out whether 5.0 is significant, go to Table E-5 and look at the column labeled "3" because you have three means you are comparing. Then, go down and look at row 21 because you have 21 degrees of freedom in your error term (as you can see by looking at the original ANOVA table). The value in that table is 3.57. This is the critical value that you will use in all your comparisons. If your Tukey statistic for a pair of means is larger than this critical value, there is a significant difference between conditions. Because 5.0 is greater than 3.57, your result is significant at the .05 level.

But, do blue and yellow differ? To find out, compute the Tukey statistic.

$$\frac{10.0 - 8.0}{\sqrt{(8 \times 1/8)}} = \frac{2.0}{\sqrt{1}} = \frac{2.0}{1.0} = 2.0$$

Because 2.0 is less than our critical value of 3.57, the difference between blue and yellow is not statistically significant at the .05 level.

Do yellow and green differ?

$$\frac{8.0 - 5.0}{\sqrt{(8 \times 1/8)}} = \frac{3.0}{\sqrt{1}} = \frac{3.0}{1.0} = 3.0$$

Because 3.0 is less than our critical value of 3.57, the difference between yellow and green is not statistically significant at the .05 level.

Directions for Using Table E-6

If you are doing an experiment, you can use Table E-6 to randomly assign participants to treatment condition. If you are doing a survey, you can use Table E-6 to generate a random sample.

Randomly Assigning Participants to Groups in an Experiment

STEP 1: Across the top of a piece of paper, write down your conditions. Under each condition, draw a line for each participant you will need. In this example, we had three conditions and needed 12 participants.

GROUP 1	GROUP 2	GROUP 3
_____	_____	_____
_____	_____	_____
_____	_____	_____
_____	_____	_____

STEP 2: Turn to Table E-6. Roll a die to determine which column in the table you will start at.

STEP 3: Assign the first number in the column to the first space under Group 1, the second number to the second space, and so on. When you have filled the spaces for Group 1, put the next number under the first space under Group 2. Similarly, when you fill all the spaces under Group 2, place the next number in the first space under Group 3.

Table E-6 — Table of Random Numbers

5	28	80	31	99	77	39	23	69	0	15	49	100	2	22	64	73	92	53
29	71	48	4	87	32	17	90	89	9	99	34	58	8	61	73	98	48	89
90	94	19	80	70	36	2	17	48	63	82	39	85	26	65	27	81	69	83
62	66	48	74	86	6	66	41	15	65	6	41	85	57	84	64	70	39	64
67	54	3	54	23	40	25	95	93	55	59	46	77	55	49	82	26	8	87
75	27	62	15	81	36	22	26	69	42	44	91	55	0	84	48	68	65	5
70	19	7	100	94	53	81	76	73	40	22	58	49	42	96	18	66	89	8
75	7	9	20	58	92	41	42	79	26	91	44	63	87	45	21	23	15	6
55	70	10	23	25	73	91	72	29	47	93	58	21	75	80	52	9	12	36
83	42	62	53	55	12	11	54	19	2	45	43	67	13	5	74	30	93	11
94	20	76	23	65	72	55	27	44	19	10	72	50	67	83	18	67	22	49
51	10	72	9	59	47	66	32	17	6	75	8	54	22	37	3	46	83	95
99	50	22	2	92	9	98	9	40	23	34	8	63	58	49	31	70	39	83
9	12	3	23	2	0	82	75	36	63	71	19	78	26	66	63	16	75	7
20	40	50	29	51	82	81	47	73	69	74	100	80	37	14	67	1	90	92
90	92	54	52	74	0	88	71	45	49	38	54	80	2	85	42	75	47	20
25	6	92	30	19	31	22	41	0	22	79	87	84	61	6	19	67	97	60
13	12	94	76	29	61	50	67	29	76	27	70	97	16	83	88	100	22	48
91	77	51	3	92	85	46	22	0	58	84	64	87	93	94	94	13	98	41
29	12	39	35	32	47	30	81	40	32	37	8	48	81	50	77	18	39	7
43	96	86	14	91	24	22	85	16	51	42	37	41	100	94	76	45	50	67
57	44	72	45	87	21	7	29	26	82	69	99	10	39	76	29	11	17	85
63	10	10	76	7	75	19	91	2	31	45	94	54	72	10	48	52	7	12
34	28	11	95	4	82	51	7	69	53	93	36	81	66	93	88	15	73	54

Source: This table is taken from the random numbers table in Appendix D of *Foundations of Behavioral Research,* 3rd ed. (pp. 642–643) by F. N. Kerlinger, 1986, New York: Holt, Rinehart and Winston. Copyright (c) 1986 by Holt, Rinehart and Winston. Reprinted by permission.

GROUP 1	GROUP 2	GROUP 3
12	20	63
39	*3*	64
53	37	95
29	*1*	18

STEP 4: Assign the first person who participates in your study to the condition with the lowest random number. The second participant will be in the condition with the second lowest random number, and so on. Thus, in this example, your first two participants would be in Group 2 and your third participant would be in Group 1.

Using Table E-6 to Get a Random Sample

STEP 1: Determine how large your sample will be.

STEP 2: Get a list of your population and put a line next to each individual's name.

STEP 3: Turn to Table E-6. Roll a die to determine which column in the table you will start at.

STEP 4: Assign the first number in the column to the first name on your list, the second number to the second space, and so on.

STEP 5: Put your participants in order based on their random number. Thus, the individual with the lowest random number next to his or her name would be the first on the list, the individual with the second lowest random number would be the second, and so on.

STEP 6: Go down the list to get your sample. If your sample will be 50, pick the first 50 individuals on the list. If it is 100, pick the first 100 individuals on the list.

Glossary

A–B design The simplest single-*n* design, consisting of measuring the participant's behavior at baseline (A) and then measuring the participant after the participant has received the treatment (B).

A–B–A reversal design See *reversal design.*

Abstract A short (fewer than 120 words), one-page summary of a research proposal or article.

Analysis of variance (ANOVA) A statistical test for analyzing data from experiments that is especially useful when the experiment has more than one independent variable or more than two levels of an independent variable.

Archival data Data from existing records and public archives.

Baseline The participant's behavior on the task before receiving the treatment. A measure of the dependent variable as it occurs without the experimental manipulation. Used as a standard of comparison in single-subject and small-*n* designs.

Between-groups variance (mean square treatment, mean square between) An index of the degree to which group means differ. An index of the combined effects of random error and treatment. This quantity is compared to the within-groups variance in ANOVA. It is the top half of the *F*-ratio. If the treatment has no effect, the between-groups variance should be roughly the same as the within-groups variance. If the treatment has an effect, the between-groups variance should be larger than the within-groups variance.

Bias Systematic errors that can push the scores in a given direction. Bias may lead to "finding" the results that the researcher wanted.

Blind (also called *masked*) A strategy of making the participant or researcher unaware of what condition the participant is in.

Blocked design A factorial design in which, to boost power, participants are first divided into groups (blocks) on a subject variable (e.g., low-IQ block and high-IQ block). Then, participants from each block are randomly assigned to experimental condition. Ideally, a blocked design will be more powerful than a simple, between-subjects design.

Carryover (treatment carryover) effect The effect of a treatment administered earlier in the experiment persists so long that it is present even while participants are receiving additional treatments. It is often a problem with single-subject and within-subjects designs because you do not know whether the participant's behavior is due to the treatment just administered or to a lingering effect of a treatment administered some time ago.

Ceiling effect The effect of treatment(s) is underestimated because the dependent measure is not sensitive to psychological states above a certain level. The measure puts an artificially low ceiling on how high a participant may score.

Central limit theorem If numerous large samples (30 or more scores) from the same population are taken, and you plot the mean for each of these samples, your plot would resemble a normal curve—even if the population from which you took those samples was not normally distributed.

Chi square (χ^2) test A statistical test you can use to determine whether two or more variables are related. Best used when you have nominal data.

Coefficient of determination The square of the correlation coefficient; tells the degree to which knowing one variable helps to know another. Can range from 0 (knowing a participant's score on one variable tells you absolutely nothing about the participant's score on the second variable) to 1.00 (knowing a participant's score on one variable tells you the participant's exact score on the second variable).

Conceptual replication A study that is based on the original study but uses different methods to assess the true relationships between the treatment and dependent variables better. In a conceptual replication, you might use a different manipulation or a different measure.

Confounding variables Variables, other than the independent variable, that may be responsible for the differences between your conditions. There are two types of confounding variables: ones that are manipulation irrelevant and ones that are the result of the manipulation. Confounding variables that are irrelevant to the treatment manipulation threaten internal validity. For example, the difference between groups may be due to one group being older than the other rather than to the treatment. Random assignment can control for the effects of those confounding variables. Confounding variables that are produced by the treatment manipulation hurt the construct validity of the study because even though we may know that the treatment manipulation had an effect, we don't know what it was about the treatment manipulation that had the effect. For example, we may know that an "exercise" manipulation increases happiness (internal validity), but not know whether the "exercise" manipulation worked because people exercised more, got more encouragement, had a more structured routine, practiced setting and achieving goals, or met new friends. In such a case, construct validity is harmed because we don't know how properly to label the "exercise" manipulation.

Construct A mental state such as love, intelligence, hunger, and aggression that cannot be directly observed or manipulated with our present technology.

Construct validity The degree to which a study, test, or manipulation measures and/or manipulates what the researcher claims it does. For example, a test claiming to measure aggressiveness would not have construct validity if it really measured assertiveness.

Content analysis A method used to categorize a wide range of open-ended (unrestricted) responses. Content analysis schemes have been used to code the frequency of violence on certain television shows and are often used to code archival data.

Content validity The extent to which a measure represents a balanced and adequate sampling of relevant dimensions, knowledge, and skills. In many measures and tests, participants are asked a few questions from a large body of knowledge. A test has content validity if its content is a fair sample of the larger body of knowledge. Students hope that their psychology tests have content validity.

Control group Participants who are randomly assigned to *not* receive the experimental treatment. These participants are compared to the treatment group to determine whether the treatment had an effect.

Convenience sampling Including people in your sample simply because they are easy (convenient) to survey. It is hard to generalize the results accurately from a study that used convenience sampling.

Convergent validity Validity demonstrated by showing that the measure correlates with other measures of the construct.

Correlation coefficient A number that can vary from −1.00 to +1.00 and indicates the kind of relationship that exists between two variables (positive or negative as indicated by the sign of the correlation coefficient) and the strength of the relationship (indicated by the extent to which the coefficient differs from 0). Positive correlations indicate that the variables tend to go in the same direction (if a participant is low on one variable, the participant will tend to be low on the other). Negative correlations indicate that the variables tend to head in opposite directions (if a participant is low on one, the participant will tend to be high on the other).

Counterbalanced within-subjects design Design that gives participants the treatments in different sequences. These designs balance out routine order effects.

Covariation Changes in the treatment are accompanied by changes in the behavior. To establish causality, you must establish covariation.

Crossover (disordinal) interaction When an independent variable has one kind of effect in the presence of one level of a second independent variable, but a different kind of effect in the presence of a different level of the second independent variable. Examples: Getting closer to people may increase their attraction to you if you have just complimented them, but may decrease their attraction to you if you have just insulted them. Called a *crossover interaction* because the lines in a graph will cross. Called *disordinal interaction* because it cannot be explained by having ordinal rather than interval data.

Debriefing Giving participants the details of a study at the end of their participation. Proper debriefing is one of the researcher's most serious obligations.

Degrees of freedom (*df*) An index of sample size. In the simple experiment, the *df* for your error term will always be two less than the number of participants.

Demand characteristics Characteristics of the study that suggest to the participant how the researcher wants the participant to behave.

Demographics Characteristics of a group, such as gender, age, social class.

Dependent-groups *t* test A statistical test used with interval or ratio data to test differences between two conditions on a single dependent variable. Differs from the between-groups *t* test in that it is to be used only when you are getting two scores from each participant (within-subjects design) or when you are using a matched-pairs design.

Dependent variable (dependent measure) The factor that the experimenter predicts is affected by the independent variable; the participant's response that the experimenter is measuring.

Descriptive hypothesis A hypothesis about a group's characteristics or about the corrrelations between variables; a hypothesis that does not involve a cause–effect statement.

Dichotomous questions Questions that allow only two responses (usually "yes" or "no").

Direct (exact) replication Repeating a study as exactly as possible, usually to determine whether or not the same results will be obtained. Direct replications are useful for establishing that the findings of the original study are reliable.

Discriminant validity When a measure does not correlate highly with a measure of a different construct. Example: A violence measure might have a degree of discriminant validity if it does not correlate with the measures of assertiveness, social desirability, and independence.

Discussion The part of the article, immediately following the results section, that discusses the research findings and the study in a broader context and suggests research projects that could be done to follow up on the study.

Disordinal interaction See *crossover (disordinal) interaction.*

Double-barreled question A statement that contains more than one question. Responses to a double-barreled question are difficult to interpret. For example, if someone responds, "No," to the question "Are you hungry and thirsty?" we do not know whether he is hungry, but not thirsty; not hungry, but thirsty; or neither hungry nor thirsty.

Double-blind technique A strategy for improving construct validity that involves making sure that neither the participants nor the people who have direct contact with the participants know what type of treatment the participants have received.

Empty control group A group that does not get any kind of treatment. The group gets nothing, not even a placebo. Usually, because of participant and experimenter biases that may result from such a group, you will want to avoid using an empty control group.

Environmental manipulation A manipulation that involves changing the participant's environment rather than giving the participant different instructions.

Eta squared (η^2) An estimate of effect size that ranges from 0 to 1 and is comparable to *r* squared.

Ethical Conforming to the American Psychological Association's principles of what is morally correct behavior. To learn more about these guidelines and standards, see Appendix C.

Ex post facto research When a researcher goes back, after the research has been completed, looking to test hypotheses that were not formulated prior to the beginning of the study. The researcher is trying to take advantage of hindsight. Often an attempt to salvage something out of a study that did not turn out as planned.

Experiment A study that allows researchers to disentangle treatment effects from natural differences between groups, usually by randomly assigning participants to treatment group. In medicine, such studies may be called controlled clinical trials or randomized clinical trials.

Experimental design A design in which (a) a treatment manipulation is administered and (b) that manipulation is the only variable that systematically varies between treatment conditions.

Experimental group Participants who are randomly assigned to receive the treatment.

Experimental hypothesis A prediction that the treatment will cause an effect.

Experimental (research) realism When a study engages the participant so much that the participant is not merely playing a role (helpful participant, good person).

Experimenter bias Experimenters being more attentive to participants in the treatment group or giving different nonverbal cues to treatment group participants than to other participants. When experimenter bias is present, differences between groups may be due to the experimenter rather than to the treatment.

Exploratory study A study investigating (exploring) a new area of research. Unlike replications, an exploratory study does not follow directly from an existing study.

External validity The degree to which the results of a study can be generalized to other participants, settings, and times.

Extraneous factor Factor other than the treatment. If we cannot control or account for extraneous variables, we can't conclude that the treatment had an effect. That is, we will not have internal validity.

***F* ratio** Analysis of variance (ANOVA) yields an *F* ratio for each main effect and interaction. In between subjects experiments, the *F*-ratio is a ratio of between-groups variance to within-groups variance. If the treatment has no effect, *F* will tend to be close to 1.0.

Face validity The extent to which a measure looks, on the face of it, to be valid. Face validity has nothing to do with actual, scientific validity. That is, a test could have face validity and not real validity or could have real validity, but not face validity. However, for practical/political reasons, you may decide to consider face validity when comparing measures.

Factor analysis A statistical technique designed to explain the variability in several questions in terms of a smaller number of underlying hypothetical factors.

Factorial experiment An experiment that examines two or more independent variables (factors) at a time.

Fatigue effect Decreased performance on a task due to being tired or less enthusiastic as a study continues. In a within-subjects design, this decrease in performance might be incorrectly attributed to a treatment.

File drawer problem A situation in which the research not affected by Type 1 errors languishes in researchers' file cabinets, whereas the Type 1 errors are published.

Fixed-alternative question Item on a test or questionnaire in which a person must choose an answer from among a few specified alternatives. Multiple-choice, true–false, and rating-scale questions are all fixed-alternative questions.

Floor effect The effects of treatment(s) are underestimated because the dependent measure artificially restricts how low scores can be.

Frequency distribution A graph on which the frequencies of the scores are plotted. Thus, the highest point on the graph will be over the most commonly occurring score. Often, frequency distributions will look like the normal curve.

Functional relationship The shape of a relationship. Depending on the functional relationship between the independent and dependent variable, a graph of the relationship might look like a straight line or might look like a U, an S, or some other shape.

Hawthorne effect When the treatment group changes their behavior not because of the treatment itself, but because they know they are getting special treatment.

History Events in the environment—other than the treatment—that have changed. Differences between conditions that may seem to be due to the treatment may really be due to history.

Hypothesis A testable prediction about the relationship between two or more variables.

Hypothesis-guessing When participants alter their behavior to conform to their guess as to what the research hypothesis is. Hypothesis-guessing can be a serious threat to construct validity, especially if participants guess right.

Hypothesis testing The use of inferential statistics to determine if the relationship found between two or more variables in a particular sample holds true in the population.

Hypothetical construct See *construct*.

Illusory correlation When there is really no relationship (a zero correlation) between two variables, but people perceive that the variables are related.

Independence Factors are independent when they are not causally or correlationally linked. Independence is a key assumption of most statistical tests. In the simple experiment, observations must be independent. That is, what one participant does should have no influence on what another participant does and what happens to one participant should not influence what happens to another participant. Individually assigning participants to the treatment or no-treatment condition and individually testing each participant are ways to achieve independence.

Independent random assignment Randomly determining for each individual participant which condition he will be in. For example, you might flip a coin for each participant to determine to what group he will be assigned.

Independent variable The variable being manipulated by the experimenter. Participants are assigned to a level of independent variable by independent random assignment.

Inferential statistics Procedures for determining the reliability and generalizability of a particular research finding.

Informed consent If participants agree to take part in a study after they have been told what is going to happen to them, you have their informed consent.

Instructional manipulation Manipulating the treatment by giving written or oral instructions.

Instrumentation bias The way participants were measured changed from pretest to posttest. In instrumentation bias, the actual measuring instrument changes or the way it is administered changes. Sometimes people may think they have a treatment effect when they really have an instrumentation effect.

Interaction When you need to know how much of one variable participants have received to say what the effect of another variable is, you have an interaction between those two variables. If you graph the results from an experiment that has two or more independent variables, and the lines you draw between your points are not parallel, you may have an interaction.

Internal consistency The degree to which each question on a scale correlates with the other questions. Internal consistency is high if answers to each item correlate highly with answers to all other items.

Internal review board (IRB) A committee of at least five members—one of whom must be a nonscientist—that review proposed research in an effort to protect research participants.

Internal validity The degree to which a study establishes that a factor causes a difference in behavior. If a study lacks internal validity, the researcher may falsely believe that a factor causes an effect when it really doesn't.

Interobserver (judge) agreement The percentage of times the raters agree.

Interobserver reliability An index of the degree to which different raters give the same behavior similar ratings.

Interval scale data Data that give you numbers that can be meaningfully ordered along a scale (from lowest to highest) and in which equal numerical intervals represent equal psychological intervals. That is, the difference between scoring a "2" and a "1" and the difference between scoring a "7" and a "6" are the same not only in terms of scores (both are a difference of 1), but also in terms of the actual psychological characteristic being measured. Interval scale measures allow us to compare participants in terms of how much of a quality participants have—and in terms of how much more of a quality one group may have than another.

Interview A survey in which the researcher orally asks questions.

Interviewer bias When the interviewer influences participant's responses. For example, the interviewer might verbally or nonverbally reward the participant for giving responses that support the hypothesis.

Introduction The part of the article that occurs right after the abstract. In the introduction, the authors tell you what their hypothesis is, why their hypothesis makes sense, how their study fits in with previous research, and why their study was worth doing.

Known-groups technique A way of making the case for your measure's convergent validity that involves

seeing whether groups known to differ on the characteristic you are trying to measure also differ on your measure (e.g., ministers should differ from atheists on an alleged measure of religiosity).

Laboratory observation A technique of observing participants in a laboratory setting.

Law of parsimony The assumption that the explanation that is simplest, most straightforward, and makes the fewest assumptions is the most likely.

Leading question Question structured to lead respondents to the answer the researcher wants (such as, "You like this book, don't you?").

Levels of an independent variable When the treatment variable is given in different kinds or amounts, these different values are called *levels*. In the simple experiment, you only have two levels of the independent variable.

Likert-type item Item that typically asks participants whether they strongly agree, agree, are neutral, disagree, or strongly disagree with a certain statement. These items are assumed to yield interval data.

Linear relationship A relationship between an independent and dependent variable that is graphically represented by a straight line.

Loose-protocol effect Variations in procedure because the written procedures (the protocol) is not detailed enough. These variations in procedure may result in researcher bias.

Main effect See *overall main effect*.

Manipulation check A question or set of questions designed to determine whether participants perceived the manipulation in the way that the researcher intended.

Matched-pairs design An experimental design in which the participants are paired off by matching them on some variable assumed to be correlated with the dependent variable. Then, for each matched pair, one member is randomly assigned to one treatment condition, and the other gets the other treatment condition. This design usually has more power than a simple, between-groups experiment.

Matching Choosing your groups so that they are similar (they match) on certain characteristics. Matching reduces, but does not eliminate, the threat of selection bias.

Maturation Changes in participants due to natural growth or development. A researcher may think that the treatment had an effect when the difference in behavior is really due to maturation.

Mean An average calculated by adding up all the scores and then dividing by the number of scores.

Median If you arrange all the scores from lowest to highest, the middle score will be the median.

Median split The procedure of dividing participants into two groups ("highs" and "lows") based on whether they score above or below the median.

Mediating variable Variables inside the individual (such as thoughts, feelings, or physiological responses) that come between a stimulus and a response. In other words, the stimulus has its effect because it causes changes in mediating variables, which, in turn, cause changes in behavior.

Method section The part of the article immediately following the introduction. Whereas the introduction explains *why* the study was done, the method section describes *what* was done. For example, it will tell you what design was used, what the researchers said to the participants, what measures and equipment were used, how many participants were studied, and how participants were selected. The method section could also be viewed as a "how we did it" section. The method section is usually subdivided into at least two subsections: participants and procedure.

Mixed design An experimental design that has at least one within-subjects factor and one between-subjects factor.

Mode The score that occurred most often; the most frequent score. For example, 2 is the mode of the following data set: 2, 2, 2, 6, 10, 50.

Moderator variable Variable that can intensify, weaken, or reverse the effects of another variable. For example, the effect of wearing perfume may be moderated by gender: If you are a woman, wearing perfume may make you more liked; if you are a man, wearing perfume may make you less liked.

Mortality (attrition) Participants dropping out of a study before the study is completed. Sometimes, differences between conditions may be due to participants dropping out of the study rather than to the treatment.

Multiple-baseline design A single-subject or small-*n* design in which different behaviors receive baseline periods of varying lengths prior to the introduction of the treatment variable. Often, the goal is to show that the behavior being rewarded changes, whereas the other behaviors stay the same until they too are reinforced.

Multiple regression A statistical technique that can take data from several predictors and an outcome variable to create a formula that weights the predictors in such a way as to make the best possible estimates of the outcome variable given those predictors. In linear multiple regression, this equation is for the straight line that best predicts the outcome data. Often, with multiple regression, you not only are able to predict your outcome variable with accuracy, but you are also able to tell which predictors are most important for making accurate predictions. For more information on multiple regression, see Appendix D.

Naturalistic observation A technique of observing events as they occur in their natural setting.

Negative correlation An inverse relationship between two variables (such as number of suicide attempts and happiness).

95% confidence interval A range in which you can be 95% sure that the population mean falls.

Nominal-dichotomous item A question that presents participants with only two—usually very different—options (e.g., "Are you for or against animal research?"). Such questions are often yes/no questions and often ask the participant to classify herself or himself into one of two different categories.

Nominal scale numbers Numbers that do not represent different amounts of a characteristic but instead represent different kinds of characteristics (qualities, types, or categories); numbers that substitute for names.

Nonequivalent control-group design A quasi-experimental design that, like a simple experiment, has a treatment group and a no-treatment comparison group. However, unlike the simple experiment, random assignment does not determine which participants get the treatment and which do not.

Nonreactive measure Measurement that is taken without changing the participant's behavior; also referred to as *unobtrusive measure*.

Nonresponse bias The problem caused by people who were in your sample refusing to participate in your study. Nonresponse bias is one of the most serious threats to a survey design's external validity.

Nonsignificant results See *null results*.

Normal curve A bell-shaped, symmetrical curve that has its center at the mean.

Normal distribution If the way the scores are distributed follows the normal curve, scores are said to be normally distributed. For example, a population is said to be normally distributed if 68% of the scores are within one standard deviation of the mean, 95% are within two standard deviations of the mean, and 99% of the scores are within three standard deviations of the mean. Many statistical tests, including the *t*-test, assume that sample means are normally distributed.

Null hypothesis The hypothesis that there is no relationship between two or more variables. The null hypothesis can be disproven, but it cannot be proven.

Null results (nonsignificant results) Results that fail to disconfirm the null hypothesis; results that fail to provide convincing evidence that the factors are related. Null results are inconclusive because the failure to find a relationship could be due to your design lacking the power to find the relationship. In other words, many null results are Type 2 errors.

Observer bias Bias created by the observer seeing what the observer wants or expects to see.

Open-ended question Question that does not ask participants to choose between the responses provided by the researcher (e.g., choosing "a," "b," or "c" on a multiple-choice question or choosing a number between 1 and 5 on a rating scale measure) but instead asks the participant to generate a response. Essay and fill-in-the-blank questions are open-ended questions.

Operational definition A publicly observable way to measure or manipulate a variable; a "recipe" for how you are going to measure or manipulate your factors.

Order The place in a sequence (first, second, third, etc.) when a treatment occurs.

Order (trial) effects A big problem with within-subjects designs. The order in which the participant receives a treatment (first, second, etc.) will affect how participants behave.

Ordinal scale numbers Numbers that can be meaningfully ordered from lowest to highest. Ranks (e.g., class rank, order in which participants finished a task) are ordinal scale numbers.

Overall main effect The overall or average effect of an independent variable.

$p < .05$ **level** A traditional significance level; if the variables are unrelated, results significant at this level would occur less than 5 times out of 100. Traditionally, results that are significant at the $p < .05$ level are considered statistically reliable and thus replicable.

Parameter estimation The use of inferential statistics to estimate certain characteristics of the population (parameters) from a sample of that population.

Parameters Measurements describing populations; often inferred from statistics, which are measurements describing a sample.

Parsimony See *law of parsimony*.

Participant bias Participants trying to behave in a way that they believe will support the researcher's hypothesis.

Participant observation An observation procedure in which the observer participates with those being observed. The observer becomes "one of them."

Placebo treatment A fake treatment that we know has no effect, except through the power of suggestion. It allows experimenters to see if the treatment has an effect beyond that of suggestion. For example, in medical experiments, participants who are given placebos (pills that do not contain a drug) may be compared to participants who are given pills that contain the new drug.

Plagiarism Using someone else's words, thoughts, or work without giving proper credit.

Population The entire group that you are interested in. You can estimate the characteristics of a population by taking large random samples from that population.

Positive correlation A relationship between two variables in which the two variables tend to vary together—when one increases, the other tends to increase. (For example, height and weight have a positive correlation: The taller one is, the more one tends to weigh; the shorter one is, the less one tends to weigh.)

Post hoc test Usually refers to a statistical test that has been performed after an ANOVA has obtained a significant effect for a factor. Because the ANOVA says only that at least two of the groups differ from one another, post hoc tests are performed to find out which groups differ from one another.

Post hoc trend analysis A type of post hoc test designed to determine whether a linear or curvilinear relationship is statistically significant (reliable).

Power The ability to find differences or, put another way, the ability to avoid making Type 2 errors. The ability to find significant differences when differences truly exist.

Practice effect The change in a score on a test (usually a gain) resulting from previous practice with the test. In a within-subjects design, this improvement might be incorrectly attributed to receiving a treatment.

Pretest–posttest design A before–after design in which each participant is given the pretest, administered the treatment, then given the posttest.

Probability value (p value) The chances of obtaining a certain pattern of results if there really is no relationship between the variables.

Proportionate stratified random sampling Making sure that the sample is similar to the population in certain respects (for instance, percentage of men and women) and then randomly sampling from these groups (strata). Has all the advantages of random sampling with even greater accuracy.

Psychological Abstracts A useful resource that contains abstracts from a wide variety of journals. The *Abstracts* can be searched by year of publication, topic of article, or author. For more about the *Abstracts,* see Web Appendix B.

Psychological construct See *construct.*

PsycINFO The computerized version of *Psychological Abstracts.*

Quadratic relationship A relationship on a graph shaped like a "U" or an upside down "U."

Quasi-experiment A study that resembles an experiment except that random assignment played no role in determining which participants got which level of treatment. Usually, quasi-experiments have less internal validity than experiments.

Questionnaire A written survey instrument.

Quota sampling Making sure you get the desired number of (meet your quotas for) certain types of people (certain age groups, minorities, etc.). This method does not involve random sampling and usually gives you a less representative sample than random sampling would. However, it may be an improvement over convenience sampling.

Random assignment See *independent random assignment.*

Random digit dialing Finding participants for telephone interviews by taking the area code and the 3-digit prefixes that you are interested in and then adding random digits to the end to create 10-digit phone numbers. You may use this technique when (a) you cannot afford to buy a list of phone numbers and then randomly select numbers from that list or (b) you want to contact people with unlisted numbers.

Random error Variations in scores due to unsystematic, chance factors.

Random sampling A sample that has been randomly selected from a population. If you randomly select enough participants, those participants will usually be fairly representative of the entire population. That is, your random sample will reflect its population. Often, random sampling is used to maximize a study's external validity. Note that random sampling—unlike random assignment—does not promote internal validity.

Randomized within-subjects design As in all within-subjects designs, all participants receive more than one level or type of treatment. However, to make sure that not every participant receives the series of treatments in the same sequence, the researcher randomly determines which treatment comes first, which comes second, and so on. In other words, participants all get the same treatments, but they receive different sequences of treatments.

Ratio scale data The highest form of measurement. With ratio scale numbers, the difference between any two consecutive numbers is the same (see *interval scale*). But in addition to having interval scale properties, in ratio scale measurement, a zero score means the total absence of a quality. (Thus, Fahrenheit is not a ratio scale measure of temperature because 0 degrees Fahrenheit does not mean there is no temperature.) If you have ratio-scale numbers, you can meaningfully form ratios between scores. If IQ scores were ratio (they are not; very few measurements in psychology are), you could say that someone with a 60 IQ was twice as smart as someone with a 30 IQ (a ratio of 2 to 1). Furthermore, you could say that someone with a 0 IQ had absolutely no intelligence whatsoever.

Regression (toward the mean) The tendency for scores that are extremely unusual to revert back to more-normal levels on the retest. If participants are chosen because their scores were extreme, these extreme scores may be loaded with extreme amounts of random measurement error. On retesting, participants are bound to get more-normal scores as random measurement error abates to more-normal levels. This regression effect could be mistaken for a treatment effect.

Reliability A general term, often referring to the degree to which a participant would get the same score if retested (test–retest reliability). Reliability can, however, refer to the degree to which scores are free from random error. A measure can be reliable, but not valid. However, a measure cannot be valid if it is not also reliable.

Repeated-measures design See *within-subjects design.*

Replicable Repeatable. A skeptical researcher should be able to repeat another researcher's study and obtain the same pattern of results.

Replicate Repeat, or duplicate, an original study.

Research journal A relatively informal notebook in which you jot down your research ideas and observations. The research journal can be a useful resource when it comes time to write the research proposal. Note: Despite the fact that they sound similar, the term "research journal" is not similar to the term "scientific journal." The term "scientific journal" is used to distinguish journals from magazines. In contrast to magazines, scientific journals tend (1) not to have ads for popular products, (2) not to have full-page color pictures, (3) to have articles that follow APA format (having abstract, introduction, method, results, discussion, and reference sections), and (4) to have articles that have been peer-reviewed.

Researcher effect Ideally, you hope that the results from a study would be the same no matter who was conducting it. However, it is possible that the results may be affected by the researcher. If the researcher is affecting the results, there is a researcher effect.

Researcher expectancy effect When a researcher's expectations affect the results. This is a type of researcher bias.

Response set Habitual way of responding on a test or survey that is independent of a particular test item (for instance, a participant might always check "agree" no matter what the statement is).

Restriction of range To observe a sizable correlation between two variables, both must be allowed to vary widely (if one variable does not vary, the variables cannot vary together). Occasionally, investigators fail to find a relationship between variables because they study only one or both variables over a highly restricted range. Example: comparing NFL offensive linemen and saying that weight has nothing to do with playing offensive line in the NFL on the basis of your finding that great offensive tackles do not weigh much more than poor offensive tackles. Problem: You compared only people who ranged in weight from 315 to 330.

Results section The part of an article, immediately following the method section, that reports statistical results and relates those results to the hypotheses. From reading this section, you should know whether the results supported the hypotheses.

Retrospective self-report Participants telling you what they said, did, or believed in the past. In addition to problems with ordinary self-report (response sets, giving the answer that a leading question suggests, etc.), retrospective self-report is vulnerable to memory biases. Thus, retrospective self-reports should *not* be accepted at face value.

Reversal design (A–B–A design, A–B–A reversal design) A single-subject or small-*n* design in which baseline measurements are made of the target behavior (A), then an experimental treatment is given (B), and the target behavior is measured again (A). The A–B–A design makes a more convincing case for the treatment's effect than the A–B design.

Scatterplot A graph made by plotting the scores of individuals on two variables (e.g., each participant's height and weight). By looking at this graph, you should get an idea of what kind of relationship (positive, negative, zero) exists between the two variables.

Selection (or selection bias) Apparent treatment effects being due to comparing groups that differed even before the treatment was administered (comparing apples with oranges).

Selection by maturation interaction Treatment and no-treatment groups, although similar at one point, would have grown apart (developed differently) even if no treatment had been administered.

Self-administered questionnaire A questionnaire filled out in the absence of an investigator.

Semistructured interview An interview constructed around a core of standard questions; however, the interviewer may expand on any question in order to explore a given response in greater depth.

Sensitive, sensitivity The degree to which a measure is capable of distinguishing between participants who differ on a variable (e.g., have different amounts of a construct or who do more of a certain behavior).

Sensitization After getting several different treatments and performing the dependent variable task several times, participants may realize (become sensitive to) what the hypothesis is. Sensitization is a problem in within-subjects designs.

Sequence effect Participants who receive one sequence of treatments score differently than those participants who receive the same treatments in a different sequence when you have a sequence effect.

Simple experiment A study in which participants are independently and randomly assigned to one of two groups, usually to either a treatment group or to a no-treatment group. It is the easiest way to establish that a treatment causes an effect.

Simple main effect The effects of one independent variable at a specific level of a second independent variable. The simple main effect could have been obtained merely by doing a simple experiment.

Single blind To reduce either subject biases or researcher biases, you might use a single-blind experiment in which either the participant (if you are most concerned about subject bias) or the person running participants (if you are more concerned about researcher bias) is unaware of who is receiving what level of the treatment. If you are concerned about both subject and researcher bias, then you should probably use a double-blind study.

Single-*n* designs See *single-subject design*.

Single-subject design Design that tries to establish causality by studying a single participant and arguing that the covariation between treatment and changes in behavior could not be due to anything other than the treatment. A key to this approach is to prevent factors other than the treatment from varying.

Single-*n* designs are common in operant conditioning and psychophysical research. See also *A–B design, A–B–A reversal design, multiple-baseline design*.

Social desirability bias A bias resulting from participants giving responses that make them look good rather than giving honest responses.

Spurious When the covariation observed between two variables is not due to the variables influencing each other, but because both are being influenced by some third variable. For example, the relationship between ice cream sales and assaults in New York is spurious—not because it does not exist (it does!)—but because ice cream does not cause assaults, and assaults do not cause ice cream sales. Instead, high temperatures probably cause both increased assaults and ice cream sales. Beware of spuriousness whenever you look at research that does not use an experimental design.

Stable baseline When the participant's behavior, prior to receiving the treatment, is consistent. Single-*n* experimenters try to establish a stable baseline.

Standard deviation A measure of the extent to which individual scores deviate from the population mean. The more scores vary from each other, the larger the standard deviation will tend to be. If, on the other hand, all the scores are the same as the mean, the standard deviation would be zero.

Standard error of the difference An index of the degree to which random sampling error may cause two sample means representing the same populations to differ. In the simple experiment, if we are to find a treatment effect, the difference between our experimental-group mean and control-group mean will usually be at least twice as big as the standard error of the difference. To find out the exact ratio between our observed difference and the standard error of the difference, we conduct a *t* test.

Standard error of the mean An index of the degree to which random error may cause the sample mean to be an inaccurate estimate of the population mean. The standard error will be small when the standard deviation is small, and the sample mean is based on many scores.

Standardization Treating each participant in the same (standard) way. Standardization can reduce both bias and random error.

Statistical regression See *regression (toward the mean)*.

Statistical significance When a statistical test says that the relationship we have observed is probably not due to chance alone, we say that the results are statistically significant. In other words, because the relationship is probably not due to chance, we conclude that there probably is a real relationship between our variables.

Stimulus set The particular stimulus materials that are shown to two or more groups of participants. Researchers may use more than one stimulus set in a study so that they can see whether the treatment effect replicates across different stimulus sets. In those cases, stimulus sets would be a replication factor.

Stooge Confederate who pretends to be a participant, but is actually a researcher's assistant. The use of stooges raises ethical questions.

Stratified sampling. See *proportionate stratified sampling*.

Straw theory An oversimplified version of an existing theory. Opponents of a theory may present and attack a straw version of that theory, but claim they have attacked the theory itself.

Structured interview An interview in which all respondents are asked a standard list of questions in a standard order.

Subject bias (subject effects) Ways the participant can bias the results (guessing the hypothesis and playing along, giving the socially correct response, etc.).

Summated score When you have several Likert-type questions that all tap the same dimension (such as attitude toward democracy), you can add up each participant's responses to those questions to get an overall, total (summated) score.

Survey A nonexperimental design useful for describing how people think, feel, or behave. The key is to design a valid questionnaire, test, or interview and administer it to a representative sample of the group you are interested in.

Systematic replication A study that varies from the original study only in some minor aspect. For example, a systematic replication may use more participants, more standardized procedures, more levels of the independent variable, or a more realistic setting than the original study.

t **test** The most common way of analyzing data from a simple experiment. It involves computing a ratio between two things: (1) the difference between your group means, and (2) the standard error of the difference (an index of the degree to which group means could differ by chance alone). If the difference you observe is more than three times bigger than the difference that could be expected by chance, then your results are probably statistically significant. We can only say "probably" because the exact ratio that you need for statistical significance depends on your level of significance and on how many participants you have.

Temporal precedence The causal factor comes before the change in behavior. Because the cause must come before the effect, researchers trying to establish causality must establish that the factor alleged to be the cause was introduced before the behavior changed (temporal precedence).

Test–retest reliability A way of assessing the amount of random error in a measure by administering the measure to participants at two different times and then correlating their results. If the measure is free of random error, scores on the retest should be highly correlated with scores on the original test.

Testing effect Participants score differently on the posttest as a result of what they learned from taking the pretest. Occasionally, people may think the participants' behavior changed because of the treatment when it really changed due to testing.

Theory A set of principles that explain existing research findings and that can be used to make new predictions can lead to new research findings.

Time-series design A quasi-experimental design in which a series of observations are taken from a group of participants before and after they receive treatment. Because it uses many times of measurement, it is an improvement over the pretest–posttest design. However, it is still extremely vulnerable to history effects.

Trend analysis See *post hoc trend analysis*.

Type 1 error Rejecting the null hypothesis when it is in fact true. In other words, declaring a difference statistically significant when the difference is really due to chance.

Type 2 error Failure to reject the null hypothesis when it is in fact false. In other words, failing to find a relationship between your variables when there really is a relationship between them.

Unobtrusive measurement Recording a particular behavior without the participant knowing you are measuring that behavior. Unobtrusive measurement reduces subject biases such as social desirability bias and obeying demand characteristics.

Unstructured interview When the interviewer has no standard set of questions that he or she asks each participant—virtually worthless approach for collecting scientifically valid data.

Valid Usually, a reference to whether a conclusion or claim is justified. A measure is considered valid when it measures what it claims to measure. See also *construct validity*, *internal validity*, and *external validity*.

Variability between group means See *between-groups variance*.

Within-groups variance (mean square within, mean square error, error variance) An estimate of the amount of random error in your data. The bottom half of the *F*-ratio in a between-subjects analysis of variance.

Within-subjects design (repeated-measures design) An experimental design in which each participant is tested under more than one level of the independent variable. The sequence in which the participants receive the treatments is usually randomly determined. See also *randomized within-subjects design* and *counterbalanced within-subjects designs*.

Zero correlation When there doesn't appear to be a linear relationship between two variables. For practical purposes, any correlation between $-.10$ and $+.10$ may be considered so small as to be nonexistent.

References

Abelson, R. P. (1995). *Statistics as principled argument.* Mahwah, NJ: Erlbaum.

Abelson, R. P. (1997). On the surprising longevity of flogged horses: Why there is a case for the significance test. *Psychological Science, 8,* 12–15.

Ainsworth, M. D. S., & Bell, S. M. (1970). Attachment, exploration, and separation: Illustrated by the behavior of one-year-olds in a strange situation. *Child Development, 41,* 49–67.

Alexander, C. N., Langer, E. J., Newman, R. I., Chandler, H. M., & Davies, J. L. (1989). Transcendental meditation, mindfulness, and longevity: An experimental study with the elderly. *Journal of Personality and Social Psychology, 57,* 950–964.

Ambady, N., & Rosenthal, R. (1993). Half a minute: Predicting teacher evaluations from thin slices of nonverbal behavior and physical attractiveness. *Journal of Personality and Social Psychology, 64,* 431–444.

American Psychological Association. (1982). *Ethical principles in the conduct of research with human behavior.* Washington, DC: Author.

American Psychological Association. (1996a). *Guidelines for ethical conduct in the care and use of animals.* Washington, DC: Author.

American Psychological Association. (1996b). *Task force on statistical inference initial report.* Washington, DC: Author.

American Psychological Association. (2001). *Publication manual of the American Psychological Association* (5th ed.). Washington, DC: Author.

American Psychological Association. (2002). Ethical principles of psychologists and code of conduct. *American Psychologist, 57,* 1597–1611.

Anastasi, A. (1982). *Psychological testing* (5th ed.). New York: Macmillan.

Anderson, C. A., & Bushman, B. J. (2002, June/July). Media violence and the American public revisited. *American Psychologist, 57,* 448–450.

Anderson, C. A., Carnagey, N. L., & Eubanks, J. (2003). Exposure to violent media: The effects of songs with violent lyrics on aggressive thoughts and feelings. *Journal of Personality and Social Psychology, 84,* 960–971.

Anderson, C. A., Lindsay, J. J., & Bushman, B. J. (1999). Research in the psychological laboratory: Truth or triviality? *Current Directions in Psychological Science, 8,* 3–9.

Antill, J. K. (1983). Sex role complementarity versus similarity in married couples. *Journal of Personality and Social Psychology, 45,* 145–155.

Aronson, E. (1990). Applying social psychology to desegregation and energy conservation. *Personality and Social Psychology Bulletin, 16,* 118–131.

Aronson, E., & Carlsmith, J. M. (1968). Experimentation in social psychology. In G. Lindzey & E. Aronson (Eds.), *Handbook of social psychology* (2nd ed., pp. 1–79). Reading, MA: Addison–Wesley.

Asch, S. E. (1946). Forming impressions of personality. *Journal of Abnormal and Social Psychology, 41,* 258–290.

Asch, S. E. (1955). Opinions and social pressure. *Scientific American, 193,* 31–35.

Ayllon, T., & Azrin, N. H. (1968). *The token economy: A motivational system for therapy and rehabilitation.* New York: Appleton-Century-Crofts.

Banaji, M. R., & Crowder, R. G. (1989). The bankruptcy of everyday memory. *American Psychologist, 44,* 1185–1193.

Baron, R. M., & Kenny, D. A. (1986). The moderator-mediator distinction in social psychological research: Conceptual, strategic, and statistical considerations. *Journal of Personality and Social Psychology, 51,* 1173–1182.

Basson, R., McInnes, R., Smith, M., Hodgson, G., & Koppiker, N. (2002). Efficacy and safety of sildenafil citrate in women with sexual dysfunction associated with female sexual arousal disorder. *Journal of Women's Health and Gender Based Medicine , 11,* 331–333.

Beins, B. C. (1993). Using the Barnum effect to teach about ethics and deception in research. *Teaching of Psychology, 20,* 30–35.

Berkowitz, L. (1981, June). How guns control us. *Psychology Today,* 11–12.

Berlyne, D. E. (1971). *Conflict, arousal, and curiosity.* New York: McGraw-Hill.

Bernhardt, P. C., Dabbs, J. M., Jr., Fielden, J. A., & Lutter, C. D. (1998). Testosterone changes during vicarious experiences of winning and losing among fans at sporting events. *Physiology and Behavior, 65,* 59–62.

Bernieri, F. J. (1991). Interpersonal sensitivity in teaching interactions. *Personality and Social Psychology Bulletin, 17,* 98–103.

Berscheid, E., Dion, K., Walster, E., & Walster, G. W. (1971). Physical attractiveness and dating choice: A test of the matching hypothesis. *Journal of Experimental Social Psychology, 7,* 173–189.

Blough, D. S. (1957). Effect of lysergic acid diethylamide on absolute visual threshold in the pigeon. *Science, 126,* 304–305.

Brady, J. V. (1958). Ulcers in executive monkeys. *Scientific American, 199,* 95–100.

Brennan, C. (2005, March 24). E-mail surveys may be first step in effort to cripple progress of Title IX. *USA Today,* p. D5.

Brescoll, V., & LaFrance, M. (2004). The correlates and consequences of newspaper reports of research on sex differences. *Psychological Science, 15,* 515–520.

Brewer, C. L. (1990). *Teaching research methods: Three decades of pleasure and pain.* Presentation at the 98th Annual Convention of the American Psychological Association, Boston.

Briggs, C. S. (2001). *Supermaximum security prisons and institutional violence: An impact assessment.* Unpublished master's thesis. Southern Illinois University, Carbondale, Illinois.

Broad, W. J., & Wade, N. (1982). Science's faulty fraud detectors. *Psychology Today, 16,* 50–57.

Brown, J. D. (1991). Staying fit and staying well: Physical fitness as a moderator of life stress. *Journal of Personality and Social Psychology, 60,* 555–561.

Burke, J. (1978). *Connections.* Boston: Little, Brown.

Burke, J. (1985). *The day the university changed.* Boston: Little, Brown.

Bushman, B. J., & Anderson, C. A. (2001, June/July). Media violence and the American public: Scientific facts versus media misinformation. *American Psychologist, 56,* 477–489.

Buss, D. M. (1994). *The evolution of desire.* New York: Basic Books.

Byrne, B. M. (2004, July). *A beginner's guide to structural equation modeling: Basic concepts and applications.* Workshop presented at the meeting of the American Psychological Association, Honolulu, HI.

Byrne, D. (1961). Interpersonal attraction and attitude similarity. *Journal of Abnormal and Social Psychology, 62,* 713–715.

Byrne, D. (1971). *The attraction paradigm.* New York: Academic Press.

Campbell, D. T., & Stanley, J. C. (1963). *Experimental and quasi-experimental designs for research.* Chicago: Rand McNally.

Carrere, S., & Gottman, J. (1999). Predicting divorce among newlyweds from the first three minutes of marital conflict discussion. *Family Process, 38,* 292–301.

Carroll, R. T. (2003). *The skeptic's dictionary.* Hoboken, NJ: Wiley.

Chapman, L. J., & Chapman, P. J. (1967). Genesis of popular but erroneous psychodiagnostic observations. *Journal of Abnormal Psychology, 72,* 193–204.

Cialdini, R. B. (2005, April). Don't throw in the towel: Use social influence research. *APS Observer, 18,* 33–34.

Clark, H. H. (1973). The language-as-fixed-effect fallacy: A critique of language statistics in psychological research. *Journal of Verbal Learning and Verbal Behavior, 12,* 335–359.

Cohen, J. (1976). Random means random. *Journal of Verbal Learning and Verbal Behavior, 15,* 261–262.

Cohen, J. (1990). Things I have learned (so far). *American Psychologist, 45,* 1304–1312.

Cohen, J. (1994). The earth is round ($p < .05$). *American Psychologist, 49,* 997–1003.

Cohen, J., & Cohen, P. (1983). *Applied multiple regression/correlation analysis for the behavioral science.* Hillsdale, NJ: Erlbaum.

Coile, D. C., & Miller, N. E. (1984). How radical animal activists try to mislead humane people. *American Psychologist, 39,* 700–701.

Coleman, E. B. (1979). Generalization effects vs. random effects. *Journal of Verbal Learning and Verbal Behavior, 18,* 243–256.

Coles, C. D. (1993). Saying "goodbye" to the "crack baby." *Neurotoxicology and Teratology, 15,* 290–292.

Condry, J., & Condry, S. (1976). Sex differences: A study of the eye of the beholder. *Child Development, 47,* 812–819.

Cook, T. D., & Campbell, D. T. (1979). *Quasi-experimentation: Design and analysis for field settings.* Chicago: Rand McNally.

Cronbach, L. J. (1957). The two disciplines of scientific psychology. *American Psychologist, 12,* 671–684.

Cumming, G., & Finch, S. (2005). Inference by eye: Confidence intervals and how to read pictures of data. *American Psychologist, 60,* 170–180.

Custer, S. (1985). *The impact of backward masking.* Presented at the Thirteenth Annual Western Pennsylvania Undergraduate Psychology Conference in Clarion, Pennsylvania.

Danner, D., Snowden, D., & Friesen, W. (2001). Positive emotions in early life and longevity: Findings from the nun study. *Journal of Personality and Social Psychology, 80,* 804–813.

Darley, J., & Batson, D. (1973). From Jerusalem to Jericho: A study of situational and dispositional variables on helping behavior. *Journal of Personality and Social Psychology, 27,* 100–119.

Darley, J., & Latané, B. (1968). Bystander intervention in emergencies: Diffusion of responsibility. *Journal of Personality and Social Psychology, 8,* 377–383.

Davis, D., Shaver, P. R., & Vernon, M. L. (2004). Attachment style and subjective motivations for sex. *Personality and Social Psychology Bulletin, 30,* 1076–1090.

Dawes, R. M. (1994). *A house of cards: Psychology and psychotherapy built on myth.* New York: Free Press.

Dawkins, R. (1998). *Unweaving the rainbow: Science, delusion, and the appetite for wonder.* Boston: Houghton Mifflin.

De Leeuw, E. (1992). *Data quality in mail, telephone, and face-to-face surveys.* Amsterdam: TT Publications.

Dermer, M. L., & Hoch, T. A. (1999). Improving descriptions of single-subject experiments in research texts written for undergraduates. *The Psychological Record, 49,* 49–66.

Diener, E., & Diener, C. (1996) Most people are happy. *Psychological Science, 3,* 181–185.

Diener, E., & Seligman, M. (2004). Beyond money: Toward an economy of well-being. *Psychological Science in the Public Interest, 5*(1) (November), 1–31.

Dillman, D. A. (1978). *Mail and telephone surveys: The total design method.* New York: Wiley.

Dillman, D. A. (2000). *Mail and internet surveys: The tailored design method.* New York: Wiley.

Dillon, K. (1990). Generating research ideas; or, that's Salada tea. . . . *High School Psychology Teacher, 21,* 6–7.

Doherty, P. (2002). In M. Thomas (Ed.), *The right words at the right time* (p. 89). New York: Atria Books.

Edwards, T. (1990, July 23). Marketing grads told to take a reality check. *AMA News,* p. 9.

Ehrenberg, R. G., Brewer, D. J., Gamoran, A., & Williams, J. D. (2001). Class size and student achievement. *Psychological Science in the Public Interest, 2,* 1–30.

Elias, M. (2005, March 7). Study: A happy marriage can help mend physical wounds. *USA Today,* p. D7.

Elicker, J., Englund, M., & Sroufe, L. A. (1992). Predicting peer competence and peer relationships in childhood from early parent-child relationships. In R. D. Parke & G. W. Ladd (Eds.), *Family-peer relationships: Modes of linkage.* Hillsdale, NJ: Erlbaum.

Emmons, R. A., & McCullough, M. E. (2003). Counting blessings versus burdens: An experimental investigation of gratitude and subjective well-being in daily life. *Journal of Personality and Social Psychology, 84,* 377–389.

Estes, W. K. (1997). Significance testing in psychological research: Some persisting issues. *Psychological Science, 8,* 18–20.

Faurie, C., & Raymond, M. (2005). Handedness, homicide, and negative frequency-dependent selection. Proceedings of the Royal Society of London B.

Festinger, L., & Carlsmith, J. M. (1959). Cognitive consequences of forced compliance. *Journal of Abnormal and Social Psychology, 58,* 203–210.

Field, T. (1993). The therapeutic effects of touch. In G. C. Brannigan, & M. R. Merrens (Eds.), *The undaunted psychologist: Adventures in research.* New York: McGraw-Hill.

Fisher, R. A. (1938). Presidential Address to the First Indian Statistical Congress.

Fiske, D. W., & Fogg, L. (1990). But the reviewers are making different criticisms of my paper! Diversity and uniqueness in reviewer comments. *American Psychologist, 45,* 591–598.

Fitzsimons, G. M., & Kay, A. C. (2004). Language and interpersonal cognition: Causal effects of variations in pronoun usage on perceptions of closeness. *Personality and Social Psychology Bulletin, 30,* 547–557.

Forer, B. R. (1949). The fallacy of personal validation: A classroom demonstration of gullibility. *Journal of Abnormal and Social Psychology, 44,* 118–123.

Forsyth, D. (2004, Fall). IRBism: Prejudice against Institutional Review Boards. *Dialogue, 19,* pp. 14–15, 20.

Frank, M. G., & Gilovich, T. (1988). The dark side of self- and other perceptions: Black uniforms and aggression in professional sports. *Journal of Personality and Social Psychology, 54,* 74–85.

Franz, C. E., McClelland, D. C., & Weinberger, J. (1991). Childhood antecedents of conventional social accomplishment in midlife adults: A 36-year prospective study. *Journal of Personality and Social Psychology, 60,* 586–595.

Frederickson, B. L., Roberts, T., Noll, S. M., Quinn, D. M., & Twenge, J. M. (1998). That swimsuit becomes you: Sex differences in self-objectification, restrained eating, and math performance. *Journal of Personality and Social Psychology, 75,* 269–284.

Frederickson, N. (1986). Toward a broader conception of human intelligence. *American Psychologist, 41,* 445–452.

Frijda, N. H. (1988). The laws of emotion. *American Psychologist, 43,* 349–358.

Garner, D. M., & Garfinkel, P. E. (1979). The eating attitudes test: An index of the symptoms of anorexia nervosa. *Psychological Medicine, 9,* 273–279.

Gesn, P. R., & Ickes, W. (1999). The development meaning contexts of empathic accuracy: Channel and sequence effects. *Journal of Personality and Social Psychology, 77,* 746–761.

Gilovich, T., Vallone, R., & Tversky, A. (1985). The hot hand in basketball: On the misperception of random sequences. *Cognitive Psychology, 17,* 295–314.

Gladue, B. A., & Delaney, H. J. (1990). Gender differences in perception of attractiveness of men and women in bars. *Personality and Social Psychology Bulletin, 16,* 378–391.

Glass, D. C., & Singer, J. E. (1972). *Urban stress: Experiments on noise and social stressors.* New York: Academic Press.

Glick, P., Gottesman, D., & Jolton, J. (1989). The fault is not in the stars: Susceptibility of skeptics and believers in astrology to the Barnum effect. *Personality and Social Psychology Bulletin, 15,* 559–571.

Goldman, B. A., & Mitchell, D. F. (1990). *Directory of unpublished experimental mental measures* (Vol. 5). Dubuque, IA: Wm. C. Brown.

Gosling, S. D., Vazire, S., Srivastava, S., & John, O. P. (2004). Should we trust web-based studies? A comparative analysis of six preconceptions about Internet questionnaires. *American Psychologist, 59,* 93–104.

Gottman, J. M. (1993). *What predicts divorce? The relationship between marital processes and marital outcomes.* Hillsdale, NJ: Erlbaum.

Greenberger, E., & Steinberg, L. (1986). *When teenagers work: The psychological and social costs of adolescent employment.* New York: Basic Books.

Greenwald, A. G. (1975). Significance, nonsignificance, an interpretation of an ESP experiment. *Journal of Experimental Social Psychology, 11,* 180–191.

Greenwald, A. G. (1976). Within-subjects designs: To use or not to use? *Psychological Bulletin, 83,* 314–320.

Greenwald, A. G., Gonzalez, R., Harris, R. J., & Guthrie, D. (1996). Effect sizes and *p* values: What should be reported and what should be replicated. *Psychophysiology, 33,* 175–183.

Groves, R. M., & Kahn, R. L. (1979). *Surveys by telephone: A national comparison with personal interviews.* New York: Academic Press.

Haack, S. (2004, July/August). Defending science—within reason: The critical common-sensist manifesto. *Skeptical Inquirer,* pp. 28–34.

Hadaway, C. K., Marler, P. L., & Chaves, M. (1993). What the polls don't show: A closer look at U.S. church attendance. *American Sociological Review, 58,* 741–752.

Hagen, R. L. (1998). A further look at wrong reasons to abandon statistical testing. *American Psychologist, 53,* 801–803.

Harker, L., & Keltner, D. (2001). Expressions of positive emotion in women's college yearbook pictures and their relationship to personality and life outcomes across adulthood. *Journal of Personality and Social Psychology, 80,* 112–124.

Harris, R. J. (1997). Significance tests have their place. *Psychological Science, 8,* 8–11.

Haselton, M. G., Buss, D., M., Oubaid, V., & Angleitner, A. (2005). Sex, lies, and strategic interference: The psychology of deception between the sexes. *Personality and Social Psychology Bulletin, 31,* 3–23.

Hays, W. L. (1981). *Statistics* (3rd ed.). New York: Holt, Rinehart and Winston.

Hebl, M. R., King, E. B., & Lin, J. (2004). The swimsuit becomes us all: Ethnicity, gender, and vulnerability to self-objectification. *Personality and Social Psychology Bulletin, 30,* 1322–1331.

Hebl, M., & Mannix, L. (2003). The weight of obesity in evaluating others: A mere proximity effect. *Personality and Social Psychological Bulletin, 29,* 28–38.

Hedges, L. (1987). How hard is hard science, how soft is soft science? *American Psychologist, 42,* 443–455.

Helliwell, J. F. (2003). How's life? Combining individual and national variables to explain subjective well-being. *Economic Modeling, 20,* 331–360.

Henderson, M. A. (1985). *How con games work.* Secaucus, NJ: Citadel Press.

High-handed professor's comments called hot error. (1985, August). *USA Today,* p. C2.

Hill, C. A. (1991). Seeking emotional support: The influence of affiliative need and partner warmth. *Journal of Personality and Social Psychology, 60,* 112–121.

Hilton, J. L., & Fein, S. (1989). The role of typical diagnosticity on stereotype-based social judgments. *Journal of Personality and Social Psychology, 57,* 201–211.

Hilton, J. L., & von Hippel, W. (1990). The role of consistency in the judgment of stereotype-relevant behaviors. *Personality and Social Psychology Bulletin, 16,* 723–727.

Holmes, D. S., & Will, M. J. (1985). Expression of interpersonal aggression by angered and nonangered persons with Type A and Type B behavior patterns. *Journal of Personality and Social Psychology, 48,* 723–727.

Honomichl, J. (1990, August 6). Answering machines threaten survey research. *Marketing News,* p. 11.

Huberty, C. J., & Morris, J. D. (1989) Multivariate analysis versus multiple univariate analyses. *Psychological Bulletin, 105,* 302–308.

Ickes, W. (2003). *Everyday mind reading: Understanding what other people think and feel.* Amherst, NY: Prometheus Books.

Ickes, W., & Barnes, R. D. (1978). Boys and girls together and alienated: On enacting stereotyped sex roles in mixed-sex dyads. *Journal of Personality and Social Psychology, 36,* 669–683.

Ickes, W., Robertson, Tooke, W., & Teng, G. (1986). Naturalistic social cognition: Methodology, assessment, and validation. *Journal of Personality and Social Psychology, 51,* 66–82.

Injury quiets Rams. (1984, August 6). *USA Today,* p. C7.

Iyengar, S. S., & Lepper, M. R. (2000). When choice is demotivating: Can one desire too much of a good thing? *Journal of Personality and Social Psychology, 79,* 995–1006.

Jackson, J. M., & Padgett, V. (1982). With a little help from my friend: Social loafing and the Lennon-McCartney songs. *Personality and Social Psychology Bulletin, 8,* 672–677.

Jackson, J. M., & Williams, K. D. (1985). Social loafing on difficult tasks: Working collectively can improve performance. *Journal of Personality and Social Psychology, 49,* 937–942.

Jolley, J. M., Murray, J. D., & Keller, P. A. (1992). *How to write psychology papers: A student's survival guide for psychology and related fields.* Sarasota, FL: Professional Resource Exchange.

Kay, A. C., Jimenez, M. C., & Jost, J. T. (2002). Sour grapes, sweet lemons, and the rationalization of the status quo. *Personality and Social Psychology Bulletin, 28,* 1300–1312.

Kenny, D. A., & Smith, E. R. (1980). A note on the analysis of designs in which subjects receive each stimulus only once. *Journal of Experimental Social Psychology, 16,* 497–507.

Keyser, D. J., & Sweetland, R. C. (Eds.). (1984). *Test critiques.* Kansas City, MO: Test Corporation of America.

Kiesler, C. A. (1982). Public and professional myths about mental hospitalization: An empirical reassessment of policy-related beliefs. *American Psychologist, 37,* 1323–1339.

Kiesler, C. A., & Sibulkin, A. E. (1987). *Mental hospitalization: Myths and facts about a national crisis.* Beverly Hills, CA: Sage.

Kimble, G. A. (1990). A search for principles in principles of psychology. *Psychological Science, 1,* 151–155.

Kincher, J. (1992). *The first honest book about lies.* Minneapolis, MN: Free Spirit.

Kirsch, I., Moore, T. J., Scoboria, A., & Nicholls, S. S. (2002). The emperor's new clothes: An analysis of antidepressant medication data submitted to the U.S. Food and Drug Administration. *Prevention & Treatment, 5,* Retrieved July 23, 2002, from http://journals.apa.org/prevention/volume5/toc-jul15-02.htm

Klarreich, E. (2004, December 4). Take a chance: Scientists put randomness to work. *Science News,* pp. 362–364.

Kline, R. B. (1998). *Principles and practice of structural equation modeling.* New York: Guilford Press.

Kohlberg, L. (1981). *The meaning and measurement of moral development.* Worcester, MA: Clark University Press.

Kohn, A. (1988). You know what they say: Are proverbs nuggets of truth or fool's gold? *Psychology Today, 22*(4), 36–41.

Kosko, B. (2002, June 7). Scientific jargon goes over heads of judges, jurors. *The Atlantic Journal-Constitution,* p. A23.

Kramer, J. J., & Conoley, J. C. (Eds.). (1992). *The eleventh mental measurements yearbook.* Lincoln, NE: Buros Institute of Mental Measurements.

Krosnick, J. A., & Schuman, H. (1988). Attitude intensity, importance, and certainty and susceptibility to response effects. *Journal of Personality and Social Psychology, 54,* 940–952.

Kuehn, S. A. (1989). *Prospectus handbook for Comm 352.* Unpublished manuscript.

Langer, E. J., Blank, A., & Chanowitz, B. (1978). The mindlessness of ostensibly thoughtful action: The role of "placebic" information in interpersonal interaction. *Journal of Personality and Social Psychology, 36,* 635–642.

Langer, E. J., & Rodin, J. T. (1976). The effects of choice and enhanced personal responsibility for the aged: A field experiment in an institutional setting. *Journal of Personality and Social Psychology, 34,* 909–917.

Lardner, R. (1994, Feb. 21). Common nonsense: The age of reason (1974–1994). *The Nation, 258,* 232–234.

Latané, B., & Darley, J. M. (1968). Group inhibition of bystander intervention in emergencies. *Journal of Personality and Social Psychology, 10,* 215–221.

Latané, B., & Darley, J. M. (1970). *The unresponsive bystander: Why doesn't he help?* New York: Appleton-Century-Crofts.

Latané, B., Williams, K., & Harkins, S. (1979). Many hands make light the work: The causes and consequences of social loafing. *Journal of Personality and Social Psychology, 37,* 822–832.

Lawson, T. J. (1999). Assessing critical thinking as a learning outcome for psychology majors. *Teaching of Psychology, 26,* 207–209.

Lehman, D. R., Lempert, R. O., & Nisbett, R. E. (1988). The effects of graduate training on reasoning: Formal discipline and thinking about everyday-life events. *American Psychologist, 43,* 431–442.

Levitt, S. D., & Dubner, S. J. (2005). *Freakonomics: A rogue economist explores the hidden side of everything.* New York: William Morrow.

Levy-Leboyer, C. (1988). Success and failure in applying psychology. *American Psychologist, 43,* 779–785.

Lewis, D., & Greene, J. (1982). *Thinking better.* New York: Rawson, Wade.

Liberman, V. Samuels, S. M., & Ross, L. (2004). The name of the game: Predictive power of reputations versus situational labels in determining prisoner's dilemma game moves. *Personality and Social Psychology Bulletin, 30,* 1175–1185.

Lin, H. Y. (2004, August). Responses on anonymous and computer administered survey: A good way to reduce social desirability effect. Poster session presented at the annual meeting of the American Psychological Association, Honolulu, HI.

Loftus, E. F. (1975). Leading questions and the eyewitness report. *Cognitive Psychology, 7,* 560–572.

Luo, S., & Klohnen, C. C. (2005). Assortative mating and marital quality in newlyweds: A couple-centered approach. *Journal of Personality and Social Psychology, 88,* 304–326.

MacCallum, R. C., Zhang, S., Preacher, K. J., & Rucker, D. D. (2002). On the practice of dichotomization of quantitative variables. *Psychological Methods, 7*(1), 19–40.

Maslow, A. H. (1970). Cited in S. Cunningham, Humanist celebrate gains, goals. *APA Monitor, 16,* 16.

McNulty, J. K., & Karney, B. R. (2004). Positive expectations in the early years of marriage: Should couples expect the best or brace for the worst? *Journal of Personality and Social Psychology, 86,* 729–745.

Medvec, V. H., Madey, S. F., & Gilovich, T. (1995). When less is more: Counterfactual thinking and satisfaction among Olympic medalists. *Journal of Personality and Social Psychology, 69,* 603–610.

Milgram, S. (1974). *Obedience to authority: An experimental view.* New York: Harper and Row.

Milgram, L., Bickman, L., & Berkowitz, L. (1969). Note on the drawing power of crowds of different size. *Journal of Personality and Social Psychology, 13,* 79–82.

Miller, E. T., Neal, D. J., Roberts, L. J., Baer, J. S., Cressler, S. O., Metrik, J., & Marlatt, G. A. (2002). Test–retest reliability of alcohol measures: Is there a difference between Internet-based assessment and traditional methods? *Psychology of Addictive Behaviors, 16,* 56–63.

Miller, R. L., Wozniak, W. J., Rust, M. R., Miller, B. R., & Slezak, J. (1996). Counterattitudinal advocacy as a means of enhancing instructional effectiveness: How to teach students what they do not want to know. *Teaching of Psychology, 23,* 215–219.

Mitchell, J. V. (Ed.). (1983). *Tests in print III: An index to tests, test reviews, and the literature on specific tests.* Lincoln, NE: Buros Institute of Mental Measurements.

Moerman, D. E. (2002). "The Loaves and the Fishes": A Comment on "The emperor's new drugs: An analysis of antidepressant medication data submitted to the U.S. Food and Drug Administration." *Prevention & Treatment, 5.* Retrieved July 23, 2002, from http://journals.apa.org/prevention/volume5/toc-jul15-02.htm

Morris, J. D. (1986). MTV in the classroom. *Chronicle of Higher Education, 32,* 25–26.

Moskalenko, S., & Heine, S. J. (2003). Watching your troubles away: Television viewing as a stimulus for subjective self-awareness. *Personality and Social Psychology Bulletin, 29,* 76–85.

Myers, D. G. (1999). *Social psychology* (6th ed.). New York: McGraw-Hill.

Myers, D. G. (2002a). *Social psychology* (7th ed.). New York: McGraw-Hill.

Myers, D. G. (2002b). *Intuition: Its powers and perils.* New Haven, CT: Yale University Press.

Mynatt, C. R., & Doherty, M. E. (1999). *Understanding human behavior.* Needham Heights, MA: Allyn & Bacon.

Neisser, U. (1984). *Ecological movement in cognitive psychology.* Invited address at the 92nd Annual Convention of the American Psychological Association in Toronto, Canada.

Nickell, J. (2005, May/June). Alleged Reagan astrologer dies. *Skeptical Inquirer, 29,* 8–9.

Nisbett, R. E., & Ross, L. (1980). *Human inference: Strategies and shortcomings of social judgment.* Englewood Cliffs, NJ: Prentice-Hall.

Nisbett, R. E., & Wilson, T. D. (1977). Telling more than we can know: Verbal reports on mental processes. *Psychological Review, 84,* 231–259.

Nosek, B. A., Banaji, M. R., & Greenwald, A. G. (2002). E-Research: Ethics, security, design, and control in psychological research on the Internet. *Journal of Social Issues, 58,* 161–176.

Orne, M. (1962). On the social psychology of the psychological experiment: With particular reference to demand characteristics and their implications. *American Psychologist, 17,* 776–783.

Park, R. L. (2000). *Voodoo science: The road from foolishness to fraud.* New York: Oxford University Press.

Pennebaker, J. W., Dyer, M. A., Caulkins, R. S., Litowitz, D. L., Ackerman, P. L., Anderson, D. B., & McGraw, K. M. (1979). Don't the girls get prettier at closing time: A country and western application to psychology. *Personality and Social Psychology Bulletin, 5,* 122–125.

Pettijohn, T. F., & Jungeberg, B. J. (2004). *Playboy* playmate curves: Changes in facial and body feature preferences across social and economic conditions. *Personality and Social Psychology Bulletin, 30,* 1186–1197.

Pfungst, O. (1911). *Clever Hans.* New York: Henry Holt.

Phillips, D. P. (1979). Suicide, motor vehicle fatalities, and the mass media: Evidence toward a theory of suggestion, *American Journal of Sociology, 84,* 1150–1174.

Pliner, P., Chaiken, S., & Flett, G. L. (1990). Gender differences in concern with body weight and physical appearance over the life span. *Personality and Social Psychology Bulletin, 16,* 263–273.

Plomin, R. (1993). Nature and nurture: Perspective and prospective. In R. Plomin, R. McClearn, & G. E. McClearn (Eds.), *Nature, nurture, and psychology.* Washington, DC: American Psychological Association.

Porter, T. M. (1997). *Trust in numbers: The pursuit of objectivity in science and public life.* Princeton, NJ: Princeton University Press.

Prentice, D. A., & Miller, D. T. (1992). When small effects are impressive. *Psychological Bulletin, 112,* 160–164.

Provine, R. F. (2004). Laughing, tickling, and the evolution of speech and self. *Current Directions in Psychological Science, 13,* 215–218.

Ralof, J. (September 19, 1998). The science of museums. *Science News,* 184–186.

Ranieri, D. J., & Zeiss, A. M. (1984). Induction of a depressed mood: A test of opponent-process theory. *Journal of Personality and Social Psychology, 47,* 1413–1422.

Reifman, A. S., Larick, R. P., & Fein, S. (1991). Temper and temperature on the diamond: The heat-aggression relationship in Major League Baseball. *Personality and Social Psychology Bulletin, 17,* 580–585.

Reis, H. T., & Stiller, J. (1992). Publication trends in JPSP: A three-decade review. *Personality and Social Psychology Bulletin, 18,* 465–472.

Richter, M. L., & Seay, M. B. (1987). ANOVA designs with subjects and stimuli and random effects: Applications to prototype effects on recognition memory. *Journal of Personality and Social Psychology, 53,* 470–480.

Robins, C. J. (1988). Attributions and depression: Why is the literature so inconsistent? *Journal of Personality and Social Psychology, 54,* 880–889.

Robinson, D. N. (Speaker). (1997). *The great ideas of psychology, part 1, minds possessed: Witchery and the search for explanations.* (Cassette Recording). Washington, DC: The Teaching Company.

Robinson, M. D., Vargas, P. T., Tamir, M., & Solberg, E. C. (2004). Using and being used by categories: The case of negative evaluations and daily well-being. *Psychological Science, 15,* 515–520.

Roethlisberger, F. J., & Dickson, W. J. (1939). *Management and the worker.* Cambridge, MA: Harvard University Press.

Rogers, C. R. (1985). Cited in S. Cunningham, Humanists celebrate gains, goals. *APA Monitor, 16,* 16.

Rosa, L. R., Rosa, E. R., Sarner, L. S., & Barrett, S. B. (1998). Close look at therapeutic touch. *Journal of the American Medical Association, 279,* 1005–1010.

Rosenthal, R. (1966). *Experimenter effects in behavioral research.* New York: Appleton-Century-Crofts.

Rosenthal, R. (1992, Fall). Computing contrasts: On sharpening psychological science. *Dialogue,* p. 3.

Rubin, Z. (1970). Measurement of romantic love. *Journal of Personality and Social Psychology, 16,* 265–273.

Ruchlis, H., & Oddo, S. (1990). *Clear thinking: A practical introduction.* Buffalo, NY: Prometheus.

Rucker, D. D., & Petty, R. E. (2003). Effects of accusations on the accuser: The moderating role of accuser culpability. *Personality and Social Psychology Bulletin, 29,* 1259–1271.

Sagan, C. (1993). *Broca's brain.* New York: Ballantine.

Sargent, M. J. (2004). Less thought, more punishment: Need for cognition predicts support for punitive responses to crime. *Personality and Social Psychology Bulletin, 30,* 1485–1493.

Saucier, D. A., & Miller, C. T. (2003). The persuasiveness of racial arguments as a subtle measure of racism. *Personality and Social Psychology Bulletin, 29,* 1303–1315.

Scarr, S. (1997). Rules of evidence: A larger context for the statistical debate. *Psychological Science, 8,* 16–17.

Schachter, S. (1959). *The psychology of affiliation.* Stanford, CA: Stanford University Press.

Schmit, J. (2005, May 31). A winded FDA races to keep up with drug ads that go too far. *USA Today,* 1A, p. A4.

Schultz, D., & Schultz, S. (1990). *Psychology and industry today: An introduction to industrial and organizational psychology* (5th ed.). New York: Macmillan.

Schwarz, N. (1999). Self-Reports: How the questions shape the answers. *American Psychologist, 54,* 93–105.

Seligman, M. E. P. (1975). *Helplessness: On depression, development, and death.* San Francisco, CA: Freeman.

Seligman, M. E. P. (1990). *Learned optimism: How to change your mind and your life.* New York: Pocket.

Seligman, M. E. P. (2002). *Authentic happiness.* New York: Free Press.

Semon, T. (1990, April 16). Beware of bedazzling number mongers. *Marketing News,* p. 13.

Shedler, J., & Block, J. (1990). Adolescent drug use and psychological health: A longitudinal inquiry. *American Psychologist, 45,* 612–637.

Shefrin, H. M., & Statman, M. (1986). How not to make money in the stock market. *Psychology Today, 20,* 52–57.

Sherman, L. W., & Berk, R. A. (1984). The specific deterrent effects of arrest for domestic assault. *American Sociology Review, 49,* 262–272.

Sherman, S. J. (1980). On the self-erasing nature of errors of prediction. *Journal of Personality and Social Psychology, 39,* 211–221.

Shorter, E. (1997). *A history of psychiatry.* New York: Wiley.

Shrout, P. E. (1997). Should significance tests be banned? Introduction to a special section exploring the pros and cons. *Psychological Science, 8,* 1–2.

Sigall, H., & Mills, J. (1998). Measures of independent variables and mediators are useful in social psychology experiments: But are they necessary? *Personality and Social Psychology Review, 2,* 218–226.

Skinner, B. F. (1948). "Superstition" in the pigeon. *Journal of Experimental Psychology, 38,* 168–172.

Slovic, P. S., & Fischoff, B. (1977). On the psychology of experimental surprises. *Journal of Experimental Psychology: Human Perception and Performance, 3,* 455–471.

Snyder, M. (1984). When belief creates reality. In L. Berkowitz (Ed.), *Advances in experimental social psychology, Vol. 18.* New York: Academic Press.

Stanovich, K. E. (1990). *How to think straight about psychology.* Glenview, IL: Scott, Foresman.

Steele, C. M., Southwick, L. L., & Critchlow, B. (1981). Dissonance and alcohol: Drinking your troubles away. *Journal of Personality and Social Psychology, 41,* 831–846.

Steinberg, L., & Dornbusch, S. M. (1991). Negative correlates of part-time employment during adolescence: Replication and elaboration. *Developmental Psychology, 27,* 304–313.

Stern, P. C. (1993). A second environmental science: Human-environmental interactions. *Science, 260,* 1997–1999.

Sternberg, R. J. (1986). *Intelligence applied: Understanding and increasing your intellectual skills.* New York: Harcourt Brace Jovanovich.

Sternberg, R. J. (1994, Spring). Love is a story. *The General Psychologist, 30,* 1–11.

Stirman, S. W., & Pennebaker, J. W. (2001). Word use in the poetry of suicidal and non-suicidal poets. *Psychosomatic Medicine, 63,* 517–522.

Stone, J., Aronson, E., Crain, A. L., Winslow, M. P., & Fried, C. (1994). Introducing hypocrisy as a means of encouraging young adults to use condoms. *Personality and Social Psychology Bulletin, 20,* 116–128.

Stone, P. J., Dunphy, D. C., Smith, M. S., & Ogilvie, D. M. (1966). *The general inquirer: A computer approach to content analysis.* Cambridge, MA: M.I.T. Press.

Surowiecki, J. (2004). *The wisdom of crowds.* New York: Doubleday.

Swann, W. B., Jr., & Rentfrow, P. J. (2001). Blirtatiousness: Cognitive, behavioral, and physiological consequences of rapid responding. *Journal of Personality and Social Psychology, 81,* 1160–1175.

Swets, J. A., & Bjork, R. A. (1990). Enhancing human performance: An evaluation of "new age" techniques considered by the U.S. Army. *Psychological Science, 1,* 85–96.

Thomas, G., Fletcher, G., & Lange, C. (1997). On-line empathic accuracy in marital interaction. *Journal of Personality and Social Psychology, 72,* 939–850.

Thomas, M. (Ed.). (2002). *The right words at the right time.* New York: Atria Books.

Tversky, B. (1973). Encoding processes in recognition and recall. *Cognitive Psychology, 5,* 275–287.

Twenge, J. M. (2002). The age of anxiety? The birth cohort change in anxiety and neuroticism, 1952–1993. *Journal of Personality and Social Psychology, 79,* 1007–1021.

Ward, W. C., & Jenkins, H. M. (1965). The display of information and the judgment of contingency. *Canadian Journal of Psychology, 19,* 231–241.

Wedell, D. H., & Parducci, A. (1988). The category effect in social judgment: Experimental ratings of happiness. *Journal of Personality and Social Psychology, 55,* 341–356.

Weiten, W. (1992). *Psychology: Themes and variations.* Pacific Grove, CA: Brooks/Cole.

Wickens, T. D., & Keppel, G. (1983). On the choice of design and of test statistic in the analysis of experiments with sampled materials. *Journal of Verbal Learning and Verbal Behavior, 22,* 296–309.

Wike, E. L., & Church, J. D. (1976). Comments on Clark's "The language-as-fixed-effect fallacy." *Journal of Verbal Learning and Verbal Behavior, 15,* 249–255.

Wilkinson, L., & The Task Force on Statistical Inference. (1999). Statistical methods in psychology journals: Guidelines and explanations. *American Psychologist, 54,* 594–604.

Williams, K. D., Nida, S. A., Baca, L. D., & Latané, B. (1989). Social loafing and swimming: Effects of identifiability on individual and relay performance of intercollegiate swimmers. *Basic and Applied Social Psychology, 10,* 73–81.

Williams, K. D., & Sommer, K. L. (1997). Social ostracism by one's coworkers: Does rejection lead to loafing or compensation? *Personality and Social Psychology Bulletin, 23,* 693–706.

Williams, R. L., & Long, J. D. (1983). *Toward a self-managed lifestyle* (3rd ed.). Boston: Houghton-Mifflin.

Wilson, M., & Daly, M. (1985). Competitiveness, risk taking, and violence: The young male syndrome. *Ethology and Sociobiology, 6,* 59–73.

Wilson, T. D. (2002). *Strangers to ourselves: Discovering the adaptive unconscious.* Cambridge, MA: The Belknap Press of Harvard University Press.

Wilson, T. D., & Schooler, J. W. (1991). Thinking too much: Introspection can reduce the quality of preferences and decisions. *Journal of Personality and Social Psychology, 60,* 181–192.

Wohlford, P. (1970). Initiation of cigarette smoking: Is it related to parental smoking behavior? *Journal of Consulting and Clinical Psychology, 34,* 148–151.

Woods, N. S., Eyler, F. D., Conlon, M., Behnke, M., & Wobie, K. (1998). Pygmalion in the cradle: Observer bias against cocaine-exposed infants. *Developmental and Behavioral Pediatrics, 19,* 283–285.

Zajonc, R. B. (1965). Social facilitation. *Science, 149,* 269–274.

Zajonc, R. B. (1968). The attitudinal effects of mere exposure. *Journal of Personality and Social Psychology, 9,* 1–27.

Zajonc, R. B., & Sales, S. M. (1966). Social facilitation of dominant and subordinate responses. *Journal of Experimental Social Psychology, 2,* 160–168.

Zebrowitz, L. A., Montepare, J. M., & Lee, H. K. (1993). They don't all look alike: Individual impressions of other racial groups. *Journal of Personality and Social Psychology, 65,* 85–101.

Zimbardo, P., Haney, C., Banks, W. C., & Jaffe, D. (1975). The psychology of imprisonment: Privation, power, and pathology. In D. Rosenhan & P. London (Eds.), *Theory and research in abnormal psychology* (pp. 272–287). New York: Holt, Rinehart and Winston.

Zuckerman, M. (1993). Out of sensory deprivation and into sensation seeking: A personal and scientific journey. In G. C. Brannigan & M. R. Merrens (Eds.), *The undaunted psychologist: Adventures in research.* New York: McGraw-Hill.

Index

TO THE OWNER OF THIS BOOK:

We hope that you have found *Research Design Explained,* Sixth Edition, useful. So that this book can be improved in a future edition, would you take the time to complete this sheet and return it? Thank you.

School and address:_____

Department:_____

Instructor's name:_____

1. What I like most about this book is:_____

_____

_____

2. What I like least about this book is:

_____

_____

3. My general reaction to this book is:

_____

_____

4. The name of the course in which I used this book is:

_____

5. Were all of the chapters of the book assigned for you to read?_____

   If not, which ones weren't?_____

6. In the space below, or on a separate sheet of paper, please write specific suggestions for improving this book and anything else you'd care to share about your experience in using this book.

_____

_____

_____

_____

THOMSON
WADSWORTH

BUSINESS REPLY MAIL
FIRST-CLASS MAIL   PERMIT NO. 102   MONTEREY CA

POSTAGE WILL BE PAID BY ADDRESSEE

Attn: *Vicki Knight, Psychology Publisher*

Wadsworth/Thomson Learning
60 Garden Ct Ste 205
Monterey CA 93940-9967

OPTIONAL:

Your name: _____ Date: _____

May we quote you, either in promotion for *Research Design Explained,*
Sixth Edition, or in future publishing ventures?

Yes: _____   No: _____

Sincerely yours,

Mark L. Mitchell and Janina M. Jolley